QUESTIONING THE SECULAR STATE

Questioning the Secular State

The Worldwide Resurgence of Religion in Politics

edited by
DAVID WESTERLUND

ST. MARTIN'S PRESS, NEW YORK

St. Martin's Press, Scholarly and Reference Division, 175 Fifth Avenue, New York, N.Y. 10010

Printed in India

ISBN 0-312-12522-4

Library of Congress Cataloging-in-Publication-Data

Questioning the secular state/ [edited] by David Westerlund. — 1st ed.
          p.   cm.
      Includes bibliographical references and index.
      ISBN 0-312-12522-4 (cloth)
         1. Relegious fundamentalism—Case studies.   2. Secularism—Case studies.   3. Religion and politics—Case studies.   I. Westerlund, David.
   BL238.047   1996
   200′.9′045 — dc20   95–19152
                                                                        CIP

PREFACE

In recent decades secularism, or the separation of religion and state, has become increasingly questioned by various religious movements and organizations in different parts of the world. The aim of this book is to present casestudies of such groups – which in the West are often referred to as 'fundamentalist' – in a global perspective. Special attempts have been made to focus on movements which have not previously been given much attention in comparative works on 'fundamentalism'.

The book is one of the results of a research project on the political aspects of the current Islamic revival in Africa, which has been financed by the Bank of Sweden Tercentenary Foundation. In addition to Africa, cases from the Americas, Europe and Asia are also presented here. The extensive introduction to the volume presents a theoretical model of different policies of religion, discusses the concepts of fundamentalism and anti-secularism and introduces the subsequent casestudies.

In editing this book I have been assisted by several people. I particularly wish to acknowledge my debt to Eva Hellman, who has provided an important basis for some parts of the introduction. Carl Fredrik Hallencreutz has offered many significant views on the contents of the case studies. Without mentioning each one of them, I also wish to express my gratitude to many other colleagues at Uppsala University for constructive discussions and for providing a stimulating research environment.

Uppsala   DAVID WESTERLUND
June 1995

v

CONTENTS

THE CONTRIBUTORS

Ishtiaq Ahmed is Associate Professor in the Department of Political Science, Stockholm University. His research focuses particularly on issues of religion and politics in South Asia. His numerous publications include *The Concept of an Islamic State: An Analysis of the Ideological Controversy in Pakistan* (1987) and *Sikh Separatism in India* (1993).

Sven Cederroth is Associate Professor in the Department of Social Anthropology, Göteborg University, Sweden, and Senior Research Fellow at the Scandinavian Institute of Asian Studies, Copenhagen. Cederroth has carried out fieldwork in Indonesia and Malaysia, and has published several books, including *The Power of Mekkah and the Spell of the Ancestors: A Sasak Community on Lombok* (1981) and *The Meaning of Death: Essays on Mortuary Rituals and Eschatological Beliefs* (1988), which he co-edited with Jan Lindström and Claes Corlin.

Simon Coleman is a Lecturer in Anthropology, University of Durham, England. His major research interests are Christian evangelicalism, pilgrimage and social movements, and his current area interests are Sweden, Germany and England. He has published many articles in international journals and, with Helen Watson, *An Introduction to Anthropology* (1990). Currently he is completing a book, with John Elsner, on pilgrimage in the world religions.

Mattias Gardell, a Ph. D. of the Department of Comparative Religion, Stockholm University, is trained in the anthropology of religion and is particularly interested in issues of religion and politics. He is currently completing a work on the Nation of Islam in the United States.

Virginia Garrard-Burnett, Lecturer at the Institute of Latin American Studies and Department of History, University of Texas, Austin, is a specialist on religion in Guatemala. She has published extensively and recently edited, with David Stoll, *Rethinking Protestantism in Latin America* (1993).

Paul Gifford, Leverhulme Research Fellow, jointly at the School of Oriental and African Studies, University of London, and the Department of Theology and Religious Studies, University of Leeds, England, is a specialist on issues of Christianity and politics in various parts of Africa. He has published the books *The New Crusaders: Christianity and the New Right in Southern Africa* (1991) and *Christianity and*

Politics in Doe's Liberia (1993) and edited *New Dimensions in African Christianity* (1992, 1993).

Mikael Gravers, Senior Lecturer in Ethnography and Social Anthropology at the University of Aarhus, Denmark, has done fieldwork among the Karen in Thailand. His research is focused on ethnicity, nationalism and religion, and his numerous publications include *Nationalism and Political Paranoia in Burma: An Essay on the Historical Practice of Power* (1993).

Carl F. Hallencreutz is Professor of Mission Studies and Dean of the Faculty of Theology, Uppsala University. His research interests include ecumenical issues, inter-religious dialogue and questions of religion and politics, and he has published numerous books and essays. With Ambrose Moyo, he edited *Church and State in Zimbabwe* (1988).

Eva Hellman is a Lecturer of Religious Studies at the University of Falun, Sweden. Her research areas are modern Hinduism and Buddhism in South Asia, particularly issues of religion and politics, and in addition to several articles, she has published *Political Hinduism: The Challenge of Visva Hindu Parisad* (1993).

Roman Loimeier, Research Fellow at the Department of Islamic Studies, University of Bayreuth, Germany, is a specialist in West Africa who has dealt with problems of religion and society in Nigeria and Senegal. His publications include *Islamische Erneuerung und politischer Wandel in Nordnigeria. Die Auseinandersetzungen zwischen den Sufi-Bruderschaften und ihren Gegnern seit Ende der 50er Jahre* (1993), now translated into English.

Frieder Ludwig, is a research fellow in Church History at the University of Munich. An English version of his first German doctoral thesis, *Church in a Colonial Context: Anglican Missionaries and African Prophets in Southeastern Nigeria, 1879-1918*, was published in 1992, and he has completed a second doctoral thesis, *Das Modell Tauzania: Untersuchungen zum Verhältnis zwischen Kirche und Staat während der Ära Nyerere (1961-1985)* (1994).

Mohamed Mahmoud, a lecturer at the Oriental Institute, Oxford University, has concentrated since the mid-1980s on Islamic studies. He has published numerous papers on the problems of reading the Quranic text and the intellectual discourse of modern Islamism. His publications have appeared mainly in Arabic in journals such as the London-based quarterly *Mawaqif* and the Cairo-based *Kitabat Sudaniyya*.

Bruce Matthews is C.B. Lumsden Professor of Comparative Religion at Acadia University, Nova Scotia, Canada. His research interest is Theravada Buddhism in the modern age focusing on Sri Lanka and Burma, and among his recent titles are *Craving and Salvation: A Study in Buddhist Soteriology* (1983); *Religion, Values and Development in*

Southeast Asia, with Judith Negata (1986); and *The Quality of Life in Southeast Asia: Transforming Social, Political and Natural Environment* (1992).

Asta Olesen, Senior Lecturer at the Institute of Anthropology, Copenhagen University, did extensive fieldwork in Afghanistan in the 1970s, studying problems of ethnicity and development issues. Her work *Islam and Politics in Afghanistan* (1994) deals with the role of Islam and religious leaders in Afghan politics since 1880. She has also carried out research on Euroislam and been coordinator of the Islam in Denmark project sponsored by the Danish State Research Council of the Humanities.

Thomas Parland, Research Fellow at the Department of Political Science, Helsinki University, has focussed on problems of racism (particularly anti-semitism) and urbanization, and questions of religion and Russian nationalism. He has published numerous articles and his doctoral thesis *The Rejection in Russia of Totalitarian Socialism and Liberal Democracy: A Study of the Russian New Right* (1993).

Melissa A. Pflüg, Assistant Professor of Anthropology at the Department of Sociology and Anthropology, University of Wisconsin, Eau Claire, has done extensive fieldwork among the Odawa (Ottawa) in northern Michigan and Ontario since the later 1980s. Her research interests include myth and ritual, revitalization movements, religious retention and transformation. A book, *The Seventh Fire: Myth and Ritual in Odawa Revitalization*, is forthcoming.

Susan Rose, Associate Professor and Chair of Sociology at Dickinson College, Carlisle, Pennsylvania, moved from studying North American evangelicalism to examine the growth and nature of this movement in the so-called Third World, particularly in Guatemala, the Philippines, Korea and South Africa. She has published *Keeping Them Out of the Hands of Satan: Evangelical Schooling in America* (1988), and is currently finishing a book, *Fundamentalism's Mission in the Third World*.

Leif Stenberg, a doctoral candidate in the History of Religions at the Department of Theology and Religious Studies, Lund University, Sweden, is particularly interested in contemporary discussions of the function of Islam in relation to modernity. In a forthcoming doctoral thesis he analyses discourses concerning the Islamization of science, especially the natural sciences.

David Westerlund, Associate Professor at the Department of Comparative Religion, Stockholm University, and Senior Lecturer in the History of Religions at the Department of Theology, Uppsala University, is engaged in research on indigenous African religions, Islam in Africa and problems of religion and politics. His numerous publications include

Ujamaa na Dini: A Study of Some Aspects of Religion and Society in Tanzania, 1961-1977 (1980) and *Culture, Experience and Pluralism: Essays on African Ideas of Illness and Healing* (1989), co-edited with Anita Jacobson-Widding.

INTRODUCTION

ANTI-SECULARIST POLICIES OF RELIGION

Carl F. Hallencreutz and David Westerlund

In recent years a considerable number of scholarly works have appeared dealing with so-called fundamentalist movements in different religions and regions.[1] Many of them focus on the Middle East, while other regions, such as Africa south of the Sahara, are frequently overlooked. For instance, the well-known and comprehensive Fundamentalism Project of the American Academy of Arts and Sciences has a strong emphasis on the Middle East.

This volume, by contrast, concentrates largely on groups and areas which have hitherto received little attention in comparative works on 'fundamentalism'. However, well-known and especially significant cases, such as conservative Christianity in the United States and the Islamic Salvation Front in Algeria, are included too. This book, moreover, differs from many other works on contemporary 'fundamentalism' in having a clear focus. The specific theme is how, according to so-called fundamentalist or anti-secularist groups in various religions, the state should relate to the religious entities within its area. Hence the main questions dealt with are how and to what extent anti-secularist movements, organizations and individuals oppose secularism, and how they wish to strengthen the role of religion in political life. With these questions in mind our primary focus is on developments during the 1980s and early 1990s.

Since secularism – i.e. the pursuit of politics irrespective of predominant religious interests – is the most widely established policy on religion in the world today, anti-secularists normally form opposition groups. In his book *The New Cold War? Religious Nationalism Confronts the Secular State* (1993), Mark Juergensmeyer identified the issue of whether the state should be secular or religious as a major conflict in contemporary international politics. His examples, however, are almost all Asian. Our perspective is more global, since it also includes case studies of countries in North and Central America, Europe and Africa. Before introducing these studies, however, we will first present a theoretical model of various policies of religion and discuss some of the problems of terminology involved in cross-religious studies of anti-secularist policies.

1

Policies of Religion

The term 'policy of religion' is used here primarily to define the position of the state in relation to the religious traditions within its sphere of jurisdiction. The issue has at least three interacting aspects. First, there is the question of individual and corporate freedom of religion. Individual religious liberty is the right of the individual to choose and practise a certain religion or to abstain from such practices. Corporate religious freedom concerns the extent to which religious groups may organize themselves, practise their faith, establish social and political programmes and proclaim their message inside as well as outside their own fold. Often individual religious freedom is given more generous recognition than corporate religious freedom. The second aspect of the issue concerns the role played by different religious communities as partners of the state in the implementation of certain national policies, e.g. in education and health care. In some societies, schools and hospitals run by religious organizations are of great significance. Some regimes, however, may see religious communities as ideological threats to be fought as obstacles in the national political process. A third and more complex aspect of special importance in this context, concerns the way the government sees itself in relation to religious traditions, particularly if its allows such traditions to inspire and inform its own policies. There can be a clear demarcation between religion and politics, with religion seen as a private matter or a group interest subordinate to what happens at the political level. However, religious institutions and values may also be regarded as sources of inspiration for the state. A government may even subordinate its policies to the specific truth-claims, norms and structures of one religious tradition.

In a comparative model of different policies of religion we can identify three main types, which may be further qualified in more detailed analyses. They can be illustrated in the following way:

POLICIES OF RELIGION: A COMPARATIVE MODEL

Confessional	Generally Religious	Secular
Strict/Modified		Liberal/Marxist

In countries with a confessional policy of religion, a certain religious tradition or community is politically established, with a more or less intimate interaction between religion and politics. This alternative is the predominant one in Muslim countries. In European history confessional policies of religion are a legacy from the time when there were national states that were uniform in religion. Religious states, which in some contexts may be considered as theocracies, pursue strictly confessional policies of religion. The Islamic Republic of Iran is an example of such a state: here the state apparatus is subordinate to Islam and religious leaders have a decisive say in political affairs. In other countries with a Muslim majority, as well as in some predominantly Christian and Buddhist countries such as Sweden and Thailand, there is a modified confessional policy. In countries with almost exclusively Muslim populations Islam is generally the state religion and is privileged in certain ways, but religious leaders and institutions are to some extent subordinate to the interests of the state.

The secular policy of religion evolved particularly after the American and French revolutions of the late eighteenth century and is now adopted in many countries all over the world. This alternative presupposes that there is at least a formal separation of religion and the state. There is a tendency to limit the role of religion to a 'religious' sphere of society. In liberal forms of the secular policy of religion, however, religion is seen as a societal resource. Individual as well as corporate religious freedom is provided for to a greater or lesser extent, and thus religion may in practice have a significant role in political life. In many such cases different types of 'civil religion' have developed, where religious symbols and practices are used politically to foster national integration. Marxist versions of the secular religious policy, established in the Soviet Union in 1917 and in China in 1949, are characterized by an ideologically-defined negative view of religion. Countries whose regimes are inspired by a Marxist critique of religion have a strong ideological divide between religion and politics, and corporate religions freedom may be subordinate to the prerogatives of political organizations.

The generally religious policy on religion is vaguer than the other alternatives. Here the state, while guided by religion in general, is not institutionally tied to any specific religious tradition. The best example of this middle option is Indonesia, where one of the five pillars of the state ideology, *Pancasila*, refers to belief in God as one of the bases on which the Indonesian nation should be built. This position, with its vague reference to belief in God, is very similar to 'civil religions' in other multi-religious states. However, whereas the generally religious policy of religion in Indonesia is an *official* policy, 'civil religion' is not *formally* recognized.

In order to understand the current growth of new anti-secularist and politically committed religious movements, the tool of analysis of different policies of religion which we have advanced, and which is predominantly constitutional, must be seen in relation to the leading actors in the religious and political field. Thus during the colonial era, Western powers introduced secularism in their dependencies, and in post-colonial times the secular policy of religion often proved useful as a means of national integration in new multi-religious states. In India the option of a secular policy of religion proved important, although it provoked Pakistan to opt for a more confessional policy. In Vietnam a Marxist type of secular policy was chosen, while the policy that developed in Japan after the Second World War was more liberal.

Secularism was strongly supported by many ruling élites to avoid religious conflicts and promote national coordination in countries with religious divisions. Such élites were usually western-educated and tried to implement Western political ideals. In practice, the officially recognized secular policy often encouraged the evolution of various kinds of civil religion. Nigeria and Tanzania, for instance, are examples of such developments. However, during the last few decades new revivalist religious groups have increasingly challenged the secular as well as the generally religious policy models. Many politically oriented religious movements thus consciously reject the secular ideals which have dominated national policies, and appear as champions of confessional options. This is a characteristic element in the 'fundamentalist' protest, as the case studies in this volume clearly illustrate.

Fundamentalism or Anti-secularism?

In the West an all-inclusive term, 'fundamentalism', has come to be used, particularly in the media, to designate different religious movements in various parts of the world. However, this broad use of the term has become increasingly irrelevant. As a derogatory concept, tied to Western stereotypes and Christian presuppositions, it easily causes misunderstandings and prevents the understanding of the dynamics and characteristics of different religious groups with explicit political objectives. The aim of the above-mentioned Chicago-based Fundamentalism Project is to establish a mutually acceptable vocabulary for dialogue between different faiths and peoples at a time when misinformation and misunderstanding exacerbate national and international conflicts. It seems likely, however, that use here of the term 'fundamentalism' as a key concept goes against this excellent aim; and many non-Christian scholars and others have for good reasons objected strongly to its continued use.[3]

Within Christian history the term 'fundamentalism' has been used both as a proud self-designation and as a nickname by outsiders to designate a specific inter-denominational Protestant movement.[4] It has also been used more generally to refer to a specific view and use of the Bible. Since many people have erroneously defined the fundamentalist way of reading the Bible simply as a literal reading of the text, it is important to stress that the point of conflict between fundamentalists and others was not literalness but *inerrancy*. In Christian tradition the fundamentalist movement is characterized by the latter approach to the Bible. The movement started in the second decade of the twentieth century as a reaction against the adoption of Biblical criticism within some American denominations. Between 1910 and 1915 twelve pamphlets called *The Fundamentals* were written and distributed *en masse*. They propagated what was seen as five non-negotiable elements of true and authentic Christianity, namely: the inerrancy of the Bible; the deity of Jesus Christ and the historicity of the virgin birth; the atonement based on the substitutionary death of Jesus Christ; the bodily resurrection of Christ from the dead; and the second coming of Christ. In 1919, the important World's Christian Fundamentals Association was founded and the continued expansion of fundamentalism led to a polarization among Baptists, Methodists, Presbyterians and other Christian denominations. After the Second World War, fundamentalism developed in somewhat different directions, and one important change, of special interest here, is that in recent years many fundamentalists have begun to challenge the basically apolitical views of the older fundamentalists. Well-known examples of what may be called neo-fundamentalism are Jerry Falwell and his organization Moral Majority, formed in 1979.

'Fundamentalism' became common as a label for distinct Muslim movements with articulate political objectives, particularly after the Islamic revolution in Iran in 1979. For many Americans and other Westerners, Muslim 'fundies' have replaced 'commies' as the archenemy. No doubt, the idea of the Islamic world as a threat against the Christian or secular Western world has contributed greatly to the derogatory use of the word. It appears that in some Muslim countries, regimes have consciously used the tactic of branding political opponents 'fundamentalists' and depicting them as serious threats in order to gain support from the West and soften criticism of their own authoritarian and repressive rule. The current power relations in the world suggest that the notion of an 'Islamic threat' is ill-founded; yet in the minds of many Westerners it is a powerful and historically deeply-rooted enemy image.[5] The view of Islam as the main ideological enemy is common among American fundamentalists – William Shepard has written: 'US fundamentalists are part of a society that was and is imperialist in various senses, and generally they share the attitudes that underlie that imperialism', whereas Muslim 'fundamentalists' 'are part of societies that have suffered from imperialism and are anti-imperialist, often stridently so'. Shepard rightly concludes that the common label 'fundamentalist' is likely to obscure this basic contrast.[6]

While the political and religious reasons for the habit of labelling certain Muslims and other non-Christians 'fundamentalist' are fairly obvious, it is more difficult to find adequate scholarly reasons for it. As already noted the term in its original Christian context referred to a set of 'fundamental' doctrines and above all to a specific view of the Scriptures. In Islam, however, correct behaviour has always been a more central concern than correct doctrines. In this, so-called Muslim fundamentalists are not an exception. Nor is their view of Holy Scripture easily comparable to the Christian fundamentalist view with its Protestant basis. According to Muslim 'fundamentalists', as well as to the great majority of Muslims, the Quran cannot be isolated from the tradition, or Sunna; hence their view of Scripture is more similar to an Orthodox or Catholic Christian position than to the fundamentalist Protestant one. In addition, the idea of the inerrancy of the Quran is not exclusive to Muslim 'fundamentalists' – it is a basic tenet common to virtually all practising Muslims.

In many works, 'fundamentalism' has been contrasted to modernism or what is conceived of as modern. For instance, the subtitle of Bruce B. Lawrence's book *Defenders of God*, in which he deals with Christian, Muslim and Jewish 'fundamentalists', is *The Fundamentalist Revolt against the Modern Age*.[7] Similarly, Thomas Meyer writes about 'fundamentalism as "the world-wide insurrection against the modern" '.[8] Here it is important to stress the distinction between the concepts of modernism and the modern, which are sometimes confused.[9] It is not modernity as such which is opposed by so-called 'fundamentalists' but *secular modernity* or *modernism*. They reject the idea that consensual norms and ultimate values can be located in a secular or non-religious source. In Christian contexts the term 'modernism' was originally associated with a reform movement which started within the Catholic Church at the end of the nineteenth century. Because it supported historical critical research on the Bible and evolutionist ideas, it was condemned in 1907 in a papal encyclical. This denunciation of modernism was supported by the integrist movement – the Catholic dichotomy of modernism/integrism corresponding roughly to the Protestant dichotomy of liberalism/fundamentalism.

Within, and particularly outside, religious contexts modernism is associated with the philosophical values of the Enlightenment, which are regarded as anti-religious and are thus naturally refuted by Muslim 'fundamentalists'. However, they are clearly not against modern technological and scientific achievements. They do not see an opposition between reason and religion – many Muslim 'fundamentalists' are students at or alumni of faculties of science and medicine. They do not aim to reestablish some form of medieval society, although the earliest period of Islamic history is an important source of their inspiration. Their goal is to 'Islamize' the modern world, not to reject it. This can be achieved by practising *ijtihad*, that is, an independent interpretation or analysis of the Quran and Sunna. In this they differ from more traditionally oriented Muslims who believe that 'the gates of *ijtihad*' were closed more than 1,000 years ago. Reformist movements that champion the principle of *ijtihad* have appeared time and again in Islamic history. Hence one should be careful not to over-emphasize the issue of 'fundamentalism v. modernism'. It should be noted, also, that in the age of postmodernism, feminism and other new Westernisms, modernism is no longer very modern.[10]

Like the early Christian fundamentalists, some traditionalist Muslims have a basically apolitical orientation, but among Muslim 'fundamentalists' the political dimension of their aims and activities is most prevalent. Although the creation of Islamic societies may be the short-term objective, the ultimate goal is the establishment of Islamic states based on Islamic law, *sharia.* In their reaction against Western secularism and the 'privatization' or depoliticization of Islam, Muslim 'fundamentalists' aim at restoring or revitalizing the role of Islam as a complete societal and political order. 'The heart of contemporary revivalism is this ideologization of Islam; Islam is interpreted as a total ideology that provides the basic framework of meaning and direction for political, social, and cultural life.'[11]

However, the issue of 'extra-Christian fundamentalism' is not limited only to the Muslim world. Occasionally, Vishva Hindu Parishad (VHP) – a leading organization campaigning for a Hindu India – has similarly been referred to as 'fundamentalist'. Is this a label that increases our understanding of the religious and political phenomenon that the VHP represents? A closer look at the characteristics of this group shows that here too 'fundamentalism' is a misnomer. According to the VHP, none of the classical Hindu Scriptures or traditions of interpretation provide relevant and sufficiently detailed guidelines for contemporary Hindu life and society. Moreover, the VHP opposes the idea that there are immutable norms, laws and institutions – for instance, they do not accept the orthodox Manu's law but argue that it is antiquated and obsolete as a guide for modern India. VHP members also work actively for the integration of so-called Untouchables into the Hindu community. The rejection of Manu's law and the support of Untouchables are challenges against more orthodox Hindu groups.[12] Like Islamists, but unlike many Christian fundamentalists, VHP supporters are deeply involved in politics. Like Islamists, too, they do not reject Western science and technology, but often point out that there are scientists who have declared their respect for Indian wisdom. According to the VHP, what Westerners have discovered are actually rediscoveries of elements in the Hindu tradition. Moreover, VHP supporters, like Islamists and other 'fundamentalists', largely use modern audiovisual facilities in order to spread their message and ideology.

However, the VHP's openness towards science and technology contrasts sharply with its attitude to certain scholarly views on Indian history: for example, it does not accept the idea of an Aryan immigration to India but argues that this theory, which originated in the nineteenth century and which has become accepted by Western scholars, was launched by the British for political reasons, i.e. to support the claim that the 'Aryans' (Hindus) were not the original inhabitants of India and thus had no obvious right to rule it. Sources like the Purana texts and the Mahabharata are used to dismiss the theory of an 'Aryan' immigration. In other words, mythology is historicized, and the conclusions arrived at used for political goals.

The examples we have cited point to some of the problems created by the use of the term 'fundamentalism' as a cross-religious concept. Similar and more diverse problems are also found in the context of other religions such as Buddhism and Sikhism. To many Westerners 'fundamentalism' implies a monolithic threat that in reality does not exist. According to Juergensmeyer, 'the only thing that religious activists around the world have in common, aside from their fervor, is their rejection of Westerners and those like us who subscribe to modern secularism'. He refers to such activists, who strive for a revival of religion in the public sphere, as religious nationalists. In his view, the chief problem with the term 'fundamentalism' is that it carries no political meaning. Religious nationalists 'are concerned about the rationale for having a state, the moral basis for politics, and the reasons why a state should elicit loyalty', and they strongly dismiss 'secular nationalism as fundamentally bereft of moral and spiritual values'.[13]

Given the limited scope here – the focus on the issue of religion and state – the theme of anti-secularism occurs in the title of this introduction. Most of the movements and organizations studied are anti-secularist in the sense that they oppose the idea of a secular state and want to strengthen the political role of religion. Some groups aim at a far-reaching confessionalization of the state, while others have more limited goals. Christian fundamentalists still often accept the principle of secularism, although there is, as has already been noted, an increasing political awareness and level of involvement among many Christian neo-fundamentalists.

The Americas and Europe

The contributions to this book are divided regionally into three main parts, concerning the Americas and Europe, Africa and Asia respectively. The first case-study, by *Simon Coleman*, deals with conservative Christians in the United States. Coleman argues that conservative Protestants have attempted to gain widespread cultural and political legitimation by appropriating and thereby redefining the symbols of North American civil religion. In the process the rhetoric of both the secular and the religious Right has, in certain ways, been mutually enforcing, since both have challenged liberal definitions of the American polity. These developments are shown to have had consequences beyond the United States itself, an example of this international influence being a conservative Protestant group in Sweden related to the international Rhema network, which shows how the characteristics and political orientation of conservative American civil religion can be adapted to new cultural and religio-political circumstances.

Coleman's chapter provides an important background to the studies of new Christian groups in the so-called Third World. The existence of conservative Christianity in Latin American, African and Asian countries is largely a consequence of changes in American missionary work in the wake of the anti-modernist or anti-liberal protest which is reinforced by neo-fundamentalist and other conservative Christian groups. Older mainline missionary societies have become divided and new often interdenominational, organizations have developed. In particular, the chapters by Virginia Garrard-Burnett on Guatemala, Paul Gifford on Africa and Susan Rose on the Philippines illustrate the great significance of new American missionary endeavours. The use of modern media techniques and the influence of the American 'Cold War' mentality have inspired the rise of new and indigenous religious movements and conservative political groups. In some regions there are clear connections between the new, often strongly anti-Catholic and anti-Muslim Protestant missionary initiatives and American political influences.

Within the United States there are certain religious minorities, sometimes labelled 'fundamentalist', that voice a strong protest against conservative Christians as well as against secularism and the whole American political system. One such group, the Nation of Islam (NOI), is described by *Mattias Gardell*. In the United States, in contrast to several African and Asian countries, Islam lies outside the realm of 'civil religion', which is discussed in the chapters by Coleman and Gardell. For the members of NOI, Islam is an expression of black protest. The African-Americans are the true people of God and within the NOI, demands for the creation of a separate state for black people have been raised. In preparation for anticipated changes, a 'theocratic shadow cabinet' and a separate legal system have been formed. In addition, the NOI has its own army and national symbols in the form of a flag and an anthem. However, the creation of a separate state is only an interim solution until the end of the world, when God will destroy the devilish rule of the white people and transform the world into a black and eternal paradise. Gardell stresses the importance of this apocalyptic perspective within the NOI – which is comparable to the significance of eschatology among, for instance, Tibetan Buddhists.[14] Both black Muslims in the United States and Tibetan Buddhists face opponents much stronger politically than themselves. A pronounced emphasis on eschatology has also characterized Shia Muslims, who in most Muslim states have lived as politically inferior minority groups under Sunni rule. It is noteworthy that in Iran today, following the establishment of Islamic Shia rule, eschatological aspects have been somewhat eclipsed by the concerns of the present religious state, although this state is regarded as an interim solution before the return of the twelfth Imam.

The eschatological element is significant also in *Melissa Pflüg's* chapter on the Odawa Indians of Michigan. The revitalization of traditionalist Odawa Indian religion is voiced in a myth that anticipates the advent of a transformed world, when non-Indians and all their values will be destroyed. Odawa traditionalists view the secular US legal system as an artificial order created by Euro-Americans to protect their own interests. The advent of the transformed world will occur when all Odawa follow the 'Old Ways'. Unlike some Odawa 'accommodationists', traditionalists refuse to give in to the US authorities and to be supervised by the Bureau of Indian Affairs. Their goal is total sovereignty, and in their struggle for autonomy the issues of religion and language as well as of land rights are crucial.

Indigenous religious movements have often been vital in the struggle of North American Indians to preserve or regain their lands and ways of life; thus there are many examples of a revitalization of the Indian religious heritage. Unlike the case of the Odawa traditionalists, some of these have a pan-Indian orientation. However, charismatic Christianity has also spread widely and rapidly on North American Indian reservations since the 1960s, mainly in Pentecostal denominations. This development, as well as the imprisonment in the 1970s of some activist leaders from the American Indian Movement, who had on occasions taken up arms against the superior authorities, have reduced the occurrence of more acts of rebellion.[15]

While there are cases of a revival of traditional values among certain minorities in the United States, religious developments in Latin America have been marked by a far-reaching polarization between Catholic liberation theology and US-inspired neo-fundamentalist movements. The spread and impact of these movements have lead to a situation which has caused some sociologists of religion to contemplate whether Latin America is 'turning Protestant'. Guatemala is an especially notable case in point. In her study *Virginia Garrard-Burnett* adopts a long historical perspective on Catholic developments in what many claim to be the most 'religious' country in Latin America. Against the background of liberal policies and a Catholic Church institutionally weak since the late nineteenth century, she traces a contradictory Catholic development. On the one hand, the institutional establishment was reinforced, but on the other there was an expansion of more formal expressions of liberation theology as well as of contextualized or politicized rural Catholicism among oppressed Indians.

On the Protestant side, Garrard-Burnett explores a gradual development in three stages. First there has been an expansion since the 1950s of Protestant church movements in urban environments. From around 600,000 in the early 1960s, the population of Guatemala City had grown to more than 2 million inhabitants by the 1990s. The percentage of Protestants – of various denominations – has in the process grown from 2 to about 30 per cent. The second phase focuses on General Efraín Ríos Montt, who combined conservative Evangelical convictions with anti-communism and managed to enlist both ecclesiastical and economic US support from March 1982 until he was ousted by his minister of defence, Oscar Mejía Victores, in 1983. General Montt upheld the confessional policy of religion of the Guatemalan government and favoured the fundamentalist advance, while his successor Mejía Victores claimed a lower-profile confessional policy. Even so the consolidation of Guatemalan fundamentalism continued through the 1980s. The third phase, which is more involved and difficult to assess, started even before Ríos Montt's period of rule. It concerns the so-called conversions of the Quiche Indians, who had to adjust to pressures from both guerrillas and the national army. If the situation is viewed purely in terms of church growth, it is easy to overlook the fact that the process reflects the indigenous strategies of survival of an oppressed minority. However, Garrard Burnett does not delve further into that particular dimension of the resacralization of Guatemalan politics since the 1960s.

After the demise of the Soviet Union and the decline of Marxist-Leninist ideology, Orthodox Christianity in association with Russian neo-nationalism has appeared as the most important political alternative to a Western liberal democratic development in Russia. In the final chapter of the first part, *Thomas Parland* shows how this religiously-coloured neo-nationalism link up with an old tradition of embittered resistance against the Western-inspired modernization and secularization of Russian society. The 'counter-reformist' ideology that conservative circles use as a weapon against Western influence is based on the idea that Russia should follow its own model of development. In practice this has led to an adherence to the old imperial and theocratic monarchy and dissociation from the secularized Western rule of law. The Soviet parenthesis in Russian history is interpreted and condemned primarily in terms of a destructive state atheism. The contemporary phenomenon of 'clerical fascism' is manifested in a resurgence of additional confessionally oriented anti-Semitism. Another current phenomenon is the political marriage of convenience between atheist Stalinists and Orthodox anti-communist patriots. It is noteworthy that many former Marxists have converted to Orthodox Christianity.

The case of Russia may be seen in the wider context of an Orthodox 'Byzantinist commonwealth'. In his much discussed essay 'The Clash of Civilizations', Samuel Huntington refers to the 'Slavic-Orthodox' civilization as one of the major civilizations which, he hypothesizes, will dominate the development of global politics in the near future.[16] As in Russia, there exists in countries like Serbia, Bulgaria, Rumania and Greece a distrust of the West and of the Catholic Church, and in several parts of eastern Europe religious nationalism now appears as an important alternative to communism. Russia's sympathy for the Serbian side in the civil war of former Jugoslavia is well-known.

In western Europe and in the struggle for a European political union the role of Catholic and Protestant Christianity is difficult to evaluate. However, there appears to be a religious component in the strong popular resistance to the European Community in northern Europe. Given the strength of 'Catholic' countries in the European Community and of Christian Democratic Parties dominated by Catholics, there are those who regard the enlargement of the Community as a 'Catholic threat'. Many fundamentalists who interpret the European union in the light of the Book of Revelation are highly critical of any striving for political unity. Some among them, and indeed some non-fundamentalists with other religious ideals, see the move towards European unity as a threat against the idea of national or state churches.

Africa

One of the most important anti-secularist Islamic movements in contemporary Africa is the Front Islamique du Salut (FIS) (Islamic Salvation Front) of Algeria. In the local elections of 1990 FIS won a clear majority, but the ruling Front de la Libération Nationale (FLN) (National Liberation Front) then postponed the first round of the parliamentary elections till December 1991. However, when the FIS won this election too, the process of democratization came to a halt and FIS members soon became objects of fierce repression. In the first chapters of the second part, *Leif Stenberg* explores the ideals and objectives of FIS, which aims to establish an Islamic state based on the *sharia*, and more specifically, deals with the use and interpretation of Islamic terminology, particularly in the Quran and Sunna, among Algerian Islamists. In addition, he provides comparative notes on other Islamist movements in the Middle East.

Several scholars have argued that one of the reasons for the success of the Islamic movement in Iran was that the religious institutions and leaders were not completely, or even largely, incorporated into and controlled by the state. Hence, it retained the possibility of autonomous action and organization. A striving for institutional or organizational independence from the state is a typical feature of the Islamic revival. Particularly in countries without a democratic tradition, Islamist organizations can provide important channels for political opposition.[17] Certainly Algeria is one of the countries where Islamists have succeeded in 'liberating' the 'religious sphere' from the state control established by secularist socialists. The number of non-authorized mosques, often built on private land and without officially employed religious leaders, has increased rapidly. The ideology and politics of the FLN regime have been criticized in hundreds of such 'roadside mosques'.

Stenberg stresses, among other things, the importance of lay people in the FIS. There are frequent conflicts between traditionally oriented *ulama* and more reformist and radical Islamist lay leaders. Another example of this is touched on in the chapter by *Muhammad Mahmoud* on the Muslim Brotherhood in Sudan, the African country where Islamists have been most successful in achieving far-reaching Islamization. In the 1970s President Nimeiri abandoned his socialist policies in favour of a gradual Islamization, culminating in the introduction of the so-called September laws of 1983. After the coup in 1989 the position of the Muslim Brotherhood was much strengthened, and Muslim Brothers were given several key posts in the administration. In the early 1990s Khartoum developed into an important international Islamist centre.[18] However, due to the serious economic situation and the violent conflicts with secularist-oriented non-Muslims in southern Sudan, the political situation remains unstable.

Mahmoud deals, in particular, with the ideas and policies of the internationally established leader Hasan al-Turabi, according to whom secularism is a devilish system in that it compartmentalizes Islam – that is, it separates religion from politics and other aspects of society. Through a process of Islamization an Islamic society should be developed before the establishment of the Islamic state – the Islamic state being the political expression of that Islamic society. The attempts to create Islamic societies as a preparation for and in anticipation of Islamic states typically characterize Islamist organizations. The development of Islamic schools, hospitals, clinics, pharmacies, banks, insurance companies etc. has probably contributed substantially to the advance of the Islamic movement. Like other Islamists, al-Turabi is opposed to the conservatism or traditionalism of many *ulama* and Sufi leaders.[19] Historic forms of Islamic society should not be copied, although they may be important sources of inspiration.[20] Mahmoud elaborates, for instance, on al-Turabi's attempts to question and reform traditional Islamic views on religious minorities and the segregation of the sexes.

In West Africa there are now many Islamist groups challenging non-Islamic regimes. The case of Senegal, where more than 90 per cent of the population are Muslims, is studied by *Roman Loimeier*. In addition to their struggle against secularism, Senegalese Islamists are involved in a sometimes harsh conflict with Sufism, the form of Islam to which the great majority of Senegalese Muslims adhere. As in other countries, Islamists in Senegal are frequently well-educated people – many have studied in Arab countries – who oppose the '*neo-jahiliyya*' (ignorance) of Sufism. This new period of *jahiliyya* is in a sense considered worse than the situation of religious ignorance before the time of Muhammad, when the Quran and Sunna had not yet been revealed. The 'clerical' role of Sufi leaders, or *marabouts*, as intermediaries between God and human beings, as well as their disregard for the *sharia*, are criticized by the Islamists. For instance, they oppose the practice of leading *marabouts* of marrying more – sometimes considerably more – than four wives, and champion the ideal of monogamy.[21] As noted by Loimeier, the modern Islamic schools set up by Islamist organizations have forced the powerful Sufi fraternities to follow suit and to establish modern schools of their own. In their attempts to fight back, the *marabouts* are also consciously establishing themselves in urban areas, where the Islamist groups have their strongholds.[22] Leading politicians continuously seek support from prominent marabouts, who have been less reluctant to accept the principle of secularism and to co-operate with the powers that be. It should be noted, also, that the Islamist *literati* are somewhat alienated from the mass of Senegalese peasants and workers and do not have resources comparable to those of the *marabouts* for providing a nation-wide 'welfare system'.[23]

In his overview of the political role of the mushrooming fundamentalist and charismatic churches in Africa, *Paul Gifford* concludes that the members of these churches officially keep a low political profile. As a rule, they claim to be completely apolitical and interested only in 'taking the continent for Jesus'. However, Gifford argues that in practice this ostensibly non-political concentration on evangelism becomes very political indeed. Togo, Sierra Leone, the Central African Republic, Liberia and Kenya are mentioned as examples where autocratic rulers have used conservative churches to keep themselves in power.[24] The significance of American missionary endeavours on the rapid growth of conservative fundamentalist and charismatic Christianity in Africa, as elsewhere in the 'Third World', has already been indicated. Christian bookshops are stocked with American materials, churches are organized on American lines, choirs sing American gospel music, Bible colleges are accredited by American institutions, and American evangelists often preach in Africa. New African denominations that propagate the 'gospel of prosperity' have close links with supporters in the United States; one organization that has been particularly successful in promoting this gospel is the Full Gospel Business Men's Fellowship International.[25]

In some countries, according to Gifford, the neo-fundamentalist kind of Christianity may be inclined more consciously to enter the political arena where there is a 'Muslim threat' to counteract. There are several indications that charismatic groups in Nigeria are increasingly renouncing their apolitical views and more actively supporting Christian political candidates. Another African country with more or less equal numbers of Christians and Muslims is Tanzania, where President Ali Hassan Mwinyi has pursued the inclusivist secularist religious policy of his Christian predecessor Julius K. Nyerere. However, some new Islamist organizations and leaders have challenged this policy; for instance, certain Muslims have demanded a reintroduction of separate *sharia* courts. Zanzibar, where Islam is deeply rooted and some Muslims would prefer to see the union between Zanzibar and mainland Tanzania dissolved, has been a particular problem. Partly in response to this intensified Islamic orientation, some Christians have been more outspoken, and the relationship between Muslims and Christians in general has tended to become polarized. As elsewhere, the inter-religious conflicts tend to be exacerbated by international involvement. Whereas Christian groups receive much support from anti-Islamic denominations in the United States and other Western countries, the Islamic movement receives both financial and moral support from Muslim regimes and organizations, many of them markedly anti-Western.

Asia

In the 1950s and '60s many observers of the political and religious scene in South Asia took it for granted that religion would be reduced to the private sphere, with secular, democratic and socialist India being seen as a model of the expected development. The years immediately after India's independence have been characterized as the time of nation-building: industries and infrastructure were developed, agriculture was modernized and the education system extended. Separate regional and religious interests were subordinated to the interests of the nation. During Jawaharlal Nehru's period as prime minister (1947-64) the government developed different strategies to balance the ideals of pluralism and national integration. The search for unity and the optimistic prospects for socio-economic development compelled organizations championing separate Hindu, Sikh or Muslim demands to lie low. As a rule, they were not able to influence policy.[26]

In more recent years, however, the situation has greatly changed. Militant movements fighting for a Hindu India, a Sikh Khalistan, a Muslim Kashmir and a Christian Nagaland have grown in strength. Their activities have provoked clashes with the government and contributed to violent confrontations between adherents of different religions. The years of growing religious activism have illustrated the continued potential of religion to shape identity and ideology. The Indian case clearly exemplifies the difficulties of firmly establishing secularism in non-Western areas. However, anti-secularist tendencies are not limited to India but can be seen in other parts of South Asia.[27] Movements demanding a homeland for a religiously defined group are found in a number of countries. In Hinduism, Sikhism and Buddhism, as well as in Islam, the concept of religion is comprehensive and tends to cover all spheres of life, including politics. Inter- as well as intra-religious exclusivism can easily breed intolerance, and there are many examples of violent confrontations between those with different beliefs.

In the discussion of issues of terminology above, references were made to the *Vishva Hindu Parishad. Eva Hellman's* chapter on anti-secularist Hinduism in India explores the ideas behind this movement. In particular, she presents and discusses the key concepts of *dharma* (law, principle, norm, righteousness), *Hindu samaj* (Hindu society, the collective of Hindus) and *Bharat* (India), which refer both to the sacred or divine and to the mundane or social sphere. Thus the VHP represents a challenge to the Western-influenced secularism of the Indian state. Hellman points out that these key Hindu concepts have been reformed and adapted by the VHP, which thus represents a new development – a 'dynamic Hinduism'. The organization holds that the role and responsibility of the *Hindu samaj* is to actualize *dharma* in *Bharat*. The holy land and nation is personified in the form of the goddess *Bharat Mata* (Mother India). Hellman argues that the establishment of a Hindu nation is the VHP's ultimate concern, which is thus located in the mundane or temporal sphere. The political and social role that, according to the VHP, should be accorded religious leaders or *sadhus* (good or holy men) may be compared to the decisive role of *fuqaha*, religious specialists in law, in the Islamic Republic of Iran. What *dharma* means in terms of norms of behaviour should be decided by a Religious Parliament, *Dharma Samsad*, with *sadhu* members ideally representing all Hindu denominations. Members of the VHP work systematically to arouse a Hindu identity so as to create an electorate voting 'Hindu'. Census figures show that this may not be an easy task. According to the 1981 census, 82 per cent of the Indian population was Hindu, but this included 'Untouchables' (15 percent). Moreover, for *savarna* Hindus (members of the four basic castes) identity based on caste, class or region may sometimes be more important than a Hindu identity. The attempts by the VHP to create a Hindu majority are associated with its role as an opposition movement, which aims to replace the present secular state with a confessional Hindu state. In the struggle for this state, political and metaphysical dimensions are equally important.

A basic distinction in terms of theology of religion may provide some possibilities for co-operation with Sikhs, Jains and Buddhists, who like Hindus are regarded as adherents of 'dharmic' religions.

Muslims and Christians, however, are members of 'non-dharmic' religions, and Muslims in particular are regarded as a serious threat to the struggle for a Hindu nation.[29] This religio-theological distinction notwithstanding, relations not only between Hindus and Muslims but also between Hindus and, among others, Sikhs have deteriorated in recent time. In his case study of Sikh religious nationalism in India *Ishtiaq Ahmed* emphasizes that the credibility of the Indian state as a secular-democratic polity has suffered a setback among important minorities. Despite its formally secularist ideology even the Congress Party has manipulated religion in its Punjab policies.[30] The Indian attack on the Golden Temple of Amritsar in 1984 caused an uproar among Sikhs all over the world, and many of them interpreted it as an assault on their religion. Those who support the idea of a separate state, *Khalistan* ('land of the pure'), argue that India is de facto a Hindu state, which discriminates against its minorities, and fear that under present conditions the Sikh identity is endangered. It is argued that Sikhs as a Nation function on the basis of the Sikh religion and attachment to Punjabi culture; hence many envisage that in a free *Khalistan* there would be no secularism and that Sikhism would regulate all aspects of life.

In some Asian countries, such as Burma, Sri Lanka and Thailand, the association between Buddhism and indigenous cultural values has been of great importance. Since the end of the colonial era the Buddhist religion has been used as an instrument of national integration. Most recently, more or less militant movements have tried to strengthen the political role of Buddhism, partly in struggles against minority groups like the Tamils of Sri Lanka, where elements of the Theravada tradition have been used as a legitimation for exclusive Sinhalese rights to the island. A conflict ideology, of great significance for contemporary Sinhalese demands, was developed by Anagarika Dharmapala (1864-1933) who claimed that Ceylon would become a *dhammadipa*, i.e. an island where Buddhism would flourish. This prophecy was to be fulfilled by the Sinhalese people. In a chapter on Buddhist activism in Sri Lanka *Bruce Matthews* traces the rise of various Sinhalese organizations and reviews the role of the Buddhist monastic order or *sangha*. The state is still, in theory, secular although, according to the constitution, Buddhism is the foremost religion and is guaranteed protection. In practice, the concept of *jathika chintanaya* (national ideology or way of life), which is identified largely with the hard-line Sinhalese cultural exclusivism and nationalism that emerged in the 1980s, has been used by anti-Tamil and anti-Western Buddhist activists, including monks, to further their aims of strengthening the political role of Buddhism.

The following chapter, written by *Mikael Gravèrs*, deals with Buddhism and politics in Burma (Myanmar) and illustrates the flexibility or elasticity of Buddhism there. In 1960 Prime Minister U Nu, who espoused a form of Buddhist socialism, committed himself and his party to making Buddhism the state religion of the country. This was unpopular with minorities such as the Christian Karens and one of the reasons for General Ne Win's coup two years later. The military regime officially returned to the policy of separating religion and the state. As a consequence, it abolished religiously inspired legislation and discontinued state financial support for religious activities. Yet Buddhism, which has become virtually synonymous with 'genuine' Burman ethnic identity, continued to be a fundamental political issue. Democracy and human rights have been rejected as foreign inventions alien to Burmese cultural and religious values, and minorities like Christians and Muslims have been severely oppressed. Recently 200,000 Muslims were expelled from the country. Buddhists who question the religious and moral legitimation of the autocratic regime aim to combine universal ethical values with a particularly Burman approach to democracy. In the opposition against this rule Buddhist monks, particularly young ones, have played a significant role. A symbolically powerful act of protest was launched in 1990 when monks turned their rice bowls upside down and refused to accept offerings from soldiers and their relatives.

The cases of Sri Lanka and Burma exemplify the important role religion plays in the global process of formation of identities and consequent strategies. The apparently increased significance of religion must be seen partly in relation to the problems of nationalism and ethnicism. Concurrently with a proclaimed adherence to universal values, differences in terms of history and culture enter the models of society and the strategies for construction of identities. Thailand provides another example of the problems and strategies of minorities in a country where religion and politics are closely linked. For a long time Buddhism has functioned as a national religion there and has been seen as a substantial tool in the promotion of unity. The adoption of a Theravada Buddhist version of confessional policy of religion has been resisted by ethnic minorities in northern Thailand, who have either reinforced indigenous beliefs or opted for missionary Christianity. In certain cases, e.g. among the Karen, this critical response to a confessional policy of religion has been strengthened by the rise of messianic movements, which are nurtured by certain mythical traditions common to many of these ethnic minorities. Politicized religion in northern Thailand thus expresses the search for a reinforced ethnic identity in a pluralistic cultural environment, where the government makes use of the majority religion as a means of national integration.[31]

In the context of modern religious developments the Philippines is more like Latin America than its Southeast Asian neighbours. After the ousting of Ferdinand Marcos in 1986 the expansion of more militant neo-fundamentalist church movements has been remarkable. In her chapter on this country *Susan Rose* explains the background and high-lights the political and religious implications of this development. Since the early 1980s there has been an influx of new Protestant missionary agencies. This is due to more indigenized versions of Catholic liberation theology reinforcing a Catholic critique of Marcos's autocracy and Protestant mainstream churches upholding democratic ideals. Some of these agencies propagated the Prosperity gospel. The unifying objective, however, was to counteract 'communism, Muslim terrorism and Catholic idolatry', which also included liberation theology. After Corazon Aquino restored democracy and opted for a more independent political course, neo-fundamentalism in the Philippines intensified its expansive mission. The triad of enemies – 'communism, Muslim terrorism and Catholic idolatry' – is the same even after 1989. In the Philippines 'communism' equals Maoism and is still seen as a relevant cause to counteract. Rose shows how Philippine fundamentalism openly propagates US political objectives and how organizational links with the new religious and political right in the United States are very strong. References are made both to Jerry Falwell and to the more charismatic Lester Sumrall. Although this is not her main concern, Rose hints at the positive response which US-inspired neo-fundamentalism has been able to enlist among certain sectors of the Philippine military.

In predominantly Muslim Malaysia, Indonesia and Afghanistan the problem of ethnicity and religious minorities is an important factor for the varying policies of religion. *Sven Cederroth's* chapter provides a comparative discussion of the influence of Islamism in the two Southeast Asian countries Malaysia and Indonesia. Although there are great similarities between the Malays of Malaysia and Indonesians, particularly the Javanese, the political position of Islam is radically different in the two countries. Whereas it is the state religion of Malaysia, Indonesia pursues a generally religious policy of religion. This is paradoxical because Muslims form only a little more than 50 per cent of the Malaysian population, whereas they number about 90 per cent of Indonesians. Cederroth argues that the dissimilarity in religious policy must be seen in the light of different historical experiences. Unlike Indonesians, Malays have been confronted with large-scale immigration of Chinese and Indian peoples, and an increasingly orthodox form of Islam became a unifying factor that distinguished the Malays from their non-Muslim competitors. In Indonesia a more 'mixed' form of Islam, influenced by several other religions, has become deeply rooted and there are strong political forces opposed to the confessionalization of Islam championed by Islamist groups.

The political role of Islam in this part of Southeast Asia may be compared, for example, to that in Nigeria and Senegal. In Nigeria 50 per cent of the population, as in Malaysia, are Muslims, while in Senegal, as in Indonesia, they form about 90 per cent. Yet Islam seems politically less strong in Senegal than in Nigeria, where the politically well-established Hausa and Fulani peoples of the north are the prime defenders of this religion and culture. There are strong elements of more orthodox forms of Islam, and the historical heritage of the Islamic state of Usuman dan Fodio, who in the early nineteenth century established the Sokoto caliphate, provides important inspiration for Nigerian Islamists today. As shown above, Islam in Senegal is still largely dominated by the 'mixed' Islam of the Sufi fraternities.

In her chapter *Asta Olesen* points out that Afghanistan has been dominated by the Pashtun majority, and that the question of the influence of non-Pashtun minorities is continuously a thorny issue. However, in the war against communist rule and Soviet occupation Islam served as a powerful unifying ideology. This struggle was almost unanimously legitimated in religious terms as a *jihad* ('holy war'). Olesen outlines the historical and social background of the Islamic movement in Afghanistan and discusses its ideological basis and views on the Islamic state. As in other Sunni-dominated countries, Islamists here strongly condemn Sufism and are usually opposed to a politically decisive role of the *ulama*. The Islamic coalition government has introduced some Islamic regulations, but it is seriously divided on religious as well as on ethnic issues.

The case of Afghanistan illustrates the political use of the term 'fundamentalism' in the West. As long as Soviet troops occupied this country, people who resisted this occupation were seen as freedom fighters, but when they withdrew, Muslim fighters became 'fundamentalists'. After the fall of President Najibullah's regime, Hikmatyar became the fundamentalist *par excellence*, while the exalted guerrilla leader Massoud was depicted as a moderate. It appears, however, that in the Afghan struggles for power ethnic and personal conflicts are more important than Islamic ideological differences.

Notes

1. For some recent examples, see Augustine 1993; Björkman 1988; Caplan 1987; Jäggi & Krieger 1991; Kaplan 1992; Kepel 1991; Kepel 1993; Lawrence 1990; Marty & Scott Appleby 1991; Meyer 1989; Odermatt 1991; Pfürtner 1991; Riesebrodt 1990; Silberstein 1993; Westerlund 1992. An extensive list of references is found, e.g., in Stolz & Merten 1991: 109-26.
2. Starting with a volume entitled *Fundamentalisms Observed* (1991), the series editors of this project, Martin E. Marty and R. Scott Appleby, have produced six extensive

volumes, of which the third, *Fundamentalisms and the State: Remaking Polities, Economies and Militancy* (1993), is of particular interest in this context.

3. For two recent examples, see Muzaffer 1992 and D'Souza 1993.
4. It should be noted that there are still some Christians, especially in the United States, who use the term 'fundamentalism' as a proud self-designatioñ. See, e.g., Falwell 1989: 10.
5. In a recent article entitled 'The Phony Islamic Threat', Edward Said (1993: 62) convincingly argues that the prospects of an Islamic takeover are highly unlikely and therefore 'grotesquely exaggerated in the West'. See also Esposito 1992.
6. Shepard 1992: 281.
7. Lawrence 1990.
8. Meyer 1989: 65; Lawrence 1990: 229.
9. While the thesis that 'fundamentalists' are modern but not modernist is emphasized in the book by Lawrence (1990), Meyer (1989) and some other scholars are more ambivalent on that point.
10. Like Muslim and other 'fundamentalists', postmodernists and feminists are critical of certain aspects of the enlightenment project. For further discussion on Islam and postmodernism, see Ahmed 1992.
11. Esposito 1988: 169. Most of the writers who deal with Islamic groups in this book use the term 'Islamism' instead of 'fundamentalism'. The former term has become increasingly common, and one of its advantages is that it is, at least in some cases, a self-designation of Islamic groups.
12. Here we are indebted to Eva Hellman. For more detailed discussion, see Hallencreutz, Hellman & Westerlund 1992: 16 ff.
13. Juergensmeyer 1993: 4 ff.
14. For a recent study of Buddhism and politics in Tibet and among Tibetans in exile, see Hammar 1993.
15. See further, e.g., Jorgensen 1985.
16. Huntington 1993.
17. One may compare this with the important earlier role of many Sufi fraternities as channels for anti-colonial opposition.
18. For a recent study of the new 'revolutionary diplomacy' of the Sudanese Muslim Brotherhood, see Prunier 1992.
19. Mahmoud mentions, e.g., that in accordance with his 'anti-clerical' position, al-Turabi criticizes the Iranian institution of *vilayat-i faqih*, i.e. the idea that the religious leaders or specialists on the *sharia* should have a decisive political role.
20. 'Nous ne voulons pas répéter les formes historiques du passé de l'Islam. Je regarde le passé juste pour m'en inspirer, pour y prendre une certaine expérience, non pour y trouver un modèle formel' (Duteil 1992: 121).
21. A religious argument for the taking of many wives is that by doing so the *marabouts* spread their *baraka* (special divine blessing or power) to more descendants.
22. Despite the antagonism, however, there are also examples of co-operation – e.g., the Sufis sometimes have to hire Islamist teachers for their schools – and their is an increased attachment to Islamic law *within Sufism* too.
23. In this respect not even the state seems capable of competing very successfully.
24. Even an apparent exception like Zambia reinforces this picture.
25. For a study of the prosperity gospel in West Africa, see Hackett n.d.
26. Here again we are indebted to Eva Hellman. See further Hallencreutz, Hellman and Westerlund 1992: 30 ff.
27. For a special study of this geographical area, see Björkman 1988.
28. See Huntington's interesting discussion on 'the clash of civilizations' (Huntington 1993).
29. More mundane reasons for estrangement of a minority from the majority community – economic deprivation, socail discrimination and political victimization – are hardly

prevalent in this case. Rather, East Punjab is one of the most prosperous areas of India, and Sikhs are employed in disproportionately large numbers in state services.
30. Hovmeyr 1989.

References

Ahmed, A.S. 1992. *Postmodernism and Islam: Predicament and Promise.* London: Routledge.

Augustine, J.S. (ed.) 1993. *Religious Fundamentalism: An Asian Perspective.* Bangalore: South Asia Theological Research Institute.

Björkman, J.W. (ed.) 1987. *Fundamentalism, Revivalists and Violence in South India.* Delhi: Manohar.

Caplan, L. (ed.) 1987. *Studies in Religious Fundamentalism.* London: MacMillan.

Duteil, M. 1992. 'Un entretien avec Hasan al-Turabi', *Monde arabe: Maghreb-Machrek* (137), 116-22.

D'Souza, A. 1993. 'The Challenge of Fundamentalism: A Crisis in Understanding', *Annual Report 1993 of Uppsala Studies of Mission.*

Esposito, J.L. 1988. *Islam: The Straight Path.* Oxford University Press.

——. 1992. *The Islamic Threat: Myth or Reality?* Oxford University Press.

Falwell, J. 1989. 'I Am a Fundamentalist', *Fundamentalist Journal*, May 10.

Hackett, R.I. (n.d.) 'The Gospel of Prosperity in West Africa', forthcoming in R. Roberts (ed.), *Religion and the Transformation of Capitalism.* London: Routledge.

Hallencreutz, C.F., E. Hellman and D. Westerlund 1992. ' "Fundamentalism" och religionspolitik: En inledande problemorientering', in D. Westerlund (ed.), *Sekularism ifrågasatt: 'Fundamentalism' och religionspolitik i jämförande perspektiv, 11-36.* (Tro och Tanke 6.) Uppsala: Svenska Kyrkansforskningsråd.

Hammar, U. 1992. 'Buddhism och politik i Tibet och bland tibetanerna i exil', in D. Westerlund (ed.), *Sekularism ifrågasatt: 'Fundamentalism' och religionspolitik i jämförande perspektiv,* 195-208. (Tro ock Tanke 6.) Uppsala: Svenska Kyrkansforskningsråd.

Hovemyr, A.P. 1989. *In Search of the Karen King: A Study in Karen Identity with Special Reference to 19th Century Karen Evangelism in Northern Thailand.* (Studia Missionalia Upsaliensia 49.) Uppsala: Swedish Institute of Missionary Research.

Huntington, S.P. 1993. 'The Clash of Civilizations', *Foreign Affairs*, Summer, 22-49.

Jorgensen, J.G. 1985. 'Religious Solutions and Native American Struggles: Ghost Dance, Sun Dance, and Beyond', in B. Lincoln (ed.), *Religion, Rebellion, Revolution: An Interdisciplinary and Cross-Cultural Collection of Essays.* London: Macmillan; New York: St. Martin's Press.

Juergensmeyer, M. 1993. *The New Cold War? Religious Nationalism Confronts the Secular State.* (Comparative Studies in Religion and Society 5.) Berkeley, Los Angeles: University of California Press.

Jäggi, C.J. and D.J. Krieger 1991. *Fundamentalismus: Ein Phänomen der Gegenwart.* Zürich: Orell Füssli.

Kaplan, L. (ed.) 1992. *Fundamentalism in Comparative Perspective.* Amherst: University of Masachusetts Press.

Kepel. G. 1991. *La Revanche de Dieu: Chrétiens, juifs et musulmans à la reconquête du monde.* Paris: Seuil.

Kepel, G. (ed.) 1993. *Les politiques de Dieu.* Paris: Seuil.

Lawrence, B.B. 1990. *Defenders of God: The Fundamentalist Revolt against the Modern Age.* London: I.B. Tauris.

Marty, M.E. & R. Scott Appleby (eds) 1991. *Fundamentalisms Observed.* (The Fundamentalism Project 1.) University of Chicago Press.

Marty, M.E. & R. Scott Appleby (eds) 1993. *Fundamentalisms and the State: Remaking Polities, Economies, and Militance.* (The Fundamentalism Project 3.) University of Chicago Press.

Meyer, T. 1989. *Fundamentalismus: Aufstand gegen die Moderne.* Reinbek bei Hamburg: Rowohlt.

Muzaffar, C. 1992. 'Fundamentalist Fallacy', *Far Eastern Economic Review,* 23 April, 23.

Odermatt, M. 1991. *Der Fundamentalismus. Ein Gott – eine Wahrheit – eine Moral?* Zürich: Benziger.

Pfürtner, S.H. 1991. *Fundamentalismus. Die Flucht ins Radikale.* Freiburg im Breisgau: Herder Spektrum.

Prunier, G. 1992. 'Frères musulmans soudanais. Une nouvelle diplomatie révolutionnaire', *Islam et Sociétés au Sud du Sahara* 6, 5-16.

Riesebrodt, M. 1990. *Fundamentalismus als patriarchalischer Protestbewegung: Amerikanische Protestanten (1910-29) und iranische Shiiten (1961-79) im Vergleich.* Tübingen: Mohr.

Said E.W. 1993. 'The Phony Islamic Threat', *New York Times Magazine,* 21 Sept., 62-5.

Shepard, W. 1992. 'Comments on Bruce Lawrence's *Defenders of God'*, *Religion* 22, 279-85.

Silberstein, L.J. (ed.) 1993. *Jewish Fundamentalism in Comparative Perspective: Religion, Ideology, and the Crisis of Modernity.* New York University Press.

Stolz, F. and V. Merten (eds) 1991. *Zukunftsperspektiven des Fundamentalismus.* (Religion – Politik – Gesellschaft in der Schweiz 6.) Freiburg: Universitätsverlag.

Westerlund, D. (ed.) 1992. *Sekularism ifrågasatt. 'Fundamentalism och religionspolitik i jämförande perspektiv.* (Tro och Tanke 6.) Uppsala: Svenska Kyrkansforskningsråd.

Part I
THE AMERICAS AND EUROPE

CONSERVATIVE PROTESTANTISM, POLITICS AND CIVIL RELIGION IN THE UNITED STATES

Simon Coleman

'When a religion seeks to found its sway only on the longing for immortality equally tormenting every human heart, it can aspire to universality; but when it comes to uniting itself with a government, it must adopt maxims which apply only to certain nations. Therefore, by allying itself with any political power, religion increases its strength over some but forfeits the hope of ruling over all.'

– Alexis de Tocqueville[1]

This chapter deals with two important and striking features of North American religious activity: civil religion and the recent resurgence of conservative Protestant Christianity.[2] The juxtaposition of these two phenomena might initially appear to be paradoxical. Civil religion, after all, is concerned with the celebration of national values in a religious idiom that, at least in theory, can be understood and shared by all the citizens of the state. Ideally, it is a means of complementing sectarian or denominational religious faiths by providing an overarching and uncontroversial means of referring to transcendent norms. Conservative Protestantism, on the other hand – especially in its more fundamentalist varieties – has been marked throughout most of the twentieth century by a confrontational attitude towards other faiths and denominations. Thus, while civil religion is, by definition, mainstream, with an organic relationship to the history of the United States, conservative Protestantism has in its recent past been isolated from centres of power or general legitimacy within society as a whole.

Despite these differences, these two features of religion in the United States have become ever more intertwined since the late 1970s. There is extensive literature on both subjects which demonstrates the ways in which the generalized symbols of a nation can become appropriated by a particularistic religious movement as it aims to gain influence and power in both political and religious realms of society. We examine here, as an essential part of the equation, the changing attitudes of many conservative Protestants to the relationship between their faith and the notion of an active participation in politics. This issue is especially salient at a time when such religion has undergone a revival over the last few years, a revival that has taken many foretellers of the inevitable spread of secularization by surprise.[3]

Finally, the scope of the chapter is widened by discussing an important but little considered question regarding the fate of North American civil religion: given the global activities of many conservative Protestant missionaries, to what extent will the civil religious aspect of their message be reproduced or, alternatively, transformed in novel politico-religious contexts? This issue is addressed by means of a case study based on the activities of the Word of Life Foundation (*Livets Ord*) in Sweden. As an almost direct 'import' of American evangelical ideology to Scandinavia, the Word of Life retains orientations towards church-state relations which reflect many of the aims and experiences of conservative Protestants in the United States, but of course it expresses them in a very different institutional and cultural context.[4]

Civil religion in theory and practice

Before I move to an analysis of the history and contemporary activities of conservative Protestants, I must discuss further the concept of civil religion, and in the process describe some of the features of church-state relations in the United States. The term 'Civil Religion' was first used by Jean-Jacques Rousseau in *The Social Contract*. While it was therefore employed as early as the 18th century to refer to the religious dimension of a polity, it has become an important concept within the sociology and anthropology of religion through the work of a contemporary American scholar – Robert Bellah.[5] In a highly influential article originally published in 1967, 'Civil Religion in America',[6] as well as in subsequent publications, Bellah has attempted to define the notion of a civic faith and assess its significance in the history of the American republic. Essentially, it is seen as the generalized religion of the American way of life, existing with its own integrity alongside the more particularistic faiths of the denominations.[7] Robbins and Anthony summarize it as 'a complex of shared religiopolitical meanings that articulate a sense of common national purpose and that rationalize the needs and purposes of the broader community'.[8] Thus, while the religious and political spheres are structurally differentiated in the United States, civil religion provides a symbolic means of uniting the two in a separate realm of existence. Bellah notes, along with de Tocqueville himself, that the American political experience is founded on a fundamental ambiguity regarding the role of the state with regard to conditions of public morality: the notion of a virtuous republic in which the state regulates public morality conflicts with the *laissez-faire* ideal of a state acting merely as a neutral legal mechanism, restricting itself to maintaining the minimum framework of public order, According to this view, the inherent conflict has in the past been resolved by an assumption that the churches, along with civil religious values, will maintain a disciplined moral consensus. However, one of the great questions of the present, according to Bellah, is whether either institution will have the strength to continue to hold the republic together in the fact of increasing utilitarian individualism.

Specifically, American civil religion posits the notion that a democratic United States is the prime agent of God in history. The particular location and history of the country are linked to notions of transcendent meaning and legitimation in a way that is this-wordly and activist in its implications. The Puritan belief that America is renewing a covenant with God, and has a millennial calling to establish a Christian commonwealth, is combined with a doctrine uf religious liberty, and an optimistic Enlightenment belief in progress. Significant events within the history of the republic are interpreted and redefined in terms of such expectations: the Revolution can be seen as indicating a form of biblical exodus from Europe; with the Civil War, a theme of sacrifice and rebirth is incorporated, symbolized by the life and death of Lincoln.

For our purposes, four potential interrelated functions of civil religion are to be stressed. First, civil religion can provide a public manifestation of religion, as opposed to the more privatized orientations of particular faiths. Benton Johnson has argued that the increasing structural differentiation of private from public sectors, characteristic of contemporary societies, makes the general acceptance of a uniform sacred cosmos and moral order unlikely.[9] This claim raises the question of whether such a process is inevitable, and the extent to which it can be combated by the general normative canopy of civil religion.

Secondly, civil religion is ideally a means by which citizens of a nation-state represent their shared identity to themselves in symbolic, often ritualized, ways.[10] In the United States, the Stars and Stripes (the flag) is seen as a sacred object; a ritual calendar is provided by celebrations on Memorial Day, the Fourth of July, Thanksgiving, etc.; other important rituals involve the inauguration of Presidents, the President's annual address, and many sports events such as the Super Bowl; cemeteries to war dead or monuments like the Lincoln Memorial are important locations for civic piety; the founding myth of the country involves accounts of the travails of the Pilgrim Fathers and the revolt from European oppressors; finally, the sacred texts confirming national identity and aims are provided by the Declaration of Independence and the Constitution.

Thirdly, according to Bellah, civil religion is the medium through which citizens can maintain faith in common values in a society explicitly predicated on ideals of mutual tolerance and religious and cultural pluralism. Peter Berger[11] asserts that American society in the past has combined religious pluralism with moral unity, but that in the present such unity is threatened by the growth of disputes over moral issues such as abortion and the role of the military. As in point number one (above), this situation, if accurately characterized, poses a fundamental question: Is civil religion likely to be undermined, or will the latter's function become more important as a means of combating the fragmentation of national morality?

Finally, civil religion may provide one means by which to combat the forces of secularization by investing allegiance to the state with religious values. Berger argues that processes of secularization and pluralism reinforce each other: 'Secularization fosters the civic arrangements under which pluralism thrives, while the pluralism of world views undermines the plausibility of each one and thus contributes to the secularizing tendency.'[12] However, by taking cultural and religious pluralism into account, yet also celebrating the sacred nature of the nation, civil religion has at least the potential to provide a form of religious practice that can co-exist with the secularization of other areas of society.[13]

Church-state relations in the United States

As will be clear from the above, American civil religion has a complex relationship to the polity – a relationship that reflects the history of the United States. The separation of church and state specified in the Constitution guarantees the freedom of religion. In contrast to the formal situation in many European countries, therefore, the principle of *Cuius regio, eius religio* is explicitly undermined.[14] However, the United States is, in terms of both practice and belief, one of the most religious industrialized nations in the Western world. In contrast to many European countries no established symbols of the policy exist in the form of a monarchy or state church[15] and yet the values and rituals of civil religion provide a diffuse and unofficial means of articulating national identity.[16] Bellah states; 'Americans were a religious people and their public life ever gave expression to that fact, but they avoided any hint of establishment by opting for a neutral religious language that could give offense to none'.[17]

Such language is intended to be available for use by all in the political sphere since religion is not associated with any single political or religious stance.[18] Bellah's initial essay, indeed, concentrates on the use of religious imagery in the speeches of American presidents. For instance, in Kennedy's inaugural address of 20 January 1961, God is mentioned in three places. Bellah notes that Kennedy, born a Catholic, avoids any particularistic reference to Christ or Moses in favour of a suitably ambiguous and consequently all-embracing term for the deity.

Clearly, Bellah's concept of civil religion emerges out of a Durkheimian tradition. It stresses the notion that, from its earliest years, the American republic has articulated a collection of beliefs, symbols and rituals with respect to sacred things which provide a patriotic form of *conscience collective* – or at least its modern successor. However, such convictions should not be seen as a mere justification, on a transcendental plane, of American society: while the god of civil religion is believed to have a special concern for America, the country must act in such a way as to preserve its divinely-ordained covenant. It must, in other words, *deserve* to be a light to other nations. Without an awareness that the nation stands under a higher judgment, the tradition of civil religion is seen as potentially dangerous: the vision of America as the new Israel can provide a justification for mere imperialism.[19]

One of the problems with this notion of 'higher judgment' lies in the issue of who precisely is to decide what such higher ideas are, and whether particular forms of behaviour uphold or contradict their essential tenets. In addition, the civil religious tradition, as Bellah acknowledges, can under certain circumstances be appropriated by extreme or marginal groups. This latter realization highlights one of the problems of a Durkheimian sociology which stresses the close connection between religious ideas and the social order but fails to incorporate a theory of conflict between competing ideologies or interest groups within the same society. Robbins and Anthony assert: 'The decline of civil religiosity has set the stage for a sectarian reassertion of the ideal of the virtuous republic transformed into an explicitly theocratic version of itself'.[20] In the following we examine the extent to which conservative Protestants provide an example of such sectarian activity.

Civil religion and conservative Christianity: some initial comparisons

Though stripped of their particularistic connotations, the symbols and myths of civil religion retain a strong Judaeo- Christian flavour.[21] Such biblical themes as the establishment of a covenant with God, the acceptance of a missionary role in the world, and the coming of the millennium, parallel those emphasized in conservative Protestantism. Indeed, many of the elements of civil religion are echoed in rather more extreme forms among conservatives: the conviction concerning the exemplary nature of the country becomes instead a dualistic division of the world into forces for evil or good; the stress on the transcendent significance of historical events can be used to reinforce an eschatology implying the imminence of the 'Last Days'; the desire to articulate a public morality is converted into an insistence that conservative standards of behaviour are the only ones acceptable to a properly virtuous America.

The key difference between civil religion, as defined by liberal intellectuals such as Bellah, and much conservative ideology lies in their respective attitudes to cultural pluralism in general, and religious pluralism in particular. The liberal form of civic piety attempts to combine the expression of fundamental moral consensus with a recognition that a truly democratic religio-political context has to embrace differing, even conflicting, views. The logic of its conservative counterpart implies that a single moral and religious truth exists – and moreover one that, according to some believers, can be converted into political doctrines and actions. An irony is therefore evident with regard to the position of many conservatives, especially fundamentalists: their movements are permitted to exist and even flourish in a context of institutional pluralism, even when their views may be interpreted as being fundamentally opposed to the principle of tolerance.

For any group that is committed to widespread cultural revitalization, the symbols of nationhood can provide a tremendously powerful resource. Like all symbols, they are inherently ambiguous – and therefore open to multiple interpretation and appropriation – but also emotionally charged, since they define the moral centre of a differentiated and complex society. The anthropologist Victor Turner has noted that a symbol has the power to condense a rich diversity of meanings within the same physical form.[22] In Western societies such richness is derived from the historical resonances the symbol – manifested in physical form or as an idea – can accrue over time. Thus, conservative Protestants can adopt such civil religious symbols as the flag, the notion of the nation's missionary calling, or the blessing of the Founding Fathers, and attempt both to profit from their considerable resonances in the United States and to interpret such symbols in particularistic ways. In doing so, they can deny that they are presenting unusual or novel ideas, since they can claim they merely wish to move the nation back to 'traditional' mainstream values which are in danger of being forgotten.[23] The danger of this approach, as we shall see, is that it runs the risk of being severely criticized by those who can present radically different interpretations of the same central symbols. Like Bellah, conservatives are likely to agree that the 'divine covenant' is in danger of being broken, and that key areas of socialization and therefore moral revitalization involve the family, schools and churches – but their remedy is rather different from his vision of a pluralist yet unified republic.

The history of conservative Protestantism

We should now fill out the broad claims made above with a more detailed analysis of the reasons for conservative Protestantism's new-found confidence and motivation in the public sphere of American society. Initially, it must be stressed that conservatives do not in fact form a unified, homogeneous movement.[24] Conservative Protestantism contains within it a number of different, sometimes conflicting, some-times complementary, religious orientations – fundamentalist, evangeli-cal, Pentecostalist and charismatic. Fundamentalism has generally been marked by a stress on the need for biblical knowledge and an assertion that the words of the Bible are inerrant, i.e. literally true. Evangelicalism, according to most definitions, involves an acceptance of the Bible as the word of God but incorporates a slightly more flexible attitude towards its interpretation. Pentecostalism is the product of a revival that developed at the beginning of the 20th century. While its adherents tend to be fundamentalist in their attitude towards the Bible, they also stress the possibility of gaining the Gifts of the Spirit such as speaking in tongues. For present purposes, charismatics may be regarded as Christians who, like Pentecostalists, believe in the power of present manifestations of the Holy Spirit, but who choose to stay in 'mainline' congregations.

Overall, conservative Protestantism can be differentiated from liberal Christianity in the sense that it tends to see the Bible as without errors and directly applicable to present circumstances rather than the product of a particular time and culture. As a consequence, it tends to regard the complex hermeneutic approaches of many intellectual liberals as unnecessary or even dangerous, since they appear to value human in-terpretation above divine revelation.[25]

The emphasis on biblical authority, devotional piety, voluntarism, individual conscience and conversion has a long history in American culture, as is indicated by the 'Great Awakenings' of the eighteenth and nineteenth centuries. During much of the nineteenth century it formed a dominant stream in American religious life. However, urbanism, the growing power of scientific explanation and the emergence of new, critical methods of studying the Bible provided potential threats to such religion, and around the turn of the century those Christians who came to be known as fundamentalists began to set themselves apart, in op-position to the prevailing culture. By the 1920s conservative Protestants, and especially fundamentalists, had become ideological strangers in their own land.[26] Fundamentalists were marked by their scholasticism, strong ad-vocacy of biblical inerrancy, strident opposition to modernism, and mistrust of political attempts to better the social order. While many of the revivals of the 19th century were postmillennial, stressing the possibility of creating the millennium on earth, fundamentalists often preferred a premillennial notion that the world would inevitably decline until it came to an end, with only the just being saved from destruction. This encouraged a concern with creating an internally pure culture, sheltered from modernizing influences with its own schools, Bible colleges and radio stations.

In general an increased withdrawal of religious institutions from the public sphere occurred in the United States from the 1920s, and it is certainly the case that from this period evangelicals and fundamentalists were on the cultural and religious defensive. The ridicule poured on fundamentalism after the famous Scopes or 'Monkey' trial of 1925, which juxtaposed fundamentalist with evolutionary views of creation, did not encourage a desire to compromise with secular forces in society. However, this is not to say that conservative Protestants were inactive. Fundamentalism grew considerably during the 1930s, and radio programmes such as Charles Fuller's 'Old Fashioned Revival Hour' proved highly popular. Billy Graham became famous from the time of the Second World War as a broadly evangelical preacher who was to become respectable enough to act as an adviser to a number of presidents. Carl McIntire, the founder of the fundamentalist American Council of Christian Churches in 1941, spent the subsequent three decades attacking such perceived threats as ecumenism, Communism and Catholicism. The concern over Communism, especially, resonated with secular political concerns during and after the McCarthy era.[27] Nevertheless, up until the 1970s conservative Protestants were still either too internally fragmented or too concerned with maintaining internal purity to become an effective political force.

New-found confidence

In recent years, the movement known as the NCR (New Christian Right) or NRPR (New Religious and Political Right) has clearly managed to motivate enough conservatives to give its message a firm and recognizable profile in contemporary America.[28] Although by no means representing all of conservative Christianity, it constitutes a politically active orientation which has gained a new-found confidence within the national public arena. The reasons for such a rise in public profile are many, and involve a combination of aspects of American religious and political culture, historical events, the development of new media technologies and characteristics of conservative Protestantism itself.

Initially, it is possible to indicate certain features of contemporary America that have caused particular concern to such Christians, and served to unite them against the forces of 'secular humanism'. The latter has become, indeed, a catch-all term for what are perceived to be the evils of the contemporary world. Supreme Court judgments since the 1950s have increasingly taken religious pluralism into account, and decisions that have been intended by courts to be seen as religiously neutral have been interpreted by fundamentalists and evangelicals as specifically opposed to conservative aims. Private prayer, for instance, has been removed from the syllabus in state-run schools. In addition, signs of sexual permissiveness are perceived to be evident in the spread of pornography, the apparent decline in the nuclear family and the legalization of abortion.

Such apparent indicators of moral decline have occurred at a time when the United States in general has suffered considerable blows to its self-esteem. The countercultural movements of the 1960s, Vietnam and the Watergate scandal have provided even secular patriots with considerable food for thought, as they contemplate the country's allegedly exemplary role in world history. The historian of fundamentalism, George Marsden, has argued that conservative Protestants actually benefitted from the emergence of countercultural movements in the 1960s, since the latter questioned the legitimacy of the mainline liberal establishment without providing a lasting counter-establishment of their own: 'Confronted with the crisis in authority in a changing and pluralistic society, evangelicals could point to the sure certainty of the word of God.... Evangelicals generally could draw on the immense residual prestige of the Bible in America as a firm rock in a time of change.'[29] The religio-political conservative revival can therefore be seen as providing a form of reinvigorated populism at a time when patriotic sentiments have been under threat. It has gained strength, in other words, from being a kind of 'counter-counter-culture'. Furthermore, when an evangelical, Jimmy Carter, became President in the mid-1970s, this indicated that such a firm personal religious belief was not a fatal liability in standing for national public office.[30] According to Flowers, Carter was very concerned to separate private faith from public office – a distinction that was generally less important to Ronald Reagan, as we shall see.[31]

Apart from the general contextual points mentioned above, it should be emphasized that certain factors have recently allowed conservatives to make their voice heard in unprecedentedly strident ways. The South – traditional stronghold of conservatives – has became more affluent in recent decades, partly owing to the spread of industry from the North into cheaper and less regulated areas of the country. More and more conservatives have been able to purchase the media technology necessary for widespread evangelization, and have been inclined to take advantage of such technology to a much greater extent than liberals. The latter, less committed to overt spiritual evangelization, have tended rather to become involved in social work projects, and often mistrust 'simple' unnuanced ways of broadcasting the message of the Gospels. Many conservatives, on the other hand, are more than willing to use both radio and television to evangelize, given their belief in the saving powers of the Word[32] and their willingness to engage in rationalized forms of revival.[33] Furthermore, even if the actual numbers of conservative Protestants make up a relatively small minority of the total population,[34] those who are committed to using the public airways can of course give the impression of representing a huge constituency of followers.

As we shall see, for many conservatives, engagement in politics or the accumulation of wealth are no longer seen as compromises with the secular world: rather they are the means by which to take over secular institutions, and assimilate them to fundamentalist or evangelical ends. This view has encouraged conservatives to become more explicit in their adoption of a more positive orientation towards material success and optimism regarding progress. Such a shift in position has been especially evident through the emergence of the so-called Faith Movement, which is committed to the notion of 'Prosperity Theology' and what one of its leaders, Kenneth Copeland, calls the 'Laws of Prosperity'. The Bakkers, while making their name as TV evangelists, also set up a huge Christian theme park, on the model of Disneyworld, called 'Heritage USA'. Even the doctrine of Creationism, the totemic marker of fundamentalist separation in the 1920s, has been renamed Creation Science in an attempt to make it fit the categories of wider society. Rather than making a virtue out of being a misunderstood and isolated minority – their orientation for much of this century – many conservatives have come to regard the resources of 'the world' as neutral, and therefore able to be put to good or evil uses. Money, music, politics and the symbols of national piety, such as those that make up the complex of ideas behind civil religion, are waiting to be claimed for God's purposes.[35]

Nevertheless, it must be emphasized that not all conservative Protestants have chosen to re-enter the public sphere. Some prefer to wait for the millennium, content to remain aloof from what is seen as a corrupted and corrupting world. In a sense, of course, political or other public activity provides a dilemma for those premillennialists who believe in the inevitable decline of morality until the Second Coming. As Cox puts it, 'Fundamentalism has never been able to decide whether to gather at the river and await the rapture or to invade the citadels of sin with the Sword of the Lord in hand.'[36] Falwell himself, the leader who for some time came most of all to represent the involvement of fundamentalism in political life, denied in his early career that he could ever become involved in anything other than 'preaching the pure saving gospel of Jesus Christ.'[37] Pat Robertson, presidential candidate for the 1988 election, denied at least as late as 1983 that he was seriously interested in politics.[38]

The battle to define civil religion

The aim of activist conservative Protestants is essentially to establish a complementary relationship between piety and patriotism.[39] Just as the Founding Fathers of the republic can be presented as directly reflecting the will of God, so can the conservatives of the present. Traditional morality, a combination of biblical and American virtues, is seen as a fixed and unambiguous point of reference:

> The Movement remains committed to synthesizing selected Christian theological judgments with specific conceptions of how a democracy ought to function. In working toward this objective, the New Right believes that it carries the authority of both the Bible and the guiding philosophical principles of the nation's Founding Fathers.[40]

In constructing a vision of America's past which in effect legitimates action in the present, conservatives construct a 'counter mythology' to the interpretation of American history put forward by liberals.[41] This involves considerable mutual accusation: 'Within each coalition one may note the claims or the implication that they are the true patriots or, conversely, that the other has un-American, antidemocratic, and even totalitarian tendencies.'[42]

The attempts of conservative Christians to re-enter the public realm of American life have been greatly aided by their skilful use of the mass media, as well as the setting up of pressure groups aimed at lobbying government institutions. The public profile of the NCR has been spearheaded in many respects by TV evangelists of varying persuasions, who may not represent the views of all conservatives but who have access to the most significant means of symbolic production. According to Packard, the TV gospel shows combined may reach a total of sixty-one million people per year, but such estimates are notoriously hard to make.[43] Many of these gain purely local constituencies within certain states or regions, but in this chapter I am concentrating on those preachers who have developed their media ministries throughout the whole nation. Although they are often classed together, in fact such evangelists represent varying theological persuasions: Jerry Falwell is a fundamentalist who is neither Pentecostal nor charismatic, and has publicly critized the practice of speaking in tongues; Jimmy Swaggart, Pat Robertson and Jim Bakker are 'fundamentalist Pentecostals'; Oral Roberts is charismatic but not a Pentecostalist as such; Robert Schuller is actually a Reformed Church Minister who would not class himself as fundamentalist but who preaches a form of 'possibility thinking' that echoes the assumptions behind much of prosperity theology. While Falwell is both a minister of a local church and a media evangelist, a preacher like Robertson now concentrates on para-church activity, in effect locating his ministry within the media.

Falwell has been a key figure in the construction of a political face for the NCR, acting as a mediator between fellow conservative Protestants, between Protestants and religious conservatives from other faiths, and between religious and political activists. He was a friend of Menachem Begin and frequently expresses his love for Israel. Having started his ministry in a bottling plant in Lynchburg, Virginia, in 1956, he has built up a church with a membership of many thousands, as well as a Christian school, a Baptist college and a home for alcoholics.[44] In 1981 services from his church were broadcast to 392 TV stations and 600 radio stations. He is most famous for co-founding and becoming the president of the Moral Majority in 1979. This was an organization based in Washington DC which built up a network of some 72,000 pastors and 40,000 lay members.[45] As its name implies, the aim of the organization was not only to put moral issues on the public agenda, but also to imply that its values and attitudes were both populist and popular within the country as a whole. Rather than accepting a status as a misunderstood minority group, it wished to present itself as representing the traditional, mainstream values of the nation. Accordingly, it attempted to mobilize conservative Christians politically, both by encouraging them to vote *en bloc* on highlighted issues, and by recruiting Christians who were willing actually to stand for public office. Numerous related organizations were set up under its umbrella, with such names as the Committee for the Survival of a Free Congress, Young Americans for Freedom and the National Conservative Political Action Committee. After the success of Reagan in the 1980 election, the Moral Majority was able to claim that it represented a powerful political force, and felt encouraged enough to introduce a rating system of political candidates.[46] The means of testing the moral standards of candidates included such questions as: 'Do you agree that this country was founded on a belief in God and the moral principles of the Bible? Do you consider that this country has been departing from those principles and needs to return to them?' Such activity seems, as noted earlier, to contradict the old fundamentalist emphasis on the reform of individual hearts and souls; it is accepted, apparently, that society-wide legislation is also important in creating the America of the future.

One of the most significant aspects of the Moral Majority, apart from its activist approach to politics, was its aim of attracting a constituency beyond that of conservative Christianity *per se*. Its leaders tried to construct an identity and therefore an appeal which transcended any single denominational affiliation. Accordingly, Falwell chose, as far as was possible, to keep his role as a fundamentalist minister separate from his involvement in the organization, even though the latter's grass-roots support came primarily from evangelicals and fundamentalists. This attempt to articulate a generally conservative religious organization over and above denominational ties ultimately did not succeed in divesting itself of its purely fundamentalist origins. Bruce has pointed out that such interest-groups as conservative Catholics shared NCR positions on abortion, tax-relief for Christian schools and opposition to gay rights; but they could not forget the previously anti-Catholic statements of Protestant NCR supporters.[47] The Moral Majority also received criticism from fundamentalists themselves, such as strictly separatist organizations like Bob Jones University. As Billy Graham had been before him, Falwell was accused of diluting the uncompromising message of the Gospels. By 1986, the Moral Majority had changed its name to the Liberty Federation.

Other conservative Protestant groups were founded in the same year as the Moral Majority, which in combination with its activities attempted to assert an influence beyond the purely religious realm. The Christian Voice, based in Pasadena, California, was formed in order to lobby in the political sphere and enable conservative candidates to win election to public office. Such ambitions were aided by the Christian Broadcasting Network (CBN), Pat Robertson's television company, which granted it free advertizing time. It claimed to have enlisted both Catholic and Protestant ministers, and to have enrolled not far short of 200,000 members. Various conservative members of Congress have served on its advisory committee. Bruce quotes from some of its literature:

America was founded by men of faith on Biblical principles! Virtually all of our founding fathers recognized the crucial importance of religious morality as the foundation for our liberty and social well-being.... Not only is it our civic duty but, more importantly, our Biblical imperative to be God's standard-bearer in the affairs of our nation.[48]

The Religious Roundtable, meanwhile, based in Arlington, Virginia, was founded in September 1979 by Ed McAteer, a southern Baptist. The organization has consisted of a select group of fundamentalist leaders and leaders of the New Right in general, and acted as a think tank for conservative ideas.

The most direct foray into the political realm has been provided by Pat Robertson, who has made his name through the leadership of CBN. As early as April 1980 he co-chaired Washington for Jesus Day with Bill Bright, President of the Campus Crusade for Christ. This attracted an attendance of some 200,000 and was marked by its repeated equation of America with Israel. Capps describes Robertson's general position as follows: 'A blending of American aspirations and Protestant Christian faith, Robertson's message is calculated to be strongly appealing to an electorate that cherishes boldness, strong convictions, resolute authority, and... protection of the American way of life.'[49] Robertson showed sufficient confidence in the widespread popularity of his message to put himself forward as a presidential candidate for the Republican Party. Interestingly, however, in this capacity he chose to represent himself not as a sectarian religious leader but as an ideal American citizen in secular as well as spiritual terms. This involved stressing his non-religious qualifications – as an entrepreneur, the son of a senator, a soldier in Korea and a graduate of Yale. He went so far as to relinquish his ordination in order to mitigate the potential liability of being labelled a Pentecostalist preacher, while Paul Weyrich, his political strategist, attempted to present his vocation as a profession just like any other.[50] Presenting Washington as corrupt yet 'redeemably bad',[51] he attempted to ensure that his attacks on crime, schools and illegitimacy did not appear simultaneously to be attacking blacks (that is, a vulnerable minority group). Unfortunately for Robertson, scandal over the activities of the Bakkers emerged during his campaign and he found it extremely difficult to disassociate himself from the criticism aimed at televangelists evident at this time.

The strategies of both Falwell and Robertson demonstrate a wider trend among activist conservative Protestants – a renewed sensibility to their public image as they have moved the boundaries of acceptable activity more and more into the conventionally secular realm. In effect, they are concerned with the production of a Goffmanesque presentation of a 'civic self' that is likely to appeal not only to members of fundamentalist or evangelical denominations but to other citizens within American society.[52] They have learned to tone down their more 'offensive' aspects, such as accusing others of sin, heresy, and immorality, and have publicly underplayed elements of absolutism in order to pander to pluralist ideals present in the society as a whole. To combat such a strategy, liberal pressure groups, such as People for the American Way, deliberately monitor statements made by preachers like Falwell, Robertson and Swaggart in order to point to differences they perceive between the public and private faces of such men.

The alliance between religion and politics

Just as the relatively deregulated nature of the American media has allowed religious conservatives to take over radio and cable TV stations, so the decentralized nature of the political system has permitted the targetting of local political elections by well-organized interest groups.

What matters in such contexts is the ability to activate a sufficiently large and dense network of people who are prepared to cast their votes in the same way. Certainly, one of the factors behind the recent prominence of conservative Protestantism has been its relative willingness to align itself with secular conservatives in a marriage of mutual convenience. Two of its chief organizers – Richard Viguerie, a fundraiser and expert in direct mailing techniques, and Paul Weyrich – have strong contacts within the realm of secular politics. In effect, therefore, the NCR (New Christian Right) must be seen in the wider context of the growth of the NR (New Right).

Both secular and religious conservatives are concerned at the apparent threat to regional autonomy posed by the increasing power of the state, and yet both benefit from the technology which has acted as one of the chief means by which such centralization is occurring. Both wish to assert a new form of patriotism after the disillusionments of the 1960s and '70s, and are in favour of more military spending but less funding for welfare programmes. Furthermore, many of the preachers represent fine exemplars of the conservative American dream, as their ministries can be presented as enterprises built up by hard work and entrepreneurship from few resources.[53]

Many religious conservatives support the separation of church and state to the extent that they are unlikely to recommend the creation of an exclusively Christian party as such. However, they do with their moral agenda influence the existing political parties:

> By combining the ideological themes of economic libertarianism, special traditionalism, and militant anti- Communism with an organizational strategy featuring extensive networking, independent political initiative such as political action committees, and an aggressive direct mail campaign, the New Right courts a growing constituency of corporate conservatives and Americans worried about the nation's perceived economic and moral decline.[54]

While the religious periphery, in the form of fundamentalists and evangelicals, have therefore moved closer to the political and economic centres of power, in some ways the centre has also moved to the periphery in order to accommodate them. When Ronald Reagan won re-election in 1984, he cultivated votes by suggesting – without wishing to appear overtly sectarian – that he favoured the causes of the NCR. For instance, he gave leading pastors, including Falwell, prominent positions in the Dallas nominating convention. In addition, both he and conservative Christians were keen to be seen together in photographs or in the media generally. It is, however, difficult to assess to what extent this apparent support from Reagan had more to do with the cultivation of an electorally successful image than any personal spiritual conviction, and it is certainly the case that, with regard to federal legislation, the NCR has had little success over the reintroduction of private prayer into schools or the prevention of abortion. Admittedly, such conservative colleagues as Senators Jesse Helms and Orrin Hatch attack liberal and 'secular – humanist' policies by making it difficult for Congress to give financial support to such causes. However, Warner notes that the impact of politicized evangelicalism on the elections of 1980 and 1984 has often been exaggerated (not least by evangelicals themselves as well as their opponents) even if religious conservatives did help to win some congressional races.[55]

In the latest election campaign, the rhetoric of the Religious Right has again made its presence felt. 'God', as Wills memorably puts it,[56] 'was the favorite delegate' at the Republican convention – a convention at which Pat Buchanan, himself an original challenger to Bush for their party's nomination, gave a speech remarkably similar to one he had delivered only a few months earlier at Falwell's Liberty College. Most significantly for the purposes of this chapter, Pat Robertson had participated in conducting a rally at the convention, perhaps signalling his readiness to be considered as a serious candidate for the 1996 elections. Overall, Wills stresses the way Republican campaigns have moved their main line of attack, in a post-Cold-War world, to focus on the *internal* enemies of conservative America, as exemplified by the pro-minority values of the Clintons, and such a horror of liberal attitudes continues to fall easily into line with NCR principles.

The globalization of civil religion

Recent events have not, admittedly, proved entirely favourable for the NCR in the United States. The Republicans have been removed from the White House, and the collapse of the Communist states of Eastern Europe, while apparently providing proof of the unworkability of atheist ideologies, has also of course removed a 'significant other' against which conservative Protestants have been able to articulate a powerful sense of identity and mission. However, the past few years have also demonstrated the essential flexibility of the NCR's civil religious message, illustrating its ability to incorporate and, in effect, mythologize occurrences in the present. Most obviously, the Gulf War and the subsequent victory parade in Washington have confirmed the moral and military superiority of the United States, while also justifying its citizens' continued duty to intervene in events far beyond its own shores.

Furthermore, the exploitation of modern media technologies as well as opportunities to travel facilitate the spread of the evangelical message to cultural contexts far *beyond* America itself. This situation raises an intriguing question regarding American civil religion, as expressed by fundamentalists or evangelicals: what will happen as the symbols of national identity developed for use within the United States are carried to other countries as part of the ideological package of conservative Protestant doctrine? In other words, how can a parochial mythology, constructed to celebrate the transcendent qualities of a particular nation state, be adapted to a globalizing process (in this case, evangelization) which bypasses national boundaries?

This is a question that cannot be answered fully here. However, I wish to give a preliminary indication of the issue involved by describing the case of the Word of Life foundation, based in Uppsala, Sweden – an organization within which I have carried out fieldwork since 1986.[57] The group maintains extensive connections with one branch of the north American NCR – the 'Faith' movement – both inviting preachers from the United States to speak at its conferences and selling considerable quantities of books, cassettes and videos manufactured by such preachers as Kenneth Hagin, Kenneth Copeland and Lester Sumrall.[58]

The doctrines and aims of the Word of Life, as expressed by Swedish preachers such as Ulf Ekman, in effect represent a form of 'internationalization' of American civil religion, as it has been articulated by conservative Protestants. Notions of a national 'calling', the significance of the millennium, and the creation by spiritual 'pioneers' of widespread moral revitalization, are taken up and relocated to have salience in the Swedish context. Of course, these notions are all contained within the broad Judaeo-Christian heritage, but what is striking is the way the Word of Life, in common with American groups, combines them with an orientation towards society that I have defined as 'assimilationist' rather than isolationist. Furthermore, while it is inappropriate for the Swedish group to refer to specific aspects of American history, it has adopted an attitude towards religious and economic entrepreneurship that is clearly American in origin. The following is a passage taken from a conference sermon given by Ekman in 1987:

> The Lord's glory shall come from north, south, east and west. North means here. The Lord's glory will... run like syrup down to Europe. South is South Africa... Preachers from the west... have come here from the USA. The east – you know what is happening in South Korea.... The Gospel will reach the whole world through TV, radio, preachers, etc.[59]

One implication of this statement is that a world-wide revival is under way. In addition, however, it implies that such a revival is being constructed through an evangelical division of labour, according to which each part of the globe is the responsibility of a particular set of preachers. As Ekman says elsewhere:

> God has given people different areas of the earth to look after. He's

given us Sweden. When God gives people responsibility for something. He also gives them pride in their responsibility. That's what
we call nationalism.... Just as people have a specific identity so
do nations, and we need to rediscover that identity. God has given
Sweden a special responsibility and a special task. We are a little
country in terms of population, but our influence is, and has always
been, considerable over the world around us. God has made sure
of that. So we must understand that and take our responsibility.[60]

These ideas are graphically illustrated by the cover of the group's newsletter for September 1985, which shows a picture from a recent conference
held by the Word of Life. On the podium stand participants at the
conference, each waving the national flag of a different country. Ekman
stands at the front with the Swedish flag, with the American preacher
Jim Kaseman close beside him, waving the Stars and Stripes.

At the end of his original essay on civil religion, Bellah speculates
on the possibility of a world civil religion one day coming into existence.[61]
In a sense, the Word of Life demonstrates one of the ways in which
this can occur, but does so in a way that is not in accordance with
Bellah's expectations. The group encourages the particularistic celebration of a nation state, Sweden, while providing a functional equivalent
to the conservative Protestant version of American civil religion. Sweden
is thus presented as having its own special vocation within a world
order of revitalized nation states.

However, if the United States is notable for its pluralism, re–
publicanism and separation of church and state, Sweden has retained
a relative cultural homogeneity, a monarchy and an established church.
The Word of Life's message of organizational autonomy, positive thinking and prosperity, while perhaps adapted to the style of many American
denominations, has little grass-roots support or resonance in the Swedish
religio-political context as it is constituted at present.[62]

Proponents of the NCR in the United States have attempted to gain
influence in society by linking their aims and actions to mainstream
forms of influence, including politics. One of the methods used to
legitimate such actions has involved explicit or implicit appeal to the
ideals of American civil religion: conservative Protestantism is said
to defend the 'traditional' values of the Founding Fathers, and celebrate
true American patriotism in defiance of the secular forces of Communism
or other threatening ideologies. The message is also expansionist, as
we have seen, both in the sense that it implies that the United States
has a 'calling' to influence other nations and in the sense that its civil
religious message can be adapted to local cultural circumstances far
from the United States itself.

A movement like the NCR has become of general interest to scholars not only because of its visibility, but because it has attempted to make its activities relevant to areas of life other than those that can be classed as purely religious. While surprisingly successful in the short term, there is no doubt that this attempt is marked by a number of internal contradictions. First, as we have seen, the American context is marked by an explicit commitment to pluralism – which permits movements such as the NCR to exist, but is unlikely to give widespread legitimation to its aims. Secondly, while conservative Protestants appeal to notions of a golden age unmarked by the secular ravages of modernity, they use the most up-to-date products of technology in highly rationalized ways in order to articulate this message. As a result of such 'para-church' activities, they run the risk of reinforcing the very problems they seek to redress. Televangelism, for instance, cannot provide a functional equivalent for the bonds of community ideally created by a neigh- bourhood church, nor can it assess the extent to which its aim of achieving a moral consensus among its consumers is achieved in practice. Thirdly, in order to achieve influence – or the appearance of it – in a democratic society, any minority group has to be able to claim that it has the backing of a substantial constituency. In line with this, groups such as the Moral Majority have attempted to recruit non-Protestants to lend their support to morally conservative issues. In doing so, they establish a contradiction between their internal aims of world-wide conversion to an exclusive, coherent and particularistic faith and their externally oriented strategy of suppressing certain characteristics of their message in order to be able to co-operate with others. And fourthly, within conservative Protestantism, especially fundamentalism, the attempt to improve the world by human means contradicts the belief held by some that the material world is inevitably doomed to decline and destruction, and therefore should be ignored rather than transformed.

All of these contradictions relate to the fact that the NCR represents a minority pressure group attempting to make its voice heard in a society it cannot control. The anthropologist Shirley Ardener has noted that 'muted', or minority, groups are often forced to adopt dominant modes of expression if they wish others to hear or even comprehend their points of view.[63] It can be argued that the attempt by the NCR to appropriate the symbols of civil religion represents just such a situation, and therefore contains the inherent dangers of this strategy. In being translated into terms acceptable to others, the conservative message may be transformed to a possibly irrevocable degree – to the extent that some conservatives may come to regard it as a travesty of their values and aims. As we have seen, Bob Jones University will have little truck with Falwell's 'ecumenical' attempts to gain influence. In addition, the more the message of the NCR is heard, the more it can be challenged by others who can also use the open conditions of American society to make their own case heard. If Young Americans for Freedom are challenged by People for the American Way, which one represents the 'true' America?

We have seen that conservative Protestantism, as a whole, is not a unified movement – rather, it contains a number of differing, often mutually contradictory, orientations. If it is difficult to characterize the movement itself in simple terms, it is even harder to compare it to other so-called religious revivals or fundamentalisms, such as those evident in the Islamic world. However, it seems that such revivals raise some broadly similar issues for scholars concerned with religion. Increasingly, they force us to re-consider the nature of religious authority in contemporary nation-states. In addition, we are obliged to explore the many ways in which a religion that stresses rigid internal coherence and consensus on a doctrinal level can be maintained in a world that is increasingly becoming subject to cultural fragmentation and ideological pluralism.

Notes

1. Toqueville 1969: 294. Also quoted in Myers 1986: 9.
2. For the purposes of stylistic brevity, 'America' refers in this paper to the United States.
3. See Cox 1984: 11.
4. For a detailed discussion of this issue, see Coleman 1993.
5. Somewhat ironically, Bellah himself has now stopped using the term 'Civil Religion'. In 1989: 147 he argues that the definitional debate over the term has prevented discussion of the substantive issues involved.
6. This article first appeared in *Daedalus* 96: 1 – 21.
7. Herberg's *Protestant, Catholic, Jew* shows how mainstream religious sentiment in the United States has been prevented from taking a purely Christian direction by the influence of Judaism in the country.
8. Robbins and Anthony 1982: 10.
9. Johnson 1982: 51-66.
10. Connerton 1989: 64 makes the point that the principle of 'modernity' denies the idea of life as a structure of celebrated recurrence, since integral to it is 'the transformation of all signs of cohesion into rapidly changing fashions of costume, language and practice'.
11. Berger 1982: 18. See also the main thesis of Herberg 1955.
12. Berger 1982: 15.
13. As David Westerlund has pointed out to me, such an orientation walks a tightrope between resisting secularization and accepting its widespread diffusion.
14. Implying, in other words, that religious legitimacy is appropriated by the temporal power. See also Wood 1983.
15. Hill 1983: 110 – 12.

16. John Wilson 1979 criticizes Bellah for never satisfactorily specifying whether civil religion can be seen as a separate, constant, differentiated religion in itself or rather a more general dimension of society as a whole.
17. Bellah 1975: 45.
18. As will be made clear later in this chapter, whether such an intention is realized is open to question.
19. Bellah was writing, of course, in the shadow of Vietnam.
20. Robbins and Anthony 1982: 19.
21. This is a point made by Gamoran 1990: 254.
22. Turner 1967: 45 – 46.
23. Compare Hobsbawm and Ranger 1983: 1 – 14.
24. The term 'conservative Protestant' contains some ambiguity. Originally, the conservatism of such groups could be characterized as largely theological as opposed to political, i.e. reacting in opposition to liberal interpretations of the Bible.
25. Bruce 1984; Forstorp 1990: 163.
26. Compare Hill 1983: 112 – 22.
27. Marsden 1982: 155.
28. The word 'movement' is a slightly misleading way to describe what is in reality an internally-differentiated network of groups, many of whom distrust the notion of centralized authority.
29. Marsden 1982: 157.
30. It may be that the Jesus Movement played a significant part in making enthusiastic, charismatic worship more acceptable in wider circles than ever before.
31. Flowers 1983.
32. See Coleman 1991b: 14.
33. See Frankl 1987.
34. Bruce notes: 'Very roughly speaking, of the approximately 33 million members of the twelve largest Protestant denominations, one third were in evangelical, fundamentalist, or pentecostal denominations' (1990: 22). Nielsen ratings from 1986 give the various individual televangelists audiences of between nearly 2,000,000 to a little under 350,000.
35. Attitudes towards the secular world do vary. Falwell, for instance, although accepting the need for material wealth in order to evangelize, disapproves strongly of what he considers to be immodest styles of dress, or inappropriate popular music.
36. Cox 1984: 48.
37. Marsden 1982: 55.
38. Bruce 1988: 129.
39. Conservative Protestants have not been the only religious activists to use a civil religious idiom. In recent years, the Moonies have produced their own version of the sacred mission of the United States.
40. Capps 1990: 3.
41. See e.g. Heliz 1983; Wuthnow 1988.
42. Hunter 1883: 160.
43. Packard 1988: 170 – 180. See also Bruce 1988: 47; 1990: 96 – 106.
44. In 1988 Falwell invited Oliver North, whom he describes as a true patriot, to address his Liberty University.
45. Described in Wood 1980.
46. See Packard 1988: 205.
47. Bruce 1988: 87.
48. Bruce 1988: 83.
49. Capps 1990: 159.
50. Capps 1990: 174.
51. Wills 1990: 65.
52. Compare Coleman 1989: 229.

53. This is a point made by Falwell in his book *Listen, America!* in which he explicitly states that the free enterprise system is recommended in the Bible.
54. Liebman and Wuthnow 1983: 6.
55. Warner 1988: 297-301.
56. Wills 1992: 12.
57. Coleman 1991b; 1993.
58. Although the 'Faith' movement has tended not to be explicitly political, it nevertheless has stressed the strategic importance of the United States as an exemplary force for good throughout the globe.
59. Also quoted in Gustafsson 1987: 56.
60. Ekman 1985: 1.
61. Bellah 1967: 18.
62. For more detailed discussions, see Coleman 1989: 1991a; 1991b.
63. Ardener 1978.

References

Ardener, S. 1978. *Defining Females: The Nature of Women in Society*. London: Croom Helm.

Barker, E. 1984. *The Making of a Moonie: Choice or Brainwashing?* Oxford: Basil Blackwell.

Bellah. R. 1967. 'Civil Religion in America', *Daedalus* 96, 1-21.

——. 1970. *Beyond Belief: Essays on Religion in a Post-Traditional World*. New York: Harper and Row.

——. 1975. *The Broken Covenant*. New York: Seabury.

——. 1989. 'Comment on 'Twenty Years After Bellah: Whatever Happened to American Civil Religion?' by James A. Mathison, *Sociological Analysis* 50 (2), 147.

Berger. P. 1982. 'From the Crisis of Religion to the Crisis of Secularity', in M. Douglas and S. M. Tipton (eds), *Religion and America: Spirituality in a Secular Age*, 14-24. Boston: Beacon Press.

Bruce, S. 1984. *Firm in the Faith*. Aldershot: Gower.

——. 1988. *The Rise and Fall of the New Christian Right: Conservative Protestant Politics in America 1978-1988*. Oxford: Clarendon Press.

——. 1990. *Pray TV: Televangelism in America*. London: Routledge.

Capps, W.H. 1990. *The New Religious Right: Piety, Patriotism and Politics*. Columbia: University of South Carolina Press.

Coleman, S.M. 1989. 'Controversy and the Social Order; Responses to a Religious Group in Sweden'. Unpublished Ph.D. thesis, Cambridge University.

——. 1991a. 'Broadcasting the Faith: Evangelicalism and Modernity in Sweden', *Religion Today* 6 (1), 15-18.

——. 1991b. ' "Faith which Conquers the World": Swedish Fundamentalism and the Globalization of Culture', *Ethnos* 56, 1-2, 6-18.

——. 1993. 'Conservative Protestantism and the World Order: The Faith Movement in the United States and Sweden', *Sociology of Religion* 54, 4 (1993), pp. 353-73.

Connerton, P. 1989. *How Societies Remember*. Cambridge University Press.

Ekman, U. 1985. 'Vilket Sverige Vill Du Ha?', *Livets Ords Nyhetsbrev*, Aug., 1-2.

Falwell, J. 1980. *Listen, America!* New York: Doubleday.

Flowers, R.B. 1983. 'President Carter, Evangelicalism, Church-State Relations, and Civil Religion', *Journal of Church and State*. 25 (1), 113-32.

Forstorp, P.-A. 1990. 'Receiving and Responding: Ways of Taking from the Bible', in G. Hansson (ed.), *Bible Reading in Sweden: Studies Related to the Translation of the New Testament 1981*, 149-69. Stockholm: Swedish Bible Society.

Frankl, R. 1987. *Televangelism: The Marketing of Popular Religion*. Carbondale: Southern Illinois University Press.

Gamoran, A. 1990. 'Civil Religion in American Schools', *Sociological Analysis* 51 (3), 235-56.

Gustafsson, O. 1987. 'Ornen har landat – utkast till ett forskningsprojekt', *Svensk Missionstidskrift* 75 (3), 45-59.

Heinz, R. 1983. 'The Struggle to Define America', in R. Liebman and R. Wuthnow (eds), *The New Christian Right: Mobilization and Legitimation*, 133 – 149. New York: Aldine.

Herberg, W. 1955. *Protestant, Catholic, Jew: An Essay in American Religious Sociology*. Chicago University Press.

Hill, S.S. 1983. 'The New Religious-Political Right in America', in E. Barker (ed.), *Of Gods and Men. New Religious Movements in the West*, 110 – 23. Macon, GA: Mercer University Press.

Hobsbawm, E. and T. Ranger (eds). 1983. *The Invention of Tradition*. Cambridge University Press.

Hunter, J.D. 1983. 'The Liberal Reaction', in R. Liebman and R. Wuthnow (eds), *The New Christian Right: Mobilization and Legitimation* 150 – 160. New York: Aldine.

Johnson, B. 1982. 'A Sociological Perspective on the New Religions', in T. Robbins and D. Anthony (eds), *In Gods We Trust: New Patterns of Religious Pluralism in America*, 51-66. New Brunswick, NJ: Transaction.

Liebman. R and R Wuthnow (eds) 1983, *The New Christian Right: Mobilization and Legitimation*. New York: Aldine.

Marsden, G.M. 1982. 'Preachers of Paradox: The Religious New Right in Historical Perspective', in M. Douglas and S.M. Tipton (eds), *Religion and America: Spirituality in a Secular Age*, 150-68. Boston: Beacon.

Myers, R.J. 1986. 'Preface to 'Religion and the State; The Struggle for Legitimacy and Power', *The Annals of the American Academy of Political and Social Science* (483), 9-11.

Packard, W. 1988. *Evangelism in America: From Tents to TV*. New York: Paragon House.

Robbins, T., and D. Anthony (eds) 1982. *In Gods We Trust: New Patterns of Religious Pluralism in America. New Brunswick: Transaction*.

de Tocqueville, A. 1969. *Democracy in America*. New York: Anchor.

Turner, V. 1967. *The Forest of Symbols: Aspects of Ndembu Ritual*. Ithaca, NY: Cornell University Press.

Warner, R. 1988. *New Wine in Old Wineskins: Evangelicals and Liberals in a Small-Town Church*. Berkeley: University of California Press.

Wills, G. 1990. *Under God: Religion and American Politics.* New York: Simon and Schuster.
——. 1992. 'The Born-Again Republicans', *New York Review of Books* 24,. Sept.
Wilson, J. 1979. *Public Religion in American Culture.* Philadelphia: Temple University Press.
Wood, J.E. Jr. 1980. 'Religious Fundamentalism and the New Right', *Journal of Church and State* 22 (3), 409-21.
——. 1983. 'Religious Encounter in a Religiously Plural World', *Journal of Church and State* 25 (1), 5-11.
Wuthnow, R. 1988. *The Restructuring of American Religion: Society and Faith since World War II.* Princeton University Press.

BEHOLD, I MAKE ALL THINGS NEW!

BLACK MILITANT ISLAM AND THE AMERICAN APOCALYPSE

Mattias Gardell

Islam is the most rapidly expanding religion in the world. This is also true in the United States, where Islam is expected to pass Judaism as the second largest religion in the country during the present decade. The large majority of American Muslims keep a relatively low political profile. Whatever sympathies exist for the rising surge of Islamic 'fundamentalism' in the Muslim world are largely expressed within the confines of the community and do not reach the outer society. However, vociferous exceptions do exist, mainly within the African American community, where Islam has made a highly significant inroad.

This chapter focuses on the most renowned and controversial of these groups, the Nation of Islam (NOI). This organization was established during the Great Depression in the rapidly expanding inner-city ghettos of the industrial North. The Nation was from the very beginning exclusively Black and had emphatic political demands. The United States was depicted as the Empire of Evil soon to be destroyed by the wrath of God, whereupon the Blacks would ascend to their predestined position as world rulers. The movement produced some of the leading Black nationalists of the twentieth century: Elijah Muhammad, Malcolm X and Louis Farrakhan. The controversial positions of the Nation drew the attention of both the media and the domestic intelligence agencies. Infiltrated and investigated by the FBI since the Second World War, when the Nation supported Japan in what was seen as a war against white world supremacy, the movement strengthened its position as the largest Black nationalist organization in the United States. The politico-religious influence the Nation undoubtedly has in the African American community does not cease to hold the official United States in abhorrence.

The present leader of the NOI, Minister Louis Farrakhan Muhammad, repeatedly makes the headlines. He accepts financial aid from Libya, expressed sympathy for Noriega and gave his support to Saddam Hussein in the Gulf War. Speaking out during the Los Angeles uprising of 1992 – the century's bloodiest riot with fifty-eight deaths – Farrakhan said violence was the only resort of the oppressed and stressed that unless justice is done, America will be doomed: 'The worst is yet to come.'[1]

Farrakhan is said to be an 'inverted racist', an 'anti-Semite', a 'Black Hitler' and an 'Islamic fundamentalist'. Despite the much-debated position of the Nation, almost no research has been done on the movement. Studies on the Nation have with two notable exceptions been based on secondary sources of information due to the unwillingness of the NOI to be an object of academic inquiries.[2]

Based on field research, recorded interviews and taped lectures, the present study aims to correct this. The main section deals with the Nation after 1977, when Louis Farrakhan took office. The political aspects of the religion will be stressed, including a discussion of the aforementioned controversial aspects.[3] Since the Nation operates in a multi-religious society, its various relations to other religions will be discussed. Besides Christianity, Judaism and mainstream Islam, the discussion includes what has been called 'American civil religion'. The essay will begin with a discussion on the latter *religion of status quo* which constitutes a part of the context in which the emergence of Black Islam should be understood.

Civil religion and Islam

When European immigrants from various cultures and religious persuasions engaged in the societal construction that was to be known as the United States, a new super-national community was forged. In its search for a unifying answer to the fundamental question of the meaning of being an American, what has since Rousseau been termed 'civil religion' was gradually formulated as the new, all-embracing American identity emerged.

Freedom of belief was from the very beginning an important principle for the Founding Fathers. Equally essential was making religion operative in society. This is provided for by the civil, or civic, religion which lends the secular national identity a religious dimension. In its American formula, civil religion can be understood as a fusion of selected elements from Protestantism, Catholicism and Judaism projected on a higher level of abstraction, where it constitutes a unifying, transcendent 'Americanism'.

As noted by Bellah and Rouner, Biblical symbols and themes are used in the historiography of the United States.[4] The Americans are identified as the 'chosen people', who through an 'Exodus' from Europe reached the 'Promised Land' and there founded the 'New Jerusalem'. American civil religion has its own prophets (Benjamin Franklin, Thomas Jefferson, George Washington); its own martyrs (Abraham Lincoln, the Kennedys, all soldiers killed in war); its own sacred events (the Declaration of Independence, the Boston Tea Party); its own sacred places to which pilgrimage is made (Gettysburg, the Tomb of the Unknown

Soldier, the Lincoln Memorial); its solemn rituals of commemoration (Memorial Day, Thanksgiving Day, Veterans' Day); and its sacred symbols (the Stars and Stripes, the White House, the Statue of Liberty).

American civil religion preaches all the values, norms and ideals associated with *the American way of life*. The United States is the defender of freedom and decency and the safeguard against Communism and barbarism.[5] Civil religion is the sacred expression of the American Dream. The United States is the fortress of individual liberty where each man can reach success. The legend of Horatio Alger is described by Ortner as a key scenario from American culture, both formulating the American notion of success – wealth and power – and suggesting a strategy for its achievement. The exemplary story – well-known from an endless series of Hollywood productions – runs: 'poor boy of low status, but with total faith in the American system, works very hard and ultimately becomes rich and powerful'.[6] The ideology of Americanism pays homage to the lonely individual with trust in God and denies the existence of collective injustices.

Civil religion is by definition unifying and ecumenical. It formulates *one* community, as opposed to the church which only constitutes one community among others. Initially, inter- Protestant divisions were transgressed. During the late 19th century, the concept of Christendom was broadened to include Catholicism, which until then had been regarded with suspicion. As a logical consequence, abstracted elements from Catholicism were incorporated into civil religion. After the end of the Second World War, the definition was further expanded as Judaism was assimilated and the 'Judaeo-Christian tradition' became the underlying foundation of American society and its religion of *status quo*.[7]

Islam was never incorporated. Muslim immigration started in 1860 with migrants from Greater Syria. Well aware of the traditional Christian antagonism toward Islam, they chose to keep a low profile, unwilling to put the constitutional freedom of belief to the test. The bulk of early American Muslims, however, did not arrive as voluntary migrants but as slaves. Allan Austin estimates that approximately 10-15 per cent of the total of captured Africans brought as slaves to the shores of North America were Muslims.[8] Despite the fact that more than one tenth of the slave community was Muslim, Islam did not survive as an organized religion except in isolated instances.[9] The substantial Islamic advance in the present century cannot, therefore, be described as the emergence of a hidden tradition, even though the early history of Islam in America has its given role in modern Black Muslim rhetoric.[10] A far more significant reason for the Islamic tide is the process of cultural revitalization that has successively transformed Black self-understanding since the end of the last century.

When African American intellectuals searching for their roots rediscovered Africa, they encountered Islam. They found great Islamic civilizations in West Africa and made note of the relatively harmonious integration of Islam in the various local African cultures.[11] The single most powerful symbol for the connection between Africa and Islam is Bilal Ibn Rabah. He was a Black slave of Abyssinian origin owned by Ibn Khalaf of the mighty Ummayyah clan in Mecca. Bilal was one of the first historical Muslims and was severely brutalized when his master tried in vain to force him to apostatize. He was then ransomed by Abu Bakr and became a close companion to the Prophet Muhammad. Bilal had a melodious voice and became Islam's first *muadhdhin*, reciter of the call to prayer. The fact that a Black former slave was the prototype for the Muslim call that resounds five times a day from the minarets of the mosques is given a tremendous symbolic significance: it is the Black man who leads humanity to God.

Islam could thus be presented as an indigenous *African religion* in contrast to Christianity, which was introduced by colonialism.[12] In addition, Islam was regarded as traditionally opposed to European expansion and racial discrimination.[13] The descendants of Africa and Islam found themselves placed in a parallel relation of opposition to the American Dream. Islam was never assimilated in the unifying Judaeo-Christian tradition that would constitute the basis of American civil religion, and African Americans were not included in the liberty preached by this faith. Islam could thus successfully be formulated as a Black *religion of resistance*, which found its most militant expression in the Nation of Islam.

Black God and white devil

The 'Black fundamentalism' of the Nation aims to present a positive solution to the problem of identity, so central for the post-emancipation Black community. They were Africans and yet not Africans. They were Americans and yet not Americans. Who were they? Black nationalists have suggested various secular concepts for the perceived identity, none of which has so far been met with universal acceptance. The heat in the debate of whether or not they should be called Negroes, Colored or Blacks, Negro-Saxons, Anglo-Africans, Euro-Africans, Afro-Americans, African-Americans or most recently African Americans highlights the emotional significance of the dilemma. Black religious nationalists have added the crucial question '*why?*' Why did they have to go through the cataclysm of slavery? Was there a *meaning* to this incomparable suffering? The answers given differ in detail and elaboration, but have a certain structure, a specific and basic theme in common, based on a mystical and cyclic interpretation of history.

The Blacks, being the true people of the covenant, are held to have a special relationship with God. Their original culture inhabited a golden age long past and was the cradle of civilization. For various reasons, not least their own people's sins, the Blacks lost world hegemony to other races and were put to 'sleep' – a metaphor for unawareness of the true identity of self. But the course of history is cyclical. What has been shall be again. White supremacy is a vicious but necessary lesson to learn before the pale-skinned tools of God have served their purpose. Thereafter – in the 'hereafter', which is a concrete, earthly concept in this context – the wheel of history will turn and the Black nation will regain its original position. Slavery is thus but a baptism of fire, strengthening the leaders-to-be.

With this theme as their basis, labelled 'Ethiopianism' by some scholars, Black religious nationalists have created their own concepts of identity, frequently replacing the secular bipolar concepts with a unitarian one that reflects the perceived divine meaning of the nation. Thus, we find religious groups asserting that Blacks in reality are *Ethiopians* (Rastafarians, various 'Ethiopian' or 'Abyssinian' churches), *Moors* (the Moorish Science Temple), *Jews* (various Black Hebrew groups), *Nubians* (the Ansaaru Allah Community) or *Bilalians* (American Muslim Mission).

This cyclical interpretation of history was in general combined with a specific theory of race which, influenced by European theoreticians like Herder, Schleiermacher, Guizot and von Trietsche, was to dominate even the more secular branch of classical Black nationalism. The *race*, or, as we would say today, the *nation* or the *ethnic group*, was perceived as an *organic entity* with specific features differentiating it from other race-organisms. The race-entity was seen as a hierarchic, authoritarian corporate body, in which all members think and act unanimously, directed by a leader who governs the race-organism as the brain governs the human body. A restoration of this 'natural unity' became a pressing goal, at times perceived as a necessary prelude to regaining the divinely-assigned position of world community leaders.

The Nation of Islam adheres to this tradition, arguing that African Americans belong to an Original Black Asiatic Islamic Nation. God is not an invisible mystery ghost, but a Black Man. The Black Nation is created from His substance. They share a common nature, and man thus has the potential to become God, as declared in the Scripture: 'Ye are all Gods, children of the Most High God'. The history of mankind is like the life-cycle of an individual; a process of maturity aiming to fully develop the inherent qualities. Decisive in this process is the Quranic saying 'enjoining what is right and forbidding what is wrong'.[14]

In the cosmogonic act, God created the positive and the negative. This duality is integrated in all things created, from the finest particle of matter to the largest planet. The dialectic of good and evil was thus present within the Original People. God made nature submit to Islam, the Natural Law by which the negative is controlled, but gave mankind freedom of choice. In the aboriginal society, a tendency to underestimate the power of evil arose, which reduced the understanding of the necessity of Islam. God, whose plan is the perfection of mankind, decided in His omniscience to conduct an experiment to teach the Original People their innate potential for good and evil. Through self-knowledge, blacks can ennoble their divine capacity and become like Gods, but first they must learn to recognize evil and how to defeat it.[15]

A dissatisfied Black scientist named Mr Yacub worked 6,600 years ago. He was obsessed with the idea of constructing a force terrible enough to transform the original harmony into its opposite. God let him think that he acted in rebellion while in reality he was used to implement the divine scheme. Mr Yacub withdrew with a band of followers to the island of Patmos. By an elaborate process of gene-manipulation he found out how to drain the divine substance out of the Original People. At 200-year intervals he grafted the brown, red and yellow races until his task was accomplished, and a race of extracted and concentrated evil, was produced whose members were by their very nature incapable of thinking good or acting decently. In Quran 2:30, the Original People, the angels, abhor the idea of an evil vice-regent on earth and ask God: 'Wilt Thou place therein one who will make mischief therein and shed blood?' God replies: 'I know what ye know not', and the *blond, blue-eyed white devil* was a fact in world history.

The Original People were put to 'sleep'. They 'died' mentally and God gave the devil 6,000 years to rule. The Era of Evil explains the African-American social experiences in the New World: slavery, racism, ghettos and poverty. Christian fundamentalists believe the world was created 6,000 years ago. Their intelligence is as limited as their time in power. God will in the near future erase them from the face of the earth. The final phase was initiated in 1555, when the white devil John Hawkins anchored the slave-ship *Jesus* off the shores of West Africa. He kidnapped the twelfth tribe, headed by Imam Shabazz – Scripturally known as Abraham – and brought them as chattels to the *Wilderness of North America*. The slave-ship was a Trojan horse carrying the People of God into the stronghold of the devil. The event is described in Genesis 15:13-14 where God informs Imam Shabazz:

> Thy seed shall be a stranger in a land that is not theirs, and they shall serve them; and they shall afflict them for four hundred years; And also that nation, whom they will serve, will I judge: and afterward shall they come out with great substance.

Doomsday is approaching. God descended in Detroit in 1930 in the guise of a door-to-door salesman. Known as W. D. Fard or Master Farad Muhammad, He established the *Nation of Islam*. He met Elijah Poole, of a Southern rural background, whom He anointed as His Messenger: Elijah Muhammad. Three years later, He was able to return to the place from where He oversees mankind, leaving His Nation in the care of His Messenger. The mission of Elijah Muhammad was to accomplish the mental resurrection, to re-animate the dry bones. The black sleeping beauty shall awaken through the touch of love from the divine Messenger and re-ascend the throne.

A notion of the primacy of ideas is implied in this conception of reality. The Nation of Islam has in its own manner reached the same conclusion as Michel Foucault did when he inverted the old adage thus: 'The soul is the prison of the body.'[16] It is *mental chains* that lock African Americans as so-called Negroes at the bottom of society. Only ontological misconception of self prevents them from rising out of their degradation. When they realize their innate divinity, the outer world will automatically change accordingly.

The Blacks have been oppressed by themselves, by their own capacity for evil manifested as the white devil. They now must separate themselves from evil and return to God. Never again will they underestimate the potential power of evil. Never again will they let loose the devil within – he will for eternity be mastered by Islam. The white devils will have served their purpose as pedagogical tools and can as historical waste be thrown into the lake of fire.

The NOI emphasis on the cardinal quality of ideas offers an escape route for the white man. 'You cannot reform a devil. All the prophets tried and failed. You have to kill the devil', Farrakhan declared in a sermon. But, he continues, 'it is not the *color* of the white man that is the problem. It is the *mind* of the white man that is the problem. The mind of white supremacy has to be destroyed.'[17] Should the devil, however, prove unwilling to commit his mental suicide there is no alternative to the physical end of the world. Farrakhan confesses a deep pessimism in this respect:

> Unfortunately, the world rulers are so upset over their loss of power that they really don't give a dog about a new world reality. If they're gonna lose power they'll take the whole world down with them.[18]

The Messianic age has begun

In 1975 the eschatology moved dramatically closer to fulfilment. On 25 February, the congregation received news of the Messenger's death. He was succeeded by his son, Wallace D. Muhammad, who with astonishing speed initiated a process of transformation, moving the Nation towards mainstream Sunni Islam.[19] Imam Muhammad argued that it was necessary for the Nation to get rid of 'the hangover from yesterday of "Black Nationalist" influence...because it [is] in conflict with the open society and democratic order of an Islamic community.'[20]

Master Farad was de-deified, the whites de-demonized and Elijah Muhammad had to give up his position as the Messenger of God to Muhammad Ibn Abdullah, the last Messenger of mainstream Islam. The former condemnation of American society died away. Imam Muhammad considers himself a loyal patriot in a society built on an *Islamic* foundation. He tries to fuse elements abstracted from Islamic teachings with American civil religion by emphasizing the Muslim mind of the Founding Fathers: 'The Constitution of the United States is basically a Quranic document. Its principles were presented to the world over 1,400 years ago by Prophet Muhammad.'[21]

The process of transformation was accomplished at the cost of the movement's unity. Farrakhan argues that 'Elijah Muhammad never intended for us to follow completely what is called orthodox Islam',[22] and points to the existing racism in the Muslim world to show that mainstream Islam would not be a sufficient solution for his people. Black Americans need the specific divine message they were given, which is why he, in 1977, declared his intention to resurrect the Nation of Islam.[23]

Farrakhan regards himself as the true heir of Elijah Muhammad and as the defender of the Messenger's life-work against his unfaithful son who, like a modern-day Absalom, seeks to destroy the father's kingdom. The argument is supported by a newly developed creed. An element of spontaneous scepticism was voiced as soon as the Messenger's death was first announced. 'We who believe', a follower stated when receiving the news, 'won't accept anything until we see his body.'[24] Sister Tynetta Muhammad, a leading theologian in the Nation, describes a vision she received on the evening of 25 February 1975:

> I dreamed that the Honorable Elijah Muhammad sat upright on the funeral bench where he had been lain with the sheet wrapped across his body in the style of the Ihram garments worn by the Pilgrims during Hajj. When I saw him sitting in this position, I exclaimed several times, he is not dead![25]

The Messenger of God did not die but hid to escape a lethal conspiracy. As the *hidden one*, the true identity of Elijah Muhammad has thereby been revealed. He is the awaited Saviour of the three world religions, Islam, Christianity and Judaism. Farrakhan declares that this is 'the crux of the theology that I represent: the Messiah is alive. He is in the world. The power of God is present in America with me.'[26] As the mouth-piece of the Messiah, Farrakhan has been entrusted with an important mission:

My work is to make his great commission known. To say to the Jews who are looking for the Messiah, to say to the Muslims who await the Mahdi, that Elijah Muhammad is not Messenger of God. That he is the Messiah that the whole world is looking for. And that I and my work in America is the witness that the Messianic age has in fact begun.[27]

Initially, this doctrine was founded exclusively on exegetical argument. Pressed by followers of Imam Muhammad, who accused him of preaching what he knew was a lie, Farrakhan received a vision that confirmed the truth of his creed.[28] On 17 September 1985, Farrakhan was in the tiny Mexican village of Tepotzlan. In the vision, Farrakhan climbed a nearby mountain on top of which is the ruin of a temple dedicated to Quetzalcoatl. As he reached the top, a UFO appeared calling Farrakhan to come closer. Farrakhan immediately realized the importance of the moment. According to the cosmology of the Nation, God is aboard a giant man-made planet – known in the Bible as the Wheel of Ezekiel – whence he directs the destiny of mankind. On the planet are the armed spacecraft-carriers that will stage the Final Battle and an entirely new civilization – the New Jerusalem – that will descend to earth following the coming war of annihilation. The spacecraft transported Farrakhan to this heavenly abode, where, after docking, he was escorted to a room, empty except for a speaker in the ceiling. The well-known voice of Elijah Muhammad sounded through the speaker authorizing Farrakhan as guide for the Original People and instructing him to direct a final warning to mankind. As the Messiah spoke to him, a scroll with the full message of God in cursive writing was rolled down and placed in the back of Farrakhan's brain, whereupon Farrakhan was taken back to earth. The scroll makes the message of Farrakhan the message of God. Farrakhan is a modern kind of prophet,[29] surrounded by a staff who record all his utterances. It is God who through His vessel has announced that America must repent or prepare for her doom.

The devil is fully aware of the threat from outer space. That is the reason why NASA classifies all UFO reports as top secret. Moreover, the government of America invests billions of dollars in military space-technology, including a seemingly unreasonable budget for the Strategic Defense Initiative, despite the fact that the Russians have reduced their nuclear arsenal. This proves that SDI never was intended as protection against the secular missiles of the former Soviet Union, but as a devil's shield against the holy missiles of divine retribution.

When the space shuttle *Challenger* was to be sent out into space in 1986, its true mission was to gather intelligence in a native quest to prevent the destruction of Babylon. But, as God states in the Holy Quran 86: 15-16: 'they are but plotting a scheme, and I am planning a scheme'. The 'spy-ship' that sought to challenge God exploded seven-

ty-two seconds after take-off. This is no coincidence, but refers to the
72nd Surah of the Quran where the incident is recorded in verses 8
– 9:

> And we pried into the Secrets of Heaven: But we found it filled
> with stern guards and flaming fires. We used, indeed, to sit there
> in [hidden] stations, to [steal] a hearing; but any who listens now
> will find a flaming fire watching him in ambush.

The devil's pathetic endeavour to survive by means of massive military
mobilization is doomed to failure. The world as we know it is coming
to an end. With the arrival of al-Mahdi (Master Farad Muhammad)
and the Messiah (Elijah Muhammad), the Final Battle has already begun.
The present mental phase of Armageddon, in which Lazarus, the Black
Man, is resurrected, will imminently pass on to the physical phase
unless the devil voluntarily surrenders world domination.

The apocalyptic perspective permeates the Nation of Islam and explains its position on a number of current topics. The following topics
will be discussed separately below: the relationship between the Nation
and mainstream Islam and to Christianity, the alleged co-operation between Farrakhan and white extreme nationalists, and finally the political
role the Nation believes it has God's mandate to resume in the present-day
United States.

The sun of Islam will rise in the West

The theology of the Nation is, as we have seen, in some respects essentially different from mainstream Islam. It grew out of the tradition
of Black religious nationalism and held initially only vague ideas of
what Islam meant for the rest of the Muslim world. Through studies
of the Holy Quran and dialogue with mainstream Islamic theologians,
a process of Islamization was initiated. Upon the departure of the Messenger of God, his son Wallace Muhammad completed this process
of transformation by purging all remnants of heterodox traits.

As described above, this caused a split in the movement due to
Farrakhan's insistence on the legitimacy of the divergent features in
the teachings of Elijah Muhammad. Farrakhan is, however, neither un-
aware of nor unaffected by criticism from mainstream Muslims.[30] Since
the 1990s, the Nation of Islam has had working relations with radical
Muslim organizations and states. This co-operation, along with Islamic
studies and the sometimes fierce criticism from American or foreign
Islamic organizations, has brought about a process of outward accom-
modation to Islamic orthopraxy while refining the reasons for rejecting
Islamic orthodoxy.

Concerning *orthopraxy*, the NOI has largely adopted mainstream

Muslim forms of prayer, fast and pilgrimage. To avoid alienating new adherents to the movement, a gradual approach is used. Open meetings, for instance, are held on Sundays in church- like facilities making for first-timer feel at home and not put off by 'exotic' elements. Members are successively introduced to the Islamized parts and may participate in internal meetings in facilities with mosque-styled interiors in which Friday Prayer can be led by African guest Imams.

Concerning *orthodoxy*, the distinguishing features of the NOI creed are legitimized by theological arguments. The interpretative differences between the NOI and mainstream Islam are in some respects so far apart that one or the other has to give in and accept reform. The apocalyptic perspective makes Farrakhan confident enough to argue that before long 'we shall see who is misguided'. It is 'the scholars of the old world of Islam' who 'must be reformed. They must be guided back to the right path' by 'the people that Allah has chosen'.[31]

The NOI shares the basic perspective of both modernist and Islamist movements, even though the conclusions drawn differ. It argues that the message that God gave humanity through Muhammad Ibn Abdullah was *eternal in its principles* and at the same time *time-specific in its details*. The reason for the present backwardness of the Muslim world is the failure to make this distinction. When conservative-minded Muslim scholars denounced the possibility of reinterpretation (*ijtihad*) in favour of imitation of the past (*taqlid*), they blocked the gate to divinely intended progress. Should not God understand that the world He created is in a process of constant evolution? If religion does not develop accordingly, it ceases to be a source of guidance and turns into a hampering and stagnating element. That is what has happened in the traditional Islamic heartlands. That the former guides have become blind could be seen clearly in the senselessly bloody conflict between Iran and Iraq, in which both camps claimed that God was on their side.

The Muslim world has long expected these days to come. The rightly-guided who at the End of Time will raise the banner of freedom, justice and equality – that is, Islam – will not be found in the Orient, but in the Occident. Muhammad Ibn Abdullah speaks in a *hadith* of the Final Days as the time when 'the sun of Islam will rise in the West'. Another *hadith* points to the people who will fulfil the prophecy – Prophet Muhammad said: 'I heard the footsteps of Bilal going into Paradise ahead of my own.' The interpretation is, Farrakhan states, obvious:

> He didn't mean his own personal footsteps. He was white. He was an Arab. And he was saying that it is the Blacks who are going to lead the Arab world back to the faith that they had forsaken, and lead them into the Paradise their God promised to them by the prophet Muhammad (PBUH) and the Quran.[32]

The racism that in the Era of Evil has permeated every religion, Islam included, bars the road to salvation opened with the coming of the Messiah. As in Christianity, Islam has come to understand the Saviour in racial terms, putting, Farrakhan argues, each Believer to a severe test:

> Would your latent or dominant racism stop you from accepting your salvation? That is the greatest trial of all for the whole world. Can you accept Mahdi and Messiah as Black people? If you can't, then you go out with this world as it goes out.[33]

In addition to the theological argument that God in the Person of Master Farad Muhammad descended to establish the NOI, which is why the Nation's interpretation of Islam indisputably has to be the correct one, a specific scriptural exegesis is used to prove its position. As do many other Islamic groups, mainly within Sufism and Shiism, the Nation acknowledges the existence of *two* Qurans: one manifest, exoteric, and one hidden, esoteric. The latter is the most significant and its hidden message can, according to the Nation, be revealed through 'the Mathematical Code of the Holy Quran's Revelation'.[34] Using the method worked out by the recently murdered computer-Sufi Dr. Rashad Khalifa, the NOI theologians can support their heterodox matters of belief, like the existence of the Wheel and the true nature of Master Farad and Elijah Muhammad.

The mathematical code provides yet another argument against the Arabs and others who have tried to monopolize Islam. Farrakhan claims that although they have had the Quran they do not possess the key to its proper understanding. They can be likened to the market donkey carrying a cargo of gold on its back: the ass does not realize the value of the load, which is why it becomes a burden. Meddlesome mainstream scholars deny the existence of the Code and can be repudiated by the words of God in the Holy Quran 3:70: 'Ye People of the Book! Why reject ye the Signs of God?'

Christians at the cross-roads of Salvation or Doom

The Nation of Islam was from the start inimical to Christianity, with significant portions of the NOI teachings appearing to be constructed as negations of Christian doctrines. The Bible was branded as 'the Poison Book'.[35] 'Christianity is a curse to us' Elijah Muhammad wrote, 'and is full of slavery teaching.'[36] By means of a morbid cult centred around a dead body nailed to a cross, the devil conquered the world. Christianity dupes the African American into turning the other cheek, hoping in vain for reward in Paradise. But there exists no such place-without-sorrows beyond the grave. Elijah Muhammad declared: 'There is no such thing as dying and coming up out of the earth and meeting those who died before you. I say get out of such slavery teachings. It keeps you blind, deaf and dumb to reality... When you are dead, you are DEAD.'[37] Heaven and Hell are *conditions* on earth. The Whites live in heavenly affluence while the Blacks experience hell right here and now. The resurrection and the hereafter promised by the prophets signify, respectively, the awakening of the Blacks out of their mental death and the world after the approaching battle of Armageddon.

Two prominent reasons for this criticism of Christianity are immediately discernible. The first acknowledges the racism that permeates parts of the history of Christianity. During the days of colonialism and slavery a specific Christian colour-symbolism evolved, in which God, Jesus, Mary, the apostles and the Angels were all portrayed as white. 'White' came to symbolize the divine, the clean, the innocent and the good. The opposite of white became identified as the opposite of good. 'Black' came to symbolize the devil, the evil, the sinful, the dreadful. 'Black magic' was malevolent, 'white magic' benevolent. African Fathers of the Church became Hellenized Greeks and embarrassing facts such as the existence of Black saints were explained away by theological rationalization. St. Benedict the Moor, patron saint of slaves, for example, was considered to be originally White. To avoid temptations from the opposite sex, St. Benedict prayed that God might make him ugly – God granted his request and made him Black.[38] The colour symbolism of the Nation constitutes a mirror to the context in which it operates.

The second major reason for the criticism of Christianity is related to the role of the Black Church in American society. Initially, the Black Church was radical. It was the only independent space for the African American and a significant institution in the struggle for emancipation. In the course of the twentieth century, the socio-political position of the Black Church became increasingly more conservative.[39] 'The greatest miracle Christianity has achieved in America', wrote, Malcolm X 'is that 22 million black people have not *risen up* against their oppressors'.[40] Seen in this context, Elijah Muhammad taught that Christianity and Islam represented two clashing camps – that of the devil and that of God – which would soon come together on the battlefield for a showdown.[41]

For a long time, the Messenger's religious interpretation of African American history was a voice crying in the wilderness: 'The only *distinctively* Black theological reflection in written form that anyone was aware of prior to 1964 was produced by... the Nation of Islam.'[42] Inspired by the Nation and by the rising demands for Black power, Black Christians, such as Albert B. Cleage and James H. Cone developed a Black Theology of Liberation. 'The task of Black Theology', Cone wrote, 'is to analyze the nature of the gospel of Jesus Christ in the light of oppressed Black people so they will see the gospel as inseparable from their humiliated condition, bestowing on them the necessary power to break the chains of oppression.'[43] God cannot be colourblind in the American context because he is a God of the oppressed.

The theological rebellion brought Black Christianity closer to the black Muslim position. Black, as a theological key-concept, transcended doctrinal differences between the religions, allowing extensive co-operation to be initiated. Farrakhan now argues that essentially, Islam and Christianity are one and the same.[44] Black theologians are invited to the Mosques of the Nation and Muslim Ministers are common guests in Black churches. In a Black Christian magazine, Farrakhan is described as the criterion of God, whose mission in America is likened to that of Moses in Egypt, Daniel in Babylon and Jesus of Nazareth in the Roman Empire.[45] A sign of the new interreligious Black unity came on 24 October 1993, when Rev. Ben Chavis, executive director of NAACP, mounted the rostrum of Farrakhan at Mosque Maryam, with the Bible and the Quran in his hands. Reading from both Holy Scriptures, Rev. Chavis spoked on the necessity to build bridges and described the event as a Holy moment in Black history, a final re-unification of God's people.[46]

Nazis, fascists and the Nation of Islam

The Nation of Islam has been described by some observes as constituting a kind of Black Nazism, related to the so-called 'Third Position', that is, a leftist-oriented national socialism. In support of this argument, observers direct attention to Farrakhan's alleged anti-Semitism and to the links between the NOI and white extreme nationalists.

The National Front (NF) of Great Britain hailed Farrakhan in their papers *National Front News* and *Nationalism Today*.[47] The latter paper was also 'particularly pleased' to publish a longer article by Abdul Wali Muhammad, spokesman of the NOI.[48] NF militants sold the Muslim paper *Final Call* along with their own papers'[49] and in 1988 the NF visited the Washington D.C. branch of the NOI.[50] Farrakhan is said to have accepted a symbolic donation from Tom Metzger, leader of the Ku Klux Klan at that time.[51] For some years, White nationalist support for the Nation seemed unilateral, but in the 1990s a discernible shift can be noted. In 1990, *Final Call* published an article by Gary Gallo, spokesman for the National Democratic Front in the United States, along with this Third Positionist White nationalist organization's declaration of principles.[52] With the conflict in the Gulf escalating, the NOI representative Abdul Alim Muhammad participated in a LaRouche Conference in December, 1990,[53] and, together with German Nazis, expressed support for Saddam Hussein. In 1991, *Final Call* hailed LaRouche as a freedom-fighter imprisoned for his 'outspokeness'.[54] Also in 1991, NOI signed a British Movement appeal for racial separation that was distributed as a leaflet.[55]

Reports like these made journalists speculate on the establishment of a 'new alliance' between 'right-wing extremists' and 'Islamic fundamentalists'.[56] These speculations gave rise to the media's presentation of the NF proposal for 'a New Axis', linking the NF together with Libya and the NOI, as something more than a unilateral idea.[57] Even though the above-mentioned connections do exist, the 'alliance-theory' is based on incomplete knowledge of the religious rationale behind the NOI position.

From a short-term perspective the positions of the Nation and the aforementioned white nationalist organizations are in congruence. Both camps preach racial pride, race-endogamy and separation. They cry in unison about the need to keep the black race black and the white race white. The NOI position, however, can only be fully understood from the long-term apocalyptic perspective.

The Nation argues the necessity for African Americans to awake from their mental slumber. They must fully realize the diabolical nature of the white man and separate themselves from evil, not fraternize with it. This signifies an essential eschatological phase and a prerequisite for the war of Armageddon. The skinheads of the National Front and the sneaky attackers of the Ku Klux Klan are pedagogically useful as manifest devils, confirming the veracity of the NOI's teachings. The white extreme nationalists unknowingly accelerate the final solution. Though Farrakhan does not approve of their violence against Blacks, he deems it an expression of White nature and a foretold step in the eschatology: 'Their violence is prophetic. It is fulfilling prophecy to make it uncomfortable for Black people to stay here....[It] is all part of the drama. The world wide drama the prophets foretold.'[58]

The apocalyptic perspective also explains Farrakhan's unequivocal support for the former anti-Islamic Baath ideologist, Saddam Hussein. According to the revealed eschatology of the Nation, the Final Battle begins with a conflict in West Asia between opposite global camps. It is to be followed by a European civil war, beginning in eastern Europe, and will reach its final stage with the doomsday trumpet blast as the Messiah arrives with the battle-fleet from space. Living constantly in the day before doomsday, Farrakhan made what would seem to be a hasty pronouncement at the outbreak of the Gulf War: 'This is Armageddon.'[59]

Come out of her, my people

The ideologists of the Nation frequently focus on the prime symbols of American civil religion, which are given a revised and reversed meaning in order to expose the diabolical nature of American society. The *American Dream* turns into a nightmare. The golden door of the Statue of Liberty proves to be the iron bars of a prison cell.[60] The Stars and Stripes does not symbolize freedom but suffering, slavery and death.[61] Independence Day is seen as the festival of hypocrisy because the Founding Fathers denied the African Americans their independence. The 4th of July is still of paramount importance for the African American because God chose that day for His coming to His people in Detroit in 1930. He came as a thief in the night on a day of great significance. Elijah Muhammad wrote: 'It is their day of great rejoicing. As with former people and their governments, their destruction took place when they were at the height of their rejoicing.'[62]

America is, according to Farrakhan, on the road to self-destruction. She is a 'declining civilization', displaying all the signs of the 'breakup of society' with 'the social fabric beginning to pull apart'.[63] Drugs, criminality, unemployment, poverty and pornography are all signs of the Final Days. America is identitied as the Babylon of Revelations whose fall is imminently impending. Any moderate Black political call for equal integration with the foul spirits in the habitation of devils is not only insane but a suicidal policy. The only reasonable course of action is to follow the divine command in Revelations 18:4: 'Come out of her, my people, that ye be not partakers of her sins, and that ye receive not of her plagues.'

While awaiting Armageddon, NOI demands the establishment of a separate Black state in an area fertile and rich in minerals, as compensation for all the centuries of unpaid slave labour.[64] The creation of an independent Jewish state and the reparations paid by Germany is here seen as a juridical precedent.[65] Summing up the suffering of the African American, Farrakhan holds that America is indebted well beyond her assets: 'Add it up, white man. The whole world belongs to the oppressed, if you add it up. But we're not asking for the whole thing... just give us some of it and let us go to build a nation for ourselves.' Fair compensation lies in the white man's own interest. Should he prove himself unwilling, he qualifies for the wrath of God: 'Add it up. If it's a life for a life, then God is justified to kill everybody who refuses to submit.'[66]

The organizational structure of the Nation reflects a conscious effort to function as a theocratical shadow cabinet – as a state within the state. It has a separate administration of justice, complete with separate laws, prescribed conduct and sanctions. Penalties range from community service to suspension from the Nation for a specified period of time. When suspended from the Nation, the offender is ignored even by his closest friends and relatives. For severe crimes, the suspension lasts for ever; as was the case with a convicted rapist whom Farrakhan himself sentenced and 'forbade his father, his mother, his sisters and his brothers to have anything more to do with him for the rest of his life'.[67] When conditions permit, Farrakhan wants to impose harder penalties for such a crime:

> As we get stronger and stronger, and Islam becomes more and more powerful in America, I promise you we will put to death every violator of our women. And we really don't give a damn what the white man says. Even if it's your father, we will kill him.[68]

In addition to the punishments mentioned above, the military cadre of each mosque acts in part as an internal police force and deals with offenders in its own way. Similarly to most independent nations, the NOI has created a military defence organization, which it calls the *Fruit of Islam* (FOI). The highly disciplined soldiers are seen as the fruit of NOI teachings, carrying the seed to the future transformation of the world. In an internal FOI pamphlet, Farrakhan expounds:

> What is the meaning of FOI?... The name given to the military training of the men who belong to Islam in North America. Military training implies tactics. Military training implies manoeuvers. Military training implies going behind the lines in enemy territory. Military training implies establishing a beachhead in enemy territory and then proceeding to take control. Military training implies WAR.[69]

Besides using symbolic means to stress the desired national independence, such as the adoption of a national anthem or the hoisting of a separate national banner, the NOI purposefully acts to promote the building of a separate Black infrastructure. During the regime of Elijah Muhammad, the Nation prospered economically, establishing enterprises in various areas. According to C. Eric Lincoln, the NOI developed to become 'the most potent organized economic force in the black community'.[70] At the succession of Wallace Muhammad, the assets of the Nation were estimated at US $60 – $80 million.[71] Among the methods of reorientation initiated by Imam Muhammad was a sweeping process of company privatization which resulted in a dismantling of the financial empire. A prime priority of Farrakhan is to rebuild the economic base of the Nation. In 1985, the NOI launched the POWER program (People Organized and Working for Economic Rebirth) 'for the absolute purpose of restoring Black people in America to their original industrial and commercial greatness'.[72] A wide variety of enterprises has been established, including shampoo and skin-cream ranges, publishing firms, restaurants, hotels, agribusiness, food imports and banking.[73] These developments notwithstanding, the New Nation is still a long way from its former economic strength.

Despite the militant separatist rhetoric that characterizes the message of the Nation, an analysis shows the movement's adoption of conservative American middle-class values. The social programme can be seen as *a project of auto-civilization*. From this perspective, the spokespersons of the Nation act as *agents of acculturation*, who – if successful – will adjust their segment of African American ghetto culture to the basic norms and patterns of behaviour of the surrounding society. Applauding conservative pillars such as God, Nation and the Nuclear Family, the NOI depicts its members as the knights of morality pitted against the dragon of decadence. The moral level of present-day Blacks is, according to Farrakhan, way below the standards of the Original Civilization: 'We are living a criminal life, a very wicked and savage life here in America. Though we have the potential to be wonderful Muslims our condition is such that no civilized society wants us to be a member.'[74] The life-style of young Black Americans is harshly condemned: 'Your heads are full of reefers, your veins so full of heroin and your noses so full of cocaine or you're so busy at the party chasing one another sexually that you become a modern Rome.'[75]

Farrakhan has the Muslim military to back up the acute actions he finds necessary. Beginning in 1988 FOI intervened as *Dopebusters* in rundown Black neighbourhoods in Washington DC, acting to clear the streets of dealers and prostitutes. Besides such 'taking-back-the-streets' actions, the Nation has been widely acknowledged for its work with drug addicts and criminals. Minister Don Muhammad – responsible for the NOI East Coast co-ordination – is only one among many Muslims awarded for successful NOI rehabilitation programmes for inmates and ex-convicts.[76]

The improvement in social conditions accomplished by the Nation is an expression of the power of God, says Farrakhan: 'God raised a group from among us [the decaying black community] and gave us life, and we are the witnesses of Elijah Muhammad. Clean-cut, sharp, disciplined, non-smoking, non-drinking, non-dope using, strengthening the family.'[77] The African American has divine potentials that will be realized if he is freed from the grip of the devil. Addressing the Congress, Farrakhan urged, 'Let our Black brothers out of prison, give us your poor... give them to me – Let my people go.'[78] This would, he emphasized, benefit all parties:

> We can reform the convict, you can't. We reform the drug addict, you don't. We reform the alcoholic and the prostitute. You don't. We take the poor and give them hope by making them do something for themselves. You don't. We are your solution.[79]

The above statement reflects the conviction that the nature of the problem is on a level way beyond the competence of traditional politicians: 'No politician can save anybody', Farrakhan stated, 'politicians are in no saviour business. Politicians are hoodlums. No whore can save you.'[80] He repeatedly displays dissatisfaction with the mainstream Black American political and religious leaders, arguing that they have sold their souls to the devil and made 'a covenant with death and an agreement with hell'.[81]

Traditionally, the NOI has stayed aloof from Babylonian politics, refusing to drop their vote in the ballot box of the devil. The Jesse Jackson campaign of 1984 marked a first shift in orientation. The well-organized cadre of the Nation joined the Jackson machine and soldiers of the FOI functioned as body guards for the Black candidate. The Original People registered to vote for the first time.[82] Convinced of having the mandate of God to lead America, the NOI's next step was to run its own candidates. 'We need a Muslim politician', Farrakhan argued, 'The Scripture says, "What man having a light would hide it under a bushel basket?" No, take your light out from the bushel basket and you place it on a hill. What hill? Capitol Hill!'[83]

George X. Cure and the commander of the *Dopebusters* mentioned above, Abdul Alim Muhammad, Minister of Mosque no. 4, Washington DC, ran for Congress in 1990. While the outcome was modest for George X, who gained 5 per cent of the vote in the DC General election, Minister Muhammad fared better: he received 21 per cent of the vote in the 5th district of Maryland. Though the high expectations were unfulfilled, the fact that one in five voted for a Muslim candidate must be considered noteworthy.[84]

The sudden involvement in the democratic procedures of the devil will in all probability never alter the main strategy for the transformation of American society. The true solution is separatism as a method for re-creating the organic unity of the race, and this, when accomplished, will automatically bring about the downfall of the devil. According to the ideologists of the NOI, the devil has long feared the generation of redeemers carried in the wombs of Black women. Desperate so prolong his era of power, the devil has developed different counter-strategies.

For decades the domestic intelligence units of the FBI have tried to neutralize every organized body of black dissidents that emerges. FBI Director J. Edgar Hoover, with presidential approval, initiated a campaign in the late 1950s to crush the NOI but it was curtailed ten years later. In 1967, the NOI was among the groups targeted by the FBI COINTELPRO, whose explicit aim was to 'expose, disrupt, misdirect, discredit or otherwise neutralize the activities of black nationalist, hate type organizations and groupings, their leadership, spokesmen, membership and supporters...'[85] FBI agents became involved in a series of covert actions. The premises of the Nation and the homes of prominent spokespersons were bugged. An extensive network of infiltrators and informants was created. Bogus mail, false jacketing and strategically placed informants were used to plant the seeds of dissension within the NOI. Similar methods were used to create animosity and conflicts between the Nation and other black nationalist organizations, such as the Black Panther Party and the Republic of New Africa. Loyal journalists were used to channel whatever information the FBI thought desirable to present – fabricated or not – to the American public. While generally successful in its efforts to neutralize most black nationalist organizations, the programme directed against the Nation was an overall failure. It seems that the activities of the FBI were largely counterproductive: the agency fitting nicely into the eschatology of the Nation, fulfilling the expected role of the forces of evil in the latter days. The FBI's activities were turned into a powerful argument, proving the truth of the NOI teachings.

The representatives of the Nation argue that the FBI only constitutes one part of a much wider conspiracy. Farrakhan claims that the government, the police, the media and the Jews are acting together to plot his death, just as they did in the time of Jesus. Due to the fact that the Final Days have already begun, single acts of murder are unable to alter the course of history. With Armageddon approaching, the devil steps up the preventive measures. Farrakhan uses the Scriptures to reveal these evil schemes: 'When you read your Bible about Herod, when you read about Pharaoh, you are reading about the mind of the administration in Washington DC.'[86] As Herod's fear of confronting the redeemer of the oppressed made him kill all male babies, so the government of America seeks to escape its destiny by a carefully planned genocide. Methods in use include programmes for contraception and abortion and the spread of artificial diseases such as AIDS. Governmental programmes to kill Black youth through the distribution of narcotics and weapons have, according to the NOI, been fatally effective. The gang wars so characteristic of the past few years are also part of the scheme: 'So they plan your removal. How? Create gangs. Feed weapons to the gangs and make them kill each other; just confine the killing to the Black neighborhood, don't let it spill over to the white neighborhood.'[87]

Farrakhan and the Nation of Islam have made their most significant inroads among African American youth. Evidence of Farrakhan's rapport with urban youth was apparent in the early 1990s. Confronting communities on the brink of a civil war, Farrakhan urged Black gangs to stop the killing and unite 'as one family as an army of God movin' for the liberation of our people'.[88] His appeal was successful, and 'Bloods' and 'Crips', the two largest federated gangs in Los Angeles, signed a cease-fire truce in May 1992, declaring their intention to halt criminal activities and in the words of 'Crips'-member Daud, turn into a 'human rights movement'.[89] The Los Angeles example was followed by similar peace treaties in several urban African American and Hispanic communities during the summer and autumn of 1992.[90]

Islam has become a Black urban youth cultural phenomenon during the last ten years. Besides the appeal of the NOI message and the magnetism of its harbinger, one explanation for its success is to be found in music. As the spread of the Rastafarian faith in the 1970s can be related to reggae, so the rise of Black Islam is related to rap music. Most of the top hip-hop artists, such as Public Enemy, Africa Bambaataa, Brand Nubian, Ice Cube, Prince Akeem, Divine Styler, Queen Latifah, Lakeem Shabazz, and Poor Righteous Teachers, are either members of or sympathizers with the NOI or other related Black Muslim groups.[91] Chuck D., ideologist of perhaps the most well-known of these rap-groups, Public Enemy, says he puts rhythm to the essential teachings of Minister Farrakhan and turns it into rap music.[92] Through music, the NOI creed becomes a part of the everyday life of Black youths. Farrakhan stresses the importance of this.

You don't wanna come here sit 'n' listen to Farrakhan for two hours, that's a little bit too much. But turn on the box and the [Public Enemy] are getting to you with the Word, and whities sayin' 'Oh, my God, we gotta stop this'! But it's too late now, baby! When you got it – it's over, when the youth got it – it's over... the white world is coming to an end.[93]

The End is approaching, and as the devil seems unwilling to give up his world supremacy, God has no choice but to initiate the physical phase of Armageddon. Divine retribution will finally set the score whereupon the Original Man will experience the promised hereafter:

And I saw a new heaven and a new earth; for the first heaven and the first earth were passed away... And I saw the holy city, New Jerusalem, coming down from God out of heaven, prepared as a bride adorned for her husband. And I heard a great voice out of heaven saying:...God himself shall be with them, and be their God. And God shall wipe away all tears from their eyes; and there shall be no more death, neither sorrow, nor crying, neither shall there be any more pain: for the former things are passed away. And he that sat upon the throne said, Behold, I make all things new.[94]

Notes

1. Farrakhan 1992.
2. The Black sociologist of religion, C. Eric Lincoln, published an excellent thesis entitled *The Black Muslims in America* in 1961 (rev. edn 1973). The Nigerian political scientist Essien-Udom published his *Black Nationalism* in 1962. Martha F. Lee published *The Nation of Islam: An American Millenarian Movement* in 1988, but she overlooked the religious rationale of the NOI. A few articles of high quality have been written (notably Mamiya 1982; 1983). See also Gardell 1994.
3. This paper does not discuss the alleged anti-Semitism of the NOI due to two reasons. Firstly, most of the accounts written on Minister Farrakhan and the Nation in the 1990s make the anti-Semitic charge a chief issue as if that is what the Nation is all about. Secondly, a long section in my dissertation, 'Countdown to Armageddon: Minister Farrakhan and the Nation of Islam in the Latter Days', is dedicated to the subject and will give a far more indepth understanding of this complex controversy than would be possible to convey within the limits of this chapter.
4. Bellah 1967: 18; Rouner 1986.
5. Following the fall of the Soviet and East European Communist regimes, the United States can no longer meaningfully define itself in opposition to 'the empire of evil'. During the past few years we have witnessed a return to an older pattern, in which the Western world finds its *raison d'être* through an oppositional position *vis-à-vis* Islam. The United States is still the safeguard against totalitarianism, but the symbols of evil are now found in the Islamic world. Saddam Hussein and Mu'ammar al-Qadhdhafi are depicted as super-crooks of a magnitude worthy of a novel by Ian Fleming. This is done despite the facts that Hussein, as a leader of the secularist, national socialist Baath Party represses Islamist tendencies in Iraq, and Qadhdhafi, because of his modernist liberalist attitude towards established Islamic traditions, is considered something of a heretic in many camps throughout the Islamic world.
6. Ortner 1979: 95.
7. Wilson 1986: 115ff.
8. Austin 1974: 29-36.
9. As could possibly have been the case in the Sea Islands, Georgia. See Austin 1974; Raboteau 1978.
10. The existence of Muslim slaves on Selapo Island, GA, and especially the excerpts of a Maliki treatise in Arabic, written by Bilali in the early 19th century, is taken by Isa al Mahdi of the Black Nationalist Ansaaru Allah Community, Brooklyn, as 'evidence that the first language of the Black slaves residing today in America was Arabic and that Al Islaam was their true way of life' (1989: 330).
11. Central for this process were two Black nationalist pioneers, Edward Wilmot Blyden (1832-1912) and Bishop Henry McNeal Turner (1834-1915). See Blyden 1887; Lynch 1967; Moses 1978; Redkey 1969.
12. It is interesting to note that Christianity, when discussed in this context, is presented as a predominately *alien*, white religion. The very same debators can in other contexts focus on the African contribution to early Christianity: Mary is hailed as a black Egyptian; the African Christian civilizations of East Africa are proudly accounted for, as are the great African thelogians Clement, Origen, Tertullian, Cyprian, Dionysius, Athanasius, Didymus, Augustine and Cyril, who made important contributions to the theological formulation of the universal Church from the third to the fifth century.
13. Concerning the professed anti-racist stand of Islam, no critical examination was ever made (except by small splinter-groups such as the Ansaaru Allah Community). Lewis (1990) has in an important scholarly work shown that a racist sentiment in Islam developed over the centuries. But, what is essential to understand here is that it was *the image of Islam* and *not the reality of Islam* that influenced African American thinking.
14. The Holy Quran 3:110, translated by Yusuf Ali.

15. See, for example, J. Muhammad 1985; L. Farrakhan, speech 1991.
16. Foucault 1979 (1977): 30.
17. Farrakhan, 1989a.
18. Farrakhan, interview 1989a.
19. For more information concerning this Islamization process, see Lincoln 1983; Gardell 1988 and 1994.
20. W.D. Muhammad 1988: 82.
21. Sharif 1985: 118.
22. Farrakhan, interview 1989b.
23. L. Muhammad 1977: 5.
24. McClory 1975: 16.
25. T. Muhammad 1986: 84.
26. Farrakhan, interview 1989a.
27. Farrakhan, interview 1989a.
28. Farrakhan, interview 18 May 1989; compare to Farrakhan 1989a.
29. Farrakhan is a prophet in the terminology of the phenomenology of religions. He is called 'prophet' by certain followers, as in the Public Enemy tune *Bring the Noise*, but I have never heard him call himself by this epithet which, of course, would violate the traditional Islamic understanding of Muhammad Ibn Abdullah as the Seal of the Prophets.
30. See, for example, Farrakhan, speech 1984 and 1990a.
31. Farrakhan, interview 1989b.
32. Farrakhan, interview 1989a.
33. Farrakhan, interview 1989a.
34. T. Muhammad, 1986: 81.
35. E. Muhammad, 1965: 94.
36. E. Muhammad 1973: 169.
37. E. Muhammad 1965: 168.
38. Bastide 1967: 317.
39. Wilmore 1986: 135ff.
40. X, M. 1965: 247.
41. E. Muhammad 1973: 203ff.
42. Wilmore 1979: 67.
43. Cone 1970: 23.
44. Muhammad, A.W. 1990.
45. Walker 1989.
46. James Muhammad 1993.
47. See, for example, *National Front News* (NFN) no. 84, 1987, pp. 4-5; NFN no. 93, August 1987, front page; p. 5; June 1988, p. 3; no. 94, pp. 4-5; NFN no. 105, p. 3; *Nationalism Today* (NT) no. 22, p. 7; no. 29, May 1985, p. 17; no. 37, March 1986, p. 7; no. 44, Jan. 1989, pp. 6-7.
48. *Nationalism Today* (undated), no. 39: 1, 16-20.
49. *Nationalism Today* no. 46, July 1989, 25.
50. *Nationalism Today* no. 44, Jan. 1989: 4-5.
51. *Searchlight* b,'Farrakhan...' (1986). *Searchlight* does not mention any sum of money. According to *Nationalism Today* it was purely symbolic, USD 100.
52. Gallo 1990.
53. Berlet 1991: 12.
54. Muhammad, A.W. 1991: 7.
55. *Brand*, 'Fascistmos' 1991: 29.
56. Lindeborg 1991: B2; Lodenius and Larson 1991: 157ff.
57. 'New...' 1987: 3.
58. Farrakhan, interview 1989b.
59. Muwakkil 1991:8. I wrote 'seem' because *Final Call* warns its readers against ques-

tioning whether this really was Armageddon. In an editorial, the reader is asked if he realizes 'the tremendous impact, the ripple effect against America, that the devastation of Iraq is causing throughout the so-called Third World'. The reader is assured that the Final Battle between good and evil, black and white, is not over yet – because soon 'the oppressed mass of humanity, the darker peoples of the earth who are writhing under poverty and deprivation are being moved by the hand of God to explode like a human volcano' (1991: 14).

60. Farrakhan 1983a: 9.
61. E. Muhammad 1965: 238.
62. E. Muhammad 1973: 69.
63. Farrakhan, speech 1989b.
64. E. Muhammad 1965: 161. The area does not necessarily have to be in America. Africa is frequently mentioned as an alternative.
65. Farrakhan, interview 1989b.
66. Farrakhan, speech 1990b.
67. Farrakhan, speech 1990c.
68. Farrakhan, speech 1990c.
69. Farrakhan 1983b: 1.
70. Lincoln 1973: 97.
71. Mamiya 1982: 144.
72. NOI...1985.
73. 'Farrakhan Returns With POWER'.
74. Farrakhan, interview 1989a.
75. Farrakhan, speech 1989b.
76. D. Muhammad, interview 1989.
77. Farrakhan, interview 1989b.
78. Farrakhan, speech 1989a.
79. Farrakhan, interview 1989b.
80. Farrakhan, speech 1989c.
81. Farrakhan 1989b: 16ff.
82. Strausberg 1984: 3.
83. Farrakhan, speech 1990d.
84. Vote results taken from *Washington Post* 3 Sept. and 8 Nov. 1990.
85. FBI 1967.
86. Farrakhan, speech 1989c.
87. Farrakhan 1990: 19.
88. Farrakhan, speech 1990e.
89. X M. 1992.
90. Gardell 1992; for a follow-up, see X M. 1993.
91. Among those groups, the two most important are the Five Percent Nation of Islam and the Ansaaru Allah Community. The first was established in Harlem, NY, by Clarence 13X in 1963. It is largely an East Coast youth organization and explicitly militant in appeal. In the past they criticized the NOI but have during the last ten years sought and found reconciliation and co-operation with Farrakhan. A large number of artists and musicians are to be found among the Five Percenters. The Ansaaru Allah Community was established in 1970 by As Sayyid Al Imaam Isa Al Haadi Al Mahdi, who claims to be the Holy Spirit manifested to reinstate the Nubians (as the Blacks properly should be called) as world leaders. The Ansaars too, have had a history of clashes with the NOI, but since the late 1980s have been on good terms with Farrakhan. Under the name of Dr York, Imaam Isa is himself a musician and has drawn a large number of Black artists to the movement.
92. Chuck D., interview 1990 (partly published in Gardell 1990).
93. Farrakhan, speech 1989a.
94. Revelations 21: 1-5.

References

Recorded interviews
Chuck D. 1990. Interview, Stockholm, 31 March.
Farrakhan, L. 1989a. Interview, Chicago, 11 May.
——1989b. Interview, Chicago, 18 May.
Muhammad, D. 1989. Interview, Boston, 8 June.

Recorded speeches
——. 1989a. 'The Origin of the White Race: The Making of the Devil', delivered at Mosque Maryam, Chicago, 23 March.
——. 1989b. 'A Time of Danger: The Signs of the Fall of America', delivered at the University of Maryland, 29 March.
——. 1989c. 'The Crucifixion of Jesus: The Destruction of Black Leadership', delivered at Mosque Maryam, Chicago, 26 March.
——. 1990a. 'The Three Rules that Prove there is no God but Allah and Muhammad is His Messenger', delivered at Mosque Maryam, Chicago, 14 Jan.
——. 1990b. 'Stop the Killing', delivered at the Omni, Atlanta, GA, 28 Apr.
——. 1990c. 'The Nature of the Black Man', delivered at The Muhammad University of Islam, Chicago, 20 June.
——. 1990d. 'Muslims Ready to Serve Community', delivered in Washington DC, 5 May.
——. 1990e. 'Stop the Killing II', delivered in Los Angeles, 2 Feb.
Farrakhan, L. 1989. 'The Arab Press Conference', delivered at Howard Inn, Washington DC, 17 Aug.

Literature
Austin, A.D. 1974. *African Muslims in Antebellum America*. New York: Garland.
Bastide, R. 1967. 'Color, Racism and Christianity', *Daedalus* (2).
Bellah, R.N. 1967. 'Civil Religion in America', *Daedalus* (1).
Berlet, C. 1991, Strange Alliances, *In These Times*, 30 Jan.
Blyden, E.W. 1967 (1887) *Christianity, Islam and the Negro Race*. Edinburgh University Press.
Cone, J.H. 1970. *A Black Theology of Liberation*. Philadelphia: J.B. Lippincott.
Essien-Udom, E.U. 1962. *Black Nationalism*. University of Chicago Press.
Farrakhan, L. 1983a. *Warning to the Government of America*. Chicago: Honorable Elijah Muhammad Educational Foundation, Inc.
——. 1983b. *The Meaning of F.O.I.* Chicago: Honorable Elijah Muhammad Educational Foundation, Inc.
——. 1989a. *The Announcement: A final warning to the U.S. Government*. Chicago: Honorable Elijah Muhammad Educational Foundation, Inc.
——. 1989b. 'Your Agreement with Hell Will Not Stand', *The Final Call*, 31 Dec.
——. 1990. 'Brothers, how did you become a gang? (Death Plan part II)', *The Final Call*, 29 Jan.
——. 1992. 'The Worst is Yet to Come', *The Final Call*, 5 June.
'Farrakhan and his fellow travellers'. 1986. *Searchlight*, Dec.

'Farrakhan Returns with POWER', *The Final Call*, special edition.
'Fascistmos'. 1991. *Brand* (2).
FBI, File 100-448006-(?) From Director, FBI to SAC, Albany, 25/8/67.
Foucault, M. 1979 (1977). *Discipline and Punish: The Birth of the Prison.* Harmondsworth: Penguin Books.
Gallo, G. 1990. 'What do "white" nationalists believe?', *Final Call*, 21 March.
Gardell, M, 1988. 'Religiös nationalism och nationalistisk religion', *Svensk Religionshistorisk Årsskrift*, 3. Uppsala.
——. 1990. Interview with Chuck D., Stockholm, 31 Mar., published in part in 'Rappens Rebeller. Brand möter Public Enemy', *Brand*.
——. 1992. 'No Justice – No Peace', *Brand* (4).
——. 1994a. 'Halvmånen och Stjärnbanéret' in *Majoritetens islam: am muslimer utan för arabvärlden.* D. Westerlund & I. Svanberg (eds). Stockholm: Arena.
——. 1994b. 'The Sun of Islam will Rise in the West' in Y. Haddad and J. Smith (eds), *Muslim Communities in North America.* Albany, NY: State University of New York Press.
Lee, M. F. 1988. *The Nation of Islam: An American Millenarian Movement.* Lewiston, NY: Edwin Mellen Press.
Lincoln, C.E. 1973. *The Black Muslims in America.* Boston: Beacon Press.
——. 1983. 'The American Muslim Mission in the Context of American Social History' in E.H. Waugh, B. Abu-Laban and R.B. Qureshi (eds),*The Muslim Community in North America.* Edmonton: University of Alberta Press.
Lindeborg, L. 1991, 'Antisemiter på frammarsch', *Dagens Nyheter*, 2 Feb.
Lewis, B. 1990. *Race and Slavery in the Middle East.* Oxford University Press.
Lodenius, A.L. And S. Larsson, 1991. *Extremhögern.* Stockholm: Tidens Förlag.
Lynch, H. 1967. *Edward Wilmot Blyden: Pan-Negro Patriot.* Oxford University Press.
al Mahdi, I.H. 1989. *The Ansaar Cult.* Brooklyn: The Original Tents of Kedar.
Mamiya, L. 1982. 'From Black Muslim to Bilalian. The Evolution of a Movement', *Journal for the Scientific Study of Religion*, vol 2, no. 6.
——. 1983. 'Minister Louis Farrakhan and the Final Call: Schism in the Muslim Movement' in Waugh *et al.* (eds), *The Muslim Community in North America*, Edmonton: University of Alberta Press.
McClory, R. 1975. 'City in Tribute to Muhammad', *Chicago Defender*, 26 Feb.
Moses, W.J. 1978. *The Golden Age of Black Nationalism.* Oxford University Press.
Muhammad, A.W. 1990. 'Muslim/Christian relationships: One faith, one religion', *Final Call*, 21 Mar.
——. 1991. 'Mr Bush, New Dictator', *Final Call*, 22 Apr.
Muhammad, E. 1965. *Message to the Blackman.* Philadelphia: Hakim's Publications.
——. 1973. *The Fall of America.* Chicago: Muhammad's Temple of Islam 2.
Muhammad, J. 1985. *Farrakhan: The Traveller.* Phoenix: PHNX SN & Co.
Muhammad, James. 1993. 'Farrakhan, Chavis unite: Fulfilling a unity pledge, NAACP leader is guest at Mosque Maryam', *The Final Call*, 10 Nov.
Muhammad, L. 1977. 'New Farrakhan thrust', *Chicago Defender*, 3 Dec.

Muhammad, T. 1986. *The Comer By Night*. Chicago: Honorable Elijah Muhammad Educational Foundation.

Muhammad, W.D. 1988. *Focus on al-Islam*. Chicago: Zakat Publications.

Muwakkil, S. 1991. 'Peaceful desires unite religious blacks', *In These Times*. 6/2/91.

'The New Axis', 1987. *Searchlight* (147), Sept.

Ortner, S.B. 1979. 'On Key Symbols' in W.A. Lessa and E.Z. Vogt (eds), *Reader in Comparative Religion*, New York: Harper and Row.

Raboteau, J.A. 1978. *Slave Religion*. Oxford University Press.

Redkey, E.S. 1969. *Black Exodus*. New Haven and London: Yale University Press.

Rouner, L.S. 1986. 'To be at Home: Civil Religion as Common Bond' in L.S. Rouner (ed.), *Civil Religion and Political Theology*. Notre Dame, IN: University of Notre Dame Press.

Sharif, S.R. 1985, *The African American (Bilalian) Image in Crisis*. Jersey City: New Mind Productions.

'So, you think the war is over?' 1991. Editorial, *The Final Call*, 11 Mar.

Strausberg, C. 1984. 'Muslims get into politics', *Chicago Defender*.

Walker, M. 1989. 'A Voice Crying in the Wilderness', *The Platform*, May/June.

Wilmore, G.S. 1979. 'Introduction' to 'The Attack on White Religion', in G.S. Wilmore and J.H. Cone (eds), *Black Theology*. Maryknoll, NY: Orbis Books.

———. 1986. *Black Religion and Black Radicalism*. Maryknoll, NY: Orbis Books.

Wilson, J.F. 1986. 'Common Religion in American Society', *Civil Religion and Political Theology*. Notre Dame, IN: University of Notre Dame Press.

X, M. 1965. *The Autobiography of Malcolm X*. New York: Ballantine.

X, R.M. 'Truce called by LA gangs', *Final Call* 5 June.

———. 1993. 'L.A. gang truce strong as ever...', *Final Call*, 28 July.

'THE LAST STAND'?

ODAWA REVITALIZATIONISTS VERSUS U.S. LAW

Melissa A. Pflüg

Three years of fieldwork with the Algonkian-speaking Odawa Indians of the state of Michigan revealed factors inherent in their contemporary socio-religious movement. To understand what is happening within this Odawa society, it is necessary to realize that this is a community struggling with two embattled strategies for cultural survival.[1] The Odawa as a whole have formulated two distinct strategies for asserting their identity: one that participants themselves call 'traditionalist' and another that I call 'accommodationist'. Although traditionalists do not have a name of their own for this counter-strategy – nor do the proponents of it – accommodationists tend to be members of organizations that are recognized as legitimate political entities by the federal and state governments or of groups that aspire to such a status. Their strategy for cultural survival is characterized by a pan-Indian philosophy of ethnic and political identity, and followers are willing to embrace the US government's definition of them as 'domestic dependent nations' – especially through the US Bureau of Indian Affairs (BIA) as arbitrating agency – in exchange for badly needed economic subsidies. In effect, accommodationists maintain enough Indian-ness to establish relations with the authorities. In their own ways, both strategies seek to respond constructively to pressures of secularism that emanate from the non-Indian community and from the opposed faction of Indians. This chapter focuses on the strategy of traditionalists, whose goal is to revitalize Odawa identity by faithfully applying religious tradition to a changing social context. The core of the traditionalists' perspective lies in retaining Odawa language, myth and land in contradistinction to obliging secular trends which they fundamentally question: US law, federal Indian policy, and Indian accommodationists.

To explain what is implied in the traditionalists' response to secularism, the general nature of revitalization movements is outlined, which demonstrates that their particular movement both conforms to a typology of revitalization and has parallels with 'fundamentalism'. The Odawa's move towards revitalization stems from the pressures of secularism, of which the accommodationists' reaction forms a part, and

75

which is especially articulated by US Law. Consequently, an inherent conflict in Odawa – US government relations is revealed by focusing specifically on the secular arena of US law from a traditionalist perspective. What is important at the outset is to acknowledge that traditionalists strive for 'sovereignty' which they take to mean recognition by others of their total cultural autonomy and unique identity, especially as reinforced by language and land. Their aim is to translate this sovereignty into an everyday meaning.

The traditionalists' revitalization and sovereignty efforts are constructive actions to counter 'ethno-stress' or social crisis. Pressures of secularism threaten them with socio-cultural marginalization – within and among both the wider non-Indian Euro-American society, and among their own Indian, Odawa, and socio-cultural peers. Traditionalists are marginalized on three fronts: from the accommodationists and their representative political organizations, from the state government, and from the federal government. Their marginalization is also reinforced by the self-imposed socio-cultural invisibility they adopted as part of their survival strategy in the past as a means of maintaining an autonomous identity.

The social crisis for Odawa traditionalists partly results from historical pressures of acculturation, State-building, and frequently-changing U.S. federal Indian policy. Today, these sources of ethno-stress are coupled with pressures associated with factionalism between Indian groups that are federally recognized and those that are not. For traditionalists, ethno-stress is defined within the context of an 'us-and-them' dichotomy, with the emphasis lying in the complexity of interrelated factors that cut across their own cultural self- identity, interfering with it and demanding response. They identify two hypothetical responses: to give in to these pressures and lose their autonomy, as they see the accommodationists doing; or to overcome the stress creatively, which they see themselves being charged to do. The traditionalists respond to the pressures of secularism on their own terms; they face threats to their identity in an 'Odawa' manner. They recognize that their only weapon to combat secularism is their unique identity. They also choose not to use treaties and other American-produced legal devices for any purpose other than reinforcing their own special ethos.

Unlike accommodationists, traditionalists tend to be members of bands that are not recognized as legitimate political entities by the federal and state governments or by other recognized Indian groups. Traditionalists do not aspire to the status of 'domestic dependent'. They strive for total cultural and political sovereignty by revitalizing their own unique band identity and autonomy.

Traditionalists are accomplishing this cultural revitalization and this sense of sovereignty by retaining religious traditions and by applying religiously charged values to socio-political activism. This strategy's essential values include, but are not limited to: retaining the Odawa language; establishing proper relationships based on reciprocity; maintaining the contention that life is continuously changing for good or ill but that one can influence that change through quiet persistence in acting ethically; maintaining respect for, and reciprocity with, the earth or land; commitment to the person's and the group's transformation through establishing a powerful connection with the land; establishing a connection with the power of the earth to promote social solidarity and ethnic identity; commitment to the authority of myth. The key factors among these values are language, which establishes and maintains identity, and land, which gives a sovereign base for maintaining and presenting that identity. Both language and land, as the essential sources of identity, are validated by myth.

By practising these values, traditionalists view autonomy, independence, liberation, equality, power, freedom, and sovereignty as concepts that are cyclical in their interconnection. They contend that through quiet persistence, proper interpersonal relationships can be (re-)established, and with sovereignty, the 'circle of life' will be completed. By these means they renew ethnic identity and social solidarity. Today, in their attempt at revitalization and sovereignty, Odawa traditionalists are reinterpreting and reapplying central religious values, which are voiced mythologically and ritually, to combat the stress of secularism, especially as it derives from the pressures of US law. For these Odawa, myth and ritual are significant components in the action dimension of their traditional perspective.

Traditionalists interpret US law as consistently stressing differences between Indian and non-Indian religious doctrines and as upholding the non-Indian emphasis on historicity, which continually undermines the Odawa's focus on the mythological ordering of the world. For them, how to adapt to this worldview is problematic. Traditionalists respond by structuring their revitalization within a framework of fundamentalism; a fundamentalism that reinforces the values of their own world view. They regard the US legal system as framed by the concept of arbitration. Traditionalists believe that for US lawyers, the Law actually exists as an existential reality which is static, impersonal and hostile to negotiation. Furthermore, traditionalists interpret the legal system as an artificial order created by Euro-Americans to protect themselves from others. According to one Elder: 'The American legal system is a lot of absolute rules and regulations made up by lawyers, which they use to control others.' In direct contrast, the world for Odawa traditionalists is structured by a flexible, yet formalized, gift-economy that reinforces social unification, revitalizes their lives, and is contained within certain fundamental paradigms.

The Odawa's ethos and worldview are structured by the conjunction of three existential postulates: Person – Gift – Power. The interconnection of the values, ethics and behaviours that are related to these postulates forms a system for mediating with others who are dangerous, thereby transforming them from foes to friends.[2] The key word in this process is 'mediate'. The Odawa's enacting Gift maintains proper relationships by mediating interpersonal distance and overcoming differences. Mediating disagreements through gift-exchange reinforces the idea that ethical acts of responsibility ultimately bond people together in dynamic relationships. Mediation through gift-exchange highlights ethical acts of responsibility. With such an ethos and worldview structured by the characteristics of a gift-economy and an ontology structured by extended social relationships, Odawa traditionalists view acts that address interpersonal disagreement not as a matter of arbitration or adversarial litigation, but as just and ethical mediation or negotiation through interpersonal reciprocation. They see the US legal system as having a fundamentally opposite perspective derived from market-exchange principles. An Elder noted: 'I don't think the US legal system asks us what our needs are. The law just decides for us what programs are going to be started in our own backyards, without our representation'. Because it is not framed within a system of gift-giving, US law is viewed by the Odawa as legitimizing the continuing attempts by American policy-makers to suppress Odawa sovereignty efforts.

The Odawa respond to this suppression by enacting gift-exchange as a source of power. Today, the prerogative of power is voiced through the call for social transformation via their myth of the Seventh Fire.[3] The ability to use power to transform the quality of life also is voiced in ritual activities that produce social solidarity, as in the annual *Gi-be* feast.[4] Myths and their ritual enactment express both the ethical challenge of achieving kinship solidarity and the greater challenge of expanded social solidarity, which aims for sovereignty.

The aim of many non-recognized, traditionalist Odawa bands is to establish a proper sovereign relationship with their ancestors, with the federal and state governments, and with various other Indian organizations, especially those that by virtue of having federal recognition, directly affect legal policy. However, without the benefit of federal recognition, these non-recognized bands are particularly vulnerable to federal policy, especially as reinforced by US courts. The decisions by reviewing courts are crucial to Odawa – US government relations generally, and threaten the traditional values placed on land both as a means of asserting sovereignty and expressing identity.

Some non-recognized Odawa bands have managed to progress toward their goal of sovereignty by implementing a strategy of asserting traditionalism. The traditional precedents for using ethical behaviour to establish proper relationships are set by the great figures of mythology, who achieved their status of greatness and became empowered through exemplary acts of co-operation expressed through giving. The threatening characters of mythology are those who consciously and consistently withhold, and for Odawa traditionalists, these threatening mythological characters have their secular counterparts. As one Elder put it: 'The US says that legally we're citizens. But citizens of what? They've taken our lands and taken our rights. And what have we received in return? Lines and boundaries and reservations.' Another Elder said: 'The US uses laws to try to protect itself and to control others. And we all know that what it controls, it thinks it owns – right down to our ancestors'. Clearly, traditionalists view US law as an institutional system that withholds: an act which is, to them, the worst sort of unethical behaviour and is not their own idealized way of doing business. Their commitment to fundamental values, ethics and behaviour regarding proper means of establishing and restoring relationships drives their current revitalization and sovereignty efforts. For Odawa traditionalists, the last stand for cultural continuity and, therefore, survival is whether an agreement can be mediated between their religiously-charged system of justice and secularized US law.

Justice versus U.S. law

The statutory enactment of Euro-American society was the adoption of the US Constitution, which stems from a model for structuring the legal system based on the dictum 'Equal Justice Under the Law'. The Constitution includes the Right of Due Process and the Right to Equal Protection. An Odawa attorney argued: 'The US has always claimed to use the Right of Equal Protection to support treaty negotiations and provisions'. However, the attorney argued, if treaties were negotiated before the implementation of the US Constitution, the relationship is not Constitutionally established but is based on a political relationship bounded only by the Northwest Ordinance, which allowed the original British colonists to claim lands 'in the name of the Crown'. Thus, this attorney concluded that through the earliest treaties and the resulting relationship 'lands could be claimed for US ownership without Equal Protection and reimbursement'.

The decisions by the US Supreme Court in two cases are particularly important regarding this issue of land claims and of sovereignty generally. *Johnston* v. *MacIntosh* (1823)[5] implied that Indians as a collective have no right of traditional custodianship of the lands they inhabit and cannot handle such lands without federal government consent. *Cherokee Nation* v. *State of Georgia* (1832)[6] established that Indian groups are not sovereign foreign nations but are domestic dependent nations under the legal jurisdiction of the US Constitution. With *Cherokee Nation*

v. *State of Georgia*, a federal Indian policy emerged based on a guardian
– ward relationship. More than 100 years elapsed after these two prece-
dent-setting cases before US law addressed the issue of the religious
rights of Indians.

Congress passed the American Indian Religious Freedom Act (1978)[7]
as a measure intended to reaffirm the federal government's commitment
to maintaining the ethnic identity of Indians, and to provide a means
of documenting cultural continuity and integrity to meet the Bureau
of Indian Affairs' recognition stipulations. Section I of the AIRFA states:
'the United States [will act] to protect and preserve for American Indians
their inherent right of freedom to believe, express, and exercise [their]
traditional religions...', especially by guaranteed right-of-access to sites,
use and possession of sacred objects, and freedom to worship through
ceremonies. Considering the First Amendment of the US Constitution,
why was the Freedom of Religion Act necessary?

The answer is that the First Amendment is not absolute. It reads
in part that: 'Congress shall make no law [1] respecting an establishment
of religion, or [2] prohibiting the free exercise thereof; or abridging
the freedom of speech, or of the press; or the right of people peaceably
to assemble, and to petition the government for a redress of grievances'.
Thus, Americans are guaranteed the right to gather collectively, to speak
freely, and to practise religion. The First Amendment, ratified in 1791,
contains two provisions regarding the relationship between Church and
State: the Establishment Clause and the Free Exercise Clause. Although
written to limit Congressional powers, these two religion clauses also
apply to states through the Fourteenth Amendment's Due Process Clause,
which was ratified in 1868. According to the Establishment Clause,
Congress cannot pass laws 'respecting the establishment of religion',
which calls for a broad separation between Church and State. Neither
the federal government nor a state can create a church, and neither
can pass laws supporting one religion or all religions or establish
preference for one over another. Basically, this clause was inserted
to create a wall of separation between Church and State, an act consistent
with the Colonists' wish to curtail the rise to political power of religious
organizations such as the Church of England. With the Free Exercise
Clause, the government cannot forbid religious services, punish people
for having particular religious beliefs, or exclude members of a religious
community from public service, as these actions would limit religious
freedom. Essentially, the Free Exercise Clause was a direct result of,
and response to, the European Reformation experience. The intent was
to prevent discrimination against dissenting religious denominations and
to establish general freedom of conscience.

Yet, the free exercise of religion is not absolute: special privileges
cannot be granted because of religion if they undermine public interests

underlying the law. Consequently, for example, in 1879 the Supreme Court decided that Congress could outlaw polygamy among Mormons, even though for them the practice was a religious duty. So, in theory, the First Amendment must be neutral: it cannot be used to show favour, or disfavour on religious grounds. But, in practice, if the government can neither outlaw religious belief nor burden the exercise of that belief, then the courts must at times determine whether an asserted religious belief is sincerely held. If it is found to be sincere, the burden on individual worship is balanced against the state's interest in restricting it. If the state's interest is compelling, it outweighs individual interest. The key words in this legal process are *individual* and *belief*. What about collective practice?

In theory, with the granting of citizenship to Indians (1924),[8] no need for special legislation to protect religious freedom existed because such rights were constitutionally guaranteed. Federal courts simply judged separate cases by analyzing the applicability of the First Amendment Free Exercise and Establishment Clauses. For Indians, the determining factor in cases related to the practice of religion under the Free Exercise Clause is whether they have a *collective* right of access to sacred lands under federal jurisdiction. R. Michaelsen[9] states the issue clearly:

> The sacred site cases pose the question of survival in poignant fashion. While the general doctrine of broad applicability may be useful to American Indian free exercise litigants, there has been, among the various free exercise cases decided in the American courts, no exact precedent on which to rest Indian sacred site claims.

The courts approach the issue in terms of the right of Indian peoples to collectively access lands when those lands are subject to competing land use.

One case is particularly noteworthy for the Supreme Court's interpretation of Free Exercise: *Wisconsin* v. *Yoder* (1972).[10] The Court held that the Free Exercise Clause is only implicated if the government coerces an individual to act against his or her beliefs. If free exercise is not jeopardized, the government does not have to provide a compelling reason for its actions, and no collective organization can claim exclusionary right of land access and use based on religious beliefs. John Petoskey, an Odawa attorney explains the effect of *Wisconsin* v. *Yoder*:

> ...It is the Court's bench mark for claims of free exercise impairment. Under Yoder's analysis, a free exercise claim must first prove that the government has burdened important religious interests. Once this is established, the burden of proof shifts to the government.[11]

Petoskey interprets the *Yoder* decision as reinforcing the policy that the federal government must prove a religious practice would harm the state's interest.[12] However, federal and state officials – and individuals with special interests, especially land-developers – continued to deny Indian peoples communal access to sacred lands to practise collective rituals.

The lower courts have tried more than twenty-four cases concerning the American Indian Religious Freedom Act and land-use rights. Almost half of these cases address the issue of land-use rights and Indian communal access to, and protective custodianship of, sacred lands. Most of the decisions have overruled right-of-access, a fact demonstrated in *Sequoyah* v. *Tennessee Valley Authority* (1980),[13] *Bandoni* v. *Higginson* (1981),[14] *Fools Crow* v. *Gullet* (1982),[15] and *Wilson* v. *Block* (1983).[16] These cases are examples of claims to land-use rights based on the Free Exercise Clause, and they illustrate the federal agenda that Indian groups must prove their existence and the legitimacy of their religions before land-use rights are considered Constitutionally bound. The decisions by the reviewing courts resulted in the Cherokee, Navajo, Cheyenne and Lakota, and Navajo and Hopi, respectively, being denied communal access to use and protect federally owned sacred sites. The *Bandoni* case is especially disturbing because the decision implied that the American Indian Religious Freedom Act may be unconstitutional.[17] Most cases related to the AIRFA, result from Indian claims to their right of collective custodianship of sacred lands. An Odawa Elder voiced this concern: 'We hope to be acknowledged, but we'll never be satisfied with the status of "domestic dependent nation". We want acknowledgement through our traditional practice of custodianship of land by the band'. To date, however, no Indian claims have succeeded. Reviewing courts have stubbornly and consistently weighed the Establishment Clause over the Free Exercise Clause.

The Odawa identify the self-defensiveness of US law not only throughout the above policy statements, but also in the American Indian Graves Protection And Repatriation Act (1990). Based on several statements made by Odawa Elders to non-Indian museum curators during a session on repatriation at the 1991 annual meeting of the Michigan Museum Conference, the Odawa have two key concerns about the Repatriation Act. Their first concern is that objects eligible for repatriation must be defined and inventoried, and the information must be made available to Indian groups who may be interested in making their own claims, within a five year period. These claims will be adjudicated by a seven-member board of Indians and non-Indians funded through the National Park Service (NPS). The Odawa understand this to mean that the burden of proof for identification and reclamation falls to separate, and potentially competing, Indian groups, and they fear that preference will go to those organizations with federal recognition. The second concern is that the functioning of the Act will be under the auspices of the NPS, but that the Department of Interior, as umbrella agency for the NPS, had yet to begin to seek funding eighteen months into the programme. The Odawa can only sit and wait patiently.

Two Odawa Elders at the 1991 meeting voiced questions arising from the wording of the Act. They wanted to ascertain the credentials of the groups involved in defining objects of concern. They wanted to know whether there can, or will, be a system ensuring equity of adjudication. They wanted to know whether there is a fiduciary responsibility. Given that the NPS is initially responsible for funding, the Elders wanted to know where available funding is to be found. They wanted to know whether the Act applied to private collectors. They also inquired about timing, about what groups are eligible to make claims, what definitions apply, how the criteria for repatriation will be balanced with the requests, and whether there is the assurance of a balance of ideologies (for example, between and within Indian groups).

Many Odawa interpret the Act to mean that it is the responsibility of institutions such as museums to prepare inventories and make notifications so that Odawa groups can make claims. The Odawa do not see repatriation as a matter for legal arbitration but as an express right. An Elder at the meeting said:

> What we want is simple. We want the bones and associated grave goods of our ancestors to be returned for reburial – period. Artifacts taken by a non-Indian community that were not found in burials will be returned for our Elders to use. The issue is central to our identity, self-definition, and self-determination. It's a means of retaining our traditions and of keeping our identity alive.

His statement captures the extent to which cultural and material artifacts that are now 'owned' by others are powerful symbols for mobilizing traditionalist communities. Repatriation of such materials is very much a part of Odawa social activism and sovereignty efforts. However, there is much scepticism as to whether the United States will give the Odawa what they want. 'I'll believe it when I see it', said another Elder. 'The government has made many promises, and we've continually been disappointed. Another law. More big talk. But, nothing ever gets done. I won't hold my breath about ever seeing our ancestors returned to the earth where they belong.'

Underlying efforts to affect legislative policy is a split in philosophy between Odawa accommodationists and traditionalists. Those groups who have been granted federal recognition – the accommodationists – also have high political and social visibility. To these Odawa, the acquisition of a status as 'domestic dependent nations', which complies with federal law and is maintained by a non-traditional pattern of centralized government, seems a fair exchange for the economic and social benefits that result. Those groups that are not federally recognized – the traditionalists – have been socially invisible, and have adopted this invisibility as part of their strategy for achieving the goal of autonomy and independence. Typically, non-recognized groups work to gain sovereign status by emphasizing a traditional value of quiet persistence, and by implementing decentralized band councils consisting of Elders, pipe-carriers and other acknowledged religious functionaries who mediate disagreements by consensus.

While formerly the methodological approach of the traditionalists was invisibility leading to autonomy, independence, liberation, and finally sovereignty, today the invisibility factor is on the wane because of their greater understanding of, exposure to, and participation in the US legislative and judicial structures. They understand that policy is debated in the arenas of the elected bodies, the courts, and the 'streets' and that the legislative agenda is set by the elected bodies agreeing on the essential issues and establishing laws for addressing them. The Odawa know that policies not won in the legislature move to the courts, and that the court arena differs fundamentally from the legislative arena: they see it as a battlefield based on opposition instead of consensus. Odawa traditionalists counter opposition with their commitment to fundamental values, ethics and behaviour related to proper means of establishing and restoring right relationships: it is the restoration of the right relationship that drives their current revitalization and sovereignty efforts.

Features of traditionalists' revitalization

Theoretical works regarded by scholars as seminal in identifying revitalization movements among American Indian peoples typically focus on socio-religious reactions to Euro-American contact, and their own economic derivation.[18] However, revitalization results more specifically from socio-cultural marginalization; that is, one group is marginalized from the cultural network by another group, resulting in a sense that its traditional culture and social identity are in decline, which provokes members of the group to respond with constructive intentions. The standard feature of revitalization movements is that they present a developmental process in which symbolic actions are purposeful responses to events. These actions are then manipulated to produce specific results; that is, they aim for a particular destination. A general typology of revitalization can be constructed, which can be used as a comparative base for the Odawa.

Revitalization movements are actions directed to a series of events. There is an initial event of intrinsic and extrinsic crisis. There are new technological and cultural influences. There is a redefinition of territory. There is economic decline. There is a loss of language and cultural identity. Total cultural decline threatens. A shift in value patterns occurs due to dominance and suppression. Time becomes perceived as disrupted. These events can be characterized simply: they produce the marginalization of one group by another.

Actions are then taken by the marginalized group to rectify the events. Attempts are made to (re-)establish a unique identity. Actions are taken to get and maintain power manifest in underlying ideologies. Traditional ideals and values are asserted. Ritual and myth are codified and linked with a pre-existing apocalyptic tradition. An individual or group is charged with the supreme task of setting time and the world to rights. Like the events leading to them, these actions can also be characterized simply: they are examples of the constructive use of conflict.

Being constructive, actions have two purposes: they intend to define group identity and they are directed to generating salvation and rebirth through either total transformation or partial redemption. The purpose of the actions taken to counter events, then, is generally to achieve positive change, leading the group to a specific destination, including destruction or alleviation of the extrinsic source of conflict, decreased influence of non-indigenous values, group solidarity, and a positive future. In other words, these actions seek to attain cultural unification, or sovereignty, such as existed before disruption, but now require re-establishing and recovering in the face of new threats to their autonomy. Testing the Odawa's socio-religious movement against this general typology of revitalization requires, first, establishing that they have experienced the event of marginalization.

The Odawa's experience of marginalization partly results from significant treaties, signed in the eighteenth and nineteenth centuries, that have continued to define Odawa relations with the state of Michigan and the federal government. These treaties resulted in the transfer of lands from Indian custodianship to American ownership, allowing the Michigan Territory to be established as a state and thus developed for non-Indian settlement and for agriculture and lumbering pursuits. The 1855 Treaty of Detroit was a particularly critical event for the Odawa of northern Michigan because it removed their rights to their traditional lands, and stripped them of any further collective dealings with the US federal government.[19]

The entire treaty phenomenon resulted from the eighteenth- and nineteenth-century federal policy of removal, or reservationism, of all Indians west of the Mississippi River. The Odawa, although having sacrificed their traditional land-base, managed to avoid being removed by upholding their tradition of political decentralization, especially through governance by councils that upheld the integrity of separate bands.

Following the removal era, government policy shifted in the late nineteenth century. The United States realized the dire economic consequences of supporting Indian reservations and of losing both the land and the resources they held. Consequently, policy shifted to one based on the allotment of small parcels of land to individual heads-of-household who, after gaining title, had to pay taxes. This allotment policy held until the 1950s, when the Eisenhower Administration implemented a policy of termination, which was intended to promote the assimilation of Indian peoples into mainstream, industrial, urban society with a consequent loss of Indian cultural and social identity. The policy of termination remained in force until the implementation in the 1970s of the current policy of 'self-determination', in which Indians are supposed to have autonomy and power to determine their own 'destiny'.

'Self-determination' is a misnomer, as a group's 'success' actually depends on its recognition by the federal government as a legitimate political organization based on proven ethnohistorical precedent established by 'an historian, anthropologist, or other qualified scholar'.[20] 'Recognition' means being under the supervision of the U.S. Bureau of Indian Affairs, and traditionalists view accommodationists as giving in to the government, sacrificing traditional councils which govern by consensus, in order to access federal and state economic subsidies. One Elder from a non-recognized band explained:

> One of the recognized groups organized itself, acquired their land base, and is operating without ever having a consensus of all the northern Odawa leaders. They've centralized their governmental organization, rather than following our traditional ways. They split off from the other local bands, voluntarily fragmenting themselves for their own self-interest, mainly controlling the 1836 treaty-stipulated waters for fishing. The leaders from the different bands were never consulted. They even combined with Ojibwe groups to increase their power. They're just down there setting themselves up at our expense, without the approval of the Elders.

Another Elder from a non-recognized group complained: 'The reserved Indians, who are recognized, are selling out to the government to get money and things they don't really need. I refuse to be accountable, just to get money.' A third Elder from a non-recognized band remarked about a recognized organization: 'They're afraid of our organizing ourselves independently because they think that the available sources of funding are limited, and they're threatened by the thought that if we get any there'll be less to go around.' This last statement is particularly telling of intergroup and intragroup conflict and factionalism: newly organized non-recognized bands threaten groups already recognized by virtue of being reservationed; reservationed groups feel that the success of these other bands means decreased disbursements available for them.

In addition to shifting federal policy, the Michigan state government has a profound effect on the organization and success of Odawa traditionalists. When the state asks who is 'Indian' in Michigan, it does so in terms of the its own unique definition; it is political membership and affiliation, not socio-cultural identity, that forms the basis of this definition.

Currently, three criteria define an 'Indian' from the state's perspective, compliance with one of which is necessary for recognition as 'Indian': 1. a person must be a member of a group which is federally recognized and must carry a card showing such affiliation; 2. a person must be a member of the Confederation of State Historic Tribes,[21] or; 3. a person must be a member of a recognized group from another state. This third criterion is important because there are Indian peoples living in urban centres in the southeast part of Michigan – the area with the highest total Indian population – who represent sixty-one separate Indian groups from throughout the U.S. All three criteria require extensive federal and genealogical records to substantiate an individual's inclusion so that the burden of proof does not lie with the state.

Thus, the only means of communicating with the state are to meet the state's criteria for 'Indian' status, to accommodate the state through constitutions and elected officials that centralize a hierarchical governing structure, and to produce genealogical reconstruction of membership. For groups that are not recognized, this situation becomes a problem that defies its own solution. Members of non-recognized groups perceive that, without state recognition, they receive no funding. They ask, as one Elder put it: 'Without funding, where is the money supposed to come from to produce the genealogical and ethnohistorical documentation?' Elders are particularly resentful of not being regarded as having the authority to substantiate their own cultural integrity. Clearly, non-recognized groups of Odawa traditionalists have been marginalized both by the federal and state governments, and also by the recognized groups. An Elder commented: 'Not only is the government trying to overtly destroy us by keeping us fragmented, it's sitting back and letting us – maybe hoping that we will – self-destruct by adopting non-Indian ways'.

Odawa marginalization has resulted from conflicting values between Law and Justice, and between ownership and custodianship, especially of land. It is land that provides the locus of Odawa identity. They respond to the event of marginalization by constructively using conflict with the American government and with accommodationists to enhance group identity and cohesion. Traditionalists recognize that their survival depends upon their own initiative. Traditionalists also exhibit an element of radicalism as they fight for the ideals and values that they regard as defining *Odawa*, and consequently they are intolerant of the departure from this central identity exhibited by accommodationists. For traditionalists, action is purposeful: it is directed at changing the imposed non-Indian values that they see as corrupting. The goal of their purposeful action is total sovereignty: they want a unique identity, language and land, along with shared values and politico-economic autonomy. Their experience of marginalization, their actions of constructive conflict, their purpose of positive change, and their destination of sovereignty leading to cultural unification put their socio-religious activism squarely within the typology of revitalization.

Odawa traditionalists, moreover, are engaged in a socio-religious movement that not only conforms to the typology of revitalization but also shares essential elements of 'fundamentalism', as this term is commonly understood: traditionalists charge themselves with the responsibility to drive the revitalization movement; the movement is framed by an authoritative myth and ritual; and participants use their past to inform the present and the future by restructuring a new historical consciousness within a traditional mythological framework. Let us look at each one of these in turn, first of all considering the religious underpinnings and legitimations for their revitalization activities. Traditionalists have reinterpreted and restructured traditional myths of healing and a traditional mortuary ritual, and have reapplied them to the contemporary context.[22] The central myth and its accompanying ritual are the ammunition that traditionalists use to struggle against the crisis of secularism.

The Odawa goal of socio-religious revitalization is voiced in a myth that anticipates the Seventh Fire, in which it is prophesied that the advent of a transformed world will occur only when all Odawa follow the 'Path of Life', and that the practice of the Old Ways will both empower them and bring about the destruction of all non-Indians along with all values associated with them. In this mythic model, fire symbolizes energy, life and, ultimately, socio-cultural metamorphosis. A Pipe-carrier related the myth:

> Let me tell you about the Seventh Fire. The World was created with seven layers, each with its own fire that illuminates and contributes to the specific lifestyle of that level, giving it power. Each fire represents a world and a people. Life at the beginning, during the first fire, was perfect. But, for some reason, the ancestors failed to follow the Path of Life that Ki-je Manido, our Great Grandfather, made for their own good. The world changed. Ki-je Manido was not pleased with any of the changes. People were no longer following the Red Path, the Path of Life. So, the original perfection was

destroyed. Then, having destroyed the first world and people, Ki-je Manido felt a little bad. So, he sent Nanabozho [the Odawa culture-hero] to make a new life – people, and plants, and animals – everything – and to teach people how to live properly, with respect for all things. Nanabozho gave us another chance to prove ourselves. All this happened during the Second and Third Fires. Then our prophets taught that the Fourth Fire would be a time when White Faces would appear, and that they would either be friends, or bring death. It was death that came – physical and spiritual – to the Odawa. The present world is somewhere in between the Fourth and Seventh Fires. But, Grandfather promised that by returning to the Red Path, and Path of Life – the traditional ways – that the life of the Seventh Fire will come, and we will return to the way things were in the beginning. With the Seventh Fire, the circle will be mended, the Old Ways will return, and my people will return to a better life. Ki-je Manido will again destroy the imperfect world, including all people not following the traditional ways – those who stubbornly insist on following the Path of Technology. Those of us following the Path of Life will return to perfection, and we will be reunited with our ancestors. Our great hope is that the community currently living – tomorrow's ancestors – will be wise enough to follow the Right Path leading to this unity: the Red Path, and not the Path of Technology. Our prophets also have taught that the world of the Fifth and Sixth Fires are to prepare and strengthen us. No one knows when the Seventh Fire will happen. It's part of the Great Mystery. It may be in my generation. Things are very powerful now... It may be that we are just fanning the embers of it, and it will be for my children...or grandchildren... The world and people of the Seventh Fire will only be when all Odawa have faithfully returned to the Red Path, destroying all non-Indian values and all people who follow them. We'll know of the Seventh Fire when a young man appears who will show us where to find the ancient and original Midewiwin birchbark scrolls which were buried during our long migration from the East, and our spiritual and physical illness will once again be overcome.

The myth asserts that non-Indians, and their obsession with technology, are destroying the earth and that only faithfulness to Odawa traditions can set it right. Like the classic role of the shaman, traditionalists are charged with purifying society and thereby establishing the setting for this total transformation and empowerment.

This myth, which explains the adversity of the technological, secular world, and highlights the terrible consequences of not following the traditional ways, is a classic example of new revitalistic myth-making. It also shares features of fundamentalism by depicting the traditionalists as the authorities who drive revitalization, and by depicting an ideal past to inform a constructive future. Also, because time/history is simultaneously cyclical and progressive in the myth, a new kind of historical consciousness is voiced in which the Odawa traditionalists will triumph.

This myth presents the model for proper ethical behaviour and anticipates cultural and even global transformation. A related ritual implements the model and, at least for the duration of the ritual, achieves the goal of cultural unification.[23] It is during the annual communal *Gi-be* feast, or 'Ghost Supper', a modified form of the ancestral ritual 'Feast of the Dead', when the implicit aim of the Odawa's revitalization movement is experienced: *the restoration of the right relationship.*

Living in a world constructed by extending social relationships through giving, the fundamental question that traditionalists face is 'who causes?' rather than 'what causes?' Events necessitate action for the Odawa because events are always personally motivated for good or ill. Because events are so motivated, they require and expect either an affirming or a resisting response. This expectation about behaviour is embodied in the myth of the Seventh Fire by Ki-je Manido (the concentration of power: *Ki-je* means 'great', *manido* means 'power') and by the culture-hero Nanabozho. Both mythological figures establish constructive interdependence as the goal of ritual and enjoin people with the ritual responsibility to work toward the balanced life that the contemporary Odawa understand as interpersonal solidarity. The Odawa's view that history results from personal actions instead of impersonal causes shows how they can reinterpret and reapply the 'Feast of the Dead' as a contemporary vehicle for creating and maintaining new forms of interband, intragroup, and intergroup solidarity, expanding and redefining social identity in the process.

While the *Gi-be* feast is a modified and simpler form of the 'Feast of the Dead', both rituals derive from the Odawa's conviction that their identity depends on their interdependence with each other and with their ancestors. The community is empowered by reinterpreting and reapplying both the instrumental exchanges in the Feast of the Dead and their expressive, or symbolic, meanings. Thus, the purpose of the feast is to contribute to the destination of community unification and sovereignty, the ritual event consisting of the actions of sharing and eating food that bonds the living community together and that group with its ancestors.

Today, the ritual event itself, which includes the action of sharing and eating food, expresses the rationale of unification. Sharing and eating not only unite the people, living and dead, but also unite two disparate levels of meaning. Sharing food is a gift of empowerment. By elaborating the symbolic content one step further, food itself becomes the medium for uniting people in compassionate and nurturing associations. The action of sharing food represents a conception of the ways that the community can be sustained, unified and thus become autonomous. The *Gi-be* feast involves a conceptual chain that highlights the ethical character of gift-exchange: Food as gift = sustenance = empowerment = unification = sovereignty.

Odawa traditionalists simultaneously enhance social solidarity and direct changing socio-religious experience through myth and its related discourse. They look to myth as the source for knowing how to respond to the changing social circumstances that have created a sense of crisis. For them, myth is a powerful medium for social orientation, maintenance, building and transformation, while simultaneously reinforcing the traditional religious structure. Myth voices traditional values, and the periodic transformation in social experience. Using questions implicit in myths as models for ethical behaviour, the Odawa subtly adapt their definitions of themselves and other people by asking, 'with whom should proper interpersonal relations be established?', 'how should interpersonal distance be mediated?', and 'to whom should the identity of dangerous foe be attributed?' Definitions of ethical people and behaviour are mapped by the actions of the great figures of mythology who present the values, ethics and behaviours that govern Odawa life, and the models for revitalizing a sovereign culture.

For Odawa traditionalists, communal access to sacred sites and the use of land for ritual activities are the most important steps towards achieving cultural revitalization and therefore sovereignty. But their successes gained through the workings of the law – the courts and Congressional Acts, especially the American Indian Religious Freedom Act and the American Indian Graves Protection and Repatriation Act – have been few. The law's continual denial of their land rights and collective religious expression is not only a 'structural' deprivation, it is the fundamental destructive act of annihilating traditionalists and their culture.

Odawa traditionalists view US law in terms of 'fences', 'lines', and 'ownership': that is, they see the Law as a defensive mechanism for others to create territorial or state or national boundaries, and to establish moral and civil mandates that separate a human being from himself, from others, and from the universe of ethical persons. The Odawa see the United States, which is framed within the law, in opposition to their model for establishing and maintaining proper interpersonal relationships. For Odawa traditionalists, proper relations are ordered and guided by gift-giving, which they understand to be a continuum of sharing and reciprocity, but for them the United States has never reciprocated anything. Consequently, they interpret relations with the United States as completely asymmetrical, and see US law as behaving with a total lack of exchange: the law owns and its withholds.

For Odawa traditionalists, then, the paramount questions are: 'how do we respond to such unethical behaviour?' and 'how do *we* establish proper relations with *them*?' Answering these questions is problematic because they interpret an absolute conflict between the operative metaphor that voices the US ethos and worldview through its concept of Law and the operative metaphor that voices the Odawa ethos and worldview through its concept of justice. The Odawa do not approach the world through the motto 'Equal Justice Under Law' but through the opposite: 'Equal Laws Under Justice'.

The Odawa occupy themselves with the skill of using power ethically to achieve social justice. Today, the prerogative of power is voiced through their call for social transformation in terms of the narrative of the Seventh Fire. It is also voiced in ritual activities – notably the *Gi-be* feast – that produce social solidarity. Because for them the organizational precepts of the traditional religious system are inseparable from all facets of the social matrix, it becomes paramount to apply those traditional religious values to legal endeavours to achieve ethnic solidarity. Yet, in reviewing Indian case law, we immediately recognize a clash in the operational metaphors guiding the concepts of law and justice between the non-Indian and Odawa cultures.

Milner S. Ball[24] is correct in identifying the predominant metaphor structuring the US legal system as 'law is the bulwark of freedom', and in warning of the hazards of such a defensive imagery. It is a metaphor rooted in the early Euro-American doctrine of discovery-and-conquest and extending to the present doctrine of ownership. The doctrine of discovery-conquest-ownership rests on a unique and distinctive Euro-American myth of 'progress'. This myth of progress could not be more removed from the mythological precepts guiding the operational metaphor that structures the Odawa ethos and worldview. Person-Gift-Power is the Odawa's system of mediating between co-operating and competing others. The key word in this process is 'mediates'. Mediating disagreements through gift-exchange reinforces the ideology that ethical acts of responsibility ultimately bond people together in dynamic relationships. The US metaphor 'law as bulwark' captures how non-Indian power rests on division, privatization and accumulation. The social world for the Odawa, however, derives from giving, which extends interpersonal relations. 'The twenty-one feathers on the tribal flag at powwows reminds us of the Twenty-one Instructions that guide our life', said a Pipe-carrier, 'They keep us in harmony. They're not laws. They weren't created by people. They were a gift to us from Ki-je Manido, our Great Grandfather. They bring us together'. Clearly, traditionalists view justice as a gift from the great figures of mythology, powerfully generating social unity, and they see this ontology as a sharp contrast to a world structured by laws that were made by people and are used for social control.

The US metaphor 'Law is the bulwark of freedom' voices the goal of protection against danger, especially dangerous others. The Odawa well understand this aspiration. However, their goal now is to protect themselves from a controlling United States by working through that very system. This seems to be an anomalous and impossible task in which success is not guaranteed. The Odawa battle in the courts is between *Law* v. *Gift as the Source of Protecting Against Chaos*. The metaphor 'law is the bulwark of freedom' reflects a reality in absolute conflict with the reality voiced by the metaphor structuring Odawa life. The Odawa see all too clearly that, in a system without true justice, laws become the source of power for those behind that system: 'The more laws, the merrier the mighty.' 'Law is the means by which White society can dominate and suppress,' said an Elder. This is the legal process Odawa traditionalists are trying to adapt to by relying on the existential value of using power ethically to transmute 'state of being', both in personal status and in ethnic identity. Understanding the power of metaphorical reinterpretation and reapplication, the Odawa can rework the central image of the American legal system. After all, events (marginalization) lead to actions (conflict) that have a purpose (positive change) directed to a specific goal (sovereignty). Once the legal system's controlling stance is rejected, a gift-cycle can be initiated based on exchange between the religious sphere and the social, economic, political and legal spheres. The Odawa world can be transformed if the aim of law is to mediate interpersonal distance and overcome a sense of otherness; that is, to mediate between disagreeing peoples through negotiation, as the councils have traditionally done. If the legal system becomes a channel for proper ethical action and response to social stress, it can open the door to communication and, therefore, to mediation which would result in positive change and ultimately to Odawa sovereignty.

The precedent for just and ethical action to produce positive change is apodictically laid out in Odawa myth. Within the contemporary myth of the Seventh Fire and its related ritual discourse, fire represents energy and life. Today, fire is the core symbol of vital energy, or power, and by extension, positive change, which will culminate in sovereignty. For the Odawa, fire is a focal point for conflicts that can be overcome only if the Law becomes a mediating and transparent medium – like fire – instead of a defensive and static arbitrating agency. In their 'last stand', Odawa revitalizationists, as they creatively work to achieve the Seventh Fire, have the most fundamental, and religiously dictated, weapon for achieving their goals of cultural continuity and sovereignty.

Notes

1. Because of the sensitivity of the Odawa's current socio-political activism, and the factionalism associated with it, it is essential to keep confidential the identity of the specific groups involved and of the individuals whom I consulted.
2. Pflüg 1992: 247-58.
3. Pflüg (forthcoming).
4. Pflüg 1992: 247-58.
5. *Johnston* v. *MacIntosh* [21 US 543: 1823].
6. *Cherokee Nation* v. *State of Georgia* [US 1: 1832].
7. American Indian Religious Freedom Act [AIRFA: PL-95-341, 92 Stat. 469, codified at 42 USC: 1978].
8. *Indian Citizen Act* [43 Stat. 253: 1924].
9. Michaelsen 1986: 251, 252.
10. *Wisconsin* v. *Yoder* [406 US 205, 214: 1972].
11. Petoskey 1985: 223.
12. Ibid.: 224.
13. *Sequoyah* v. *Tennessee Valley Authority* (480 F. Supp. 608 [ED Tenn.]: 1979; 620 F 2d 1159, 164 [6th Cir.] cert. denied, 449 US 953: 1980).
14. *Bandoni* v. *Higginson* (455 F. Supp. 641 [D. Utah]: 1977; 638 F. 2d 172, 180 [10th Cir.]: 1980; cert. denied, 452 US 954: 1981).
15. *Fools Crow* v. *Gullet* (541 F. Supp. 785 [DSD]: 1982).
16. *Wilson* v. *Block* (708 F. 2d 735, 742, n. 3 [DC Cir.]: 1983).
17. Petoskey 1985: 227.
18. See Lewis Coser, *The Functions of Social Conflict*, 1956. London: Routledge and Kegan Paul; James Mooney, *The Ghost Dance Religion and Wounded Knee*, [1896] 1973, New York: Dover; Philleo Nash, 'The Place of Religious Revivalism in the Formation of The Intercultural Community of The Klamath Reservation,' 1937, unpublished Ph. D. thesis, University of Chicago; Ralph Linton, 'Nativistic Movements', in *American Anthropologist* 45 (1943): 230-40; Anthony F.C. Wallace, 'Revitalization Movements', in *American Anthropologist* 58 (1956): 264-81; Peter Worsley, *The Trumpet Shall Sound: A Study of Cargo Cults in Melanesia*, 1957; London: MacGibbon and Kee; David Aberle, 'The Prophet Dance and Reactions to White Contact', in *Southwest Journal of Anthropology*, 15, 1 (1959): 74-83; Kenneth Burridge, *Mambu: A Melanesian Millenium*, 1960, London: Methuen, and *New Heaven, New Earth: A Study of Millenarian Activities*, 1969, New York; Schocken Books; Weston LaBarre, *The Ghost Dance: The Origins Of Religion*, 1970, Delta; Bryan R. Wilson, *Magic and the Millenium*, 1973, New York: Harper and Row; Ralph Thornton, *We Shall Live Again: The 1870 and 1890 Ghost Dance Movements as Demographic Revitalization*, 1986, Cambridge University Press; Robert H. Ruby and John A. Brown, *Dreamer-Prophets of The Columbia Plateau: Smohalla And Skolaskin*, 1989, vol. 191 of the Civilization of the American Indian Series, Norman: University of Oklahoma Press; Richard D. Hecht and Melissa A. Pflüg, 'The Great Lakes Odawa and Israel's Gush Emunim: Two Cases in Search of Adequate Theory – Revitalization and Fundamentalism' (in progress).
19. See Phillip Mason, *United States* v. *State of Michigan. Civil Action No. M 26-73. United States District Court: Western District of Michigan. Treaty of July 31, 1855. Summary Report* 8, 1978b, Detroit, MI: Wayne State University Reuther Archives.
20. See pt. 82 of the *Federal Code of Regulations*.
21. A confederation of bands not federally recognized, but in existence when Michigan was chartered as a state in 1837, and who operate under the Michigan Commission on Indian Affairs as umbrella agency in arbitrating with the state.
22. Pflüg (forthcoming).
23. Ibid. Also see Pflüg 1992: 247-58.
24. Ball 1985.

References

Ball, M.S. 1985. *Lying Down Together: Law, Metaphor, and Theology.* Madison: University of Wisconsin Press.

Michaelsen, R.S. 1986. 'Sacred Land in America: What is it? How can it be Protected?', *Religion* 16, 249-68.

Petoskey, J. 1985. 'Indians and the First Amendment', in V. Deloria, Jr. (ed.), *American Indian Policy in the Twentieth Century, 221-38.* Norman: University of Oklahoma Press.

Pflüg, M.A. 1992. ' "Breaking Bread": Ritual and Metaphor in Odawa Religious Practice', *Religion* 22 (3) 247-58.

—— (forthcoming). *The Seventh Fire: Myth And Ritual In Odawa Revitalization,.* Norman: University of Oklahoma Press.

RESACRALIZATION OF THE PROFANE

GOVERNMENT, RELIGION, AND ETHNICITY
IN MODERN GUATEMALA

Virginia Garrard-Burnett

Guatemala is, perhaps, one of the most 'religious' nations in Latin America. In 1990, its population was divided into three broad Catholic factions consisting of orthodox, practising Catholics; adherents of a highly syncretic mixture of Christian and indigenous beliefs practised by the nation's majority Maya Indian population; and of Catholics who by design or disinterest fall into neither of these former categories. Guatemala also claims one of Latin America's largest Protestant populations. Protestantism, particularly non-denominational Pentecostalism, cuts across class, ethnic and spatial lines in Guatemala. One-third of its people call themselves Protestants; of these, the vast majority have converted to Protestantism from some variation of Catholicism since the 1960s. Since 1982, Guatemala has had two Protestant heads of state.

This is unparalleled elsewhere in Latin America, where even the states which employ ideologically anti-Catholic rhetoric are governed by Roman Catholics, or even by professed atheists, but never by adherents of non-Catholic faiths. The importance of a Catholic identity for political advancement in Latin America is most obvious is the case of Alberto Fujimori, the president of Peru. Fujimori, the son of Japanese Buddhist immigrants, went to great pains during his 1991 presidential campaign to emphasize his Roman Catholicism. The purpose of this chapter is to explain how such a thing might happen, and, in doing so, to examine how Guatemalans have deconstructed the secular state.

The legacy of liberalism

Despite (or perhaps because of) this highly-charged religious culture, the government of Guatemala has been stridently secularized since the consolidation of the modern state in the late nineteenth century. Although obviously unversed in the writings of classical theorists of the then-emerging sociology of religion, Guatemala's first reformer, General Justo Rufino Barrios, followed a blueprint of nation-building and the expansion of state hegemony that equated the secularization of the state with modernization. For Barrios and many of his counterparts in the rest of

Latin America during the late nineteenth century, France – latinate, formerly Catholic, but eminently modern – served as a template.[1]

The philosophical nexus of the Barrios regime, and of the liberal governments which succeeded him, almost without interruption until the mid-twentieth century was Liberalism. Late nineteenth-century Liberalism in Guatemala was an eclectic mix of percolated ideas of the French Enlightenment, overlaid by the positivist ideology of France's Auguste Comte. Like its intellectual progenitors, Liberalism was profoundly anti-clerical – in his first year of office alone, Barrios banned holy orders, secularized cemeteries, sold off church properties, and effectively stripped the Catholic Church of all its political and economic power. The following year, he evicted foreign (mainly Spanish) members of monastic orders, placed a limit on the number of Catholic clergy who could reside in the country, and passed a decree of 'freedom of religion' that not only permitted but encouraged Protestants to enter the country.[2]

Many scholars have argued that Barrios's anti-clerical reform was intended solely for the purpose of nation-building – to weaken the agency that competed most efficiently with the state for the hearts and minds of the populace, not to mention strategic political and economic resources. I submit that Barrios's policies were not merely anti-clerical, but specifically anti-Catholic. Evidence of this lies in the fact that Barrios's anti-clerical policies intruded more on the practice of worship than did those of his Liberal counterparts such as Benito Juarez or Porfirio Díaz in Mexico, who were generally content to reduce the Church's temporal power, but not impinge upon its spiritual hegemony.[3] The implications of this are twofold. First, Barrios and his successors believed that secularization – and specifically, the divorce of the public sphere from Catholicism – and modernization, as defined in positivist terms of 'order and progress' were intrinsically linked. Second, the historical record (in the form of preferential legislation, enticements and police protection for Protestant missionaries and the like) indicates that Guatemala Liberals believed that the introduction of Protestantism into the cultural discourse, might, in a Weberian sense, contribute to the furtherance of both.[4]

In terms of this first implication, the Liberal era, which, with the exception of a decade-long hiatus in the 1920s, lasted until 1944, was largely successful in secularizing the Guatemalan state – and in emasculating the institutional Church at large. Although Guatemala's anti-clerical decrees were similar to legislation enacted at the turn of the century in many nations across the region, it was unique both in how adamantly those laws were enforced and, as John Lloyd Mecham has noted, how long they persisted without change.[5] By the middle of the twentieth century, from an institutional perspective, Guatemala seemed to have lost its faith. The episcopal structure of the Church, while maintaining some ties with urban, elite sectors of the population, was almost entirely absent in many parts of the densely-populated, pre–dominantly Indian western highlands. As a number of ethnological studies have eloquently shown, very little institutional, orthodox Catholic in-fluence has penetrated many Indian communities, in some cases since the early years of this century.[6] Catholic missionaries to the remote but densely- populated Indian districts of Huehuetenango and San Marcos in the early 1940s found not a single priest present in either department.[7] Tight government restrictions, rigorously enforced, severely limited the number of priests who could enter the country, even for a short visit, and capped the number of domestic clergy to be permitted to take their vows. Even as late as 1945-54, only three priests were ordained in Guatemala, and the ratio of Catholics to priests was a top-heavy 16,039:1.[8]

The institutional weakness of the Catholic Church in Guatemala masked the great strength of organic Catholicism during this period, a point we shall return to later. Yet, by mid-century the political alienation of the institutional Church was significant but not complete, as shown by the reaction and influence of the Catholic hierarchy to Guatemala's 'ten years of Spring' – a period of political and social experimentation between 1944 and 1954.[9] The revolutionary governments of this era repudiated Liberalism, dabbled in socialism, and were eventually ousted by a CIA-backed coup, thus making Guatemala one of the first 'victories' in the Cold War, and marking the beginning of the ardently anti-communist reign of generals that characterized that nation until 1986. The literature and historical debate on Guatemala's decade of revolution is vast, but on the issues of state secularization and church marginalization the revolutionaries varied little from the liberal predecessors they so despised. While the anti-clericalism of Barrios and his successors (all liberal neo-positivists) was philosophically grounded in Voltaire and Comte, that of the revolutionary presidents Arévalo and Arbenz owed more to Durkheim and Marx.

In terms of secularization, what does distinguish the revolutionary period is the reaction of a key group of conservative ultra-orthodox Catholics to a government that it perceived as being the 'opening wedge of communism'. Important opponents of the regime in the institutional Church included the reform-minded but ardently anti-communist Archbishop Mariano Rossell y Arellano, as well as an influential Catholic group affiliated to the Spanish falangists, who denounced the revolu-tionary government from paper and pulpit. They also openly supported the oppositional Movement for National Liberation (MLN), which used as its emblem a cross and sword.[10] When the MLN successfully ousted the revolutionary president Jacobo Arbenz in 1954, the new military government vowed to reward the hierarchy for its support by restoring the Church to its ancient position of political and economic prominence.

However, save for the restitution of the Church's juridic personality, the restoration of some church property, and an end to the quota on the number of clergy permitted into the country, this new status never fully materialized.[11] Indeed, the entry of new clergy into the country, which is controlled by the Vatican rather than a national diocesan see, had the impact of actually weakening the local hierarchy's control over affairs of the national church.[12] Thus, the Church retained its position of political disarticulation; a status which it retains, to some degree, to the present.

While some have credited the failure of the military to re-empower the Church – that is, the military government feared that the Church might become a potential contender for power and allegiance – I would argue that the opposite circumstances prevailed. The Church was not restored to power because it had, effectively, already been relegated to its own sphere, and its power did not extend beyond those parameters. As an institution the Church was, explicitly, *not* a contender for power and allegiance, and for that reason, the military government had no reason to admit it into its own hegemony. This would seem to confirm the central paradigm of modernization theory: that as society becomes more complex and specialized in function, religion becomes less diffused through society and more confined to its own limited arena.[13]

Popular religiosity and indigenous religious movements

If the institutional history of Catholicism in Guatemala through this period seems to bear out the paradigms of modernization and secularization, however, the history of the popular church(es) does not. Implicit in theories of secularization is that modernization either marginalizes religion to the very fringes of society, or that religion dies out entirely. But in Guatemala, the 'secularization' of the institutional Church seems to bear a direct and inverse correlation to the strength of popular religious movements and organizations, especially in indigenous sectors. Yet because popular religious movements and even formal para-religious organizations have not always conformed to the form and content of orthodox Catholicism, the institutional Church itself has been reluctant to tap – or even recognize – the power vested in such groups.

Popular Catholicism, as opposed to the more formal, orthodox institution of the Church, has always been vital at a capillary level in Guatemala. Since colonial times, the ratio of priests to people who call themselves Catholics has been small and the presence of the institutional Church slight, especially in the Indian western highlands, where in the past the majority of the population has lived. The incursions of Liberal reform only accentuated these tendencies. Day-to-day religious observance had, since late colonial times, been maintained by religious brotherhoods, known as *cofradias*, which had their origins in Spain, but which had evolved in the New World into confessional loci of ethnic identity. By 1910, many Indian communities retained only the most tenuous ties to the formal Church; most lacked the presence of a resident parish priest, and many were only sporadically able to enlist the talents of itinerant clergy to fulfil their sacramental needs.[14] Yet the lack of clergy did not imply a religious lapse. To the contrary, indigenous communities developed highly complex confessional societies, run by the *cofradias*, and ideologically centred on a syncretic blend (*costumbre*) of orthodox Christianity, Mayan beliefs and religious forms, shamanism, and politico-religious ritual. It is important to note that most practitioners of *costumbre* considered themselves to be '*muy católico*', although their beliefs and practices often strayed far beyond the confines of European Christianity.[15]

By the late 1940s, the influence and heterodoxy of the *costumbristas* was such that the institutional Church launched a systematic program of 'revitalization' to reassert its ideological hegemony over Indian religion, under the aegis of the Catholic Action movement.[16] The timing here is hardly accidental in that it coincides with the political and economic reforms of the revolutionary period, when Indian communities were embroiled in the intricacies of land reform, expanded educational opportunities, and, for the first time, participation in politics on a national level. Thus, the impulse for Catholic revitalization in Indian communities is reflective of the clerical *bête noire* of modernization, based as it was on the experience of Western Europe. In this sense, the Church's push for orthodoxy through Catholic Action was a preemptive strike against its own marginalization in Indian society, where the fear was that as society became more 'developed', in a subjectively Western sense, religion would be increasingly relegated to the periphery. Secondly, it was through Catholic Action that the Church sought to solidify its influence in religious space at a time when bourgeoisie liberalism and rhetorical Marxism threatened to complete the fissure between the religious and the political spheres.

The ethnohistorical record is replete with evidence that the Catholic Church was in no way prepared for the bitter resistance it encountered in indigenous communities to Catholic Action, perhaps because the Church had itself assumed that the modernizing programmes of the Guatemalan government had already diffused the intense religiosity of Indian society.[17] Just as Maya religious icons had been secreted away during the Spanish conquest, *cofradia* members brought statues of saints to new and secure sacred spaces and, when possible, banished converts to orthodox Catholicism (catechists) from society and kin. Some communities refused to allow local chapels to be used by priests affiliated to Catholic Action, while in at least one instance, government military forces – in an unlikely convergence of common interests – put down a riot incurred by the efforts of a parish priest to move into the local church.[18] But ultimately, the effect of Catholic Action, from a structural view point, was to shatter the local hegemony of *costumbre*. In dividing indigenous communities into factions of catechist and traditionalist, to paraphrase Peter Berger, the sacred canopy was rent, thus creating an opening for new religious and political ideologies.[19]

A 'bombardment of twentieth century forces' and Protestant growth

The time was ripe for such an opening, for by the early 1960s Guatemala was undergoing profound socio-economic change. Many scholars attribute these changes to the unrelenting struggle between leftist guerrillas and the military-controlled government that has defined Guatemala's political reality since 1961; indeed the violence, displacement and human cost of the government's cyclical efforts to purge the country of leftists and their supporters have had a profound impact on the nation's collective psyche.[20] Nevertheless, it is too facile to credit Guatemala's crisis solely to what Guatemalans euphemistically refer to as *la política*.[21] The crisis that began in the 1960s, accelerated in the 1970s, and erupted in the early 1980s was at heart based on the transition to the long-coveted goal of 'modernization'. So profound and traumatic has this process been in Guatemala that Sheldon Annis has referred to it as a 'bombardment of twentieth-century forces'.[22]

It is outside the scope of this chapter to offer a detailed description of this period, other than to offer up some statistical milestones. During the 1960s, Guatemala experienced a 'green revolution', when the introduction of pesticides and fertilizers, and crop diversification away from a virtually monocultural dependence on coffee, gave a tremendous boost to its export economy, which by the 1970s was one of the most dynamic in all Latin America.[23] Second, improvements in medicine and public health services promoted a significant population boom. Between 1950 and 1973 the national population nearly doubled, increasing from 3 to 5.6 million people; by far the most rapid population growth was in the indigenous sector.[24] The combined effects of dramatic population increase coupled with the diversion of additional lands for export crops precipitated an acute land shortage for indigenous people. With this came concomitant stresses to traditional patterns of land ownership, community and kinship obligations and loyalties, and even to religious identity.

For some these issues together with simple economic expediency forced them to abandon the ancient loyalties of place and community and relocate themselves to urban areas. Like many Latin American capitals, Guatemala City

grew dramatically after 1960; by 1990 it was home to 2 million inhabitants, compared to 600,000 only thirty years before.[25] The influx
of migrations to the city was greatest during those times when warfare
in the countryside was most intense; thus, in the 1978-82 and 1982-3
periods, when as many as one million Guatemalans were displaced
and tens of thousands died, migration to the capital surged. The dual
impact of forced displacement and urban migration is extensive and
complex, but what is germane to our purposes here is its effect on
religiosity.

As Edward Cleary notes: 'The dislocations of many persons from
ties to local communities and the reforging of personal relations, including
religious ones, opened the way to renegotiation of allegiances to traditional institutions.'[26] The clearest evidence of this type of renegotiation
could be found in the sudden proliferation of Protestant churches which
sprang up in poor sections of Guatemala City in the mid-1960s. One
simple statistic offers dramatic testimony to this growth: in the 1960s
an informal national census placed the number of Protestants in
Guatemala at less than 2 per cent of the population. By 1990 that
figure had grown to more than 33 per cent.[27] The rapid and precipitous
growth of poor, urban and usually Pentecostal Protestant churches was
remarkable, especially given the fact that Protestant missionaries had
toiled in Guatemala since the time of Barrios and had failed to make
any substantial number of converts or to influence national life in any
substantial way prior to the 1960s. Of even greater significance is the
fact that the meteoric rise of Protestantism did not take place in the
institutional missionary-based denominations, but in independent, often
autochthonous Pentecostal congregations, which typically had few or
no direct ties to a larger denominational structure, either in Guatemala
or elsewhere, such as in the United States.

There is an extensive body of literature that attempts to describe
the sudden and spontaneous growth of Protestant churches in Guatemala
and in Latin America in general, and it is beyond the scope of this
chapter to offer an extensive review of those works. Yet the phenomenon
that David Martin calls 'a Protestant explosion' does demand some
explanation here. In accounting for the growth of Protestantism in urban
Guatemala, we may still rely on the classic work of Bryan Roberts,
a sociologist who, in a study published in 1967, was the first academic
to note the proliferation of Protestant churches in Guatemala, the vast
majority of which both then and now were both 'fundamentalist' and
Pentecostal.[28] Roberts credited the growth of Protestant churches to
a variety of factors, tied primarily to urban migration and social dislocation. He argued that Protestant churches were functional substitutes
for lost bonds of kinship and community, and were more effective
as such than the Catholic Church due to its shortage of priests and

general lack of apostolic presence in poor areas. He also suggested that 'Protestant values' lent a paternalistic order and discipline to new migrants' lives, particularly through their censures, like the prohibitions against sinful activities such as smoking, drinking and gambling. In Roberts' words: 'Sect doctrine... provides them practical means to alleviate dangers of economic insecurity'.[29]

What was unique about Roberts' work is that he was the first to identify and interpret the growth of Protestantism in urban Guatemala. In his analysis of why such growth occurred and its consequences, however, Roberts shared the theoretical limelight with other sociologists, such as Christian Lalive d'Epinay and Emilio Willems, who covered much of the same theoretical ground in their studies of similar phenomena of Protestant growth in Chile and Brazil.[30] All three of these pioneering works suggested that the expansion of Protestantism in Latin America was directly linked to the consequences of modernization. Moreover, all three authors, heavily influenced by Weber, predicted that the construction of Protestantism in Latin America would be identical to that of Europe: that is, symbiotically fused to the inexorable processes of modernization, capitalism and social secularization. While this analysis offers a valuable model for understanding motives for conversion in urban areas, it is not an especially satisfactory explanation for that rapid proliferation of Protestant denominations, sects and autonomous movements that spread dramatically through rural Guatemala in the 1970s and '80s. We shall return to this point later.

The dramatic and very visible growth of Protestantism during this period overshadowed an equally important renegotiation of religious alliances within the Catholic Church. The vortex of transformation was again the Guatemalan Catholic Action movement, which, after the conciliar sea-changes of Vatican II (1962-5), became associated with the politically-charged praxis of Liberation Theology. The interests of these two movements, which might seem at first to be contradictory, nonetheless converged through the work of foreign Catholic missionary societies during the 1960s. In the late 1950s and early '60s, orders such as the Maryknolls, the Jesuits and the Sacred Heart brothers began to send fairly large numbers of clergy into Indian areas, with the twin objectives of bringing their flock into line with contemporary Catholicism and introducing them to new economic arrangements, such as farming co-operatives.[31] As the decade progressed, the focus of Catholic Action in Guatemala slowly shifted away from the fight against heterodoxy to that against economic, ethnic and political injustice.

Catholic political activism and the Guatemalan civil war

As Ricardo Falla and Key Warren have described in some detail, the mid-to late-1970s saw a political awakening among Indians of the highlands, particularly after 1976 when a devastating earthquake literally laid bare the worst social and political inequities in the nation. In part, this mobilization was nurtured by the government's heightened political and social repression following the earthquake, and the revitalization of the guerrilla movement. Seen in one light, Indian political mobilization appears to be an example of emergent class struggle, following a classic Marxist and conspicuously secular model. Yet the entry of Indians (either as combatants or, as was much more often the case, as passive sympathizers) into the political struggle carried with it a distinctly confessional subtext, in that indigenous peoples were often politicized in the crucible of the Catholic Action movement. Catechists, who had rebelled against the traditional order in their communities, now challenged the system at large.[32]

The popular church in western Guatemala suffered gravely during this period. Fourteen priests were murdered, as were hundreds of lay catechists, but the murder of its people provoked no formal protest from the national church.[33] At the same time, Protestant churches and microdenominations spread rapidly and spontaneously throughout the Indian highlands, riding the crest of a trend of rural growth that had begun after the 1976 earthquake. Again, the reasons behind this surge of conversions have been the subject of much scholarly conjecture. Most hypotheses hinge in some way on the economic and political expediency of conversion and the effects of the violence; in short, most view conversion to Protestantism as a strategy of survival.[34] This view, to my mind, is overly reductionist in that it diminishes the notion of religious allegiance to simple economic and political rationality, but the theory does underline an essential fact: Protestants, while not immune to the violence during this period, were not nearly as likely as Catholic catechists to be labelled 'subversives' and thus eliminated.

Guatemalan catechists, unlike their counterparts in El Salvador, had no champion in the Archdiocese, nor did they enjoy any support or protection from the Church hierarchy. In part this was because the most politically active catechists tended to be poor and ethnic, the armed conflict was in the hinterland, and the clergy involved tended to be from foreign orders and therefore outside of the control of the Archibishopric. However, an exception was the archbishop, Mario Casariego, who declined to endorse the protest by the Bishop of El Quiché, a large diocese in one of the most egregious zones of conflict, who 'closed' his diocese in 1980 to protest at the atrocities that the Guatemalan army had committed against his clergy and lay catechists. Instead, the archbishop lent his support to the military government, perhaps to protect the tiny bit of political and social space that the institutional church retained *vis-à-vis* the state at large.[35]

The holy war of General Efraín Ríos Montt

It was not until 1982 that the artificial construct of separation of Church and State began to crack, and only then under the blow of an unlikely iconoclast. In March 1982, Efraín Ríos Montt, a general and born-again Pentecostal, took power in a military coup. Although Ríos Montt remained in power for less than eighteen months (he was himself ousted by his fellow military officers in August 1983), his brief tenure as head of state continues to cast a long shadow over Guatemala's political discourse.

Ríos Montt's enduring notoriety results as much from what he stands for as it does from what he accomplished. As president, his achievements were both efficacious and deadly. By demanding an end to 'cadavers on the roadside', he clamped down on Guatemala City's rampant urban crime and paramilitary assassinations; by forcing government officials to take a vow of honesty and by monitoring their performance, he greatly diminished graft in the national bureaucracy. But what Ríos Montt is most remembered for is his successful counter-insurgency war against the guerrillas. In the summer of 1982, the Guatemalan army, under Ríos' orders, launched an extensive scorched-earth campaign in the Indian western highlands to flush out and eliminate the guerrillas, their supporters and even neutral parties not actively loyal to the government's cause.

As a military strategy, the campaign was so successful that it is fondly recalled in Latin American military circles as 'the Guatemalan solution'. The guerrillas, whose numbers never exceeded a few thousand combatants, were decimated though not wiped out completely. The human cost of the campaign was horrific, especially among the indigenous population: 100,000 children became orphans, whole villages disappeared, perhaps as many as one million people went into internal and external exile, and communities were forced into resettlement camps and obligatory service in civil patrols.[36]

Despite the extremes of this period, the military aspects of Ríos Montt's programs differed from those of his predecessor in intensity, but not in kind. Guatemala has had more than its share of military strongmen, of which Ríos Montt was only one of a long series. Between 1966 and 1968, a fellow officer, Col. Carlos Arana Osorio, had presided over a sweeping counter-insurgency campaign that rivalled Ríos Montt's in its bloody efficiency.[37] What did distinguish General Ríos Montt from his fellow generals was the way in which he slashed through a century of state secularism to proclaim the war a holy crusade, not only against godless Communism but also against superstition, backwardness and the secular sins inherent in unbridled modern development.

Ríos Montt's message of salvation from Communism and the devil – which he delivered each Sunday night on national television – was met with scepticism and even ridicule in sectors of the Guatemalan elite, the Army and the Catholic Church. Outside these groups, Ríos Montt enjoyed considerable support, at least in the cities, where the civil war was not so evident and where common crime had been reduced to a bare minimum under his aegis. Not surprisingly, he enjoyed great support from most – though not all – his fellow evangelicals, who believed that Ríos Montt's political emergence (which fortuitously coincided with the centenary of the arrival of the first Protestant missionaries in the country) marked the beginning of their own social and, to a lesser extent, political ascendency.[38]

A fair amount has been written in the popular press about Ríos' strident Protestant identity, the Army's repression of Catholic catechists, and the role that Protestant denominations played in the 'reconstruction' of the country during his regime. While there is ample evidence for all of this, I would argue that Ríos Montt's agenda was formed less by evangelical beliefs than by the cold, pragmatic calculations of an ardently anti-communist general. To wit: Ríos Montt's counter-insurgency campaign, for all its pious language, was planned and executed by the Army High Command, an extremely secular body. His pogrom purged Protestants as ruthlessly as it did Catholics when the situation seemed to demand it; moreover, the Army granted equal access to both Catholic and Protestant relief agencies to work in resettlement villages. Most importantly, there was nothing identifiably 'Protestant' about Ríos Montt's pacification programme, save the rhetoric of salvation from evil (communism), and his largely unsuccessful efforts to enlist financial assistance from conservative fundamentalist groups in the United States.[39]

The same cannot be said, however, about his anti-graft campaign for government employees, and his anti-crime campaign. These programmes were highly moralistic in tone, and 'Protestant' in the sense that Ríos Montt openly equated Catholicism with stasis and corruption. It was largely because of the success of the anti-graft programme (and the resulting reduction in bureaucrats' take-home pay) that Ríos Montt was ultimately ousted from office. An apocryphal tale reports that as Ríos Montt was evicted from the National Palace, his escort mockingly paraphrased the motto of the anti-corruption campaign ('I don't steal, I don't lie, I don't abuse privilege'): 'The government that doesn't steal,' Ríos was told, 'doesn't govern.'

In a secular or liberal society, Ríos Montt's political fortunes might have resembled those of Jimmy Carter, the president of the United States from 1976 to 1980, whose personal conviction and confessional approach to governing were sadly out of step with the spirit of the times in America. But where Jimmy Carter quietly withdrew from politics as a failure, Ríos Montt continues to hold important political currency in Guatemala. His enduring legacy lies less in his programme than in the fact that he abandoned the ideal of secular government. In openly and purposefully basing his government and policies on religious precepts (if even only in rhetoric), Ríos Montt reconnected Guatemalan politics with ancient precedents that reach back far beyond medieval Spain and Tecúm Uman, the priest-king of the Quiché Maya. That Ríos Montt's personal religion is Protestant is important, but less so than the fact that he reconstructed national political discourse in such as way as to permit religion, both Catholic and Protestant, to play an overt role.

Sacralization of the profane: Guatemalan national politics since 1983

Since 1983, politics and, equally important, political perceptions have increasingly defined themselves along religious lines. This is not to imply a simple dichotomy between liberal (leftist) Catholics and conservative (rightist) Protestants. This is true in part because Guatemala's Protestants are a notoriously divisive lot, who have well earned the moniker 'protest-ant'. The large Protestant population in Guatemala is divided within itself by class, ethnicity, geography, theology, political opinion, and it also includes a large faction who believes that political participation of any kind is profane. For nearly ten years, wealthy urban Pentecostals have made a concerted effort to create a confessional-based political bloc, but the fissures inherent within Guatemalan Protestantism, coupled with a lack of a single, overarching 'Protestant' ideology, have thus far rendered these efforts ineffective.

But despite this lack of coherence, 'Protestant', used as an adjective instead of a noun, has an important social and political cachet in Guatemala in the post-Ríos Montt era. The lingering aura of Ríos Montt's regime, now given a softer edge in popular memory, has caused Guatemalans, both Catholic and Protestant alike, to associate Protestantism with desirable and modern (and distinctly Weberian) traits like honesty, integrity, discipline and personal initiative. In popular lore, stories abound of job applicants lying about their church affiliation in the belief that they are more likely to be perceived as 'honest and trustworthy' if employers think they are Protestant. In another variation on this theme, visitors are said to carry Bibles openly with them on visits to local prisons, in the hope that capricious guards will be more likely to trust Protestants than Catholics for admission into prison compounds.[40]

The presidential election of 1990 offers the clearest example of how religion, and specifically, a minority faith, had become the defining element in national politics. This election was particularly important, in that it marked Guatemala's first peaceful transition of power from one civilian president to another in the twentieth century.[41] It also marked the first time that candidates from parties from the political left and centre left had freely competed against parties of the centre right and far right. Although a few of these competing factions, such as the Christian Democratic Party, carried some religious association, none was explicitly affiliated to a specific church or denomination.

Midway through the presidential campaign, however, Efraín Ríos Montt threw his own hat into the political arena. He did not attempt to run as a 'Protestant candidate' *per se*, but he made it clear that his second term as President would strongly reiterate the themes of the first, particularly in his calls for 'Protestant values', such as discipline and law-and-order. Ríos Montt quickly dominated the field of candidates, gaining strong support across all social sectors. Most surprising of all, he was the leading presidential contender even in areas where voters were themselves survivors of Ríos Montt's scorched-earth campaigns (and, perhaps not coincidentally, where Protestantism had expanded significantly over the ensuring years).

The possibility that Ríos Montt might actually win the presidency was so great that the Guatemalan Supreme Court eventually ruled his candidacy illegal. Yet the battle lines of confessional politics had already been drawn. In early 1991, Guatemalans elected as their president Jorge Serrano Elías, a centre-right businessman, whose lacklustre campaign had floundered until Ríos Montt left the race. Until that time, Serrano had been politically indistinguishable from most of the other candidates, but he was the only Protestant on the ballot.[42] His election could only be seen as proof of popular demand to further strengthen the political role of religion – or at least of religious identity – in Guatemalan society.[43]

But what of the Roman Catholic Church? Serrano could not have been elected without the solid support of Catholic voters, who still comprise two-thirds of the national population. Still, in 1990, a clear-cut Catholic political identity was still inchoate. Guatemalan Catholicism, as we have seen, has never been monolithic, and within the institutional Church a variety of different, and sometimes conflicting, political and religious ideologies have long coexisted. Yet the repression of sectors of the Church over the past two decades, coupled with the rephrasing of the political idiom, is forcing the Church to redefine its place in a society that is moving away from the ideal of secularism. But the irony is that it is Protestantism, and not Catholicism, that has already set the stakes. Thus the 'Mother Church' finds its new political identity in opposition – a role normally reserved to minority faiths in confessional or generally religious societies.

The Roman Catholic Church is moving cautiously but decisively out of this marginalized position. In a break with precedent, the archbishop who succeeded Casariego after his death in 1983, Próspero

Penados del Barrio, has issued a series of bold pastoral letters that unabashedly seek to win back the moral high ground from the Protestants, and reassert the Catholic Church's ethical hegemony over the hearts and minds of Guatemalans. Three of these letters articulate the new political vision of the Church. Two, *Clamor por Tierra* (Cry for Land) (1988) and *Pastoral Indígena* (Pastoral Letter on Indigenous Peoples) (1992) stand in strident opposition to long-standing government policies on land tenure and ethnic rights, two issues on which the institutional church has in the past been noticeably silent. A third, *Signo de Verdad y Esperanza* (Symbol of Truth and Hope – 1989), asserts that the Catholic Church is 'moving toward a moment of special vitality', as it reestablishes its position of authority in Guatemalan society.[44] This assertion is not as premature as it may appear, even given the Protestant onslaught; for the first time in the more than one hundred years since the liberal reform, Guatemala's Catholic seminaries are filled to overflowing.[45] In post-secular Guatemala, both Protestantism and Catholicism flourish.

The case of Guatemala has a unique place in the discourse of secularism. If, as Durkheim, Weber and Gramsci all agree, religion is a datum of social reality, then it should come as no surprise that the dramatic changes in Guatemala's social landscape that have taken place over recent decades should have had a dynamic impact on religion. What is surprising, perhaps, is the form that religious change has taken.

First, and perhaps most obvious, is the rise of Protestantism in Guatemala. That Protestantism would accompany 'modernization', the expansion and maturation of capitalism, rapid urbanization, and the like is fully congruent with Max Weber's equation of the relationship between economic rationality and religious ethic. What is less obvious is that the variety of Protestantism – Pentecostalism – that has taken hold in Guatemala would not seem to inculcate the types of 'Protestant virtues' like Puritanism and rationality that Weber associates with the 'spirit of capitalism'. On the contrary, may Guatemalan converts value Pentecostalism for its very 'irrationality' and otherworldliness, two traits that seem eminently at odds with a 'modern' *Weltanschauung*. And yet, non-Pentecostals perceive their brethren to be very Puritan-like: trustworthy, frugal, honest and no-nonsense. Do these qualities, either real or perceived, point to that which Zeitlin calls the 'elective affinity' between Protestantism and capitalism?[46] There can be no doubt that in many large 'health and wealth'-oriented neo-Pentecostal churches, the affinity is both elective and eagerly sought after. But is it also true for Indian churches in the countryside, where many Pentecostal congregations have become new foci of small-group and even ethnic identity? If the answer is no, then we must accept the possibility that the dynamic and function of Pentecostalism, or even Protestantism in general, is quite different in this context; that is both moulds and is moulded by a distinctly non-Western cultural milieu.

A second point to be drawn from the Guatemalan example is the way in which society, at least on a meta-level, has shifted from pious to secular, and then back again. This pattern runs counter to most of the canon of literature on secularization, which, at least until the late 1960s, looked to France as a model, particularly for Catholic (or formerly Catholic) countries.[47] In the French example, the Catholic Church placed itself on the wrong side of the French Revolution in the eighteenth century and has lost power, privilege and moral authority to the state civil society since that time. By the mid-twentieth century, many scholars agree, the Church in France was moribund.[48] A less particular way of framing this set of circumstances has been to take a structural approach towards modernization. Such a model postulates that, as society becomes more complex, a division of labour emerges whereby institutions become more highly specialized and increasingly in need of their own technicians. As this happens, an agency that once performed multiple functions, like the Church, which formerly influenced spheres as diverse as medicine, government, and gender relations, becomes more and more circumscribed to its own area of expertise – in this case, the spiritual realm.[49] In this model, the process is linear and immutable.

The case of Guatemala runs aground on both of these models. What the forgoing case study makes abundantly clear is that the political marginalization of the institutional Church has strengthened the influence of popular religious movements, which may or may not be associated with the Catholic Church at large. One might speculate, with tongue firmly in cheek, that if religion has been relegated to its own sphere, the religious sphere is unusually large in Guatemala. A second place where Guatemala differs dramatically from the models is in the fact that here the process of secularization has been neither linear nor ir-reversible, as demonstrated by the presidencies of Ríos Montt and Serrano Elías, and the political reawakening of the Catholic Church at large.

There are two factors which make Guatemala unique from, say Iran, where religious technicians turned a secular nation into a rigidly con-fessional country virtually overnight. One is that neither Ríos Montt nor Serrano Elías were, after all, priest-kings, whose agendas were framed strictly around religious precepts – although the 'air of sanctity' of both was an important measure of their political potency. Secondly, the resacralization of Guatemalan government has been wrought thus far by Protestants, and not by the church that still claims, on at least some level, the loyalty of most of the nation's people. Thus, as Guatemala moves towards 'religious' society, it does so in a most general sense. This is not a nationalistic effort to summon forth the ghosts of a mythical

Catholic past (as in Spain under Franco) nor to fend off the demons of modernism (as in Saudi Arabia).

A final essential point which the case of Guatemala brings to the fore is the matter of the institutional Catholic Church's new political articulation. The tenor of the Church's new political voice – of formal, official, and recognized opposition – calls to mind the predictions of Gramsci, who wrote, 'religion...will be part of a comprehensive... process... for bringing the masses closer to the intellectuals in the construction of a social and individual discipline and for using the everyday experience of humans in the construction of hegemonic consensus'.[50] In Guatemala this process is reversed: the Church is opening its own hegemonic borders to include interests and concerns that once lay beyond its periphery. Indeed, it is the masses themselves who may bring the intellectuals into their own construction of hegemony. Under circumstances such as these, secularization does not herald the decline of religion, but it does usher in processes which force religion to dramatically redefine (and perhaps even expand) its place and function within society.[51]

In his work *Tongues of Fire* David Martin has suggested that one reason for the way in which modernization and secularization have paralleled one another in Europe is because religious monopoly in Europe inhibited the adaptability of religion to social change. By comparison, he argues, in the United States, where not one religion was related to a particular body of élites or to the state, 'religion adapts quite successfully to the changing world'.[52] We would argue that adaptability, rather than monopoly, is the key to understanding the Guatemalan case. Since colonial times, religion (in its most inclusive sense) in Guatemala has exhibited a marvelous elasticity. It has shown an enduring ability to expand, contract and take new shapes and contours, while retaining its fundamental density. The end of religious monopoly has offered new variations in religious adaptation, and new opportunities for socioreligious innovation. In short, as Guatemala evolves into a post-secular society, both Catholic and Protestant religion alike may become, in Daniel Levine's words, a 'convenient place from which to begin...cultural reconstruction'.[53]

Notes

1. There is a fairly extensive body of literature which deals with the Liberal Reform under Barrios, but few works focus sharply on liberal relations with the Church. A sampling of the best would include: Burgess 1926; Mecham 1966; and Miller 1971. For a broader view of Guatemalan society in the same period, see McCreery,

Rural Guatemala, 1760-1945 (1994). A book that provides a useful conceptual framework for understanding the 'nation-building' project of the late nineteenth century is Anderson 1983.

2. Barrios's desire for a Protestant presence in Guatemala was so great that when no Protestant denomination sent a missionary to Guatemala for ten years, he personally travelled to New York in 1883 to enlist the services of a Presbyterian minister to come to Guatemala.

3. For amplification of the Mexican case, see Baldwin 1990, and Bastian 1990. Juarez did, however, lend his support to a group of dissident Catholic priests, who briefly and unsuccessfully attempted to establish a reformed, autonomous Catholic Church. Their objective was to have 'the organization of a reformed church, intended to be national, liturgic, and having its foundations laid in the scriptures and its Apostolic pattern'. (Baldwin 1990: 14).

4. Garrard-Burnett 1990: 13-31 and Garrard-Burnett 1989c: 127-42.

5. Mecham 1966: 370, cited in Cleary and Stewart-Gambino, 1992.

6. The anthropologists who first mapped the ethnography of highland Guatemala in the middle years of the twentieth century left a substantial body of 'thick description' of what was then considered to be Indian folk Catholicism. The most influential of these studies were: Adams 1957; Bunzel 1952; Oakes 1951; Tax 1953.

7. Cleary 1992: 170.

8. Ibid., 170.

9. Juan José Arévalo, a civilian, served as president of the republic from 1944 until 1951. His administration was based on principles that he defined as 'spiritual socialism', which allowed open political expression, granted rights to organized labour, and stressed education. Arévalo was succeeded in office by Col. Jacobo Arbenz who attempted to address the terrible inequities in land ownership by expropriating large landholdings and redistributing the properties to landless peasants. In 1954, after Arbenz expropriated land from the nation's largest landholder, the US-owned United Fruit Company, he was ousted in a coup. For further reading on this period, see Gleijeses 1991; Immerman 1982; Schlesinger and Kinzer 1983.

10. See Frankel 1969; Garrard-Burnett 1989a: 205-33

11. Calder in Adams 1970: 259-60, 310-11.

12. Warren 1978: 93.

13. Cleary 1992: 197-8. Cleary states that the theoretical approaches to modernization are well described in Wuthnow 1988 and Wuthnow 1991. An essential critique of modernization theory is David Martin 1978.

14. McCreery 1992.

15. The classic work which outlines the structural function of the *cofradia* is Wolf 1957: 1-18.

16. The Catholic Action movement originated in the late 1920s in Europe. Because the notion of religious revitalization is so broad, the direction of Catholic Action's foci have varied dramatically from one country to the next, or even from one era to the next. Catholic Action has been associated with such diverse political tendencies as Opus Dei and Liberation Theology, as well as with such urban middle-class renewal movements as Cursillo and Marriage Encounter.

17. There are three masterful studies which describe the growing friction between practitioners of *costumbre* (*traditionalistas*) and catechists in the post-1950 period. These include Brintnall 1979; Falla 1978; and Warren 1978.

18. Cleary 1992: 172.

19. Berger 1967.

20. In Carmack (ed.) 1988, the authors attempt to use the case of Guatemala to pose a model in which violence becomes so endemic that the society devolves into a measurable 'culture of violence'.

21. Although Guatemala's political struggle is ongoing, there were four periods when

the human cost of this struggle was especially high, corresponding to specific military counter-insurgency campaigns. These were 1962-93, 1966-7, 1978-82, and 1982-3.

22. Annis 1987: 140.
23. Cleary 1992: 171.
24. Ibid.: 171.
25. Carmack 1988: 295.
26. Cleary 1992: 174.
27. Statistical information on church growth is systematically collected by SEPAL, a Protestant-run data bank in Guatemala City. Although the figures reported by this agency have come under some criticism (in part because they use a formula for tabulating Protestant populations which uses a multiplier of 2.5), their figures are corroborated by those gathered by independent Catholic sources. See Evans 1990.
28. In 1980 a national survey identified more than 200 separate Protestant denominations, of which fewer than ten were tied to traditional, non-Pentecostal institutional denominations; 85% were Pentecostal. See PROCLADES 1981.
29. Cleary 1992: 175. See Roberts 1968: 753-67.
30. Lalive d'Epinay 1969; Willems 1967.
31. Cleary 1992: 173; see also Calder 1992.
32. A new and definitive study of the impact of Indian mobilization and Army recriminations in northern Quiché province is Falla 1992.
33. Manz 1988: 35.
34. I am guilty of this myself. See Virginia Garrard-Burnett 1989b. There are, however, several excellent studies which bring to light new aspects of this functionalist interpretation. See Stoll 1990; Martin 1990; Green in Garrard-Burnett and David Stoll 1993.
35. For a look inside the institutional church during this period, see Calder 1992 and Berryman 1994.
36. Manz 1988: 30.
37. During Arana's campaign 8,000 peasant were killed in a two-year period. See Black, Jamail and Stoltz Chinchilla 1984: 22.
38. This nascent political coalescence is articulated best in a booklet published by urban Pentecostals supportive of Ríos Montt who called themselves the Congreso Amanacer [Daybreak] [19]84.
39. Stoll 1993; Garrard-Burnett 1988: 85-105.
40. Author's interview, Edmundo Madrid, 1991.
41. In 1985, the Army permitted free elections and a return to civilian rule. Marco Vinicio Cerezo, the Christian Democratic candidate, was elected President and took office in early 1985. Despite numerous coup attempts against him, Cerezo successfully filled out his term of office.
42. Serrano Elías served as President of the Council of state during Ríos Montt's administration, and is a member of a large and affluent Pentecostal denomination based in Guatemala City. There is less collusion of interests between Serrano and Ríos Montt, however, than these facts might indicate. First, Serrano's position under Ríos Montt lay outside the executive branch of government. Second, the church that Serrano attended at that time, Elim, has a long history of hostility towards Ríos Montt's church, Verbo, over doctrinal and liturgical differences.
43. On 25 May 1993, Jorge Serrano attempted an 'autogolpe', in which he dissolved the National Assembly and the Supreme Court and suspended the national constitution. On 1 June 1993, amid accusations of corruption and autocracy, he was forced to resign the presidency. In 1994, Ríos Montt was elected head of Congress, and at the time of writing was attempting to abrogate a constitutional ruling which would prevent him from seeking the presidency in the next elections.
44. Berryman, 1994: 265.
45. In 1972 only 69 students attended Catholic seminaries in Guatemala. In 1987 that

figure had grown to 483, an increase of 637 per cent. *Statistical Yearbook of the Church* 1987; *Catholic Almanac* 1975, cited in Cleary 1992: 186.
46. Zeitlin 1968: 129-130 in Torres 1992: 30.
47. See Leger 1990, in Cleary 1992: 168.
48. Martin 1978: 16.
49. Cleary 1992: 197-8.
50. As cited in Torres 1992: 25.
51. Cleary 1992: 168
52. Martin 1990: 295.
53. Levine 1991: 21-2, in Cleary 1992: 219.

References

Adams, R. N. 1970. *Crucifixion by Power: Essays on Guatemalan National Social Structure, 1944-1966*. Austin: University of Texas Press.
——. 1957. *Cultural Surveys of Panama, Nicaragua, Guatemala, El Salvador, Honduras*. Washington, DC: Scientific Publications no. 33, Pan American Sanitary Bureau.
Anderson, B. 1983. *Imagined Communities: Reflections on the Origin and Spread of Nationalism*. New York: Verso.
Annis, S. 1978. *God and Production in a Guatemalan Town*. Austin: University of Texas Press.
Baldwin, D. 1990. *Protestants and the Mexican Revolution: Missionaries, Ministers, and Social Change*. Chicago: University of Illinois Press.
Bastian, J.-P. (ed.) 1990. *Protestantes, liberales y francmasones: sociedades de ideas y modernidad en América Latina, siglo XIX* Mexico: Comisión de Estudios de Historia de las Iglesia en América Latina [CEHILA].
Berger, P. 1967. *The Sacred Canopy*. Garden City, NY: Doubleday.
Berryman, P. *Stubborn Hope: Churches, Revolution, and Counterrevolution in Central America*. Maryknou, NY: Orbis.
Black, G., M. Jamail, N. Stoltz Chinchilla, 1984. *Garrison Guatemala*. New York: Monthly Review Press.
Brintnall, D. 1979. *Revolt Against the Dead: The Modernization of a Mayan Community in the Highlands of Guatemala*. New York: Gordon and Breach.
Bunzel, R. 1952. *Chichicastenango, a Guatemalan Village*. Locust Valley NY: American Ethnological Society no. 22.
Burgess, P. 1926. *Justo Rufino Barrios*, New York: Dorranca.
Calder, B. J. 1970. 'Growth and Change in the Guatemalan Catholic Church, 1944-1966', in Richard N. Adams (ed.), *Crucifixion by Power: Essays on Guatemalan National Social Structure, 1944-1966*. Austin: University of Texas Press.
——. 1992. 'The Catholic Church in the Context of Guatemalan Politics, Society and Culture from 1940 to the Present', paper presented at the Latin American Studies Association International Congress, 24 Sept.

Carmack, R. (ed.) 1988. *A Harvest of Violence: The Mayan Indians and the Guatemalan Crisis*. Norman: University of Oklahoma Press.

Cleary, E., and H. Stewart-Gambino (eds) 1992. *Conflict and Competition: The Latin American Church in a Changing Environment*. Boulder, CO: Lynne Rienner.

Congreso Amanacer [Daybreak] [19]84. 1983. *La hora de Dios para Guatemala* [God's Hour for Guatemala]. Guatemala: Ediciones SEPAL.

Evans, T. E. 1990. 'Religious Conversions in Guatemala'. Unpublished Ph. D. thesis, University of Pittsburgh.

Falla, R. 1992. *Masacres de la selva, Ixcán, Guatemala, 1975-1982*. Guatemala: Editorial Universitaria.

——. 1978. *Quiché rebelde: estudio de un movimiento de conversión religiosa, rebelde a las creencias tradicionales, en San Antonio Illotenango, Quiché (1948-1970)*. Guatemala: Editorial Universitaria de Guatemala.

Frankel, A. 1969. 'Political Development in Guatemala, 1944-1945: The Impact of Foreign Military and Religious Elites'. Unpublished Ph.D. thesis, University of Connecticut.

Garrard-Burnett, V. 1989. 'God and Revolution in Guatemala, Protestant Missions in Revolutionary Guatemala, 1944-1954', *The Americas* 46 (2), 205-33.

——. 1989. 'Jerusalem Under Siege: Protestantism in Rural Guatemala, 1960-1987', Texas Papers on Latin America, University of Texas.

——. 1988. 'Onward Christian Soldiers: Guatemala, 1954-1984', *SECOLAS, Annals*. 19: 85-105.

——. 1990. 'Positivismo, liberalismo e impulso misionero: misioners protestantes en Guatemala, 1880-1920', *Mesoamerica* 19, 13-31.

——. 1989. 'Protestantism in Rural Guatemala, 1872-1954', *Latin American Research Review* 24 (2), 127-42.

—— and David Stoll (eds) 1993. *Rethinking Protestantism in Latin America*. Philadelphia: Temple University Press.

Gleijeses, P. 1991. *Shattered Hope: The Guatemalan Revolution and the United States, 1944-1954*. Princeton University Press.

Green, L. 1993. 'Experimenting with Protestantism: Mayan Widows in Guatemala' in V. Garrard-Burnett and D. Stoll (eds), *Rethinking Protestantism in Latin America*. Philadelphia: Temple University Press.

Immerman, R. H. 1982. *The CIA in Guatemala: The Foreign Policy of Intervention*. Austin: University of Texas Press.

Lalive d'Epinay, C. 1969. *Haven of the Masses*. London: Lutterworth Press.

Leger, D. H. 1990. 'Religion and Modernity in the French Context: For a New Approach to Secularization', *Sociological Analysis* 51.

Levine, D. 1991. 'Protestants and Catholics in Latin America: A Family Portrait', paper prepared for Conference on Fundamentalism Compared, the Fundamentalism Project, University of Chicago, Nov.

Madrid, E. 1991. Author's interview.

Manz, B. 1988. *Refugees of a Hidden War: The Aftermath of Counterinsurgency in Guatemala*. Albany: State University of New York Press.

Martin, D. 1978. *A General Theory of Secularization*. Oxford: Basil Blackwell.

——. 1990. *Tongues of Fire: The Explosion of Protestantism in Latin America*. Oxford: Basil Blackwell.

McCreery, D. 1992. 'Caja, Cofradia and Cabildo: The Transformation of "Broker"

Institutions in Nineteenth Century Guatemala', paper presented at Ethnicity and Power in Mexico and Guatemala conference, University of Texas, March 27.

——. 1994. *Rural Guatemala, 1760-1945.* Stanford University Press.

Mecham, J. L. 1966. *Church and State in Latin America: A History of Politico-Ecclesiastic Relations*, 2nd edn. Chapel Hill: University of North Carolina Press.

Miller, H. J. 1971. *Iglesia y estado en el tiempo de Justo Rufino Barrios.* Guatemala: Universidad de San Carlos.

Oakes, M. 1951. *The Two Crosses of Todos Santos.* Princeton University Press.

PROCLADES 1981. *Directorio de las iglesias, organizaciones y ministerios del movimiento protestante: Guatemala.* San Jose, Costa Rica: PROCLADES.

Roberts, B. 1968. 'Protestant Groups and Coping with Urban Life in Guatemala City', *American Journal of Sociology* 73, 753-67.

Schlesinger, S., and S. Kinzer. 1983. *Bitter Fruit: the Untold Story of the American Coup in Guatemala.* Garden City, NY: Anchor Press.

Stoll, D. 1993. *Between Two Armies.* New York: Columbia University Press.

——. 1990. *Is Latin America Turning Protestant? The Politics of Evangelical Growth.* Berkeley: University of California Press.

Tax, S. 1953. *Penny Capitalism: A Guatemalan Indian Economy.* Washington, DC: Smithsonian Institution Institute of Social Anthropology no. 16.

Torres, C. A. 1992. *The Church, Society, and Hegemony: A Critical Sociology of Religion in Latin America*, trans. by Richard A. Young. Westport, CT: Praeger, 1992.

Warren, K. B. 1978. *The Symbolism of Subordination: Indian Identity in a Guatemalan Town.* Austin: University of Texas Press.

Willems, E. 1967. *Followers of the New Faith.* Nashville, Tenn.: Vanderbilt University Press.

Wolf, E. 1957. 'Closed Corporate Communities in Mesoamerica and Central Java'. *Southwestern Journal of Anthropology* 13, 1-18.

Wuthnow, R. 1988. *The Restructuring of American Religion.* Princeton University Press.

——. 1991. 'Understanding Religion and Politics', *Daedalus* (Summer), 1-200.

Zeitlin, I. 1968. *Ideology and the Development of Sociological Theory*, Englewood Cliffs, NJ: Prentice-Hall.

CHRISTIAN ORTHODOXY AND CONTEMPORARY RUSSIAN NATIONALISM

Thomas Parland

Russia's protracted and painful transition from traditional to modern society can be said to serve as a general frame of reference for this chapter. The ideological struggle between Western-style reform and Russian tradition has already been going on for three centuries, beginning with the attempts of Peter the Great to Europeanize Russia. The resistance of traditional and Orthodox Russia against secularization, and democratic and economic reforms has been so strong that all earlier attempts to modernize the country have either failed or ended up as half measures. The absence of a strong and independent middle class as well as of competing centres of power in Russian history probably explains why liberal and moderate attitudes favouring compromises have been so unsuccessful in that country.

Historically the idea of establishing a specifically Russian path of development differing from the Western pattern has served as the main argument against attempts to introduce political democratic reforms and liberalize the economy in Russia. Being closely connected with the Orthodox view of the world, this thinking was elaborated on in the 1830s and '40s and resulted in the so-called 'Russian idea' (*russkaia ideia*) as the historical ideology of counter-reform movements. Today it is defined by Yanov as 'the theoretical nucleus of the Russian New Right's ideology'.[1] Its essence is, as Szamuely puts it, 'the conviction that Russia has been entrusted with the divine mission of resuscitating the world by sharing with it the revelation that had been granted to her alone'.[2]

The theoretical discussions in the 1830s and '40s leading to this political doctrine took place in literature, the only forum for social, political and philosophical debate in tsarist Russia. The dividing line was between radical Westernizers and more or less conservative Russian Slavophiles. Later, at the turn of the nineteenth century, the same intellectual confrontation spilled over into political activity when liberal and socialist movements pursued fundamental democratic reforms and social change, while statist Russian nationalists defended the tsarist theocratic regime. Half a century later, in the post-Stalin era of the

Soviet Union, liberal reformers and conservative nationalists were fighting each other inside as well as outside the Communist Party. The struggle between old and new is going on even now, but the process of modernization of Russian society is already drawing to its final conclusion. The political and economic emancipation of Russian society has made a good start and continues to thrive.

The dramatic events of August 1991, the subsequent disintegration of the Soviet Union in December 1991, President Yeltsin's spectacular victory in the violent confrontation with the conservative Russian parliament in October 1993 as well as the adoption of a new constitution through a referendum in December 1993, have greatly contributed to this development. At the same time, the years of social change since 1985 have made the Russian nationalists emerge as a totally independent political force with a counter-reform ideology. Before 1985, it should be remembered, they could exist only in a disguised way within the establishment, or openly at *samizdat*-level. The striking success Zhirinovsky's ultra-nationalistic Liberal Democratic Party had in the parliamentary elections in December 1993 testifies to a growing anti-Western and chauvinistic mood in large sections of the Russian population.

The present Russian nationalists, commonly known as National Patriots (*natsional-patrioty*), resist all efforts to introduce a Western-style market economy and create democratic political institutions.[3] They adhere to the afore-mentioned 'Russian idea' (*russkaia ideia*), which holds the prospect for a uniquely Russian path of development, inspired by the theocratic tsarist model rather than by secularized social systems of Western provenance such as liberal democracy (jurocracy) – which is based on the rule of law – and a utopian ideology like Marxist communism (ideocracy). The Soviet era is considered an un-Russian parenthesis in the history of the Russian nation. The National Patriots' contemporary interpretation of the 'Russian idea' equates it with autocratic rule, preservation of the empire and revival of Christian Orthodoxy as the ruling state ideology. These ambitions are coloured by an overt anti-Westernism and anti-Semitism.

Russian Patriotic Nationalism is in most cases intertwined with Orthodox Christianity, the official religion of Russia for more than 1,000 years. The Russian national identity has been associated with this branch of Christianity for centuries. Being considered the only pure and true religion, Orthodoxy has often been used as an argument against the secularized and superficial West, where Catholicism is based on the heritage of pagan Rome and Protestantism has led to excessive individualism.

Historically speaking, there have always been two versions of Russian nationalism. On the one hand, there is the official statist nationalism, including the so-called National Bolshevism in its atheist and Orthodox varieties;[4] and, on the other hand, there is the more or less ethnic and cultural interpretation of the 'Russian idea' encouraged by non-conformist Orthodox sects of the rural periphery. The Russian author Alexander Solzhenitsyn and the academician Igor Shafarevich are typical representatives of the latter variety,[5] while the party leader Vladimir Zhirinovsky and the Metropolitan Ioann of St Petersburg and Ladoga stand for statist nationalism.[6] In view of the growing political importance of the Orthodox Church in contemporary Russian society, this chapter will deal mainly with the different aspects of its influence on statist nationalism. The latter is considered to represent an obsolete imperial and anti-democratic tradition in contrast to the various nationalistic movements with democratic programmes in the former Soviet republics outside the Russian Federation. When necessary, complementary references will be made to Solzhenitsyn and Shafarevich as their writings have greatly influenced all National Patriotic thought, including that of the nationalistic wing of the Russian Orthodox Church.

The Russian national awakening since the 1960s

In Russia the revival of Orthodoxy has been closely connected with the new ideological climate that has been more or less prevailing since the mid-1960s. At that time, interest in Russian pre-revolutionary past had been awakened as a consequence of the serious ideological and economic crisis that affected post-Stalin society. A deep disillusionment about socialism, along with Khrushchev's chronic agricultural problems, had made an increasing number of Russians look for more tenable ideals in Russia's history before 1917 and, thus, for their original national identity.

Once an object of contempt, the Russian countryside became an object of serious discussion among Russian intellectuals. Rural Russia with its centuries-old traditions, was held up as the one and only tenable ideal in Russian history. This was the ideological climate that gave birth to the so-called 'countryside' or rural literature (*derevenskaia proza*) of the 1960s and '70s. Transgressing officially sanctioned barriers, it served as the voice of Russian national consciousness. Alexander Solzhenitsyn's short story *Matriona's House (Matrenin dvor)* was the first literary piece in this style. Well-known writers like Valentin Rasputin, Fedor Abramov, Vasilii Belov, Viktor Astaf'ev and Sergei Zalygin have established themselves within the same literary tradition.

There were also other manifestations of this wave of national romanticism: a growing interest in Russia's history and in the preservation and restoration of national monuments, primarily churches, and the call for a return to the traditional names of buildings, streets and cities, with which the Bolsheviks had tampered. The author Vladimir Soloukhin and the painter Il'ia Glazunov were some of the most active in this movement. Rasputin, Zalygin, Belov and Bondarev were among the authors and publicists who joined forces with the movement for the protection of the environment that emerged in the Soviet Union in the early 1970s.

The Russian national awakening was accompanied by a religious revival in all strata of society, notwithstanding the fact that the traditional anti-religious state policy continued in the form of repressive measures against organized religious life outside the four walls of the church. From the end of the 1960s the official debate about restoration of old churches also included suggestions that they be returned to their original function.

The kind of Russian nationalism that was spreading throughout Russia gradually developed into an overt opposition, offering an alternative to the official ideology of the Brezhnev regime. It was a political dissident movement, but a dissident movement with ideological ramifications deep in the political establishment, where it challenged the officially sanctioned brand of Marxism-Leninism. In fact, Russian National Patriotism comprised statist nationalists (*gosudarstvenniki*) of the National Bolshevik variety within the establishment, and also ethnic or cultural nationalists (*pochvenniki*),[7] represented mainly by Russian-minded dissidents, whether disguised or open. Before 1985 the rural authors as well as literary critics and publicists belonging to the latter category used to circumscribe Orthodox Christianity by referring to the centuries-old ethical traditions of the Russian people. Unable to blame Marxism-Leninism openly for the moral decay and the spiritual crisis in Soviet society, they chose to talk about the dangerous influence of Western culture and cosmopolitanism on the moral health and cultural heritage of the Russian people.

The late 1960s saw the first open ideological debate between Marxism and Russian nationalism. The main protagonists were *Novyi mir* (New World), a cultural and political periodical which represented the liberal Marxist point of view, and *Molodaia gvardiia* (Young Guard), a periodical representing the national, or rather the National Bolshevik, point of view.[8] The National Patriots and the neo-Stalinists co-operated and came out on the winning side. The outcome of the 'Iakovlev affair' also proved that the National Patriots were arguing from a position of strength within the state and party hierarchy.[9]

The Russian dissident nationalists who operated at *samizdat*-level could openly declare their ideas which were often coloured by anti-communism and anti-Semitism. In the late 1960s dissident author Siniavskii, serving his prison term in *GULAG*, was shocked by the open anti-Semitism among the prisoners, many of whom had belonged to the clandestine All-Russian Social Christian Union for the Liberation of the People (*Vserossiiskii Sotsial'no-Khristianskii Soiuz Osvobozhdeniia Naroda*, also known under the abbreviation VSKhSON).[10]

The National Patriots, in fact, gravitated toward the extreme anti-Semitic Right in the 1970s and '80s, regardless of their attitude towards the communist regime. With a programme calling for Orthodox theocracy and corporatism with certain liberal safeguards, the VSKhSON of the 1960s had in fact been a moderate organization. Its role was taken over by *Veche* (1971-4), an underground publication that had taken the name of the local assemblies in such medieval Russian cities as Novgorod and Pskov.

Veche's editorial staff with Vladimir Osipov as editor-in-chief was more or less national-liberal,[11] while its anti-intellectual readers represented chauvinistic and anti-Semitic views. The former tried to play the role of a loyal opposition to the Soviet regime and emphasized how important it was for Russia to isolate itself from the rest of the world's dangerous influences. In his famous letter to the Soviet leaders in 1973, Alexander Solzhenitsyn suggested that Russia should be allowed to develop according to its own national peculiarities.[12] This implied the ex-urbanization of society, or more specifically, the restoration of peasant and Orthodox Russia.[13] Although *Veche* and its sympathizers, including Solzhenitsyn, condemned bureaucracy and censorship and called for certain basic human rights, they were not in favour of pluralist Western democracy. Political opposition was considered to be a consequence of 'foreign' and 'alien' influences.[14]

The anti-intellectual readers of *Veche*, on the other hand, called for resolute action against 'cosmopolitanism' and 'Jewishness' in Russia. One of these numerous readers, Mikhail Antonov, wrote a long letter to the editor in which he pointed out the irreconcilable opposition between Western and Russian views in all spheres of life. In his view, the Russian Westernized intelligentsia were contaminated by a false 'Jewish-Puritanical worldview', and therefore all Jews should be weeded out from their positions of influence. A union of Russian Orthodox Christianity with Leninism was needed to consolidate the forces of the nation.[15]

The idea of co-operation between the CPSU and Orthodox nationalists was followed up by another Russian extreme nationalist, Gennadii Shimanov, who interpreted the Soviet system as a divine instrument for constructing a new Christian world.[16] As time went by, the Communist party would transform itself into an Orthodox Christian party and embrace the notion of Orthodox theocracy. Theocracy was a *sine qua non* for the Russian people to fulfil its historical mission: 'The issue should be the Orthodoxization of the entire world resulting in a certain Russification of it'.[17]

During the second half of the 1970s and the early part of the 1980s, the unofficial National Patriotism went through a semi-fascist stage of development that reached a climax with the formation of the *Pamiat'* movement in 1985. *Pamiat'* was the first independent political organization outside the CPSU, and signified the first official manifestation of the unofficial extreme Right.

Within the establishment, a similar development could be observed. The military build-up of the Brezhnev era had paved the way for a National Bolshevik revival. The army and the security services did, after all, rank among the leading forces of the strongly militarized Soviet society. In the late 1970s, something of a 'fascistization of young functionaries' of the party, *Komsomol* and the state apparatus could be observed. Books about the Third Reich were becoming valued by an increasing number of these officials.[18]

After 1985 the above-mentioned National Bolshevism manifested itself in a number of ways, including periodicals like *Molodaia gvardiia,* Elementy (Elements) and, in 1991-3, the semi-fascist paper *Den'* (The Day). *Den'* was banned after the October events in 1993, but reappeared wth the new name *Zavtra* (Tomorrow). In 1990, the *Soiuz* (Union) faction of the Supreme Soviet – the Soviet parliament that was elected in 1989 and ceased to exist in the autumn of 1991 – was founded as a rallying point for statist nationalists, neo-Slavophiles (also called *pochvenniki*) and adherents of the Stalinist version of community-fascism (*Kommuno-fashizm*), and as a voice of the Soviet military-industrial complex and its imperial ambitions.[19]

Needless to say, this 'marriage of convenience' between Stalinists and Russian nationalists could never remove their fundamental disagreements on basic issues concerning the Soviet era, including the Bolshevik policy of the 1920s and 1930s. The nationalists condemned collectivization and the repressive measures taken against the Church, whereas the Stalinists defended this policy.[20]

Russia today: two contrasting tendencies

What can be said about the spiritual and ideological atmosphere in Russia today? There are two contradictory tendencies that characterize contemporary Russian society. On the one hand, there are the obvious signs of a rapid Westernization of life, especially in metropolises like Moscow and St Petersburg, as well as in other large cities. On the other hand, this development is paralleled by something that could be called a clericalization of the whole country (*klerikalizatsiia vsei strany*).

The ongoing introduction of a market economy has along with an overall commercialization of life given birth to a 'wild capitalism' which has not yet been regulated by law. The polarization of society between the *nouveaux riches* and the poor is striking. The Russians are now experiencing something of a Klondyke or Wild West, and organized crime is a rapidly growing problem. A Russian National Patriot, the painter Ilya Glazunov, has complained that everything – honour, culture faith and loyalty – is now for sale in 'the crucified Russia'.

Russian urban society is now flooded with Western entertainment culture. In 1990 Alexander Solzhenitsyn criticized the Iron Curtain in an unexpected way: '[It] did not reach the bottom, permitting the continuous seepage of liquid manure – the selfindulgent and squalid "popular mass culture", the utterly vulgar fashion, and the byproducts of immoderate publicity – all of which our deprived young people have greedily absorbed. Western youth runs wild from a feeling of surfeit, while ours mindlessly apes these antics despite its poverty. And today's television obligingly distributes these streams of filth throughout the land.'[21]

Western lifestyle, with its limitless freedom of choice and its philosophy of entertainment, is considered to be immoral and disastrous for man in that it is devoid of any ethical guidance. Christianity in its Russian Orthodox interpretation provides the ethical guidance needed. This explains the religiously-inspired National Patriotic aversion against the Soviet system and the West alike: 'The two worlds are atheistic, and not so very alien to each other.'[22]

All in all, the nationalists view Russia's revival of past national traditions as being seriously threatened by the ongoing Westernization process, which must be stopped. Political life has, correspondingly, been affected by the introduction of a new centre of power; that is, that of an elected president with considerable power, and by the new role of the mass media, which have started to voice many different political views and have thus become symbols of ideological pluralism. The dissolution of the old Parliament in October 1993, and the election of a new one – the so-called Federal Assembly (*Federal'noe sobranie*) – along with the adoption of a new constitution, marked another important step towards the creation of a more Western-style political system.

The tendency towards Western-style secularization and commercialization is, however, counterbalanced by the influence of the Russian Orthodox Church, which celebrated its millennium in 1988. Ironically, seventy years of official atheism under Soviet rule has only strengthened the position of the Church as a moral authority in society. The role of martyrdom that has accompanied the Church since 1917 should not be underestimated when accounting for its recent rise in popularity.

The historical reconciliation between state and church in 1988 basically meant that the state relinquished its monopoly on truth. Long before, in the late 1960s when Soviet society was affected by a Russian national awakening, Orthodoxy had begun to strengthen its influence among the population. In 1988 it gained a status of unparalleled prominence in Soviet society. In a sense, it returned to its ancient historical role as a theocratic institution for moral guidance: The turn towards Christianity became something of a trend in a context where Marxism-Leninism, the official state doctrine, was no longer taken seriously. In 1991, the overwhelming majority of the mass media considered Orthodox Christianity as a new guiding ideology in society.[23] Even the inner circles of the Soviet Communist Party were strongly affected by it.[24]

The changed intellectual climate manifested itself in diverse ways. Several political leaders and top-level officials, including Yeltsin, began to attend important religious ceremonies conducted by the Russian Orthodox Church. All the new political parties that emerged in 1990-91 openly declared their adherence to or at least expressed profound respect for Orthodox Christianity. Significantly, even a conservative communist like Ivan Polozkov, the leader of the newly-founded Russian Communist Party with Stalinist leanings, preferred to use a biblical metaphor in Pravda in August 1990. He lashed out against the Jews without mentioning them by name by referring to 'the pharisees and hawkers whom Jesus had driven out of the temple, but who had subsequently been rehabilitated by the Pope in Rome'.[25]

In post-Soviet Russian society the aforementioned fashion of adhering to Orthodoxy has manifested itself in a sort of 'clericalization' of culture in society. The democratic newspaper *Nezavisimaia gazeta* (Independent newspaper) published an article in September 1992 in which the author described this process as a new danger: instead of the former party – state monopoly, there was now a 'clerical – state monopoly' as a result of the Russian Orthodox Church's coming into being.[26] As one of the most striking examples of this phenomenon, the article mentions the practice of restoring to the Church property that was confiscated in the Soviet era. In reality, however, this has led to a clericalization of culture: national works of art including pictures, sculpture and architecture, having always belonged to the state, are now being handed over to Orthodox parishes. Likewise, the Church is acquiring lands and buildings that have in fact never belonged to it.[27]

This practice has become possible through a certain clericalization of the local authorities. In trying to please the Church, the latter turn over property to it even when they have to evade the law to do so. Another form of clericalization can be seen in the practice of baptizing all children in many day-care centres, or in that of including the gospels in school syllabuses, even though the Church is officially separated from the state.[28]

Finally, a new kind of censorship is making itself felt, especially in the field of scientific research. It has become extremely difficult to publish research material where the conclusions do not coincide with the opinion of scholars of the so-called clerical school.[29] A similar tendency can be seen in literary criticism where various moralistic criteria coloured by Orthodoxy have become fashionable.[30] This would imply that the Soviet practice of supervising science, as well as art and culture in general, has not disappeared. The Communist Party has simply been replaced by the Church.

How can we explain this existence of two totally opposite tendencies in contemporary Russian society? In a broader historical perspective we can see that Russia has been a divided society ever since Peter the Great's reforms. In times of great crisis, the confrontation between endeavours to introduce Western-style reforms and anti-Western nationalist Orthodox resistance come into the open. That is exactly what we are witnessing now in Russia. Politically, President Yeltsin and the democrats in power have represented the forces of Westernization, while the Russian Nationalists supported by conservative communists have played the role of traditionalists advocating a 'genuinely, Russian path' of development instead of Western-style reforms. Since the December parliamentary elections in 1993, however, the government's composition and policy has changed and become more nationalistic.

Orthodoxy and National Patriotism in the 1990s

The deepening political, economic and spiritual crisis in Russia is a result of the bankruptcy of Marxism-Leninism and the fall of the Soviet regime. The feeling of humiliation following the break-up of the Soviet empire has aggravated the fear that even the Russian Federation will meet the same fate. These events, along with the ruling democrats' efforts to copy Western economic and cultural models, have caused a grave identity crisis among many Russians. In looking for more tenable ideals than Marxism-Leninism, a Russian-minded intellectual could not help but turn to his country's own past and its traditions and, thus, discover Christian Orthodoxy. It should be noted that traditionally many Russians have regarded Orthodox Christianity as virtually synonymous with Russia itself.[31]

Already in the years of *perestroika* the dividing line between statist nationalists of the atheist National Bolshevik variety (*gosudarstvenniki*) within the establishment, and the former underground anti-communist nationalist-oriented dissidents who advocated Orthodoxy and Russian peasantry traditions (*pochvenniki*), had become more and more blurred. The non-religious kind of National Bolshevism was superseded by the growing popularity of the Orthodox Church in the early 1990s. Many National Bolsheviks had become very critical of almost all of the Soviet era, and started to convert to, or at least to pay homage to, Orthodox Christianity.[32] The editorial policy of the National Patriotic periodical *Nash sovremennik* (Our Contemporary) since 1990 would seem to suggest that Stanislav Kuniaev, the new editor-in-chief, is one of the recent converts to Orthodox Christianity.

The fact that many atheist statist nationalists have become Christians does not necessarily mean that all of them have become believers by conviction. We know from history many examples of conversions that have been dictated by reasons of political expediency. On the other hand, we should never forget that there are also those who have become believers in the real sense of the word. This seems to be true of contemporary Russia where the system of values of the bygone Soviet era has collapsed.

As a specific Russian phenomenon, Orthodox National Bolshevism was, before August 1991, an attempt to unite Marxism-Leninism with Orthodoxy with the aim of establishing a state of peace and harmony between the Soviet government and the Church. The National Bolsheviks wanted for the most part to restore the conditions that had prevailed in Stalin's Russia during and shortly after the Second World War. This position, as has been noted earlier, made them prone to co-operation with the Stalinists and other conservative communists.

After 1991, this kind of statist nationalism began to lose the last traces of its former socialist state ideology, while, generally, Russian Orthodoxy took over as the main denominator of imperial Russian National Patriotic thought.

In the late 1990s, the former dissident nationalists were allowed to enter the political scene and voice their Orthodox and anti-Marxist viewpoints openly. This could be seen in 1989, when the works of the famous anti-communist National Patriot Igor Shafarevich were published in *Nash sovremennik*.[33] By 1990, in the words of the literary critic Alla Latynina, 'stylized Orthodoxy' (*stilizovannoe pravoslavie*) had developed into something approaching the official ideology of National Patriots.[34]

Other political movements, including those of a democratic orientation were also more or less affected by Orthodoxy. The most surprising change in attitude, however, could be seen among numerous Stalinists and conservative communists. In March 1990 the front page of the conservative newspaper *Pravda* carried a huge photograph of two Orthodox nurses or 'charity sisters' (*sestry miloserdiia*), who were praised for nursing and encouraging patients at a hospital in Minsk.[35] This was an example of the charity tradition being revived in society at the express wish of the authorities. In coping with social dropouts, the Russian Orthodox Church was now considered an extremely important ally by the Soviet regime, which had previously persecuted Christians and attempted to wipe out religion.

Later, in the period 1991-3, the co-operation between extremist National Patriots and conservative communists was more and more coloured by Orthodox ideas. As a by-product, an increasing number of Russian-minded communists converted to Russian Orthodox Christianity, probably due to the total bankruptcy of their former 'religion' Marxism-Leninism and their desperate need for another suitable identity.[36] The close interaction of communists and nationalists culminated in the origin of the so-called red-brown movement, in the form of the Front of National Salvation (*Front national'nogo spaseniia*) that was founded in the autumn of 1992.[37] The former Stalinist newspaper *Sovetskaia Rossiia* (Soviet Russia) now appeared as a mouthpiece of the new ideology by producing the supplement *Rus' pravoslavnaia* (Orthodox Russia). The editorial staff of the latter was headed by the Metropolitan Ioann of St. Petersburg and Ladoga, and consisted of some high-ranking clerics like the Metropolitan Gideon of Stavropol and Baku, and the bishop Tikhon of Novosibirsk and Barnaul.[38] Significantly enough, the socialist and Marxist slogans in *Sovetskaia Rossiia* have been more and more overshadowed by nationalist and Orthodox visions.

In post-Soviet Russian society, the political and ideological position of National Patriotism has, as we have seen, been strengthened, especially in its Orthodox version. This was a natural consequence of the dissolution of the Soviet empire, and of the threatening prospect of a further disintegration of the Russian Federation. Three parties left the Democratic Russia movement (*Demokraticheskaia Rossiia*) at the end of 1991: the Democratic Party of Russia under its leader Nikolai Travkin, the Party of Constitutional Democrats (the Cadets) under Mikhail Astaf'ev, and the Christian Democratic Movement under Viktor Aksiuchits.[39] The last two parties moved to the right and joined the moderate National Patriots. In the same manner, some outstanding democrats like Iurii Vlasov, an author, and Stanislav Govorukhin, a film director, 'defected' and joined the anti-Western Orthodox nationalists.

The 25 million ethnic Russians now living outside Russia as national minorities in other republics became a hotbed of National Patriotism, to the extent that nationalist organizations like Vladimir Zhirinovskii's Liberal Democratic Party and Dmitrii Vasil'ev's National Patriotic Front 'Pamiat' produced propaganda defending their interests.[40]

As society was, and still is, politically divided by democratic reformers on the one hand and nationalist and communist traditionalists on the other, so was, and is, the Orthodox Church. The two contrasting currents of Orthodox thought within the Church are represented by the so-called national-liberals and by the extreme National Patriots. The former, who advocate ecumenicalism and religious tolerance and emphasize the roots of Russian culture, are ideological descendants of the original Slavophiles. The most famous representative of these Russian national-liberals is Gleb Iakunin, a priest. He supports the implementation of democratic reforms in Russia and contacts with the West, while his ideological adversaries, the Orthodox extreme nationalists, advocating a sort of cultural isolationism, oppose all attempts to Westernize the country.[41] The latter are heirs of the Russian chauvinist pan-Slavism of the late nineteenth century, and the Russian anti-Semitism of the turn of the century. Some radical democrats have coined the term 'clerical fascism'[42] in characterizing these Orthodox extreme nationalists. Another, and perhaps more appropriate, concept to describe this phenomenon would be Orthodox fundamentalism.

In September 1990, Alexander Men', an Orthodox priest of Jewish origin, was assassinated. The murderer has never been identified. Father Men' espoused a universalistic Orthodox Christianity with no trace of nationalism. Being in fact ecumenical in his unconventional teaching, he had become one of the most hated people within Russian-minded clerical circles. Three days before his death, he issued a warning against an alliance between Russian fascists and a part of the Orthodox clergy.[43] This would seem to suggest that he entertained no illusions about his own security.

The level of political polarization in the Soviet Union in 1990 put pressure on the Orthodox Church to take a clear stand in the overall ideological struggle. It pledged its adherence to *glasnost* and *perestroika*, but was this out of true conviction or was it just paying lip service? Over the centuries – and all the way up to the Russian revolution in 1917 – the Orthodox Church had been part of a conservative 'resistance movement' against Western influences and models of development.

The Russian Orthodox Church has throughout the history of Russia played an important political role in society, notwithstanding its claims of an apositical stance. In the autumn of 1993, the Patriarch himself tried to mediate between the democrats represented by Yeltsin and his government, and the conservative political forces headed by the vice-president A. Rutskoi and the Parliament speaker R. Khasbulatov. This attempt, however, failed.

Generally, the Moscow Patriarch Aleksii has tried to balance national liberalism and rightist chauvinism within the Church. At the time of the armed coup in Moscow in October, however, there were several representatives of the clergy, including some members of the Union of Orthodox brotherhoods (*Soiuz pravoslavnykh bratstyv*) – the Patriarch himself being their chairman – who defended the White House, weapon in hand.[44] This seems to indicate that the Church is to some degree leaning more towards Russian National Patriotism than towards the democrats. This can also be seen in the Patriarch's support of an attempt by the Russian parliament in summer 1993 to pass a law blocking missionary work conducted by Western churches in Russia.[45] This law, however, did not come into force, as Yeltsin refused to confirm it.[46]

A decision taken by the Holy Synod after the October events is also significant here. Priests and bishops were not allowed as candidates in the parliamentary elections held in December 1993. As a result, the democratic candidate Gleb Iakunin was deprived of his rights as a priest for defying this decision.[47] This event seems to suggest that the Church is seeking to distance itself from Yeltsin and his reforms and move more towards the right.

The growing clerical nationalism, or Orthodox fundamentalism

This period of transition in Russia has obviously put the Russian Orthodox Church in an extremely difficult position. The ongoing Westernization process in society runs contrary to almost all the traditions of Russian Orthodoxy and aggravates the acute national identity crisis that has stricken the Russians in the 1990s.

The problem of Russian national identity has clearly been a stumbling block for the democratic wing of clergy. We have already noted the contrast between Orthodox Christianity and the Western philosophy of entertainment. Obviously, the nationalist 'fundamentalist' wing of the clergy cannot but strengthen its position within the Church as a result of what has happened during the last few years in Russia.

The breakup of the Soviet Union (that is, the historical continuation of the Russian empire as it was before October 1917) was a logical consequence of the democratic revolution in August 1991. As a result, ordinary Russian people and the Church were stricken by a loss of the former imperial identity. Traditionally, the Church has had its congregations and parishes in all parts of Russia. Today, millions of Orthodox Russians live in former Soviet republics outside the Russian Federation. Obviously, a considerable part of the Russian clergy cannot help but be affected by the National Patriots' call for a restoration of the empire.

In the post-Soviet era, the principle of *glasnost* was extended to include revelations about the inter-relations between the Church and KGB. Allegations concerning a direct collaboration between the two institutions were corroborated by empirical evidence.[48] Arrangements of this kind of system of mutual contact are not without historical precedent. At the turn of the century, the Union of the Russian People (*Soiuz Russkogo Naroda*),[49] the security police, the local police and parts of the clergy were acting in collusion to further common goals.[50] In the early 1920s, there were certain interrelations between the so-called 'Living Church' (*Zhivaia tserkov*')[51] and the GPU, the Soviet security police. The Ecclesiastical Regulation (*Dukhovnyi Reglament*) issued by Peter the Great in 1721 was the origin of this tradition of regular collaboration between Russian priests and the police.[52] Today, however, with their harsh criticism of these activities after 1917, the democrats have impaired their relations with the Church. The latter, feeling its prestige threatened, seems to be ready to establish closer contacts with some of the Russian nationalist organizations and movements.

The continuing liberalization and democratization process in society has created another grave problem for the Church. The new political pluralism has also been accompanied by a 'confessional pluralism'. The 'free competition' in missionary work that has become possible in Russia has included different branches of Christianity represented by several Western churches. The Russian Orthodox Church Abroad (*Russkaia Pravoslavnaia Tserkov' Za Rubezhom*) has already established itself in Russia with several communities including that of Suzdal' and its neighbouring area.[53] These communities have formed an umbrella organization named the Free Orthodox church.[54] A serious split within the Church of the Moscow patriarchate occurred as early as 1989 with the Ukrainian Orthodox Church's assertion of its autonomy.

A dangerous rival to Patriarch Aleksii II's Church, the Russian Orthodox Church Abroad is dominated by semi-fascist Russian emigrants including the priests Aleksii Averintsev and Oleg Steniaev who have had close contacts with Pamiat'.[55] In Laqueur's words, 'Various right-wing spokesmen have shown a preference for the Church Abroad over the Moscow patriarchate, in view of the fundamentalism and the more ouspoken national sentiments of the former.'[56] This has forced the Russian Church to take more of its own nationalist wing in order to neutralize the influence of this formidable rival.

Who are the real Orthodox 'fundamentalists', then? Their most remarkable representative is without doubt Metropolitan Ioann of St Petersburg and Ladoga, the second highest-ranking official after the Patriarch Aleksii II within the Church hierarchy. The Holy Synod seems to be influenced more by National Patriotic thought than by democratic viewpoints.[57] The same could be said of the Union of Orthodox Brotherhoods, with Patriarch Aleksii II as its chairman.

In 1990 the so-called Orthodox Popular Movement was founded by several extremist organizations including Vasil'ev's National Patriotic front Pamiat'. This new forum for Orthodox nationalists called for co-operation with the extreme right in Europe in the common struggle against Zionism. The Church, however, has refused to consort with Pamiat' and other right-wing extremist organizations. On the other hand, the Orthodox Church supports numerous organizations which could be considered to embody both Russian nationalism and Orthodox 'fundamentalism'. Above all, the Russian Party (*Russkaia partiia*), Russia (*Rossiia*), the Union of the Russian People (*Soiuz Russkogo Naroda*), the Fatherland (*Otechestvo*), the Union for Christian Renaissance (*Soiuz 'Khristianskoe vozrozhdenie'*) and the Slavonic Forum (*Slavianskoe sobranie*) deserve mention.[58] The democrats, however, dismiss all of them as openly fascist organizations.

The Orthodox nationalists have provided a platform for themselves in established National Patriotic periodicals like *Nash sovremennik* and *Moskva*. Furthermore, they have founded a number of papers, like *Zemshchina* (the term dates back to the reign of Ivan the Terrible and denotes a province with an autonomous local administration), *Slavianskii vestnik* (the Slavonic Messenger) and *Voskresen'e* (the Resurrection). The first, serving as a mouthpiece of the Union for Christian Renaissance, is led by Vladimir Osipov, the former editor-in-chief of the *samizdat* publication *Veche* in the 1970s. A one-time national liberal, Osipov has turned into a fully fledged sympathizer of 'clerical fascism'. Advocating absolute monarchy, *Zemshchina* condemns the French Revolution of 1789 as an expression of collective madness. Assessing the revolutionary development in Russia in terms of the execution of Tsar Nicholas II and his family, the paper refers to it as a cabalistic ritual, in order to convey the impression that Jews were responsible.[59]

Some positions of the Orthodox nationalists

The notion that the West is – and indeed always was – at the source of harmful influences on the Russian people is shared by Russian nationalists of a somewhat different shade. The rejection of the West and its political culture is an integral part of the classical Slavophile heritage of the 1840s and 1850s.

The notion of a Jewish conspiracy crystallized at the turn of the century with allegations published within the notorious *Protocols of the Elders of Zion*. Originally designed to serve the interests of the extreme right in Russia, the pamphlet played an important role in the anti-Jewish propaganda of German national socialism in the 1930s and 1940s. Now, used by the Pamiat' movement and several other nationalist organizations as well as by the nationalist wing of the Church, it appears in different versions coloured by either traditional confessional Russian anti-Semitism or by its modern equivalent. For all their dissimilarities, the current Russian anti-Jewish conspiracy theories start from the same premise: the Jews and the Freemasons, who run errands for the Jews, are branded as foreign elements, guilty of all sorts of destructive social experiments – such as the Marxist experiment in Russia and its capitalist equivalent in the countries of the West.

The *Protocols of the Elders of Zion* was publicly 'revived' in Russian society after 1985 when Pamiat', as the first nationalistic and rightist organization, started to use it in its anti-Semitic propaganda. In the beginning, this conspiracy theory was coloured by more or less atheistic National Bolshevism. Following the 'rehabilitation' of the Russian

Church and Orthodox Christianity in 1988, however, the evaluation of Russia's disasters in the twentieth century by many National Patriots, including Dimitrii Vasil'ev, was getting more and more religiously inspired. As a result, the modern secularized anti-Semitism harboured by traditional National Bolsheviks was partly overshadowed by a more traditional anti-Semitism coloured by Orthodoxy.

How did religious National Patriots like Dimitrii Vasil'ev interpret the Soviet era? For him and other monarchists, who used the *Protocols of the Elders of Zion* as a starting point for analyses, the October revolution and the concept of Soviet power stood as truly un-Russian phenomena. The communist regime was the work of the Devil – that is, the Jews and Freemasons who, occupying many leading posts in the Soviet establishment, were the real rulers of the country. They were aiming at world domination by the year 2000.[60] This view is nothing but a modification of the medieval idea of Satan and the coming of the Antichrist.[61] Extremist National Patriots interpreted everything as a struggle of life and death, between God and Satan, between the God-chosen Russian people and Evil, in the form of 'Zionists', at home and abroad. The latter had already paralyzed the West with their cosmopolitan Godless philosophy, their moral relativism, spiritual poverty, spineless democracy and crass materialism. The God-fearing Russians stood as the only force capable of resisting and thwarting the plans for worldwide hegemony of the Jews and the Freemasons.

The nationalistic wing of the Orthodox Church harbours a similar conspiracy theory, which, however, appears in a slightly more sophisticated form. The ancient tradition of anti-Semitism, which is now being revived within the Church, is based on the notion of a 'cosmic conspiracy against Russia, against the Orthodox Church and against mankind in general'.[62] The Metropolitan Ioann of St Petersburg prefers to disguise his anti-Semitism by referring to Freemasonry as 'one of the most mischievous and Satanic pseudodoctrines in the history of mankind'.[63] In his view, all the principles applied and all the methods used by the Bolsheviks to destroy Russia are very close to those of the Masons. A publicly announced number of 110.7 million people killed in the period 1917-59 revealed to the world, in his words, 'the secret of lawlessness in Russia in all the horror and disfigurement of its diabolical appearance'.[64]

The internationalistic Bolsheviks spearheaded by Trotsky and Kaganovich, however, failed to accomplish the destruction of Russia. Today, in the National Patriots' view, there is a new attempt to force Russia to choose a path of artificial development, that of Western liberal democracy and market economy. Godless communism has been replaced by irresponsible democracy.[65] Universal suffrage serving as the political basis of democracy is considered to be immoral and destructive. Ordinary people become the object of dishonest and cynical manipulation spread by the modern mass media. Why has nobody suggested electing a surgeon, a judge, a driver or an air pilot with the aid of universal suffrage?[66]

All National Patriots seem to favour a strong authoritarian rule, which rests on an ancient Russian Orthodox tradition. Originally, there existed the ideology of royal absolutism, developed by clergymen who felt that the interests of religion and church were best served by a monarch with no limits to his power.[67] Thus, Montesquieu's principle of the separation of powers is considered unacceptable by contemporary National Patriots. As even a moderate nationalist like Alexander Solzhenitsyn said, 'the three separate powers need to operate within some unifying framework, perhaps an ethical rather than a structural one.'[68] This statement is based on the assumption that man cannot be left on his own without moral guidance, and we should note that, in the early days of Russian history, this assumption was used to justify autocracy and theocracy, while in the Soviet era, it provided a rationale for ideocracy and dictatorship by the party leader.

But what about human rights – the very foundation of Western democracy? By virtue of their religiously inspired nationalism, the National Patriots put the interests of the nation first and those of the individual second.[69] They refer to 'obligations' rather than rights, for the latter serve to promote irresponsibility, arbitrariness and anarchy. These obligations or duties are of a national or ethical character.[70] 'Our duty must always exceed the freedom that we have been granted.'[71]

Paying tribute to the primacy of national cohesion and unity, the National Patriots reject Western pluralism and tolerance as dangerous sources of inspiration within the Russian cultural context with its emphasis on time-honoured spiritual traditions. Solzhenitsyn's pamphlet *Our Pluralists (Nashi pliuralisty)* is the most eloquent manifestation of this attitude:

If diversity becomes the highest principle, there can be no universal human values... If there is no right and wrong, what restraints remain? If there is no universal basis for it, there can be no morality. 'Pluralism' as a principle degenerates into indifference, superficiality: it spills over into relativism, into tolerance of the absurd, into a pluralism of errors and lies.[72]

What do the National Patriots have to offer in place of pluralism? They generally reply by referring to the ancient Slavophile *sobornost'* principle, with its emphasis on consensus between the rulers and the ruled. Originally, this principle of collectivism, or communality, was cultivated within the Church.[73] The Western principle of legalized opposition is dismissed as contrary to Russia's time-honoured history of autocracy.

The efforts by the democrats to introduce a Western-style capitalism in Russia have been harshly criticized by all National Patriots. Even a moderate Orthodox nationalist like Viktor Aksiuchits, leader of the Christian Democratic Movement, condemned in 1992 the policy of 'shock therapy' as serving the interests of 'the ruling anti-national nomen–klatura', foreign swindlers and the Mafia.[74] Aksiuchits, for his part, seems to advocate a type of national capitalism with exclusively Russian face.

In 1993, extremist Orthodox nationalists, like the Metropolitan Ioann, preferred to talk about evil plans to transform Russia into something approaching a colony of the West.[75] The ruling democrats in Russia were thought to play the role of a 'fifth column' in collusion with the Western transnational financial oligarchy, a dangerous force paving the way for the establishment of a Masonic world government.[76] This kind of argument can be traced back to the well-known conspiracy theory.

Since the elections of December 1993, the Russian New Right, in-cluding traditional Orthodox as well as modern nationalism, has appeared to exert a very strong influence on the cultural and political debate in society. As the Church distanced itself from these elections, it has no representative of its own within the Duma, where the modern nationalists spearheaded by Zhirinovsky are very influential. This being the case, Orthodox nationalists will probably try to use the Church as their political forum, particularly in view of the rift between the radical democrat Gleb Iakunin and the Patriarch in February 1994. Iakunin published in the newspaper *Nezavisimaia gazeta* an open letter to Patriarch Aleksii II, whom he criticized for accepting and supporting the 'ecclesiastic *nomenklatura*' (*tserkovnaia nomenklatura*) with its many privileges. Condemning the practice of tolerating fascist activities within the Church, along with the publication of anti-Semitic literature by the Church's printing houses, Iakunin declared his readiness to work for a profound democratic reform of the Church.[77] This action could, in fact, signify the first step towards a serious ecclesiastic schism within Russian Orthodoxy.

This being the case, the Patriarch might feel compelled to try to preserve the present *status quo* within the Church by moving closer to the right, in which case the Orthodox nationalists will see a chance to transform the Church into another centre of political activity outside the Russian parliament. This aspect has so far been ignored by Western mass media who have focused exclusively on what is going on in the Duma.

Notes

1. Yanov 1987: 19.
2. Szamuely 1974: 69.
3. As will be elaborated below, the National Patriotic alternative to the democrats' reform projects is 'national capitalism' and authoritarian rule based on Russian traditions.
4. Statism (Fr. *étatisme*) signifies primacy of the state in social, economic and political development. See the title-word "Étatisme" in Scruton 1982. In the Russian context, statist nationalism signifies preoccupation with the imperial idea too. National Bolshevism established itself as a nationalist and anti-Semitic shadow ideology behind the officially sanctioned, omnipotent, Marxist ideology of state as early as the 1920s. For more information, see Agurskii 1980 and Chalidze 1988. Originally and officially, the National Bolsheviks were pro-Communist atheists, but they did not adopt an antireligious posture (see Dunlop 1983: 263). Before 1985, on the *samizdat* level, some of them even tried to unite Marxism-Leninism and Orthodox Christianity. This tendency grew in strength after 1985 and resulted in something of an Orthodox Christian National Bolshevism. Today, in addition to this current of thought, an anti-communist Orthodox statist nationalism has established itself in society, notably within the Church, in the shape of the Metropolitan Ioann of St. Petersburg and Ladoga.
5. Both Solzhenitsyn and Shafarevich glorify the Russian peasant traditions and advocate a traditional development of the countryside without great industries. In particular, Solzhenitsyn has in many statements expressed his sympathies for the Old Believers (*staroobriadtsy*); that is, those numerous Orthodox Christians who preferred to leave the Church before accepting the Patriarch Nikon's reforms in the seventeenth century.
6. Zhirinovsky is a typical modern statist nationalist who cares little about religion, even if he, like President Yeltsin and other top level officials as well as political leaders, has begun to attend religious ceremonies conducted by the Orthodox Church. His ideological statements are coloured by geopolitics and could in a certain sense be classified as a Russian version of National Socialism. For more information, see Zhirinovsky 1993. The Metropolitan Ioann, for his part, is a representative of the statist version of traditional, that is, clerical Orthodox Russian nationalism.
7. *Gosudarstvenniki* is a derivative of *gosudarstvo* (state), and *pochvenniki* ('the soil-bound') is a derivative of *pochva* (soil).
8. The fight between *Novyi mir* and *Molodaia gvardiia* signified, in fact, a duel between Marxism and Russian nationalism. The outcome of this fight testifies to the strong position the National Patriots had in the Establishment. After *Novyi mir* had attacked the National Patriots in an article full of appropriate Marxist arguments, the response came in the form of a devastating counter-attack. A joint letter, signed by eleven National Patriotic and Stalinist authors, posed the rhetorical question: 'What is *Novyi mir* fighting?' (*Protiv chego vystupaet 'Novyi mir'*?) The letter – which accused *Novyi mir* of cosmopolitanism of a kind reminiscent of the suspect and 'subversive' Chech mass media prior to the invasion in 1968 – was published in *Ogonek*, a contemporary periodical with a solidly conservative reputation (see Yanov 1987: 115; Solzhenitsyn 1975: 274; Protiv 1989: 175-89). The campaign against *Novyi mir* continued in other papers and periodicals and had far-reaching consequences for the editorial staff. Tvardovskii, the liberal-minded editor-in-chief and author, lost his most competent collaborators, to which he responded by resigning towards the end of 1969. As a result, *Novyi mir* lost its liberal profile.
9. In 1972, Alexander Iakovlev, the Communist party's chief ideologue, used *Literaturnaia gazeta*, the mouthpiece of the writers' union, as a platform for an all-out attack against the Russian nationalists. He made his statements as a representative of the official party line; and they were not rebuked by the official media. Yet *Veche*, the underground publication of dissident nationalists, published a rejoinder (see Stranitsy

1993: 171-8). Iakovlev's reference to Lenin's conclusions about the nation's right to self-determination was rejected on the grounds that this logic might justify the dissolution of the entire Soviet Union (see Yanov 1987: 121 ff.). 'In 1918 the Soviet Republic was reduced to the dimensions of the Muscovite kingdom during the time of Ivan III. This is what the Russophiles' prosecutor dreams of' (Stranitsy 1993: 177). Shortly thereafter, Iakovlev unexpectedly left his high position within the party hierarchy for an appointment to an ambassadorship in Canada. This also marked the end of the official campaigns against the National Patriots. Iakovlev was brought back to Moscow under Yurii Andropov in 1983, and in the summer of 1985, shortly after Gorbachev came to power, he was given back his post as head of the Central Committee's Propaganda Department. In 1987 he was made a full member of the Politburo. Iakovlev has become known as the main architect of the policy of *glasnost*.

10. VSKhSON set out to overthrow the Soviet regime, and it pledged itself to Orthodox theocracy with corporate institutions rather than political parties. The party programme nevertheless had several liberal features, including the call for citizens' rights.

11. The national liberals represent the kind of moderate nationalism that joined forces with Yeltsin's democratic movement before as well as after the dramatic events of August 1991. They welcomed the liberalization and democratization of the Soviet Union and clearly do not qualify as National Patriots.

12. See Solzhenitsyn 1974.

13. See Yanov 1987: 135f.

14. Ibid.: 133.

15. Ibid.: 138f.

16. Ibid.: 236.

17. Chalidze 1988: 92 (quotation published).

18. See Yanov 1987: 254.

19. Kiva 1991: 3.

20. See Andreeva 1988.

21. Solzhenitsyn 1991: 40.

22. Soljénitsyne 1979: 29.

23. See Shikalev 1991: 14.

24. Radyshevskii 1991: 16.

25. Parland 1990: 557.

26. Vdovin 1992: 7.

27. Ibid.

28. Ibid.

29. See Ivanitskaia 1992: 7.

30. Ibid.

31. See Szamuely 1974: 64.

32. Katys 1990: 26.

33. See Shafarevich 1989a.

34. Latynina 1990: 5.

35. Sestry 1990: 1.

36. See Krakhmal'nikova 1993: 3.

37. 'The Front of National Salvation' included not only National Bolsheviks and conservative communists, but also anti- communist Orthodox nationalists and monarchists like Igor' Shafarevich, as well as certain national-liberals, who had moved to the right, like M.G. Astaf'ev, leader of the Constitutional Democrats, and V.N. Osipov, chairman of the Union for Christian Renaissance (*Soiuz 'Khristianskoe vozrozhdenie'*). See Obrashchenie 1992: 1.

38. See *Rus'* 1993.

39. See Tolz-Teague 1992: 7; McFaul 1992: 34.

40. See Grafova 1992: 9.

41. See Bodin 1993: 600.

42. See Rogatshi 1992: 69.
43. Pomerants 1991: 11.
44. Babasian 1993: 37.
45. See Bodin 1993: 600.
46. Buida 1993: 36.
47. Aleksii 1994: 1.
48. See Senderov 1992: 6f.
49. The Union of Russian People (*Soiuz Russkogo Naroda*) was the most important political party of the extreme Right to enter the political scene in 1905. It served as an umbrella organization of paramilitary troops known as 'the black hundreds' (*chernosotentsy*), who initiated pogroms and eliminated Jewish deputies of the Duma.
50. See Carter 1990: 29-32; Agurskii 1980: 52f.
51. The 'Living Church' was an unsuccessful reform movement inside the Russian Orthodox Church in the period 1922-45.
52. See Pipes 1974: 242.
53. See Bychkov 1993: 7.
54. Laqueur 1993: 227.
55. See Bychkov 1993: 7.
56. Laqueur 1993: 230.
57. See Buida 1993: 50.
58. See Rogatshi 1992: 71.
59. See Pudozhev 1991: 164f.
60. See Carter 1990: 110.
61. See Laqueur 1993: 54 ff.
62. Zelinskii 1991: viii.
63. Ioann 1992.
64. Ibid.
65. Ioann 1993.
66. Ibid.
67. See Pipes 1974: 232.
68. Solzhenitsyn 1991: 65 f.
69. See Shafarevich 1989: 174.
70. Ioann 1993.
71. Solzhenitsyn 1991: 48.
72. Solzhenitsyn 1985: 2.
73. See Szamuely 1974: 70.
74. See Aksiuchits 1992: 2.
75. See Ioann 1993a.
76. Ibid.
77. Aleksii 1994.

References

Agurskii, M. 1980. *Ideologiia natsional-bolshevizma*. Paris: YMCA-Press.
Aksiuchits, V. 1992. 'V plenu novykh utopii', *Nezavisimaia gazeta*, 23.10.
Aleksii II. 1994. 'Otvechaet Iakuninu cherez Rybkina', *Nezavismiaia gazeta*, 12 Feb.

Andreeva, N. 1988. 'Ne mogu postupat'sia printsipami.', *Sovetskaia Rossiia*, 13 Mar.

Babasian, N. 1993. 'Blazhenny mirotvortsy…', *Novoe vremia*, 43.

Bodin, P.-A., 1993. 'Den ryska ortodoxa kyrkan och nationalismen', in *Finsk Tidskrift*, 9-10.

Buida, I. 1993. 'Bog i kesar': kto blizhe?', *Novoe vremia*, 43.

Bychkov, S. 1993. 'Voskresen'e mifa', *Moskovskie novosti*, 7 Mar.

Carter, S.K. 1990. *Russian Nationalism Yesterday, Today, Tomorrow*. London: Pinter.

Chalidze, V. 1988. *Natsional'nye problemy i perestroika*. Benson, Vermont.

Dunlop, J.B. 1983. *The Faces of Contemporary Russian Nationalism*. Princeton University Press.

Grafova, L. 1992. 'Zalozhniki imperii', *Russkaia mysl'*, 31 Jan.

Ioann, Metropolitan of St Petersburg. 1992. ' Taina bezzakoniia', *Sovetskaia Rossiia*, 10 Oct.

——. 1993. 'Sviashchennoe i strashnoe delo – vlast', *Sovetskaia Rossiia*, 16 Dec.

——. 1993a. 'Chtushchii da razumeet', *Sovetskaia Rossiia*, 30 Apr.

Ivanitskaia, E. 1992. 'Evangelie na sluzhbe u kritiki', *Nezavisimaia gazeta*, 3 Dec.

Katys, M. 1990. 'Toska po Stalinu, ili 'novyi avangard marksizma'. *Ogonek*, 13.

Kiva, A. 1991. '"Soiuz" oderzhimykh', *Izvestiia*, 11 Mar.

Krakhmal'nikova, z. 1993. 'Kamen' Iudy', *Nezavisimaia gazeta*, 2 Nov.

Laqueur, W. 1993. *Black Hundred: The Rise of the Extreme Right in Russia*. New York: HarperCollins.

Latynina, A. 1990. 'Fantazmy pravye i levye', *Russkaia mysl'*, 3 Aug.

Mc Faul, 1992. 'Russia's Emerging Political Parties', *Journal of Democracy*, 3 Jan.

'Obrashchenie le grazhdanam Rossii orgkomiteta Fronta Natsional' nogo Spaseniia' 1992. *Sovetskaia Rossia*, 1 Oct.

Parland, Th. 1990. 'Rysk nationalism – förr och som en kraft i framtiden', *Finsk Tidskrift*, 9-10.

Pipes, R. 1974. *Russia under the Old Regime*. London: Weidenfeld and Nicolson.

Pomerants, G. 1991. 'Sto tysiach pochemu', *Literaturnaia gazeta*, 16 Sep.

'Protiv chego vystupaet "Novyi mir"?' 1989 (A letter to Ogonek in 1969), *Nash sovremennik* 1, 1989.

Pudozhev, V. 1991. '…putem samosoznaniia', *Nash sovremennik*, 9.

Radyshevskii, D. 1990. 'Budushchie pastyri Rossii', *Moskovskie novosti*, 7 Apr.

Rogatshi, I. 1992. 'Katsaus Nykyvenäjän poliittisten puolueiden kirjoon', *Ulkopolitiikka*, 2.

Rus' pravoslavnaia, 1993. *Sovetskaia Rossiia*, 16 Dec.

Scruton R. 1982. *A Dictionary of Political Thought*. London: Pan Macmillan.

Senderov, V. 1992. 'Govorit' vsiu pravdu edinstvennyi put' Tserkvi', *Russkaia mysl'*, 28 Feb.

'Sestry miloserdiia', 1990. *Pravda*, 23 Mar.

Shafarevich, I. 1989. 'Rusofobiia', *Nash sovremennik*, 6.

——. 1989a. 'Dve dorogi k odnomu obryvu', *Novyi mir*, 7.

Shikalev, L.G. 1990. 'Est' li v Rossii put' krome bolshevizma i pravoslaviia?', *Literaturnaia gazeta*, 13 Feb.

Soljénitsyne, A.I. 1979. *Message d'exil*. Paris: Seuil. Interview with BBC, 3 Feb.

Solzhenitsyn, A.I. 1974. *Pis'mo vozhdiam Sovetskogo Soiuza*. Paris: YMCA, Press.

———. 1975. *Bodalsia telenok s dubom*. Paris: YMCA Press.

———. 1985. 'Our Pluralists', *Survey*, 29 (2).

———. 1991. *Rebuilding Russia*. London: Harvill.

Stranitsy samizdata. 1993. 'Bor'ba s tak nazyvaemym rusofil 'stvom, iii Put' gosudarstvennogo samoubiistva', *Moskva*, 7-8.

Szamuely, T. 1974. *The Russian Tradition*. London: Secker and Warburg.

Tolz, V. and E. Teague 1992. 'Is Russia likely to turn to Authoritarian Rule?' *RFE/RL Research Report* 1, 4, 24 Jan.

Zelinskii, V. 1991. 'Daby uveroval mir...' Spets. prilozhenie k gaz. *Russkaia mysl'*, 13 Sep.

Vdovin, G. 1992. 'Plius Klerikalizatsiia vsei strany', *Nezavisimaia gazeta*, 19.9.

Yanov, A. 1987. *The Russian Challenge and the Year 2000*. Oxford: Basil Blackwell.

Part II
AFRICA

THE REVEALED WORD AND THE STRUGGLE FOR AUTHORITY

INTERPRETATION AND USE OF ISLAMIC TERMINOLOGY AMONG ALGERIAN ISLAMISTS

Leif Stenberg

Only three years after being recognized as a political party, the *Front Islamique du Salut* (FIS) (*al-jabhat al-islamiyya li-l-inqadh*) in Algeria was more or less poised to assume control of the National Assembly. Then the army intervened and cancelled the forthcoming elections. This action and the concomitant banning of FIS have forced the movement to work in a clandestine fashion. However, it is unlikely that this has stemmed its influence.

The appeal of the movement has often been presented as that of an antidote to the many years of one-party misrule by the former governing party, the *Front de la Libération Nationale* (FLN).[1] Support for the movement is usually regarded as a reaction arising out of despair and a desire for change among Algerians.[2] Consequently, it seems desirable to make an attempt to grasp the actual message and essential ideas of this movement, the growth and appeal of which took most people in Europe and North America by surprise.

In order to explain and substantiate how FIS operates in its political struggle for authority – without deviating from the requirement of conformity to the dogma of the 'Revealed Word' – the purpose of this chapter is to examine a text in which the Algerian mass movement FIS presents its political programme.[3] The 'Revealed Word' means the Quran and the Sunna.[4] In particular, the use of Islamic terminology, and the movement's interpretations of the Quran and the Sunna, will be emphasized. To this end translations of some parts of the political programme and paraphrases of several others are given in order to make easier reading. It is our intention to demonstrate the power of the 'Revealed

Word' and the strength of statements supported by quotations from the Quran at first hand. The main source is (parts of) a FIS political 'charter' as it is presented in *nass al-barnamaj as-siyasi li-l-jabhat al-islamiyya li-l-inqadh* (The Political Programme of the *Front Islamique du Salut*). In addition, there are some observations on the function of religion in Algeria and more general references to Islamic movements in the Middle East.

The reader's map

First, we shall consider the use of the Arabic language in religio-political texts. The FIS document that we study shows that the phrases are not primarily constructed to give the reader a cognitive meaning of the text. We can see that they consist of sets of slogans and prestige words. The most important of such words and axioms are picked out of the Islamic sacred sources; the Quran and the Sunna. Hence, the use of Islamic terminology creates a form of Islamic jargon. The expression 'jargon' is used in this chapter to describe a way of interpreting religious texts and symbols. The aim is to create a 'language' and to formulate a religio-political standpoint. A jargon is not necessarily formulated with the conscious intention of manipulating people. Hence, the FIS leadership can sincerely believe that their aim is to interpret the sacred sources in a just manner. One method can be the appropriation of meanings of words and verses in the Quran and Sunna. The function of this jargon is to evoke 'Islamic' emotions and/or to give the reader of the document 'Islamic' associations on the basis of which he will view the present social, political, economic or religious situation. Jargon as a means of comunication is thus directed towards the receiver of the message. However, as will be shown below, a major fallacy in this use of jargon is that while it has proved effective as a mobilizing force in the creation of public support for FIS, it is unlikely to contribute to a better understanding of the current social, political, economic and religious situation among FIS's followers.

In other words, FIS's usage of the 'Revealed Word' does not actually reveal much about the causes of the socio-economic difficulties experienced in contemporary Algeria. The examination of most Islamic movements' ideologies typically reveals a clear statement of what they are against, but only a vague idea of what they would do if they gained power.[5]

To further elucidate the role of Islamic jargon, FIS will be considered as comprising a 'core' section and a 'periphery'.[6] The core is composed of the FIS leadership and its dedicated adherents. The periphery consists of followers not fully committed to the cause, but willing to support

FIS if the movement can help them achieve their material goals. In this context, words or slogans from the sacred sources function as the link between the nucleus of the movement and its more loosely connected followers, mobilizing the latter's support. This relation will be further discussed in the analysis of the programme.

To define phenomena such as a party and a mass movement is a difficult task. In this article 'party' is defined as a formalized, but voluntary association or group framing issues and putting forward candidates in elections. One of its aims is to gain power and influence over the government. A 'mass movement' is a more loosely constructed entity. FIS acts both as a formalized political party with supporters and as a mass movement embracing a larger group of people. In both of these cases the adherents in the 'periphery' can support FIS openly or in secrecy.

The programme of the Front Islamique du Salut

FIS's programme is found in several sources.[7] One version is presented in Ghanim's book *al-harakat al-islamiyya fi-i-jazair wa azmat 'l-dimuqratiyya* (The Islamic Movement in Algeria and the Crisis of Democracy) published in 1992, and in the pamphlet *ath-thawra islamiyya fi-l-jazair* (The Islamic Revolution in Algeria) which appeared in 1991.[8] There is also one abbreviated version in a publication by Gamal al-Banna, *risala ila ad-dawat 'l-islamiyya* (A letter to those who call to Islam), 1991. Al-Banna's version excludes those parts which discuss the role of the army and foreign affairs. It is to be noted that all three texts were published in Egypt. Two possible reasons for this are, firstly, the relative freedom of the press in Egypt and, secondly, the trend of regimes in the Middle East to host dissidents from other, and neighbouring, countries, while persecuting their own internal opposition.[9] Al-Banna describes the document as a proposal for a political programme, and says that it was published in the *Front*'s paper *al-munqidh* in Algeria but is uncertain about which volume. He gives two possibilities; the first suggestion is that it was published in March 1989, and the second that it appeared in *al-munqidh* in October/November 1989. Al-Banna also remarks that FIS presented the programme in a pamphlet of about 40 pages[10] and it is therefore possible that he is referring to the pamphlet mentioned above.

The intentions behind the various presentations of FIS's programme may differ. Ghanim is reputed to be secular, a political scientist, whereas the other two publications are most likely linked to movements supportive of the message of the document. The actual text of the 'charter' is given in its original version in all three editions. In the following presentation I will use Ghanim's version, since it seems to be the most widely available text. Ghanim's work also includes the programmes of the Algerian *Hamas* movement,[11] The Movement for Islamic Renaissance (*an-nahda 'l-islamiyya*)[12] and a letter from shaykh Abd Allah Jab Allah, the leader of the *Nahda*, to the Algerian president Chadli Benjedid written in November 1988.[13] Moreover, the last part of the book gives some examples of political cartoons that appeared in the Algerian press between 1991 and 1992 and some of the official 'pro–clamations' (*nada*) and 'statements' *(bayan)* presented by Islamic movements in Algeria.[14]

The content of the programme is briefly as follows: It is claimed that the foundation of FIS's programme is the *sharia*, the Islamic law. The political ideology[15] of the movement is, accordingly, based upon the sources of Islam. The introduction emphasizes the significance of the Quran and the tradition of the prophet Muhammad in the life of Muslims in general. Then follows a passage in which the programme is related particularly to the Algerian people and their history. The next section deals with economic policy and includes paragraphs on agriculture, industry, commerce and the financial situation. Then there is a paragraph on social politics and civil rights. The next part deals with educational matters, of instance how to finance education, an outline of the discipline of pedagogics and the training of teachers. In subsequent parts of the 'charter' domestic and foreign policies are outlined. One of the paragraphs in this section is entitled 'The Features of Reformation [of Algerian society] are in the Girdle of the Islamic *Sharia' (islah-as-sirra 'l-jaza 'iriyya fi nitaq ash-sharia 'l-islamiyya).*[16] This part is followed by a paragraph entitled 'The Complete Social Reformation' (*islah al-ijtimai ash-shamil*). Next is a section on health, politics, followed by another on culture. The last part deals with the army and, finally, there is a more specific treatment of foreign affairs.

Some of the sections on the political goals of FIS, especially those which deal with the question of legitimate executive power, will now be looked at in detail. At the beginning of the programme, in a part preceding the introduction, there is a short passage establishing the foundation of the political platform of FIS. After the usual praise to God and the statement that there is no deity except God and that Muhammad is the servant and messenger of God, the programme quotes four verses from the Quran. These verses emphasize the omnipotence of God and the significance of being a Muslim.[17] After these verses, the authority of 'the Book of God' and 'Muhammad's guidance' is underlined. It is stressed that 'innovations' (*bid'a*) which are not in accordance with established holy traditions carry Muslims away from the straight path and lead them to 'hell-fire' (*an-nar*).[18] The introduction to the section on the political goals of FIS is divided into five parts. The importance of the just Islamic legal order, *sharia*, is substantiated by quoting from the Quran.[19] In Ghanim, the Quranic quotations are accentuated by being printed in extra bold types. The second part deals with the importance of acquiring knowledge and technology in creating the future Islamic society, and Quranic verses are cited, stating that the pursuit of knowledge is a commendable action.[20] The third part expresses the desire for a society free from 'colonialism' (*istimar*).[21] This shall be achieved through the Islamic faith and submission to the will of God.[22] It is further underlined that in order to implement the political agenda of the programme it is important to carry out the work in close cooperation with the Algerian people. Hence, the fourth part stresses the necessity to establish a political 'project' (*mashru*). The 'project' will work as an incentive for the political actions of FIS. The last passage in the fourth part says:

> Truly, the Front Islamique du Salut, with its characteristic methods, does not work in isolation from the people, but always starts from the principle of working with it in every step of the historical process. The implementations [of the methods] are fruits of its 'endeavour' [*lijahdihi*] and 'struggle' [*jihadihi*]. And this was the method of the Companions of the Prophet (may God be pleased with them) as they said: 'If you had set forth before us the sea, and you had dived into it, we should certainly have dived with you, and no one of us should have stayed behind you'.[23]

Thus, the 'method' (*manhaj*) is to follow the actions of Muhammad and the Companions of the Prophet. In the quotation above the Arabic root 'to endeavour' or 'to strive' (*jahada*) is used, and it forms the basis of a whole range of technical terms in Islamic terminology.[24] The most important is *jihad*, often translated as 'holy war', in the sense of war against unbelievers as a religious duty in accordance with the regulations for such a war set down by Islamic law. The term is also applied to the individual's personal struggle for Islam. The fifth part of the introduction emphasizes and repeats statements made in the earlier parts.

The next section, 'The Doctrinal Frame', emphasizes the history of Islam in Algeria. Islam is described as significant for Algerian history and culture. The political doctrine and ideology governing Algerian society should thus be drawn from the sphere of Islam: 'Islam is the most solid doctrinal girdle for the political project that has the power to confront the crises'.[25] This argument is supported by reference to several verses in the Quran.[26] These quotations all stress that Islam is the straight path and the true religion.

The following section of the document is on the 'Political Axis' (*al-mihwar as-siyasi*) of the system outlined and desired by FIS. The *sharia* is once more said to be the foundation of the whole system.[27] As the basis of FIS's standpoint, it is used in an effort to achieve truth (*al-haqq wa al-haqiqa*) and 'justice in compulsion' (*adl al-ilzam*). According to the FIS document, the implementation of the policies is based on 'conviction' (*iqna*') and not on 'subjugation' (*qahr*) among the Algerian people. This principle is based on the supposed close relationship between the Algerian people and Islam. Furthermore, a part of the Quranic verse 2:111 – 'Say: Produce your proof if you are truthful' – is quoted to support the right of FIS to formulate this very programme. This is followed by other verses warning men that there is no other god than God and that nothing can be placed side by side with God.[28] The 'truthful' in the above quotation is perceived as FIS; hence, its interpretations of the Islamic tradition are to be followed. The other verses cited warn men that the 'true' interpretation has to be observed. The FIS programme continues:

> It [the political policy of FIS] builds on the possibility to 'choose' [*ikhtiyar*] without 'coercion' [*ajbar*] according to his word, the most high: 'Say, the truth [*haqq*] is from your Lord. Let him who will believe and let him who will be an infidel'…[29] [Part of verse 18:29]. And his word, the most high: 'If it had been thy Lord's will, they would all have believed, – all who are on earth! Wilt thou then compel mankind, against their will, to believe!' [10:99]. Insist on the 'consultation' [*shura*] to do away with 'arbitrariness' [*istibdad*], the most high said:…'Their affairs by mutual consultation'…[the central part of verse 42:38]. And his world the most high:… 'and consult them in affairs [of moments]'…[a part of verse 3:159].[30]

This quotation will be dealt with extensively below in the analysis of the programme. It is an expressive example of a statement supported by various Quranic words and verses to substantiate its accuracy. The section outlining the political agenda of FIS continues with a presentation of the ideas promoted by the movement in order to overcome the problems arising from the influence of foreign political ideas. In the first paragraph the idea of consultation (*shura*) is once more stressed. This is an important term in Islamists' notions of democracy in general.[31] The 'arbitrariness' (*istibdad*) in the political process is to be eradicated. *Istibdad* is often regarded as a secular term denoting a state of despotism.[32] The political, economic and social monopoly of the ruling party (FLN) is to be eliminated. Instead, equality shall be applied in society to overcome these problems and do away with the suppression of public freedom. The programme states that FIS works to make room for popular initiatives and that it will endeavour to accomplish a free and equal society. Moreover, the movement is said to be striving for an advancement of the collective Islamic spirit in society, and condemns selfishness and favouritism – which amounts to a condemnation of corruption in

Algerian society.[33] Corruption is a widespread phenomenon in the Middle East and to accuse the regime of it is a common trait in the propaganda of Islamist movements.[34]

Under the heading 'The Political Axis' there are twelve paragraphs constituting the basis for the Front's work to 'restore the political order to health' (*tashih an-nizam as-siyasi*). The first paragraph refers to two verses from the Quran; the first reference is as follows: '[The desire of FIS is] to make the political legislation subject to the rules of the law [*sharia*] according to his word, the most high: "What! Have they partners (in godhead), who have established for them some religion without the permission of God?" '[35]

The Quranic part of the quotation is the first passage of verse 21 in 'The *sura* of Consultation' (*sura ash-shura*). As perceived by FIS, the usage of the sacred source in this paragraph serves to uphold the view that a situation where the state is governed by secular[36] legislation is to be vehemently condemned. A secular legislation where man promulgates the laws is, according to this interpretation, to associate a companion with God (*shirk*) – that is, to worship another besides God (polytheism). The programme continues with another verse from the Quran. 'And his word, the most high: Do they then seek after a judgement of (the days of) ignorance? But who, for a people whose faith is assured, can give better judgement than God?'[37] The quotation is the complete verse 5:53 of the Quran. This verse is often interpreted as expressing an 'Islamic mission'. The aim of the mission is to divert man from false attitudes and selfishness and direct him towards the supposed true Islamic spirit of unity, i.e. an equal society.[38] Thereafter, it is stated in the document that recent phases in the development of the nation have to be taken into account, and that there are a great number of institutions which have to participate in the reform of Algeria. It starts with the National Assembly, all district councils and municipal councils, and the work of reform will continue until all institutions are based on Islamic law (*sharia*). The very foundations of the Algerian Muslim people, it is stated in the programme, lie in their dedication to the Islamic law.[39]

Many of the following paragraphs of the document are brief, imprecise and vague. For instance, the ninth paragraph of the programme calls for the re-examination of agricultural policies. The support of the farmers should be secured, but it is never clearly expressed in what way. Several of the other paragraphs mention problems such as administrative malpractice, but as to what action should be taken to remedy this, nothing is said. The eleventh paragraph discusses the courts of justice:

> The reform of the judicial ranks is to take place by the return of the respect for the independence of justice and the immunity of the judge [*qadi*], just as the Islamic *sharia* defines it. This is in

order to raise the abode of the divine justice [*al-adl al-rabbani* – *rabb* implies a notion of God as owner of the world], which the oppression [*zulm*] has not tarnished, and the disgrace of injustice has not dishonoured, due to the fact that the 'Justice' [*adl*] is the foundation of the Islamically legal policy and the justification of the power and the aim of the political order.[40]

The quotation stresses the fact that FIS wishes to increase public confidence in law officials and the courts of law. The political platform presented in al-Ahnaf and originally published in FIS's paper *al-munqidh* also underlines the need to strengthen the position of the juridical apparatus in general.[41] The last of the twelve paragraphs also includes several instances of Islamic terminology. The paragraph says:

Securing for the freedom of the *umma*[42] and the right of expression of its will is accomplished with the soundest of methods, and the most flawless as to right and legality. The view, therefore, returns to the law of elections. It [FIS] does not put trust in anything but the rightly guided, such as the fool or the infant does, or one who is without legal justice. It does not force anyone to choose either of the [representatives of the] military service or the security official or the administration and the like, so all people can vote in genuine freedom.[43]

It is to be noted that FIS does not put *trust* in anything but the 'rightly guided'. The real meaning of this is likely to retain a certain fluidity – especially when the movement regards itself as the sole and rightful interpreter of the Quran and Sunna (see above). It is also interesting that the term *umma* does not refer to the traditional meaning of the word as the 'Nation' of Islam in general, but to Algeria in particular. In the above quotation, FIS supports the principles of the right of expression and the right to hold general elections. This discussion continues under the heading 'The Right of Election, Nomination of Candidates and Participation in the Running [of the election campaign]' (*haqq al-intikhab wa 'l-tarshih wa 'l-musharaka fi 'l-tasyir*).[44] In the first part of the section, Islam is described as the religion of freedom (*din al-hurriya*). Islam is said to be founded on responsibility, inasmuch as responsibility is an expression of the good will (*al-irada al-khayra*) of man's upright consciousness. The content of the belief and the strength of its morality and ethics are regarded as evidence for the statement that Islam is the religion of freedom. This statement is supported by reference to the Quran and to a tradition from Muhammad. The Quranic verse 30:30 says: '[Establish] God's handiwork according to the pattern on which He has made mankind: No change [let there be] in the work [wrought] by God....'[45]

After this verse a statement by the Prophet is quoted: 'Everyone born into the world is born according to the *fitra* (*ala 'l-fitra* – man's inborn nature, created by God).[46] The conception of *fitra* in the text is a justification for Islam as the natural religion – a condition including a state of freedom for the individual. The statement 'Islam is the religion of freedom' is finally verified with a reference to an utterance made by one of Muhammad's leading companions, the second caliph Umar ibn al-Khattab: 'How can you enslave people when their mothers delivered them as free.'[47] The paragraph maintains that this is a profoundly Islamic view of man. Thereafter, four fundamental rights in the field of law are affirmed. The first right is that of election, to choose leadership; the second is the right to be accepted as a candidate in elections. This is possible as long as one fulfils a set of premises: 'Islam' (*al-islam*), 'rightmindedness' (*al-qadwa*), 'suitability' (*al-Kafa'a*), and 'fitness and qualification' (*jadara*). The following is the third right:

> The right to administer [*taysir*], i.e. to take on the administrative and professional responsibilities, is founded on ability, suitability and competence only. So in accordance with that, the civil servant or the one appointed to the responsibilities shall be responsible before God, before the *umma* and before the authority which controls it, or is in charge of it, so that the trust is not ruined by the ruin of the responsibility; as the most high says: 'God doth command you to render back your trusts to those whom they are due.'[48] He [Muhammad] said: 'Everyone of you is a guardian and all of you are responsible for his flock.'[49]

The aim of this passage is to establish popular confidence in Algerian public institutions. The method used to create such a trust in government offices is to make civil servants responsible for their actions before God. How this will work in practice is not explained in the document. In the fourth right it is stated that trust in the administration will increase if officials fulfil the above-mentioned premises.

FIS's political programme also includes a section on 'Social Policy' (*as-siyasa al-ijtimaiya*).[50] It refers to several verses in the Quran and it deals with the rights of subjects within the state. In the first paragraph of the section, the social policy of the *Front* is said to emanate from the respect for man expressed in the following verse in the Quran: 'We have honoured [*Karramna*] the sons of Adam; provided them with transport on land and sea; given them for sustenance things good and pure; and conferred on them special favours, above a great part of our creation.'[51] This is verse 17:70 in its entirety. According to the document, the verse constitutes a starting-point by guaranteeing the rights and liberties which the judicious revelation (*al-shar*) ensures. These rights are interpreted in the document as a good model for the *umma*, bringing equality to all people. It is looked upon as a blueprint for mutual societal solidarity (*takaful*), which is itself hindered by the struggle between classes and groups. (*Takaful* is often translated as 'cooperation', but here it is better rendered as 'social solidarity' due to Marxist Influence on FIS rhetoric.) The section is then divided into two parts. The first discusses 'the right of existence' (*haqq al-wudjud*) and points out that man's right to existence is founded on 'divine respect' or 'honouring the Lord' (*at-takrim ar-rabbani*). The Quranic verse cited above speaks about God's 'honouring' of man which is derived from the principle of man's right to existence – that is, man's right to life. This is emphasized by the use of the following Quranic verses: 'I have only created jinns and men, that they may serve me (51: 56), No sustenance do I require of them, nor do I require that they should feed me (51: 57), for God is he who gives [all] sustenance, lord of power, steadfast [for ever] (51: 58).'[52]

These verses stress that the meaning of human existence is to serve God and that man is dependent upon God for his livelihood. The programme maintains that God has legitimized human existence in terms of 'service' (*bil-ibada*), and not profit. The latter is regarded as the outcome of modern ideologies 'from Malthus to Marx'.[53] The meaning of 'service' as expressed in the document is that the value of human existence or human dignity lies in the relation between man and God, and not in that between man and those things under his authority. That is to say that Muslims should use no ideology that is not subordinated to the power of God.[54] This argument is supported by a quotation from verse 49: 13 of the Quran: 'The most honoured of you in the sight of God is [he who is] the most righteous of you.'[55] The verse expresses how the tenets of Islamic society can be implemented by the individual in accordance with just Islamic practice. It is then stated that man is the axis of existence due to his capacity, which is different from the capacity of the animals. The actions of man also have cultural dimensions which make the human being a maker (*sani*) of culture within civilization and not just a tool in it.

The programme continues by reiterating that man is the axis of existence. Therefore, the *umma* claims to give security to its subjects and everyone in society is regarded as being born equal. The second paragraph under the heading 'The Social Policy' is entitled 'The Right of the Subjects and the Right to Social Security' (*haqq ar-riaya wa 'l-inaya*). It outlines the rights of the Algerian people in all stages of the country's progress, from seed to the utmost phase of guidance and perfection. The developed society corresponds to the peak of human existence, because it is regarded as an existence with a 'message' (*risaliyan*) from God to man. Hence, the possibility of establishing this perfect society is linked to the degree in which its Muslim inhabitants behave in a correct Islamic manner. The message is claimed to carry historical and cultural significance – the right to education, for instance, being contained within it. 'The revealed text makes a connection between the right of existence and the right of education in order to guarantee the "message" [*risala*]; as a sign that the message is one of the reasons for the creation and that this right is guaranteed for all.'[56]

Moreover, the right to education presupposes that every mother is responsible on matters of importance for the education of her children. The latter is supported by the Quranic quotation: 'Read! In the name of thy Lord who created – created man out of a clot.'[57] Considered to be the first revelation to Muhammad, this is often used in discussions to verify a positive Islamic position towards, for instance, new educational programmes.[58] The last paragraph under the heading 'The Social Policy' sums up FIS's position and serves as a distillation of the whole programme: 'Therefore the policy of the Front Islamique du Salut is founded on principles in accordance with the postulates on equality in Islam.'[59] Once again FIS's positive attitude towards equality is emphasized, but with the proviso that this equality shall be in accordance with the movement's idea of an 'Islamic equality'.

An analysis of the programme

Islam is comprehended as the foundation for every action in all fields of society, individual or collective. This supposition, and several of the other themes expressed in the FIS document, are shared by other Islamic movements in the Middle East.[60] From the point of view of FIS the actions recommended in the political programme, therefore, can be characterized as acts of worship (*ibadat*). Behind the notion of Islam lies the understanding of 'the oneness of Allah in all its meanings' or 'monotheism' (*tawhid*).[61] *Tawhid* is intimately connected with the concept of an ideal Islamic society or Utopia. The term implies the idea of a society based on Islamic principles, a society where no contradictory meanings exist. It can be characterized as an undivided organic totality. Thus the movement strives to unite the Algerian *umma* on principles to be found in the Quran and in the Sunna, which are normative sources. More explicitly, the '*tawhidic*' notion leads to a view where there can exist no other legislation than *sharia* and no other legislator than God. The meaning of *tawhid* is further illustrated in the document by its antithesis *fitna*, which signifies disagreement or the disruption of the Muslim community.

The programme does not accept 'innovations' (*bida*). They are not considered to be part of the Islamic tradition. The interpretation of the Islamic tradition is based not only on the Quran: according to the document, the perfect models to be followed for the creation of a just Islamic society are the actions of the Prophet Muhammad and his Companions. The utterances and actions of Muhammad and the first Muslims are also used to elucidate questions whose solutions are not explicitly expressed in the Quran. The application of the sources of Islamic tradition is thus used to legitimize the claims of FIS. In the document *sharia* is the foundation for the political system.[62] The Islamic system is regarded as the true order for Algerian society and to implement it is a legitimate act sanctioned by the highest authority – God. Many paragraphs underline the role of Islam as a religion founded on equality giving man all possible rights. Islam is perceived as the foremost and the most comprehensive of all world views.

A society where laws are instituted by, for instance, a parliament where several diametrically opposed ideologies compete, such as communism or liberalism, would be an expression of 'idolatry' or 'to associate something with God' (*shirk*). Ideologies from the 'outside', therefore, are viewed as a threat to the true Islamic order because they are not subordinated to the power of God. This is further exemplified in the programme through the claim that man has a free will and a right to elect the leadership of a state, and is further buttressed by a quotation from the Quran and strengthened by reference to a prophetic tradition.

A candidate in an election must fulfil certain demands. The first demand is to be a Muslim. The possibility of electing a non-Muslim is not mentioned in the text. The fulfilment of the other qualifications – to be just, an exemplary person and a fit and qualified Muslim – are measured according to the Islamic yardstick. The Algerian Islamic order can, in FIS's understanding, be said to encourage general elections; however, the ideal choice is not between political parties representing different ideologies, but between the most qualified Muslim individuals.

The use of language and terminology by FIS can be elucidated further by taking a closer look at the quotations (see page 145) concerning man's right to choose without coercion. The first Quranic verse cited in that context states that the truth is from God, but man has the right to make the decision to be a Muslim or not. The most important word in the passage is 'truth' or 'right' (*haqq*). God gives man the right to choose between religions. The next quotation from the Quran expresses the omnipotence of God and his ability to make all human beings Muslims. Despite God's power, He did not force all of mankind to believe in Islam. Thus the policy of FIS is that one should insist on the principle of 'consultation' (*shura*) to do away with 'arbitrariness' (*istibdad*). The accuracy of the standpoint is underlined by citing parts of two Quranic verses. The possibility to embrace any religion therefore shifts to mean the possibility to choose among individuals taking part in a general election. The choice of the most qualified Muslim individual will lead Algeria away from arbitrariness. Arbitrariness here signifies the presence within a society of despotism or competing ideologies where none of them is subordinated to the will of God.

'Consultation' (*shura*) in its traditional meaning signifies a mutual, first-hand consultation between high-level religious and worldly officials.

It has also been used to designate parliaments in the Middle East and North Africa. The consultative council established by FIS when it was officially legalized in 1989 was called *shura*.[63] In the programme 'consultation' means allowing the people to choose their Muslim representatives to the National Assembly. The document explicitly expresses a desire that these representatives, due to the qualifications they have fulfilled, should be united in the decisions they make in the Assembly. This is the aim, despite the increase of participants taking part in the actual decision-making. The purpose is to maintain 'consensus' (*ijma*)[64] within the *umma*. 'Arbitrariness', often translated as 'despotism' or 'autocracy' – related to the term 'oppression' (*zulm*) – is in opposition to this struggle for consensus in society.[65] A consequence of this standpoint is that laws shall not be promulgated by the Assembly. The Islamic law (*sharia*) already exists, and is to be applied through interpretation. This form of government is sometimes described as a '*shuracratie*'.[66]

Hence, in the Algerian context, 'arbitrariness' refers to decision-making that is not subordinated to the Revealed Word; that is, the sovereignty of God and, especially, the law of Islam. The programme can, therefore, be seen as an outline for a constitution where the idea of consensus and a supposed democracy within the Algerian community legitimizes the interpretation and application of the *sharia*, but also the actions of FIS in the eyes of the Western world. However, the word democracy (*dimuqratiyya*) is seen by the FIS leader Ali Belhadj as a neologism alien to the Arabic language.[67]

In Muslim terms, FIS's technique of argumentation can be characterized as traditional in terms of style and structure.[68] Statements and demands are substantiated by quotations from the Quran, although it is sometimes difficult to discover the connection between the statement and the Quranic passage. In some examples the Sunna is used to back up the proclaimed view and to elucidate the meaning of a verse cited.[69] One function of the sacred sources is to create an impression that the claims made in the programme are just, and of an Islamic nature. In spite of the traditional method of presentation, many of the views presented in the programme are not shared by religious scholars or the political leadership in Algeria.

The meanings of terms and their fields of association clearly shift in the document from the 'traditional' to those that bear a closer relation to the current situation in Algeria. In a typical Muslim – and Islamist – fashion, the words of the Quran and Sunna are re-interpreted with the aim of finding the 'true' purpose of God's word. Islamic movements in the Middle East often express the opinion that society's problem is not Islam in general, but the way the religion is practised.[70]

The possibility of electing representatives to the Assembly from among suitable Muslim individuals – and thereby to give the term 'consultation' a different meaning – is not an idea accepted by many religious or political leaders, at least not currently. Even if *shura* is a word often used to designate parliaments, the level of 'consultation' can be questioned. The elite class of traditionally-educated religious scholars (*ulama*) regard themselves having the exclusive right to interpret religious texts. Many leaders of FIS do not belong to this class of religious leaders, and they do not hold top-level positions. Even if the structure and style of interpretation of Islamic terminology can be seen as traditional, one of the striking features of FIS's interpretation is the fact that it is made by laymen outside the control of the traditional, top-level religious leaders.[71] It is, for instance, possible to relate the emphasis on education to the profession of one of the founders of FIS, Abbasi Madani, who is a Professor of Pedagogics.[72] The interpretations of the Islamic texts are clearly related to the contemporary situation in Algeria. Current problems such as corruption, unemployment, administrative malpractice and lack of public confidence in state institutions, influence the choice of quotations of Quranic verses or parts of verses. They also affect the choice of prophetic traditions to be cited. The verses from the Quran and the sayings quoted from the Sunna are taken out of context, conveying the idea that every word and letter of the Quran are 'God's own words' (*kalam Allah*), applicable at all times and in all circumstances. This notion of the status of the Quran makes it imperative to fulfil its commandments. In the programme, the 'traditions' (*hadith*) function in the same way, but with less significance: for instance, the words of the companions uttered at the battle of Badr in 624 CE in order to underline the loyalty of the 'helpers' (*ansar*) to Muhammad, are said in the document to express FIS's method of working, and the inference is that the movement is, accordingly, loyal to the people. Two sayings from the 'traditions' quoted in the programme can be found in several sources. In Bukhari's collection, the utterances about 'man's inborn nature' (*fitra*) and 'everyone of you are a guardian and all of you are responsible for his herd' have to do with traditions concerning the ritual at funeral prayers. In their new context, the sayings are supposed to mobilize the Algerians into supporting the interpretation of the Islamic tradition of the *Front* – Islam as a religion of freedom – and recognizing it as the true interpretation. The meaning of a term or a word from the sacred sources is thus appropriated and conceptualized – a form of philosophical realism in the traditional meaning of the word.

Engineers and university teachers – who are among the most prominent representatives of FIS – face particular problems which cause their interpretation of Islamic tradition to differ from that made by the elite group of religious scholars.[73] This laymen's interpretation expresses an endeavour to play a part in the decision-making process, and its widespread appeal suggests that these problems are also the problems of the people. Focusing on religious values in its propaganda, FIS also appeals to the people's ethical and psychological needs. The aim is to inspire individual loyalties to the 'true' values and principles of Islam as defined by FIS. These values are the platform from which followers of FIS are mobilized for moral, social and political action. Ultimately, the goal is to create an Islamic state founded on a divinely-guided political authority. Hence, the Islamic movements in Algeria are posing a political, but also a moral challenge to the regime.

The Islamic jargon can be summed up as a link between the 'core' of FIS and the 'periphery'. The latter consists of followers who, although they may not be willing to establish the Islamic Republic of Algeria and to accept living in accordance with FIS's interpretation of the Islamic law, are willing enough to support the movement as an alternative to the politics of the present regime. Neither the 'core' nor the 'periphery' can be characterized as homogeneous groups. Primarily, those belonging to the 'periphery' seek to achieve goals such as better housing and employment.[74] In order to secure the support of the 'periphery', statements by FIS, for instance by its leaders in the documents presented here or in the movement's paper *al-munqidh*, are closely linked to the sacred sources. The quotations and references to the Quran and the Sunna do not only evoke 'Islamic' emotions and associations, but also substantiate the actual message of FIS in the eyes of the adherents to the movement. That is to say that the usage of the Revealed Word and of religious symbols serve to legitimize the standpoints of FIS, and also function as a religio-political language understood by most Algerians.

Even though the FIS document is concerned with individual and state morality and ethical questions, the programme is, basically, part of a political discourse. It is of a rhetorical nature, but despite that, the document can be characterized as a draft constitution. The thoughts and images expressed by FIS and other Islamic religio-political movements include some common patterns. Most such movements in the Middle East and North Africa apprehend Islam as a world view containing an eternal and normative social order that can be applied as a political system in a state. The first measure in the establishment of the Islamic state is to define and to apply the *sharia*. The Islamic movements strive to outline the function of religion in society in general. In their ideologies they often point out that Islam is an *objective* truth. The religion is independent of 'ordinary' people's belief and interpretations of it. If leaders of the movements find the *absolute meaning* or the *correct truth* of words or verses in the Quran they can thereby establish the 'true' Islamic order and the 'real' Islamic society. In the Algerian context, the self-image of FIS is that the movement's ideology is the only correct interpretation of the Revealed Word.

Functions of religion in Algeria

In the Middle East and North Africa religious reform movements have been the vehicle for political renewal and change since the early days of Islam. Throughout the history of the region, Islamic reformers have propagated the overthrow of governments because of their supposed deviation from the true Islamic path.[75] In the contemporary Muslim World 'The Muslim Brotherhood' (*al-ikhwan al-muslimun*) is a well-known movement. It has, since it was founded in the late 1920s, striven to enhance Islam's influence on the whole of society. Many of the more militant groups established in the 1970s and 1980s can be viewed as offshoots of what militants regard as an institutionalized Brotherhood.[76]

In the Algerian context, Islam has functioned as a unifying force since the country was colonized by the French in the 1830s. This is, of course, a simplified account of Algerian history. Von Sivers describes it more fully, especially four revolts between 1849 and 1879 which he terms 'apocalyptic'. He points out: 'Apocalyptic inspiration must be regarded as a cause distinct from political, economic and social causes. Even though these causes were often simultaneously operative, it is imperative that they not be reduced to each other.'[77] Von Sivers' remarks are of significance also in the general analysis of the contemporary situation. Could the inspiration behind FIS be termed 'apocalyptic'? Another question to discuss further is: what characterizes the religious inspiration of FIS, and what is the relation between economy, religion and social matters in its standpoint? For example, to what degree is the 'religious force' distinct from the economic or the social? However, this is a matter for further research.

One of the most prominent Islamist movements appeared in Algeria during the 1930s – the *Salafiyya* movement – and one important aim of the ideology of the *Salafiyya* was to establish a national identity based on Islam.[78] The function of Islam as a unifying force and an 'ethnic marker' was again emphasized during the war which ended the French colonization of Algeria in 1962.[79] To overcome parochial identification and to create a broader Islamic sense of identity have been the goals of Islamic movements since the nineteenth century throughout North Africa.[80]

Despite the recent setbacks, when the first multiparty election in the history of the country was nullified in 1991, one can easily conclude that political Islam has been, and still is, an important oppositional force to the political leadership since the foundation of the modern Algerian state. Another such force is that centred round the Berber community. Different Islamic groups have emerged since the mid-1960s calling for a more visible role of Islam in society. The movements have all been suppressed by the regime.[81] According to Choueiri, however, the situation has not always been as simple as that: in a comment on the Boumedienne regime (1965-78) he says:

> About a third of the state budget was spent on education, and the promotion of a new cultural policy of Arabization and Islamicization. The regime, moreover, revived the legacy of the Islamic reformist, Ibn Badis, and sought the assistance of Egyptian Muslim Brethren in teaching religious and historical subjects. Thus, by monopolizing the economy and the religious arena, the Algerian government has managed to contain political opposition, forcing its Islamic radicalists to act in a diffuse and disorganized fashion.[82]

During the regime of Boumedienne, the economic reform programme was combined with the objective of strengthening the position of Islamic tradition in society. The policy was not successful. Akacem describes the structure of the Boumedienne regime in general as a replica of the former Soviet power model.[83]

Even though Algeria was generally described as a calm and stable state until the early 1980s, the situation changed rapidly towards the end of that decade.[84] Observers noted that the political culture of the elite was different from the political culture of the Algerian people.[85] The secular ideology of the political and socio-economic elite was not supported by the masses. The majority of the people still identified themselves with Islam and its religious symbols as the significant foundation for political action.[86] The limited role of Islam in the state constitution does not diminish Islam's importance in the society outside the state: in this context it has the 'potential for the reconstruction of modern states in Islamic or neo-Islamic terms'.[87] This is not solely an Algerian phenomenon. The regimes in the Middle East have to manoeuvre constantly to bridge this gap, and occasionally the secular policy of the regime is associated in the eyes of the people with failure, primarily in the field of economic policy.

The editor of the Egyptian magazine *Ruz al-yusuf*, Abd El Satar El Tawila, notes, when he talks about the growing appeal of the Islamic standpoint among the middle and lower classes: 'The petite bourgeoisie are asking themselves: What is left? Nasserism has failed, Communism has failed. Perhaps Islam *is* the solution?'[88] The latter is a view certainly featured in FIS propaganda. The economic and social frustration among the population in Algeria is, of course, an instigating force working in support of the Islamic movements.

The FIS programme presented above contains a serious critique of socio-economic conditions in Algerian society. Despite the criticism, the documents do not present a comprehensive analysis of the problems facing the Algerians. In practice, the movement has worked to establish itself as an organization dedicated to solving the everyday problems of the Algerian people. In the capital city Algiers, FIS started several community projects, including building schools, starting local housing authorities and making areas of Algiers safe for their inhabitants. The welfare activities of FIS have involved the distribution of food, clothes and money. Hence, FIS was active in helping the victims of an earthquake in northern Algeria in October 1989.[89] One reason for these actions may be to challenge the government and stress the commonly-held notion that the masses are ignored by the establishment.[90] After the local and regional elections in 1990 and the overwhelming victory of FIS, the movement's challenge to the government has been partly weakened. The newly-elected 'Islamic' councils are more concerned with 'symbolic issues such as dress, alcohol consumption and gambling than with radical changes in state, society and economy'.[91]

The democratization process started in Algeria in the aftermath of the riots in 1988. According to Akacem, the protests were against the miserable social conditions and, in the beginning, not about democracy and less about an Islamic republic.[92] The new constitution of 1989 established a multiparty system, and one of the results was the emergence of dozens of new parties.[93] FIS was officially founded in the beginning of 1989.[94] The supporters of the movement are primarily found in cities, with their socio-economic problems such as unemployment and housing shortages.[95] The adherents of the movement are found in all groups of society, but FIS is particularly well represented among students and the educated classes. According to Ghanim, supporters come from all layers of society and likewise from all districts of Algeria. He also estimates the adherents of the movement to number three million Algerians.[96] This is equivalent to the number of votes cast for FIS in the first round of the aborted elections.[97] The Islamists' appeal for social justice 'proved irresistable to the ranks of young men who have nothing better to do than prop up the wall all day'.[98] They constitute a significant base of support for FIS. The political, economic and social problems pose a dilemma for all classes in society, which may be one reason why individuals from all social strata are turning to Islam in its function of a religiously-motivated and justified opposition.

Among the new parties to appear were several founded on Islamic ideology. In addition to FIS, two of the more important ones were the previously mentioned *Hamas* and *an-Nahda*. The support for these movements increased rapidly, and in the local (*commune*) and regional (*wilaya*) elections in June 1990 FIS received almost 60 per cent of the votes. FIS took control of 55 per cent of local councils and two-thirds of the regional councils.[99] In the first parliamentary elections in December 1991, FIS prevailed, winning the first round.[100] The *coup d'état* in January 1992 stopped the democratization process, and the second round of the elections never took place. A common argument among the Islamists in the Maghreb region, and probably in the rest of the Middle East and North Africa, is that even the Prophet Muhammad had some setbacks in his struggle for the Islamic state, and that is what they are facing at the moment. The adherents of FIS have interpreted the *coup* as the only way for the repressive regime to stop them establishing the just, rightful and true Islamic state.[101]

Contemporary Algeria is bordering on civil war. The attempts at reconciliation have not succeeded and FIS has changed into an underground movement fighting against the 'non-Islamic' state from new positions. Several members have left the country and FIS's organizations in France and Germany have been more active, with *al-munqidh* appearing in a European version, published by an executive association headed by Rabih Kabir. This change is so significant that FIS can no longer be defined as purely Algerian but rather as an Algerian-French-German Islamic movement. The future will show if the strengthened position of FIS's European and US branches will cause a split from within the movement. In contemporary Algeria the voice of the Berber community has been heard in the media.[102] The Berbers are in opposition to the government and have a complex relationship with Islamism.[103] The media have also given some attention to demonstrations against the regime and FIS. One in favour of dialogue and reconciliation took place in May 1994, partly organized by *Hamas*.[104] It is possible that the 'new' forces in the Algerian arena will affect the leadership of FIS and its standpoint. For example, the GIA (Groupe Islamique Armée – al-Jamaa al-Islamiyya al-Musallaha) has attracted much attention with its radical and militant stance in the conflict; it can be seen as an extremist offshoot of FIS.

The use of the Revealed Word in the FIS document can be characterized as evocative; that is, verses from the Quran and/or parts of the Sunna act as 'symbols' presenting a possible line of action for the people to meet the situation in contemporary Algeria. The sacred sources and Islamic terminology are a political language understood by the people, and in opposition to the mistrusted FLN, with the form of Islamic secularism. The interpretation of the sacred sources by FIS's leadership is also tied to social predicaments. The Algerians' response to the Islamic jargon can thus be seen as one of the possible explanations why FIS received the support of large portions of the voting public and won a landslide victory in the elections – even though many people in Algeria, due to illiteracy and lack of (religious) education, are not familiar with the minutiae of Islamic religio-political doctrine.

In spite of the support obtained, the FIS's conscious usage of the Revealed Word does not give a clear indication of a concrete programme to remedy the problems of Algeria. However, there would seem to be sincerity in it, and the Islamic jargon is believed – at least by the 'core' – to be more than just another strategy to win political power.

In the political discourse of Algeria, Islamism can function as the instrument by which a supposedly lost 'Islamic' identity is regained, and a political language for the Muslims provided. Reviewing the document, the 'colonial theme' is clearly expressed and it is Islam as an 'ethnic marker' that is to give the Algerians their 'true' identity; that is, the FIS's programme and the interpretation of Islam, its sacred sources and its history, are closely related to the contemporary situation – a form of theorizing on Islam in the specific circumstance of the present time. FIS's interpretation of history is guided by a kind of 'deductive' method. For example, the aim is to establish the correctness of Islam. Here the term *umma* comes to denote the Algerian Muslim community.

Elucidation of the texts emphasises the dominance of Europe and North America when it comes to forming political systems. Taking over categories or terms such as 'democracy' from the political language of present-day Europe symbolizes this dominance. Therefore, the interpretations of Islam made by FIS are reflecting contemporary notions and occurrences, and the emphasis in interpretation and, for example, choice of Quranic verses will probably shift in the future. In an imaginary situation, where FIS is in power, another possible example is the term *bida* (innovation). Under such conditions the term could be expected to shift in meaning from the repudiation of 'innovations' of a general character to the repudiation of 'theological innovations'. The point of the shift would be to make room for 'innovations' in the field of technology and natural sciences in the desired Islamic Republic of Algeria. This shift in meaning of Islamic terminology can clearly be seen as an ongoing process in the history of the movement, in spite of FIS's present 'underground' position. The term *jihad* is, for example, emphasized in the Islamic jargon of the movement's paper *al-munqidh*, published in Europe since the banning of FIS in Algeria.[105]

Finally, the usage of the term *shura* to construct an Islamic form of democracy is stressed throughout the programme. The principle of *shura*, translated to mean majority decisions, is an instance of a Quranic word being given a political meaning. However, *shura* is used in a vague and imprecise manner in the document. In the perception of *shura*, and the function of Islam in general, participation in the development of an 'Islamic' political system is the religious duty of the individual as well as of the community. The participation in elections by the Muslim individual is therefore seen as the responsibility of the citizen in the Algeria *umma*. The obligation of the parliament in FIS's outline is primarily to apply *sharia* – the Islamic law in society. To be noted in this context is that the premises that a Muslim should fulfil in order to become a member of parliament do not require that he should be a religious scholar. Hence, in the opinion of FIS, to apply the *sharia* is also a matter for the layman.

Although the political system outlined in the FIS document cannot be described as an expression of equality (for instance, on religious matters, between the sexes and on liberalism), there are elements of democracy in it. In spite of the condemnation of a system based on political parties representing different ideologies the programme, for example, encourages general elections, but in the framework of Islam. Another point stressed in the document is government accountability. Therefore, it is possible to view the programme as at least a step on the road to pluralism. The *coup d'état* stopped this process. Up to that moment in January 1992, FIS had worked 'within' the political system in Algeria, playing by the rules and forming a political alternative based on its interpretation of the function of Islam. In this alternative, Islam functioned as a vehicle for a pluralistic society, at least in theory. Now, with FIS an underground movement, more or less involved in a civil war, Islam will probably be interpreted along different lines – an example of this being the emphasis on the term *jihad* in the above-mentioned issue of *al-munqidh*, revealing as it does a shift in the movement made to meet new conditions.

Notes

1. See, for instance 'The Mosque goes Underground', *The Middle East*, April 1992: 12; Deeb 1992: 53f.
2. 'The Mosque goes Underground', *The Middle East*, April 1992: 12.
3. For a more general analysis of FIS and the contemporary situation in Algeria, see Burgat 1993: 247-305.
4. Sunna is the normative practice – the received custom. The ideal model for a Muslim to imitate is the Prophet Muhammad. Sunna is primarily founded on the *hadiths* (traditions). A 'tradition' is a narration of actions and utterances of Muhammad and his companions.
5. Ibrahim 1982: 23; Lobmeyer 1991: 412ff. For bibliographies and overviews of Islamist's thought, see Haddad *et al.* 1991; Lawrence 1989; Hussain 1983. For Islamism in North Africa, see Burgat 1993.
6. For the idea of FIS as composed of 'core' and 'periphery', see Akacem 1993: 54ff.
7. Ghanim 1992, *The Islamic Revolution in Algeria* 1991 and in al-Banna 1991. There is also a presentation in al- Ahnaf, Botiveau and Frégosi 1991 including fifteen paragraphs which constitute a platform of the political claims of FIS, 'Plate-Forme

des Revendications Politiques du FIS'. This platform was originally published in the Front's paper *al-munqidh*, 'The Saviour' no. 16, see al-Ahnaf *et al*. 1991: 49ff.

8. In general, Islamic movements do not designate themselves as revolutionaries, but, rather, as saviours redeeming society. See Deeb 1992: 55.

9. For the case of Egypt, see Ibrahim 1982: 93ff. Another example is Syrian Islamists; for instance, Said Hawwa lived and published books in Cairo and Jordan. See Lobmeyer 1991.

10. Al-Banna 1991: 166.

11. *Hamas* is an Arabic 'acronym' for *harakat 'l-mujtama 'l-islami* (the Movement for an Islamic Society). In Arabic *Hamas* also means 'zeal' or 'enthusiasm'.

12. Ghanim 1992: 93-147.

13. Ibid.: 151-67.

14. Ibid.: 185-90.

15. The word 'ideology' is used here in its widest sense, as designating the jargon and ideas expressed in the programme.

16. The term *islah* is often translated 'reform' or 'reformism' and many of the movements intending to reform the Muslim world during the 19th and the 20th centuries were labelled *islah* movements. Two of the most prolific writers representing these movements are Muhammad Abduh and Rashid Rida. They both consider themselves to be disciples of the reform movement *Salafiyya*. See also note 78. Concerning the term *islah,* see Ahmad 1978: 141-71.

17. The verses are 3:102, 4:1 and 33:70-1. The quotatons from the Quran are from the translation made by Yusuf Ali. The verses are numbered in accordance with the Egyptian edition.

18. Ghanim 1992: 93.

19. Ibid. The Quranic verse is 45: 18.

20. The verses are a part of 2:269 and the end of 20:114.

21. The platform presented by al-Ahnaf *et al*. includes a paragraph emphasizing the necessity of improving relations between Algeria and countries with a large Algerian population, such as France. The paragraph stresses that relations should be based on justice and that the immigrant should be held in esteem. See al-Ahnaf *et al* 1991: 50.

22. Ghanim 1992: 94.

23. Ibid. The last part of the quotation is an *hadith*. The 'tradition' in the quotation refers, according to Islamic tradition, to the battle of Badr where the Prophet fought his first battle against the non-Muslim Meccans in 624. A large part of Muhammad's army was constituted of those who became Muslims after Muhammad's migration to Medina (the so-called 'helpers', *ansar*). According to *Sahih Muslim* the Prophet consulted his Companions when they heard about the coming of the larger Meccan troop. One of the Companions is said to have uttered the saying cited above. It is considered to be a test of the loyalty of the Companions, and above all the 'helpers'. *Sahih Muslim* 'The Book of *jihad* and campaigns' (*kitab al-djihad wa 'l-siyar*), chapter 732, on the Battle of Badr: 975.

24. The term *jihad* is significant in the *hadith* collections. See, for instance, the reference to *Sahih Muslim* in note 23 above.

25. Ghanim 1992: 94. The political claims in the platform presented originally in *al-munqidh* also express a need to stop unemployment, the emigration of the educated, the population explosion and crime. See al-Ahnaf *et al.* 1991: 50.

26. Cited are parts of verses 4:125, 3:19, 2:132, 5:52 and the complete verse 3:85.

27. The head of state should also be engaged in the effort to apply Islamic *sharia* as long as he rules a Muslim people. This is one of the paragraphs in the platform presented in al-Ahnaf *et al.* 1991: 50.

28. The verses are 88:21 and 22.

29. The word 'infidel' is in its imperfect from *yakfiru* (to be an infidel, irreligious,

non-believer) and is here translated as 'infidel' and not as one who just rejects the belief. The end of the verse is in Yusuf Ali's translation of the Quran: 'Let him who will, Believe, and let him Who will, reject it'.

30. Ghanim 1992: 95.
31. Krämer 1993: 3, 7.
32. Ibid.: 6. Krämer refers here to a secular notion of the term as opposed to a religious one. The latter denotes the taking of other gods than God alone (*taghu*).
33. Ghanim 1992: 95. In the fifth paragraph of the political platform presented by al-Ahnaf *et al*, FIS aims at restoring the 'National Audit Bureau' and establishing a status of immunity for its officials. These claims are concerned with an attempt to let institutions of the state gain public confidence. See al-Ahnaf *et al*. 1991: 49.
34. For an example of Islamist propaganda in Syria, see Lobmeyer 1991: 404.
35. Ghanim 1992: 95.
36. 'Secular' here denotes a legislation where laws are promulgated by human beings.
37. Ghanim 1992: 95.
38. See, for instance, the commentaries on verse 5:53, note 763, in Yusuf Ali's translation of the Quran.
39. Ghanim 1992: 95f. The third paragraph of the platform in al-Ahnaf *et al* suggests the establishment of a political authority which shall be independent of different political parties, and whose objective is to control the National Assembly and to guarantee the integrity of the district and municipal elections (al-Ahnaf *et al*. 1991: 49).
40. Ghanim 1992: 96f.
41. al-Ahnaf *et al*. 1991: 49.
42. *Umma*: 'nation', 'people' or 'community' of Islam – 'the sum of all Muslims treated as a community'.
43. Ghanim 1992: 97.
44. Ibid.: 110.
45. The translation of the Quranic verse includes the root *fatara* which in some forms also refers to nature and a natural disposition.
46. This tradition, in the collection of Bukhari, has to do with the funeral prayers: for instance, if a prayer should be offered to children delivered by non-Muslims, or if the child is born dead. In Bukhari's collection there is also a reference to the verse (30:30) quoted above. See *Sahih al-Bukhari*, 'The Book of Funerals' (*kitab al-janaiz*), chap. 440, 247.
47. I have not been able to locate this tradition.
48. These are the first lines of the verse 4:58 in the Quran.
49. Ghanim 1992: 110. The tradition in the last part of the quotation can be found in several chapters of Bukhari. See for instance Bukhari, 'The Book of Funerals' (*kitab al-janaiz*) Chapter 32: 208. In it the utterance of the Prophet has to do with a person's behaviour when visiting a grave.
50. Ibid.: 106f.
51. Ibid.: 106.
52. Ibid.
53. Ibid.
54. The notion of modernism as the 'evil of evils' and completely alien to Islam is an argument often repeated by Islamists. Modernism in this context is regarded as consisting of 'imported ideas'. See Sivan 1990: 138.
55. Ghanim 1992: 106.
56. Ghanim 1992: 107.
57. Ibid.: 107. The quotation is verse one and two from *sura* 96.
58. The importance of education is also emphasized in paragraph 14 in the political platform presented in al-Ahnaf *et al*. The aim is to reform the system of education,

and the goal is to guarantee social justice and equality in education and to preserve the integrity and authencity of the Nation. See al-Ahnaf *et al.* 1991: 50.

59. Ghanim 1992: 107.
60. See Ibrahim 1982: 23; Krämer 1993: 4.
61. *Tawhid* is often translated as 'belief in the unity of God' – 'monotheism'.
62. In Syria one of the Islamists' programmes does not include the demand for the introduction of Islamic law. This leads the author to the conclusion that the document is not of a religio-political kind, but a politico-economic one. See Lobmeyer 1991: 412ff.
63. Deeb 1992: 57.
64. Lewis has translated the term *idjma* 'climate of opinion'. His translation indicates that the 'climate' can change over time. See Lewis 1988: 29.
65. Related to the term 'consensus ' is also the term *khalifa*, meaning man as a representative of God on earth. As *khalifa* he is responsible for God's creation and is obliged to maintain the godly order on earth.
66. For a discussion on the notion of '*shuracratie*' see al-Ahnaf *et al.* 1991: 84ff.
67. Al-Ahnaf *et al.* 1991: 85. For a description of Ali Belhadj, see Burgat 1993: 276.
68. One example of a non-traditional or radical technique of argumentation is the views expressed by a Muslim women's organization called Sisters in Islam. It is particularly their hermeneutical attitude which differs from the approach of FIS. The Sisters of Islam reject traditional interpretations of Islamic tradition and argue, for instance, that the Quran is determined by the social conditions of its time.
69. This technique is used by Islamists in Syria. See Lobmeyer 1991: 414.
70. For example, see the ideas of Sayyid Qutb presented in Choueiri 1990: 93-5.
71. This is a characteristic trait of Islamic movements in general (Haddad 1986: 162ff). The criticism of top religious leaders is also a common trait. For example, in interviews with Islamists arrested after riots in Egypt in 1977, religous scholars were described as 'pulpit parrots' (*babghawat al-manabir*). See Ibrahim 1985: 500.
72. It is sometimes stated that Islamic movements have stressed the importance of education, literate knowledge and commitment to Islamic social goals in search of an Islamic identity in North African countries since the nineteenth century. See Lapidus 1992: 24. For a description of Abbasi Madani, see Burgat 1993: 275.
73. On the forces promoting Islamization in the universities in North Africa, see Burgat 1993: 91-3.
74. Akacem 1993: 54.
75. For an introduction to the origins of political Islam, see Butterworth 1992.
76. For a detailed study of the history of the Brotherhood see Mitchell 1969. John O. Voll (1991: 354), states: 'Yet the fundamentalists who would arise in the urban centers of the twentieth century did have at hard a repertoire of symbols and concepts developed by revivalist leaders of the Sunni past'.
77. Sivers 1973: 48.
78. Choueiri 1990: 47f. *Salafiyya* (the word has to do with 'predecessors', 'ancestors' and 'forefathers') was founded by Djamal ad-Din al-Afghani and Muhammad Abduh. Its influence was centred on Egypt, but it had a profound impact throughout the Muslim world. The movement can be described as an Islamic reform movement.
79. For the function of Islam as an 'ethnic marker' in Algeria, see Hjärpe 1993, 209ff.
80. Lapidus 1992: 24.
81. Deeb 1992: 55f.
82. Choueiri 1990: 74.
83. Akacem 1993: 51.
84. Melasuo 1993: 56. There were clashes between Muslim and left-wing students on university campuses in the early 1980s. See also Deeb 1992: 56.
85. The patterns of association in general in the Algerian political elite are to a large extent based on the patron-client relationship. It is possible that this relationship

has varied through history, but it has not changed its basic structure. It is not within the limits of this article to address this subject, but only to make the reader aware of it.

86. Entelis 1980: 423.
87. Lapidus 1992: 24.
88. 'Behind the Veil', *The Jerusalem Report*, 3 June 1993: 29.
89. The information is from a TV programme on Algeria made in 1990 by Swiss television and broadcast on Danish TV.
90. This is to be compared with the actions taken by the Muslim Brotherhood in Egypt after the earthquake in October 1992.
91. Entelis and Arone 1992: 29.
92. Akacem 1993: 52.
93. Melasou 1993: 56.
94. For the birth of FIS, see Burgat 1993: 273ff.
95. Unemployment has reached 75 per cent among people under 30 years of age: 'The Islamisation of Modernity', *The Middle East*, February 1993: 20. According to official figures, 20 per cent of the active population is unemployed: 'Taking Responsibility', *The Middle East*, April 1993: 17.
96. Ghanim 1992: 29.
97. 'The Mosque goes Underground', *The Middle East*, April 1992: 12.
98. 'Taking Responsibility', *The Middle East*, April 1993: 17; Akacem 1993: 52. In Algeria all these young unemployed men have a nickname, they are called *hittistes*, 'those who support the wall'. The name is based on the Arabic word for wall (*hayt*).
99. Entelis and Arone 1992: 28.
100. According to Entelis & Arone, FIS won 188 of 430 seats in parliament. See Entelis & Arone 1992: 33.
101. 'The Islamisation of Modernity', *The Middle East*, Feb. 1993: 19.
102. 'Looking for Scapegoats', *The Middle East*, May 1994: 21.
103. Burgat 1993: 247.
104. 'Looking for Scapegoats', *The Middle East*, May 1994: 21.
105. See, for example, *al-munqidh*, nos 3-4, Sept.-Oct. 1993.

References

Ahmad, A. 1978. 'Islah', *Encyclopedia of Islam* 4, 141-71. Leiden: E.J. Brill.

al-Ahnaf, M., B. Botiveau and F. Frégosi 1991. *L'Algérie par ses islamistes*. Paris: Karthala.

Akacem, M. 1993. 'Algeria: In search for an Economic and Political Future', in *Middle East Policy II*, 50-60. Washington, DC: Middle East Policy Council.

al-Banna, G. 1991. *Risala ila ad-dawat 'l-islamiyya* (A letter to those who invite to Islam). Cairo: Dar al-fikri 'l-islami.

'Behind the Veil' 1993, *The Jerusalem Report*, 3 June.

Burgat, F. 1993. *The Islamic Movement in North Africa*. Center for Middle Eastern Studies, University of Texas at Austin.

Butterworth, C.E. 1992. 'Political Islam: The Origins' in C.E. Butterworth and

I.W. Zartman (eds), *Political Islam*, 26-37. (Annals of the American Academy of Political and Social Science) London: Sage.

Choueiri, Y.M. 1990. *Islamic Fundamentalism*. London: Pinter.

Deeb, M.-J. 1992. 'Militant Islam and the Politics of Redemption', in C.E. Butterworth and I.W. Zartman (eds), *Political Islam*, 52-65. (Annals of the American Academy of Political and Social Science) London: Sage.

Entelis, J.P. 1980. 'Democratic and Popular Republic of Algeria' in D.E. Long and B. Reich (eds), *The Government and Politics of the Middle East and North Africa*, 415-36. Boulder, CO: Westview Press.

—— and L.J. Arone 1992. 'Algeria in Turmoil', in *Middle East Policy I*, 23-36. Washington DC: Middle East Policy Council.

Ghanim, I.B. 1992. *Al-harakat 'l-islamiyya fi 'l-jaza'ir wa azma 'l-dimuqratiyya* (The Islamic Movements in Algeria and the Crisis of Democracy). Cairo: Umma brisa.

Haddad, Y. 1986. 'Muslim Revivalist Thought in the Arab World: An Overview', *The Muslim World* (3-4).

—— *et al.* 1991. *The Contemporary Islamic Revival: A Critical Survey and Bibliography*. New York: Greenwood Press.

Hjärpe, J. 1993. 'Islam, Nationalism and Ethnicity', in H. Lindholm (ed.), *Ethnicity and Nationalism: Formation of Identity and Dynamics of Conflicts in the 1990s*, 207-33. Göteborg: Nordnes.

Hussain, A. 1983. *Islamic Movements in Egypt, Pakistan and Iran: An Annotated Bibliography*. London: Mansell.

Ibrahim, S.E. 1982. *The New Arab Social Order: A Study of the Social Impact of Oil Wealth*. Boulder: Westview Press.

——. 1985. 'Egypt's Islamic Militants', in N.S. Hopkins and S.E. Ibrahim (eds), *Arab Society: Social Science Perspectives*, 494-507. Cairo: American University in Cairo Press.

Islamic Revolution 1991. *Ath-thawra 'l-islamiyya fi 'l-jazair an-nass al-kamil li-l-barnamadj as-siyasi li-jabhat 'l-inqadh 'l-islamiyya* (The Islamic Revolution in Algeria: The Complete Political Programme of the Islamic Salvation Front). Cairo: Yafa.

'The Islamisation of Modernity', 1993. *The Middle East*, February,.

Krämer, G. 1993. 'Islamists' Notion of Democracy', in *Middle East Report*, July/August. Washington, DC: Middle East Research and Information Project (MERIP).

Lapidus, I.M. 1992. 'The Golden Age: The Political Concepts of Islam', in C.E. Butterworth and I.W. Zartman (eds) *Political Islam*, 13-25. London: Sage. Annals of the American Academy of Political and Social Science).

Lawrence, B.B. 1989. *Defenders of God: The Fundamentalist Revolt against the Modern Age*. San Francisco: Harper and Row.

Lewis, B. 1988. *The Political Language of Islam*. University of Chicago Press.

Lobmeyen, H.G. 1991. 'Islamic Ideology and Secular Discourse: the Islamists in Syria', *Orient,* 32, (3).

'Looking for Scapegoats', *The Middle East*, May, 1994.

Melasuo, T. 1993 'How to Understand Islamism in Algeria?', in H. Palva and K.S. Vikor (eds), *The Middle East – Unity and Diversity*, 56-70. (Nordic Proceedings in Asian Studies no. 5). Copenhagen: NIAS.

Mitchell, R.P. 1969. *The Society of the Muslim Brothers*. Oxford University Press.

'The Mosque goes Underground' 1992. *The Middle East*, April.

al-Munqidh (3-4), Sept.-Oct. 1993.

Quran. Translation and commentary by Yusuf Ali, Dar al- Arabia, Beirut.

Sahih al-Bukhari. Vol. II, Arabic-English, trans. by Muhammad Muhsin Khan. Cairo: Dar al-Fikr.

Sahih Muslim. Vol. III, transl. by Abdul Hamid Siddiqi. Beirut: Dar al-Arabia.

Sivan, E. 1990. *Radical Islam: Medieval Theology and Modern Politics*. New Haven: Yale University Press.

Sivers, P. von. 1973. 'The Realm of Justice: Apocalyptic Revolts in Algeria (1849-1879)', *Humaniora Islamica: An Annual Publication of Islamic Studies and the Humanities* I, 47-60. The Hague: Mouton.

'Taking Responsibility' 1993. *The Middle East*, April.

Vatikiotis, P.J. 1991. *Islam and the State*. London: Routledge.

Voll, J.P. 1991. 'Fundamentalism in the Sunni Arab World: Egypt and the Sudan', in M.E. Marty and R. Scott Appleby (eds), *Fundamentalism Observed*, 354-402. University of Chicago Press.

——. 1991. *Are Women and Men Equal Before Allah*? (pamphlet). Sisters in Islam.

THE DISCOURSE OF THE
IKHWAN OF SUDAN AND SECULARISM

Muhammad Mahmoud

The beginnings of the *al-Ikhwan al-Muslimun* (henceforth, *Ikhwan*) movement in Sudan may be traced back to the mid-1940s. This period witnessed the emergence of small student and popular-based groups.[1] As far as the latter are concerned we find that their commitment was the outcome of two direct influences: the interest that the Egyptian *al-Ikhwan al-Muslimun* was taking in Sudan (owning partly to the fact that Egypt was a partner alongside Great Britain in the Condominium arrangement) and the ferment of the Sudanese nationalist movement that expressed itself partly in terms of an Islamist and Arabist identification. However, the most pressing matter for these forerunners of the *Ikhwan* was not the issue of secularization or Islamic polity but rather the national question of determining the country's future. In contrast, the student group showed a more pronounced ideological orientation, and this may be attributed to the specific circumstances of its inception as it grew largely in reaction to the growth of the communist left among the students. What made Marxism uninviting for them was its atheism. They argued that Islam was a 'comprehensive' religion that addressed the concerns and problems of this world (as opposed to the 'hereafter'), and in insisting upon an intrinsic complementarity between the religious and the worldly in Islam they were decidedly anti-secularist.

However, their hostility to Marxism did not prevent them from borrowing considerably from its sources and so they maintained that Islam was a 'socialist' religion and formulated a programme that called for the abolition of feudalist and capitalist relations of production in the Sudan and for taking the means of production into social ownership. The confrontation with the communists had thus produced an 'Islamist' left – a situation that was bound to invite a backlash. By the early 1950s the mainstream of the Islamist student movement was showing determined signs of distancing itself from the 'socialist' rendering of Islam and, when in 1954 a founding conference was convened, a conservative trend emerged as the victor and the decisive shaping force of the *Ikhwan*'s *political destiny*.

The first stiff challenge that the nascent *Ikhwan* movement had to face was the constitution debate between 1955 and 1958. The *Ikhwan* called for an 'Islamic constitution' and promulgated a model for this. The salient Islamic features in this document were provisions for Islam as the state religion, for *sharia* (Islamic canonical law) as the source of legislation, the prohibition of *riba* (usury), and the charging of the state with the collection of *zakat* (alms tax).[2] The document was clearly modelled on Western constitutions and based on the acceptance of the Sudanese state within its recognized territorial boundaries, without insisting on a distinctive 'Islamic' concept of state.

The *Ikhwan's* campaign during this period succeeded in grafting its discourse on to the wider national political discourse. The extent of this success was evident in 1968 when the Draft Permanent Constitution was produced, turning out to be 'more Islamic than the 1958 draft'.[3] To understand this development we must take into account the overall context of the Sudanese political scene between 1964 and 1969. This was a time of multi-party democracy and the *Ikhwan* was gradually growing out of its pressure-group phase and entering a party formation phase. Its major achievement was spearheading a vigorous campaign that led to the dissolution of the Sudanese Communist Party in December 1965. The pretext for this highly political act was 'religious': the communists were atheists. The hitherto secularized nature of the dominant political discourse in the country, notwithstanding the religious basis of the two major parties, *al-Umma* and the Democratic Unionists, underwent a radical shift after this event. Henceforth, the politics of 'Islamization', and particularly in its strident *sharia* version, grew into an active, aggressive component in the political struggle, so much so that by the mid-1980s *sharia* became the foremost divisive issue in Sudanese politics.

The May 1969 *coup d'état* of Colonel Jaafar Nimeiri started off as a left-oriented affair but ended up veering in the opposite direction and adopting *sharia*. The bloody confrontation between the regime and its opposition in the *Umma* Party, the Democratic Unionists and the *Ikhwan* led eventually to a reconciliation between the regime, the *Umma* Party and the *Ikhwan* in 1977. It was, however, the *Ikhwan* which profited most from this development. The movement assumed a decidedly capitalist nature, channelling a great deal of its energies into banking and commercial activities, while conducting an extensive, low-profile campaign to win over new recruits. The dramatic shift occurred, however, in September 1983 when President Nimeiri announced the implementation of *sharia* with immediate effect. By April 1984, the process had gathered full momentum and a state of emergency was announced. With the *Ikhwan* acting as the regime's judicial right-hand, Northern Sudan was plunged into a full *sharia* rigour and by March 1985, when the regime was brought down, there had been 106 amputations of hands including seventeen cross-limbs (i.e. amputation of right hand and left foot), the number of floggings ran into thousands,[4] and Ustadh Mahmoud Muhammad Taha, the founder of the Islamic Republican Party who had called for a blend of social democracy and mysticism, was hanged on a charge of apostasy.[5] The civil war in the South was in full swing, with a mounting civilian and military death toll and an unprecedented harrowing displacement of ever-growing masses of people.

Between 1985 and 1989, the North-South divide was reduced to the question of *sharia*. This bestowed upon the *Ikhwan*, who emerged as the third parliamentary force, a unique political significance. The prevalent political balance and the momentum of the secular campaign against the Islamization of the law led, however, to a moratorium on *sharia*. When it became evident that this state of affairs and other political developments might favour a dismantling of Islamic law, the *Ikhwan* swiftly moved in and staged a *coup d'état* in June 1989.

A blueprint for an Islamic state

In exploring the *Ikhwan's* ideological perspective, we shall concentrate on the writings of Dr Hasan Abd Allah al-Turabi (b. 1932), the movement's political leader and principal ideologue. Turabi's formal education was entirely secular, since he had studied law at the Universities of Khartoum, London and Paris. Since 1965 he has dominated the movement and succeeded in moulding it in his own image. He has been greatly helped in this by his personal abilities and by the weakness of the representation of the *ulama* (theologians and experts on *sharia*) class in the movement. This section will deal with Turabi's concept of the Islamic state, his project concerning the reform of Islamic legal thinking, and his position on women, which is meant to demonstrate his practical *fiqh* (Islamic jurisprudence) and the constraints which are placed on it.

The *Ikhwan's* set purpose has been the establishment of an Islamic state, which is projected as the highest expression of an Islamic society. Secularization as a process that separates the practice of politics and the running of government from the concepts, precepts, values and injunctions of the religion of Islam has always been anathematized by the *Ikhwan*. In explaining the dialectic that relates state to society, Turabi says:

> The state is only the political expression of an Islamic society. You cannot have an Islamic state except insofar that you have an Islamic society. Any attempt at establishing a political order for the establishment of a genuine Islamic society would be the superimposition of laws over a reluctant society.[6]

Turabi establishes a clear sequence here: as an 'expression' the state comes after the creation of a genuine Islamic society.

But how does such a genuine Islamic society come into being in the first place? According to Turabi, this takes place in the course of a natural and relentless process of pervasive 'Islamization' that constitutes the destiny of all Muslim societies. Its substance is an assertive 'religious energy' and it is through political organization that this process assumes its historical expression.

In expounding the ideological foundations of his state, Turabi points out that the Islamic doctrine of *tawhid* (God's unity) is the creedal basis that determines its intrinsically religious nature and makes it decidedly anti-secular. In elaborating this, he asserts: 'All public life in Islam is religious, being permeated by the experience of the divine. Its function is to pursue the service of God as expressed in a concrete way in the *shariah*....'[7] He is certainly aware of what he describes as 'elements of secularisation in the political conduct of Muslims', but he is quick to point out that the redeeming virtue of Muslims (as opposed to Christians) is that they often recognize the 'gap' between their practice and the Islamic 'ideal' as enshrined in the Quran and the Sunna (Prophetic guidance).

In dealing with his state's physical attributes, Turabi addresses himself to: a. people; b. territory; and c. sovereignty. In the light of the Islamic concept of *umma* (the community of believers), he finds the phrase 'Islamic state' a bit of a misnomer, since the state is 'only the political dimension of the collective endeavour of Muslims'.[8] This judgement is based on the way *sharia* is supposed to operate, since it depends only partly on the state's sanctions and is mostly left to the 'free conscience of believers' or (maybe more effectively) to the 'informal means of social control'. In placing this final emphasis on *sharia* and in stressing its relative independence from the state, Turabi adopts a minimalist position in portraying his state. With *sharia* as an ultimate source of the *umma's* cohesiveness and the state's legitimacy, it seems that Turabi's logic implies that *sharia* is the foundational element in defining his state; it is the element through the agency of which the neutral/secular category of 'people' is transformed into the Islamic category of *umma*.

However, Islam being a universal religion, there is only *one umma* and consequently *one* state. The *umma's* unity is predicated on the unity of God and hence nationalism cannot be accommodated within Turabi's scheme. Likewise, territory has no place since the Islamic state is theoretically not limited by any territorial boundaries. Furthermore, the centrality of *sharia* makes Turabi's state one that is neither absolute nor sovereign.

Turabi characterizes his state as republican and as a representative democracy. He is, however, careful to emphasize that an Islamic republic is not 'strictly speaking a direct government of and by the people; it is a government of the *sharia*'.[9] Bearing his Western readership in mind, Turabi chooses his words carefully in order to play down the 'theocratic' nature of his state, which is supposed to represent divine will as opposed to the will of the people. *Shura* (consultation) is the Islamic formula for democracy as it guarantees a fair distribution of political power, which should coalesce with a fair distribution of wealth. Turabi's state is a *Sunnite* state that does not allow for an Iranian-like *vilayat-i faqih* (guardianship or government by the expert theologians), which he derides as an 'elitist or theocratic government'.[10] In addition, the Islamic state according to his scheme is not a patriarchal affair that excludes women.

Turabi does not rule out a multi-party system outright, but he prefers what amounts to a one-party system that seeks to govern through consensus politics. An important feature that brackets his state with modern states and decidedly distances it from the classical Islamic state is his suggestion that it establish complete legal codes. The legal codes would no longer emanate from the jurists as in the past, but from the state.[11] The implication of his minimalist leaning is abandoned here in favour of direct governmental and centralized intervention. Showing the influence of his own education and inspired by the example of early Muslims who had to cope with the problems of their expanding imperial realm, Turabi adopts a flexible approach to legislation:

> Any form or procedures for the organisation of public life that can be ultimately related to God and put to his service in furtherance of the aims of Islamic government can be adopted unless expressly excluded by the *shariah*. Once so received, it is an integral part of Islam whatever its source may be.[12]

In dealing with the status of religious minorities within his state, Turabi assures them the sanctity of their basic rights and invokes the example of the Medina state under Prophet Muhammad.

Addressing the same theme of the Islamic state in a paper presented in Khartoum in 1987, Turabi treats his subject with a different approach. His tone is characterized this time by an intense sense of self-righteousness and his statements exhibit a marked disdain for some of the concepts he had previously espoused, such as democracy. He maintains that all Muslim governments subsequent to the Medina state deviated from the prescribed norm and that all existing Muslim governments are devoid of legitimacy owing to their 'irreligiosity'.[13] The influence of the Egyptian Islamist Sayyid Qutb is evident in this tendency to hereticate existing governments and to demand the acceptance of the Islamist project as a precondition for accepting their legitimacy. Another significant Qutbite feature is Turabi's commitment to the elitist 'vanguard' formula, whereby an Islamist vanguard organizes itself with the express intention of 'Islamizing' the rest of society (and of course, ultimately, the whole of mankind). All means are open to this vanguard, including *jihad* (war in the cause of Islam, whether offensive or defensive) against its enemies.[14] He argues that once this vanguard has taken power and once Islam has governed, then all human ills will find their solutions – secular ideologies like democracy and socialism have failed and the only feasible formula is that of the Islamist programme, the twin pillars of which are *tawhid* and *sharia*.

Turabi poses a 'universal model' which is largely divorced from the concrete history of the Islamic state from its foundation under the Prophet to the dissolution of the Caliphate. An example that is dear to his heart is the way non-Muslims fared under the Prophet's state. It is noteworthy that his references to the status of Jews and non-Muslim Arabs during that period consistently expurgate the problems experienced during it and the bloody confrontation that led to the virtual eradication of Jews from the Arabian Peninsula and the forcible imposition of the new religion on the Arab polytheists.

When Turabi turns to inter-state or international relations, he is at his weakest and vaguest due to his assumption that his state is an embodiment of a divine plan and as such its frontiers must coincide with those of the world. As soon as he shifts to the non-homogeneous terrain of non-Muslims, his scheme shows less confidence and this is quite evident in the emotional nature his argument assumes when he addresses Christians living under his Islamic state:

> Christians in particular who now, at least, do not seem to have a public law, should not mind the application of Islamic law as long as it does not interfere with their religion. It is a moral based on values which are common and more akin to Christian values than any secular law – Caesar's law.[15]

In dealing with Christians and non-Muslims Turabi avoids the use of terms such as *dhimmis* (non-Muslims subject to the Islamic state), *kharaj* and *jizya* (taxes exacted from non-Muslims). This gives an idea of the change that his movement's discourse has perceptibly undergone. Though he stated triumphantly in 1979 that his movement had eliminated secularism in Sudan,[16] the movement's discourse and some of its stated policies clearly demonstrate the inroads of secularism. Two examples may suffice in this connection: the first concerns non-Muslims and their holding of public offices under *sharia*. Contrary to their formerly-stated position about the ineligibility of a non-Muslim to hold positions of legal power over Muslims or become president of the republic, the *Ikhwan* announced in a document that appeared in 1987 under the title 'Sudan Charter: national unity and diversity' that 'none shall be barred from any public office, only because of his adherence to any religious affiliation'.[17] The second example concerns the federal formula which the movement had put forward in the aforementioned Charter and which constitutes the basis of the movement's proposed plan for the ending of the present civil war in Sudan. According to this plan, the implementation of a federal system entails a legal division whereby Northern Sudan (mainly Muslim) shall be subject to *sharia* while Southern Sudan (subscribing mainly to traditional African religions and Christianity) shall be subject to secular laws. Consequently, Muslims who reside in the South shall be outside *sharia* jurisdiction, whereas non-Muslims who live in the North shall be subject to *sharia*. Though this proposal is rejected by non-Muslims in the Sudan because of the discriminatory nature of *sharia*, it undoubtedly represents a daring break on the part of the *Ikhwan* with *sharia* as it has been historically practised and conceived.[18] Since there is a powerful secular trend in Sudan that opposes and abhors discrimination on the basis of religion, it is reasonable to assume that the *Ikhwan* was directly influenced by it on both counts. However, to make this position plausible, Turabi and his movement had to argue from within the Muslim tradition in terms of a different perspective.

The necessity for a revitalized fiqh

In his writings and talks, Turabi does not just present himself as an advocate for the revival of Islam or as a fundamentalist in the sense of simply going back to 'fundamentals,' but primarily as an exponent of *tajdid* (renewal, reform). He does not of course conceal his dissatisfaction with the decadent and abject conditions of contemporary Muslims and does not fail to point out the role of imperialism in this. He is, however, equally critical of the internal problem of juridical and intellectual stagnation and rigidity on the part of the Islamic schools of *fiqh*.

In a seminal tract entitled *Manajiyyat al-Tashri fi al-Islam* (The Methodology of Legislation in Islam, 1987) Turabi maintains that the condition of Islamic decadence has degenerated to such a level that it no longer suffices to open the gate of *ijtihad* (independent judgement) but that it is necessary to address the central question of methodology. An established methodology approved by present-day Muslims would serve as a general framework within which *ijtihad* could be exercised and as a yardstick against which opinions could be verified and differences harmonized.

He draws the traditional sharp distinction between the Quran and the Prophetic Sunna on one hand (as the two permanent, most reliable sources that are not subject to the mutability of history and that constitute the essence of the Divine plan for the guidance of man) and *fiqh* on the other hand, which is a human response to the problems arising within a specific historical context. The body of *fiqh* and its devised foundations are human *kasb* (acquired knowledge) which retain authority insofar as they respond adequately to human needs. The classical science of *usul al-fiqh* (the foundations of jurisprudence) was largely influenced by Greek formal logic and was such a highly formalized and abstract activity that it soon divorced itself from its social environment, thus failing to produce a living and adaptable *fiqh*. Turabi recognizes that the Muslims are nowadays under the cultural hegemony of modern Western culture, with what he describes as its 'logical positivist, relativist, and empirical methodologies', a circumstance that is bound to affect them. Just as the Muslim jurists opened themselves to Greek influences in the past, he is quite willing to follow their example of *istishab* (preference) and open his *usuli* blueprint to Modern Western influences.[19]

In outlining his position, Turabi starts off from the familiar Islamist assertion that all activities comprising the totality of human life should be subjected to religious legislation. This he bases on the Islamic premise of a unity of God. The criticism that he levels against classical *fiqh* is based on his preference for an all-embracing *fiqh* scope. He lashes against the classical jurists for having produced a *fiqh* system that tended to operate exclusively within the sphere of private life. *Fiqh*, consequently, grew less and less concerned with public issues pertaining to the running of the state. Turabi thus envisages a *fiqh* that extends to politics as well.[20]

Who is going to produce such a *fiqh*? As one might expect, Turabi, seasoned politician that he is, would be reluctant to leave this crucial matter with its vital role in his projected Islamic polity solely in the hands of the specialized class of *fiqh* scholars and to the independent internal mechanisms of the discipline. He would rather control and direct the *fiqh* process himself. In Turabi's Islamic state the *sultan*, or the executive power, is not only charged with taking decisions but can also make laws and, as such, actively contribute to the making of *fiqh*. In the power structure he outlines, *fiqh* scholars outside the governmental judiciary system are not formally recognized. Furthermore, he advances a populist view designed to undermine the status and the role of the *ulama*. He argues that Islam does not recognize a specialized class of scholars who are invested with the powers of instructing Muslims and legislating for them. This anti-clerical position may be encountered in the pronouncements of many modern Islamists and Turabi uses it in order to forestall any potential discord or threat that an independent *ulama* body might pose to his state.[21]

In dealing with problems such as the appeal to authority as opposed to the appeal to reason, or the dependency on received tradition as opposed to the freedom of innovation, Turabi is careful not to dissociate himself altogether from the traditional *Sunnite* position, while stressing at the same time the necessity for adopting a more flexible and open attitude.[22]

The position he propounds makes no appeal to any of the existing juridical schools. On the contrary, Turabi believes that the challenges facing Muslims today and the pressure of Islamic resurgence make it incumbent upon Muslims to throw their respective schools to the winds and seek a unitarian position.

It may be argued that the weakness in Turabi's proposed methodological perspective is that, despite his constant awareness of the historical relativity of *fiqh* and its schools, he does not apply the same measure to the Quranic text and the Sunna traditions which are treated as meta-historical frames of reference. This places a clear limit on his attempt at renewal and modernization which claims to derive its authority from these sources. To make a better assessment of his dilemma, we will turn to his treatment of a specific problem in order to explore the nature of his *fiqh*.

Women as a case in point

In 1973, Turabi brought out a tract entitled *Al-Marr'a fi Taalim al-Islam* ('Women in the Teachings of Islam'). This tract came out in the atmosphere of a heightened political and ideological confrontation between the *Ikhwan* and the Left on the campus of the University of Khartoum in the early 1970s. It was clear for Turabi that the movement's subscription to the traditional Islamic position of insisting on the inferiority of women and their marginalization was doing it a great deal of damage and that it was losing the battle with feminism. Owing to the sensitivity of the subject and the entrenched Islamic conservatism attached to it, Turabi circulated the tract before its publication, by way of testing the water without putting his name to it. It was reportedly shown to the influential Egyptian Islamist, Muhammad al-Ghazali, an Azharite scholar, who gave it his seal of approval.[23]

Turabi's line of argument is 'fundamentalist' in the sense that he assumes an 'original' Islamic condition where women enjoyed an 'ideal' status of equality and active social and political involvement. This ideal condition was followed by a 'fall' which characterized Muslim societies, allowing for the creeping in and dominance of deep-rooted prejudices against women. The 'original' Islamic condition is enshrined in the pronouncements of the Quran and epitomized by the Prophetic tradition. The Medinan model Islamic society set by the Prophet was later deviated from and betrayed, the Quranic and Prophetic precepts ignored and distorted, and so the Islamic feminist revolution never really came of age.

In the course of his argument, Turabi moves on two levels: creedal and juridical. On the creedal level he asserts that the call of Islam is addressed to both male and female, that religious duties and obligations constitute personal responsibilities that cannot be performed by proxy, and that on the Day of Judgement women earn reward or punishment on the basis of their individual accountability. On the juridical level, Turabi dismisses the *hijab* (veil) and argues that it is an anomalous institution meant only for the Prophet's wives owing to their distinctive status as 'mothers of the believers'. Consequently, he fervently argues in favour of desegregation which he deems the 'normal' Islamic condition.[24]

To drive his point home and prove his case, Turabi marshals his evidence. During the Prophetic era, women were allowed to participate in congregational prayer and they took an active role in military expeditions. They took part in the *tawaf* (circumambulation) ritual alongside men, during the pilgrimage, were present at public festivals, and were free to receive guests in their homes and entertain them. A Muslim woman may own property, take an active part in the community's economic life, and has the right to acquire education. When the opinions of Muslims were sought to decide on the favourite caliph after the assassination of Umar Ibn al-Khattab, women were included in the consultation process.[25]

In dealing with the vexed question of whether it is permissible to greet women by shaking hands, Turabi is on the liberal side, though he cautiously warns that it should take place in a 'chaste' atmosphere. The tradition deployed by the conservatives, in which the Prophet is reported to have said, 'I do not shake hands with women', is discounted by Turabi as referring to a practice that is unique to the Prophet and not applicable to the rest of the *umma*.

Nevertheless, Turabi upholds many of the restrictions laid down by *sharia*. So, women should dress in strict accordance with what is stipulated in the Quran: covering the whole body except the face and the hands. Men and women should not meet in private, and in the absence of her husband a woman should not meet a man except in the presence of one or two other men. Men and women are not allowed to gaze at each other lest illicit sexual desires be aroused. In congregations where men and women gather, a distance between them should be maintained. This distance should also be rigidly maintained in public thoroughfares where women should not walk in the middle of the road but keep to the sides. In mosques, women should have a special entrance. Closely allied to women's potential sexual seductiveness is the stipulation that they should not pass by men when wearing perfume.[26]

It is noteworthy that Turabi's treatment circumvents the discomfiting issues that testify to some aspects of *sharia* discrimination against women. The legal capacity of a woman to be head of state is never discussed. It is doubtful whether any modern Muslim can discuss the question of women credibly without bringing up the issue of their political role.[27] As a movement, the *Ikhwan* did in fact come to terms with the political role of women in Sudan, but up to now it has not addressed the wider juridical implications of this role.[28]

Like the rest of Islamic revivalists, Turabi offers up the Prophetic society of Medina as an ideal model for every time and every place. In may, however, be argued that this proposed ideal presents modern Muslims with a problematic situation. Let us, for instance, take Turabi's reference to the participation of women in congregational prayers as a model of desegregation and examine it more closely.

The Medina mosque was in fact a tripartite space of ritualized and sexist segregation where men occupied their designated front space and women occupied their assigned rear space, with an empty space in the middle dividing the two sexes. It is thus unlikely that the Medina mosque would be looked upon as a viable model of desegregation in the modern sense, where desegregation means the free movement of men and women within a shared space. An important question related to women and congregational prayer is whether they can lead the prayer. Though the issue has not been conspicuously raised by Muslim feminists, one may envisage that they might put it forward at some point in the future. Just as this question proved to be problematic and divisive in the contexts of modern Judaism and Christianity, so it is likely to be, if not more so, in the context of modern Islam.

Furthermore, other issues concerning problematic aspects of the status of women under *sharia* are disregarded by Turabi: for example, the question of their testimony is never discussed. A woman's testimony in Islamic law is deemed to be half that of a man's in civil lawsuits, whereas her testimony is not accepted at all in criminal lawsuits. Neither can a woman function as a judge according to the majority of scholars. One school of *fiqh* maintained, however, that women can act as judges in civil but not criminal courts.[29] The secular nature of the Sudanese educational system has produced a good number of women lawyers and judges, and this is likely to present the *Ikhwan's* Islamist project with a practical challenge if it moves in the direction of barring women from the legal profession.

The question of inheritance is one of those issues on which Turabi is likewise silent. His assertion that women can own property and take an active part in economic life raises questions about their legal rights as active economic agents who contribute their share in the creation of social wealth. The fact that Sudanese women have been an active productive force in the traditional sector and that an increasingly growing number of them are gaining education and becoming part of the productive force in the modern sector is bound to highlight the problem of the present inheritance laws.[30] Hence, any Islamist reform programme is likely to find itself under great pressure to take this into account.

Turabi is at his best when he writes about family law. It may, however, be argued that the ideal image he projects of the Muslim family is rooted far more in the values of the educated, urbanized middle class of Sudan rather than in those of seventh-century Islamic Arabia. In such a family, polygamy, for instance, is anathematized and is described as a 'thing of the past'. And in such a family the beating of a wife for 'disobedience', a measure enjoined by the Quran, is unacceptable. Both the problems of polygamy and beating as a corrective measure are notably absent from Turabi's treatment.

The multi-religious context of Sudan also raises a problem that does not figure in Turabi's discussion: namely, whether a Muslim woman has the right to marry a non-Muslim. In many African countries the *sharia* stipulation that a Muslim woman can marry only a Muslim has been flouted, and there are examples of this in Southern and Western Sudan.[31]

Turabi's treatment is characterized by a serious deficiency in his failure to take into account the scope of the change in the status of women and some of their most pressing needs. It should, however, be pointed out that his education and physical and intellectual contact with the West have made him more amenable to the pressures and exigencies of modernization and hence he demonstrates a higher degree of awareness of the dilemmas of *sharia vis-à-vis* women. He tries to meet the modernist challenge at a point of his own choosing in order to avoid a calamitous collision. However, he is entangled in the poignant predicament of many a Muslim reformer: the pressing challenges posed by the 'outside' (modernization being one of its manifestations) are so pervasive and overwhelming, that a systematic coming-to-terms with them will lead to perceptible divergences from the received tradition which is constantly projected as comprehensive and capable of tackling all problems irrespective of time or place.

The Islamist impulse has always expressed itself in terms of an 'idealist' project, in the sense of aspiring and striving to transform existing social reality by subordinating it strictly to a given 'ideal'. In the demonology of Islamists, secularism has come to represent a 'grand Satan' since it 'compartmentalizes' Islam and excludes it from politics and the organization of social life in accordance with its precepts. Secularization is further held responsible for the fragmentation of the *umma* into 'nations', thus serving the designs of the enemies of Islam.

Although the *Ikhwan* movement in Sudan subscribes to the Islamist universalist ideal, its leaders have been pragmatic enough to insist on indigenizing their movement and giving it a distinctly 'Sudanese' character.[32] This earned the movement political success, but in the process another perceptible transformation took place. When the movement started in the 1950s and 1960s it saw itself as a 'moral force' that aspired to 'religionize' politics. By the late 1970s and 1980s the movement had established itself as a political, economic and social force to be reckoned with, but the more it submerged itself in the quagmire of power politics, the more it became evident that the movement was, rather, about 'politicizing' religion. The nature of Sudanese Islam, which is characterized by its tolerance and disregard for *sharia* except in the areas of personal status law and inheritance, and Sudanese politics, which has inclined towards secularism as an acceptable and fair formula that accommodates the country's religious, cultural, and ethnic diversity, have together created a context that inheres powerful resistance to Islamization whether in its revivalist or fundamentalist versions.

Between 1985 and 1989, the *Ikhwan* made repeated assurances that it accepted liberal democracy as a framework within which it wanted to push its programme through. In June 1989, it turned its back on those assurances and decided to impose its 'ideal' through the naked and brutal force of a military regime. The manner of the *Ikhwan's* seizure of power and the way in which it has so far run the country, do not demonstrate any intrinsic differences between their 'Islamic' regime and other military regimes in developing countries.

Sudan's great diversity and its present intractable political, economic and social problems have confronted the *Ikhwan* with serious dilemmas that are increasingly proving recalcitrant. The harsh irony may turn out to be that the *Ikhwan* are in a better position to thrive (and even flourish under certain circumstances) as long as they hold up an 'idealised' and 'unrealised' promise of a 'final Islamic solution', but that once in power, they are very likely to lose their appeal rapidly and their Islam-based ideological authority may be seriously questioned and challenged.

Notes

1. Ahmad 1982: 6-15; al-Turabi 1991a: 27ff; el-Affendi 1991: 46-52.
2. Ahmad 1982: 46f.

3. Kok 1991: 240.
4. Khalid 1990: 310.
5. For more discussions of the period of Islamization under Nimeiri, see Khalid 1985, Esposito 1988, Delmet 1990, Fluehr-Lobban 1990, and Warburg 1990. For an informative and balanced account of the execution of Ustadh Mahmoud Muhammad Taha, see Abdullahi Ahmed An-Na'im's introduction in Taha 1987.
6. Turabi 1983: 241.
7. Ibid.: 242.
8. Ibid.: 243.
9. Ibid.: 244.
10. Ibid.: 244.
11. Ibid.: 246.
12. Ibid.: 249.
13. al-Turabi 1987b: 23.
14. Ibid. 50-7. The leaders of the *Ikhwan* were apprehensive about the revolutionary implications of Sayyid Qutb's ideas and so they distanced themselves from them. Nevertheless, Qutb continued to exert a considerable influence and some of his ideas were incorporated into the *Ikhwan's* active discourse. See al-Turabi 1991a: 241 and Hamid 1989: 138.
15. Turabi 1983: 250.
16. Quoted in Voll 1983: 135.
17. Quoted in Niblock 1991: 264.
18. This observation should, however, be qualified. In the nineteenth century the Ottomans engaged in a legal reform that modified some aspects of *sharia* in favour of *dhimmis*. The reform was limited but it provided a basis for a new approach to the question of religious minorities. For a discussion see Ye'or 1985: 56f.
19. al-Turabi 1987a: 14.
20. Ibid.: 19.
21. The *ulama* have generally tended to ally themselves to the state and this association has earned them the bitter scorn of the radical Islamists in many countries. For the disenchantment of the *Ikhwan* in Egypt and Syria with the *ulama*, see Sivan 1985: 50-53.
22. al-Turabi 1987a: 37-43.
23. See Turabi 1991b: 2.
24. Ibid.: 27.
25. Ibid.: 20.
26. Ibid.: 32-5.
27. For an investigative and polemical treatment of the issue of women and political power in Islam, see Mernissi 1991. The Moroccan author's feminist consciousness crossed a new threshold when she decided to grapple with this theme and her views express an emerging feminist sensibility that questions the image of women in traditional Islamic sources and most of what has been produced by modern revivalists.
28. For a recent account of the gender politics of the Sudanese *Ikhwan*, see Hale 1992.
29. See al-Zuhayli 1984: 482f.
30. For a good account of women's education and its social impact, see Hall and Ismail 1981: 50-79, 213-22.
31. For an example of a court case involving a marriage between a Muslim woman and a non-Muslim, see Fluehr-Lobban 1987: 132f.
32. The movement's constitution mentions explicitly its 'Sudanese' nature. See Makki 1990: 371. For the differences between the Sudanese and the Egyptian *Ikhwan* movements over the question of amalgamation into a pan-Islamist movement, see Hamid 1989: 121.

References

Affendi, A. el- 1991. *Turabi's Revolution*. London: Grey Seal.

Ahmad, H. Makki M. 1982. *Harakat al-Ikhwan al Muslimin fi al-Sudan 1944-1969 (The Movement of the Muslim Brothers in Sudan 1944-1969)*. Khartoum: Institute of African and Asian Studies.

——. 1990. *Al-Haraka al-Islamiyya fi al-Sudan 1969-1985: Tarikhuha wa Khitabuha al-Siyasi* (The Islamic Movement in Sudan. 1969-1985: Its History and Political Discourse). Khartoum: Mahad al-Buhuth wa al-Dirasat al-Ijtimaiyya and Bayt al-Marifa.

Delmet, C. 1990. 'La Place de la loi islamique dans le système judiciare soudanais, évolution et perspectives', *Afrique Contemporaine* 156 (4), 273-83.

Esposito, J.L. 1988. 'Sudan', in S.T. Hunter (ed.), *The Politics of Islamic Revivalism: Diversity and Unity*, 187-203. Bloomington and Indianapolis: Indiana University Press.

Fluehr-Lobban, C. 1987. *Islamic Law and Society in the Sudan*. London: Frank Cass.

——. 1990. 'Islamization in Sudan: A Critical Assessment', *The Middle East Journal* 44, 610-23.

Hale, S. 1992. 'The Rise of Islam and Women of the National Islamic Front in Sudan', *Review of African Political Economy* 54, 27-41.

Hall, M., and B.A. Ismail 1981. *Sisters under the Sun: The Story of Sudanese Women*. London and New York: Longman.

Hamid, T.A. 1989. 'Islam, Sectarianism and the Muslim Brotherhood'. Unpublished Ph.D. thesis, University of London.

Khalid, M. 1985. *Nimeiri and the Revolution of Dis-May*. London: Kegan Paul International.

——. 1990. *The Government They Deserve: The Role of the Elite in Sudan's Political Evolution*. London: Kegan Paul International.

Kok, P.N. 1991. 'Conflict over Laws in the Sudan: From Pluralism to Monolithicism', in H. Bleuchot, C. Delmet and D. Hopwood (eds), *Sudan: History, Identity, Ideology*, 235-52. Reading: Ithaca Press.

Mernissi, F. 1991. *Women and Islam: An Historical and Theological Enquiry*. Oxford: Basil Blackwell.

Niblock, T. 1991. 'Islamic Movements and Sudan's Political Coherence', in H. Bleuchot, C. Delmet and D. Hopwood (eds), *Sudan: History, Identity, Ideology*, 235-52. Reading: Ithaca Press.

Sivan, E. 1985. *Radical Islam: Medieval Theology and Modern Politics*. New Haven: Yale University Press.

Taha, M.M. 1987. *The Second Message of Islam*. Trans. by Abdullahi Ahmed An-Na'im. Syracuse, NY: Syracuse University Press.

Turabi, al-, H. 1983. 'The Islamic State', in J.L. Esposito (ed.), *The Voices of Resurgent Islam*, 241-51. Oxford University Press.

——. 1987a *Manajiyyat al-Tashri fi al-Islam* (The Methodology of Legislation in Islam). Khartoum: Dar al-Fikr.

——. 1987b 'Al-Mujtamaal-Islami wa Abaduhu al-Siyasiyya (Islamic Society and its Political Dimensions) in H. al-Turabi and M.S. Al-Awwa (eds), *Min Maalim al-Nizam al-Islami* (Some Features of the Islamic System), 19-58. Khartoum: Islamic Thought and Culture Group.

——. 1991a. *Al-Haraka al-Islamiyya fi al- Sudan* (The Islamic Movement in the Sudan). Cairo: Al-Qari al-Arabi.

——. 1991b. *Women in Islam and Muslim Society.* London: Milestones.

Voll, J.O. 1983. 'The Evolution of Islamic Fundamentalism in Twentieth Century Sudan' in G.R. Warburg and U.M. Kupferschmidt (eds), *Islam, Nationalism, and Radicalism in Egypt and the Sudan*, 113-42. New York: Praeger.

Warburg, G.R. 1990. 'The Sharia in Sudan: Implementation and Repercussions, 1983-1989', *Middle East Journal* 44, 624-37.

Ye'or, B. 1985. *The Dhimmi: Jews and Christians under Islam.* London and Toronto: Associated Universities Press.

Zuhayli, al-, W. 1984. *Al-Fiqh al-Islami wa Adillatuhu* (Islamic Fiqh and its Proofs). Damascus: Dar al-Fikr.

THE SECULAR STATE
AND ISLAM IN SENEGAL

Roman Loimeier

Senegal, like many other African states, adopted the political system of the former colonial power, France, with its independence in 1960: the constitution of the Fifth Republic, the bureaucratic centralism, the 'laicistic' school, the organization of the trade unions, the legal system based on the Code Napoléon, down to the rules for regulating traffic. This system has been conserved in Senegal with only minor modifications to the present day. Thus, Article 1 of the Senegalese constitution says: 'The Republic of Senegal is laicistic, democratic and social', a formula that was taken over from the French constitution of 1958 which was again based on the 'Law of the Separation of Church and State' of 5 December 1905, where the French state defined itself as 'non-confessional'.[1] Yet Senegal is a country with a ninety-five per cent Muslim population. Islam has a long history going back almost 1,000 years and Islamic religious norms have considerably influenced the different societies in Senegal. Nevertheless, the Western and secular model of the state established in colonial times has pushed aside other forms of social organization. The Senegalese democracy is seen in the African context as a model for other states and is also accepted by the strongest religio-political movements in Senegal itself – the Sufi brotherhoods of the *Tijaniyya* and the *Muridiyya*. Criticism of this state-model thus emanates almost exclusively from within the ranks of the Senegalese 'Islamists'. Since the 1950s, they have wanted to replace the existing secular state by an ideal 'Islamic State' based on the *sharia* (Islamic law) and want to resolve all existing social problems by the recourse to Islam. The development of the relationship between the Senegalese state and the Islamists can be divided into three phases: from the 1950s to the coup against Prime Minister Mamadou Dia in 1962; from 1962 to the end of the era of President Senghor in 1979-80; and since Abdou Diouf's takeover in 1981.

Cheikh Touré and the Development of the Union Culturelle Musulmane

The evolution of the Islamist movement in Senegal is closely connected

183

with the person of Cheikh Touré. Touré (b. 1925) came from a respected family of religious scholars connected with the *Tijaniyya*. He went through the customary education in diverse Quranic schools and thereby developed a growing aversion towards the system of '*maraboutage*' – submission to the absolute authority of a Sufi leader, a *shaykh* – a phenomenon also described by Amar Samb. in his novel *Matraqué par le destin* and by Cheikh Hamidou Kane in his book *L'aventure ambiguë*. The categorical rejection of laicism and Western education forced the old *marabouts* to assert their authority in an often arbitrary way. The more absurd their argumentation was, the weaker their authority became. This loss of authority intensified the strain of tyranny in their pedagogy. Amar Samb describes how an old *marabout*, in a discussion with his nephew, a young student attending a French school, maintained that the world was flat and that it ended at the horizon. When his young relative objected, he was punished by his uncle with a slap in the face. This violent physical reaction can be understood as a direct manifestation of the essential helplessness of the existing Islamic educational system as far as the demands of the modern times were concerned.[2] The rigidity of Islamic education as it was described by Amar Samb and experienced by Cheikh Touré contributed to the formation of an Islamic reform movement that tried to develop modern forms of Islamic education as one of its major objectives. Cheikh Touré, the founder of this Islamic reform movement, established a modern Islamic school immediately after leaving school himself.

After completing his education in the Quranic schools of Fass Touré in 1944, Cheikh Touré went to St Louis, the capital city of the colony at that time, to continue his education. In St Louis he met the Mauritanian scholar and employee at the *Institut Français d'Afrique Noire* (IFAN), Mukhtar ould Hamidoun, who made him familiar with the writings of the North African reform movement, the *Salafiyya*.[3] In 1949 Cheikh Touré was able to take his *Examen de brevet d'etudes franco-arabes* at the *Institut d'Etudes Islamiques* in Boutlimit (Mauritania). After his return to St. Louis he started his first *école franco-arabe*, a school where Arabic and Islamic sciences were taught in addition to the official curriculum.[4] Together with some other Senegalese students he took part in a qualification programme in Algeria in late 1952 despite the opposition of the French colonial authorities. In Algeria he came into contact with leading representatives of the *Association des 'Ulama' Musulmans Algériens* (AUMA), one of the most influential anti-colonial movements in North Africa, an Islamic organization which had es-tablished a modern Islamic school system of its own in Algeria. After a few months of further education at the *Institut Bin Badis* in Constantine, he was forced by the French colonial authorities to return to Dakar, with the other Senegalese, where in 1953 he established the *Union*

Culturelle Musulmane (UCM) after the model of the AUMA. In addition he also founded a newspaper of his own, *Le réveil islamique*.[5]

Many urban Muslims especially in Dakar, St Louis and Thies joined the UCM in the 1950s. Through their activities in the UCM they saw an opportunity to oppose colonial power and at the same time to maintain their identity as Muslims independent of the system of *maraboutage*. In opposition to the colonial administration, the UCM succeeded in establishing a number of modern schools in the 1950s and to publicize its goals through newspapers, conferences and seminars. The UCM had a theatre group of its own which performed pieces such as *Le cadeau politique* or *L'heure de la vérité*. The former piece was directed against the activities of the *Service des Affaires Musulmanes* (SAM), a section of the French Security Service (*Deuxième Bureau*). The SAM was responsible for the supervision of Muslims but also tried to compromise the *marabouts* politically by granting them certain favours.[6]

The first *Congrès fédéral* of the UCM took place in Dakar from 22 to 25 December 1957. Delegations came from many other West African countries such as Guinea, Mali, Senegal, Upper Volta or Ivory Coast. Cheikh Touré was elected first President of the federal UCM and after the congress he became thoroughly involved with the organization of new regional units of the UCM. Another major preoccupation of the UCM was the French West African colonies' struggle for independence. Cheikh Touré and the UCM agitated for a vote for immediate independence at a referendum held in 1958 concerning the future position of the African colonies within a *Communauté Française*. However, as the colonial administration was supported by the Sufi brotherhoods, they lost the vote. In the face of the ongoing attacks from the *marabouts* and the animosities of the colonial administration, Cheikh Touré was to travel abroad for some time after 1958, where he concentrated his efforts on the establishment of the UCM in West Africa.[7]

With Senegal's independence in 1960 and the administration of Mamadou Dia, who as a Prime Minister influenced the internal development of the country in a decisive way until 1962, the prospect for the realization of the reform programme of the UCM improved. Dia was a friend of Cheikh Touré's uncle Hady Touré, a renowned religious scholar, and had shown distinct sympathies for the activities of the UCM in the 1950s. His ideas of social reform were almost identical with those of the UCM and after independence, Dia continued to support the UCM: the *Service des Affaires Musulmanes* was dissolved,[8] and a new official newspaper called *L'ère nouvelle* was founded and edited by Cheikh Touré. Cheikh Touré was also appointed Director of the *Section de Presse Arabe* in the Ministry of the Interior. In this function he was, among other things, responsible for a radio programme in

Arabic and for the translation of government correspondence into Arabic.[9] The Dia administration acknowledged the *Certificat d'études primaires* of the UCM schools and increased the number of grants of studies in Arab countries. In 1961, the Dia administration even started working on a new personal law codex 'concurring with the *sharia*'.[10] Dia also planned to set up a *Conseil Supérieur Islamique* in order to overcome the splits within the different Muslim communities in Senegal. This new Supreme Islamic Council was supposed to be responsible for all problems concerning Muslims in Senegal, such as the organization of the pilgrimage, the development of a new family code on the basis of the *sharia*, the establishment of a modern system of Islamic education, and the organization of Islamic festivals. In addition, the Dia administration intended to develop an *Institut Islamique* in Dakar, 'that was to become an institute for research and training, an embryo of a future faculty of science and Islamic theology'.[11]

However, Dia's policy of structural reform soon provoked opposition, in particular from the ranks of the powerful Sufi brotherhoods who were afraid that Dia's reforms would infringe upon their sinecures. *Marabouts* of both *Muridiyya* and *Tijaniyya* resented the idea of a Supreme Islamic Council, fearing for their autonomy. Also, they felt threatened by Dia's efforts to set up farmers' co-operatives, a process which reached its decisive stage in 1962: in that year collective fields were formed out of the *alarbar*-fields that were traditionally cultivated by farmers for the *marabouts*. The *Murides* especially were afraid that they would lose their clientele to the new co-operatives. Furthermore, the Dia administration had reduced funds and favours for the *marabouts* and introduced a strategy of granting credits only for well-defined projects.[12] This change of financial policy touched the relationship between government and *marabouts* at its very heart: the exchange of services between both parties came to an end and the government set about extending its control over hitherto uncontrolled territories. Dia's enemies used these reform programmes to alienate Dia from the *marabouts* with whom he had been closely connected since the 1940s, when he had organized Senghor's *Bloc Démocratique Sénégalais* (BDS) in the rural areas. When the conflict between Dia and Senghor, the two major opponents, thus came to its climax in the course of the constitutional crisis in December 1962, the *marabouts* dropped Dia and gave their support to Senghor.[13]

The fall of Mamadou Dia and the takeover by President Senghor in late 1962 initiated a new phase in the relationship between the state and the Islamists. Cheikh Touré and the UCM lost all backing from within the government, their publications were discontinued or censored, Cheikh Touré himself was vastly restricted in his functions, and in addition had to submit to the supervision of Dahiru Dukuré, Senghor's advisor on Islamic affairs. The UCM was gradually taken over by forces loyal to Senghor and, by the mid-1970s, had lost its character as an independent, critical, Islamic movement of reform.[14] Under Senghor, the first initiatives towards an Islamic reform policy were discontinued, and the secular character of the state was once again emphasized. This change in orientation became especially clear in the context of the elaboration of the new family law, the *Code de la famille*, which was continued in 1965 under new auspices.

The Senegalese family law

The codification of the new family law started under the Dia administration with a decree of 12 April 1961, whereby a commission for its codification was created. The work of the commission began with the distribution throughout the country of questionnaires containing about 400 sets of questions concerning the existing norms and customs in Senegal in relation to personal law.[15] These questionnaires were evaluated by the commission in 1961, yet the work could not be finished as answers were insufficient and incomplete, and the Dia government was ousted in 1962. In 1965 Senghor again nominated a *Comité des options pour le code de la famille* which was ordered to examine all existing legal customs in Senegal. A particular problem for this commission was the unification of the different forms of law, as a number of indigenous legal practices coexisted with the established law of French origin and the *sharia* in the form of the Malikite school of Islamic law. Another problem that complicated the work of the *Comité* was the existence of a great number of customary laws, usually mixing indigenous legal practices with parts of the *sharia*. After six years of work the new *Code de la famille* was finally presented to the Senegalese public in 1972. The *Code* was characterized by four major principles: the will to unify the law, the will to strengthen the secular/laicistic character of the society, the acknowledgement of the principles of individual rights and the principle of the equality of all citizens.[16]

As the new family law left the possibility of an option between secular law and the *sharia* only in the sphere of personal law and inheritance, the *Code* was rejected by all important Muslim movements, organizations and personalities, including the Sufi brotherhoods. On account of the strengthening of the position of women the *Code* was soon called the *Code de la femme*. A number of *Muride marabouts* spoke out against the *Code* as early as 1966. Their argument was that the new law was not in accordance with the Quran and the Sunna in some respects, such as divorce or the position of women and children.[17] Yet the Quran and the Sunna of the Prophet comprised the only binding law for Muslims. All Muslims were warned against leaving the path of the *sharia* and following an 'atheist, heathen and unjust' road. Those who refused to acknowledge the *sharia* and those who attacked God and His Prophet should not be regarded as believers. Furthermore it should not be the task of a government to change Islamic law. If the rulers, such as the 'secular government of Senegal', were to deviate from the straight path, the faithful would then no longer be obliged to obey this government.[18] A communiqué of the *Conseil Supérieur Islamique* under the chairmanship of the *Tijani* scholar al-Hajj Seydou Nourou Tal, published on 3 January 1971, adopted a similar line of argument and went so far as to enumerate every single article of the *Code* that was to be rejected from an Islamic perspective.[19]

Despite continuing criticism of the *Code de la famille*, the Senghor administration enacted the new law in 1972 and thus underlined the secular orientation of the state. With the enactment of the new *Code de la famille* the Senghor government, however, accepted that two different legal systems continued to coexist in Senegal: whereas the new *Code* is commonly practised in urban areas, it is ignored in those rural areas under the influence of the religious scholars. Thus the supreme leader of the *Murides, Khalifa Général* 'Abd al-Ahad Mbakke, said that the *Code de la famille* would not be valid in the holy city of the *Muridiyya*, Touba, since the only law that would apply there was the Quran and the laws of God.[20] The *Khalifa Général* of the *Tijaniyya*, 'Abd al-'Aziz Sy, characterized the *Code* as a system of rules that would violate Muslim identity.[21] This attitude of protest lead the President of the Senegalese Supreme Court, Keba Mbaye, to remark in 1977 that, 'the *code de la famille* is not rigorously employed in our country'.[22] Nevertheless the Senghor administration rejected a revision of the *Code* on 19 November 1977, and the government of Abdou Diouf was also not prepared to make concessions to the Muslims in this respect. Criticism of the *Code de la famille* has thus continued to be one of the most important topics in the Islamic discourse.

Secularism and religious education

With the takeover of power by Abdou Diouf on 1 January 1981, a third phase in the development of the relationship between the state and the Islamists began. This period was characterized by a significant increase in the activities of Islamist groups in contrast to their stagnation in the 1960s and 1970s. The criticism of Islamist groups was directed in particular against the *Code de la famille* and the secular setup of the state. The secular character of the state was attacked in numerous speeches and publications; 'laicity' was condemned as 'the most dangerous weapon in the anti-religious arsenal of Western civilization'.[23] In particular Cheikh Touré's new periodical, *Etudes Islamiques* (established in 1979), published a number of trenchant articles against the 'laicity' of the Senegalese state,[24] and Cheikh Touré personally wrote a harsh critique of the Senegalese ruling establishment:

Alienated and affected by blind mimicry and anti-Islamic laicity these imitators are worse than the 'ceddos' and slavers of yesterday. Like them they pillage our resources, corrupt the workers, but, even worse, their actions in particular contribute to contain the people in a state of colonializability, vulnerability, obedience and servitude in respect of Western imperialism which imposes them on us.

However, in contrast to their masters they don't believe in the concepts which they gargle: liberty, respect of human rights, women's rights, children's rights, democracy, *égalité*, brotherhood, laicity etc., and which they just instrumentalize in order to fight their opponents, in particular Islam and its values which obviously have become integral features of the Black African culture.

Thus, the present rulers of Africa in their majority constitute enemy number one of the people. They are the major obstacles for the peoples' aspirations towards liberty, unity, dignity and development, and, consequently, they are the most hostile opponents of the liberating forces of Islam which, being at the disposal of the people, cannot but denounce their criminal treason and resist their efforts to instrumentalize Islam.[25]

In the face of such criticism Abdou Diouf tried to play down the laicity of the Senegalese state in a number of public statements. Thus in a speech on 31 December 1983, he claimed in the national daily newspaper *Le Soleil*: 'Laicism is neither atheism nor anti-religious propaganda'. He would rather understand the Senegalese state as an Islamic society whose values are protected and defended by the secular state. On the other hand there could be no 'policy of Islamization' by the state, as 'there is no coercion in religion'.[26] The different Islamist groups have reacted to this policy of mitigation by the state by referring to the increasing social and economic problems of Senegal's development: crime, prostitution, alcoholism, drug abuse, Westernization, unemployment and so on, in order to win the support of the people for an 'Islamic alternative'.[27]

Senegal's secular school system was at the centre of the attacks by the Islamists in the 1980s. This school system was taken over from the French after independence and has remained compatible with the French school system to the present day. As in France, there is no religious teaching in Senegal's secular state schools. Apart from the official school system there are, however, private schools managed either by the Catholic Church or Islamic organizations. The Islamic private schools are, like the Catholic schools, supported financially by the state, provided that they teach the official curriculum in addition to Arabic and Islamic studies. The efforts of the stat to organize and control the Islamic system of education in Senegal date back to the nineteenth century: in 1857 the *Ecole des Otages* was founded in St Louis as a school for the sons of local notables. This school was transformed into a Franco-Arab '*medersa*' (*madrasa*) in 1908. At this '*medersa*' Arabic and Islamic sciences such as *fiqh* (law), *hadith* (traditions of the Prophet) and *kalam* (theology) were taught, yet the curriculum was fixed by the French colonial administration. The major goal was to train indigenous teachers and employees as well as a *corps de marabouts officiels*.[28] In 1903, 1906 and 1911 the French colonial administration in a number of restrictive decrees also tried to bring the existing Quranic schools under its control.[29] However, this policy failed because of resistance by the population and due to the fact that the colonial administration was dependent on co-operation with the *marabouts*.[30]

Senegal's politicians recognized the importance of the *marabouts* in their efforts to achieve independence as early as the 1940s. Senghor, as well as Dia, respected the Quranic schools and in the 1960s even introduced the teaching of Arabic in official primary schools.[31] In this decade they supported the establishment of grants for selected students to study in Morocco, Tunisia or Egypt. Thus in 1962, eighty-three Senegalese students were staying at *al-Azhar* in Cairo,[32] and in 1977-8, altogether 989 Senegalese students were studying in Arab countries.[33] In 1965 a *Collège National d'Enseignement Franco-arabe* was founded but has remained the only official secondary school in the Franco-Arab sector of education. This college was established primarily in order to train teachers of Arabic for the primary schools.[34] To this day, however, Senegal does not have a Franco-Arab *lycée*, although plans exist to transform the *Collège* into such a school which would enable its students to continue their education up to a *baccalauréat franco-arabe*. At present, graduates from the *Collège* have to sit special examinations in order to be accepted as students at the *Département d'Arabe* at the *Université Cheikh Anta Diop de Dakar*.[35]

From the very beginning the Franco-Arab system of education in Senegal was handicapped by not having a unified and binding curriculum. President Diouf thus convened the *Etats Généraux de l'Education et de la Formation* in January 1981 in order to discuss the future educational system of the country. In addition to a stronger integration of the six officially recognized indigenous languages – Wolof, Sereer, Fulfulde, Malinke, Diola and Sarakolle – and a revaluation of Arabic, the commission in particular demanded the introduction of religious education in state schools.[36] In 1985, a seminar organized by UNESCO recommended the use of *Wolofal*, the Arabic transcription of Wolof, in order to improve the process of alphabetization in the Quranic schools. In reaction to this seminar, a national meeting of Senegalese experts on alphabetization in May 1986 supported the use of Arabic for the transcription of the national languages and started work on the homogenization of the different local forms of transcription. This task was achieved by 1987. In the same year the first pilot curriculum for Quranic schools was published, providing for the teaching of the Quran (24 hours a week), reading and writing (2½ hours), mathematics (2 hours), manual work (1 hour) and 'civic education' (30 minutes). This pilot curriculum was adopted by two Quranic schools, Malika (near Dakar) and Latmengue (near Kawlax), both constituting a 'pilot project for the improvement of Quranic schools'.[37] Since then the development of modern state-supported Quranic schools has stagnated, due not only to the chronic lack of government funds but also due to the resistance of many *marabouts*: they fear that a Quranic school reform programme, sponsored by a UN organization and carried out under the auspices of the government, might lead to stricter government control over Quranic schools. As control of the *marabouts* and their schools had been a major object of French colonial policy,[38] state intervention in the sphere of Islamic education is seen as very problematic by many *marabouts*.

Six years after the *Etats Généraux* of 1981, a 'national conference for the organization of the Islamic system of education', instituted by the Minister of Education, Iba Der Thiam, finally began to work. In five working parties a new school law, new curricula, the production of teaching material for different age groups, new examination guidelines, and the translation of didactic material into Arabic were discussed. These proceedings led to the formulation of a uniform curriculum for primary and secondary schools, as well as the publication of a didactic for the teachers of the Franco-Arab schools up to 1990.[39] Nevertheless, a binding curriculum for all official and private Franco-Arab primary and secondary schools has not been authorized,[40] thus blocking the further development of modern Islamic education in Senegal.

The state and the Islamists in the 1980s

Who are Senegal's Islamists today? As we have seen, Senghor's policy of controlling the UCM in the 1960s and 1970s by taking over control of the organization with the help of loyal forces led to a rift between these forces on one side and Cheikh Touré and his supporters on the other. Cheikh Touré and his friends finally left the UCM and founded a new independent organization in 1979: the *Jama'at 'Ibad ar-Rahman* (JIR, 'The society of the servants of God'). A number of other Islamic organizations were founded in the 1980s, but most of these were never able to achieve the same significance throughout the country as the JIR.

The majority of these organizations were also soon captured by forces loyal to the regime of Abdou Diouf. In 1988, however, a union of independent Islamic organizations was established under the name of the *Organisation de l'Action Islamique* (OAI) and placed under the patronage of Cheikh Touré.[41] These independent Islamic organizations can be understood as constituting a movement towards a new national and Islamic identity for Senegal, a movement that is in opposition to the secular state and its efforts to 'capture' and manipulate Islam for its own ends. The Islamists see Islam not only as a *contre-pouvoir* and as an alternative model to a Western-oriented, secular state, but also as a refuge for the victims of the economic policy of the Senegalese state.[42]

The JIR in particular organized itself in the 1980s into an active and successful organization. The movement was founded in Thies on 7 January 1978 and was officially acknowledged on 30 January 1979.[43] First Chairman and President of the organization was Alioune Diouf, an old friend of Cheikh Touré, who had been in Algeria together with him in 1952-3 and who led the movement until 1983.[44] The JIR is represented by local groups in all regions of Senegal, in particular Cap Vert, Thies and Kaolack. The JIR also has a youth group and a women's wing of its own since 1988. The activities of the organization concentrate on the establishment and improvement of Arabo-Islamic education and *dawa* (mission) which includes conferences, seminars or meetings, holiday camps for children, the organization of cultural events and discussions, social activities such as the construction of health centres and wells, aid for the needy and support for the refugees from Mauritania who flooded into Senegal in 1989. Of great importance for the social mobilization potential of the JIR is the network of mosques, nurseries and schools that has been set up in the last years.[45] The organization owns its own newspaper, *Le Musulman*, which since 1993 has also been available in an Arabic edition. According to Muhammad Sall, the Secretary General of the JIR, the major goal of the movement is to achieve an 'Islamic revival' among the Muslims.[46] The JIR schools have taken on the task of teaching children not only the compulsory subjects taught in secular schools, but also Arabic and Islamic sciences, in a way that stresses the understanding of the religion and as such is far removed from the mere memorization of religious texts as was practised in the old Quranic schools.[47] The dynamism of the JIR and other Islamist organizations in the sphere of modern Islamic education has forced the *marabouts* to follow suit in order not to lose their followers to their opponents: 'The marabouts don't wish to be outdistanced by the reformists.'[48] Since the early 1980s, the number of modern Franco-Arab schools have thus increased considerably, and even towns like

Touba, the religious centre of the *Muridiyya*, now boast several modern Islamic schools.[49]

The policy of President Abdou Diouf concerning the Islamists has since the 1980s relied on methods which had proved to be reliable in colonial times and the Senghor era. These methods were essentially based on an 'exchange of services'[50] between the government and the *marabouts*: the religious leaders provided for the regular payment of taxes, the cultivation of the major cash crop – namely groundnuts, the recruitment of soldiers for the colonial army, and the political support for the government at the time of election. In exchange, the government did not meddle with the internal affairs of the Sufi brotherhoods, guaranteed legal protection in disputes with other groups, distributed money for the construction of mosques, and donated gifts and decorations to *marabouts* who had proved to be particularily reliable.[51] Through their collaboration with the colonial administration and, later, the Senghor government, the *marabouts* succeeded in consolidating their authority as politico-religious leaders of the great majority of Muslims in Senegal. However, if the *marabouts* became too assertive or went so far as to demand a share in the making of political decisions, the administration would stir up the existing conflicts within the Sufi brotherhoods and play off the different *marabout* networks against one another. Religious leaders who threatened to become too critical of the government lost their privileges, their financial and legal support and were even in some cases imprisoned.[52] Furthermore the government was able to point to the existence of the reformists around Cheikh Touré who, as has already been mentioned, had started to severely criticize the *marabouts* in the 1950s. However, as the *marabouts* were important for the stability of the regime in recurring cases of crisis on account of their strong support from within the rural population, they were to maintain their political importance after Senegal's independence.

For the governments of both Senghor and Diouf, close connections with the religious leaders were of great importance. Senghor as well as Diouf thus put great emphasis on a symbolic presence of the state at all important Islamic festivities, such as the annual pilgrimage of the *Murides*, the *Magal* in Touba, or the corresponding event in Tivaouane, the *Gamou* of the *Tijanis*. These considerations aside, both governments were dominated by secular principles: the *Code de la famille* was revised several times but not with a view to giving more weight to the *sharia*, the Islamic courts lost all power in the administration of the law during the 1970s, the *hajj* (pilgrimage) to Mecca was closely controlled by the state, and the Franco-Arab schools have still not obtained a uniform curriculum.

President Diouf, a *Tijani* married to a Catholic, in addition tried to legitimize his rule by establishing an 'auréole islamique',[53] and by presenting Senegal to the Islamic countries as part of the Islamic world.[54] Thus Dakar was the seat of the annual conference of the 'Organization of the Islamic Conference' (OIC) in 1991 and Abdou Diouf became Chairman of this important Islamic organization in that year. The ban on the import of Salman Rushdie's *Satanic Verses* should be seen in the same context.[55] The educational and social activities of selected Islamic organizations were financed or supported by the state, leading representatives of Islamic movements who had proved to be loyal were nominated ambassadors or advisors to the President, and personal relations between the President and the great marabouts were cultivated.

Yet Diouf still expanded the state's room for manoeuvre by not only cultivating his connections with the different networks of the Sufi brotherhoods but also by allowing the establishment of a great number of Islamist organizations in the 1980s. These new organizations not only fought against each other for influence and supporters, but could also be used against the *marabouts* of the Sufi brotherhoods if the need arose. Thus the state was in a position to show the *marabouts* that they were not alone in claiming the right to represent Islam in Senegal.[56] In 1992, for instance, the state and some Islamic organizations led a media campaign against the system of education in the traditional Quranic schools, a campaign that was directed predominantly against the system of '*maraboutage*', the 'vagabondizing of begging Quranic-school students',[57] and supported by UNICEF.[58] The campaign against the Quranic schools had the additional function of expanding the authority of the state into a social field which had until then been outside its influence.

Diouf's policy was characterized, as already mentioned, by the effort to expand the influence of the state into areas which had not until then been controlled by the state directly. This was true not only for initiatives concerning Islamic education, but also for administrative and economic reforms that were in turn influenced by World Bank strategies, as well as the policy of regional decentralization, the structural reforms in the agricultural sector and the establishment of new forms of rural organization, such as co-operatives. These initiatives demonstrated the intention of the state address the rural population directly and therefore to deprive the *marabouts* of their role as intermediaries.[59] In this context the Islamist movements with their diverse reform programmes were of some importance to the state as a counterweight to the Sufi brotherhoods. However, despite the increasing encroachment of the state in rural areas, the *marabouts* have not yet revised their fundamental co-operation with the state: 'After all, the Sufi saints have still nothing to complain about':[60] they still receive 'services' from the state and are honoured as partners of the government.

It may be said that not only the Sufi brotherhoods but also the Islamist movements have integrated themselves to a certain degree into the system of 'exchange of services' that has been in existence since the early twentieth century. The Islamists provided the state with support in the implementation of internal reform programmes, they contributed actively to the presentation of Senegal to the Arab countries as an 'Islamic State' and they served the state as a counterforce to the Sufi brotherhoods. In exchange, the Islamists were given jobs in the administration, they were allowed to set up schools of their own, were entrusted with diplomatic missions and had a certain say in reform programmes. In order to gain access to this '*jeu politique*',[61] many Islamists were prepared to suspend their principles temporarily or to give them up entirely. One of the advisors to President Abdou Diouf, Ousmane Paye, even remarked that some of the Islamist organizations which had been founded in the 1980s had been set up purely for the purpose of being co-opted sooner or later into this '*jeu politique*', thereby gaining access to resources.[62] This political game will continue to work as long as both sides, the state and the Muslim interest groups, are able to profit from it. Even a weakening of the economic foundations of the state will not immediately have serious effects on this '*contrat social sénégalais*'.[63] The state has always only dealt with the religious elites, and used these to gain access to the rural and urban populations. The Sufi saints in turn had the task of convincing their supporters of the soundness of this policy of exchange of services. If they succeeded in their task, they were rewarded, if they failed or refused to co-operate, they were punished and cut off from the government's purse strings.

Notes

1. Sow-Sidibe 1991: 192.
2. Glinga 1987: 460.
3. Interview with Cheikh Touré, 13 April 1992.
4. Ibid.
5. Ibid.
6. Diouf 1988: 102.
7. Interview with Cheikh Touré, 13 April 1992.
8. The files of the SAM were transferred from the Ministry of the Interior to the office of the President (Dia 1985: 131).
9. Interview with Cheikh Touré, 13 April 1992.
10. Dia 1985: 131.
11. Ibid.: 131.
12. Ibid.: 121.
13. See Dia's detailed description of these events in his memoirs: Dia 1985: 132ff.

14. Interview with Cheikh Touré, 13 April 1992.
15. Guinchard 1980: 36.
16. Ibid.: 38.
17. Mbakke 1966: 1.
18. Ibid.: 3.
19. Mbaye 1976: 570.
20. Coulon 1981: 274.
21. Ibid.: 274.
22. Ibid.: 273.
23. Momar Kane in *Etudes Islamiques* 23, 1984.
24. See *Etudes Islamiques* 23, 33, 34, 40, 41.
25. Touré 1993: 5.
26. *Le Soleil*, 31 Dec. 1983.
27. Timera 1985: 48.
28. Ndiaye 1986: 136.
29. Behrman 1970: 39.
30. Ibid.: 55.
31. Ndiaye 1982: 136.
32. Coulon 1983: 99.
33. Ka 1978: 107.
34. Interview with the Director of the Collège, Abdoulaye Lo, 5 April 1993.
35. Ibid.
36. Thiam 1984: 23.
37. Prinz 1991: 26.
38. See Ndiaye 1982.
39. Ka 1991: 5.
40. Interview with Abdoulaye Lo, 5 April 1993.
41. *Etudes Islamiques* 41, 1990.
42. Fall 1986: 62.
43. *Le Musulman* 37, 1991.
44. Interview with Cheikh Touré, 27 March 1993.
45. *Le Musulman* 37, 1991.
46. Interview with Muhammad Sall, 30 March 1993.
47. Ibid.
48. Coulon 1983: 109.
49. *Wal Fadjri* 169, 23 June 1989.
50. An expression used by Behrman 1970: 50.
51. Ibid.: 51.
52. Ibid.: 95.
53. Coulon 1983: 192.
54. Ibid.: 102.
55. Gomez-Perez 1990: 173.
56. Interview with Ousmane Paye, adviser to the President, 13 April 1992.
57. Coulon 1983: 105.
58. *Le Soleil*, 8 April 1992.
59. Fall 1986: 56.
60. Ibid.: 65.
61. Interview with Ousmane Paye, 13 April 1992.
62. Ibid.
63. Cruise O'Brien 1992: 11.

References

Behrman, L. 1970. *Muslim Brotherhoods and Politics in Senegal*. Cambridge, MA: Harvard University Press.

Coulon, C. 1981. *Le Marabout et le Prince*. Paris: A. Pedone.

——. 1983. *Les réformistes, les marabouts et l'état*. Paris: Mémoires du centre d'études sur les relations entre le monde arabe et l'Afrique (CERMAA) 2, 91-123.

Cruise O'Brien, D.B. 1992. 'Le contrat social sénégalais à l'épreuve', *Politique Africaine* 45, 9-20.

Dia, M. 1985. *Mémoires d'un ancien militant du Tiers Monde*. Paris: Publisud.

Diouf, M.H. 1988. 'Contribution à l'étude des associations islamiques au Sénégal'. Mémoire de maitrise, Faculté de lettres, Université de Dakar.

Fall, M. 1986. *Sénégal: l'état sous Abdou Diouf ou le temps des incertitudes*. Paris: L'Harmattan.

Glinga, W. 1987. 'Literatur in Senegal – Geschichte, Mythos und gesellschaftliches Ideal in der oralen und schriftlichen Literatur'. Unpublished thesis (*Habilitationsschrift*), University of Bayreuth.

Gomez-Perez, M. 1990. 'L'affaire des "versets sataniques" au Sénégal', *Islam et Sociétés au Sud du Sahara* 4, 173-8.

Guinchard, S. 1980. *Droit patrimonial de la famille au Sénégal*. Paris: Librairie Générale de Droit et de Jurisprudence.

Ka, Th. 1978. 'La place de la langue arabe dans la société sénégalaise'. Mémoire de maitrise, Département de l'Arabe, University of Paris IV.

——. 1991. 'Nahw islâh at-ta'lîm al-islâmî fî-s-sunughâl'. *Al-Asdâ'* 9, 5.

Kane, M. 1984. 'Pourquoi Etudes Islamiques?', *Etudes Islamiques* 23, 4-7.

Mbakke, Ch. A. 1966. *Kallimatu Allâhi hiya al-'ulyâ* (pamphlet) Dakar.

Mbaye, R. 1976. 'L'Islam au Sénégal'. Thèse de 3ème cycle, Faculté de Lettres, Université de Dakar.

Ndiaye, M. 1982. *L'enseignement arabo-islamique au Sénégal*. Istanbul: Centre de recherches sur l'histoire, l'art et la culture islamiques.

Prinz, M. 1991. 'Kulturtragende Institutionen des Senegal'. Unpublished ms. Neuss/Bayreuth.

Sow-Sidibe, A. 1991. *Le pluralisme juridique en Afrique. L'exemple du droit successoral sénégalais*. Paris: Librairie Générale de Droit et de Jurisprudence.

Thiam, Iba Der 1984. 'L'école nouvelle', *Waraago* 7, 22-3.

Timera, M. 1985. 'Religion et vie sociale. Le renouveau islamique au Sénégal'. Dakar: Mémoire de maitrise, Faculté de lettres, Université de Dakar.

Touré, Ch. 1993. *L'Islam en Afrique*. Dakar: Centre Islamique Sérigne Hady Touré.

CHRISTIAN FUNDAMENTALISM, STATE AND POLITICS IN BLACK AFRICA

Paul Gifford

Before any discussion of fundamentalism in Africa, there is some need to clarify terms. First, the term 'fundamentalism' here is not used to suggest any distinction from 'Pentecostal'. Even though in the West, and particularly in the United States, this distinction is often important, in Africa today these two terms seem virtually interchangeable. Hence most African fundamentalists are Pentecostal as well. In what follows, the term 'fundamentalist' will always be used to include Pentecostal Christians. But, more importantly, in its classical Christian sense of denoting some belief in the Bible as inerrant,[1] almost all African Christianity is fundamentalist, for nearly all African Christians approach the Bible rather uncritically. In general, they love to quote it, refer to it, support any position by alluding to it. This is true of Christians of the mainline churches, and is doubly true of what are called the African Independent or Instituted Churches (AICs). This was well expressed in a report on the history and theology of a group of Independent Churches, written by the Independent Churches themselves. After writing of how seriously they take the Bible, they continue: 'Some people will say that we are therefore "fundamentalists". We do not know whether that word applies to us or not... We do not have the same problems about the Bible as White people have with their Western scientific mentality.'[2] Thus the phrase 'Christian fundamentalism' has less precision in Africa than in the West.

There is, however, a sector of Christianity that is assuming an ever-higher profile in Africa and to which the adjective 'fundamentalist' applies in a strict sense. The same fundamentalist Christians who within the last fifteen years have become so prominent in the United States have made great missionary advances in Africa. They have established countless ministries, fellowships and churches of their own kind, and (through their workshops, literature and media involvement) have profoundly influenced already existing churches. So Africa now has a rapidly growing sector of Christianity which is closely related to and heavily dependent on US fundamentalism, and it is this sector that we will focus on in this chapter.

When these US-influenced groups operate in Africa, they find themselves functioning in a context considerably different from that in the United States. In that country there are particular issues that focus their energy and around which fundamentalists mobilize – issues like abortion, homosexuality, the equal rights amendment, 'welfare', the teaching of evolution in schools, New Age movements, the alleged humanism of the supreme court and the media and the educational system. In Africa, whatever the policy of religion enshrined in a particular constitution, few of these are significant. In almost all African states, governments are very opposed to abortion, 'gay rights' are not an issue, women are very subservient, welfare systems most inadequate, and the courts usually very subservient to the executive. Also, the electronic technology (cable TV, free-phone networks, computerized mailing), which has been an inseparable part of the emergence of the US fundamentalist coalition, simply does not exist in Africa. Just as significant, the freedom of speech that enables US fundamentalists to denounce their government for all sorts of alleged inadequacies is not widely honoured in Africa. Consequently, strong public denunciations are out of the question in most of Africa.

As a result, most of these 'fundamentalist' churches normally keep a low profile politically, claim to be completely non-political, interested only in evangelization or 'taking the continent for Jesus'. This is certainly the most obvious characteristic of African fundamentalism's attitude to government. Yet, paradoxically, this ostensibly non-political concentration on evangelism becomes very political indeed. To illustrate this I will initially focus on Reinhard Bonnke; although German and not American, he and his organization Christ for all Nations (CfaN) nevertheless personify this kind of Christianity, and he is representative of the countless Western evangelists to be found operating in Africa today.

Reinhard Bonnke

In the June 1988 edition of his magazine *Revival Report*, it is stated of Bonnke's recent Kenya crusade:

> The attendances at the crusade began to grow steadily as the final weekend approached and as thousands received Jesus as their Saviour each night. News of the fact that the State President, His Excellency Daniel T. arap Moi, had requested an audience with Reinhard Bonnke was greeted with great joy even as the news came through that the President would attend the Thursday evening crusade himself and would sit in the crowd to hear the Word of God. *The President was accompanied by the Vice-President, eight of his Cabinet Ministers and by a number of Permanent Secretaries who all listened intently to the Gospel. Three Cabinet Ministers responded by receiving Jesus*

into their lives... The President informed the crusade team that *he had ordered the Ministry of Information and Broadcasting to broadcast the final two crusade meetings LIVE across the nation on television and radio*. This privilege had never before been granted for anything other than official state occasions and can only be seen as a mighty miracle in the declaration of the Gospel. The broadcasts went out for three hours live on each day to the entire nation of 22 million people... Reinhard Bonnke and the team have been personally invited by his Excellency the state President to return frequently to continue declaring the Message of Life to the nation of Kenya.[3]

Similarly, Bonnke writes of his 1991 crusade in Lomé:

The whole nation was moved by the Gospel of Jesus Christ – from the State President right down to the man on the street. It was such a privilege for me to meet the President of Togo three times. On one occasion he gave us a banquet that would have been worthy of the Queen of England. Before I left the country, he gave me a beautiful leather-bound stamp-album of Togo with the inscription: 'To Rev. Reinhard Bonnke, for the outstanding service rendered to the Togolese people', and then the signature of President Eyadema. I had an opportunity to pray with him, his wife and some of their children.[4]

Elsewhere the same issue of the magazine states: 'The President of Togo, General Gnassingbe Eyadema, invited Reinhard Bonnke to the presidential residence three times during the course of the week. The president himself was so ecstatic over the meetings that he personally invited the CfaN team to return, to preach and pray for the sick in the Northern portion of Togo, next year'. And in the same article, CfaN's vice-president is quoted as saying: 'During our time with President Eyadema...he told us that he had telephoned the leader of a neighbouring West African country to give an excellent report.'[5]

Earlier, in March 1990, during a six-day crusade in Ouagadougou, the capital of Burkina Faso, President Campaore gave Bonnke his own car and invited him to his home twice in six days, on one occasion with press and TV coverage. The next year, when Bonnke returned for another crusade, 'the State President sent his personal representative to welcome the team back into his country. A presidential car was assigned to Reinhard for the three hour drive from the capital to Bobo-Dioulasso.'[6]

In Freetown, Sierra Leone, Bonnke conducted a crusade 3-8 December 1991. As Bonnke's magazine stated: 'It was the first time that a state president had officially opened a Reinhard Bonnke crusade. "Sierra Leone Shall Be Saved is a theme well chosen," announced the president,

Major-General Joseph S. Momoh, as he heartily endorsed Reinhard Bonnke's mandate from heaven for what was about to take place in his nation.' The article goes on:

> Having been made an honorary ambassador upon his arrival, Reinhard Bonnke soon found himself privileged once again to be invited to stand before 'kings and rulers' to address members of the House of Parliament. (The last time he had such an opportunity was in the African nation of Malawi.) He of course, relished the chance to influence the nation's lawmakers for Jesus Christ and made the most of the opportunity and privilege by preaching an effective Gospel message and extending an altar call... It was touching to note that every man and woman in that room lined up for the ministry of prayer and the laying on of hands.[7]

In February 1992 Bonnke conducted his first crusade in the Central African Republic. Wherever he goes, he normally makes a courtesy call on the German ambassador, but the German ambassador to Bangui refused to see him, calling him a 'troublemaker'. But Bonnke's magazine reports:

> The President, André Dieu-donné Kolinga, saw it differently. He received the team twice, once at an official meeting and later at a private dinner. At this time, Reinhard had the opportunity to explain the Gospel personally and to pray with the president as well as his family. As a result of the president's God-ordained receptivity to the Gospel, Reinhard was invited yet again to address a nation's Parliament. Imagine a preacher being given the opportunity to thunder the Gospel in the British Parliament or in the American Congress, and imagine all those lawmakers responding positively to the Gospel! Yet that is exactly what happened in Bangui, by the grace of God, as the statesmen, led by Prime Minister Eduard Franck, received salvation and the prayer for the sick with the laying on of hands.[8]

The most significant thing about the attitude revealed in these examples is that it does not care about the record of governments. All the examples cited show this clearly. Consider Sierra Leone. In 1991 the United Nations Development Programme declared Sierra Leone to be the most underdeveloped country in the world – number 160 on its list of 160 nations. This was not because the country is poor. Far from it; it is fertile, and rich in natural resources like diamonds, gold, bauxite and rutile. It is poor because of the political system, which has been built on corruption[9] – corruption on the part of the very politicians who queued up to attend Bonnke's crusade and so impressed him with their readiness to 'line up for the ministry of prayer and the laying on of hands'. The irony is that the edition of Bonnke's magazine that covered his

Freetown crusade (its cover showed President Momoh opening the crusade) had scarcely reached its readers before the government was overthrown in April 1992, and most of the ministers put on trial for misappropriating public funds.

It is the same in the case of Togo. President Eyadema came to power through a coup in 1967. His rule was brutal and corrupt. Opposition attempts to introduce democracy were harshly repressed, culminating in April 1991 when twenty pro-democracy demonstrators were killed and their bodies dumped in a lagoon. Soon afterwards a pro-democracy national conference appointed Kokou Koffigoh, a lawyer, as head of a transitional government and stripped Eyadema of most of his political authority and proscribed his political party. But Eyadema retained the loyalty of most of Togo's 12,000 soldiers, who are mainly from his own ethnic group, and he used the army in a sustained and bloody attempt to retain power, which he succeeded in doing through a very dubious election in mid-1993. The nature of Eyadema's rule was common knowledge long before Bonnke's crusade.

In Kenya, President Daniel arap Moi came to power after the death of Kenyatta in 1978. Kenya's political structures have become so characterized by corruption and mismanagement that in November 1991 external donors refused further aid, pending the introduction of some system of accountability. Moi's own part in the corruption was widely acknowledged.[10] Yet, just after the widely rigged election of 1988, Bonnke's magazine could declare of Kenya: 'It truly is a great privilege for a country to be ruled by a born-again head of state.'[11]

But the shortcomings of these corrupt and dictatorial regimes mean little to fundamentalist Christianity. Only one thing matters for this Christianity, and that is evangelization. These regimes had not only allowed evangelization, but had encouraged and fostered it. That is all that was required. This was clearly evident in the words of the Kenyan chairman of Bonnke's 1991 crusade in the Nairobi slum of Mathari Valley: 'Thank God, under the wise leadership of His Excellency the President [Moi], we have freedom of worship. Because of that we can have this crusade. We got the permit. Pray for the government that peace continues in Kenya. That is the only way Bonnke can come again.'[12] And Bonnke himself has written, in a thinly veiled attack on the socio-political involvement of some churches:

> The church has one aim to concern itself with – the war with Satan and the campaign for souls... Many churches are very active, but active doing what? To fiddle about with secular issues is one way to look impressively busy and 'relevant'... But to bring the Gospel to a dying world is the true relevance. The command to evangelise is all that matters, snatching men from the flames.[13]

Liberia furnishes further examples of this. During the presidency of Samuel Doe (1980-90), Liberia was characterized by massive corruption, oppression and mismanagement, which led directly to the civil war which devastated the country. Yet fundamentalist churchmen seemed to set no importance on this. Visiting preachers vied with one another to meet government officials. Lester Sumrall of South Bend, Indiana, one of America's most travelled faith-preachers, visited Liberia for a crusade in 1989 and several times in his talks stressed that he had seen the Vice-President who told him how he had been miraculously cured when young. Sumrall reported many of the 'fine things' the Vice-President had told him. He recounted, to wild applause, how the Vice-President had 'prayed the sinner's prayer' with him. Obviously, for Sumrall, this meant that the Vice-President had done all that was required of him. Similarly, the pastor of Liberia's Potter's House, a denomination originating in Prescott, Arizona, in a report on their outreach in Liberia, wrote that he and the preacher of their first outdoor crusade had had 'the privilege of meeting with and praying for the Vice-President of Liberia'. In the denomination's American magazine, this was plucked out to be the heading of the whole article; obviously it was regarded as the most significant event in the report.[14] There was no idea here that government officials could be answerable to their people, no understanding that governments exist to secure the rights of their subjects. For this kind of Christianity, the government has just one task, and that is to allow evangelization. Obviously, Vice-President Moniba, a regular attender at the Episcopal Church, had, as one of his functions, to pray with visiting evangelists.

As the only important responsibility of government is to allow unrestricted evangelization, all freedoms are reduced to religious freedom. Thus, these fundamentalists could refer to Liberia as 'this free country'. Sumrall solemnly preached: 'This nation was born and conceived in liberty; we want it to remain that way.' The following day in another sermon, he referred to the fact that he was preaching in the Centennial Pavilion, where 'every president in this nation' had been inaugurated. 'You wouldn't get three nations on earth where we could do this. There's a lot of freedom here. You and I as God's children can come and praise God here. We ought to thank the government for this honour. It is an honour.' This attitude was characteristic not only of the faith movement; Robert Coleman, leader of a Billy Graham mission to Liberia in 1989, spoke in a sermon of 'this land of liberty'. Another member of this Billy Graham team, in the closing remarks of their conference, described Liberia as 'not only the first free country in Africa, but also in the forefront of spiritual freedom'. In the circumstances of Liberia under Doe, this claim was quite bizarre. The freedom of the press, of the courts, the freedom of speech, the freedom to associate, these things were trampled on daily. But in this fundamentalist Christianity, none of these is even an issue for discussion. When a government grants the freedom to evangelize, nothing more need be said.[15]

It was not only fundamentalist evangelists visiting Liberia who took this line. Local evangelical churches echoed this attitude, often in coded attacks on Liberia's mainline churches which were hesitantly challenging the government on its record of corruption and oppression. Thus under the headline 'Leave Politics with Politicians – Church Leaders urged', Liberia's main newspaper reported an evangelical telling 'church leaders to perform their spiritual duties and leave politics with politicians'. He reminded 'spiritual leaders who are out to politicise religious affairs that the passages in the Bible are mainly intended to win souls, saying that the passages are not intended to create confusion, disorder and destabilisation'.[16] Under the headline 'Religious Leaders advised to Shun Politics', another newspaper reported an evangelical spokesman telling church leaders 'to stop using the pulpit to express their political views and instead strive to win more souls to Christ'.[17] Another newspaper story quoted the Vice-President of the Association of Evangelicals of Liberia at an ordination ceremony urging 'Christian leaders to do away with discriminating acts and politicking. He admonished them to get on their feet for the total evangelisation of Liberia'.[18]

Political support

It is obvious from what has been written above that this fundamentalist Christianity resolutely refuses to challenge government authorities on their record, or to engage in any social analysis of political structures. But we can go further. Because it diverts attention from their deficiencies, governments use this Christianity for the support it offers them in their attempts to stay in power. In the countries we have mentioned, it is probable that Momoh, Doe, Eyadema, Campaore, and Kolinga consciously set out to co-opt this sector of Christianity to their own advantage. This suspicion is all the more likely because, at the time, all of them were under increasing pressure to become more democratic and accountable. This conclusion that fundamentalist Christianity is used for the political support it can offer is almost inescapable in the case of Kenya; we will illustrate this at more length.

Kenya's state-controlled media continually portray Moi as a God-fearing leader, guided by his Christian principles of 'peace, love and unity'. Every Sunday evening the first item of KBC TV news is Moi's attendance at church that morning. Often this takes half the time devoted to national news. Sometimes he is just shown singing hymns and listening attentively to the sermon; at other times the message is quite clear. One Sunday in February 1992, when he was under considerable internal and external pressure to lift his ban on opposition political parties, Moi attended the Gospel Redeemed Church (the same church that had sponsored Bonnke's Mathari Valley crusade), and that evening the television news carried lengthy coverage of the church leader's sermon. The leader was shown preaching: 'In heaven it is just like Kenya has been for many years. There is only one party – and God never makes a mistake.' He continued: 'President Moi has been appointed by God to lead the country and Kenyans should be grateful for the peace prevailing... We have freedom of worship, we can pray and sing in any way we want. What else do we need? That's all we need.'[9]

In return for such preaching, Moi attended a *harambee* (communal fundraising) of the Gospel Redeemed Church a few weeks later. An enormous flag of the Kenyan Africa National Union (KANU), Moi's political party, flew over the platform, dwarfing the Kenyan flags elsewhere round the ground. The church leader (echoing the rhetoric of KANU politicians) delivered a ringing denunciation of Kenya's socially involved clergy. The party daily summed up his sermon thus: 'Some churchmen masquerading as bishops and reverends had turned into rebels and were preaching their own gospel and not that of Christ. Some churchmen were drunk with the spirit of evil politics.' The bishop told his flock to stay out of politics: 'People should shut up, accept the present leadership and prepare to go to heaven.'[20] Moi then spoke for fifteen minutes, stressing the freedom of worship he allowed in Kenya, and noting that some of the emerging opposition parties would not allow this because they believed in witchcraft: 'Others visit witchdoctors, while we in KANU believe in the God of Abraham, Isaac and Jacob. Other gods do not appeal to KANU.' After the service came the fundraising. Moi contributed 400,000 shillings ($13,000), and – from the entourage that he brought with him – the Vice-President and Minister of Finance George Saitoti gave 20,000 shillings, four cabinet ministers and the Nairobi KANU chairman and the Nairobi police chief each gave 10,000 shillings, and three assistant ministers and the Attorney General gave 5,000 shillings each.

It is obvious that financial rewards like these are an important consideration in determining the political attitudes of these churches. It is the African Independent Churches, lacking the enormous resources of the mainline churches, and of those directly related to American parent bodies, that are particularly (though not exclusively) prone to preaching a politically acceptable gospel. Sometimes they succumb totally. For instance, at the end of March 1992, at a time when the government was under sustained criticism from several sources, the Africa Church of the Holy Spirit held a special service in Nairobi to pray for the government. During the service, over 1,200 followers registered as KANU members and the leader Bishop Kisanya registered as a KANU life member. The church resolved to support KANU and President Moi.[21]

This Africa Church of the Holy Spirit is a genuine AIC. The Gospel Redeemed Church mentioned above is a local African Church, but one which has established close links with Western 'parents'. Yet American expatriate fundamentalist missionaries are characteristically just as outspokenly supportive. Above, in writing of Liberia we met the Potter's House, one of the newer denominational-type American implants in Africa. This denomination has had considerable success in Kenya, too. In the midst of widespread agitation for multi-party democracy which Moi was resisting strenuously, the following appeared in the country's biggest daily under the heading 'Back the Government, says Clergyman'. The report stated:

> A pastor [of the Potter's House] said yesterday that Christians should be praying for the government instead of criticising it. 'As an American citizen who has lived in Kenya, I do not believe that a multi-party political system will work at this time in Kenya' [the pastor said]. He said he had been to many developing countries and Kenya was one of the fastest-developing he had been to. 'I believe that this is the result of good leadership. I want to thank President Moi, Vice-President Saitoti and the rest of the leaders of Kenya for the outstanding job they have done,' [the pastor] said.[22]

The international President of the Seventh Day Adventist (SDA) Church provides another example. (The SDAs would be considered as a 'cult' by most fundamentalists in the United States. In Africa they can often have quite close relations with more fundamentalist churches.) On a visit to Kenya, where the SDA has a particularly wide following, the church president paid a courtesy call on Moi. The party daily covered the visit. It reported that Moi took the opportunity to commend

> ...the SDA Church for their role in preaching the gospel and for being good missionaries. He urged the church to continue praying for peace in the country, noting that national development depended on stability. [In the Kenyan context, that was the standard coded attack on the social preaching of the National Council of Churches of Kenya (NCCK).] In his reply, the Church President commended President Moi whom he described as a champion of religious freedom and expression. [He] said that through the *Nyayo* philosophy of peace, love and unity, President Moi was a renowned world mediator and peacemaker. He assured President Moi that the SDA Church would continue supporting the government. [He] further said the followers of his church would continue being loyal to the Government and were peace-loving model citizens.[23]

At the very time of the elections, there were blatant instances of fundamentalist support for Moi. The United Evangelical Churches of Kenya (UECK) is an umbrella body of about 250 pastors representing about sixty different churches. Most of them are of the newer American-influenced fundamentalist wave, although about sixty of the pastors would be classified as of the traditional AICs. The UECK also illustrate another characteristic of so many African churches, in that in 1992 they effectively placed themselves under a parent body in the US by affiliating with the United Evangelical Churches of America, a group of 1,000 pastors under the Rev. Charles Hardin of Georgia. In November 1992 Hardin and a group of Americans came to Kenya for a major convention. This was only a month before Kenya's long-awaited general election, and, just before the convention, Hardin and his colleagues and the Kenyan leadership paid a visit to President Moi, to confer and to pray with him. Moi took the occasion to advise them to avoid ungodly behaviour, to defend the faith without compromise, to have no antagonism to the state, and to stay out of politics. Moi went on to note how the World Council of Churches (WCC) had betrayed the full Gospel message by accommodating to the world – and he spontaneously promised to loan six buses from his Nyayo Bus Company to ferry participants to the UECK convention. In the Kenyan context Moi's message was quite clear, for by this time the mainline Protestant NCCK (the local equivalent of the WCC) and more lately the Catholic Church had come out with statements on the political scene which were harshly critical of Moi. Moi's message (and patronage) was not lost on the UECK, and their ensuing convention became something of a promotion of Moi, and led to a statement signed by UECK leaders challenging the negative comments of the NCCK churches.[24] And again, two days after the elections, which Moi won, but through such irregularities that the opposition and the NCCK were still debating whether to challenge the results, the UECK leaders went on TV rebuking the NCCK and urging the opposition to accept the results.

And so it continues. Paul Yonggi Cho, the pastor of what is reputed to be the biggest church in the world, Yoido Full Gospel Church of Seoul, came to Nairobi for a crusade 25-31 March 1993. Although not from the United States his message is the classic faith gospel. He had a well-publicized reception with President Moi at State House, where Moi referred to his preaching as a 'blessing' for Kenya. The media printed pictures of Moi and his entourage attending the closing day of the crusade. A report noted that Cho preached on

...the blind man healed by Jesus (Mk 10: 46-52) and called on Kenyans to have faith in God in order to be delivered from the economic crisis facing the country. He said that Kenya was a blessed country because it had a God-fearing leader. The South Korean preacher urged Kenyans to trust in Jesus in order to prosper... The President who acknowledged the preaching with an occasional nod, listened attentively as the preacher told the crowd that with God all things are possible... [Dr Cho said] that God gave the President wisdom to lead the country.[25]

To appreciate just how political this preaching was, it is necessary to understand that exactly that week, on 22 March, Moi had reversed Kenya's economic liberalization programme, showing, according to London's *Financial Times*, 'the stranglehold corruption has over' the Kenyan economy, and 'the power wielded by a handful of politicians who have stolen millions of dollars by manipulating economic controls in their personal favour'.[26] At a time when foreign and even the Kenyan press were pointing out that the root cause of Kenya's parlous economic situation was the unbridled corruption of the ruling clique, a visiting 'man of God' was preaching to thousands, amid great publicity, that Moi was ruling with wisdom given by God himself, and that it was only the deficient faith of Kenyans themselves that was preventing a glorious and prosperous future for Kenya. Cho's preaching may or may not have been a blessing for Kenya, but it certainly was for Moi personally.

Apparent exceptions

We have argued that the normal attitude to government on the part of the fundamentalist churches is an avowed non-political stance, which on closer inspection seems very like one of unquestioning support, provided there is the freedom to evangelize. However, there are some facts which seem to nuance this picture.

It is true that Africa's fundamentalist Christianity now professes to be closely concerned with the particularities of Africa. Fundamentalist preachers readily talk about Africa's social, economic and political ills. This is often evident in the massive conventions which are becoming such a feature of Africa's major cities. Take the Zimbabwe Assemblies of God Africa (ZAOGA) 'summit' held in the Harare International Conference Centre, 9-14 February 1993. This was staged with great fanfare, and at considerable cost – the conference centre cost Zim $17,000 (US$5,000) a day, and the participants' meals cost $50,000 a day. The speakers at this conference often spoke about the ills of Africa, its needs, its problems, and Christianity's role in meeting them. ZAOGA's founder, the impressive and widely-respected Archbishop Ezekiel Guti, continually referred to the specific conditions of Africa: the poverty, dependency, economic collapse, civil wars, unemployment, hunger, the colonial past. He continually uttered phrases like 'Now is Africa's time', and 'Africa must rise up'. He was insistent that the Independent Churches (he called ZAOGA one, although it is debatable whether his church should not now more properly be classed with the recent American implants) should cease to focus exclusively on the next life and begin to grapple with the problems of this life. But he was equally insistent that the causes of Africa's problems are spiritual: 'We see the spiritual. The world sees just the physical. We know spiritual sources make things happen. We see people working, but because of the spirit of poverty, they cannot prosper. You have to be delivered from the spirit of poverty before you can prosper.' He spoke of African countries being 'spirit-controlled': 'We know in Africa, [there are] poverty, civil wars, drought. Some say it is natural. We don't see it that way. We know that there are spirits somewhere. I spoke about our devalued [Zimbabwe] dollar. The USA has a debt of trillions. But their dollar is never devalued. Our dollar is finished. What do you think? Use your brain.' (From the context it was obvious that he saw Zimbabwe's devaluation as caused by demonic powers.) He was equally clear about the remedy: 'We need God, we need God, we need God. We must do something. The people who know their God must pray.' And they must pray for leaders, with no complaining: 'History has taught me, if you involve yourself [in political activity], you have no time to pray; you become angry... You must support your government as much as you.'[27]

This was the main message of the conference. Myles Munro of the Bahamas, perhaps the convention's key speaker, spoke several times and always stressed the contextualization of his theology, insisting that he was totally oriented to the third world: 'The value of something is determined by where it came from, not by your opinion of it. We in the Third World need to learn this. Many of us here have lived under oppression, and our values have been destroyed. We have been told that we are less than other people. We believe that and treat each other that way. I want you to realise that God has placed in us himself.' Such contextualization was conscious, and is, I think, rather novel in this Christianity.[28] But this did not lead him to confront the root causes of so many of Africa's ills – its iniquitous political structures. Politically his approach was not so different from what we have considered above. In a key address entitled 'The Church and Social Responsibility or Social Change', he stated: 'I worked as Assistant Secretary in my government, and at present am advisor to government and sit on many advisory boards. I discovered that politics can never solve our problems.' He continued:

A nation can only be delivered by leadership, and the only agency that can produce this leadership is the church... When God looked at the earth he did not send a politician, so according to God we do not have a political problem. He sent a saviour, redeemer, so his solution identified our problem. Jesus is God's prescription to

[our] problem. Jesus came with one goal in mind, this is the answer to our social problems. Jesus came to give us the Holy Spirit... Our problem is a spiritual problem... Social problems in our countries are the result of not having the Holy Spirit.

Then with considerable originality and colour (arguing from the colonial system – therefore 'Americans cannot understand this') he continued:

The Church is the only agency that has the answer to our social problems. If you fill people with the Holy Spirit, you won't need law, the police, government, judges, lawyers. The church has the answer to all social problems. The church is the only agency that can introduce people to the Holy Spirit, and the Holy Spirit will release people from the law... If every leader in every nation received the Holy Spirit we could have a different world.

The solution then is to have a born-again president in every country. This message, for all its seeming contextualization and its stress on Africa's particular circumstances, is – at least so far – not so very different from the standard position we have outlined above, namely the electing of a spirit-filled leader who will encourage the preaching of the full gospel. It is because they well understand this that Moi claims to be born-again, Momoh opens a crusade, and Eyadema and Doe and Campaore receive and pray with visiting evangelists. And it is significant that Munro's publications make great play of the Caribbean leaders who regularly attend his conventions.

There is one country which at first sight seems to run counter to our general tendency. This is Zambia, seemingly the one country in Africa where evangelicals have unashamedly involved themselves in socio-political movements, in co-operation with the Roman Catholics and mainline Protestants. The co-operation and involvement began in 1979 when the Zambian government tried to introduce scientific socialism (that is, Marxism) into the education system; all the churches mobilized at the prospect of this, and combined to fight the move – so successfully that the idea was dropped. The interdenominational co-operation came alive again in the late 1980s when sharply deteriorating economic conditions led to widespread dissatisfaction with the UNIP government of President Kenneth Kaunda. The churches united to play a considerable role, first in resolving problems that threatened to derail the embryonic democratization process, and then in forming the Zambia Elections Monitoring Co-ordinating Committee (ZEMCC) to oversee the elections. Thus, on the face of it, the evangelicals in Zambia have been as committed to the process of political transformation as the other churches, and in roughly the same way.

A closer look, however, reveals that there is a considerable difference in the agendas of the different branches of Christianity. For example, the Catholic Church is committed to political activity from the rationale of liberation theology, as several official statements show.[29] The same seems true of at least the leaders of the mainline Protestant denominations. Most evangelicals, however, are extremely opposed to liberation theology, out of fear of Communism. The evangelical commitment seems to have been motivated by a concern for political and economic liberalism. Secondly, their involvement seems to have been given some direction because of the candidates involved. Kaunda, although the son of a Presbyterian minister and never hesitant in professing his Christian allegiance, had the misfortune to label his political philosophy 'humanism', by which he meant a (perhaps rather idealistic and utopian) combination of Christianity and traditional African values. But for evangelicals, of course, the word 'humanism' carries the worst of connotations. As the head of the Evangelical Fellowship of Zambia (EFZ) has written in reference to the election transition: 'The political ideology of humanism was attacked by the church as a philosophy which puts man at the centre of society, instead of God. This never works. Humanism is a disaster.'[30] Also, Kaunda was opposed by Frederick Chiluba of the Movement for Multiparty Democracy (MMD), who openly professed to be a born-again Christian.[31] Many of the evangelicals claimed that the MMD had proclaimed in its manifesto that it would make Zambia 'a Christian country'. Thus the dynamics in Zambia were fundamentally not so different from those in the countries discussed above: Moi and Momoh and Doe were given unconditional fundamentalist support because they claimed to be 'true' Christians; in exactly the same way Chiluba was given support – support all the more fervent because his opponent, Kaunda, openly claimed to be a 'humanist'.

This suspicion is reinforced by the behaviour of the evangelicals afterwards. After the election, ZEMCC transmuted into the Foundation for Democratic Process (FODEP), a body established to maintain and promote interest in the democratic ideal. The Catholic Episcopal Conference of Zambia (ECZ) and the mainline Protestant Christian Council of Zambia (CCZ) became foundation members of this; the EFZ, however, did not, seemingly because other groups were admitted as well, in particular the National Women's Lobby Group. The Evangelicals were not prepared to join in such activity with non-Christian groups. (One gets the impression that the ECZ and the CCZ deliberately opted for the wider representation, including the Women's Lobby Group, knowing full well that this would involve the withdrawal of the EFZ). Further differences emerged when not long after the election President Chiluba made a statement declaring Zambia 'a Christian nation'. The ECZ and the CCZ were quite alarmed at the implications of this declaration. Although all three (the ECZ, CCZ and EFZ) signed a press release guardedly endorsing Chiluba's statement, it appears that this was written by a member of the Catholic Secretariat, and that the alarm was primarily felt by the Catholics; in general, the EFZ was delighted.[32] Again, the motivation of the evangelical churches seems to have been chiefly the election of a 'Christian president' who would support their evangelization agenda.

Other apparent exceptions are those countries where Islam is seen as a threat or as likely to become one. In these countries the very same churches that elsewhere boast of their 'non-political' stance, aggressively involve themselves with non-evangelical churches in combatting 'the Muslim threat'. The most obvious example of this is Nigeria, where all Christian bodies – including many that in other countries have almost nothing to do with one another – have united in an umbrella organization called the Christian Association of Nigeria (CAN). CAN is made up of the Catholics, the Christian Council of Nigeria (CCN), the Pentecostal Fellowship of Nigeria (PFN), the Independents, and the fellowship of the Evangelical Church of West Africa and the more mainline churches based in the North. CAN's agenda seems every bit as political as religious, given that the Babangida regime (1985-93) was perceived as a Muslim government, and (even more important) as a government determined irrevocably to shift the balance of power in favour of the Muslims. CAN has branches in nearly all states, and at least at this level the dominant influences are as likely to be fundamentalists as Christians of other traditions. In his keynote address on 27 February 1991 at their Lagos Conference, the President of the Pentecostal Fellowship of Nigeria, made his organization's stand on politics quite clear:

> All good men must ensure that narrow-minded bigots and religious fanatics whose main preoccupation is to usurp delegated authority and distribute important positions in favour of one religious group as in the past should not be allowed to find their way onto the top. It's no longer a secret that Nigeria has been smuggled into the OIC, and everything that could be done to Islamise Nigeria and bring Sharia is being done, these things are clear to everybody. But the church must arise, men of the church must arise.[33]

At this conference, half a day was devoted to closed-door sessions on the political role of PFN in Nigeria's transition to civilian rule. The secretary of the Lagos State chapter of PFN, Pastor Ladele said of born-again Christians in politics:

> Many Christians believe it is wrong to want to be in politics. But we are teaching them in our sermons, in our lectures, that if we don't take active part by helping to choose the right person, you will see that it is the enemy that is coming to rule us again... The Americans before you can become their President, the church leaders

will come, they will agree that this is their man, and they will use the church pulpit to tell all their members. So we have to do that to get the next President: we will do it, because the suffering is enough.[34]

Again, however, the aim is primarily to elect a Christian president. The Christians failed to do this in 1993, and what future developments will occur remain to be seen. It is obvious, though, that the perception of being ruled by a government hostile to Christianity has had great success in uniting and mobilizing the evangelical community in political activity. Ruth Marshall is correct in writing: 'The growing feeling that politics is something born-agains will have to reckon with if they want to protect their interests as a community is making for a degree of politicisation not often found in other parts of the continent'.[35]

The other country where similar developments could occur is Tanzania. Since 1985, when the Muslim Mwinyi replaced the Christian Nyerere as President of Tanzania, Christians of all kinds have begun to perceive themselves as discriminated against. This reached something of a crisis in February 1993 when it was leaked that Zanzibar and perhaps even Tanzania as a whole had joined the Organisation of Islamic Conference (OIC). As in Nigeria, the government declined to clarify exactly what had occurred, which served only to alarm the Christians the more. Tanzania's Christians have not been as politically outspoken as Nigeria's, but the feeling of discrimination may yet serve to mobilize them, fundamentalists included, along the same lines as in Nigeria.

Our primary focus has been on the churches recently spread so widely by fundamentalist missions from the United States. What has been said applies beyond that group, however, as these churches are assuming an increasing influence over independent churches and even over many of the more traditional evangelical churches. Their position, we have argued, is to leave unchallenged, even to support openly, any government that permits or encourages unrestrained evangelization. In countries with such a government, these fundamentalist churches have in general refused to address anything political. Even to contemplate this was denounced as a denial of true 'biblical' Christianity.

Since the Catholic and mainline Protestant churches have recently begun to challenge the deficiencies, unaccountability and human rights records of these same governments, we have here what is becoming a crucial difference between the mainline Protestant and Catholic churches on the one hand, and the fundamentalist churches on the other. In fact, in parts of West Africa, it seems widely accepted that Christianity can be divided into two forms: 'political Christianity', which is the term used derogatively to describe the Catholic and mainline Protestant churches, and 'biblical Christianity', which is the term the fundamentalist churches use of themselves. As we have seen, however, their claim to be 'unpolitical' does not withstand close scrutiny; these churches play a very political role.

This slow and belated awakening of the mainline churches is of some importance for the future of the fundamentalist churches. In Latin America, Stoll has argued, the evangelical churches have been forced to address political issues because 'their great ideological rival', liberation theology, has made this political agenda inescapable.[36] It is probable that the lack of liberation theology in Black Africa has helped the evangelical churches so resolutely to avoid this step. As the mainline churches, in the face of Africa's economic collapse, political corruption and mismanagement, become more outspoken with a critical liberation theology, they can hardly fail to have some effect on the fundamentalist churches.

The other factor affecting the political stance of the fundamentalist churches, is, we have argued, the presence of Islam. This is already forcing many of Africa's fundamentalists directly into the political arena. Their precise forms of political involvement are yet to become clear, but 'the Muslim threat' seems likely to be the most potent factor in modifying the position we have described above.

Notes

1. Barr 1980: 65.
2. African Independent Churches 1985: 26.
3. *Revival Report*, 4/88E: 8. Italics in original.
4. *Revival Report*, B/91E: 2.
5. *Revival Report*, B/91E: 5.
6. *Revival Report*, C/90E: 5.
7. *Revival Report*, A/92E: 3.
8. *Revival Report*, B/92E: 6.
9. *New Citizen*, 1 June 1991: 2; *New Shaft*, 3-9 June 1991: 5; *Daily Mail*, 3 June 1991: 1; *Progress*, 1 June 1991: 1.
10. Harden 1991: 248-68.
11. *Revival Report*, B/89E: 3.
12. Said on 7 Feb. 1991.
13. *Revival Report*, 1/90E: 12.
14. *The Trumpet*, Jan. 1989: 19-20.
15. Gifford 1993: 130-2. For Billy Graham's support for the powerful, see *ibid.*: 137.
16. *Daily Observer*, 7 Sept. 1989: 8.
17. *Herald*, 23-9 Nov. 1989: 9.
18. Ibid.
19. See also *Kenya Times*, 2 Feb. 1992: 2.

20. *Kenya Times*, 24 Feb. 1992: 1; see also *Daily Nation*', 24 Feb. 1992: 1; *Standard*, 24 Feb. 1992: 1; *Signpost*, March 1992: 1.
21. *Standard*, 30 March 1992: 4. Pobee provides several examples of African Independent Churches' supporting Ghana's government; see Pobee 1991: 76-94.
22. *Daily Nation*, 2 July 1991: 3.
23. *Kenya Times*, 1 Dec. 1990: 2. *Nyayo* ('footsteps') is the label Moi gives his political philosophy.
24. Referred to in *Target*, 15-31 Jan. 1993: 4.
25. *Daily Nation*, 1 April 1993: 26.
26. *Financial Times*, 24 Mar. 1993: 6.
27. Tapes available from P.O. Box W 68, Waterfalls, Harare, Zimbabwe.
28. This theme (blackness, Africanness) was stressed by Otabil, another of the main speakers.
29. See the statements of the ZEC: *Economics, Politics and Justice* (July 1990), *You shall be many Witnesses (July 1991), The Future is Ours* (February 1992).
30. Imakando 1992: 3.
31. Chiluba was converted at a Bonnke rally in Malawi: see *Revival Report* A92E: 12.
32. Press Statement of 16 Jan. 1992.
33. Cited in Marshall 1992: 27.
34. Ibid.: 27-8.
35. Ibid.: 28.
36. Stoll 1990: 314.

References

African Independent Churches 1985. *Speaking for Ourselves: Members of African Independent Churches Report on their Pilot Study of the History and Theology of their Churches*. Braamfontein: Institute for Contextual Theology.

Barr, J. 1980. *Explorations in Theology: The Scope and Authority of the Bible*. London: SCM Press.

Gifford, P. 1993. *Christianity and Politics in Doe's Liberia*. Cambridge University Press.

Harden, B. 1991. *Africa: Dispatches from a Fragile Continent*. London: Harper-Collins.

Imakando, J. 1992. 'The Role of the Church in the Democratic Process in Zambia' in *Civil Society and Consolidation of Democracy in Zambia*. Lusaka: Foundation for Democratic Process.

Marshall, R. 1992. 'Pentecostalism in Southern Nigeria: An Overview' in P.J. Gifford (ed.), *New Dimensions in African Christianity*, 7-32. Nairobi: All Africa Conference of Churches.

Otabil, M. 1992. *Beyond the Rivers of Ethiopia: A Biblical Revelation on God's Purpose for the Black Race*. Accra: Altar International.

Pobee, J. 1991. *Religion and Politics in Ghana*. Accra: Asempa.

Stoll, D. 1990. *Is Latin America Turning Protestant? The Politics of Evangelical Growth*. Berkeley: University of California Press.

AFTER UJAMAA

IS RELIGIOUS REVIVALISM A THREAT
TO TANZANIA'S STABILITY?

Frieder Ludwig

Until the mid-1980s, Tanzania was considered to be one of the states in Africa where there was but little tension between Muslims and Christians. Indeed, it was often quoted as an example of a country where a harmonious relationship between different religions had been realized. This has been attributed to several factors, but many writers agreed that the policy of Julius K. Nyerere, Tanzania's President until 1985 and Chairman of the ruling *Chama Cha Mapinduzi* (CCM) until 1990, was contributory. C.K. Omari stated that 'Tanzania has enjoyed the type of leadership which has worked to promote unity and to eliminate division among the people. The emphasis has been on the development of a united secular nation'.[1] The concept of African socialism which Nyerere developed is also often referred to as favouring the unification of Christians and Muslims. S. von Sicard gives a practical example of the positive relationship existing in the *ujamaa* villages founded in the 1960s and 1970s:

> In many villages where plans are made for both a church and a mosque building, it is not uncommon that the Christians help the Muslims build their mosque and that the Muslims then in turn help the Christians. It is felt that the socialist elements of ujamaa which help to bring unity to the nation as a whole exist in both Christianity and Islam. Such things as love and respect for another, sharing the basic necessities of life, etc., are emphasized.[2]

There is also agreement that Swahili as the national language has played an important part in fostering unity.[3]

However, in recent years there have been more and more reports about disruptive tendencies endangering the former peaceful relationship. In the following chapter a short general outline of these developments is given and then a more specific look at the union between Tanganyika and Zanzibar is attempted. The following sections provide some background information about Christian and Muslim revivalist groups and their relationship to the state. Finally, some possible interpretations and conclusions are put forward.[4]

216

Revivalism and religious conflicts: a short overview

Recent events. An early example of disruptive tendencies was the Maulidi celebrations[5] in Tabora in 1982 under the auspices of the Supreme Council for Muslims in Tanzania, BAKWATA (Baraza Kuu la Waislamu Tanzania). A local group influenced by *Wahhabi* doctrines was so disruptive that strong security measures had to be deployed.[6] New problems arose in 1987 when the two Tanzanian leaders of the time, Party chairman Julius Nyerere and President Ali Hassan Mwinyi, found it necessary to come out in strong defence of freedom of worship as stated in the constitution of the United Republic of Tanzania. The background to this intervention was a nation-wide tour by a group of highly educated Muslim leaders whose intention it was to spread what they described as 'comparative religion'. This tour, organized by BAKWATA and led by Alhaj Ngaliba, climaxed in May 1987 with a series of discussions on biblical and doctrinal passages between the *imams* and born-again Christians.[7] According to C.K. Omari 'they were a failure for Christians because the Muslims who took part in the debates were well prepared and made the Christians with their fundamentalist attitudes look ignorant and foolish before the audience.'[8]

From that time on, there were regular news reports about religious confrontations and religiously-motivated conflicts in Tanzania. In summer 1988 there were angry protests against statements made by the chairwoman of the Association of Tanzanian Women (UWT), Sofia Kawawa, who had urged for the abrogation of the Islamic Marriage Law and who had argued that the right of polygamy denies justice to women. In Zanzibar, several people died in the clashes.[9]

The same year saw the appointment of Professor Kighoma Malima as Minister of Education. He felt that Muslim youths had been discriminated against in the past and therefore they should now enjoy preferential treatment in the selection process for secondary education. When Malima became Minister of Finance in 1989, there was speculation, especially among Christians, that Tanzania was heading towards increased Islamist influence. At a meeting of the Christian Council of Tanzania (CCT) in Dodoma in August of that year, a delegate claimed that the 'pushing' of Muslims to high positions in the government was part of the ground work for a *jihad* (holy war) or Islamic advancement. The delegate also pointed to the propaganda which he thought was supported by Islamic radicals in Iran. Part of the strategy, he alleged, was to buy up, and thus denude the market of, as many Bibles as possible.[10]

In 1992 the tensions reached a new height when in May the government banned any kind of religious preaching outside houses of worship to curb the instigation of religious conflicts. Prime Minister and First Vice-President John Malecela explained that some believers, especially in

Dar es Salaam and Morogoro, were preaching against other religions and that this was resulting in retaliation. According to Malecela, the 'preachings of hatred' had also been recorded on tapes for distribution to unsuspecting people.[11]

A month later, Finance Minister Malima again caused concern among Christians when he included religious bodies in the category of organizations whose imports would have to be taxed. He said that only those items to be used specifically for the purposes of prayer would be spared.[12] There were protests by the churches and their development agencies, and also several members of the Parliament expressed their disapproval. Following these interventions, imports by religious bodies were once again exempted from taxation.

Two other political decisions made that year affected the relationship between Christianity and Islam. In February it became known that the government intended to return hospitals and schools nationalized in the 1970s to their former owners, which in many cases had been the churches.[13] In June 1992, the Kilimanjaro Christian Medical Centre (KCMC) was handed over to the Good Samaritan Foundation, a board of trustees in which the representatives of the Lutheran Church have a majority, and the Mkomaindo Hospital in Masasi District was taken over by the Anglican Church.[14] These changes worried parts of the Muslim community, and an article went so far as to claim this as a major success for the Christian churches and one that would have a tremendous historical impact on Tanzania.[15] In October President Mwinyi announced that schools were not to be reprivatized, but that religious associations should be encouraged to build new schools.

Even more important was the decision to introduce multi-party democracy in the summer of 1992. Although it is stressed again and again that 'the state, political parties and religious leaders must work together to promote religious harmony and social peace in multi-party Tanzania'[16] and although political parties with a basis in religion or ethnicity are not permitted, there is a tendency among some of the emerging multi-party politicians to express popular sentiments. A case in point is the leader of the Democratic Union, Reverend Mtikila, whose programme will be discussed below.

Growing tensions between Muslim and Christian groups aside, conflicts within the religious communities also developed. The Supreme Council for Muslims in Tanzania (BAKWATA) was increasingly criticized for its alleged failure to promote effective leadership and for being responsible for chaos and disunity among Muslims in the country.[17] At the same time, a rival organization, the Tanzania Council of Koran Reading (BALUKTA), gained influence.

The churches were not free from internal problems either: many Protestant dioceses were splitting up – sometimes along ethnic lines.

The most dramatic example of such a split was the 'Mount Meru crisis' of 1992: the Meru people were part of the Northern diocese of the Evangelical Lutheran Church of Tanzania (ELCT), but a group of the Meru Lutherans, led by Jackson Kaaya, demanded the formation of their own diocese. Property was taken over by violence and some people were killed in the clashes. When the 'Mount Meru Diocese' was recognized by the state authorities, the Lutheran bishops reacted with an open letter and challenged the government. The registration was withdrawn in early 1993 by the intervention of the Minister of Home Affairs, A. Mrema. Now a 'Meru Diocese', loyal to ELCT, has been formed.[18]

More general attempts to reorganize the relationship between the state and religious bodies followed in the course of 1993. In March, President Mwinyi met Catholic, Lutheran and Anglican church leaders after they had expressed their concern about developments. The Catholic bishops especially were very outspoken: 'There are... public speeches, cassette tapes and some newspapers that are constantly carrying derogatory and insulting contents. We have realised that by keeping quiet on these matters, the government is condoning the blasphemies, insults and subsequent hatred...'[19] The government tried to appease the church leaders and to play down the issue, but following the riots in April, when alleged Muslim fundamentalists attacked and destroyed three pork butchers' shops in Dar es Salaam, it took swift action. Thirty-eight activists were arrested; Sheikh Yahya Hussein, the leader of BALUKTA, who stated openly that he was the driving force behind the attacks, was taken to court.[20] BALUKTA was subsequently dissolved and a new regulation brought in stipulating that each religious organization be recognized under an umbrella association.

The uncertain future of the union

Secessionist feeling in Zanzibar has been in evidence for well over ten years. In 1982 it was reported that the *Maendeleo Zanzibar*, a political party founded by the former minister Salim Rashid in 1972, had been reactivated and was pressing for Zanzibar's independence.[21] From 1988 onwards, the Tanzanian government, for its part, became increasingly nervous about Zanzibar's semi-autonomous role in the union and the threat of moves towards independence. In January 1988, Zanzibar Chief Minister Seif Shariff Hamad was sacked from the government, allegedly for planning to overthrow the regime with aid of mercenaries from the Gulf States. A series of demonstrations and detentions followed, culminating in May 1989 with Hamad's arrest, following his call for a referendum on the union with the mainland.[22]

Since the discussions about Zanzibar's unconstitutional entry into the Organisation of Islamic Conference (OIC) in late 1992, the future of the union has been even more under question. Press reports about the issue caused alarm among church leaders. According to the Business Times, the Lutheran Bishop Peter Mwamasika said in a press interview that if it was true that Zanzibar had joined the Islamic body, there was bound to be chaos throughout the country. Bishop Sendoro (ELCT Coastal Diocese) asked: 'If Zanzibar is an Islamic State, will it continue to be part of the Union? Will the Union Parliament have any responsibility over Zanzibar or does it exist solely for Tanzania mainland?' The Lutheran Bishops challenged the government to explain the truth.[23]

The news about Zanzibar's entry into the OIC was denied by the government of the United Republic, only to be confirmed later by the island itself. In early 1993, Zanzibar's leaders began openly to defend their decision. On 24 January, the Chief Minister, Dr. Omar Ali Juma, met a church delegation in Zanzibar and tried to explain the reasons for the OIC membership. He emphasized that the 'Organisation of Islamic Conference (OIC) is perhaps the only practical block application to date of the concept of South-South cooperation'. According to Juma, the economic advantages were considerable: 'The Islamic Development Bank (IDB) alone, which is one of the organs of the OIC, has in its possession funds estimated to exceed by far the funds of IMF and the World Bank put together. And yet the conditions for benefitting from the OIC funds are so unlike and so much milder than the IMF and World Bank conditionalities'. The Minister also stated,'that the organisation is neither strictly Muslim nor Arab'. He referred to the membership of the organization, which was established in 1972: 'A case in point is Lebanon, a founder member whose constitution dictates that the President must be a Christian. Other member states like Benin, Burkina Faso, Cameroon, Guinea, Guinea-Bissau, Sierra Leone and Uganda are also led by Christian heads of state. There are member states whose population majorities are obviously non-Muslim, such as Gabon, Uganda, Burkina Faso and Benin.'[24]

Despite these explanations, opposition to the entry remained. Tanzania's parliamentary committee on constitutional and legal affairs reported to the national assembly in March that Zanzibar's unilateral decision to join the OIC was a violation of the union's constitution. The report declared that Zanzibar's membership was illegal under the pertinent articles of the 1964 union constitution, which stipulates that foreign affairs are a union matter. After stormy parliamentary and public debates, the Zanzibar Revolutionary Government decided to withdraw its membership from the OIC in mid-August 1993.[25] Soon after the announcement, former President Nyerere addressed a press conference at his Msasani residence in Dar es Salaam and told about eighty journalists that he was disturbed 'by the way the government was behaving before and after Zanzibar's entry into OIC'. Nyerere warned that the nation was bound to disintegrate if those in authority continued to violate the law, particularly the constitution. He strongly emphasized that the present system, which provided a government for the union and a government for Zanzibar, should be maintained.[26]

But this seems unlikely. During the OIC-crisis, a pressure group of mainland parliamentarians emerged who argued that confrontations with their island counterparts could be avoided by the introduction of a three-government system (Tanganyika, Zanzibar and the union), with each running its own affairs under a loose federal-type government. At the end of July, a private motion seeking the re-establishment of the government of Tanganyika was submitted by a group of forty-four parliamentarians. It claimed that most people from the Mainland were dissatisfied with the present system and that its continuation would be a threat to the union. Although the motion was opposed by the government, it was approved by a Parliament majority.[27]

Christian revivalism

'Power-crusades' and Pentecostalism. Tanzania has been noted for its marked absence of independent Christian churches. It is true that in the southern parts of the country the 'Watch tower Movement' had some influence and that some African churches were founded. Frequently, however, they were short-lived.[28] Usually Tanzanian Christianity was organized by those churches that had their origins in nineteenth-century missionary initiatives. Approximately two thirds of all Christians are Roman Catholics. Among the Protestant denominations, the Lutherans, Anglicans and Moravians are the largest.

Although some of the missions were hesitant in supporting the struggle for freedom, since 1961 these churches have been loyal to the independent state. The East African Revival movement, which spread into the north-western parts of Tanganyika from the 1930s and caused a split in 1953, was re-integrated into the Lutheran Church during the years immediately following independence; only a small fraction remained outside. Possible disruptive tendencies could therefore be controlled.[29] In general, the churches followed the government's appeal to 'play their part' and laid great emphasis on their duty to help in the process of building up the nation. They promoted unity, stability and harmony; open disagreements with political leaders were avoided, as were conflicts with the Muslim community. At least from the outside, the churches in Tanzania appeared to be quiet and somewhat defensive.[30]

This has also changed. A new feature of Tanzania's Christianity is the increasing influence of Pentecostalism and so-called power-crusades with their aggressive use of language. The charismatic preachers emphasize personal holiness and personal salvation; thus the doctrine is individualistic and exclusive.

Pentecostalism has long been present in Tanzania, but played a marginal role up to the 1970s. The Holiness Mission came to the Mbeya Region as early as 1927, and from 1949 onwards their work was taken over by the Assemblies of God. 1932 saw the arrival of the Swedish Free Mission which started evangelizing in the Tabora region, and the ELIM Pentecostal Church took up work in the Morogoro region in 1946. Many others followed.[31]

It was not until the 1970s, however, that Pentecostalism began to spread significantly. The membership of the Assemblies of God, especially, increased rapidly. This has been attributed to several factors. A Bible School in Mbeya founded in 1959 started to produce successful preachers, and evangelization campaigns were initiated in nearly every part of Tanzania. The Assemblies of God developed into a well organized institution with an archbishop as its spiritual head and a General Council as executive organ. The General Council decides on the formation of new dioceses or sections; currently there are five regions or dioceses represented by bishops and thirty-eight sections. Another reason for the success of the Assemblies of God is somewhat surprising. Rev. G.D. Lwendo, the General Secretary, referring to the political situation in the early 1970s, points out: 'The ujamaa-philosophy and the villagisation-programme helped to make our churches grow. Many villages needed preachers, and it was easier for us to go into the villages.'[32] The Catholic and mainstream Protestant churches with their long-established centres and buildings (in some cases well over eighty years old), were less flexible than the Pentecostals who could adapt themselves more quickly to the new situation. The enforced mobility probably also helped to make the people readier to accept new religious concepts and doctrines.

However, this period of success was followed by conflict and division. Within the Tanzanian Assemblies of God there was a lengthy struggle for power which culminated in the formation of the Evangelistic Assemblies of God in 1982. A similar split occurred in the second largest Pentecostal church of Tanzania, the Swedish Free Mission (SFM), at about the same time. Some churches which had belonged to SFM now formed the Pentecostal Association in Tanzania.[33] But it seems that the spread of Pentecostalism was helped rather than hindered by these divisions. It is difficult to ascertain exact numbers, since most of the Pentecostal churches do not keep records[34] and other statistics tend to neglect them,[35] but if we accept the estimate given by the largest Pentecostal church, the Assemblies of God, of about 200,000 members,[36] the total number of Pentecostals in Tanzania could be as high as 500,000.

However, the influence of the new aggressive charismatic approach goes far beyond Pentecostalism: there is also a significant impact on other Protestant denominations. The Evangelical Lutheran Church of Tanzania (ELCT), in particular, changed its attitude. Unlike in the 1960s and 1970s, charismatic gifts (visions, prophecies, healing by prayer) are nowadays widely accepted among Tanzanian Lutherans; faith healing, especially, has become more and more integrated into the church activities. Bishop Mwakisunga (ELCT Konde-Diocese) explained: 'We don't use any paraphernalia, herbs or medicines but simply prayers of faith. And thank God, many sick Christians are coming to pray instead of consulting diviners and medicine-men. Many have received healing from God, this includes those who are demonically possessed.'[37]

Open air meetings and other evangelistic campaigns are also welcomed. Since 1986, at least one big 'crusade' a year has taken place in Dar es Salaam. In order to organize a 'crusade', representatives of the Assemblies of God, the Lutheran Church, the Anglican Church and other churches work together in the 'Big November Crusade Ministries'. This organization was officially registered in 1989/90. In 1990, it began to work outside Dar es Salaam, and in 1991 there were 'crusades' in not less than twelve regions. The big 'power-crusades' go on for about 15 days, and at their peak there can be about 200,000 people attending.[38] Often preachers from abroad are invited. The German Reinhard Bonnke is now a regular visitor, and in the colourful journals of his home organization, Christ for all Nations, Tanzania is often referred to.[39] He regards Africa as afield ripe for harvest, an approach which does not leave much room for dialogue with other religions. In Tanzania he has to refrain from direct attacks, but nevertheless he uses a 'powerful' militant language. Miracles form a regular element of his campaigns and usually occur at least once or twice during an evangelization day.[40] Bonnke's evangelistic style is very successful and often imitated, and there is a feeling among pastors and members of older Christian organizations that they could learn a lot from this German preacher. The Anglican Vicar General praised Bonnke's crusade in February 1993: 'Our friend Bonnke was here. It was wonderful. I attended his fire-conference. Many people attended, and many people were saved, as they claim... People want excitement and feeling. In our churches we are still worshipping in the old ways of our forefathers, but our Christians also want to clap and sing and dance and give witness.'[41] Similar statements are made by other Protestant pastors and church leaders. Certainly there is a new element in Tanzanian Christianity.

Political opposition and Christian anti-establishment

The main channels through which the churches have traditionally negotiated with the government are the Catholic Tanzanian Episcopal

Conference (TEC) and the Christian Council of Tanzania (CCT), an umbrella-organization embracing various Protestant denominations, with Lutherans, Anglicans and Moravians as the most influential. Whenever there were major political decisions to be made which affected the church-state relationship, delegations from CCT and TEC met with the President or a minister. For a long time, therefore, these two institutions were regarded as representative of Tanzanian Christianity as a whole, although the Pentecostal and other new churches were not members of the CCT. There was a spirit of mutual mistrust between the CCT churches and those outside the organization. This is reflected, for instance, in the 1983 Annual Report of the CCT General Secretariat: 'I am not sure if we are going forwards or backwards, there is a tendency, nowadays, of groups forming new churches or church-related organisations. These groups are trying to approach the government in order to be registered. As you all know, the government registers no new church/church-related organisation without consulting CCT.'[42] CCT had the power to veto deliberately delay registration.[43] At least some new Christian groups felt rejected and dissatisfied with the *status quo* especially over the relationship between church and state.

Because of the close connection between Tanzania's political elite and the representatives of the two leading Christian organizations, the leaders of the 'established churches' did not react overenthustiastically to the introduction of multi-party democracy in the summer of 1992. Pastors were discouraged from participating in politics. When opposition parties asked them for prayers before their meetings, they were refused. Some opposition leaders even claim that they were not permitted to attend Sunday services. Thus criticism of the established churches grew: according to T. Njuu, Deputy Secretary of the Pragmatic Democratic Party (PDA), the church had become a 'yes-man' after the Arusha Declaration and 'did not say anything against the government. The churches of Tanzania lost their position, their respect and their prestige.'[44]

The criticism of the existing church/state relationship formed a common ground between the new Christian and the new political organizations. During the initial period after the introduction of multi-partyism, there was often a somewhat surprising connection between these two disparate groups: 'I am the leader of the Labour Party – but I am saved,' explained a Pentecostal politician.[45]

The best-known example of an opposition leader who is at the same time a pastor of a non-established church is the Reverend Christopher Mtikila. Because of his strongly-worded speeches against the ruling party and the court cases which sometimes follow, he is often featured in the press.[46] He sees his aim as 'unlocking the minds of the down-trodden (*walalahoi*) so that they see the reality that Tanganyika is their motherland and that they have got to sacrifice in one way or another for its rescue'.[47] Mtikila was born in Milo, Ludowa District, and grew up in a mission there. In 1966 he went to Malangali Government School in Mufindi District. After he left school he was recruited as a court clerk with the Ministry of Justice in Dar es Salaam. Later he joined the now defunct East African Airways in Nairobi as a traffic clerk and then went into business, where he claims he was 'very successful'. In 1982 he had a 'born again' experience and became a pastor of the Full Salvation Church.[48] From 1988 onwards, he began to criticize the government and the party. The main object of his attacks was President Mwinyi: 'I started to be curious about Mwinyi when he took over power. I looked at him as a man who had no ideology and no education. So I thought such a man was going to be either a tyrant or a "his master's voice" to be used by Nyerere to the worse,' he told the *Weekly Mail*. But more important in Mtikila's agenda is the issue of the union between Tanganyika and Zanzibar. To him the union is the expression of Nyerere's betrayal of his own people. He argues that the Zanzibaris are more privileged than, and are prevailing over, the indigenous Tanganyikans. He also accuses them of being great looters of the country's wealth together with the Arabs, Indians and Somalis.[49] Needless to say Mtikila's message is favoured by recent political events and the likelihood of the formation of a Tanganyikan government.

However, there is another general development among non-established groups. After the April riots, the government decided, as was mentioned above, that each religious organization should be recognized under an umbrella association. The inauguration of the Pentecostal Council of Tanzania (PCT) in June 1993 was an outcome of this decision, although some of the Pentecostal leaders had felt the need to form a unifying body long before that. It was discovered that 'there is power in unity'. The PCT aims to represent Pentecostal interests regarding, for instance, radio broadcasting and open air meetings. In order to achieve this, some form of collaboration with the government and integration into the present political system are necessary. In its constitution the council stated as one of its objectives, to 'take measures to ensure its non-involvement in politics, ensure cooperations with all persons, as well as the Government and other public organs, in its endeavours to save and deliver man from all forms of oppression and to secure the promotion of peace and national unity'.[50]

A similar stance is taken by the Big November Crusade Ministries. There were times when the government refused to allow the holding of crusades because of the fear of provocation and riots, but an agreement was reached: 'When we preach, we don't have to provoke other religions. We don't have to attack other people's faith. That is a condition. We have to promote unity – we must not preach against it'.[51]

It seems, therefore, that the radical approach of some individuals and groups can be checked by the formation of umbrella organizations which facilitate the development of more pragmatic and moderate attitudes. There is, thus, a move towards integrating Pentecostalists and 'Power-Crusaders' into the established church/state relationship from which they have been excluded for so long.

Islamic revivalism

New organizations. The main representative body of Muslims in the country, BAKWATA, has respected the party line and is recognized by the government, but it does not have the unanimous support of the Muslim community, some of whom have felt that it is no more than an instrument of the government to control the aspirations of Muslims in the country.[52] These feelings date back to the very foundation of BAKWATA in 1968 when, through the establishment of a national council, external influences were diminished.[53] According to P. Smith, BAKWATA was, throughout the 1970s, an organization with the interests of Tanzania at heart and with Islamic interests as a second priority.[54]

Other more radical Islamic movements include the *Warsha ya Waandishi wa Kiislamu* (Workshop of the Commission of Islamic Authors) which was formed 'to translate and publish Islamic books with the aim of educating Muslims'.[55] *Warsha* claims to have a considerable following in the 20 – 40 age group. Its publications include a book called *The True Way of Life*[56] and a booklet entitled *Uchumi Katika Uislam* (Economics under Islam). The latter describes communism and captalism as being 'like sister and brother who come from the same mother and father',[57] but communism is considered to be worse because it develops into 'dictatorship' and 'excessive centralism' and also because 'there is no freedom of worship'.[58] However, according to *Warsha* there is a third option: 'The only solution to solve economic problems is Islam... The meaning of Religion is the way of life, neither communism nor capitalism.'[59] *Warsha*, which had started within BAKWATA, appeared on the scene for the first time in 1982. The security forces had to be used against the new group to prevent the disruption of the Maulidi celebrations in Tabora. After this event, BAKWATA began warning the government against *Warsha*'s activities.[60]

Other rival organizations of BAKWATA are the Muslim National Conference, *Baraza Kuu*, and the previously-mentioned Tanzania Council of Koran Reading, BALUKTA. The Muslim National Conference was formed out of protest against BAKWATA which was considered not to have fulfilled its task and not to have committed itself to the needs of Muslims. *Baraza Kuu* is trying to build up its own education system and is trying to woo away BAKWATA members.[61]

BALUKTA was registered in December 1987. The Constitution stated among its aims:

1. To promote Koran Reading and Islamic propagation by supporting the present Muslim Religious schools (Madrasas) financially and materially.
2. To establish and run Muslim Religious Schools (Madrasas), Islamic Centres and Higher Institutions of religious learning.
3. To encourage and teach Muslims and Non-Muslims to learn, understand and memorize the Holy Koran.
4. To arrange religious seminars, workshops, symposiums whereof Muslim and Non-Muslim will participate in discussing and learning all the major four Books of God i.e. The Taurat, Injil, Zabur and Koran.
5. To organise and participate in Koran Reading and Memorizing competitions with in and outside the country.
6. To publish and print and distribute and to assist in the publication, production and distribution of Islamic religious books, literature, films, video and audio cassettes, pamphlets, posters, periodicals and journals.[62]

On several occasions, BALUKTA was warned by the Administrator General that the activities of the Council had to be limited to Quran reading. In August 1988 the organization was asked to return its registration document because it had not kept to the regulations.[63] However, no documents changed hands and BALUKTA became ever more aggressive. In October 1992 the Council accused CCM Vice-Chairman, Rashidi Kawawa, of swindling Muslims out of millions of shillings in his capacity as Principal Trustee of the Maulid and Idd Prayer Trust Committee and demanded Kawawa's immediate resignation.[64] In April 1993, three pork butchers' shops in the Magomeni and Manzese areas of Dar es Salaam were attacked, and BALUKTA was held responsible for the riots.[65] In June, the Council of Quran Reading was dissolved.

Other new Islamic groups include the Union of Muslim Youth, the Union of Muslim Preachers and the Union of Muslim Students. At the University of Dar es Salaam a University Muslim Trusteeship has also been founded with the object of promoting better understanding Islam as a complete mode of life, conducting research, publishing, translating and distributing Islamic literature and planning, establishing and maintaining investment projects which are compatible with Islamic practice. Its constitution suggests that this could be done, for instance, by providing facilities for further Islamic education for Muslims at all stages, or through awarding scholarships and financial assistance to well-qualified Muslim students.[66] According to S. von Sicard, some of these new Tanzanian groups have in the last ten years been sustained by organizations outside the country, most notably the *Rabitah al-Alam al-Islami* (Muslim World League) with headquarters in Jeddah, which has opened an office in Dar es Salaam.[67]

All this had its effects on the officially recognized body representing Islamic interests in Tanzania, BAKWATA. Peter Smith summarizes developments since 1985:

> Since then the Council has become more forceful than before in pursuing Islamic interests – mosque buildings, Islamic scholarships, though it also claims to be open to cooperation with other religions. However Bakwata has also recently appealed to the government for a return to the system of separate Qadi courts for Muslims... Bakwata has been strongly influenced of late by its international contacts. Many of these have been through the Union of Muslim Councils of Eastern, Central and Southern Africa which now meet annually. The meeting of 1987 was held in Dar es Salaam. Through these contacts and contacts with other international organisations Bakwata would seem to be more Islamic than nationalistic.[68]

Muslims and the state

Muslim appeals to correct or change the political system are increasing. These appeals articulate demands to reintroduce the system of separate Islamic courts, as expressed by BAKWATA, and also stress the need for separate Islamic development plans within society, as did the Ten Year Development Plan of the Tanzania Muslim Youth published in 1984. One aspect of all this is the growing emphasis on implementation of the *sharia*.[69]

The requests for change are based on two assumptions. Since 1981 there have been some groups who have maintained that Tanzania should be an Islamic state because Muslims constitute the majority of the population. Official figures which give conflicting information are questioned. In an article on 'Islam and Politics in Tanzania', Mohamed Said wrote that it is widely believed the figures in the 1967 census, with its 32 per cent Christians, 30 per cent Muslims and 37 per cent local beliefs, had been 'doctored for political reasons to show Muslims were trailing behind Christians in numerical strength'. He backed this up with reference to the 1957 population census, when Muslims had outnumbered Christians three to two.[70]

Although after 1967 the question about religion was no longer included in the censuses, attempts were made to derive statistics from the information obtained. M.A. Kettani, for instance, has claimed that according to the 1978 census, there were 18,570,000 people in Tanzania, of whom 10,210,000 were Muslims.[71] These statistics have been questioned by C.K. Omari, who describes them as 'midleading, if not false'.

Omari prefers to accept the figures given in D. Barrett's *World Christian Encyclopedia* which indicate that in the mid-1980s Christians constituted 44 per cent, Muslims 32.5 per cent and adherents of indigenous religions 22 per cent. He argues that 'the statistics of Christians are more reliable than those of Muslims because local churches record attendance every Sunday, and keep records of the new adherents and of those who have left their churches. Muslims have tended to include all with Muslim names.'[72] It should be noted that numbers provided by Christian organizations can vary.[73] But it seems fairly clear that the estimate of 50 per cent or more of the Tanzanian population being Muslim is exaggerated. Nevertheless some Muslim groups take the high figure for granted – an article which appeared in *Arabia* in 1985 started as follows: 'Although Muslims are the majority, Tanzania is now encouraging terror tactics in the repression of Islam.'[74] This also refers to the second assumption: that is, that Islam has been suppressed in Tanzania. Revisionist histories are being written today which endeavour to show that while Muslims have played a decisive part in the struggle for national freedom, Christians have taken the lead since independence.

In 1991, in the Islamic magazine *Mizani*, it was stated categorically that the whole process of demanding independence was left to Muslims. The article argued that Abdulwahid Sykes, the general secretary of the Dockworkers Union founded in 1947 and the secretary of the Muslim organization *Jamiatul Islamiyya fi Tanganyika*, had been the driving force behind the formation of TANU (Tanganyika African National Union): 'But colonialists propagated that Julius K. Nyerere was the founding father of TANU; this is not true.'[75] According to the article, Nyerere and other Christians like John Kefo, Nesno Eliufoo or John Mwakangale emerged as leaders of TANU only because the colonial government had passed a condition that only educated people had the right to vote. Because Muslims were lacking in education, Christians were favoured. The writer then continued: 'After independence, the independence government had the mission to suppress Islam and let in more Christians in the government leadership.'[76] In support of this, the article pointed to the dissolution of the Muslim party AMNUT (All Muslim National Union of Tanganyika) in 1964 and to that of the East African Muslim Welfare Society (EAMWS) in 1968. The Muslim council, BAKWATA, founded afterwards, was, in the writer's view, only an instrument of the government.[77]

Another example which is used to demonstrate the supposed suppression of Muslims is the educational system. A letter to the *Business Times* summarizes the objections:

Pre-and post-independence schools including government schools were church-oriented. It was a rule that before the beginning and after the classes ALL pupils, regardless of their beliefs, were to say Christian prayers. I myself experienced the same routine when

I joined Standard One at Murutunguru Primary School in Ukerewe. This phased some Muslims out of learning circles as some Muslims refused to send their children to school for fear of getting them converted to Christians... Schools observe the praying periods for Christians but not for Muslims. Saturdays and Sundays are both off-days... In schools and most colleges, uniforms are church-oriented... The school uniforms were (and still are) shorts for males, skirts for females and short-sleeved shirts for both. This too phased some Muslim children out of learning circles.[78]

Similar arguments are expressed in other journals and magazines. J.C. Sivalon's book *Kanisa Katoliki na Siasa ya Tanzania bara 1953 hadi 1985* (1992) has often been referred to as supporting the thesis of the suppression of Islam, although this was probably not the intention of the author and publisher. Muslims sometimes describe themselves as being the 'country's underdogs'[79] or as 'witnessing...suppression, assault and desecration of Islam'.[80]

Whether these interpretations reflect historical reality or not, they do reflect the views and feelings of parts of the Muslim community. It is clear that such a reconstruction of history has political implications. These may at times be expressed in the call for a *jihad*, but more often the demand is for a separate development plan to overcome real or supposed disadvantages.

In order to explain the new revivalist trends in Tanzania, outside factors are often referred to. P. Smith gives the following explanation:

A change in this harmonious state of affairs began to appear at a time which coincided with the election of Ali Hassan Mwinyi to the presidency as successor to Julius K. Nyerere. For an understanding of these changes it is important to recall for a moment the global situation of Islam outside of Tanzania. In the Islamic World there has been a renewed vitality which has shown itself in the strong affirmation of an Islamic identity and in an opposition to other ideologies. The heroes and role models were found in people like Colonel Gadaffi, the militancy of the P.L.O. and later in Ayatollah Khomeini. The writings of Aba A'la Mawdudi and his disciple Sayyid Qutb have also been influential. For them the Islamic model as they interpret it is no longer seen as an alternative model for society but as an imperative.[81]

S. von Sicard agrees with this and points to the influence of the *Rabitah* and to the activities of embassies from various Muslim countries. Though a Christian, he sees positive elements: 'Islam in Tanzania has rediscovered its roots and shows many signs of a dynamic vitality. It has considerable potential to contribute to a nation which owes much of its history and development to Muslims from various parts of the world'.[82] As a rule, however, writers with a Christian background are more critical and regard the external religious forces as a threat to traditional harmonious relations between Christians and Muslims.[83]

The economic aspect of this argument is elaborated by C.K. Omari: 'Some Gulf States, for example, are showing a growing interest in helping Tanzania recover from her economic problems. Such interest and solidarity is purely political but, since for some of the Muslims there is no separation between "secular and religious concerns", such solidarity may mean both.'[84] Other writers state more bluntly that 'oil wealth is now being pumped into [Tanzania]'.[85] There is some truth in this; certainly, development in Tanzania cannot be regarded as isolated from outside influence. However, this argument often seems to be over-stretched; it does not give due weight to the initiatives and decisions made by Tanzanian citizens, and their changing situation. Just as the emergence of an African Christianity cannot be explained purely in terms of gifts from rich European missions, so the new Islamic revivalism cannot be sufficiently understood by referring to 'oil wealth being pumped into Tanzania'. The argument of external influence also tends to overlook the fact that there are parallel developments in Tanzanian Islam and in Tanzanian Christianity: in both cases there are revivalist groups whose interests the established umbrella organizations – BAKWATA, TEC and CCT – do not represent.

Jumanne Wagao's interpretation of events puts more emphasis on internal factors. In a paper entitled 'Religion and Economic Policy Reforms: Tanzania', he calls for a reinterpretation of religious faiths by stressing their socio-political dimension rather than their cosmological orientation. According to the economic advisor of former president Nyerere, the 'fall of Ujamaa ideology is the main cause of growth of religious militancy in Tanzania as the people grapple for alternative ideologies to help them pull out of stark poverty'. Other factors mentioned by Wagao are 'the ideology of economic recovery programmes and the dominant liberalization theology'.[86]

Although the argument that matters concerning the economy deter-mines virtually every other aspect of life is questionable, it is not to be doubted that economic and political changes do have an impact on the way people think and express their beliefs. However, if we consider the fact that some revivalist groups have their roots in the 1970s and early 1980s (and, in exceptional cases, such as the Assemblies of God, had their main growth period during this decade), it could also be argued that the new wave of religious revivalism in Tanzania started not after, but during, the *ujamaa*-period, and is only becoming more visible now. It is possible that the increased, and sometimes enforced mobility – as for instance through the villagization programme – has helped in the spread of new ideas and new groups. This line of argument could also fit within D. Westerlund's thesis that there was a tendency during the Nyerere years to 'compartmentalize religion'.[87] As a consequence, the umbrella organizations – BAKWATA, CCT, TEC – did not overtly criticize the government or the party, and the stage was thereby set for the emergence of groups with differing views.[88]

What we can observe in post-ujamaa Tanzania is a process in which political leaders are endeavouring to find a concept to reshape the national identity, and also in which the leaders of the established religious groups are seeking to redefine the functions of their respective organizations. TEC, CCT, and BAKWATA have become much more outspoken in recent years, and 'open letters' are virtually a common occurrence nowadays. A new relationship between religion and politics is developing, and the question of whether religious revivalism will be a threat to Tanzania's stability or not will depend upon the nature of this relationship.

Notes

1. Omari 1987: 61.
2. Sicard 1978: 66.
3. Rasmussen 1993: 87-90.
4. This contribution is based on material collected during three research visits to Tanzania in 1992 and 1993 for a study on church and state relationships in post-independence Tanzania. The author is very much indebted to Professor D. Westerlund who provided further material.
5. The reading of Al-Barzanji's eighteenth-century poem *Maulidi* ('Life of the Prophet') is performed to celebrate the Prophet's birthday.
6. Sicard 1991: 8.
7. 'Tanzania: Muslim-Christian Tension Mounting', in *All Africa Press News and Features Bulletin*, 29 June 1987: 4.
8. Omari 1987: 66.
9. 'Chapter and Clause', *Africa Events*, August 1988: 37-9. The journal comments: '*President Ali Hassan Mwinyi says that they died in stampede. But eye-witness reports say that they were shot by the police...*'
10. 'Tanzania: Islamic Fundamentalism worries Churches', *All Africa Press Service – Features*, 21 Aug. 1989.
11. 'Govt bans opens air religious preaching', *Daily News*, 14 May 1992.
12. 'Move to tax religious imports under fire', *The Express*, 26 June 1992.
13. A *Memorandum of Understanding* was signed between the Christian Council of Tanzania (CCT)/Tanzanian Episcopal Conference (TEC) and the United Republic of Tanzania on 21 Feb. 1992.
14. 'Government handing over hospitals', in: *Express*, 26 June 1992
15. 'Religious memorandum worries fundamentalists', *Family Mirror*, 2 June 1992. The

Family Mirror is quoting from an article which appeared in *An annur*, an Islamic newspaper.

16. 'Multi-party Tanzania: Religious leaders must work closely – Kolimba', *Daily News*, 22 Sept. 1992

17. 'Bakwata comes under fire', *Daily News*, 16 Sept. 1991.

18. Ludwig 1993: 19.

19. 'Stop religious polemics, Catholic Church asks government', *Business Times*, 7.3.1993; 'Bishops Summoned to State House', *Drum*, April 1993; 'Religious tension in Tanzania: bishops summoned to Ikulu', *Family Mirror*, Second Issue, March 1993.

20. 'Tanzania charges Muslim activists', *Daily Nation*, 15 April 1993; 'Sheiks Yahya, Kassim in Dar courts', in: *Daily News*, 23 April 1993; 'Plot to oust Govt. revealed', *The Express*, 15-23 April 1993; '500 youths register for "jihad" ', *Family Mirror*, April 1993; etc.

21. 'Sezessionsbestrebungen auf Zanzibar', *Internationales Afrikaforum* March 1982

22. Woodsworth 1989.

23. 'Is Zanzibar an Islamic State or Not? – Bishops', *Business Times* 25 Nov. 1992.

24. The speech by Dr O.A. Juma is published in *Daily News*, 28 Jan. 1993. See also *Daily News*, 29 Jan. 1993: 4.

25. 'Isles quit OIC', in *Sundays News*, 14 Aug. 1993.

26. 'Nation warned: Nyerere in Defense of Tanzania', *Daily News*, 17 Aug. 1993.

27. 'MPs demand Bill to form Tanganyika Government', *Sunday News*, 1 Aug. 1993; 'Farewell to United Republic?', *The Express*, 2-8 Sept. 1993.

28. A survey of independent churches is given in Ranger 1970.

29. Ranger 1971: 123. For an introduction to the history of the East African Revival see Kibira 1960; Kibira 1974.

30. Ludwig 1993: 10-18.

31. A short history of the Pentecostal Movement in Tanzania is given in Gamanywa 1993: 2-3. There is also a list of 22 Pentecostal churches working in Tanzania.

32. Interview, Dar es Salaam, 22 Sept. 1993.

33. Interview with Rev. Sylvester Gamanywa, Chairman, Pentecostal's Council of Tanzania, Dar es Salaam, 21 Sept. 1993.

34. The recently-founded Pentecostal Council of Tanzania has established a Research Commission which will provide data in due course.

35. The statistics published in Barrett (1982: 660) are not sufficient.

36. Interview with Rev. Gordon D. Lwando, General Secretary, Tanzanian Assemblies of God, 22 Sept. 1993.

37. Veller 1993: 68.

38. Interview with John B. Lutembeke, Secretary, Big November Crusade Ministries, 23 Sept. 1993.

39. See for instance 'Durchbruch in Tanga/Tansania'. Christus für alle Nationen ', *Telegramm. Missionsreportage*, July 6 1993.

40. This is the impression given by the videos of Christ for all Nations as *Ein blutgewaschenes Afrika* or *Ein blutgewaschenes Afrika 2*. More information about Bonnke is provided in Gifford 1987; Gifford 1991.

41. Interview with Vicar-General Canon J.N. Mwamazi, Dar es Salaam, 23 April 1993.

42. Shauri 1983: 7.

43. The Rev. S. Gamanywa described the application of The Word and Pentecostal Organisations (WAPO) as follows: 'When I applied to register my organisation, the government sent me to the Christian Council. They delayed the issue. I went back to the government and asked them: "Why do you send there, if Pentecostals are not accepted?" CCT refused a recommendation, but we became registered in June 1990.' (Interview, 21 Sept. 1993).

44. Interview, Dar es Salaam, 22 Oct. 1992.

45. Interview with Mr Miselya, Chairman of the Labour Party, Dar es Salaam, 21 Sept. 1993. The Labour Party is not yet registered, but temporarily recognized.
46. See *Daily News*, 28 Jan. 1993: 'Mtikila, four others charged with sedition'.
47. 'Who is this man Mtikila?', *Weekly Mail*, 1 Apr. 31 May – 6 June 1993, 4-5.
48. Although the Full Salvation Church believes in baptism by the Holy Spirit, it is not recognized as a Pentecostal Church by other Pentecostal organizations. Rev. S. Gamanywa, chairman of the recently formed Pentecostal Council of Tanzania, stated: 'Mtikila's Full Salvation Church is not recognized as a Penetcostal Church. It is different. They don't believe in baptism by immersion, they believe they are being filled by the Holy Spirit with fire. They misinterpret the Scripture.' (Interview, 21 Sept. 1993).
49. See note 45.
50. *The Constitution of the Pentecostals Council of Tanzania*, June 1993, Paragraph 4.9 (4).
51. Interview with John B. Lutembeke, Secretary, The Big November Crusade Ministries, Dar es Salaam, 23 Sept. 1993
52. Sicard 1991: 7.
53. Westerlund 1980: 100-06.
54. Smith 1990: 178.
55. *Warsha* n.d.: III.
56. Sicard 1991: 10.
57. *Warsha* n.d.: 6.
58. *Warsha* n.d.: 10.
59. *Warsha* n.d.: 13-14.
60. *Daily News*, 19 Feb. 1983, quoted in Smith 1990: 179.
61. Breuer 1993: 8.
62. 'Preamble, 3. Aims and Objectives', in *The Constitution of the Registered Trustees of Tanzania Council of Koran Reading*, Dar es Salaam, 1987: 1-2.
63. *Daily News*, 17-20 June 1993, quoted in *Tansania Information* 7/93
64. 'Balukta accuses Kawawa of swindling Trust Committee', *Business Times* 16 Oct. 1993.
65. 'Plot to oust Govt. revealed', *The Express*, 15-21 April 1993: '...Sheikkh Yahya... openly declared that he is the leader of the people arrested in connection with the demolition of pork shops in Magomeni and Manzese Areas last week.'
66. Dar es Salaam University Muslim Trusteeship (DUMT), *Constitution*, n.d.
67. Sicard 1991: 7.
68. Smith 1990: 179, 181.
69. Sicard 1991: 8.
70. Said 1989.
71. Kettani 1982, quoted in Omari 1984: 1-2.
72. Omari 1984: 5.
73. A survey of some statistics is given in Haafkens 1991: 23.
74. 'Terror responses to fundamentalism fears', *Arabia* 4 (43), 1985: 30.
75. 'Historia: Uislamu na Siasa; Tanzania Chanzo Cha Bakwata' *Mizanim 19, 21 Dec. – 3 Jan. 1991*.
76. The article is continued in *Mizani* 20, 18-31 Jan. 1991.
77. The last part of the article is to be found in *Mizani* 23, 1-15 March, 1991.
78. Nyembo 1992: 8-9.
79. 'Terror response to fundamentalism fears', *Arabia* 4, 43 (1985): 30.
80. 'Chapter and Clause', *Africa Events*, August 1988: 38.
81. Smith 1990: 178.
82. Sicard 1991: 11.
83. Bahendwa 1991: 17.
84. Omari 1987: 66.

85. Anonymous Catholic writer (1992).
86. Wagao 1992.
87. Westerlund 1980: esp. 57-62.
88. More detailed studies on particular groups will be necessary to provide a more profound analysis of revivalism in Tanzania.

References

Bahendwa, L.F. 1991. 'Christian-Muslim Relations in Tanzania', CSIC Papers (Centre for the Study of Islam and Christian-Muslim Relations, Selly Oak Colleges, Birmingham) (5): 14-17.

Barrett, D. 1982. *World Christian Encyclopaedia* Nairobi: Oxford University Press.

Breuer, R. 1993. 'Report on a Journey to Tanzania 4-23 Feb. 1993'. Unpublished paper, Misereor, Aachen.

Haafkens, J. 1991. *Islam and Christianity in Africa*. Revised text of a presentation at the AACC Symposium 'Problems and Promises of the Church in Africa in the Nineties', Mombasa, 9-16 Nov. 1991.

Gamanywa, S. 1993. "Risala Ya PCT Kwa Waziri Wa Mambo Ya Ndandi Na Naibu Waziri Mkuu Mhosimiwa A.L. Mrema". Unpublished document, 19 July.

Gifford, P. 1987. ' "Africa shall be saved": an Appraisal of Reinhard Bonnke's Pan-African Crusade', *Journal of Religion in Africa* 17, 63-92.

——. 1992: 'Reinhard Bonnke's Mission to Africa, and His 1991 Nairobi Crusade', in P. Gifford (ed.), *New Dimensions in African Christianity*, Nairobi, All African Conference of Churches.

Kettani, M.A. 1982. 'Muslim East Africa: An overview', *Journal: Institute of Muslim Minority Affairs* 4 (1-2), 104-19.

——. 1985. 'Muslim East Africa: An Overview', *Journal: Institute of Muslim Minority Affairs* 6(1), 219-20.

Kibira, J.M., 1960: *Aus einer afrikanischen Kirche*. Bielefeld: Verlagshandlung der Anstalt Bethel.

——. 1974. *Church, Clan and the World*. Studia Missionalia Upsaliensia XXI, Stockholm: Almqvist and Wiksell.

Ludwig, F. 1993. 'Ethnic Identities and National Identity as Factors in Modern Tanzanian Church History'. Unpublished paper given at historical seminar, University of Dar es Salaam.

Nyembo, S. 1992. 'Sheikh Yahya shortsighted over plight of Muslim', *Business Times*, Sept. 11, 8-9.

Omari, C.K. 1984. 'Christian – Muslim Relations in Tanzania: The Socio-Political Dimension', *Journal: Institute of Muslim Minority Affairs* 5(2), 373-90; *Bulletin on Islam and Christian – Muslim Relations in Africa* 2 (2), 1-22.

——. 1987. 'Christian – Muslim Relations in Tanzania', in P.J. Rajashekar (ed.), *Christian – Muslim Relations in Eastern Africa*, 61-8. Report of a seminar/workshop sponsored by the Lutheran World Federation and the Project for Christian – Muslim Relations in Africa. Nairobi.

Ranger, T.O. 1970. *The African Churches of Tanzania* (Historical Association of Tanzania Paper no. 5). Nairobi: East African Publishing House.

——. 1971. 'Christian Independency in Tanzania', in D. Barrett (ed.), *African Initiatives in Religion*, 122-41. Nairobi: East African Publishing House.

Rasmussen, L. 1993. *Christian – Muslim Relations in Africa: The Cases of Northern Nigeria and Tanzania Compared*. London: I.B. Tauris.

Said, M. 1989: 'Islam and Politics in Tanzania'. Unpublished paper given at the *Warsha* Conference on Daawa in East Africa, Nairobi, 19-20 May.

Shauri, S. 1983. 'General Secretariat', *Chrsitian Council of Tauzania 1983 Report*, 1-13.

Sicard, S. von. 1978. 'Christian and Muslim in East Africa', *Africa Theological Journal* 7(2): 53-67.

——. 1991. 'Islam in Tanzania', CSIC Papers (5), 1-13.

Smith, P. 1988. 'An experience of Christian – Muslim Relations in Tanzania', *Africa Ecclesiastical Review* 30 (2): 106-11.

Smith, P. 1990. 'Christianity and Islam in Tanzania: Development and Relationship', *Islamochristiana* 16, 171-82.

Veller, R. 1993. 'Zeichen und Wunder – die charismatische Bewegung erfasst die evangelischen Kirchen Ostafrikas', *Weltmission Heute* 13, 60-73.

Wagao, J. 1992. 'Religion and Economic Policy Reforms: Tanzania'. Unpublished paper, given at a symposium on Islamic revivalism in Dakar, Senegal.

Warsha n.d. 'Uchumi katika Uislam'. Unpublished paper.

Westerlund, D. 1980. *Ujamaa na Dini: A study of some aspects of society and religion in Tanzania*. Stockholm Studies in Comparative Religion 18, Stockholm: Almqvist and Wiksell International.

Woodsworth, N. 1989. 'Secessionist sentiment revives the ghosts of Zanzibar's Arab past', *Financial Times*, 11 July 1989.

DYNAMIC HINDUISM

TOWARDS A NEW HINDU NATION

Eva Hellman

During the 1980s a strong current of Hindu revivalism became apparent in India. The spokespersons for a Hinduization of Indian society were numerous and often highly articulate. Sometimes they even suggested that a Hinduization of India would be good not just for the Hindu majority,[1] but for the entire nation.

The Bharatiya Janata Party's (BJP) change of policy during the 1980s, and the party's successful performances in the general elections in 1989 and 1991, can be taken as evidence of the growing Hindu resurgence. During the 1980s the BJP adopted a Hindu profile and has since progressively raised it.[2] In the *Lok Sabha* elections in 1984 the party won only two seats,[3] the number of seats increased to 85 in the 1989 elections and after the elections in May – June 1991 the BJP had 119 *Lok Sabha* representatives, thus becoming the largest opposition party.[4] Approximately 20 per cent of the electorate voted for the BJP in the 1991 elections. The BJP thereby doubled its share of the votes as compared to the 1989 election, which was itself regarded as a success by the BJP.[5]

At the same time, the polarization of Hindus and Muslims became more accentuated. During the 1980s there was a steep rise in militant confrontations between the two communities. In the process of a growing Hindu resurgence and a reinforced polarization between Hindus and Muslims, religion played a focal and multi-dimensional role. The most obvious example is the Ramajanmabhumi-Babri Masjid controversy; that is, the Hindu campaign, launched in the mid-1980s, to build a Hindu temple in Ayodhya in Uttar Pradesh, where the Babri Masjid (Babur's mosque) was located.

The Ramajanmabhumi campaign

In 1984 the idea of liberating what was called the Ramajanmabhumi, Rama's birthplace, was introduced by the *Vishva Hindu Parishad* (VHP). According to the VHP, in 1528 the Mughal ruler Babur ordered the destruction of the *mandir* (temple) in the town Ayodhya, which marked the birthplace of Lord Rama. On that spot he had the Babri Masjid raised. Critics of this view state that Babur did not himself initiate the building of the mosque.[6] Furthermore they assert that there is no historical evidence to prove that a temple associated with Rama ever existed there.[7]

The VHP projected the demand for the rebuilding of the Rama temple as an issue of religious concern, as a step towards the recreation of Hindu pride, and even as a national concern. The Ramajanmabhumi campaign was represented as a protest against symbols of foreign rule over India; Har Mohan Lal, the then General Secretary of the VHP, said that the Babri Masjid was a reminder 'of the atrocities committed on the Hindus by the Mughal invaders'.[8] In February 1986 a local court allowed the building to be opened for Hindu worship. The emphasis of the campaign then changed, with general claims, like the liberation of the temple or the handing over of the site to Hindus, being replaced by the demand for the construction of a new Rama temple at the site.

By 1989 the Ramajanmabhumi controversy had developed into a major political issue. It appeared on the political agenda of the BJP and featured as a cornerstone in the party's campaign before the general elections. At the same time the VHP arranged a nationwide campaign which culminated in the foundation-laying ceremony of the proposed Rama temple. The political potential of the issue was further demonstrated by the BJP's performance in the general elections in 1991, which clearly proved that the BJP had emerged as the political channel for Hindu dissatisfaction and enthusiasm inspired by the Ramajanmabhumi campaign. In 1992, about 100,000 *kar sevaks* (construction volunteers) responded to a call by the VHP, the BJP and the *Rashtriya Svayamsevak Sangh* (RSS)[9] to resume construction work at the planned temple. A small mob of activists stormed past guards and pulled the mosque down.

The remainder of this chapter is devoted to an analysis of politicized Hinduism as represented by the VHP, the organization which launched, organized and spearheaded the Ramajanmabhumi campaign. The focus will be on the ideological foundations of this kind of politicized Hinduism, and if and in what respects politicized Hinduism challenges the ideas underlying the Indian secular state.[10]

The Vishva Hindu Parishad

The VHP is a Hindu umbrella organization. It was founded in 1964 by S.S. Apte, a *pracharak* (full-time activist) of the RSS. If the VHP is characterized with reference to its types of activity at different times, it is reasonable to distinguish between an early consolidation phase (1964-80), a later activist one (1981-90) and a period of emerging tension within the organization.

During the early phase of the VHP, the basic structure and organization of members evolved. Several social service projects were undertaken for the improvement of the material and social conditions of *asprishyas* (Untouchables). *Paravartan*,[11] or conversion work, played an important role during this early phase as did good-will work among the *sadhus* (the holy men, the religious specialists). The VHP also initiated organizational and doctrinal reforms of Hinduism. During this phase, all the activities mentioned above continued, but additional elements were introduced which gave the VHP a changed profile. The most obvious of these new elements were the country-wide mass campaigns intended to awaken and unite Hindus. In the 1980s three campaigns were launched; one of them – and by far the most successful – was the Ramajanmabhumi campaign.

The next period opened with the Minakshipuram conversions. In February 1981, approximately 1,000 Hindu untouchables were converted to Islam in Minakshipuram, a small village of about 1,300 untouchables in Tamil Nadu. The conversions provoked a strong Hindu reaction. At the national level the event was seen as an effort to destabilize the country by increasing the number of Muslims. Hindu critics regarded the conversions as a step towards an Islamization of all countries between West Asia and the Far East.

The developments of the VHP since the early 1990s have been characterized by its political involvement and its close ties with the BJP. At the same time these developments have forced the VHP to face a dilemma. After the elections in 1991, which brought the BJP into power in Uttar Pradesh, the party toned down the issue of the Rama temple. At the same time, radical elements among the *sadhus* and within the *Bajrang Dal*, the VHP's youth wing, demanded the immediate building of the temple, and threatened to break away from the VHP if their demands were not met.[12] In November 1991 it was unclear in what way the VHP would handle this problem. Was it to listen to the moderate voice of the BJP leadership? Would it give in to the demands of the radical element among the *sadhus* and within its youth organization? Would it split into moderate and extremist factions?

I leave the chronology of the VHP at the very peak of its clash between religious and political loyalties and turn to an analysis of three key concepts of the VHP: *dharma* (law; principle; norm; righteousness), *Bharat* (India) and *Hindu samaj* (Hindu society, the collective of Hindus).

Dharma

Dharma is undoubtedly a key concept for the VHP. Declarations by leading VHP functionaries on the mission of the organization clearly indicate that this is the case. In his speech at the world Hindu convention in Allahabad in 1966, S.S. Apte, the then General Secretary of the

VHP, stressed that he regarded *dharma* as pivotal for the survival of the Hindus. He remarked that: 'Amongst the Hindus of the world a sense of duty and obligations to the society which of late is fast disappearing, requires to be regenerated on the basis of our Dharma'.[13] Apte further suggested that one of the overall aims of the convention was the rejuvenation of *dharma*: 'To fulfil the object of rejuvenating and reviving our Dharma and culture, we have set before us the primary task of inviting all the Hindus spread the world over to a Parishad'.[14] In retrospect, this VHP conference was considered a milestone in the history of the protection of *dharma*.[15] Editorials of the VHP's official monthly, the *Hindu Vishva (HV)*, call attention to the fact that the task of the VHP is to establish *dharma* and to fight *adharma* (non-*dharma*).[16] The overall aims of the VHP are to protect the righteous, to punish evil-doers, and to establish the rule of *dharma*.[17] The motto of the VHP aptly summarizes the importance given to *dharma* over the years: *dharmo rakshati rakshitah*, which in the *HV* is rendered as 'if you protect Dharma, Dharma will protect you', or 'One who protects Dharma is protected in turn'.[18]

Although the concept of *dharma* recurs frequently in declarations on the main tasks of the organization, the VHP has not yet presented any definite normative interpretation of *dharma*. The absence of a well-defined body of propositions necessitates a reconstruction of the interpretation pursued by the VHP. Since the *HV* was envisaged as a 'practical guide in the understanding of the fundamental principles of Hindu Dharma' by S.S. Apte,[19] I will concentrate on the picture of *dharma* as presented in the *HV*. What emerges is representative of the predominant strand of the VHP.

Two main aspects of *dharma* are generally emphasized in the *HV*: *dharma* is on the one hand regarded as an eternal, universal, unchangeable principle which considers divinity to be at the core of existence, and lays down the fundamental unity between the divine and everything which exists. It is on the other hand also regarded as a norm for social, as well as individual behaviour, and in this aspect it is not eternal, unchangeable or universal, but prescribes rules according to the situation. Because in its second aspect *dharma* is adaptable to changing circumstances, it is compatible with reforms of different kinds. A *samanya dharma*: that is, a set of rules to be followed by all Hindus irrespective of caste and stage in life, is laid down. It covers all aspects of daily life; among these, for instance, are rules for individual behaviour, social and political duties and the proper handling of mass actions like the Ramajanmabhumi campaign.

However, it is not sufficient to distinguish between *dharma* as principle and *dharma* as norm, if we want to understand the involved view of the VHP on *dharma* – there is also an interaction between these aspects.

An early statement by S.S. Apte on the overall aims behind the efforts towardsd common code provides the basis for a discussion of the interaction of *dharma* as principle and *dharma* as norms of behaviour:

> We have to restate the rules of life to make the whole society live as one and indivisible organism. It is necessary to prescribe the code of Hindu conduct, the obligations and duties of everyone in the society and to define the social relations in a manner which will not be inconsistent or contradictory with the basic principles on which our eternal Society has evolved its structure.[20]

First of all, Apte underlines the need for the formulation of new norms for Hindus; norms which are to be adapted to the contemporary situation. Secondly, he stresses the necessity of the norms not being inconsistent with the basic principles on which the structure of Hindu society is said to have evolved. If this statement is read in the light of the preceeding analysis of *dharma*, it follows that *dharma* as norms of behaviour necessarily must be consistent with *dharma* as principle. The picture thus emerges of an overall eternal principle framing a variety of contingent rules covering all aspects of worldly life. *Dharma* as principle is identified with the characteristics claimed to be at the core of existence: divinity and unity. These fundamentals are to be implemented in society and in the life of the individual. *Dharma* as norms of behaviour is the concrete way to put these fundamentals into practice in mundane life. This model of Hinduism as a guide for social and individual behaviour should be seen as a simplified version of Svami Vivekananda's 'Practical vedanta', which propagates an ethical and social application of the *advaita vedanta*.[21]

The understanding of *dharma* in the *HV* is thus coloured by the neo-Hindu understanding of the *advaita vedanta*. *Dharma* as principle (unity, divinity) is to be implemented in the world. Hence we can conclude that important aspects of the traditional understanding of *advaita vedanta* are missing in the *HV* discourse. To Shankara and Ramanuja, knowledge about *Brahman* and *atman* has a bearing on soteriology: he who realises the identity between these entities is liberated from *samsara* (the cycles of birth and rebirth). In the *HV*, on the other hand, knowledge of *dharma* as principle has a bearing on this-worldly matters: ethical and political directives are to be derived from it. Parenthetically it may be added that the *HV* understanding of *dharma* has a closer resemblance to Ramanuja's *vishishtadvaita* (modified non-dualism) than to Shankara's *kevaladvaita* (absolute non-dualism). *Vishishtadvaita* assigns a definite reality to the world as god's modi, whereas *kevaladvaita* insists on the illusory nature of the world.

The VHP has adopted a specific method to decide what *dharma* as norms of behaviour implies. *Dharma* as norms of behaviour is to be postulated not by any single individual or by any cultural, political or religious group, but by the consensus of *sadhus* of, ideally, all Hindu denominations. By focusing on the *sadhu* as a guide on *dharma* and mundane matters and not only on spirituality in the narrow sense, the VHP propounds a new role to be adopted by the religious specialist. He is to guide society towards perfection by determining how *dharma* as principle or truth is to be implemented in the world. Thus the *sadhu* is important primarily as a *dharmacharya* (teacher of *dharma*) and not as a *guru* (spiritual preceptor).

The VHP has launched the *Dharma Samsad* (DS) as a body to collectively, and by consensus, establish the meaning of *dharma* as norms of behaviour. The DS, which in the *HV* is rendered into English as the 'Religious Parliament', is to be made up of *sadhus* representing all Hindu *sampradayas* (religious traditions), every Indian state and Hindu community in foreign countries. The total number of DS delegates to be nominated is 1,008.[22] It is still an open question which political role the DS, or a similar body of *sadhus*, is expected to perform in the envisaged *Hindu Rashtra* (Hindu India). Is it to function as a parliament, promulgating laws and directing the course of politics? Will the announced nomination of candidates make elections and political parties unnecessary? Will the DS merely be an advisory body to a politically-elected leadership? Two months before the first meeting of the DS in 1989, an editorial in the *HV* was highly critical of democracy based on adult franchise, which was considered to undermine the impartiality of the lawmaker. The editorial further asserted that in the past, lawmaking was entrusted to *sadhus*, who viewed everyone as equal and made concession to no particular group.[23] This kind of constitutional issue, which remains unsettled, deserves to be carefully studied by social scientists interested in state-formation in the Asian context.

The concept of Hindus as being under threat from hostile forces is at the heart of the VHP discourse. The most frequently mentioned enemies are Christians, Muslims and Communists, with secularists and materialists also being denounced as inimical forces. They are said to represent threats such as separatism, anti-nationalism and disregard for spiritual and ethical values.[24] The conflict between Hindus and other groups is not restricted to a hostility between groups of ordinary people; the antagonism is cosmologized and is said to take place between divine and demonic, or dharmic and adharmic forces.[25] It is not just the Hindus who are being threatened, but the entire order of the universe. This cosmologized conflict is displayed in Indian history, geography and society, as well as in the life of individual people. It can be summarized as a conflict between dharmic forces, working for the maintenance of the cosmic order, and adharmic forces, which are seen to be inimical to the cosmic order.

Bharat: from the holy land to the the holy nation-state

Even at a quick glance at VHP's activities and *HV* articles one realises that *Bharat* (India) is of prime importance in the thought pattern of the VHP. *Bharat* is depicted as a living entity,[26] as a deity to be worshipped,[27] as the only land for Hindus to live in,[28] and as having a mission to fulfil for the whole world.[29]

In the *HV, Bharat* is repeatedly depicted as the *original* and *only* homeland of the Hindus. Authors of articles in the *HV* consequently denounce the theory of an Aryan invasion into *Bharat*. The authors allege that there is no evidence in the Vedic literature, or in the *puranas*, to substantiate the view of an invasion. They insist that this theory, which is of Western origin, has the status of a myth based on assumption and imagination.[30] Political considerations are said to have been the prime motive behind the emergence of the theory; the British are accused of having ingeniously advocated the theory in order to further their policy of divide and rule.[31] Contributors to the *HV* maintain that the Aryans, who are equated with the Hindus, were the original inhabitants of *Bharat*. This might explain why the authors of *HV* articles avoid calling tribals *adivasis* (original inhabitants), but instead refer to them as backward people or just tribals. The repudiation of the theory of an Aryan invasion is not confined to VHP, however; it has grown into an accepted view in orthodox, as well as modernist, Hindu circles. Detailed arguments against the Aryan theory have been presented by, for instance, Svami Vivekananda,[32] the former leader of the RSS M.S. Golwalkar,[33] and Bharati Krishna Tirtha, the Shankaracharya of Puri (1925-60).[34] At the beginning of the 1990s the then BJP Uttar Pradesh government initiated the rewriting of historical manuals for primary and secondary schools. The revised history curriculum approved by the BJP government insists that the Aryans were the original inhabitants of India and not immigrants.

Bharat is depicted not only as the original and only homeland of the Hindus, but also as the place where Hindu culture and civilization have developed, where the common history of the Hindus has been played out, where Hindu gods have manifested themselves and where the founders of different Hindu schools have seen glimpses of the divine.[35] In the *HV* it is presupposed that *Bharat* and the Hindus constitute a unit which cannot be dissolved. *Bharat* is a necessary condition for the preservation of Hindus and Hinduism. Thus the land gains its importance from its forming the basic requirement for an alleged Hinduness. Furthermore *Bharat* is represented as the territorial basis for *Hindu Rashtra* (Hindu India).[36]

In official VHP material we meet two contradictory views on *Hindu Rashtra*: on the one hand *Bharat* is stated to be the *Hindu Rashtra*,[37] and on the other, the necessity of transforming India as it now is into

Hindu Rashtra is stressed.[38] The distinction between nation, which is a psychological and cultural entity, and state, which is a legal and political construction, clarifies the contradictory views on *Hindu Rashtra*. Accordng to the VHP, the Hindus are already a nation in a loose sense – with a common motherland, history and culture. *Bharat*, however, is not yet a Hindu state. VHP officials have stressed the need for installing a *Dharma rajya* (a dharmic state)[39] or *Ramarajya* (Rama's rule) in *Bharat*.[40] The VHP's legitimation of political power in terms of *dharma* is a further indication of its interest in state-formation as well as making Hindus consciously identify with the Hindu nation.

Bharat as the holy land, as well as the holy *Hindu Rashtra*, is personified as the goddess *Bharat Mata* (Mother India). Two main types of argument are given in the *HV* as a means to demonstrate the alleged divinity of the land: on the one hand *Bharat Mata* is held to be the concrete manifestation of divinity, and on the other hand *Bharat* is said to be the only land where gods have been incarnated and where *gurus* of *dharma* have been born. In this way they have impregnated the land with divinity. *Bharat Mata*, who is a new goddess in the Hindu pantheon, is depicted in the traditional way:[41] she wears a richly embroidered *sari* (an outer garment worn by Hindu women, consisting of a long piece of cotton or silk worn around the body), her headgear is golden crown encrusted with jewels, she is adorned with heavy golden ornaments with gems marking the different *chakras* (centres of power), her smile is beatific and her right hand is raised in the blessing gesture (*mudra*), and in her left hand is her attribute weapon, the saffron coloured flag. The goddess is represented as standing on *Bharat*, which is her visible form, with her animal mount (*vahan*) near her. The pictorial representations of *Bharat Mata* contain elements which signal strength, force, might and sovereignty – for example there is a halo fire around her head, and the lion is her animal, while her sharp-edged flagpole is a potential spear. She stands firmly and self-confidently on *Bharat* carrying the saffron flag which is the symbol of her supremacy.

In the VHP discourse on *Bharat* there are thus two different dimensions, one political and one metaphysical. These dimensions are equally important, and they are interrelated. In the political dimension *Bharat* is important in the context of a Hindu nation-state, and in the metaphysical, *Bharat* is important as the divine and worshipful goddess *Bharat Mata*. To ensure the objective of creating a Hindu nation-state, a variety of political claims are put forth by the VHP including demands for the integration and the stability of the Indian Union, which imply a hard line towards regional separatism, a strong defence and claims which involve radical constitutional changes.

Hindu samaj: the holy people

In the VHP discourse at least two different interpretations of *Hindu samaj* are pursued: on the one hand *Hindu samaj* is depicted as the collective of present-day Hindus, and on the other as the future ideal Hindu society.

The *actual Hindu society* is represented as being torn asunder by caste conflicts, regional separatism and sectarian strife. In addition untouchability, dowry, corruption and one-sided preoccupation with the spiritual aspects of life are seen as conducive to the present weakness of Hindu society. 'Foreign'-isms (capitalism, communism, materialism), missionary endeavours from Christians and Muslims, and the infiltration of Muslims from Bangladesh and Pakistan, are mentioned as examples of external threats to *Hindu samaj*. The increase in the numbers of Muslims, who are said to have a higher birthrate than the Hindus, is presented as posing a threat to the Hindu majority. Two of the prerequisites for the strengthening of the *Hindu samaj* lies, according to the VHP, in the unification of its different sections and in the formulation and implementation of pro-Hindu political claims.

The *ideal Hindu society* is represented as a metaphysical entity which involves integrative mundane models. The VHP compares the ideal society to a body which is comprised of different parts, each part having its specific function which it has to perform perfectly in order to secure the well-being, growth and strength of the body. In the *HV* it is proclaimed that in the past *Hindu samaj* was just such an ideal society. This ideal society is referred to as *Virat Purusha*, which is translated as the 'corporate person of society'.[42] It is also designated as *Samaj Purusha*, which is translated in the same way.[43] The ideal Hindu society is said to have been the highest developed society that ever existed.[44] With a multitude of functional groups in perfect co-operation, *Virat Purusha*, or the ideal society, is described as having countless eyes, hands and heads, but only one heart.[45] Now the *Virat Purusha* is to be re-established: the 'I' of the individual is to be merged with the 'We' of the ideal society – the *Virat Purusha*.[46] This ideal is reflected in the different organizational models for Hindu society recommended by the VHP. As has been hinted at above, the VHP denounces the present caste system according to which one's position is determined by one' birth and instead wants to introduce the *varna* system in a modernist version as the basic organizational model.

In the *HV*, VHP's first General Secretary S.S. Apte has given an outline of the ideal *varna* system (caste system).[47] In his argumentation the *Purushasukta (Rigveda* 10.90) plays a prominent role. This vedic hymn describes the creation of the universe in terms of the sacrifice of *Purusha*. The parts of him become portions of the universe. Only two verses of the hymn are referred to in Apte's argument:

> When they divided Purusha, into how many parts did they dispose him? What (did) his mouth (become)? What are his two arms, his thighs, his two feet called?

> His mouth was the Brahman, his two arms were made the warrior, his two thighs the Vaishya; from his two feet the Shudra was born.[48]

According to Apte the *Purushasukta* describes the ideal society as one indivisible and integrated whole. He further asserts that the hymn mentions the four *varnas* as integral organs of the living body of the *Samaj Purusha*, which he also calls the 'corporate person of society'. The *brahmans* (priests) function as the head, or intellect, of *Samaj Purusha*, the *kshatriyas* (warriors) defend it, the *vaishyas* (farmers and merchants) produce the wealth, and the *shudras* (servants) are assigned the hard work of keeping the body of the *Samaj Purusha* in perfect order by serving, cleaning and washing. Apte concludes that the *varnas*, as described in the *Purushasukta*, are all indispensible for the upkeep of the *Samaj Purusha*, hence they are of equal worth in the task of keeping the corporate person of society living and moving.

Apte continues his interpretation of the hymn by stating that the individual belongs to a specific *varna* not because of his birth but because of his talents and virtues in the present life: 'It is only by the "sanskaras", i.e., the impacts influences, impressions, education, nursing of good qualities and performing the assigned functions, that one becomes entitled to belong to a particular class or Varna and not on account of birth.'[49] Apte recommends the introduction of the *varna* system in this modernist version in contemporary India.[50] This objective would mean a major reform of the caste system involving the abolition of untouchability and, at least theoretically, permitting mobility between *varnas*. It would also imply the introduction of a completely new social structure, characterized by the emphasis on integration and absence of conflicts, with complementary groups working for a common goal – the perfect functioning of society. In this integrative system where every individual is assigned a place according to his ability to perform the desired functions, there would be no reservation of jobs and educational opportunities for members of lower castes.

As already stated, there is a metaphysical dimension in the VHP's view of the ideal *Hindu samaj*: it is regarded as a living god and as the manifestation of *Parameshvar* ('the Almighty'). An *HV* editorial illustrates this metaphysical representation:

> Hindu society, whole and integrated, should be the single point of devotion for all of us. No other consideration whether of caste, sect,

language, province etc., should be allowed to come in the way of that devotion to society. This is the criterion of real devotion. In the devotion to our LIVING GOD, the Hindu society, all the ruling disruptive passions in our minds today have to be given up, as they come in the way of discharging the essential and foremost duty of upholding and strengthening the inherent unity of our people. May we all rise to take the life-giving message of our innate unity, transcending and submerging all other barriers, to every hearth and home and light up in every heart the effulgent flame of the realisation of the singleliving 'SAMAJA-DEVATA' throbbing with life in her multitude of glorious expressions.[51]

This short passage alludes to three interconnected theological ideas held by the VHP. First, the ideal *Hindu samaj* is identified with God. In the quoted *HV* editorial this God is referred to as *Samajdevata* (God of society) and *Pratyakshdevata* (living God).[52] As mentioned above, another editorial states that the ideal *Hindu samaj* is a manifestation of *Parameshvar*.[53] Second, this God should be the object of worship and devotion,[54] which is referred to as *samajbhakti* (worship of society).[55] Thirdly, the acts of *samajbhakti* are qualified as service,[56] or *seva*.[57] The *HV* is not explicit as to how to understand this kind of service; however, I would suggest that *samajbhakti* in the VHP discourse is equivalent to selfless activity, through which, in the VHP's understanding, the ideal *Hindu samaj* is actualized and maintained.

Dynamic Hinduism

Having given an outline of three key-concepts of the VHP: *dharma, Bharat* and *Hindu samaj*, I would like to suggest that the VHP represents a new development of Hindu tradition which I tentatively label 'dynamic Hinduism'.[58]

I will start by drawing a typology of dynamic Hinduism which can be represented in the following manner:

                future
this-worldly   present   change   outer activity   renunciation
other-worldly   past   consolidation inner activity

Five distinct characteristics of dynamic Hinduism are delineated. First, there is an emphasis on this-worldly matters. The prime objective is to build a new and ideal India which will eventually provide an exemplary model to be followed by the rest of the world. In this emphasis on mundane matters there are two interrelated dimensions which are equally important: the political and the metaphysical. In my analysis of the key-concepts of the VHP – that is, *dharma, Bharat* and *Hindu samaj* – this intermingling is demonstrated in detail: *dharma* as a metaphysical principle gives guidelines for politics; *Bharat* is the holy land as well as a prerequisite for the survival of the Hindus; *Hindu samaj* is not only the collective of all Hindus but also a potentially divine entity. Second, there is an emphasis on present conditions. Although the organization recommends the revival of past ideals and projects an ideal future, the present situation is in focus. A perspective of threat is delineated, which stresses the necessity for mobilization. Now is the time when Hindus have to wake up and defend themselves, *Bharat* and *dharma*. In the perspective of immediate threat, a metaphysical dimension has been introduced: not only are the Indian Union and the collective of Hindus depicted as being under threat from hostile forces today, but the holy land of *Bharat* is seen as being torn asunder, and the divine ideal, *Hindu samaj*, is represented as a mere potentiality. Even the fundamentals of existence are depicted as being seriously at risk at the present time. Now is the time to mobilize against the disruptive forces. Third, change is emphasized, not consolidation. It is important to stress that the vision of a global utopia is not at present in focus. The prime objective of the VHP is pragmatically limited to India, which should be transformed and renewed. Fourth, a prerequistite for the transformation of India is human effort. In this effort it is the active, not the contemplative life, which is regarded as the necessary means of bringing about the desired change. Collective efforts of various kinds are emphasized, and violence is not condemned. This activity is represented as religious acts, and is referred to as *puja* (worship), *yagya* (sacrifice), *seva* (service to God) or *bhakti* (devotion). Lastly, *tyag* (renunciation) should be the guiding principle of the activities undertaken. The individual should be totally dedicated to the cause of bringing about the change of India and should renounce his or her individual desires.

The religious and political expression of dynamic Hinduism

All religious traditions define the *summum bonum* of human life. They locate the goal which is to be strived for, and they specify how to realize this objective. This *summum bonum* is offered as the ultimate concern to the individual; its realization is held to make life worth living. Examples of ultimate concerns presented by different religious traditions include *moksa* (liberation) *nirvana* or *soteria* (salvation), *he basileia tou theou* (the kingdom of God).

With dynamic Hinduism a new ultimate concern, to be accepted by all Hindus, is introduced. In *Bharat* the Hindus should implement *dharma*, as understood by this tradition, in all walks of life. Thereby the potential divinity of *Bharat* and *Hindu samaj* will be actualized.

The final result of these efforts is represented as the sovereign and divine *Bharat Mata.*

This ultimate concern of establishing *Bharat Mata* is located within *samsara* (the cycles of birth and rebirth). It implies that *Bharat* and *Hindu samaj* should be liberated from *adharma.* This is to be seen in contrast to the traditional Hindu outlook according to which the individual should be liberated from the effects of *karma* and eventually from *samsara.* In the new context the emphasis is on the collective/societal and the this-worldly. Moreover, in the outlook of dynamic Hinduism, the divinity of the collective of Hindus is emphasized, not the divinity of the single individual.

Furthermore, when *Bharat Mata* has been actualized in *Bharat* by the collective effort of the Hindus, she is to become the model for the rest of the world. In her world-guiding function she is referred to as the *atman* (soul) of the world or as the *Jagadguru* – that is, the *guru* of the world. Hence, once the Hindus have manifested divinity in the *dharmaksetra* (field of *dharma*) of *Bharat*, they are to make the whole world divine by providing ideal patterns of life. Thus, *Bharat*, the centre of the world, is necessary for the world's liberation from *adharma* and for the actualization of divinity throughout the world.

I now suggest that dynamic Hinduism is developing its external fundamentals: that is, an alleged line of predecessors, a creed, new cultic forms, new cultic centres and common religious leaders, which should be minimally accepted by every Indian. In specifying the kinds of external fundamentals which are emerging, I refer to the *Ekatmata stotra* (the Unity hymn), which is a Sanskrit hymn in thirty-three verses. At a meeting of the central advisory board of the VHP, one of its more important members, Svami Satyamitrananda,[59] recommended that the *Ekatmata stotra* should be popularized among all Hindus.[60]

The hymn describes the fundamentals of Hinduism as conceived by this tradition. It begins with a veneration of the Supreme Lord (*paramatman*) and Nature (*prakriti*), and goes on to express veneration of *Bharat Mata.* The remaining thirty verses enumerate holy places in *Bharat*, books to be revered and women to be worshipped as mother goddesses. Further categories include great men (like Krishna and Rama), noble souls (like the Buddha and Shankara), brave warriors (like Shivaji *c.* 1600 CE) and scientists (like the materialist Caraka *c.* 100 CE). This inventory is followed by an enumeration and a veneration of devotees of *Bharat Mata (bhaktas)*; they are designated as socio-religious leaders and *viras* (heroes) who have revived Hindu society. The list begins with Ramakrishna (the founder of the Ramakrishna Mission and the *guru* of Svami Vivekananda) and includes among others Svami Dayananda Sarasvati (the founder of the reformist *Arya Samaj*), Svami Vivekananda, B.G. Tilak (the Maharashtrian revolutionary who recommended violence to be used against British colonial power), V.D. Savarkar (who launched the concept of *hindutva* – Hindu-ness), K.B. Hedgewar (the founder of the RSS) and ends with M.S. Golwakar (the RSS leader who was one of the founding fathers of the VHP).

The hymn would seem to indicate that a creed which expresses the basics of dynamic Hinduism is emerging. According to this outlook, *Bharat Mata* is a concrete manifestation of *paramatman* (God). The geography of *Bharat* is holy, and the heritage which the divine *Hindu samaj* has evolved through its history is sacred. Special attention is given to alleged defenders of *Bharat Mata*. The enumerated *bhaktas* of *Bharat Mata* or *viras* should be regarded as acclaimed predecessors of dynamic Hinduism. The alleged line of successors which is drawn by the VHP suggests that dynamic Hinduism is a *parampara* (tradition, or line of succession between teacher and pupil) in the making.

Further external fundamentals are emerging which deserve to be thoroughly studied. A new Hindu leadership is being launched. The *Dharma Samsad* represents this line of development. It is to lay down the fundamentals of a code of correct Hindu behaviour. New collective ceremonies for ensuring temporal aims are being created: *yagya*-ceremonies, *puja, rathyatra* (processions). Ceremonies for the veneration of martyrs are also appearing and new festivals are being developed. The launching of a new religious centres is recommended. Examples of such centres at the local level are the *mandirs* (temples) for collective rituals recommended by the first *Dharma Samsad*.[61] The proposed Rama temple in Ayodhya, Krishna's birthplace in Mathura, and Siva's manifestation in Benares are likely to be singled out as places of all-Indian importance.

It has been revealed that there is a strong political emphasis in the VHP's outlook, and that political claims are put forward in order to protect alleged Hindu interests. The introduction of a common civil code, the ban on cow-slaughter, the compulsory teaching of Sanskrit and Yoga in schools, the legal restraint on the conversion of Hindus and the liberation of Ramajanmabhumi are examples of such claims. To protect *Bharat* from threats, a check on illegal immigration is demanded, as is a hard line towards separatist movements. It has been maintained , moreover, that a new constitution based on *dharma* must be implemented. Thus, the political claims which are put forward range form the moderate, like the demand for a common civil code, to the far-reaching, like the introduction of a constitution based on *dharma*, in the VHP's understanding of the term.

For the communication of its message, and for the mobilization of the Hindu masses, dynamic Hinduism has adopted and developed a multitude of techniques. It is not only the written word (magazines, pamphlets, books, advertisements in the press) which are important,

but also audio-visual techniques, like videos and tapes. In the Ramajanmabhumi campaign there emerged another technique of mass communication: the well-planned, nationwide campaign drawing heavily
on Hindu motives, symbols and cultic elements. In the Ramajanmabhumi
campaign, familiar traditional Hindu elements, like the *puja* and the
rathyatra,[62] have been deliberately exploited. However, the approach
in the campaign to these elements is different from the traditional one.
The *rathyatra* and the *puja* are no longer local matters, but attain a
national dimension. The motorized *raths* (chariots) cover long distances
and pass through cities, towns and villages familiarizing crowds with
the message. The *rathyatras* and *pujas* are not primarily of spiritual
significance, but are held in order to create massive Hindu support
for the political claims put forward in the campaign. The fact that the
campaign has been intensified at important Hindu festivals has been
no doubt conducive to the massive Hindu participation. The Hindu
elements discernable in the campaign are characterized by modernism:
a traditional Hindu phenomenon appears in a new context, is given
a new content of a political character and is used for the mobilization
of Hindus. In this variant of modernism, the traditional phenomenon,
which retains much of its traditional value and appeal, transfers its
power to the new phenomenon.

Hence, in its political expression, dynamic Hinduism challenges the
established political order and legitimizes political power in metaphysical
terms. Furthermore, it uses Hindu symbols and Hindu phenomena in
a modernist shape in the formulation of its aims and in order to spread
its message.

Dynamic Hinduism and other religious traditions

Dynamic Hinduism makes a distinction between religions which have
originated in *Bharat* and the Semitic religions. The former are all said
to be based on *dharma*.[63] This is not the case with the Semitic religions
which are criticized for their alleged intolerance and exclusivism.[64] In
order to highlight this difference, we introduce the distinction between
'dharmic religious traditions', that is religions of *Bharat*, and 'non-
dharmic religious traditions'. Within the 'dharmic religious traditions'
a distinction is also made between 'core Hindu traditions' and other
traditions.

In the efforts to establish that Sikhs, Buddhists and Jains are in
fact Hindus, symbols and aspects which are, or have been, important
to the self-understanding of these religious traditions are highlighted.
Thus the Sikhs are represented as the martial defenders of *dharma*.[65]
The ideals of sacrifice and martyrdom are stressed.[66] The Buddha's
alleged rejection of caste is underlined.[67] The Jain emphasis on *ahimsa*

(non-violence) is acknowledged. However, in the context of dynamic Hinduism the implications of this Jain commandment of non-violence are severely restricted: *ahimsa* implies merely the prohibition of the killing of animals and the infliction of mental torture to one's neighbour.[68] Since these aspects, which are eulogized by dynamic Hinduism, are said to be lacking in much of contemporary Hinduism, Sikhism, Buddhism and Jainism are projected as important revitalizing forces within the Hindu tradition. Individual Sikhs, Buddhists and Jains are given definite roles within Hindu society. It is to be noted, however, that the VHP highlights only the social and moral aspects of Sikhism, Buddhism and Jainism – no attention is paid to ontology, soteriology or cultic elements.

When dharmic religious traditions other than Sikhism, Buddhism and Jainism are considered, a somewhat different picture emerges. It is suggested that representatives of 'core Hindu tradition' have served as defenders of *dharma* or reformers of *Hindu samaj*. In addition they are held to have laid down different spiritual paths conducive to the spiritual development of the individual. It is alleged that the Hindu sages and seers have seen glimpses of God, but none has seen the whole truth.[69] Therefore, it is argued, the 'core Hindu traditions' are all necessary, and equally valuable, spiritual paths leading to God or liberation.[70] The diversity in the spiritual field is reinforced. It is said to provide a spiritual path for everybody,[71] by affording the individual the possibility to choose a spiritual path appropriate to her/his disposition.[72] This approach is not controversial in contemporary Hindu thought. It is accepted within the current (orthodox) *smarta* tradition.[73]

As mentioned above, dynamic Hinduism makes a distinction between the religious traditions which have originated in *Bharat* and religions which are of foreign origin. The former are said to be based on *dharma* and to have made – and to be able to make – valuable contributions to the development of Hindu society. This is not the case with religions like Christianity and Islam. They are, among other things, accused of intolerance. Even Christians who actively strive for the indigenization of Christianity are criticized and ridiculed in the *HV*. An article entitled 'The so-called Christian Yogis and Sanyasis' claims that Bede Griffiths and Henri Le Saux 'offend Hindu religious sentiment with their syncretistic religious experiments'; also that the 'crucified yoga' taught by them is, at best, 'useful in treating frazzeled [sic] nerves and on par with hot baths, good whiskey, and Irish story-telling'.[74]

According to dynamic Hinduism, all dharmic and non-dharmic religious traditions are to be subordinated to the religious expression of dynamic Hinduism. This feature, we contend, can be understood as a subordinating inclusivism. Since the VHP makes an evaluating distinction between dharmic and non-dharmic religious traditions, this kind of inclusivism can be further qualified as subordinating, hierarchical inclusivism.

Dynamic Hinduism and Indian secularism

The preamble to the Indian constitution states that India shall be a secular state.[75] In Hindi the secular state is rendered as *dharma nirpeksha rajya*,[76] a state which is unconcerned about, or indifferent towards, religion. As is well-documented, the concept of the secular state has been assigned two different interpretations in India. On the one hand, there is the Western meaning of separating state and religion, which in the Indian context has been referred to as a Nehruvian model of secularism, and on the other hand, there is the interpretation of a state aiding all religions impartially. This has been called a Gandhian model of secularism.[77] As has been illustrated by D.E. Smith, both models have been operative in post-independence Indian politics.[78]

This section briefly asks what the fate of Indian secularism would be if dynamic Hinduism were allowed to set the agenda of Indian politics. We recall the VHP's interpretation of *dharma*. The tripartite relationships between *dharma* as principle, *dharma* as norms of behaviour and the *sadhus* as interpreters of *dharma* is important as a model of legitimation in a twofold way. First, it legitimizes prescriptions of all kinds: recommendations on morality, on social and political behaviour, laws and constitutional regulations. By stating the prescriptions to be in accordance with *dharma*, the *sadhus*, who are held to be experts on *dharma*, authorize the prescriptions. Secondly, it legitimizes political power in a specific way. The VHP has repeatedly stressed the necessity for conducting politics in conformity with *dharma* and argued that the *sadhu*, in his capacity as expert on *dharma*, should have a decisive influence on the political process.[79] According to this argument, he who follows *dharma* is the legitimate ruler. As demonstrated in the sections on *Bharat* and *Hindu samaj*, dynamic Hinduism as represented by the VHP does not restrict its discourse on the land and the people to a political dimension, but adds a metaphysical dimension. According to this outlook, the goddess *Bharat Mata* is a personification of the land as well as of the envisaged ideal Hindu nation-state. She is held to be divine and worshipful. By identifying the envisaged objective of *Hindu Rashtra* (a Hindu India) with the divine *Bharat Mata*, the VHP introduces a legitimizing element. The Hindus have a legitimate right to fight for a state which is in reality the manifestation of divinity in the temporal sphere. The VHP's representation of the ideal *Hindu samaj* as a divine organism is a conflict-reducing model which is metaphysically legitimated. It reduces actual conflicts in Indian society by providing integrative allegedly divine models for behaviour. Tribals, untouchables, women, workers, members of different castes, linguistic groups, regional groups, even Christians and Muslims, are thereby integrated into Hindu patterns of behaviour.[80]

By legitimizing political power in metaphysical terms – that is *dharma* which implies divinity – and not in secular terms, like the consent of the people, dynamic Hinduism represents a challenge to secularism in the Western or Nehruvian understanding. Since dynamic Hinduism in addition legitimizes political claims in metaphysical terms, this challenge is further strengthened.

According to the VHP, all religious traditions – Semitic ones as well as indigenous ones – should be subordinated to dynamic Hinduism, to which every Indian should subscribe. Dynamic Hinduism is thus presented as the future official national religion of India, whereas it is recommended that the other religious traditions, being of less value, should be the concern of the individual only. Gandhian secularism with its insistence on religious tolerance and official support for all religious traditions is not compatible with dynamic Hinduism.

Notes

1. Percentage of population according to community: Hindus 82.64; Muslims 11.35; Christians 2.43; Sikhs 1.96; Buddhists 0.71; Jains 0.48. It should be noted that this census excludes Assam. (Census 1981: viii.)
2. Gupta 1986: 19; Noorani 1990a: 29ff.
3. The parliament consists of the *Lok Sabha* (lower house) and the *Rajya Sabha* (upper house), members of the former being elected at least every five years, members of the smaller upper house being Presidential nominees or elected by the states.
4. General election 1991: 20. The by-elections in November resulted in 121 BJP MPs. (Agha 1991: 31.) In the *Lok Sabha* there are 545 members.
5. In the 1991 election the BJP won a substantial number of votes in the Hindi belt: in Delhi and in Uttar Pradesh the party won a good 30% of the votes, in Rajasthan and in Madhya Pradesh the figure was approximately 40% and in Gujarat a good 50% voted for this party. (General election 1991: 22.) It is noticeable that the party won 29% of the votes in Karnataka. The BJP has announced the intention of getting a foothold in south India. (Vishwanathan 1991: 19ff.)
6. Ahmed & Shukla 1986: 6-7; Babri Masjid 1990: 218f; Chandra *et al* n.d.: 3f.
7. Chandra *et al* n.d.: 3; Engineer 1990: 7-8; Noorani 1990b: 64, 67; Shrivastava 1990: 38. Bakker 1991: 91, however, supports the Hindu view that a Rama temple dating form the eleventh century was demolished before the erection of the Masjid.
8. *HV* 21 (7): 4f.
9. Of the Hindu nationalist organizations emerging during the colonial era, the one that remains the most vital today is the RSS.
10. For a more detailed and a fuller documented discussion of the Vishva Hindu Parishad and contemporary political Hinduism, see Hellman 1993.
11 In the early years of the organization, conversion to Hinduism was referred to by

the word *paravartan*,lit. to turn around (to the ancestral faith). In 1985 it was renamed *dharma prasar*, lit. the expansion or dispersion of *dharma*, an expression which is more in tune with the overall profile of the VHP. (*HV* 20 (8), 21.)

12. See Awasthi & Aiyar 1991: 14ff.
13. Visheshank 1966: 89.
14. Ibid.: 8.
15. *HV* 14 (7-8), 6f.
16. *HV* 17 (1), 3. This quotation, as well as the following one, should be regarded as paraphrases of *Bhagavadgita* 4. 7-8.
17. *HV* 24 (12), 2.
18. *HV* 20 (2), 29; 16 (1), 4. This *pada* in Sanskrit is not uncommon in the classical *smriti*- literature. See *Manusmriti* 8: 15; *Mahabharata* III: 313, 128; XII: 90, 156.
19. *HV* 5 (3), 102.
20. *HV* 4 (10), 48.
21. 'Practical vedanta' was the title of a series of lectures given by Vivekananda in London. For the lectures, see Vivekananda 1945: 289-356. It should be noted that Vivekananda pursues a new interpretation of the classical *advaita vedanta* doctrines as represented by Shankara, c.800 CE.
22. *HV* 19 (9), 37; 21 (4), 19.
23. *HV* 19 (4), 5.
24. *HV* 5 (3), 18; 5 (4-5), 4; 20 (3), 32; Warning n.d.
25. *HV* 9 (1), 5.
26. *HV* 22 (8),' 2.
27. *HV* 19 (3), 43.
28. *HV* 25 (6), 27.
29. *HV* 24 (2), 5.
30. *HV* 19 (11), 25ff; 20 (4), 17ff; 21 (3), 21ff.
31. *HV* 19 (11), 25; 20 (4), 20. In order to denounce the birthright of the Aryans (read: Hindus) to Bharat, so the argument goes, the British maintained that the Aryans invaded India.
32. *HV* 20 (4), 20, 23; Vivekananda 1946: 293, 1947: 436-7. In Vivekananda (1945: 333) a slightly different view is propounded.
33. Golwalkar 1945: 10-13.
34. Tirtha 1985: 66-8.
35. *HV* 21 (2), 8ff.
36. See e.g. *HV* 24 (2), 5. *Hindu Rashtra* can be translated literally as 'Hindu nation'.
37. See e.g. *HV* 26 (9), 2; 27 (2), 2.
38. See e.g. *HV* 24 (5), 60; 26(11), 11; 27 (3), 12; 27 (4), 3.
39. *HV* 21 (4), 21.
40. *HV* 22 (5), 22; 23 (2), 17.
41. The following account is based on Ekatmata yagya 1983; *HV* 19 (3), 74; 21 (1), 4; 21 (8), cover picture; 22 (8), cover picture.
42. *HV* 12 (12), 5 (Hindi edition); 12 (12), 5. The English version of the article is almost identical to Golwalkar 1980: 131-3. Some minor editing has been done, however.
43. Apte 1979: 108.
44. *HV* 12 (12), 5.
45. *HV* 14 (7-8), 26, 34.
46. *HV* 14 (7-8), 34.
47. Apte 1979: 108; *HV* 12 (12), 33-6. The ensuing account of Apte's argumentation is based on these articles.
48. Macdonell 1984: 200ff.
49. Apte 1979: 108.
50. *HV* 12 (12), 36; Apte 1979: 108.

51. *HV* 12 (7), 5. This article is almost identical with Golwalkar 1980: 157f. Only some minor editing has been done.
52. *HV* 12 (7), 5.
53. *HV* 13 (5), 5 (Hindi edition).
54. *HV* 13 (5), 5; 19 (3), 22.
55. *HV* 12 (7), 5; 19 (3), 22.
56. *HV* 7 (3), 51.
57. *HV* 7 (3), 51; 12 (12), 5 (Hindi edition).
58. The expression 'dynamic Hinduism' (Hindi: *gatiman hindu dharma*) has been employed as a self-referent for the kind of Hinduism which is recommended by the VHP. See *HV* 5 (3), 61; 5 (3), 56 (Hindi edition).
59. He is a VHP trustee and a former Shankaracharya of the Bhanpurapitha. In the late 1960s he renounced his office in order to work for the VHP. Hindu awakening n.d.:24; *HV* 5 (1), 47.
60. The hymn is reproduced in *HV* 21 (2) 8ff; 24 (5), 44f. (Hindi edition).
61. *HV* 19 (5), 5. See also *HV* 21 (4), 23.
62. The *rathyatra* is a common phenomenon in traditional Hinduism. To celebrate, for instance, the birthday of a god, a *yatra* (journey) is arranged. The *murti* (image), or a duplicate image, is brought out of the *mandir* (temple) on a *rath* and is drawn or carried through the streets to give *darshan* (vision) to the *bhaktas*. Within traditional Hinduism these religious processions are local rituals which are confined to the ritual/sacred sphere. On a day prescribed by the cult-calender and in a manner regulated by the cult manual of the temple, the god leaves his home and undertakes the journey. On this auspicious day the devotees are offered the opportunity of gaining merit by seeing, and being seen, by the god.
63. *HV* 5 (3), 49.
64. *HV* 5 (3), 18.
65. See Phadnis 1990: 259.
66. See Dietrich 1987: 123.
67. Caste and caste distinctions were abolished in the *sangha*, the order of ordained monks and nuns and novices, but remained among the Buddhist laity (Thomas 1971: 110).
68. *HV* 25 (3), 31.
69. *HV* 21 (11), 6.
70. *HV* 23 (3), 19f.
71. *HV* 19 (4), 4.
72. *HV* 23 (3), 20f.
73. Tirtha 1985: 53.
74. *HV* 25 (8), 37f.
75. 'We, the people of India, having solemnly resolved to constitute India into a sovereign socialist secular democratic republic... do hereby adopt, enact and give to ourselves this constitution'. Constitution 1988: Preamble.
76. Halbfass 1988: 310.
77. For discussions of the Indian interpretations of secularism, see Nandy 1985; Rao 1989; Smith 1963: 493ff, especially 498f.
78. Smith 1963: 498.
79. *HV* 20 (2), 39; 22:7, 7; 24:(2), 4f.
80. The VHP's inclusive definition of Hindu makes it theoretically possible for every Indian, including Christians and Muslims, to identify as a member of *Hindu samaj*. In order to count as a Hindu, one has merely to respect certain values which are said to have originated in the Indian peninsula. For the VHP's inclusive definition of Hindu, see *HV* 5 (3), 62.

References

Agha, Z. 1991. 'By-elections. Congress [I] scores', *India Today* 15 December: 31-2.

Ahmed, N., and R.L. Shukla 1986. *Babri Mosque or Rama Janam Temple*. New Delhi: Institute of Objective Studies.

Apte, S.S. 1979. 'Modernising the Hindu samaj and dharma', *World Hindu Conference 1979*: 98-108. Bombay: Vishva Hindu Parishad.

Awasthi, D. and S.A. Aiyar 1991. 'RSS-BJP-VHP. Hindu divided family', *India Today* 30 November: 14-21.

Babri Masjid 1990, 'Babri Masjid movement coordination committee's comments on the document presented by V.H.P. to the government of India on 6 Oct., 1989', in A.A. Engineer (ed.), *Babri-Masjid Ramjanambhoomi Controversy*, 218-24. Delhi: Ajanta Publications.

Bakker, H. 1991. 'Ayodhya: A Hindu Jerusalem', *Numen* 38 (1), 80-109.

Census 1981. *Census of India 1981, Series-1 India, Paper 3 of 1984, Household Population by Religion of Head of Household*. Delhi: Controller of Publications.

Chandra, B. *et al* n.d. *The Political Abuse of History. Babri Masjid-Rama Janmabhumi Dispute*. New Delhi: Centre for Historical Studies, Jawaharlal Nehru University.

Dietrich, A. 1987. 'The Khalsa resurrected. Sikh Fundamentalism in the Punjab', in L. Caplan (ed.), *Studies in Religious Fundamentalism*. London: Macmillan.

Ekatmata yagya 1983. *Ekatmata Yagya Yugabd 5085*. New Delhi: Vishva Hindu Parishad.

Engineer, A.A. 1990. 'Editorial. Introduction', in A.A. Engineer (ed.), *Babri-Masjid Ramjanambhoomi Controversy*, VIII, 1-15. Delhi: Ajanta Publications.

General election 1991. 'General election. What the results mean', *India Today*, 15 July, 19-22.

Golwalkar, M.S. 1945. *We or Our Nationhood Defined*. Nagpur: Bharat Prakashan (1939).

——. 1980 (1966). *Bunch o; Thoughts*. Bangalore: Jagarana Prakashana.

Gupta, S. 1986. 'Bharatiya Janata Party veering right', *India Today* 31 May: 19-21.

Halbfass, W. 1988 (1981). *India and Europe:. An Essay in Understanding*. Albany: State University of New York Press.

Hellman, E. 1993. *Political Hinduism: The Challenge of the Visva Hindu Parisad*. Uppsala: no publisher.

Hindu awakening n.d. *The Hindu Awakening: Retrospect and Promise*. Calcutta: S.L. Garg.

Hindu Vishva 2 (3-4) (Oct.-Nov. 1966)-28 (5) (Jan. 1993).

Macdonell, A.A. 1984 (1917). *A Vedic Reader for Students*. Madras: Oxford University Press.

Nandy, A. 1985, 'An anti-secularist manifesto', *Seminar* 314, 1-11.

Noorani, A.G. 1990a. 'BJP: new sights', *Frontline*, 13 October, 29-32.

——. 1990b. 'The Babri Masjid-Ramjanmabhoomi question', in A.A. Engineer (ed.), *Babri-Masjid Ramjanambhoomi Controversy,* 56-78. Delhi: Ajanta Publications.

Phadnis, U. 1990. *Ethnicity and Nation-Building in South Asia.* New Delhi: Sage.

Rao, K.R. 1989. 'Religion and secularism', in M. Shakir (ed.), *Religion and State and Politics in India,* 27-37. Delhi: Ajanta Publications.

Shrivastava, S. 1990. 'The Ayodhya controversy: Where lies the truth?', in A.A. Engineer (ed.), *Babri-Masjid Ramjanambhoomi Controversy,* 28-55. Delhi: Ajanta Publications.

Smith, D.E. 1963. *India as a Secular State.* Princeton University Press.

Thomas, E.J. 1971 (1933). *The History of Buddhist Thought.* London: Routledge and Kegan Paul.

Tirtha, Svami B.K. 1985 (1964). *Sanatana Dharma: The Eternal and Everlasting Way of Life.* Bombay: Bharatiya Vidya Bhavan.

Visheshank 1966. *Hindu Vishva Visheshank.* Bombay: Vishva Hindu Parishad.

Vishwanathan, A. 1991. 'Bharatiya Janata Party. Staking out the South', *India Today,* 31 Oct., 19-21.

Vivekananda. 1945. *The Complete Works of Swami Vivekananda,* vol. 3, Almora: Advaita Ashrama.

———. 1946.*The Complete Works of Swami Vivekananda,* vol. 4, Almora: Advaita Ashrama.

———. 1947, *The Complete Works of Swami Vivekananda*, vol. 5, Almora: Advaita Ashrama.

———. (n.d.), *Warning: India in Danger* (no place of issue, no publisher).

RELIGIOUS NATIONALISM AND SIKHISM

Ishtiaq Ahmed

According to the 1981 Census, the total population of India was 685 million. It comprised 550 million Hindus of all categories and castes (82%), 75.5 million Muslims (12%), 16.2 million Christians (2.4%), 13 million Sikhs (2%), 4.7 million Buddhists (0.7%), 3.2 million Jains (0.5%), and several thousand Zoroastrians or Parsis. The 'backward castes' of Hindus made up about 100 million (15%) of the population and the tribal population scattered in different parts of the country including the few aboriginals accounted for about 60 million people (8%). Thus the upper castes constituted 59% and the backward castes and tribes (officially designated as scheduled castes and tribes) made up 23% of the Hindu population. The overall rate of literacy was 36.2%. Of these 9.49 million held graduate and post-graduate degrees.[1]

The Indian Constitution adopted on 26 November 1949 specifies a parliamentary form of government for the Union of India, within a federal structure. The forty-second amendment of 1976 describes India as a 'Sovereign Socialist Secular Democratic Republic'. The Constitution prescribes three separate legislative lists: a Union list, a State list and a concurrent list on which both the Union and State governments can legislate. In financial and legislative matters the Constitution is heavily biased in favour of Union authority. More importantly, the federal parliament can alter the boundaries of the states, and even amalgamate them, thus setting up a unitary government. Under Article 365 the central government can, during an emergency, take over the administration of a State and impose the President's Rule in a trouble-ridden State. In the case of the centre judging that the security of India or a part of it is threatened by external aggression or internal disturbance, Parliament can confer on the Union President the power of the Legislature of the State to enact laws, thereby reducing the State government to a nonentity. It must be borne in mind that President's Rule has been imposed frequently in India: up to 1984 it had been imposed seventy times.[2] There are several laws which can be put into effect to curb civil liberties. The Preventive Detention Act (1950), the Maintenance of Internal Security Act (1971) and the Defence of India Rules (1971) have frequently been invoked during periods of social and political unrest.

Hamza Alavi asserts that in India no single ethnic group can be

259

identified as the dominant holder of power at the centre; and further, that the Congress, which has been in power at the centre during most of the post-independence period, has sought to recruit its members and leaders in the various states (that is the provinces) from among the local people. Thus the leadership and organization is locally recruited. Consequently political tension between the various parties and ethnic groups in a state has not normally taken the form of separatist movements of subordinated locals against dominant outsiders. Rather it has tended to be a bargaining game, involving, on the one hand, state governments and local group leaders, and on the other, underprivileged groups which demand quotas in jobs and educational facilities and the advanced groups which insist on such allocations being made on merit. Normally such conflict has been defused or resolved on the local level, under Congress hegemony. The conclusion thus drawn is that separatist nationalism, such as that displayed by sections of the Sikh community, is an anomaly in Indian politics.[3]

In criticism of such theorization, one can say that it does not take cognizance of the current dominant political trend in Indian politics: religious and communal revivalism among Hindus, Muslims and Sikhs. Among Hindus the idea has been gaining ground since the early 1980s that they alone are loyal to India while the religious minorities want to break up the Indian state and form independent separate states.[4] Consequently the idea of a Hindu nation has been put forward as a replacement for the notion of a composite secular Indian nation comprising the different religious and linguistic minorities residing in India, which was sanctioned by the founding fathers of modern India, Mahatma Gandhi and Jawaharlal Nehru. It is important to note that after the 1977 election defeat the formally secular Congress Party, under the leadership of Indira Gandhi, itself began increasingly to employ the religious card to win electoral support among Hindus at the expense of the minorities.[5] Among Kashmiri Muslims and Sikhs, who are concentrated in specific regions, these developments have encouraged separatist nationalism. Since the 1980s both these groups have been embroiled in bloody conflict with the Indian state. In this chapter I shall trace the evolution of the Sikh claim to the status of a separate nation in post-independence India.

The current separatist struggle by Sikh militants in the Indian Punjab is one of the main challenges to the secular credentials of the Indian state. It is important to note that sub-clause (b) of clause 2 of Article 25 of the Indian Constitution declares the Sikhs, along with Jains and Buddhists, as part of Hindu society. The framers of the Constitution, which included Sikhs, had taken this position with a view to enabling the low caste Sikhs, Jains and Buddhists to benefit from the system of reservation of seats for the scheduled castes and tribes in the various assemblies and government jobs, which was to be introduced by the government in independent India. Over the years low caste Sikhs have been beneficiaries of such policy. However, the more communal-minded Sikhs were opposed to Sikhs being categorized as a Hindu sect. Later, when separatist nationalism developed among sections of Sikh society, demands were raised for classifying Sikhs as a distinct religious community. In order to make sense of this claim we need to examine the historical origins of Sikhism.

The social and cultural origins of Sikhism

In the 9th century a reformist movement, later to become famous as the *Bhakti* movement, started in South India which emphasized a belief in one God and rejected idol worship and caste. It spread gradually from South to North India, attracting people from all Hindu castes, but gained popularity mainly among the low castes. The Islamic presence in India had been firmly established by the beginning of the thirteenth century and many peripheral tribes and lower castes had been converted to Islam. By the fifteenth century the *Bhakti* movement had even won adherents among the Muslim lower orders. Punjab, which was situated between Delhi and the north-western frontier beyond which the Muslim world in West Asia was located, was particularly reflective of diverse religious and cultural traditions. Its strategic location also exposed Punjab to warfare and plunder. Towards the end of the fifteenth century, several Muslim and Hindu brotherhood orders including the *Bhaktis* were active in Punjab. Amid such an environment the Sikh movement was initiated by Nanak Chand (1469-1539).

Nanak was a *Khatri* (that is of the *Kshatriya* caste). In Punjab *Khatris* were engaged in a wide variety of services and trade, as well as in the teaching profession, which was normally monopolized by *Brahmins* in Hindu society. Guru Nanak, as he became known in history, combined several universal principles of Hinduism and Islam and some new socio-religious tenets in his preachings. Sikhism, as this new creed came to be called, rejected the caste system and stressed the worship of one God. He advised his disciples to participate actively in societal affairs with a view to achieving salvation through hard work and piety rather than by hermetic withdrawal and solitary meditation.[6] To provide a practical example of collective welfare, Nanak founded a system of free community kitchens, and was able to persuade his followers who came largely, though not exclusively, from Hindu ranks to eat together and thus reject untouchability. However, this anti-caste measure, although a major break with caste exclusiveness, does not seem to have extended to all sectors of social life: inter-caste marriage, it seems, was not instituted as a regular practice. Nanak and his nine successors – all *Khatris* by caste – contracted marriage for themselves and their children within the caste boundary. However, notwithstanding the practical continuation of such traditional Hindu distinctions, Sikhism, with its strong emphasis on human equality, made headway largely among the agricultural and artisan castes of Punjab; castes otherwise assigned a lowly station in the Hindu social order. These strata were thereby able to achieve upward mobility.

Before his death Guru Nanak nominated one of his trusted disciples, Angad (1504-52) as his successor. This was resented by some of his followers who, instead, proclaimed Nanak's eldest son, Sri Chand, as their guru. This minor breakaway sect known as the *Udasis* was thus formed in the very early stages of the advent of the Sikh movement. The succession of most of the later gurus was also challenged by contenders and pretenders, thus creating several divisions among the Sikhs. The Sikh gurus claimed neither to be the incarnations of God, as was the case of Hindu gods, nor as prophets receiving direct revelation from God, as in the Islamic tradition. They made the modest claim of being exemplary spiritual guides who were not to be worshipped or considered infallible. However, their followers gradually haloed much of their spoken words and deeds, thus creating a Sikh dogma and orthodoxy.

Sikhism remained a peaceful reformist sect during the time of the first four Gurus; almost undistinguishable from other reformist brotherhoods. The political order of the time headed by Muslim and Hindu rulers did not look upon the early Sikhs as a particularly dangerous groups, although some apprehension was expressed from time to time about their growing numbers. The Moghul Emperor, Akbar, known for his tolerant views, was impressed by the learning of the fifth Guru, Arjun (1563-1606), and honoured him with expensive presents and grants in land and revenue. By that time many towns and villages in Punjab had come under Sikh influence. Consequently Sikh power based on peasant and petty trader support began to emerge in north-western India. With the ascent to the throne by Akbar's son, Jahangir, state policy towards the Sikhs was reversed. The new Emperor was antagonized by Guru Arjun's friendliness towards his son Khusrau who had rebelled in a bid to capture the throne. The rebellion was crushed and vengeance was wreaked on all those who were suspected of having aided Khusrau. Arjun was arrested and put in prison where the torture and humiliation he endured finally led to his death. The sixth Guru, Hargobind (1595-1644), started maintaining a regular body of troops and established fortresses in areas under Sikh influence and power. His successor Har Rai (1630-61) preferred not to antagonize the Moghuls and led a rather secluded life. The next Guru, Hari Krishen (1656-64) died in childhood. His successor Teg Bahadur (1664-75) resisted the Moghul state, but was defeated, captured and put to death on the orders of the Emperor Aurangzeb.[7]

Militant Sikhism

Teg Bahadur's teenage son, Gobind Rai (1666-1708), became the tenth and last Guru of orthodox Sikhs. He abandoned the conciliatory policy which had characterized the attitude of his predecessors. He maintained a regular army, well-trained and disciplined. Most of his soldiers came from the poorer sections of the peasantry and artisan castes. Under Gobind Rai's militant leadership the Sikh movement assumed political, military, economic and social ramifications which tended to challenge Moghul suzerainty. The Sikhs began to collect revenue and other taxes in areas under their control. Consequently the rising Sikh power came into direct conflict with the Moghul state, which intensified its persecution of Guru Gobind Rai. Subsequent events forced the Sikhs to organize themselves into mobile guerrilla bands, hiding in forests and hills from which they posed a threat to much larger armies with surprise attacks and ambush.

In 1699 Guru Gobind summoned his followers to collect at Anandpur in northern Punjab. At this gathering he decided to organize the Sikhs along distinctive lines and instituted the system of baptism. Five men, a *Brahmin*, a *Kshatriya* and three men from the lesser castes were chosen to drink out of one bowl to signify their initiation into the fraternity of the *Khalsa* (literally the pure). They were given one family name: Singh, which means a lion. The baptism meant that they had given up their previous professions and become soldiers of the *Khalsa*, abandoning all other social ties except that of the *Khalsa*, and given up rites and rituals not sanctioned by the Sikh faith. Further, five emblems were introduced: hair and the beard were to be worn unshorn all the time (*kes*); a comb was to be carried (*kangha*); knee-length breaches were to be worn all the time (*kach*); a steel bracelet was to be worn on the right hand (*kara*); and a sabre was to be carried at all times (*kirpan*). These five identity markers and some other related practices were instituted.[8] Gobind Singh further declared that there was to be no other Guru after him. The Sikh Holy book, the Granth Sahib (also known as Adi Granth), was to be the ever-present Guru from whom the Sikhs were to seek guidance. Thus the line of living Gurus came to an end.

In the course of time Sikh power became a dominant force in the politics of northern India. Gobind Rai fought many battles against both Muslim and Hindu chiefs. His campaigns, it seems, were not viewed necessarily as religious crusades by the Punjab populace: many Muslim notables opposed to Moghul supremacy sided with him, and Muslim and Hindu soldiers were to be found in substantial numbers in the Sikh armies. However, the confrontation with the Moghuls cost Gobind Rai dearly in men and material. All his four sons lost their lives in this conflict: two died in battle and two minors were executed by the Moghuls. In 1708 Guru Gobind Singh died from stab wounds inflicted by two Muslim assassins.

The *Khalsa* Sikhs became the orthodox majority. They began to be referred to as the *kesedhari Khalsa* (i.e. those-who-wear-their-hair-unshorn). Gradually the *Khalsa*, however, were sub-divided into various theological configurations as new interpretations and rival claims to leadership were put forward by the devout. The militant *Khalsa* creed from quite early times appeared particularly attractive to the vast *Jat* peasantry of middle and eastern Punjab, who were accorded low status in the Hindu caste system.[9] In western Punjab large numbers of *Jats* had gone over to Islam some centuries earlier. Under the *Khalsa* movement the *Jats* of central and eastern Punjab emerged as the new power. Thereafter, the Sikh religion came to be identified more strongly with the *Khalsa* and the Punjabi *Jat*, although sizable numbers of *Khalsa* Sikhs were not *Jats*, and not all Sikhs subscribed to the five emblems. The latter became known as the *Sahajdharis* (i.e. those-who-take-time to-adopt). On the other hand, several breakaway sects founded earlier by rival claimants to Guruhood continued to exist. New sects were founded by reformers and dissidents rejecting Gobind Singh's teaching. Some of these sects reclined into Hinduism, becoming either one of its many cults, or simply merging into its mainstream altogether. As regards the relationship between Hinduism and Sikhism, historically the lines between them were never drawn distinctly and many people continued to subscribe to a popular religion combining Hindu and Sikh beliefs. In fact intermarriage between Hindus and Sikhs of the same caste were quite common, particularly in West Punjab. Also, among some Punjabi Hindus, raising one son as a Sikh was an established tradition. This process has continued into the present times.

Some permanent centres of Sikh faith and influence were established early in its history. The most important among these is the Golden Temple established at Amritsar by the fourth Guru, Ramdas. It contains, among other things, the Akal Takht (that is the throne of the Immortal) established by the sixth Guru, Hargobind, who wore two swords signifying a link between spiritual and temporal authority (*piri* and *miri*).[10] The Akal Takht thus symbolizes Sikh aspirations to effective political influence. Five high priests preside over the Akal Takht and constitute the highest moral authority. Current separatist ideas among Sikhs emphasize the creation of a state where the supreme authority of the Akal Takht can be realized; indicating the possibility of the subordination of secular government to the ruling of high priests in a future *Khalistan*.

During the eighteenth century the Moghul Empire was delivered severe blows by a series of attacks led by Persian and Afghan invaders. First came the Persian Nadir Shah (in 1738 and 1739) who laid Punjab and the areas around the capital, Delhi, waste. A series of invasions followed under the Afghan Ahmed Shah Abdali (1747-8, 1748-9, 1751-2, 1756-7, 1759, 1762, 1764, 1766 and 1769) which played havoc with the social order of Punjab and northern India. Muslims, Hindus and Sikhs – all became victims of the genocide that followed Afghan victory. At any rate, no Moghul administrative or military structure worth the name survived those repeated onslaughts. In these circumstances, the *Khalsa* who had taken to the forest, emerged as a strong force in Punjab. The continuing confrontation with the Moghul state had forced the *Khalsa* to organize themselves into several small military units which proved effective in surprise attacks on the state. With their mobile military formations intact and with the old order a shambles, the Sikhs could now emerge as the strongest military force in Punjab.

The Sikh kingdom of Punjab

In 1799 the young leader of one of the Sikh military units, Ranjit Singh, succeeded in establishing his supremacy over the various other Sikh military units. He expelled the Afghans from Punjab and captured Lahore. Other Muslim and Hindu Rajput rivals in and around Punjab were also subdued. In 1801 Ranjit Singh proclaimed himself Maharaja (supreme king) of Punjab and began a long reign of expansion, consolidation and reform. Thus, the Sikh rise from a minor sect to the ruling community of Punjab was consummated in the creation of an independent kingdom. It is important to note, however, that despite the fact that the Sikhs became the dominant group in Punjab they remained a tiny minority of the total population of Punjab: Muslims made up 53%, Hindus 30% and Sikhs only 14%.

Although Ranjit Singh employed considerable force and terror to crush the mainly Muslim opposition in Punjab and the regions around it, once having succeeded in that purpose and in consolidating his power, he sought a broader Punjabi image for his kingdom. Muslim and Hindu notables were co-opted into the council of ministers. The Maharaja opened public dispensaries where medicine was given to the sick free of charge and without distinction of religion. Separate courts based on religious and customary laws were established for the three religious communities. Muslims and Hindus along with Sikhs were to be found at all levels within the army, including in positions of command. The Maharaja even hired European instructors to train and modernize his army. At that time the British were expanding rapidly in northern India, but, during Ranjit Singh's lifetime, avoided conflict with the Punjab kingdom and instead negotiated a peace treaty.[11] However, upon his death in 1839, a struggle for the throne erupted among different Sikh claimants. The British thereupon took full advantage of the situation and invaded Punjab. Several battles were fought between the British and the Sikh armies. Finally, in 1849, Punjab was occupied by the British.

Punjab under the British

In the late nineteenth century, nationalism was on the rise in India and this also affected Punjab. Here, besides the all-embracing nationalism of the All-India National Congress, nationalism also took the shape of religious revival among the three major communities of Muslims, Hindus and Sikhs. It all started initially as a defensive reaction to the hectic activities of Christian missionaries in Punjab. Some leading Sikhs, including Dalip Singh, a son of Ranjit Singh, had converted to Christianity. However, soon afterwards the religious revival also took the form of a religious debate among Muslim, Hindu and Sikh priests and intellectuals. It soon degenerated into an exchange of invective and abuse between them. In particular, Sikh-Hindu relations suffered a serious setback when, in the early 1900s, an acrimonious controversy erupted among Hindus and Sikh zealots over the status of Sikhism. While certain Hindu leaders tried to prove that the Sikhs were merely a Hindu sect, the *Khalsa* Sikhs asserted that they were a completely different religious community. Confusion was added to the argument when some non-*Khalsa* Sikhs themselves declared that they were Hindus.[12] These developments prompted the Sikhs to revitalize their communal institutions. At the same time the need to prepare the Sikh community in relation to other communities in Punjab for the competition for jobs, economic advancement and public office, promoted Sikh leaders to establish modern educational institutions where young men could be imparted a proper education. Similar trends were under way among Hindus and Muslims. Another aspect of the communalization process in Punjab was that elite Muslims, Hindus and Sikhs took up quite particular positions on their cultural identity. The Muslims identified themselves with the Urdu language, a northern Indian language used by Muslim upper classes all over India, the Hindus adopted Hindi and the Sikhs alone declared Punjabi as their mother-tongue. At home most Punjabis, including the elite, spoke some dialect of Punjabi. These associations were entered in the census records.

Towards the end of the nineteenth century, Sikhs from the overpopulated areas of East Punjab began to emigrate to other parts of the world in search of work. As one of the main communities serving in the British Indian Army, they had acquired considerable experience of the outside world. They went to China, Southeast Asia, East Africa, the United States, Canada and other places where British colonialism had its connexions. However, for those wishing to enter North America, considerable difficulties were created by the US and Canadian governments. Laws virtually banning the entry of Asians were passed. The immigrants protested against such discrimination but their pleas were ignored. Consequently, in March 1913 the more daring of these people decided to form a revolutionary organization called the Gadar Party (the party based on the spirit of the 1857 Uprising, called by the nationalists as the War of Independence) with the view to returning to India to start a revolution that would expel the British. However, the plot was foiled by British intelligence. Many Gadarites were arrested on their way to India; others were rounded up in Canada and on the west coast of the United States. Some of those who did manage to reach India were able to stir up parts of the Punjab countryside. However, they were betrayed by pro-British Punjabis. Many of these revolutionaries were executed while others were given long sentences and sent to the Andaman Islands.[13] Substantial numbers of Sikh youths inspired by the Gadarite spirit joined the various anti-colonial organizations. Among these were the Congress and Communist parties.

The emergence of the Akali Dal

The fear of being absorbed into Hinduism has confronted Sikh puritans throughout their short history. Early this century the Sikhs began to organize themselves in real earnest to protect their communal interests and cultural identity. In 1920, the *Akali Dal* was established with such specific purposes in sight. The initiative came when a movement was started to recover Sikh temples and holy places from the British-appointed priests called *mahants*. The *mahants* were in many cases known for not complying with the standards of piety upheld by the orthodox; some *mahants*, in fact, were not even Sikhs but Hindus. The colonial administration initially backed the *mahants* and considerable force was used against the Sikh protesters. The agitation dragged on for five years, during which many Sikhs died offering only passive resistance.[14] The moderate Sikh leadership which had hitherto supported the colonial government was shocked by British high-handed methods. Finally in 1925 the government changed its policy and handed over the temples to the Sikh community. The government passed a Sikh Gurdwara Act which placed the management of the Sikh shrines and temples under an elected Sikh body called the *Shiromai Gurdwara Prabandhak* Committee (SGPC). The SGPC took over considerable financial assets attached to the shrines. Thereafter elections to the SGPC became an important event in internal Sikh politics. The *Akali Dal* gradually took shape as a political party, and in the post-independence period became a major platform for the articulation of Sikh populist demands.

During the period between the two world wars, Punjab politics was dominated by the big Muslim, Sikh and Hindu landowners. This landed elite kept politics a closed affair within its narrow circles. However, after the Muslim League in its annual session at Lahore in March 1940 raised the demand for a separate Muslim homeland, Punjab politics gathered a populist momentum as the idea of Pakistan began to gain ground among the Muslims. At about the same time a section of the Sikh community floated the idea of a separate state: *Sikhistan*.[15] But since the Sikhs made up only about 14 per cent of the Punjab population and, except for some areas of East Punjab, were spread out thinly all over the province, their ability to press for their separate state was limited. The Sikhs were, therefore, wooed by both the Congress and the Muslim League.

The creation of Pakistan became imminent after the Muslims of India gave a clear verdict in favour of a separate Muslim state in the 1945-6 elections (franchise at that time was extended to about fifteen per cent of the Indian population; ownership of property and educational qualifications conferred the right to vote). The Muslim League leadership made efforts to win Sikh support for Pakistan. They were promised autonomy and even right to maintain their army in Sikh-majority areas.[16] But since Pakistan was going to be a state of the 'Muslim Nation' the Sikhs were wary of Muslim League overtures. On the other hand, Jawaharlal Nehru assured the Sikh leaders that they would be entitled, in democratic India, to autonomy in an area in the north where they could 'freely experience the glow of freedom'.[17] The Sikh leadership of the *Akali Dal* therefore decided to hitch their future to that of secular India.

But the problem that agonized the Sikhs most was the fate of Punjab. Was this Muslim majority province going to go to Pakistan? For the Sikhs, such a prospect was completely unacceptable. Of all the communities in Punjab the Sikhs were the most deeply rooted in its soil. Sikh identity – ethnic, religious, historical and cultural – was inseparable from Punjab. They were therefore totally opposed to any constitutional scheme that gave the entire Punjab to Pakistan. But realizing that they might not be able to stop such an eventuality completely, they demanded that Punjab be divided on religious grounds: the Muslim majority areas of West Punjab going to Pakistan and the Hindu-Sikh majority areas of East Punjab being given to India. The Congress backed this Sikh demand and Punjab was accordingly divided during Partition. Consequently, in the wake of the communal violence which broke out in Punjab, several million Sikhs and Hindus left West Punjab for India and about the same number of Muslims left East Punjab for Pakistan.

More that half a million Punjabis lost their lives in this infamous upheaval. Several hundred Sikh holy places were left behind in Pakistan, including the birthplace of the founder of the Sikh faith, Guru Nanak.

Sikhs in independent India

Sikhs constituted barely two per cent of the total population of independent India. In pre-partition Punjab, Sikhs were largely based in the rural areas. There was also a trading section among Sikhs. In northern Punjab it was comprised of *Khatris* known as *Bhapas*. Elsewhere it was mainly the *Arora* caste that was involved in trading and shopkeeping. The large majority of Sikhs belonged to the biggest agricultural caste of Punjab, the *Jats*, who made up some sixty per cent of the total Sikh population.[18] The second largest group consisted of the artisan castes. At the bottom of the social scale were the converts from Untouchables, known as *Mazhabis*.

After Partition, the *Jat* Sikh refugees from West Punjab settled in the East Punjab rural areas where they were allotted land against claims of land left behind in Pakistan. They were easily assimilated among the East Punjab *Jats* who bore similar sub-caste names to them. However several hundred thousand Sikhs from different castes were relocated elsewhere in India, too. On the other hand, often being town-dweller, West Punjabi Hindus and the Sikh *Bhapas* were inclined to look for urban areas to settle. They headed, therefore, towards the towns of East Punjab and beyond, particularly to the capital, Delhi. The artisan and menial castes among Sikhs were distributed both in the rural and urban areas. Insofar as the distribution of the Sikh and Hindu communities as a whole in East Punjab is concerned, the Sikhs were concentrated more in the villages and rural settlements while Hindus predominated in the towns and cities.[19] There was of course district-wise variation in the Hindu-Sikh proportions in the rural and urban areas. Apart from the Indian army, in which Sikhs sought employment in large numbers, many also went into the transport sector. Sikh truck and bus owners and drivers became the dominant group in the Indian transport sector. Also important to note is that emigration from Punjab received another impetus in the 1950s, when Britain started recruiting workers in large numbers from her former colonies. Thousands of Sikhs reached the industrial cities of northern England and London. This was to serve as the basis for further inflow during the 1960s and early 1970s.

Pre-Partition Punjab was a huge administrative unit created by the British. It included many non-Punjabi-speaking areas, many of which continued to be part of the post-independence Indian Punjab. The Sikhs formed a minority under this arrangement. Sikh leaders of the *Akali Dal* therefore demanded the re-establishment of Punjab borders on a linguistic basis, with the specific recognition that Punjabi be written in the *Gurmukhi* script (believed to have been created by the second Guru, Angad) and not in the *Devanagri* script used in Hindi.[20] The States Reorganization Commission, set up in 1953 to reorganize the states, had accepted linguistic criteria as the basis of establishing provinces and demarcating their boundaries. Several new states (that is, provinces) had come into being on such a basis in different parts of India. However, when it came to Punjab the Commission refused to concede to the Sikh demand for an exclusive Punjabi-speaking state. Hindi and Punjabi were not considered sufficiently distinct from each other. It was feared that the creation of a Sikh-dominated Punjab might exacerbate intercommunal relations between Sikhs and Hindus. This suspicion was based on the fact that the Sikh leader Master Tara Singh, a *Khatri* refugee from the Rawalpindi district of northern Punjab, articulated the demand for a Punjabi state in religious terms, and had consequently been opposed by the powerful Hindu communal lobby in Punjab which wanted to have Hindi declared as the official language of Punjab. The roots of such communal identification with language, as we have noted earlier, lay in the politics of pre-Partition Punjab.

Thus the Hindu communalists belonging to the *Jan Sangh* (founded 1951) and other similar organizations, advised the Punjabi Hindus to declare Hindi as their mother tongue. It is important to note that the Congress also supported the Hindu communalists. In fact many leading members of Congress were also members of Hindu communal organizations.[21] Another factor which seems to have influenced the Commission's decision not to declare Punjabi as the only official language of Punjab was the fact that Sikhs and Hindus were dispersed all over the province and this complicated the adjustment of boundaries along exclusively linguistic lines. The Commission, therefore, recommended that both Punjabi and Hindi should be the official languages of the province.[22]

In the 1950s the *Akali* Sikhs began to agitate for a separate Punjabi *Suba* (province). These essentially peaceful agitations continued into the mid-1960s. Thousands of Sikhs were arrested, many were subjected to police brutality, and some even took recourse to the Gandhian tactic of fast unto death, although in only one case did it lead to death. The Congress Sikhs led by Pratap Singh Kairon, however, showed little enthusiasm for the Punjabi *Suba* idea. Behind the government's resolve to forestall the creation of a Sikh-dominated province under the leadership of communal politicians such as Tara Singh was the figure of Nehru, who considered such a prospect vitiating to his concept of a secular India and seriously damaging to Indian unity and security. At any rate, during this long agitation Hindu-Sikh relations were severely strained.[23]

In 1965, a war broke out between India and Pakistan which was fought mainly along the Punjab border. The Sikhs, who had bitter memories of the partition riots and violence which they blamed on the Muslims, offered broad support to the Indian war effort. Even *Akali* leaders came out forcefully against Pakistan in their speeches and sermons. Furthermore, the leadership of the *Akali Dal* passed into the hands of a new leader, Fateh Singh, a *Jat* by caste. Fateh Singh dropped the religious overtones of the Punjabi *Suba* demand, projecting it as a secular demand based purely on language. In the changed atmosphere of Punjab politics in which the Sikhs had displayed unusual patriotism during the war, a basis for compromise developed between the central government and the Sikh nationalists. In 1966, when Indira Gandhi became the new prime minister of India, the Punjabi *Suba* was finally established. Some Sikh grievances, however, remained unresolved in the way territory was distributed between Punjab and the adjoining new provinces of Harayana and Himachal Pradesh. As the Hindu communalists had successfully persuaded many Hindu voters to declare Hindi as their mother tongue, large chunks of otherwise Punjabi Hindu majority areas were given to other provinces. For the Sikh communalists this meant an improvement of their ratio of the population of the new Punjab province. However, even with all these changes, the Sikhs made up a majority of only 56 per cent of the population of Punjab.[24]

The creation of Punjabi *Suba* greatly enhanced the prestige of the *Akali Dal*, yet it did not lead to a dramatic increase in its popular support. This followed from the peculiar caste and class composition of the Sikh community and the political divisions in Punjab. As mentioned earlier, the presence of a radical anti-colonial tradition among Sikhs had led many of them to join the Congress Party during the freedom movement, while the more revolutionary sections were attracted to the Communist Movement in pre-Partition Punjab. These political loyalties continued to claim the support of Sikh voters after independence. The *Akali Dal* thus competed with several parties for Sikh support in the elections. More importantly, the exploitation of religion, caste links and other primordial ties was widely practised by all the major parties; the *Akali Dal* and the Hindu *Jan Sangh* doing it more openly, while the Punjab Congress Party, the largest party in the province until 1977 and with direct links with the ruling party at the centre, adopting less obvious but no less sectional means to enhance its support among the electorate. The Communist parties adhered more consistently to secular puritanism, but were constrained to devise their electoral strategies in the light of the existing realities.

The core voters of the *Akalis* were the agricultural caste of *Jats* who constituted some two-thirds of the Sikh population. But *Jat* society comprised a vast number of independent peasant-proprietors who were ridden with factionalism resulting from disputes over property, social influence and contending ambitions for influence and power.[25] Consequently the *Akalis* were supported only by sections of *Jats*. Furthermore after the *Jat* takeover of the *Akali Dal* under Fateh Singh, the business and trading-caste Sikhs often supported breakaway factions of the *Akalis*. Similarly Sikh artisan castes rarely voted for the *Akalis*; they tended to support the Congress. The Untouchable converts (*Mazhabi* Sikhs) almost never voted for the *Akalis*, since *Jat* society looked down upon them even when canonical Sikhism predicated to the contrary. Consequently, apart from the 1977 anti-Congress wave in which Mrs Gandhi and the Congress were swept out of power in the national elections, the *Akalis* had been used to getting less than one third of the total votes.[26] Thus, both Congress and *Akali Dal*-led coalition governments had come to power in Punjab. It is interesting to note that both parties even formed coalition governments between themselves: in other words, the Akalis were never so effective as to make themselves the sole spokesmen of the Sikh community. In fact a serious challenge was mounted to *Akali* pretensions to represent Sikh religious interest by the Sikh Chief Minister of the Congress Party, Giani Zail Singh (later Home Minister and President of India), who in the period 1972-7 tried to wrest the support of religiously-minded Sikhs away from the *Akalis*. He went out of his way to appease the religious sentiments of his community, and his conduct of government was marked by an increasing adherence to Sikh rituals.[27] All this made the *Akalis* constantly look for issues that could improve their standing in Sikh society and in election results.

The contradictions of agricultural modernization and development in Punjab

At the time of independence, India faced a gigantic problem in the feeding of its teeming millions. The traditional food-grain production systems proved patently inadequate in meeting the needs of the people. India therefore initially had to rely on imports of wheat and other cereals, and on food aid. The idea of a modernization of agriculture through structural changes in production methods was promoted by the World Bank and other related international development agencies as the proper strategy to solve chronic food shortages. The idea of self-reliance in food-supply received eager support from Indian planners and the government.

Drastic land reforms had already been undertaken in the 1950s in Punjab and the old-style landlordism (called *Zamindari*) abolished. The Indian planners chose Punjab as the most appropriate region for experimentation in the Green Revolution, as this development strategy came to be known. In the 1960s a most successful transformation of the agricultural sector in Punjab was achieved. By the early 1970s, Punjab had been converted into one of the most prosperous states of India. Metalled roads, brick houses, expansion of school and university education, modern hospitals and other indicators of increasing welfare typified the Punjab countryside. Generous government loans and subsidies were available and many Sikhs borrowed beyond their means to take advantage of new opportunities. However, an important role in this transformation was also played by monetary contributions from some one million Sikh immigrants in Europe (overwhelmingly in Britain), North America, Southeast Asia and other parts of the world.[28] An important role in internationalizing the separatist conflict in Punjab was played by some diaspora Sikh leaders during the 1980s.

A rich class of modern Sikh farmers strongly entrenched in the *Akali Dal* had come into being by the 1970s. During the 1970s, *Akali* politics continued to rely on religious causes for mobilizing popular support, but the aims and objectives underlying such strategy became increasingly materialistic and temporal, most usually in compliance with vested Sikh interest. As a result *Akali* popularity began to dwindle, particularly among the poorer sections of the *Jats* who, lacking capital and influence, could not benefit from the capital-intensive Green Revolution technology. Also, the prosperity of the 1960s had enabled many a peasant to buy his children a university education. Once uprooted from their humble backgrounds, these university graduates sought office jobs. Such jobs were of course limited. Frustration naturally emerged among these new achievement-oriented Sikhs. The situation was further complicated by the fact that, by the early 1980s, the debt burden, incurred during the early phase of the Green Revolution by many middle and poor peasants, became increasingly heavy as the market for their goods did not continue to maintain its upward trend and began to fluctuate rather disturbingly. Also, the landowners and industrialists (small-scale industry was established in many parts of Punjab) had started importing cheap labour from the poorer provinces. During the great boom of the 1960s, a dearth of cheap labour had begun to occur as the Punjabi rural workers demanded higher wages. Cheap labour from outside began to damage the interests of Punjab's own poor who, despite all-round prosperity, remained a large group.[29]

In the 1970s, the *Akalis* evolved a strategy that could help restore their waning influence among Sikhs. The dramatic transformations in Punjab's economic structure had loosened the hold of the big landowners on the peasantry, thus weakening the role of the *Akali Dal* in Sikh society. The *Akali Dal* came to be seen as the party of the rich. Consequently, in 1973, the first version of the historic Anandpur Resolution was put forth by the *Akalis*, demanding several economic, political and religious concessions from the government. Among the economic demands were better prices for Punjab's agricultural products on the internal Indian market and a greater share of water resources. It demanded also, that the ceiling on ownership of agricultural land be raised to 30 acres instead of the existing limit of 17.5 acres. The political demands concentrated on the provision of substantial provincial autonomy and limitations on the constant interference in Punjab politics by the centre, directly and through its provincial branch. More specifically, the central government was to limit its jurisdiction to defence, foreign relations, currency and general communications. Among the religious rights were demands for conferring the status of holy city on Amritsar, the broadcasting of Sikh religious sermons on government radio, and a set of other such pleas – all couched in vague terms.[30]

These demands mainly reflected the interests of the landowning upper echelons of Sikh society, but were given a populist religious flavour. On the question of autonomy, the resolution took an extreme position which was almost impossible for Mrs Gandhi to accept. Over the years she had strengthened the central government and armed herself with sufficient economic, political and constitutional clout to subdue the provinces. Not surprisingly the central government labelled the Anandpur Sahib Resolution a secessionist document.[31] It is interesting to note that several versions of the Anandpur Sahib Resolution were later put forth by different Sikh factions. Most significantly, in the later version, permission to establish medium and heavy industries was included.

The Punjab conflict of the 1980s

The propagation of the Anandpur Sahib Resolution improved *Akali Dal's* standing among Sikhs and coincided well with the growing frustration among the people of India with the strongly centrist and authoritarian policies of Mrs Gandhi. It cashed in on its new-found popularity in the Punjab elections of 1977. The *Akali Dal* and the Hindu communal party, the *Jan Sangh*, were the main victors in Punjab. These two formed a coalition government during the brief *Janata* period (1977-9). However, disputes and rivalries soon cropped up among the disparate elements forming the *Janata* alliance. Mrs Gandhi, now out of power, was quick to seize the opportunity to stage a comeback. Accordingly, on the advice of her younger son Sanjay Gandhi (who died in a plane crash in 1980) and the defeated Congress chief minister of Punjab, Giani Zail Singh, she began to look for a Sikh leader who could help them against the *Akalis*. The choice fell upon Sant Jarnail Singh Bhindranwale (1947-84), a religious preacher and agitator who belonged to a poor *Jat* peasant family. Bhindranwale was opposed to the upper-class Sikh gentry in the *Akali Dal*.[32]

Initially, Bhindranwale was unsuccessful against the *Akalis*, but in

1978 he emerged as a hero when his group clashed with the minor breakaway sect of *Nirankari* Sikhs. Thirteen of his group and three *Nirankaris* were killed. Thereafter his popularity and influence increased rapidly, both in the society as well as in the Sikh-dominated Punjab administration and police. In his puritanical sermons, Bhindranwale urged Sikhs to abandon drinking and avoid immorality and to return to the strict *Khalsa* way of life. Such ideas began to attract young Sikhs in their thousands. Among his followers were also the growing body of unemployed BA degree-holders and some Naxalites (a Maoist revolutionary movement which originated in Bengal in 1967 and spread to other parts of India, including Punjab) who had survived the police terror of the late 1960s and early 1970s. Moreover, his anti-landlord rhetoric won him support form the subordinate non-agricultural castes. Some other extremist Sikh groups were also formed, but the largest following was won by Bhindranwale. In 1980 Mrs Gandhi was back in power. Punjab was under a Congress (I) government (Congress had split during the 1975 emergency. Congress (I) was led by Mrs Gandhi). She now saw in Bhindranwale a greater menace than the *Akalis*. The Congress press began to portray him as a dangerous and disruptive fanatic. Consequently violent conflicts between Bhindranwale's group and Congress (I) on the one hand, and between Sikh and Hindu extremists on the other, erupted in Punjab. Political assassinations began to loom large over the Punjab horizon. Bhindranwale was accused by the government of being behind some of the terrorist acts against Hindus, the *Nirankaris*, as well as the Sikhs opposed to him. He was arrested, but later discharged.[33] On the other hand, Hindu extremists in the neighbouring state of Harayana began to attack Sikhs living there. It is important to note that despite a drastic increase in the illegal circulation of firearms in Punjab and widespread political terrorism, communal violence between Sikhs and Hindus did not break out on a large scale. The two communities continued to live peacefully side by side in the towns and villages of Punjab.

In the meantime the various militant Sikh groups began to establish their bases in the Golden Temple at Amritsar. They also started bringing modern weapons into the Temple. On 12 June 1982, Bhindranwale and several hundred of his heavily-armed followers, including a disgraced former hero of the Bangladesh war, Major-General Shahbeg Singh, who just prior to retirement had been dismissed on corruption charges, entered the Golden Temple in search of sanctuary. From here Bhindranwale intensified his campaign against the government and began propagating the idea of a separate homeland. Simultaneously Sikh leaders based in North America and Britain gave the call· for an independent Sikh state: *Khalistan*.[34] An explosive situation began to develop, but for almost two years the government did nothing decisive to contain it. On 6 October 1983 the Congress-I government in the Punjab was dismissed and President's Rule was proclaimed. Finally, in the late spring of 1984 Mrs Gandhi took the drastic step of ordering the Indian army to prepare for a manoeuvre to oust Bhindranwale and his supporters from the Golden Temple. Operation Blue Star began in the night of 5 June under the command of a Sikh officer, Major-General Kuldip Singh Brar. Tanks, armoured vehicles and heavy artillery were employed by the army, but the Sikh militants entrenched inside the precincts of the Temple complex gave tough battle. However, by 6 June they were overwhelmed. Bhindranwale, Shahbeg Singh and several hundred other militants were slain. Many Sikh pilgrims, including women, children and old people were inside the Temple when the army action began. Several hundred were killed or injured as a consequence. Casualties among the troops also ran into hundreds.[35]

The assault on the Golden Temple caused an uproar among Sikhs all over the world. Sikh troops mutinied and many Sikh officers in the armed forces and the civil administration resigned their offices and surrendered government awards in protest.[36] Revenge for this desecration of the holiest Sikh shrine was pledged by many in the community. Thus on 31 October 1984 two of the prime minister's Sikh bodyguards shot her dead in the compound of her Delhi residence. The assassination of Indira Gandhi provoked Hindu outrage against the Sikhs on a massive scale in some parts of India. Outside Punjab, Sikhs were hunted down, stabbed or shot and their homes burned. Neither children, women nor the old received mercy. The mayhem was especially gruesome in the capital, Delhi. The police and other branches of the civil administration did nothing for three days to stop the violence. An independent inquiry committee of private citizens established clear proof of Congress involvement in the Delhi riots.[37] Similarly the London-based Amnesty International and the Minority Rights Group reported that the police let loose a reign of terror in Punjab. Sikhs suspected of terrorist connexions were captured, tortured and killed in fake encounters. It is important to remember that to this day, in spite of repeated demands, people identified and accused of being behind the Delhi riots have not been tried in a court of law.

Notwithstanding such deterioration in the maintenance of peace and order, the people of Punjab continued to reject extremism. In 1985, elections were held in Punjab. Both Congress(I) and the militants were badly defeated. *Akali Dal*, which represented the moderate course, received the majority of votes and formed the government. In July 1985 an agreement was reached between the Punjab and central governments on the restoration of normality in Punjab. The Punjab Accord, as it came to be known, conceded many *Akali* demands, including the right of people to seek employment in the army on merit rather than fixed quotas, and more importantly, Chandigarh which had been serving as the capital of both Punjab and Harayana was to be handed over to Punjab alone by 26 January 1986. Also, India was to be made a true federal republic with greater autonomy for the states.[38] However, the government reneged on the commitments and the Accord became a dead letter. Moreover, in 1987 the *Akali* government was dismissed apparently for its failure to contain terrorism. The Punjab conflict has continued to drag on over the years. According to one estimate, some 35,000 people were killed between 1984 and 1991.[39] The Indian Government has accused Pakistan of aiding the Sikh terrorists; something which the latter denies. Terrorism perpetrated both by Sikh extremists and the police continues to haunt Punjab even now.

The concept of Khalistan

The earliest ideas about a separate Sikh state in the post-independence period were put forth by Sirdar Kapur Singh, a senior civil servant who had been dismissed from service on corruption charges. His book *Sachi Sakhi*, in Punjabi, is his account of an unsuccessful attempt on his part to convince the Indian Government to give him a fair chance to prove his innocence. He alleges that the corruption charges were framed against him by the prejudiced Indian administration because he was a devout Sikh.[40] Kapur Singh began to propagate the idea of *Khalistan* in the 1960s and continued to do so until his death in 1986. However, it was the movement for a Sikh-majority Punjabi province which kept Sikh nationalists occupied during the 1950s and 1960s, and it was not until the 1970s that this idea was seriously raised again in India.

Sant Jarnail Singh Bhindranwale never directly demanded *Khalistan*, although in his rustic Punjabi he preached the inevitability of Sikh freedom from the Indian yoke. In the various audio and video cassette tapes released by Sikhs, Bhindranwale clearly enjoins his followers to resist the authority of the Indian Government. Purchasing of weapons and motorcycles is to be given priority. Employment of Sikh religious symbolism, particularly the various accounts of Sikh heroism and martyrdom, is profuse and melodramatic in his speeches.[41] It is important to note that the idea of *Khalistan* was first put forth publicly by diaspora Sikhs settled in North America and Britain. Among them, Dr Jagjit Singh Chauhan – the London-based, and for some years the self-styled, President of *Khalistan*, and Ganga Singh Dhillon of Canada, were the most prominent. The Indian government alleged that both were working in close liaison with Pakistan and members of the US Congress.[42]

In a number of interviews that I conducted with spokesmen of different Sikh factions based in Europe and North America, Guru Gobind Singh was acclaimed as the ideal political leader, both as military-political leader and as champion of the peasantry and lower castes against feudal oppression. Jagjit Singh Chauhan preferred to establish a Punjabi state on the pattern of Ranjit Singh. It was to be based on an economic system which was to respect private property. Industry which caused pollution was to be disallowed. Agro-industries were to be promoted. However, women's right to a share in agricultural property was to be banned as it conflicted with 'Sikh tradition'. Davinder Singh Parmar, holder of the portfolio of Defence Minister in the future *Khalistan*, also emphasized the golden period of Ranjit Singh and the historical rights of Sikhs to be given back Punjab which had been taken away from them by the British in 1849. Gurmej Singh Gill, holding the potential portfolio of Prime Minister, emphasized the importance of the Sikh values of tolerance. However, only those creeds that were based on a belief in God were to be allowed in *Khalistan*. Secularism and Western democracy were not to be accepted as they tended to weaken the religious basis of society and divide people. Man Mohan Singh Khalsa of the *Dal Khalsa* group laid stress on the imposition of true *Khalsa* values, while Gurdeep Singh of the *Babbar Khalsa* emphasized the militant character of *Khalsa* ideology. Dr Chanan Singh Chan and Lachman Singh Anjala, two members of the *Khalistan* Council, drew attention to the anti-feudal struggle of Guru Gobind Singh and his lieutenant, Banda Bahadur. *Khalistan* was to be a revolutionary state which was to abolish caste and big landlordism. All the proponents of the *Khalistan* idea rejected untouchability and emphasized the equal social status of women. Common to all the calls for a separate Sikh state was the accusation that India was a sham secular democracy, and that it was in fact a Hindu communal state functioning in the interest of the upper castes. Apart form this common complaint, and the conviction that *Khalistan* should be based on Sikh moral values and historical legacy, the proponents of the *Khalistan* idea differ from each other on their conception of an· ideal *Khalistan*.[43]

In December 1987, the monthly *Khalistan News*, published from Britain by the *Khalistan* Council, started serializing the 'Instrument of Charter of Khalistan', a sort of declaration of the main ideological and constitutional framework of the proposed future state of *Khalistan*. The December 1987 and January 1988 issues provide a definition of the Sikh nation: a community sharing common belief in orthodox Sikhism. From this premise is derived the conclusion that, just as Hindus were given India and Muslims Pakistan, Sikhs should have their own separate state.[44] The February 1988 issue announces the social, economic, political and foreign policy of *Khalistan*. Thus, while different interest groups will have the right of representation, there will be no room for political parties or trade unions in *Khalistan*. Religion and State will not be separated; rather, all aspects of life will be regulated according to divine commands as preserved in the Sikh faith. The economy is to be based on free enterprise. Considering that in 1988 the Cold War was very much a reality, the author(s) of the Charter make the intriguing, though somewhat odd announcement that Khalistan would 'offer to contribute with manpower for service with the North Atlantic Treaty Organisation'.[45]

In short, the concept of *Khalistan* put forth by the Sikhs derives its ideological legitimacy from the assumption that Sikhs are a nation by virtue of their religion and their specific attachment to Punjabi culture. Additionally, the existence of the Punjab Kingdom of Ranjit Singh is mentioned as historical proof of the Sikhs' claims to a separate state. As regards the territorial extent of Khalistan, it is not clear what precise boundaries are envisaged. Punjab was partitioned in 1947 and reconstituted again in 1966. Sikh advocates of the *Khalistan* scheme are divided and confused on this question. At any rate, whatever the size and shape of Khalistan it is bound to include other minorities unless wholesale forced expulsions of non-Sikhs are undertaken. There is the additional problem of the civil and political rights of freethinkers among Sikhs and of sects such as the *Nirankaris*. It is obvious that these sections of Sikh society will be subjected to censure and very probably some type of persecution. As regards the economic system, some form of capitalism with a strong bias in favour of capitalist farmers seems to be the preferred arrangement of the *Khalistanis*. There are of course many Sikhs who find the *Khalistan* project incompatible with Sikh interests. Harbans Singh Ruprah, a businessman of Southall, London, who harboured pro-Indira Gandhi sympathies, claimed that the *Khalistan* movement was engineered from abroad. Pakistan, the United States, Britain and West Germany were accused by him of being party to a conspiracy to destabilize India.[46] Similar views have been expressed by many other Sikh scholars and intellectuals.

The Sikh separatist movement has obviously survived much longer than was calculated by the government when it ordered military action against Bhindranwale and his followers entrenched inside the Golden Temple. The storming of the Temple which resulted in considerable damage to the buildings inside, including the burning-down of the library containing rare Sikh relics, and huge loss of human life was a fatal miscalculation by Mrs Gandhi. The conflict was suddenly transformed from a confrontation between extremist Sikhs and the Indian government to one between the Sikh community and a Hindu government. It was seen by many Sikhs as an assault on their religion and identity.

That the Sikh community never as a whole supported the *Akalis* can partly be explained by the divisive role which caste and class play in Sikh society, but it also reflects the inadequacy of communalism alone to rouse mass hysteria. Somehow a deep sense of unfair treatment and wounded pride has to affect the psyche of a community before it can be mobilized for sustained action against the alleged oppressor. In the case of the Sikhs, the activation of a wide array of cultural symbols and historical episodes and legends about Sikh resistance against tyranny are easily available.

Under these circumstances, great skill is required of powerholders to exercise their authority in a manner which placates the fears and apprehensions of minority groups. Since India is a multi-religious and multi-ethnic state, secularism, democratic rule, and a more radical distribution of power between the centre and the provinces are a precondition for maintaining the unity of the country through peaceful means. In the context of the Punjab, we find that, notwithstanding the formal secular ideology of the ruling Congress Party, it has been indulging in communal politics from the very onset of independence. The *Akali Dal*, the former *Jan Sangh* and now BJP (*Bharata Janata* Party), of course, have been openly communal. Yet working alliances and coalition governments between them have been possible. In the absence of a strong secular political movement cutting across communal and caste divisions, the problem of divided loyalties to the Indian state and to religious and ethnic particularities is destined to plague the course of Indian politics with disastrous consequences in the long run. In a state based on constitutionalism and democratic values, the establishment of a secular political framework requires at least three important arrangements. One, between the individual and religion: this means that he/she can freely choose a religion, or do without one. Two, between the individual and the state, which means that the religious beliefs of an individual should not subject him/her to discriminatory treatment from the state in terms of rights and duties. Three, between state and religion, which means that the state should not adopt or patronize a particular religion in favour of others. India fulfils these criteria amply in formal constitutional terms, but mainstream politics has increasingly assumed a communal character. The onus of such a negative development lies largely with the various elites that compete with one another for power and influence in the polity.

Notes

1. Khan 1989: 49-50.
2. Bhattacharya 1989: 183.
3. Alavi 1989: 222-23.
4. Gupta 1991: 573.
5. Tully and Jacob 1985: 12.
6. Singh 1963: 42.
7. Cunningham 1918: 49-66.
8. Singh 1963: 82-4.
9. Ibid.: 89.
10. *The Truth*, 1985-6: 36.
11. Singh 1985.
12. Kapur 1986: 46-7.
13. Josh 1977.
14. Mukherji 1985: 71-118.
15. Singh 1966: 258-9.
16. Akbar 1985: 144-9.
17. Ibid.: 157.
18. Jeffrey 1986: 48-9.
19. Brass 1974: 300.
20. Ibid.: 323, 343.
21. Gill and Singhal 1984: 603-8.
22. Brass 1974: 320-1.
23. Singh 1989: 113-76.
24. Akbar 1985: 175.
25. Pettigrew 1975: 121-4.
26. Brass 1974: 371-2.
27. Puri 1985: 67.
28. Helweg 1989: 313-16.
29. Gujral 1985: 42-53.
30. Akbar 1985: 179-82.
31. Tully and Jacob 1985: 50.
32. Ibid.: 57-60.
33. Singh 1984: 9-11.
34. Helweg 1989: 313-19.
35. Aurora 1984: 90-104.
36. Tully and Jacob 1985: 192-217.
37. Citizen's Commission 1985.
38. Memorandum 1985.
39. Gill 1992: 187.
40. Kapur 1986.
41. Bhindranwale's speeches.
42. White Paper 1984: 35-7.
43. Ahmed 1990: 126-32.
44. *Khalistan News* 1987.
45. Ibid.: 1988.
46. Ahmed 1990: 132.

References

Ahmed, I. 1990. 'Sikh Separatism in India and the Concept of Khalistan' in K.R. Haellquist (ed.), *NIAS Report 1990*. Copenhagen: Nordic Institute of Asian Studies.

Akbar, M.J. 1985. *India: The Siege Within*, Harmondsworth: Penguin Books.

Alavi, H. 1989. 'Politics of Ethnicity in India and Pakistan' in H. Alavi and J. Harriss (eds), *Sociology of 'Developing Societies': South Asia.* London: Macmillan.

Bhattacharya, M. 1979. 'Bureaucracy a;nd Politics in India' in Z. Hasan, S.N. Jha and R. Khan (eds), *The State, Political Processes, and identity: Reflections on Modern India.* New Delhi: Sage.

Brass, P.R. 1974. *Language, Religion and Politics in North India*. Cambridge University Press.

Cunningham, J.D. 1918. *A History of the Sikhs*, Oxford University Press.

Gill, S.S. 1992. 'Punjab Crisis and the Political Process', *Economic and Political Weekly* vol. XXVII, no. 5, 1 February, Bombay.

Gill, S.S. and K.C. Singhal 1984. *Economic and Political Weekly,* vol. XIX, no. 14, 7 April, Bombay.

Gujral, I.K. 1985. 'The Economic Dimension' in A. Singh (ed.), *Punjab in Indian Politics: Issues and Trends*. Delhi: Ajanta.

Gupta, D. 1991. 'Communalism and Fundamentalism: Some Notes on the Nature of Ethnic Politics in India' in *Economic and Political Weekly*, vol. VI, nos 11 and 12, Bombay.

Helweg, R.W. 1989. 'Sikh Politics in India: The Emigrant Factor' in N.G. Barrier and V.A. Dusenbery, *The Sikh Diaspora: Migration and the Experience Beyond Punjab*. Delhi: Chanakya Publications.

Jeffrey, R. 1986. *What's Happening to India?* London: Macmillan.

Josh, S.S. 1977. *Hindustan Gadar Party: A Short History*. New Delhi: People's Publishing House.

Kapur, R. 1986. *Sikh Separatism: The Politics of Faith*. London: Geo. Allen and Unwin.

Khan, R. 1989. 'The Total State: The Concept and its Manifestation in the Indian Political System' in Z. Hasan, S.N. Jha and R. Khan (eds), *The State, Political Processes and Identity: Reflection on Modern India*. New Delhi: Sage Publications.

Mukherji, P.N. 1985. 'Akalis and Violence' in A. Singh (ed.), *Punjab in Indian Politics: Issues and Trends*, Delhi: Ajanta Publications.

Memorandum of Settlement on Punjab, July 24, 1985, Delhi: Government of India Publication.

Pettigrew, J. 1975, *Robber Noblemen*, London: Routledge and Kegan Paul.

Puri, R. 1985. 'The Roots of the Problem' in A. Singh (ed.), *Punjab in Indian Politics: Issues and Trends*. Delhi: Ajanta Publications.

Report of the Citizens' Commission (on Delhi riots) 1985. Delhi.

Sant Jarnail Singh Bhindranwale, recorded speeches. Radio-cassette tapes 1-13; videocassette tapes 1-3.

Singh, G. 1989. *History of Sikh Struggles*, vol. I: *1946-1966*, New Delhi: Atlantic Publishers and Distributors.

Singh, K. 1963. *A History of the Sikhs,* vol. I: *1469-1839.* Princeton University Press.
——. 1966. *A History of the Sikhs,* vol. 2: *1839-1964.* Princeton University Press.
——. 1984. 'Genesis of the Hindu-Sikh Divide' in A. Kaur *et al.* (eds), *The Punjab Story.* New Delhi: Roli Books International.
——. 1985. *Ranjit Singh: Maharaja of the Punjab, 1780-1839.* New Delhi: Orient Longman.
Singh, S.K. 1982. *Sachi Sakhi,* Vancouver: Modern Printing House.
The Truth: An International Magazine on Sikhism, 2, (3-4), December 1985 and April 1986, Quebec.
Tully, M. and S. Jacob 1985. *Amritsar: Mrs Gandhi's Last Battle.* London: Jonathan Cape.
White Paper on the Punjab Agitation 1984. Delhi: Government of India Publications.

BUDDHIST ACTIVISM IN SRI LANKA

Bruce Matthews

Theravada Buddhism has been associated with Sri Lanka for over two millennia. It has become an integral part of the culture of the Sinhalese people, who make up three-quarters of the population.[1] Throughout Sri Lanka's long history, Buddhism has shown itself to be concerned with more than otherworldly goals; it has had important and lasting economic, social and political implications as well.

In the current context of Sri Lanka's various crises, not unexpectedly these latter aspects of Buddhism frequently come into focus. This is particularly so with two situations that presently confront the nation. The first is the devastating decade-long civil war between the Sinhalese and the minority Ceylon Tamil community. The second is the struggle within Sinhalese society itself to foster and project an appropriate national image (*jathika urumaya* – literally 'our heritage') in a world perceived to be largely captive to a secularist, materialist, and capitalist West.

This chapter reviews the way in which Buddhism is harnessed by various forces to respond to these issues. Many Sinhalese demand that the role of Buddhism in the destiny of the nation be given a higher public profile and greater force. Among other things, this has led to the politicization of Buddhism and to the evolution of a number of exclusivist Sinhalese 'nationalist' (*deshapremi*) organizations, some of them quite powerful.

It is tempting to call these organizations and the people who support them 'fundamentalist', a term that in part implies something that is possibly retrograde and intolerant. But as Mark Juergensmeyer has pointed out, fundamentalism is not necessarily an appropriate characterization of this phenomenon, in Sri Lanka or even elsewhere in a world marked by similar struggles.[2] A more accurate term is 'activism'. Buddhist activism in turn begets religio-cultural 'nationalists' and sometimes even religio-cultural 'revolutionaries' (for example, Buddhist monks who participated in the insurrections of 1971 and 1988). Buddhist activism may share some of the same religious indications as fundamentalism or of revivalism (arguably a less pejorative term), such as the emotional attachment to a way of being religious and reliance on the succour a religious community gives its devotees.[3] But unlike fundamentalists, Buddhist activists are not necessarily scriptural literalists nor antagonistic towards the technological features of modernity. Their world-view (*arkalpa*) is usually based on a mixture of religious, linguistic, cultural and ethnic claims. They press for a state ideology which will enshrine Sinhalese cultural exclusivism – and Buddhism is only one part of this ideology. Sadly, in this regard it is not infrequently mobilized for questionable purposes (such as the obstruction of political compromise between the Sinhalese and the Tamils). These efforts characterize Buddhism as culturally exclusivist and militant. They do disservice to a religion established on principles of non-violence, tolerance and the search for personal freedom. But the reality of modern Sri Lanka is such that it is an extremely troubled country with a recent history of poor political statesmanship and lingering crises. Not surprisingly, Buddhist activists take advantage of public cynicism about government and its complete failure to bring peace and prosperity. In this regard, it might be asked if the Buddhist activist experience in Sri Lanka is an example of the ferment of religious reassertion seen elsewhere in Asia, notably with Hinduism in India's Bharatiya Janata Party. This is an appropriate question. There are indications in Sri Lanka that Buddhism is ripe for political manipulation on a grand scale. This possibility should not be underestimated, given the notorious engagement of ethnic and religio-cultural causes by Sri Lanka's major political parties since independence in 1948. Notwithstanding the above, two important observations need to be made at this point.

First, although many monks have become involved in activist movements of one sort or another, few in my opinion do so with venal intentions. Most act out of conscience and in good faith that they are performing both meritoriously and for the honour of the community. It must be remembered that monastic education remains old-fashioned and that most monks are not fully aware of the consequences of their involvement in political affairs. They have yet to come to terms with the many irreversible changes that have taken place in their country.

Second, in Sri Lanka no political space for violence in the name of Buddhism has been enjoined. Over a million Tamils continue to live in relative peace among the Sinhalese in the south. The racial massacres of 1983 were never condoned by the monastic order, and are anyway unlikely to recur. Yet clearly, in some other ways, Buddhism has still become too politically involved in Sri Lanka, in particular with the ethnic or so-called 'national' question. In the process, as S.J. Tambiah has rightly asked, might there not also be a question of 'Buddhism betrayed'?[4]

This essay will examine Sinhalese Buddhist activism from three perspectives. First, a brief review is presented of the role of Buddhism in post-independence Sri Lankan political history. Second, Buddhist activism as it pertains to the current ethnic crisis is analyzed. Third, the Buddhist component of an extremist cultural trend in Sinhalese society identified with *jathika chintanaya* ('national ideology') warrants review.

The historical background of Buddhist activism

Turning to the first point, it was not until the 1940s and the end of the colonial era that Sinhalese Buddhism began to take stock of its impending ideological role in the new political order that came with independence. During the British period, Buddhism was in general politically quiescent, despite a prominent religious revival in the late nineteenth century.[5] Even the rise of the *Sinhala Maha Sabha* in 1937 has been explained as a mere attempt to bring the Sinhalese together culturally (divided as they were by such features as caste) with no exclusivist or triumphalist ethnic-political goal. Beneath the surface, however, a Sinhalese political consciousness lay dormant, waiting for the moment it could legitimately assert itself. In 1948 the British bequeathed to Ceylon a secular, Westminster-style polity. This also gave the majority Sinhalese the legitimate authority to introduce their own vision of nationalism, of what the new state should represent. Understandably this was based in part on a traditional Sinhalese world-view associated with a Sinhalese Buddhist understanding of Lanka as an ancient and unitary state. It also embraced elements of a profound racial sentiment linked with language and religion. Bruce Kapferer has called this an 'ontology', maintaining that it is 'beneath the level of conscious reflection, is prereflective... present in a vast array of routine cultural practises'.[6] It is, further, an extremely 'archaic' ontology shared by numerous generations of Sinhalese. William Pfaff might identify this with what he has called 'time lines' in his description of the reemergence of powerful ethnic claims in Eastern Europe.[7]

It could be argued that the Sinhalese have even older 'time lines' and that these are to be located in an unchanged, centuries-old appreciation or understanding of religious, cultural and even national identity. This last point is contentious, with some maintaining that Sinhalese 'nationalism' is something relatively new.[8] But as Steven Kemper has recently persuasively argued, although there might not have been 'nationalism' as such in Sri Lanka 1,000 years ago, 'there was something – whether one calls it a set of beliefs, practices, a discourse... ready to be transformed'.[9] The point to be made here is that, by the time of independence, a sense of Sinhalese Buddhist 'nationalism' was in place and ready to declare itself as such. Some minority communities (notably the Muslims) amicably adapted to the new reality of a Sinhala state. But the Ceylon Tamils, who claimed a historic homeland in the north and east, feared cultural and territorial assimilation. From the outset they resisted the gathering ambition of Sinhala hegemony by seeking some kind of political autonomy. Regrettably, despite many attempts to work out a peaceful solution with the Sinhalese, they were never successful.

Buddhist political involvement since independence

It was in these charged circumstances that the *sangha* became the most visible symbol of the modern Sinhalese nationalism. Monks already associated with the 'Vidyalankara Declaration' of February 1946, had marked out a broad definition of what the *sangha* should be involved in (for example, education and social work).[10] Shortly thereafter they also instigated the 'Kelaniya Political Declaration on the Freedom of Ceylon' and became involved with a number of societies to 'safeguard' Buddhist interests (*sasana-araksaka samiti*).

Perhaps the most important consequence of this activism was the establishment of the *Eksath Bhikku Peramuna* in 1956. This was an organization exclusive to monks. It had as one of its aims advice and direction to the laity on political matters. Although the movement declined in significance after the assassination of Prime Minister S.W.R.D. Bandaranaike in 1959, it nonetheless indicated that many monks challenged the notion of a secular state and wanted a visible role in social and political affairs. The Bandaranaike years were thus marked by an aggressive, militant Buddhism. Bandaranaike was reasonably successful in reining in the newly unleashed forces. He was a liberal populist who realized that there was no way of keeping a majority down. His few years of leadership may have appeared chaotic, but in fact without him the forces of Buddhist ultra-nationalism could have been much more dangerous.

Sinhalese Buddhist activism was not a prominent feature in the 1960s, although its potential to turn against a government was never to be taken lightly.[11] Further, when Mrs Sirimavo Bandaranaike returned to power in 1970, Buddhist activists found that many of their demands were either met or were about to be achieved (special status for the Sinhalese language, the take-over of Christian mission schools, the establishment of a state ministry of Sinhala culture and, in the 1972 Constitution, the recognition of Buddhism having a 'foremost place'). A brief, but serious, attempted insurrection by the radical Sinhalese movement the *Janatha Vimukthi Peramuna* in 1971 involved some Buddhist monks, but this was in essence a class and generational struggle.

This relatively quiescent period came to a close with the election of J.R. Jayewardene's United National Party in 1977. The country was completely transformed by this event. Although ostensibly a free-enterprise, right-of-centre and pro-Western government, the Jayawardene era also introduced an authoritarian executive-style presidency, concentrating power within a small cabal at the top. Parliament became more or less redundant. Further, the defeated prime minister, Mrs Bandaranaike, was unnecessarily humiliated by having her civic rights taken away. Important elements of the *sangha* were clearly distressed by this turn of events. An attempt by the government in 1981 to meet Tamil demands for political autonomy by devolving power to the districts failed completely through presidential lack of will to implement the plan. The upshot of this was the 1983 uprising of the Liberation Tigers of Tamil Eelam in the north and east, the intervention of the Indian army and an imposed Indo-Lankan Accord in 1987, and finally the resurrection of the *Janatha Vimukthi Peramuna* in the south in 1988. All of this occurred within the space of six confused years. Not unexpectedly, it produced a further rapid politicization of the *sangha* and a dramatic intensification of Buddhist activism.

Chief among the activist groups were the *Jathika Peramuna*, organized in 1985 to protest against talks between the government and Tamil secessionists. This led directly to the *Mawbima Surekeemy Vyaparaya* (Movement for the Defence of the Motherland), an important organization designed to bring monks and various Sinhalese cultural-political associations together. The *Mawbima* had as one of its principal leaders the Ven. Palipanne Chandananda, the primate of the Asgiriya chapter of the Siam Nikaya and arguably the most senior and respected monk in the country. The other leader was Mrs Bandaranaike, who participated in huge public rallies with Palipanne. This was the closest that a major politician and a monk have come to a shared office of leadership in Sri Lanka. Palipanne himself maintains that the issues at stake were 'national', not 'political', but the point is that he came forward as the chief spokesman in the 1980s for monks demanding a role in national affairs.[12]

The *Mawbima* was successful in gaining wide public attention. It brought sufficient pressure on the government to alter its policy concerning any proposed devolution of power toward the Tamils. But neither the *Mawbima* nor any other Buddhist activist group was prepared for an unexpected return of the militant Sinhalese movement, the *Janatha Vimukthi Peramuna*, in the south. The JVP quickly tried to corner the Sinhalese sense of outrage at India's intervention in Lanka. They portrayed the 1987 Indo-Lankan Accord as an affront to 'nationalism' and patriotism', thereby harnessing dark ethnic fears and rivalries to their cause. Many monks became involved, beyond the control of their monastic superiors and in despite of the traditional rule of conduct (*vinaya*). Such Buddhist activities were most visible on university campuses.[13]

Although crushed in a two-year struggle marked by extraordinary brutality, the JVP experience has been as important to the issue of continuing Buddhist activism as the civil war in the north and east. It is true that the JVP used the ethnic crisis to heighten its claim for legitimacy as a Sinhalese nationalist movement, but the party's real aim was the overthrow of the state and the introduction of a hybrid Marxist-Sinhala xenophobic rule. Although defeated for the moment, many of the social, economic and political conditions which spawned the JVP are still in place. New organizations rise from time to time to express aspects of the *jathika*, or nationalist ideology fostered by the JVP – and Buddhism, albeit indirectly, is included. Buddhist activism is still in high gear.

Buddhist activism, nationalist enthusiasm and the civil war

Sri Lanka's civil war in the north and east is now in a second phase (which began again in June 1990, after a brief lapse for negotiations and re-armament on both sides). The political demands made by the Liberation Tigers of Tamil Eelam for a separate state appear to have been somewhat reduced lately. The Tamil leader Velupillai Prabakaran now suggests that he would accept a federal model, with merged Northern and Eastern Provinces for the Ceylon Tamils.[14] Most Sinhalese politicians have come a long way in the matter of at least considering 'federalism' (although they would never use that word, which to them somehow appears tainted with secessionist goals) as a future form of government for Sri Lanka. But on the issue of the merger of the Northern and the Eastern Provinces (even if it were only a matter of a much-reduced part of the Eastern Province), Sinhalese political opinion is in general negative and unyielding. This is the only major obstacle that prevents resolution of Sri Lanka's disastrous conflict. Unfortunately, Buddhist activists acting in the name of various nationalist organizations are the chief saboteurs of any initiatives or plans to come to grips with this issue.

This conclusion can be demonstrated in three ways. First, the organizations in question are sufficiently powerful to undo presidential statesmanship. The whole issue of communicating with the Liberation Tigers of Tamil Eelam was the 'Achilles heel' of the late President Ranasinghe Premadasa. For example, in a parliamentary attempt to impeach Premadasa in September 1991, much was made of his shipments of arms to the LTTE during a brief lull in hostilities two years earlier. These arms were to be used against the Indian Peace Keeping Force, which Premadasa wanted out of the country.

Second, the Buddhist activist groups prevent anyone else from the Sinhalese community from making fruitful contact with the LTTE for purposes of political reconciliation. For example, when the Anglican Bishop of Colombo, Kenneth Fernando, met with LTTE leader Velupillai

Prabakaran in Jaffna in January 1993, his visit was vitriolically attacked in the Sinhalese and Colombo-based English language press for weeks. The bishop's attempt at least to open the line of communication was seen as turncoat and naive, and his effort to show that Prabakaran had some 'human' qualities roundly scorned.

Third, the Buddhist groups keep the whole communal question before the public on the boil as much as possible. Sometimes this is achieved through a 'branch' (*sangamaya*) of a political party, such as the *Hela Urumaya* (Sinhala National Heritage) of the Sri Lanka Freedom Party,[15] or the *Mahajana Eksath Peramuna* (a small but vociferous party whose leader, Dinesh Gunawardena, is one of the best orators in Sri Lanka's parliament). The fact is that nearly all of the Sinhalese political parties have strong pro-Sinhala lobbies supported by Buddhist activists, both clerical and lay.[16] More problematic are certain Buddhist activist associations not directly linked with a political party, but nonetheless with political agendas in mind. Some of these (for instance, the *Sinhala/Mahasammata Bhumiputra Pakshaya*, or Sinhala Sons of the Soil Party) are too small or too marginalized to make much of an impact at the moment, though their potential to come suddenly into prominence should not be underestimated.[17] Presently, however, two organizations in particular receive considerable attention in Sri Lanka. The first is the *Sinhala Arakshaya Sanvidhanaya* (Sinhala Defence League), a lay movement led by a former highly respected cabinet minister (Gamini Jayasuriya) who resigned over the issue of the 1987 Indo-Lankan Accord. Although this organization defined itself only in terms of Sinhalese culture, language and ethnic identity, it is nonetheless widely supported by various Buddhist pressure groups. Its aim is to prevent any introduction of federalism as a possible solution to Tamil claims for political autonomy in the north and east. Importantly, and to its credit, the *Arakshaya* claims not to be racist, even arguing that cultural diversity 'is one of the glories of our country and should at all times be protected and fostered'.[18]

A second powerful organization is the *Bauddha Sasanika ha Bauddha Katayuthu Adikshana ha Karya Sadhaka Mandalaya* (Task Force to Supervise Buddhist Religious Activities and Affairs). Established with the specific purpose of preventing a merger between the Northern and Eastern provinces (a key Tamil political demand as a condition for peace), the *Bauddha Sasanika* has since become actively involved in thwarting the efforts of any initiative designed to resolve the ethnic crisis. With a governing body consisting of the prelates of all three Buddhists *nikayas* and other senior clergy, as well as the chairmen of important lay Buddhist organizations such as the All Ceylon Buddhist Council and Young Men's Buddhist Association, the *Bauddha Sasanika* is well situated to be of political consequence. In conclusion, it can be argued that several Sinhalese cultural organizations are politically active in Sri Lanka, and that the 'protection' or 'fostering' of Buddhism is inseparably involved in their ideology. There are divided opinions on the relative significance or potency of these movements, but taken together they represent a widespread religio-cultural public response towards issues that are essentially political.

Jathika Chintanaya: quest for the complete Sinhalese paradigm

A third and final theme of this chapter concerns the role of Buddhism in recent attempts to define what it means to be Sinhalese. The vast majority of Sinhalese are Buddhist,[19] so not unexpectedly the subject of a Sinhalese culture (*samskrutiya*) or world-view (*arkalpa*) will include elements of Buddhism. It has already been argued that Buddhism has become politicized and involved in state affairs, especially in matters which appear to threaten the ethnic *status quo* or dominance of the Sinhalese. But even apart from the destabilizing effects of the civil war on Buddhist consciousness, there is yet another debate on whether the Sinhalese are well-served or not by continuing to uphold so many perceived Western standards and customs. Sometimes this results in Sinhalese cultural proponents urging a wholesale 'purification' of Sinhala society and institutions. Buddhist activists are easily attracted to these aims if only because they are so closely attached to their own essentially mythical vision of a glorious Sinhala past. One study cogently summarizes the roots of this popular understanding thus:

> Sinhala ideology derives from a naive understanding of the Sinhala past – of an agrarian society organized in villages and temples and reservoirs, of Sinhala peasants with free access to their own land, of a spirit of mutual help and cooperation in work, of a people who were egalitarian in their social relations and had high moral and spiritual values drawn from an adherence to Buddhism. The culture that developed in this Sinhalese – Buddhist agrarian society was held to have qualities of austere simplicity, deep religiosity and accord with nature. This society and cultural formation was now under threat from alien and corrupting values intruding from the 'decadent West'. While being anti-capitalist and anti-Western, Sinhalese ideology was also specifically antagonistic to the Tamil ethnic group. The growing nationalism of the Tamils posed a threat to Sinhalese Buddhist hegemony of society which was perceived as absolutely essential for the restoration and maintenance of the Sinhala community.[20]

Many today will insist that the specific Sinhalese ethnic heritage this passage refers to is also a 'national' heritage (*jathika urumaya*), based on a special 'social character' (*samaja chittaya*) and a particular kind of 'nationalist' economy (*jathika arthika*, a kind of updated economic model based on Prime Minister S.W.R.D. Bandaranaike's 1956 prototype). As an ideology designed to reintroduce a 'lost' Sinhalese way of life, this is politically most seductive. For example, the Democratic United National Front (*Prajathantravadi Eksath Jathika Pakshaya*), a new party formed in 1990 by estranged UNP politicians, has already set itself up to be the guardian of traditional Sinhalese religio-cultural interests. Not to be outdone, the former UNP government did everything in its power to show that *it* was the protector of the Sinhala Buddhist heritage, often with ludicrously poor taste.[21] Yet, despite their efforts, the Sinhalese political parties have not been able to 'corner the market' and thereby determine the issue of Sinhala cultural ideology.

Apart from its place in the quasi-political organizations designed only to combat Ceylon Tamil gains, the ideological question is also at the forefront of intellectual life. In this regard it is sometimes referred to as *jathika chintanaya* (national ideology or way of thinking) and identified largely with the hard-line Sinhalese cultural exclusivism and nationalism that reemerged in the 1980s. The actual phrase *jathika chintanaya* first emerged in 1984 when certain prominent Sinhalese social scientists were victims of a prolonged media attack because they had dared to challenge the myths of Sinhala origins and the rising ethnic chauvinism of the time.[22] Shortly thereafter Nalin de Silva, a Colombo university mathematics professor, and Gunadasa Amarasekera, a Colombo dental surgeon, used the phrase to help define the need for a uniquely Sinhalese educational methodology.[23]

But *jathika chintanaya* has an application far beyond the few hundred university students who currently embrace it at Colombo University. It is also popular among sectors of the urban elite and among the *sangha*. (In a perhaps somewhat far-fetched observation Nalin de Silva likes to point out that *jathika chintanaya* is also found in every village Buddhist temple.) What is particularly interesting about this 'movement' (de Silva insists it is only a 'philosophy', not an organization) is its scheme to completely restructure Sinhalese education. With that theoretically accomplished, its reforming effects on society, economy and polity would then automatically follow. De Silva's *jathika chintanaya* appears fairly straightforward (although his writings on the subject are complicated and obtuse). Essentially, he rejects the adequacy of Western epistemology for the Sinhalese, arguing that the West's 'extreme rationalism' has isolated 'the laws governing the universe', and has failed to offer a holistic understanding of reality. Further, the 'Judaic' belief in a creator God has led Western man 'to think he has a right to exploit world resources as well as women to satisfy his needs'.[24]

De Silva's aim is to introduce a specifically Sinhalese way of understanding, learning and teaching. This will require a 'revolution in the
way of thinking' (*chintanaya viplavaya*). Although ignored when at
all possible by academic administrators and political authorities, de Silva's
jathika chintanaya is by no means regarded as a crank theory by his
many followers. He has further boldly pointed out how the use of English
in the universities (a language that is now confined almost entirely
to the professional and science faculties) 'divides' (*kaduwa* – literally
'the sword') those with privileged backgrounds from those without.
University students coming from rural locations are often at a disadvantage
in this regard. De Silva's *jathika chintanaya* appeals to them greatly.
In this regard, some interpret it as a nursery for disaffected Sinhalese youth
who might formerly have been attracted to the JVP. Although *jathika
chintanaya* is not specifically a Buddhist phenomenon, it is nonetheless
easy to see how it can be used by Buddhist activists to further their aims.

We have argued first that Buddhist activism is an historic and ongoing
facet of Sinhalese life. In the post-colonial context, Buddhist activists
have had major contributions to make towards the social and political
evolution of the country. No government since 1948 has been able
to ignore the influence of Buddhist interest groups. Although the state
in theory remains 'secular', it is important to note that Buddhism is
constitutionally enshrined as the foremost religion and is guaranteed
protection. But Buddhist activists have not just been concerned with
spiritual priorities. Buddhism as a religion has always been associated
with Sinhalese culture and language. The fourfold formula of *basa,
rasadesa* and *sasansa* (language, nation, country and religion) has shown
itself to be more than a mere litany or ritual mumble. It continues
to demand that Buddhism be acknowledged in an ethnic and cultural
context, and not merely as an independent spiritual belief.

Second, in this regard it is averred that Buddhist activists frequently
have political agendas. An example is the unrelenting pressure certain
Sinhalese religio-cultural groups exert to contain Ceylon Tamil ambitions
for territorial autonomy or sovereignty. Third, because of Buddhism's
close association with Sinhala culture and language, not unexpectedly
it is part of Sinhalese attempts to re-examine the way in which that
culture expresses itself in the modern world. One example of this is
the *jathika chintanaya* initiative, which arguably can be called a kind
of cultural fundamentalism. Critics of this way of thinking are concerned
that it is an ideological step backwards at a time when most of Asia
goes forward in these matters, and that it will lead to dangerous degrees
of radicalism and fanaticism if left unchecked. Sri Lanka is one of
the most tragic countries in the world today, particularly because of

its long-term civil war. Buddhist activism is partly responsible for this, related as it is to Sinhalese obstructionism and cultural exclusivism. Admittedly the present leadership of the Ceylon Tamil cause has become fanatical and beyond the reach of moderates, but it can be shown that Sinhalese religio-cultural organizations still do much to prevent reconciliation. No Sinhalese prime minister or president has had the courage – or even the political strength – to confront and control these forces. Until Buddhism is freed from its current culturally triumphalist harness, it cannot be expected to be the true liberating force that Gotama had in mind and that the Sinhalese people deserve.

Notes

1. The other major ethnic community are the Ceylon Tamils, who make up twelve per cent of the island's population. They are predominantly Saivite Hindus, although this fact is never invoked by Tamil secessionists. Traditionally, most have lived in the Northern and Eastern Provinces, but the civil war has reduced the Tamil population in the main city of Jaffna to about 400,000. There are also about 1 million Ceylon Tamils living in the south among the Sinhalese. A further million so-called Indian or 'plantation' Tamils live in the southern hills, largely as estate workers. They are not involved in the civil war. Thus the Tamil community in Sri Lanka is highly fragmented, and the question of what its various sections should be called is always somewhat controversial. A second important minority in Sri Lanka are the Muslims (Ceylon Moors), who make up 6% of the population. Although mostly Tamil-speaking, they have long co-operated with the Sinhalese in political matters.
2. Juergensmeyer 1993: 85.
3. De Silva; Björkman 1988: 107.
4. Tambiah 1992: 1.
5. 'A deep-rooted desire to be on good terms with the established political authority was probably one of the reasons why the Buddhist 'revival' of the nineteenth century did not develop into an organized political movement for national independence'. Malalgoda, 1976: 261.
6. Kapferer 1988: 83.
7. 'The past lies in strata of human experience, never totally forgotten even when deeply buried in society's consciousness, but too often still raw at the surface. Here the time lines are crucial.' Pfaff 1992: 59.
8. Certainly the Sinhalese as a society, much less a nation, have had some late additions, including whole castes that came from south India as recently as three centuries ago. See Roberts 1979: 39. Further, some assert that the entire notion of nationalism is fairly modern. See Anderson 1983: 13.
9. Kemper 1991: 17, 72.
10. Nowhere is the motivation for this activist role more clearly expressed than in Ven. Walpola Rahula's *Bhiksuvage urumaya*, Colombo: Swastika, 1946.
11. Mrs Bandaranaike's defeat in 1964 was seen as a 'victory' for the *sangha*. Bechert quotes one senior monk commenting on the defeat: 'this government which came into power with the blessings of the *sangha* destroyed itself because it did not continue to get the blessings of the *sangha*. A government in this country needs the blessings

of the *sangha*'. Bechert 1966: 359. Although Buddhist activism was less strident during the 1960s and 1970s, nonetheless the 'four pillars' of consensual ideology that each of the major Sinhalese parties had to endorse included socialism, language, history and religion. See Jupp 1978: 356. Even today political parties must acknowledge the primacy of these features in their political platforms, as for example in the traditional Sri Lanka Freedom Party slogan: '*Sinhala rata, Sinhala jathiya, Sinhala bhasawa, Sinhala bauddha*' (Sinhala country, nation, language, religion).

12. Interview, Ven. Palipanne Chandananda, 7 Feb. 1989. Palipanne did not keep the *Mawbima* leadership for long. He was soon surpassed by far more volatile exponents of *sangha* involvement, notably Ven. Dengamuwe Nalaka Thera and Maduluwave Sobitha Thera. A continuing concern is the possible creation of an entirely new *nikaya* based on Sinhalese xenophobic aims. To prevent this, some important monks have chosen to link themselves with certain Sinhalese Buddhist organizations. One monastic group in particular is thereby prevented from monopolizing a repertoire of narrowly defined 'nationalist' issues.

13. At Peradeniya University in 1987, monks constituted about 25% of the Arts students, a not inconsiderable number. The monks 'student union' (*Bhikhsu Bala Mandalaya*) claimed no official affiliation with the JVP, but took no action to control the activities of its more thuggish members. Before the JVP closed the universities in the south for two years, monks regularly took part in JVP controlled meetings, their presence adding 'cultural weight' to JVP strategy.

14. BBC interview with Velupillai Prabakaran, 26 Feb. 1993.

15. '*Hela*' is a shortened form of 'Sinhala', but a proper noun in its own right. The *Hela Urumaya* is represented by a group of Sri Lanka Freedom Party members of parliament who are antagonistic towards their leader, Mrs Sirimavo Bandaranaike. They represent the conservative wing of a power struggle in this political party. Their pro-Sinhala ideology is based on claims that the Ceylon Tamils have a 'diabolical design' to take over the whole country. These racist assertions are taken seriously by many from all sectors of Sinhalese society.

16. There are important exceptions. For example, the politically left-of-centre *Lanka Sama Samaja* Party has recently supported Tamil demands for a merged north and east, averring that this is the only way to ensure a peaceful settlement of the communal discord. This also constitutes an outright rejection of Buddhist activism in politics.

17. Among other things, this movement argues that voting rights in Sri Lanka should be confined to Sinhala Buddhists (the only true 'sons of the soil') and that an ethnic quota system be introduced (even in the private sector) to keep the economy under Sinhalese control. The *Mahasammata Bhumiputra* is exclusively Buddhist and will not accept Sinhalese Christians into its membership.

18. *Sunday Times*, Colombo, 21 Feb. 1993.

19. The only other religion embraced by sizable numbers of Sinhalese is Christianity, with just under 8% of the population. See Roberts 1979: 30.

20. Abeysekera 1987: 3.

21. For example, at the government-sponsored 're-awakening' (*gam udawa*) of the town of Kataragama in 1991, a statue of the mythical Ravana as the 'first king' and 'true father' of the Sinhalese was unveiled by the late president, Ranasinghe Premadasa. See *Christian Worker*, 3rd Quarter, 1991.

22. This affair has become known as the *Divaina* (or *Divayina*) controversy, named after a major Sinhala language newspaper. In her cogent analysis of this event, Serena Tennekoon concludes that 'Sinhala culture thus was raised to the symbolic stature of the Buddha, effectively positioned beyond criticism and debate' (1987: 10).

23. Nalin de Silva's central work is *Mage Lokya* (My World), 1992. Much the same philosophy is found in Gunadasa Amarasekera's *Ganaduwa Madiyama Dakinemi Arunala* (I See a Streak of Light in the Thick Darkness), 1987.

24. De Silva 1992: 5.

References

Abeysekera, C. 1987. *Facets of Ethnicity*. Colombo: Social Scientists Association.

Amarasekera, G. 1987. *Ganaduna Madiyama Dakinemi Arunalu*. Nugegoda: Piyavi.

Anderson, B. 1983. *Imagined Communities: Reflections on the Origin and Spread of Nationalism*. London: Verso.

Bechert, H. 1966. *Buddhismus, Staat und Gesellschaft in den Landen des Theravada-Buddhismus*, vol. I. Frankfurt: Alfred Metzer.

Bharati, A. 1976. 'Monastic and lay Buddhism in the 1971 Sri Lanka insurgency', *Journal of Asian and African studies*, April 1976.

De Silva, K. M. 1988. 'Buddhist Revivalism, Nationalism and Politics in Modern Sri Lanka' in J.W. Björkman (ed.), *Fundamentalism, Revivalists and Violence in South Asia*. Delhi: Manohar.

De Silva, N. 1992. *Mage Lokya*, Dehiwela: Mudasaya.

Goonetilleke, H.A.I. 1975. *The April 1975 Insurrection in Ceylon: A Bibliographic Commentary*, 2nd edn. Leuven.

Juergensmeyer, M. 1993. 'Why Religious Nationalists are not Fundamentalists', *Religion*, vol. 23, no. 1.

Jupp, J. 1978. *Sri Lanka: A Third World Democracy*, London: Frank Cass.

Kapferer, B. 1988. *Legends of People, Myths of State: Violence, Intolerence and Political Culture in Sri Lanka and Australia*. Washington: Smithsonian Institute.

Kemper, S. 1991. *The Presence of the Past: Chronicles, Politics and Culture in Sinhala Life*, Ithaca: Cornell University Press.

Malalgoda, K. 1976. *Buddhism in Sinhalese Society, 1750-1900: A Study in Religious Revival and Change*, Berkeley: University of California Press.

Pfaff, W. 1992. 'The Absence of Empire', *New Yorker*, 10 Aug. 1992.

Rahula, W. 1946. *Bhiksuvage Urumaya*. Colombo: Swastika.

Roberts, M. 1979. *Collective Identities, Nationalisms and Protest in Modern Sri Lanka*. Colombo: Marga.

Tambiah, S.J. 1992. *Buddhism Betrayed? Religion, Politics and Violence in Sri Lanka*. University of Chicago Press.

Tennekoon, S. 1987. 'Symbolic Refractions of the Ethnic Crisis: the Divaina Debates on Sinhala Identity', in C. Abeysekera (ed.), *Facets of Ethnicity*. Colombo: Social Scientists Association.

QUESTIONING AUTOCRACY IN BURMA

BUDDHISM BETWEEN TRADITIONALISM AND MODERNISM

Mikael Gravers

Buddhism is a fundamental element in defining Burman ethnic and national identity in opposition to foreign, especially Western, cultural identity.[1] In Burmese history, nationalism inscribed Buddhism as an essential and primordial element of the Burman ethos. In this way Buddhism became synonymous with genuine Burman ethnic identity.[2] Thus Buddhism has become a powerful medium of antagonistic political strategies with either a universalistic (humane) or a particularistic (cultural primordialist) emphasis. Buddhism can be considered a field of political and symbolic struggle between traditionalism and modernism, and between autocracy and democracy. The use and the interpretation of Buddhism in mediating political struggles vary depending upon the social position of the agents: monks, peasants, urban elites or the military. The role of Buddhism in Burma is also part of a global process of struggles to define ethnic and national identities.[3] In this process modernist demands of human rights and democracy collide with nationalistic emphasis on traditional cultural and religious substance. And it is precisely in a political practice where religion, culture, identity and nationalism mix that we find examples of religious fundamentalism and the questioning of secular regimes in the present world order.[4] This chapter is an attempt to outline some of the main oppositional properties of Buddhism in the recent history of Burma. For definitions of the theoretical concepts applied, please see the appendix to this chapter (pp. 316-17).

Buddhism and the struggle for democracy

'To be Burmese is to be Buddhist.'[6]

This statement made by the 1991 Nobel Prize laureate, Aung San Suu Kyi, is indisputable in Burma.[7] In this section the role of Buddhism in the recent violent struggle is analysed, and especially Aung San Suu Kyi's interpretation of Buddhist concepts in formulating a strategy and a model for democracy against the autocratic State Law and Order Restoration Council (SLORC), the name of the military regime. In the writings and speeches of Aung San Suu Kyi, Buddhism is used as

297

a medium of translating universal values of human rights and democracy into Burmese concepts. This is not done merely with the intention of appealing to tradition but to explain democracy, the rule of law, and human rights to a population long denied access to these rights and to international discourse on these matters:

> The Burmese people, who have had no access to sophisticated academic material, got to the heart of the matter by turning to the words of the Buddha on the four causes of decline and decay: failure to recover that which had been lost, omission to repair that which had been damaged, disregard of the need for reasonable economy, and the elevation to leadership of men without morality and learning.[8]

Aung San Suu Kyi's interpretation of the causes of social and moral decline is a precise demonstration of how Buddhist concepts are used by the people to criticize the regime. By making statements within the religious field of absolute ethical values the speaker places her/himself above the secular debate and political violence – in a 'sacred refuge' – and by provoking the opponent, in this case the military regime, to expose its anti-democratic and inhumane practices. This specific function of religion is not particularly Buddhist or Burmese, and may be found where autocratic and totalitarian regimes have ruled for so long that civil society has almost disintegrated.

Aung San Suu Kyi has characterized Burmese society as corrupted by fear: 'Fear of losing power corrupts those who wield it and fear of the scourge of power corrupts those who are subject to it.'[9] According to Aung San Suu Kyi's interpretation of Buddhist teaching, the regime is following the wrong path. The wrong path (*agati*) comprises the four selfish qualities which corrupt the mind and obstruct enlightenment: corruption by desire, hatred, aberration due to ignorance and fear. Fear is often the root of other three selfish qualities. Indeed, no one can deny that Burma has been engulfed by violence and hatred, xenophobia and corruption. The chain of causation (*nidanas*) in Buddhism, which begins with ignorance, is easily applied to developments in Burma. While the former leader, General Ne Win, and his entourage of officers are exposed as the culprits, Aung San Suu Kyi also explains the situation as a result of passivity and fear on the part of the whole population. It has lost faith (*saddha*) in Buddhist ethics (*sila*), in justice, liberty and human rights. Faith here is not blind belief but practice according to Buddhist teaching (*dhamma*).[10]

SLORC has been ridiculing and condemning human rights and the Universal Declaration of 1948 as Western inventions alien to the Burmese tradition. Thus the regime has dismissed Amnesty International's reports on its brutality as neo-colonialism and imperialism and denied UN envoys and other observers admission to investigate human rights issues. The regime also considers democracy as a particularly Western cultural construction in total opposition to Burmese cultural values. SLORC argues that the population is not fit for political responsibility and that Western democracy is not suited to the Burmese.[11] To support its argument the regime claims that foreign enemies are trying to split the Union and thus threatening Burman culture. The influence of foreigners (*kala*) is seen as the hand behind the ethno-nationalist separatist movements among the minorities.[12] And the foreign media, especially the BBC, are rightly considered a serious enemy in a country where the population is denied access to global information. The army claims to be the only force which has been able to keep the Union from disintegrating since the coup in 1962. It points to the situation from 1948 to 1962 and argues that parliamentary democracy and the government collapsed because it released opposing ethnic and religious forces.

Aung San Suu Kyi reiterates that the Burmese population was responsive to representative government in that period despite ethnic and religious conflicts. The causes of the decline can be explained in Buddhist terms. In Buddhist cosmology and teaching everything comes under the law of impermanence (*anicca*): the self, society and even the influence of Buddhist *dhamma* (the teaching of Buddha, the law of existence). Social decline and moral decay is embedded in the cosmological cycles between the Buddha (5,000 years ago) and the coming Buddha (*bodhisatta*, 'embryo Buddha').

During the demonstrations against authoritarian rule in 1988, Aung San Suu Kyi soon discovered that the population still used the Buddhist concepts of the four causes of decline and decay to interpret the political situation. These concepts refer to the mythical Buddhist monarch – a righteous King (*dhammaraja*) who restored peace and well-being when society collapsed into chaos. The King also had the title *Mahasammata*, the name/title used in the Burmese version which was conferred 'because he is named ruler by the unanimouse consent of the people'.[13]

As a *dhammaraja*, a king or leader is expected to rule according to ten duties: almsgiving, observance of the Buddhist precepts, self-sacrifice, rectitude, gentleness, self-restraint, denial of anger, non-violence, forbearance and non-opposition to the will of the people.[14] He should avoid avarice, greed (*lobha*), ill will, hatred, anger (*dosa*) and delusion (*moha*), and rule without the use of force (*danda*) and weapons of destruction (*sattha*). Aung San Suu Kyi put a special emphasis upon the last of the ten duties: 'The tenth duty of kings, nonopposition to the will of the people (*avirodha*) tends to be singled out as a Buddhist endorsement for democracy...a strong argument for democracy...i.e. respect for public opinion and just law.'[15]

In this way traditional values serve the modern discourse of democracy and combine particular cultural concepts with universal ideals. From the duties of a *dhammaraja* it is easy to deduce that it is the right of the people to remove an unjust ruler. And rebellion against a ruler who was not a righteous monarch has occurred many times in the history of Burma. Pretenders (*mìn-laùng*, 'king-to-be') have tried to legitimize rebellions by claiming to be universal rulers (*cakkavatti*) and the coming Buddha (*bodhi-satta*), embodying the moral qualities and the symbolic power of these figures in the Buddhist cosmology. Aung San Suu Kyi refers to this tradition: 'Rebellion then is a universal right when life and welfare is threatened'. In her view it is a right equal to the preamble in the Universal Declaration of Human Rights establishing the following as a fundamental part of freedom: 'Whereas it is essential, if man is not to be compelled to have recourse, as a last resort, to rebellion against tyranny and oppression, that human rights should be protected by law.'[16] The Human Rights Declaration and Buddhism are thus based on the same fundamental and universal values transgressing frontiers of cultural differences. To Aung San Suu Kyi then, the principles of serving the people by generosity (*dana*), virtue (*sila*) and nonviolence (*ahimsa*) are equal to liberal democracy, individual freedom and human rights. They are all antidotes to fear and violence.

Within this discourse, the regime attacks her by accusing her of importing foreign values like democracy produced by Western culture to the detriment of Burmese culture. The xenophobic fear of losing cultural identity is thus added to the fear of imprisonment and torture. All who think like Aung San Suu Kyi are considered to be un-Burman and *kalas* (foreigners) and do not deserve to have equal rights. They will even be denied their citizenship and national identity as her children have been because their father is British. The regime also attacked her for saying that Buddha was an ordinary human being. They accused her of sacrilege even though Buddha is not a deity. She responded by saying that it is in the teaching of Buddhism not to lie; that is the fourth precept: 'refraining from false speech'. In this way the National League for Democracy (NLD) – the leading opposition party – and Aung San Suu Kyi have challenged the regime in an attempt to underline its legitimacy.

The military grossly violated Buddhist ethics by killing thousands during the demonstrations and by using all manner of extrajudicial measures. In July 1989 Aung San Suu Kyi was put under house arrest and at the time of writing is still living in virtual isolation. In 1990, after the landslide victory of the NLD in the elections, the regime blocked the new parliament and arrested most of the opposition leaders. In August of that year 7,000 monks in the former roval city of Mandalay decided to refuse offerings from soldiers and their relatives and declined to perform religious rites for them. This dramatic symbolic action is described as 'the power to overturn the begging bowl'. In Burman, the term for ritual boycott (*thabeit hmauk*) is used colloquially also to mean 'strike'. The term is loaded with much symbolic power, as is the religious act, and the boycott is rarely used by the monks.[17] In Mandalay it came as a reaction to the killing of demonstrators by the army and among those killed were two monks, making the killing the most extreme act of demerit. The boycott spread all over the city, where 80,000 of Burma's some 300,000 monks live. Monks in other towns in Upper Burma soon joined the boycott. Troops were sent in to raid 350 monasteries and imprisoned dozens of monks. The boycott thus came to an end but this demonstration was another severe blow to the SLORC regime and probably also to its support among the rank and file. The boycott also sent a shock-wave through Thailand.[18] The monks in Mandalay had been active during the pro-democracy demonstrations in 1988 when they maintained order in the city. Mandalay, the last royal city, has been the hub of political involvement by monks since the struggle for independence and is perhaps not representative of the whole country. Although most monks, especially the younger ones, are probably opposed to the regime, it is also likely that many are against political action – and against direct involvement in secular affairs generally. Monks should indeed refrain from participating in such affairs since attachment to worldly matters diverts attention away from religious practice, especially meditation. By renouncing the world the monk guarantees the preservation of *dhamma* and the accumulation of merit for the improvement of *karma*. We will return to this complex contradiction contained within Buddhism between the world and the renunciation of it. There can be no doubt, however, that this confrontation between the army and the monks underlined the disharmony and extreme social and moral decline in Burmese society and served to discredit SLORC despite its claims that monasteries were hiding heroin, weapons, fake monks and communists.

Buddhism as a philosophical system and as institutional religious practice is thus a major medium in the struggle between autocracy and democracy – especially when all other forms of political practice are prohibited through the use of violence. Aung San Suu Kyi's appeal to the public through the use of Buddhist concepts thus strikes at the core of everything Burman: the cosmology, the ontology and the ethical system are combined in one singular model consisting of 'timeless values'.[19] Buddhism not only appeals to belief in precepts and *karma* but to the very essence of belonging to a society through the sharing of its fundamental values. This traditional identity is expressed by Aung San Suu Kyi: 'Buddhism obviously played a large part in creating [cultural] homogeneity, but it could not be said to have supplied ideas to support nationalism; rather it provided an essential component of the self-concept, which enabled the Burmese to see themselves as different from foreigners.'[20]

This opposition of mutually exclusive culturally and religiously defined identities became manifest in modern nationalist movements in the twentieth century and has been radicalized further during the recent struggle.[21] By locating the original Burman identity in Buddhism, Aung San Suu Kyi combines the primordial sentiments of Burman cultural identity with modern liberal democratic ideals: in other words, she ascribes universal values to a particular ethos and reproduces the past in the present and in the future.

Religion and state in the history of Burma

The use of Buddhism in political struggles is not a recent phenomenon. It has been an important part of the historical changes in Burmese society and has a major role in the construction of social and cultural identity.

When Burma gained its independence in 1948, the constitution provided for religious freedom and the recognition of Buddhism, Islam, Christianity, Hinduism and Animism as equal religions. Although Buddhism was mentioned as the religion professed by the majority of the population, it was not made the state religion. Burma's leader and national hero, Aung San, made it clear that religion and politics had to be separated so as to avoid political abuse of religion and conflicts between ethnic groups.[22] In a speech addressed to the monks, he said: 'You are the inheritors of a great religion. Purify it and broadcast it to all the world so that mankind might be able to listen to its timeless message of love and brotherhood...carry the message of religious freedom – freedom from fear, ignorance, superstition.'[23]

Politics and religion as institutions are of different orders and must not be mixed – that is, the *sangha* (the monastic order) must look after religious functions and keep discipline in its own ranks. State and *sangha* must remain separated. In the pre-colonial period, the *sangha* and dynastic rule were also separate institutions. Monasteries could intervene and protect people from persecution by the King or by governors. The King, on the other hand, could initiate a purification of the *sangha* to strengthen discipline and make new editions of the sacred texts. In this way, King and monk were counterparts with complementary social functions – the former representing the 'hot' world of power and government, the latter the 'cool' life of worldly renunciation and meditation. Dynasty and *sangha* were the two central elements of the 'state' united under the *dhamma* and its laws of impermanence.[24] The King was the protector of Buddhism and the *sangha*, and since he was born to be a King he was judged to possess a strong *karma* and *hpòn* ('glory'), related to male power. *Hpòn* is the sign of merit. A monk is called *hpòngyi* in Burman ('a person of great glory'), obtained by renouncing the world.

But glory in a layman or a King is made manifest in his personal charisma. As we have mentioned, the King would be compared with the ancient ideals of a righteous monarch (*dhammaraja*), the upholder of material welfare, and a *cakkavatti* ('universal ruler'), the defender of Buddhism and the state.[25] These two were often combined in a *bodhisatta* and represented in a royal person, his titles and behaviour. But lost wars, natural disasters and a decline in welfare and morals could deprive the King of his power. He would appear as one who had exhausted his *karma* and would be challenged by a pretender (*mìn laùng*) and a rebellion. *Karma*, glory and power had to be constantly reproduced and accumulated by the building of pagodas and the giving of gifts to the monks. But the accumulation of symbolic power was always measured against the development of society.[26]

In 1886, when the British had conquered all of Burma and exiled the last King, Buddhism and the *sangha* lost the support of secular rule. During the 'pacification' of Upper Burma, several monks left the monasteries and became active in the widespread guerrilla warfare against the foreign conqueror. This caused great surprise to the British who considered Buddhist monks to be completely apolitical and unworldly. There were several reasons for this direct participation in acts of war, which constituted a clear break with monastic practice. First of all the conquest was seen not only as a political and economic subjugation but as a complete destruction of the Burman world order and its religious values, and of Burman cultural identity. It is impossible within the confines of this chapter to list all the details relating to this, but a few examples may illustrate the Burman feeling of total humiliation and loss of identity.[27] The British allowed Baptist missionaries to convert the Karen and to preach against Buddhism. The missionaries disrupted Buddhist ceremonies and warned against 'the worship of living gods'. Preachers called for a holy war against 'oriental despotism' so as to pave the way for Western civilization. The Baptists not only demanded absolute conversion but also denunciation of the cultural traditions connected with Buddhism. For example, the monasteries had a significant function as schools for male children, even if their parents were Muslims or Animists. But the Baptists did not allow any connection with Buddhist institutions or the monks. The Burmans regarded the missions as agents of Western culture – in other words not merely in terms of religious conversion but also as a force aimed at the annihilation of their ethnic identity. Today a Burman/Burmese who is not a Buddhist is viewed as peripheral in almost every sense and is sometimes even called a *kala* (foreigner).[28]

Christian Karens and some Baptist missionaries were directly involved in the military conquest and pacification. Karens decapitated monks believed to be partisans and took thousands of rupees in rewards. British soldiers used the monasteries as barracks and insisted on wearing their shoes when inside – an insult to and an extreme humiliation of Buddhism and Burman ethnic identity. Burman cultural and social identity was thus attacked and placed in extreme ethnic opposition to Western Christian civilization. Fear of losing the means to accumulate merit, to learn the *dhamma*, and to preserve ethical precepts, eroded and attacked the very essence of Burman identity. Foreign influence was seen as a threat to the rituals and ceremonies and the daily practices of giving food to the monks, obtaining spiritual advice and other functions which connected the order of the universe with individual existence. Buddhism supplied a total model – with cosmological, ontological and ideological elements – and with the universe cast askew through the appearance of social and moral decay, the time had come to resist and restore that order. In the dynastic model of the state, Buddhism created a holistic hierarchical order of monks, kings and laypeople defined by *karma* and *hpòn*. In a modernist-inspired model of the state, power is supposed to be demystified and detached from its previous religious roots, although these roots may still be used metaphorically.

From 1886 Buddhism changed and thus became the medium for more than one model of society and cultural identity. And its relationship with worldly power changed. According to Aung San, the modern state is connected with politics and society, while religion is concerned with individuals and consciousness as separate functions. As we shall see, this separation is not easily made even though the constitution explicitly names it.

In summary, Buddhism in precolonial times supplied a model of the universe including secular power and its change. A general model, of course, cannot account for every individual social action or for the changes which occurred in Burmese society. There is great variation in the understanding, knowledge and use of *dhamma* and its concepts.[29] The important point to emphasize in this generalization is that Buddhism has dominated daily practice at all levels of society in the past and the present: laypeople are born of *karma*, depend on *karma* and have to 'invest' in *karma* by accumulating merit. Merit not only improves the karmic position now and in future cycles of existence, but also provides the individual with social prestige (*goung*). To accumulate merit one has to give and share (*dana*); the collection of money for religious purposes by groups and villages is both an individual and a collective act.[30] The giving of presents to monks and monasteries is returned in merit, but it also prevents wealth from engendering greed, lust and attachment. Thus, wealth and generosity are prerequisites for the accumulation of merit. *Dana* is a neccessary act whereby material wealth is transformed into symbolic capital and power. Symbolic capital connects the social life of the past with the present and future existence.

It renders the contradictory properties of the secular world and the sacred world complementary within the same holistic model. That is why the monks are so important; they are the agents of this exchange – the field of religious merit – which is indispensible to individuals and society. And they are indispensible because everything changes – including adherence to Buddhist values. However, Buddhism and its doctrine (*dhamma*) represent a permanent symbolic power.

We could say, in Weberian terms, that Buddhism is the *Gesamthabitus* of Burman society and culture, the dominant frame of reference in the formation of identity.[31] Colonization not only confirmed this role of Buddhism but made it the basis for the construction of nationalist strategies and models for a free Burma. As it has been used by nationalists and at present by Aung San Suu Kyi, Buddhism generates a bridge across the discontinuity and disruption of history created by colonization. Buddhism reinscribes Burman self-identification in the past on to the present and renders a future beyond autocracy possible.

Buddhism and nationalism

'If Buddhism was used as a political weapon by the Burmese, it was not from Machiavellian motives, but because Buddhism was and is both the symbol and the essential ingredient of their national identity.'[32]

While Buddhism is neither the origin of nationalism nor the only substance of national identity in Burma, nationalism intervened and elevated Buddhism to the essence of Burman national identity during colonial rule. Nationalism 'fundamentalized' Buddhism as the Burman ethos was threatened by foreigners, their culture and the Christian religion. By stressing particular cultural values – and not the universal elements, as Aung San Suu Kyi has done – nationalism used Buddhism in the first decades of the twentieth century as part of a traditionalist or neo-traditionalist strategy.

The first organization to use Buddhism in opposition to colonial rule was the Young Men's Buddhist Association (YMBA) established in 1906 as a response to Christian dominance. The members of YMBA organized campaigns for 'no footwear in the pagodas'. In the 1920s the Buddhist reaction became more radical. U Ottama, a monk who had travelled in Asia, wrote nationalist articles in a Rangoon newspaper and proposed a boycott of British goods. He organized *Wunthanu Athins* ('nationalist associations') whose supporters demonstrated in homespun clothes. About 10,000 of these village associations became an alternative source of authority to that of the headman serving the colonial government. U Ottama argued that Buddhism was disappearing because the government did not support the monasteries and the schools. Christian schools dominated. He also pointed to a decline in the amount of gifts to monks and monasteries. Without novices trained in Buddhism and with less *dana* due to the impoverishment of the peasants, Buddhism was in danger he said. His organizations gained wide support and the British imprisoned him for sedition. The boycott was extended to include the 1922 election for the first legislative council in which Burmans were to be represented. The boycott was effective but the new dyarchy – i.e. the sharing of power between the British Governor and the local government – failed to develop into genuine self-determination because the powerful British Chamber of Commerce blocked Burman influence. Western democracy was brought into discredit in this period because it represented a cover for foreign colonial rule. The British repressed the boycott and punished villagers collectively for supporting *Wunthanu Athins*. Villages were destroyed and collective fines taken from the peasants, eighty-five per cent of whom incurred debts. U Ottama died in prison in 1939 and became a martyr. His strategy was a mixture of Gandhian non-violence (neo-traditionalism) and Buddhist tradition. The *sangha* reluctantly supported his efforts, and then only when the movement had spread all over the country. However, the organizations lost popular support, some when politically active monks could not resist worldly temptations: there were cases of misuse of funds, monks going to the cinema and being seen with girls. The boycott strategy had reached its limits and proved to laypeople and leaders of the *sangha* that the modern political monk was easily corrupted by attachment to worldly life. The major reason for the disintegration of the GCBA was perhaps the reluctance among many monks to support direct militant actions. Yet Buddhism had by then been reconfirmed as an important political medium.

When non-violence failed and was suppressed by a heavy colonial hand, some of the peasant leaders of *Wunthanu Athins* proposed a rebellion but did not get the support from the *sangha*. Hsaya San, a monk and a peasant, who had been involved in an investigation of the impoverishment of the peasants, became leader of a rebellion against the British in 1930. He mobilized the peasants by using the traditional symbols connected with monarchy and the Buddhist thesis on rebellion against a non-benevolent rule. He appeared as a *mìn-laùng* (king-to-be) with a great *hpòn*, and as a *cakkavatti* (universal ruler). He acted as one who would reestablish the order of *dhamma* in the universe and prepare for the coming of the next Buddha (*Ariyamettaya*). But before this could be achieved, foreigners and non-Buddhists had to be driven from the country. He proclaimed to his soldiers: 'In the name of our Lord Buddha and for the Sangha's greater glory I, Thunapannaka Galon Raja [Hsaya San's royal title], declare war upon the heathen English who have enslaved us...Burma is meant only for the Burmans – the heretics removed the King by force. They have ruined our race and religion...The heathen English are the rebels'.[33] The aim of Hsaya San was perhaps not to become King of Burma, but to challenge the British with a legitimate political authority based on the symbolic power of Buddhism and its cosmology. Another of his declarations included a secular message: 'All the inhabitants who reside in Burma: it is for the economic prosperity of monks and inhabitants, so also in the interest of religion of our Lord that I have to declare war. English people are our enemies.'[34] The rebellion spread throughout Burma and 10,000 soldiers were sent in against the poorly-armed peasants who relied on magic tattoos for protection against bullets. More than 3,000 rebels were killed or wounded; 9,000 were interned; 1,389 were given prison sentences or deported; and 125 were hanged, including Hsaya San. As a further deepening of the religious and ethnic oppositional character of the rebellion, 1,600 Christian Karen and Chin participated in hunting down the rebels.

The British government claimed that Hsaya San was a charlatan and an impostor who stirred up the ignorant and superstitious peasants. Thus, the colonial power could deny any claim that the rebellion was also part of a modern, nationalistic movement. But the Hsaya San rebellion represents the bridge between traditionalism and modern nationalism. Today Hsaya San is one of the most prominent of Burman cultural heros and is celebrated on national days. Significantly, students praised Hsaya San at a conference in 1935; they adopted the cry: 'Burma for the Burmans!' and called their organization *Dobama Asiayone* – 'We the Burman Organization'. In the 1930s members were a complex mixture of royalists, Marxists, Fabians, students, writers, workers and even some with fascist leanings. In this melting pot, revolutionary ideas and active resistance against colonial rule were united under a nationalism with modernist strategies, but still anti-Western and neo-traditionalistic in its search for a uniquely Burmese way. Aung San and U Nu, the Prime Minister from 1948 to 1962, both became famous student leaders. They took the provocative title of *thakin* ('master'; like *sahib*, used in India for a British master).

As a student in the 1930s, U Nu, among other *thakins*, believed that Marxism and Buddhism were complementary theories. Both are critical of the impact of profit, wealth and ownership and favour equality and common welfare. In their view, Marxism was concerned with the material life, while Buddhism explained the roots of delusion, attachment, greed and hatred; Buddhism locates the roots of evil in the individual and the illusion of a permanent self, while Marxism makes the relations and forces of production the determining factor. Thus some of the nationalists argued that Buddhism was a higher truth than Marxism since it explained both mind and matter. As we shall see, Marxism and Buddhism came to confront one another as antagonistic ideologies during the 1950s, each supplying opposing theories of society.[35]

In the period from 1900 to 1942, and during the Second World War, when the nationalists supported the Japanese invasion, Buddhism became integrated into nationalist ideology. Nationalism transformed the Buddhist-Burman identity into a hegemonic frame of reference for all inhabitants in the country thereby creating one common identity within its borders in opposition to all that is foreign – that is, non-Buddhist. This construction is a mixture of the three strategies mentioned above: traditionalism, neo-traditionalism and modernism. For this reason it is difficult to give the different models of society unambiguous labels. Buddhism, as stated above, contains a theory of the universe, an ontology (' a design for being in the world'), precepts of mortality and generosity and, last but not least, the identification of being a Burman in the past, present and future. However, the changes during this period elaborated and deepened oppositional and differential cultural properties connected with Buddhist-Burman identity. And every political strategy today has to face up to these properties and contradictions.

Buddhism between democracy and autocracy

With independence in 1948, Burma faced enormous problems: the destruction of war, a constitution which gave relative autonomy to some minorities but not all, and a number of insurgencies. The Karen under the leadership of the Christian dominated Karen National Union started a rebellion in 1949 and almost surrounded Rangoon before being driven back to the mountains. The Karens were bitter that they, as 'the loyal British subjects' did not gain an independent state. There was also a communist insurrection, a Muslim insurrection and a rebellion by disappointed volunteer soldiers. To complicate the situation, the Kuomintang forces defeated by Mao entered Burma with US support. All possible troubles – especially those, it seemed, initiated by foreigners – descended upon the new nation and signalled a total social and moral decline. Killing and destruction were universal.[36]

Aung San was murdered by political opponents in 1947 and his *thakin* companion, U Nu, became Prime Minister. The ruling coalition, the Anti-Fascist Peoples Freedom League (AFPFL), comprised most of the political spectrum from Left to Right. U Nu's position in the coalition was centrist; his political strategy combined Buddhism and non-revolutionary socialism. He explained the disaster of postcolonial Burma by referring to the Buddhist conception of the origin of greed and violence – according to him, property and production had to be redistributed to avoid future conflicts and moral decline (plunder, theft, corruption etc.). Property and profit lead to class-struggle which is again based on the delusion of the self. U Nu referred to the concept of non-permanence of the self (*anatta*) thus: 'To put it briefly, Buddhism is the way of the philosophy for the annihilation of the causes that give rise to the 'I' consciousness'.[37]

The root of class-struggle, then, is egoism and is illusory, since neither self, soul, property nor power are permanent according to *dhamma*. However, U Nu rejected Marxism as the ideology of the AFPFL, as a reaction to the insurrection by the Communist Party of Burma. The party's emphasis on class-struggle led to violence, bloodshed and totalitarian power, he said. Buddhism cannot even sanction acts of violence that are necessary to preserve the public order, he explained.[38] But his view of the material conditions of life still contained Marxist notions. He considered inequality to be basically rooted in moral conduct while material welfare is the instrument of securing the universal ethics of Buddhism and the implementation of *dhamma* at all levels of society. He proposed the nationalization of land and property, the lowering of tenancy rents and other measures to redistribute property. However, the changes came very slowly due to the chaotic situation. U Nu, in the launching of his plans, referred to the ancient myth about the magic wishing tree (*Padeytha Pin*): At first man did not work but lived off the unlimited amount of fruit from the magic tree and took only what he needed. This utopia disappeared when people became attached to individual possessions. Greed initiated a moral decline which was manifested in corruption, theft and plunder, as can be seen in the present era. To reestablish a social and moral order the people elected a leader, Mahathammata ('the Great Unanimously elected' – the leader Aung San Suu Kyi refers to in her book). He was supposed to make laws for the redistribution of property and products. These qualities have been ascribed to kings such as the legendary Indian King Ashoka. In Burma, King Mindon Min in the nineteenth century had these qualities of a righteous king (*dhammaraja*) and a universal king (*cakkavattin*). U Nu called his utopian welfare state *Pyidawtha* – 'Pleasant Royal Country' and a conference on the project was held in 1952.[39] The Buddhist myth was used metaphorically by U Nu as a model for a future society – and not as an argument for reestablishing the traditional monarchy. His model used tradition in a modernist discourse and he emphasized that *karma*, merit and moral actions alone did not imbue the welfare state with peace and prosperity. Democracy, rule by law and rational economic planning were essentials in his perception of a Burman welfare state.[40]

U Nu insisted on democracy as a universal ideal of freedom related to Buddhist values. It cannot be produced by academic study but only in practice and it must be adjusted to local conditions. He said: 'Democracy...requires that, while enjoying and asserting your own rights and freedom...you may also respect the rights and freedom of your neighbour.'[41] However, when U Nu tried to act as the promoter and purifier of Buddhism and mix religious and political practice, he evoked and exposed the social and political contradictions already inscribed in Buddhism by way of nationalism.

In 1954 he opened the sixth Buddhist World Council. Thousands of participants attended this important forum over the next two years. The purpose was to reinvigorate and universalize Buddhism in the year 2,500 after the *Mhaparanibbanna* (death and achievement of nirvana) of Buddha and halfway to the next Buddha. A peace pagoda and a great cave with space for 10,000 (like the first council in India) was built by 60,000 volunteers, thus acquiring merit for themselves. Relics were brought to Burma from Sri Lanka and the texts rewritten by 1,129 elder and learned monks. The Council gave the new state international stature and reconfirmed Buddhism as the essential component of Burman national identity.[42] At the same time it created expectations in the *sangha* and among laypeople that Buddhism was to be elevated to the religion of the state.

In 1950 an anti-communist propaganda war was organized with co-operation between monks and the army. Monks in Mandalay participated in a conference against communism and a programme called *Dhammantaraya*, 'Buddhism in danger', was initiated. It was supported by the Ford Foundation. This call to defend Buddhism with war was used in 1885 by the King to mobilize against the British invaders. The programme also conducted missionary work among the minorities in order to integrate them and to prevent the spread of communism.[43]

In the 1950s Buddhism became part of parliamentary resolutions and the law. Concepts like *lobha* (greed), *moha* (delusion) and *dosa* (hatred) featured in a resolution explaining the roots of the violence and destruction during the insurgency.[44] And U Nu had the slaughter of animals for the Islamic *Idd* holiday prohibited by law.[45] The political monks returned to the public scene – especially the young and more militant in Mandalay and Rangoon. They expected that Buddhism would again be placed in a hegemonic position over state and civil society and began demonstrating to make Buddhism a state religion and part of the curriculum in schools. During the Buddhist World Council in 1956 U Nu had proclaimed his intention of making Buddhism the religion of the state as an act of merit and as a help to laypeople in the accumulation of merit. Before the elections in 1960 the monks pressed him to keep his promise. His political adversaries in the now split AFPFL opposed the idea but had problems arguing against the law and not, at the same time, appearing anti-Buddhist. Reactions to the proposed law on state religion were alarming: insurgencies among the minorities increased and demands for autonomy were reiterated as a protest against what was seen as ethno-religious discrimination prohibited in the 1947 constitution. The changes in the constitution made Buddhism a part of the curriculum in schools and universities. To avoid discrimination, U Nu also made the teaching of the other major religions part of the curriculum, to the dismay of the leading monks in the *sangha*. Young monks demonstrated and in Rangoon they demolished a new mosque and killed two Muslims during the riots. Several young monks were arrested. U Nu had to release them and present them with yellow robes as *dana* after these demeritous acts. Some refused his gifts.

Following independence the *sangha* became politicized and came to form a part of every major political issue. As in the 1930s, discipline among the monks declined and political factions among young monk associations fought each other and at least two were killed. Economic problems and alienation of the minorities from the state and government were growing. Despite his good intentions, U Nu mobilized all the evil contradictions his religiously-inspired strategy tried to dissipate. He was accused of abusing religion for his own political purposes. Yet he won the 1960 elections with a huge majority. Most of the electorate, especially the peasants, saw him as a pious man and identified him as the righteous Buddhist ruler and a potential embryonic Buddha expected to appear after the year 2,500 of the Buddhist era.[46] Some leading monks also saw him in this light.[47] During the election campaign in 1959, U Nu referred to the Buddhist ideals of a righteous ruler and withdrew to meditate for long periods while tensions escalated. It is very difficult to assess how his performance was perceived by the monks. Probably many monks did not agree with his modernist egalitarian interpretation as the following statement by a leading monk indicates: 'Abolition of class is nonsense as one's present existence is determined by the law of karma.'[48]

U Nu's critics among bureaucrats and politicians considered him to be living as an Oriental ruler excercising his personal will and spending public money on ceremonies and pagodas. They claimed that he was undermining the state by evoking anti-modern traditionalism and superstition.[49] U Nu did in fact evoke all the fundamental values of Buddhist-Burman national identity and its opposition to other identities and foreign influence. He did so by mixing the particular and the universal elements of religion and internalizing them in almost all political issues and in the functions of the state administration. Every attack on either U Nu or his policy could be seen as an attack on the fundamental values of Buddhism.

As a part of this process, the use of a nationalistic interpretation of religion did 'fundamentalize' the cultural values in the social life of Burma – not because Buddhism in itself contains such properties but because its cosmological and ontological concepts were made synonymous with the national ethos of Burma as its essential and primordial values. This had occurred during colonial rule and was revoked in the subsequent confrontation between traditionalism and modernism following independence. Spiro gives the impression of an atmosphere of great expectations in 1962: 'By 1962, the Future King (*mìn laùng*) was much more than the object of a nebulous utopian belief; he was a person whose expected arrival was imminent. Indeed for thousands of Burmese (especially peasants)... he was to appear in 1965'.[50] The military intervened in what they saw as growing chaos and the 1962 coup was legitimized as a reaction against the destabilizing and 'non-rational' forces unleashed by U Nu. The religious and the secular parts of society had to be separated once again. Western parliamentary democracy had failed, General Ne Win proclaimed. The military regime abolished religiously inspired legislation: for example, the law prohibiting the slaughter of animals for religious purposes which made killings punishable by fine, flogging or one year in jail. Buddhist lay organizations and councils were also abolished and state financial support for religious activities was stopped. State and religion were separated and religious freedom proclaimed, but Ne Win's problem was – and still is – that the separation of Buddhism from the dominant political discourse is impossible. It can be subdued by force but never eliminated.

The army established a new party, the Burma Socialist Programme Party (BSPP) – the only one allowed – and its published programme of 1963 contained some Buddhist concepts and a special Burmese version of socialism which was strongly anti-communist. The programme explained that politics and religion should exist separately but in mutual correlation, as matter (*rupa*) and mind (*nama*) – that is, the physical and the spiritual aspects of life are correlated according to the ontological principles of Buddhism. The programme applies the cause-effect logic (*nidanas*) of Buddhism, which is a chain of mutually dependent ontological circumstances: spiritual-material, ignorance-wisdom, birth-death, and so on. The programme places the focus on man ('Man Matters Most'), but human reason is incomplete and must be ruled from a strong centre which can 'constantly check and control human frailties'. Otherwise evil qualities such as hatred, greed and violence are released in a destructive chain reaction. Its main concern is welfare, but egalitarianism is rejected and declared an impossibility. The programme refers to the law of impermanence but does not mention *karma*, merit and other important concepts. Here Buddhism applies the formulation of the basic and commonly known principles of the existence of man and nature purely ontologically. In fact Buddha is not mentioned in the programme at all.[51] In this way Ne Win tried to legitimate autocracy in the form of a corporate and centralized state which could eliminate all previous social and cultural conflicts generated by U Nu and foreign influence. The army already had extensive control of production and trade through the Defence Services Institute and implemented this through extensive nationalization.

The monks were against military rule and its policies. They were afraid that total nationalization and demonetarization after the coup would result in a reduction in gifts to the monasteries. The regime reacted by pointing out the necessity for purifying and disciplining the monastic order. The army said that too many bogus monks were hiding in the monasteries and that they would have to be derobed; in this way Ne Win tried to get rid of politicized monks. Demonstrations followed in 1965 but after more than 1,000 arrests a general registration of monks took place and the *sangha* withdrew from the political and worldly arena. It did not use its ultimate weapon – turning the rice bowl upside down – until 1990.

In the 1960s Ne Win seems to have supported the *Shwegyin* sect in the *sangha*. The Shwegyin sect is considered to be apolitical, ascetic and disciplined, and was supported by King Mindon in the last century. Significantly, it was against the involvement of monks in the nationalistic movements and thus a suitable partner for Ne Win in his attempt to purify the *sangha*.[52] Ne Win and the Burma Socialist Programme Party promoted their policy as a rational, modern and genuine Burman alternative to that of their predecessors – but ended as being synonomous with all the evils of non-righteous rule.[53] Few can deny that Ne Win possesses *karma* – and that is why he is difficult to challenge.

In 1980 a congregation of the *sangha* took place and Ne Win succeeded in bringing the monks under the control of the State Council by a membership register. Non-initiated persons, including women, were removed from monasteries. The successful congregation was honoured in the traditional way when Ne Win gave an amnesty to many of his political opponents.[54] U Nu was welcomed home after having led an insurrection against Ne Win. U Nu returned to his religious work preaching and re-editing Buddhist *suttas* (discourses of Buddha) but stayed out of politics.[55] Ne Win had a new pagoda built behind the great Shwe Dagon pagoda – the national monument. Donations to the new pagoda came exclusively from army personnel and, at the time of writing, it is not completed. Perhaps he felt he was running out of merit and symbolic power for he raised the top spire (*hti*) – the royal symbol of power – in 1986 before the pagoda was finished. The Government also spent 40 million kyats on gold foil to decorate the Shwe Dagon pagoda despite a deteriorating economy. However, he and the present regime cannot create even a modicum of political legitimation through any Buddhist act – they are excommunicated from this part of the political discourse for ever. Buddhism is now questioning autocracy and appearing as the real alternative, combining universal ethics with a particularly Burman type of democracy.

Power, identity and the many faces of Buddhism

We have seen how Buddhism has been used in different political struggles as a medium for various strategies. The Buddhist conceptions of the world are dominant in Burmese history although they are perceived and explained with great variation depending on social position, status and class. In the present situation it is difficult to know how Buddhism is conceived and expressed in relation to recent developments. There may be great differences, for example, between the urban population and the peasants – even in the way in which statements by Aung San Suu Kyi are received. Some monks may see her talk about a *dhammaraja* as a kind of archaic millenarianism within the folk tradition. Yet Buddhism continues as an important medium of developments.[56]

Obviously, Buddhist conceptions of the world cannot account for all actions in politics or daily life or for their motivation and cognition. But it represents the dominant ideas of symbolic power, its exchange and its accumulation. Buddhism combines the past, the present and the future in one process and places every individual in a hierarchy by ethical standards. It correlates merit with social prestige and authority. It explains social forces and their logic. And last but not least, Buddhism is the fulcrum of cultural identity – individual and public, ethnic and national. It makes 'being Burman/Buddhist' a primordial precondition of the existence of the individual and the state as defined in opposition to other foreign cultures and religions. Power is internalized in religion, and Buddhism appears simultaneously as a medium of power struggles and as the explanation of the generative forces of these struggles. Buddhism is thus a hegemonic representation of the history of Burma. Every political strategy and every model of and for a social system have to refer to Buddhism. At the same time it is a theory of the impermanence of life, of society, of morality, of identity, of power and of religion. This thesis makes Buddhism able to contain profound changes in society while continuing to be the fulcrum for new classifications of identity and new political strategies. That is also the reason why Buddhism and the monks returned to the political scene in 1988.

Buddhism is a system of exchange of symbolic power and not just a basis for the ideological legitimation of power by regimes. Everyone in Burma is compelled to enter into the discourse dominated by Buddhism if one is to explain violence, xenophobia, democracy, human rights and so on. But Buddhism is neither nationalist nor fundamentalist *per se*. In the case of Burma the tendency to elevate Buddhism to represent the very essentials and fundamentals of cultural identity is a part of nationalism and the anticolonial struggle. It reappears when social disorder, economic crises, repression and moral decline threaten the religious substance of cultural identity – that is, of genuine Burman identity. When the basis for the exchange of symbolic power is destroyed and the means of accumulating merit is threatened, then an identity crisis also becomes a religiously conceived crisis.[57]

In Burma, it will be difficult to disassociate politics from religion in the near future. And that may be a problem for Aung San Suu Kyi and the NLD. Translating democracy into a universal (moral-religious) right is one thing – another and more complicated problem is constructing a system of free democratic participation incorporating ethnic, religious and political groups. Aung San Suu Kyi expresses a high modernist and cosmopolitan world-view by integrating traditional values, human rights and her personal destiny into her political strategy. But the regime that has denied her freedom has made Burma into a 'cultural island' during thirty years of xenophobic isolation. Protecting Burman culture and religion has been a dominant part of national politics since colonial times. And defending culture and religion and their primordial qualities of identity has often been used as a strategy for denying freedom to those other than 'genuine' Burmans. The SLORC regime recently stated in the media that it is important for Burma not to become the home of an ethnic mix influenced by alien cultures: 'This is the raison d'être for the vigorous efforts being made for the preservation of cultural identity and national personality. It is a natural reaction'.[58] Culturalism and ethnocentrism are rendered natural by SLORC in an attempt to legitimize extreme repression.

Following the killing of monks in 1990, Buddhism has been reinvoked as a unifying national theme; pagodas and monasteries are being renovated. SLORC has also promoted the teaching of Buddhism in high schools. While the regime has been chasing more the 200,000 Muslim Royhingyas out of the country and destroying Christian churches in Kayah state, religion is reinvoked as the essence of cultural identity. The National Coalition Government in exile in Thailand has characterized this policy as 'Buddhist supremacist nationalism'. In 1990 the regime extended honorary ecclesiastical titles to monks. The most famous to receive a title was the Sinhalese monk Walpola Rahula, who defined Buddhism as 'part of nationalism and natural culture' in Sri Lanka.[59]

The Thai Buddhist writer and activist, Sulak Sivaraksa, has long been advocating a neo-traditionalist version of Buddhism as a middle way between Western modernism, and its content of liberalism, consumerism and materialism, and totalitarian communism. Although to be Thai is also to be a Buddhist – precisely as in the Burman-Buddhist combination – he is aware of the dangers of the culturalization of religion.

Referring to a United Nations University conference in Bangkok on Buddhism, he writes: 'It was pointed out that an obstacle to the implementation of religious principles is the mixing of culture and religion. Usually, religion has a major influence on culture, but when culture influences religion, or is equated with religion the result is often sectarianism. In some cases it becomes chauvinism and irredentism – leading to violence and slaughter in the name of religion. Religious literalism and idolatry also are the products of cultural influences.[60] He warns against putting Tibetan, Sinhalese or Thai identity before Buddhism, since the cultural particulars impede the universal ideals of Buddhism.[61] This is precisely the predicament of religion and nationalism in the new world order. Particularism can transform all universal ideas of religion into proof of the necessity for autocratic rule including control over tradition and its primordial values. And universal ideals can be evoked to subdue the xenophobia created by cultural particularism and to question autocratic rule. Buddhism not only has this Janus face but also many other changing faces, as have other religions involved in political struggle.

APPENDIX

BUDDHISM AND POLITICAL MODELS OF IDENTITY IN BURMA

High Modernism
(autocracy/democracy; universalism/particularism)

Neo-traditionalism   BUDDHISM   Modernism
(cultural particularism,   (universalism,
world renunciation)   secularism)

Traditionalism
(holistic cosmological model)

This figure is an index of identity space and a simplified condensation of concepts and keywords. As a total abstraction, it cannot account for specific strategies or actions which are much more ambiguous. Buddhism mediates between self-identity and public identification, and it connects the past, the present and the future imagined as one single process. In Burma, elements of the four models often mix in political strategies:

Traditionalism: emphasis on the eternal primordial essence of Burman culture and Buddhism; the properties of holistic Buddhist cosmology and its ethics of righteous rule is the basis of a collective identification comprising king, monks and laity.

Neo-traditionalism: traditionalism projected into modern society. The emphasis is on cultural particularism, e.g. protecting endangered culture and country against foreign intrusion and destruction; isolation from the world to achieve a self-defined and controlled modern evolution.

Modernism: nation-building, economic development, secularism. Democracy and unitary state; individual choice within a homogeneous society.

High modernism: 'new world order' by expanding modernism; more personal freedoms of action, consumption and movement; ethnic national autonomy; a global morality, e.g. human rights. And often combined with control of natural resources and political conflicts.[5]

Acknowledgement: I am grateful to Thomas Lautrup and Jens Pinholt of the Dept. of Ethnography and Social Anthropology, Aarhus University, and to Eva Hellman for valuable suggestions and comments on the first draft.

Notes

1. *Burman (Bama)* is used for the ethnic group, its members, culture and language. *Burmese* signifies what belongs to the Union of Burma. This distinction is widely used but problematic. The ethnic minorities – more than one third of the population – deny belonging to a common Burmese identity although they may be citizens of the Union. *Myanmar* as used by the present regime is an old form of *Bama* and means Burman or Burmese.
2. The concept of ethnic opposition is adapted from Scott 1990, not as an independent variable of causation of ethnic identities, but to explain the dominating logic of a specific cultural, religious and symbolic practice making Buddhism the legitimate medium of political strategies in Burma.
3. See Friedman 1992, Lash and Friedman 1992 and Giddens 1991 for a discussion of modernity and identity.
4. Fundamentalism has many negative connotations in Western discourse. Here it is used to denote a tendency in the global process outlined above and not as a particular property of any religion.
5. The figure and the concepts are modelled after Friedman 1992, Lash and Friedman 1992 and Giddens 1991 but adapted to the specific Burmese context. I prefer high modernism to late modernism. High modernism implicates a pointed modernism, especially in terms of self-identification, self-reflexion and a plurality of strategies.
6. Aung San Suu Kyi 1991: 83. The same statement can be found in Spiro 1971: 471, i.e. Buddhism is the fundament of Burman ethnic identity.
7. Aung San Suu Kyi, born 1946, is the daughter of Burma's national hero Aung San. She obtained a degree from Oxford University and lived in Britain before returning to Burma. As a leader of the National League for Democracy, which took 80% of the seats in the election in 1991, she has been held under house arrest by the regime since 1989.
8. Aung San Suu Kyi 1991: 168 f.

9. Ibid.: 180.
10. Ibid.: 178.
11. Ibid.: 168.
12. Especially the Karen under the Christian-dominated Karen National Union, The *Kachin* (Kachin Independent Organization) and the Muslim *Rohingya* in Arakan Province. See Smith 1991 on the ethnic insurgency and Gravers 1993 on nationalism.
13. Aung San Suu Kyi 1991: 169. This is a mythical explanation of the origin of ignorance, greed and violence which made it necessary to elect a strong and benevolent ruler to govern by law (Sarkisyanz 1965: 10-15). The term has been used as part of the title of the modern president of The Union of Burma (Sarkisyanz 1965: 212). The myth is recorded in Sangermano (1966: 11) and Shway Yoe (1882: 114).
14. Aung San Suu Kyi 1991: 171f. The ten royal duties are also used in Thailand. However, due to the political role of the Thai king, criticism can provoke indictment for *lèse majesté* as in the case of prominent Buddhist critic, Sulak Sivaraksa. See Sulak Sivaraksa 1991: 159-66.
15. Aung San Suu Kyi 1991: 173.
16. United Nations: Universal Declaration of Human Rights quoted in Aung San Suu Kyi 1991: 177, 182.
17. Matthews 1993: 16; Sarkisyanz 1978: 93. The rice bowl is a major symbol of ascetic life and of peace and prosperity. The monk receives his food silently, i.e. he allows the lay people to give the food and thus to accumulate merit. This reciprocity is a fundamental part of Buddhist practice.
18. Lintner 1989: 35. He quotes a Burmese saying 'dependents of army personnel tend to be even more devout than others'. To the soldiers the boycott must have been a shock since they are performing demeritous acts by killing and maiming people.
19. Aung San Suu Kyi 1991: 168.
20. Ibid.: 103. She quotes Smith 1965: 86. The secular part of the Burman ethos has been summarized in three terms: prestige, wealth (*goung*); glory, charismatic power (*hpòn*) and authority (*o-za*). Spiro 1971: 185, 474.
21. An analysis of nationalism and ethnic-religious opposition is found in Gravers 1993.
22. The constitution of 1947, paragraph 21, 4: 'The abuse of religion for political purposes is forbidden and any act which is intended or is likely to promote feelings of hatred, enmity or discord between racial or religious communities or sects is contrary to this constitution and may be made punishable by law'. Compulsory religious instruction was not allowed. Dr. Maung Maung 1961: 260 f.
23. Silverstein 1972: 55.
24. In Buddhist teaching and cosmology the three signs of being are *anicca*: impermanence, everything changes; *anatta*: no-self, the impermanence of an ego; *dukkha*: suffering, disharmony.
25. *Cakkavatti* ('turner of the wheel') signifies a ruler who will reestablish the order of the universe, drive out foreigners and bring prosperity. Greed, hate and violence will stop. He combines righteousness and power and is supposed to prepare for the coming of the next Buddha. See Spiro 1971: 174.
26. See Michael Aung Thwin 1983 on the conceptions of Burmese kinship. While Buddhism recognizes authority and power, it always emphasizes their dark sides: violence, suffering. Prestige and power represent worldly attachment, while charity and meditation are supposed to counteract this attachment.
27. On the 'pacification' of Burma, see Adas 1982 and Aung Thwin 1985.
28. Spiro 1971: 19. King Bagyidaw asked a missionary about the identity of Christian Burmans: 'Are they really Burmans?' (Judson 1823: 215.) In 1852 the Burman governor of Rangoon said to a missionary: '[Christianity] aimed to destroy every other [religion], and this was uncharitable...' (Kincaid 1852: 69).
29. Spiro (1968: 1163) explains that less than 2% of his informants knew the exact

meaning of *anatta* – non-performance of the self – but it is ingrained in common knowledge and daily practice.
30. See Spiro 1971: 470. He describes merit-making as the primary source of intra- and inter-village interaction and integration.
31. On religion, symbolic power and *habitus*, see Bourdieu 1987: 126; 1990: 131, 138.
32. Spiro 1971: 20.
33. Collis 1938: 274-9. The struggle was interpreted as a symbolic struggle between the Burmese *Galon* (the *Garuda* bird) and the British *Naga* (serpent). See also U Maung Maung 1980: the rebellion was caused by a mixture of economic, political, religious and cultural inequalities condensed during the 1930 global crisis.
34. Patricia Herbert 1982: 6. In her extremely important article, she demonstrates that British sources on the rebellion may have been deliberately distorted.
35. On the role of Buddhism in nationalism from 1900 to 1942, see U Maung Maung 1980 and 1989, Smith 1965 and Sarkisyanz 1965.
36. On Karen vs. Burman nationalism see Gravers 1993. The most detailed account of the ethnic insurgencies is Smith 1991.
37. Smith 1965: 145.
38. Sarkisyanz 1965: 219 ff.
39. On U Nu's use of Buddhism in politics see Sarkisyanz 1965; Butwell 1969; D.E. Smith 1965. On the Buddhist utopia see Shway Yoe 1882: III; Sangermano 1966: 39; Sarkisyanz 1965: 88.
40. U Nu said that modern science supported the Buddhist conceptions of decay and change.
41. Butwell 1969: 75. An example of the confusion of religion and democracy is a statement by U Ba Yi, Minister of Education. He said that Buddha was against dictatorship and for democracy while the Christian God was authoritarian and paved the way for dictators like Hitler. Sarkisyanz 1965: 193.
42. Smith. 157-65; Dalton 1970.
43. Sarkisyanz 1965: 201; Smith 1965: 20, 199.
44. Smith 1965: 146 f.
45. Butwell 1969: 66.
46. Sarkisyanz 1965: 209; Smith 1965: 138.
47. Sarkisyanz 1965: 226.
48. Smith 1965: 199. Spiro (1971: 440) quotes a monk producing a similar conclusion. And being a Buddhist Burman is considered to be superior to an Animist hill tribesman (ibid.: 430).
49. Smith 1965: 187. U Nu's party was identified as the *hpòngyi kyaung* – the monastic school party, i.e. the uneducated, the traditionalist.
50. Spiro 1971: 186. Spiro did fieldwork in Burma in 1961-2.
51. Smith (1965: 91) has called the programme a 'civil religion'.
52. Wiant (1981: 63) uses the term 'fundamentalist' for the Shwegyin sect. See also Ferguson 1978.
53. Burma Socialist Programme Party 1963. On Ne Win, see Smith 1965; Dalton 1970; and Lintner 1989.
54. See Tin Maung Maung Than 1993: 22-3.
55. U Nu formed a party in 1988 and proclaimed a new government – *his* government – to the dismay of the major opposition party NLD and Aung San Suu Kyi. He has only limited influence today.
56. See Bekker in Silverstein 1989. The number of monks is growing. Se also Matthews (1993) on the role of Buddhism and the *sangha* at present.
57. On the concept of symbolic power, see Bourdieu 1987, 1990.
58. Steinberg 1992: 228-9.
59. Matthews 1993: 14 and Tambiah 1992: 27.
60. Sulak Sivaraksa 1991. Buddhism in Thailand has also been a fundamental part of

nationalism as in the slogan 'Buddha, King and Nation'. Monks were involved in a fierce anti-communist strategy in the 1960s and 1970s. Today the Dhammakaya monastery appeals to the urban middle class with lessons in meditation supposed to improve management. A more puritan, egalitarian and neo-traditionalist movement is the *Santi Asoke* sect which is related to the influential *Palang Dhamma* political party.

61. See Tambiah (1992) on the ethno-religious violence in Sri Lanka. Buddhism was used to criticize colonialism and Christianity. Now, it is used as a basis for an anti-modern, neo-traditionalist and socialist strategy by radical monks. Tambiah (ibid.: 58) calls the Buddhist nationalism in Sri Lanka 'Buddhist fundamentalism'.

References

Adas, M. 1982. 'Bandits, Monks, and Pretender Kings: Patterns of Peasant Resistance and Protest in Colonial Burma 1826-1941', in R.P. Weller and Scott Guggenheim (eds), *Power and Protest in the Countryside*, 75-105. Durham, NC: Duke University Press.

Aung San Suu Kyi 1991. *Freedom from Fear*. Harmondsworth: Penguin Books.

Aung Thwin, M. 1983. 'Divinity, Spirit, and Human: Conceptions of Classical Burmese Kingship', in Lorraine Gesick (ed.), *Centers, Symbols, and Hierarchies: Essays on the Classical State of Southeast Asia*, 45-86. (Monograph Series no. 26.) Yale University, Southeast Asia Studies.

——. 1985. 'The British "Pacification" of Burma: Order without Meaning', *Journal of Southeast Asian Studies* 16(2), 245-61.

Bekker, S.M. 1989. 'Changes and Continuities in Burmese Buddhism', in J. Silverstein (ed.), *Independent Burma at Forty Years: Six Assessments*, 51-61. Ithaca: Cornell University Press.

Bourdieu, P. 1987. 'Legitimation and Structured Interests in Weber's Sociology of Religion', in Whimster and Lash (eds), *Max Weber, Rationality and Modernity*, 119-36. London: Geo. Allen and Unwin.

——. 1990. *In Other Words: Essays Towards a Reflexive Sociology*. Transl. by M. Adamson. Cambridge: Polity Press.

Burma Socialist Programme Party 1963. *The System of Correlation of Man and his Environment*. Rangoon.

Butwell, R. 1969 (1963). *U Nu of Burma*. Stanford University Press.

Collis, M. 1938. *Trials in Burma*. London: Faber and Faber.

Dalton, J.D. 1970 'Burma: The 1000-Year Struggle', *Far Eastern Economic Review* (5 March): 18-20.

Ferguson, J.P. 1978. 'The Quest for Legitimation by Burmese Monks and Kings: the Case of the Shwegyin Sect (19th – 20th Centuries)', in Bardwell L. Smith (ed.), *Religion and Legitimation of Power in Thailand, Laos and Burma*, 66-86. Chambersburg, PA: Anima Books.

Friedman, J. 1992. 'The Past in the Future: History and the Politics of Identity', *American Anthropologist* 94(4): 837-59.

Giddens, A. 1991. *Modernity and Self-Identity: Self and Society in Late Modern Age*. Stanford University Press.

Gravers, M. 1993. *Nationalism as Political Paranoia in Burma: An Essay on the Historical Practice of Power.* (NIAS Report no. 11.) Copenhagen.

Herbert, P. 1982. *The Hsaya San Rebellion (1930-1932) Reappraised.* Working Paper, Centre of Southeast Asian Studies, Monash University, Melbourne.

Judson, A. 1823. 'Journal', *Baptist Missionary Magazine* 4, 212-17.

Kincaid, E. 1852. 'Journal', *Baptist Missionary Magazine* 32, 68-70.

Lash, S. and J. Friedman (eds) 1992. *Modernity and Identity.* Oxford: Blackwell.

Lintner, B. 1989. *Outrage: Burma's Struggle for Democracy.* Hong Kong: Review Publishing Co.

Matthews, B. 1993. 'Burma: Buddhism under a Military Regime', *Seeds of Peace* 9(3).

Maung Maung, Dr. 1961. *Burma's Constitution.* The Hague: Martinus Nijhoff.

——. 1980. *From Sangha to Laity: Nationalist Movements of Burma 1920-1940.* New Delhi: Manohar.

Maung Maung, U. 1989. *Burmese Nationalist Movements 1940-1948.* Edinburgh: Kiscadale.

Sangermano, Father. 1966 (1833). *The Burmese Empire.* London: Susil Gupta.

Sarkisyanz, E. 1965. *Buddhist Background of the Burmese Revolution.* The Hague: Martinus Nijhoff.

——. 1978. 'Buddhist Backgrounds of Burmese Socialism', in B. L. Smith (ed.), *Religion and Legitimation of Power in Thailand, Laos and Burma*, 87-99. Chambersburg: Anima Books.

Scott, G.M. 1990. 'A Resynthesis of the Primordial and Circumstantial Approaches to Ethnic Group Solidarity: Toward an Explanatory Model', *Ethnic and Racial Studies* 13(2), 147-71.

Shway Yoe. 1882. *The Burman, His Life and Notions.* 2 vols. London: Macmillan.

Silverstein, J. 1972. *The Political Legacy of Aung San.* Data Paper no. 86. Ithaca: Cornell University.

——. (ed.) 1989. *Independent Burma at Forty Years: Six Assessments.* Ithaca: Cornell University Press.

Smith, D.E. 1965. *Religions and Politics in Burma.* Princeton University Press.

Smith, M. 1991. *Burma: Insurgency and the Politics of Ethnicity.* London: Zed Books.

Spiro, M.E. 1968. 'Buddhism and Economic Saving in Burma', *American Anthropologist* 68, 1163-73.

——. 1971. *Buddhism and Society: A Great Tradition and its Burmese Vicissitudes.* London: Geo. Allen & Unwin.

Steinberg, D. 1992. 'Myanmar 1991: Military Intransigence', *Southeast Asian Affairs 1992.* Institute of Southeast Asian Studies. Singapore.

Sulak Sivaraksa 1991. 'Buddhist Ethics and Modern Politics: A Theravada Viewpoint', in C. Wei-hsun Fu and S. A. Wawrytko (eds), *Buddhist Ethics and Modern Society: An International Symposium*, 159-66. New York: Greenwood Press.

Tambiah, S.J. 1992. *Buddhism Betrayed? Religion, Politics, and Violence in Sri Lanka.* University of Chicago Press.

Tin Maung Maung Than 1993. 'Sangha Reforms and Renewal of Sasana in Myanmar: Historical Trends and Contemporary Practice', in T. Ling (ed.), *Buddhist Trends in Southeast Asia*, 6-63. Social Issues in Southeast Asia. Singapore: Institute of Southeast Asian studies.

322/ *Mikael Gravers*

Wiant, J. 1981. 'Tradition in the Service of Revolution: The Political Symbolism of the *taw-hlan-ye-khit* ('the Revolutionary Era')', in F.K. Lehman (ed.), *Military Rule in Burma: A Kaleidoscope of Views*, 59-72. Singapore: Maruzen Asia.

THE POLITICS OF
PHILIPPINE FUNDAMENTALISM

Susan Rose

'God is preparing the Church for the greatest spiritual battle we have ever seen – the bringing down of the strongholds of the devil on our land – and will require the most concerted effort by the people of God at waging war against the real enemy, Satan.'[1]

Pastor Ramon Orosa, president of Oro International Ministries, candidate in the 1992 senatorial races and former president of City Bank, Manila, echoes the sentiments of many born-again believers in the Philippines. Increasingly active in social and political arenas, the new 'fundamentalists' (a term which here includes fundamentalists, Pentecostals, neo-Pentecostals, and charismatics) tend to take, in Niebuhr's terms, a 'Christ as transformer of culture' position rather than the old-style fundamentalist, separatist stance of 'Christ against culture'.

The symbolic war being fought by the new 'fundamentalists' in the Philippines is less against secularism and more against a Catholicism that they see as permeating the political system. The 1986 EDSA People's Revolt that ousted Ferdinand Marcos from power and installed Cory Aquino as President is illustrative of this. Claimed as a victory by the Catholic Church, EDSA was seen as a religious event inspired by religious groups and imbued with a religious ethos and ethic. Religious celebrations mingled with political ends as mass political rallies followed on the heels of High Mass. While church and state are constitutionally separate, the dynamic and dialectical interplay between religion and politics means that the Church has considerable influence in Philippine society. While Cardinal Sin encouraged his flock to join in the mass demonstrations and later celebrated the victory with President Aquino, born-again Protestants protested the erection of a statue to the Virgin Mary at the head of the Epifanio de los Santos Avenue to commemorate the event. They claimed that the real hero of EDSA was Christ himself.

Through the events leading up to the EDSA Revolt, the Catholic Church re-established itself as a relevant institution, central in the thrust towards political change and the push for a more democratic society. Evangelical positions were less clear and more mixed, though according to Lorenzo Bautista's study, an apolitical stance and conservative views were dominant.[2] The Philippine Council of Evangelical Churches, the largest association of born-again Protestant churches, which had been supportive of Marcos, took no definite policy position in relation to EDSA. Indecisive to the end, it vacillated between stressing Romans 13: 1-7, wherein Christians are called upon to obey the ruling authorities, and cautioning that civil disobedience may sometimes be an option but only after one has exhausted the judicial and constitutional processes.[3]

The dramatic events of the 1980s served, however, to politicize all factions. The Catholic Church entered into a new phase of renewal which was accompanied by a new surge of evangelical fervour – both conservative and progressive. Increasingly, the new fundamentalists are striving to go beyond mere tolerance of religious freedom to securing an active and influential political voice. Their goals are ambitious: while they hold particular concerns relevant to the Philippine context, they have joined with and are supported by the international fundamentalist movement which aims at nothing less than the Christianization of the world.

Critical of graft and corruption in government and business, insurgency, pornography, and liberalizing divorce and abortion legislation, the new fundamentalists are less likely to isolate or remove themselves from the corrupting influences of modern life, and more likely to try to influence social policy and institutional behaviour than their counterparts two decades ago. The focus on individual salvation is still central, but they are increasingly engaged in social movement activity – usually with a conservative agenda. The emphasis on individual sin and salvation rather than an analysis of structural injustice predominates, serving, as some would argue, to demobilize people and neutralize a small though significant minority of born-again Christians who have embraced transformation theology. This small group of progressive born-agains have allied themselves with progressive Catholics and environmental protection, land reform and debt release.

The majority of born-again believers, however, are very critical of liberation theology, in particular, and Catholicism in general. While they accuse liberation theology priests and nuns of being Communist subversives, they attack the established Catholic church for encouraging 'fatalism', in teaching 'the non-involvement of Christians – that you should just fold your arms and wait for Jesus, that you shouldn't be worldly'.[4]

Attributing many of the current problems in the Philippines to 'fatalistic non-involvement' promoted by the Catholic Church since Spanish colonization of the Philippines in 1512, Orosa argues that 'Christians' must engage in massive evangelization: 'What is in store for us is a spiritual victory of such proportions as to undo the devil's works of the last 450 years which have obscured and veiled the glory of the Lord in the Land.'[5] Identifying themselves as the true 'Christians', most born-again Protestants believe that Catholics (and mainline Protestants) are as much in need of salvation as Muslims or the unchurched. Strikingly similar sentiments were voiced by the first Protestants to enter the Philippines at the turn of the century. President William McKinley, in his Benevolent Assimilation Proclamation of 21 December 1898, conveniently overlooked the Catholic faith of Filipinos as he justified his programme of war and annexation to a delegation of US Methodists: 'I went down on my knees and prayed Almighty God... it came to me in this way... there was nothing left for us to do but take them all, and to educate the Filipinos, and uplift and civilize, and Christianize them, and by God's grace do the very best we could by them, as our fellow-men for whom Christ also died'.[6] And only two weeks after Commodore Dewey's victory at Manila Bay in 1898, the Presbyterian General Assembly pronounced: 'God has given into our hands, that is, into the hands of American Christians, the Philippine Islands... By the very guns of our battleships God summoned us to go up and possess the land.'[7]

From 1899 to 1954, 1,713 Protestant churches were established. By 1988, there were over 15,000 churches, with the real significant Protestant growth occurring only in the last decade, primarily among neo-Pentecostal and charismatic churches. The new Christians are on the move: 'I believe in all my heart that it is God's purpose that our nation be the spiritual *burning bush*, the beacon light of all of Asia, the last frontier of evangelism.'[8] And indeed, the 'fundamentalist' groups (as referred to by Catholic researchers) or the new wave of 'Christian' groups (as referred to by Protestant researchers) have grown significantly since 1980. A study conducted by Monsignor Bayani Valenzuela for the Archdiocese of Manila indicated that between 1980 and 1988 there was more that a 500 per cent increase in the number of non-Catholic Christian religious groups registered with the national government.[9]

Also from the viewpoint of conservative evangelical Protestants, church growth has been significant. By October 1991, the Philippine Crusades Research team for DAWN 2000 (Discipling a Whole Nation),[10] reported that they had located just over 23,000 evangelical churches operating throughout the Philippines (this would include all Protestant denominations and independent churches). Of these 23,000, approximately 9,400 had been founded between 1900 and 1980, but the majority, 13,600 churches, came into being between 1980 and 1990.[11] This reflects growth of 145 per cent in the actual number of individual churches.

This significant pattern of growth, by either measure, concerned members of the Catholic hierarchy because they felt it represented a hostile kind of Protestantism with a preponderant foreign influence. There is no question that the Philippines is one of the major sites for US evangelical missionary activity: in 1992 it ranked second in the world with 1,961 missionaries serving for four years or more, surpassed only by Brazil with 2,229 missionaries.

While some celebrate the inroads that born-again Christians are making in the Philippines, others decry their 'invasion'. About the only common ground they share is the perception that holy war is being waged. The fundamentalists tend to support the civil and military *status quo* and pro-American interests, and to challenge most directly the Catholic Church, especially its more progressive elements. In response, the Catholic Bishops' Council of the Philippines (CBCP) published a pastoral letter in January 1989 which launched a furious debate about who the fundamentalists were and what they were up to. Warning of the recent influx of fundamentalist sects, the letter fuelled religious contention that was publicly fought out in the mainstream press. The CBCP then set up 'Guidelines for Dealing with Fundamentalists':

> We ask our people not to endanger their faith through a false sense of ecumenism which often serves as the entry point of many of these sects... We must regretfully say that the fundamentalist sects, with their aggressive and sometimes vicious attacks on the Catholic Church, do not practice an ecumenism which we can trustingly reciprocate... for now, preachers and members of fundamentalist groups should not be allowed to teach in Catholic meetings even under the guise of giving witness. We also ask our faithful not to join so-called ecumenical prayer or study groups, or other meetings organized by fundamentalist groups. Our faithful must also be aware of financial enticements to join the fundamentalists.[13]

The guidelines distinguished between 'the fundamentalists' and the National Council of Churches of the Philippines with whom they declared they had 'cordial relations'. The National Council of Churches, in fact, had misgivings about the fundamentalists parallel to Catholic concerns. In a 1988 report on 'New Religious Movements in the Philippines', the NCCP warned against 'the application of religion as a campaign to preserve American interests and maintain US hegemony that has spread from Latin America to Asia, particularly the Philippines'.[14] This concern is linked to apprehensions about conservative religious support for Low Intensity Conflict (LIC), and a civil war that has been going on for some twenty years.

In such politically volatile contexts as the Philippines, labels become particularly problematic. Few conservative Filipino Protestants, even those clearly aligned with fundamentalist traditions and associations, want to lay claim to the term 'fundamentalist'. Mainstream and evangelical Protestants have an immediate aversion to the term and are very cautious about 'definitions of fundamentalism'. Most Catholics are quite ready to use the term, usually in a pejorative sense. But as a result of the media skirmish, increasing numbers of Catholic leaders are careful to distinguish between types of Protestants. By 1992 a shift in both understanding and strategy occurred, as many leading Catholic leaders decided to stop 'fueling the fire' and consciously played down the actual and potential power of fundamentalists in the Philippines.

Clearly religious semantics were a very important and politically sensitive subject at the beginning of the 1990s. In the daily newspapers, accusations and counter-accusations about the political role and agenda of the fundamentalists and Catholic Church took centre stage, at least for a while. In fact, fundamentalists, who are still a small minority of Filipinos, 80-85 per cent of whom are Catholic, probably received a disproportionate amount of attention. Why?

Reasons that immediately surface are the tremendous growth of 'fundamentalist' groups, the threat they pose to the Catholic Church from whom recruits are drawn, and the suspicions about the political as well as religious role of the new wave of 'Christians' pouring into the Philippines, especially those with US affiliations.

The new fundamentalists

The growth of the new Christian groups since 1980, which accelerated after 1986, is a cause for concern or celebration, depending upon one's predilections. In the 'Christian' camp, much rejoicing is made over the statistics on church growth, even though Protestants remain a small minority. In the Catholic camp, there is grave concern over the successes of the evangelicals.

According to a study of New Religious Movements in the Philippines, the martial law period was a time of 'steady and marked increase in the influx of evangelists both in person and [in] electronic media. There [was] no government restriction of any kind to their operations.'[15] And, according to interviews with over thirty Protestant and Catholic leaders in the spring of 1992, the new Christian groups experienced even more vigorous growth after Cory Aquino came to power. While interviewees noted the lack of concrete evidence, many were quite sceptical about the 'coincidence' of the 'invasion of the fundamentalists' and the number of attempted military coups between 1986 and 1989.

After the 1986 EDSA overthrow of Ferdinand Marcos and the election of Cory Aquino, non-Catholic Christian groups poured into the country. From 1980 to 1986, an average of twelve of these groups registered with the Securities and Exchange Commission (SEC) every month; from 1987 to 1988, this rate doubled to twenty-four a month.[16] Before 1980, only 228 of these groups were part of the religious landscape in the Philippines; by 1988, 1,676 existed.[17] As in many places in the Third World, new fundamentalist Christian groups were achieving a record 'harvest' of converts.

NUMBER OF NON-CATHOLIC RELIGIOUS GROUPS REGISTERED IN THE PHILIPPINES

	Metro Manila	Outside Metro Manila	Nationwide[18]
Before 1980	111	117	228
After 1980	836	612	1,448
Total	947	729	1,676

The numbers of actual Protestant church congregations are 1970: 5,000, 1980: 9,400 and 1990: 23,000.[19]

Consistent with the rise of fundamentalism in other politically and economically unstable places, fundamentalists in the Philippines join the cacophony of religious voices that compete with one another in the attempt to claim authority in the midst of social chaos. Fundamentalist, neo-Pentecostal and charismatic churches are proliferating in the very places where Christian base communities have been active and liberation theology has been embraced.

While the new Christians tend to be loosely organized, most often in non-denominational independent churches, many do belong to the umbrella organization of the Philippine Council of Evangelical Churches (PCEC). The PCEC is the largest organizing body of evangelical churches with a membership of 1.6 million individual members and 7,000 member churches. Established in 1965, PCEC joined the World Evangelical Fellowship (WEF) in 1974. In 1980 PHILRADS, its relief and development arm was organized and it became a charter member of WEF's Development and Relief Alliance (IRDA). The PCEC, organized to present a distinctly evangelical voice and presence, publishes a magazine, *Evangelicals Today*, which 'provides a prophetic forum to express a collective position on certain issues without legislating on its members'. Through the National Ecumenical Consultative Committee (NECC), the PCEC represents evangelical concerns about national issues to the President; through its membership in the Church and Defence National Committee (CADENCE), the PCEC 'maintains constant dialogue with the Armed Forces of the Philippines (AFP) on matters concerning peace and order, as well as Human Rights'.[20] The former General Secretary of the PCEC, Rev. Agustin (Jun) Vencer, was recently appointed as head of the World Evangelical Fellowship (the first non-Westerner to be so appointed). At virtually the same time, newly elected President Fidel Ramos appointed Vencer head of Intelligence for the Armed Forces of the Philippines. As an organization, the PCEC serves as a counterpoint to the National Council of Churches in the Philippines (NCCP).

The Catholic hierarchy suggests that while there is doctrinal similarity among the new fundamentalists, two distinct groups emerge:

...'homegrown fundamentalists' and 'US-affiliated fundamentalists'. The former are considered generally, though not always, to be relatively apolitical, though more nationalistic, and primarily concerned about conversion, individual salvation, and spiritualistic practices such as healing. The latter group is considered by many to have more of a political agenda.[21]

Protestants – even born-again Protestants – will acknowledge radical differences among themselves, which is one reason why they resist the label 'fundamentalist'. While 'apolitical' positions are still espoused by many Christians, a number of born-again groups have become increasingly politicized as a result of the political and social events of the 1980s. ('Apolitical' in this context often implies support for the *status quo*, but it was a more difficult posture to maintain given the dynamic character of political events in the Philippines in the 1980s.)

In order to obtain a better understanding of the phenomenon of the new fundamentalists in the Philippine context, we will begin by examining their theological perspectives and positions on socio-political issues.

Theological perspectives and political positions

Like their counterparts throughout the world, the new fundamentalist Christian groups in the Philippines emphasize individual salvation rather than social reform, attributing poverty and national calamities to sin and laziness. According to them, both individual and social problems are rooted in God's revenge for man's disobedience; the solution, therefore, lies in greater obedience and faithfulness to God.

Jun Vencer argues that evangelicals need to seek solutions by dealing with root causes, not just their effects. According to him, the root causes are the individual sins of people. Referring to the book of Joel, he writes:

Firstly, the sins of the people against God were the real reason for the calamity. The locusts, the drought and the fires were the tragic effects of the real cause which is rebellion against God. Secondly, the economic collapse is a sign of national sin. Because God is justly in control, and because the tragedy is due to sin, then the prophet is calling for fasting and prayer 'to spare Thy people' (Joel 2: 17).[22]

'We should pray for suffering... difficult times are transcendental times', he elaborated. In the face of national calamities: typhoons, droughts, fires, volcanic eruptions, earthquakes, 'ordinary human means will no longer work. Such crises take us to the core of deep spiritual hunger where we yearn to be with our Creator.'[23]

Orosa echoes Vencer's sentiments: 'The problems in the Philippines have resulted because people turned their back on God.'[24] He further elaborates in an article in the *Ministry Digest*:

> The ills of our nation are primarily spiritual in character, meaning that sin abounds and rules in the nation... we are a nation under judgment by God... In the Old Testament, when the nation of Israel came under judgment, there were generally three major sins prevalent. Idolatry, occultism, and great social injustice. [Religious] leaders are invited to make their own determination as to the prevalence of these issues.[25]

Although evangelical leaders acknowledged some element of social injustice, they tend to attribute peoples' suffering to their own sinfulness. Given this definition of the problem, their energies and resources go into organizing spiritual crusades and relief organizations.

Bautista argues that the development of relief organizations was primarily motivated by the availability of international funds (especially from America) rather than a fundamental concern for the poor. Nonetheless, the involvement of staff members in projects for street children, prostitutes, orphans and the sick deepened their understanding of poverty and the conditions under which people were living, and gave them a new appreciation for the social implications of their faith.[26]

What seems to characterize the position of the new fundamentalists in the Philippines is a 'concern for and duty to the poor' compared with a 'preference or option for the poor', articulated by liberation theology Catholics and Protestants. The 1989 counterpart to the Lausanne Covenant, the 'Manila Manifesto'[27] affirms that 'evangelism is primary because our chief concern is with the gospel', but it also acknowledges structural problems:

> Among the evils we deplore are destructive violence, including institutionalized violence, political corruption, all forms of exploitation of people and of the earth, the undermining of the family, abortion on demand, the drug traffic, and the abuse of human rights. In our concern for the poor, we are distressed by the burden of debt in the two-thirds world. We are outraged by the inhuman conditions in which millions live.

Nonetheless, the Manifesto clarifies that: 'Our continuing commitment to social action is not a confusion of the Kingdom of God with a

Christianized society.' Given the strength and legitimacy of liberation theology within Filipino society, the severe economic and political conditions, and yet the relatively open though volatile and dangerous political space in which such rhetoric is voiced, evangelicals have become more sensitive to and mindful of structural injustices while continuing to concern themselves primarily with individual salvation.

Prosperity theology

In the context of the Philippines, prosperity theology – that God wants you to prosper and that He will bless you with wealth – is boldly proclaimed by some. David Sumrall, nephew of Lester Sumrall, is the American pastor of the Cathedral of Praise, a charismatic congregation of some 14,000 members situated in Metro Manila. He writes about his ministry to a very poor congregation which 'had great faith in healing, but no faith for prosperity'. He describes driving a new car to church one Sunday and parking it in front of the church 'so everyone could see it. [I] smiled as the congregation expressed their amazement. That Sunday morning I preached on prosperity. The people began to see that it worked.'[28]

Critics argue that prosperity is not only boldly but crudely proclaimed. An Irish-born Columban priest in Bacolod City, Father Niall O'Brien, imprisoned in 1983 for a year for his involvement in organizing Basic Christian Communities (BCCs) and later exiled by Marcos, talked about Capalit town in Negros where 'after the bombing there was no hot water, local politicians were heading up with bars of soap with their picture and name on them. Two guys with bullhorns and their Bibles were imploring: "Give up your hunger for riches". They were selling pamphlets – it was grotesque.'[29]

Others couch the message of prosperity theology in a national and international context of development, emphasizing the power of collective prayer and the need for careful stewardship of capital. Butch Conde, pastor of the mega-church Bread of Life Ministries which established the first prayer mountain in the Philippines, refers to the prayer power of the Koreans and the rewards it has brought as a model for Filipinos:

> But the intense prayer life of the Koreans has not only resulted in their miraculous church growth; it has also brought miraculous advancement to the whole nation as well. Devastated by two major wars, Korea gradually rose from the economic shambles to become one of the most prosperous nations in the world today – a leading manufacturer of cars, ships, electronics and other products.[30]

Vencer likewise advocates prosperity theology quite explicitly both for individuals and the nation as a whole:

> National recovery may include the following blessings. God gives each one power to make wealth. He will grant the wisdom to men and women in the wheels of industry... God promises economic prosperity.[31]

Known also by its detractors as 'the Gospel of Wealth' or 'the Name It and Claim It' school, prosperity theology may serve as an evangelical pro-capitalist antidote to the BCCs. Critics argue that the brand of prosperity theology which promises that God will grant you riches if you only believe, and asks people to give when they have virtually nothing, twists the Christian message into one of consumer capital profit. In 'Kulturang Coke at Relihiyong Born-Again', the late Father Jeremias Aquino, priest of the Philippine Independent Church, drew the connections between consumerist culture and fundamentalist expansion.[32]

Believers too may question why they are not receiving the blessings that are preached to be forthcoming. In his sermon, US Pastor Tom O'Dowd of the Word of the World in Bacolod City (the Filipino branch of the Church of God, Cleveland (Tennessee), tells his poor congregation that God indeed promises financial prosperity, citing Matthew 21: 22. 'But', he says, 'God is testing the congregation – there is time between the promise and fulfillment.' The primary reason given for the 'time lag' is the interruption by evil forces who are waging spiritual warfare.

Spiritual warfare and geopolitical territories

The focus on 'Spiritual Warfare' permeates the message of the fundamentalist groups in the Philippines. It weaves its way into sermons, TV and radio broadcasts, and Christian publications. For example, the November-December 1989 issue of the evangelical magazine *Ministry Digest* is entitled 'The Church at War: Assaulting the Gates of Hell'. The special feature, 'Christians and the Coup' focused on the sixth and most violent coup that had taken place since Aquino's coming to power. Referring to the 1-8 December 1989 coup that had claimed at least 113 lives and almost toppled Aquino's government, the issue included numerous articles on spiritual warfare, including 'Prepare War! The Spirit's Call to Spiritual Warfare' by Daniel Tappeiner; 'Are You Covered? Know your place of protection in times of war!' by Gilario Romero; and 'Territorial Spirits: Identifying demonic spirits over geographical domains' by C. Peter Wagner.

In his article on 'Territorial Spirits', C. Peter Wagner, holder of the Donald McGavran chair of church growth at Fuller Theological

Seminary School of World Mission in Pasadena, California, and author of twenty-eight books on church growth, writes: 'I have come to believe that Satan does indeed assign a demon or corps of demons to every geopolitical unit in the world, and they are among the principalities and powers with whom we wrestle.'[33] Wagner's concern about spiritual warfare includes the United States, where he reports that 'former Secretary of the Interior, James Watt, through sensitivities acquired in his past association with the occult, perceives specific dark angels assigned to the White House' as well as various places in the Third World. He includes the Philippines where he cites the example of Lester Sumrall who 'cast out a spirit of an inmate in Bilibid Prison', which was 'followed by dramatic change in the receptivity of Filipinos to spiritual battle'. But Wagner cautions:

> Dealing with territorial spirits is major league warfare. It should not be undertaken casually. If you do not know what you are doing, and few whom I am aware of have the necessary expertise, Satan will *eat you for breakfast.*[35]

Further along in the issue, Brother Eddie Villanueva, the spiritual director of the 300,000-member JIL (Jesus Island) Fellowship and the national chairman of the Philippines Jesus Movement (PJM) argued that the coup was a punishment sent by God because of Filipinos' disobedience and Catholic idolatry:

> In 1986, God gave us the miracle of EDSA but look at what our countrymen have done. Instead of attributing the miracle to God, they have chosen to honor a so-called lady of peace and erected a statue and shrine for her, at the behest of Catholic religious leaders, supported by our top government officials. This is pure and simple idolatry and because of it our whole nation suffers.[36]

In 'This Will Not Be the Last Coup...' the Rev. Fred Magbanua (managing editor of the Far Eastern Broadcasting Corporation in 1989) relayed a dream he had in which God said to him:

> Ramos, Enrile, and people power... you have not given me the glory for what I have done for you. Thus, I have allowed this coup to happen. And this will not be the last. Unless you as a people will learn to give me the glory and honor, there will be more coups and problems that will come upon you as a nation.[37]

The vivid and pervasive use of military imagery in religious rhetoric is characteristic of the new fundamentalists. For example, Bill Bright, founder of Campus Crusade for Christ (CCC) which is very active in the Philippines, is quoted as saying: 'Proclaiming the gospel is like a military offensive, with the mass media serving as the Air

Force – softening up the objective – so that the ground forces can come in and capture an area.'[38] The new Christians repeatedly argue that the enemy – communists, Muslim fundamentalists, idolatrous Catholics – must be struck down. In order for this to happen, Christians must prepare themselves for war. Tappeiner (Ph. D. from Fuller Theological Seminary) writes: 'The warfare Christian... recognizes that the Lord is mustering His warriors for end-time warfare with the enemy.' To reinforce his point, he cites Joel 3: 9-10:

> Declare this to nations: Prepare war, stir up the mighty men. Let all the men of war draw near, let them come up. Beat your plowshares into swords, and your pruning hooks into spears; let the weakling say, 'I am a warrior'.[39]

It is hard to say whether or how such militaristic rhetoric leads to action or non-action, but there appears to be a curious interaction at work. After all, words have power; their messages frame the context of legitimacy or illegitimacy of particular actions. Word for the World, a charismatic Christian fellowship in Bacolod City, brought 800 souls to the Lord in six months, according to its pastor Tom O'Dowd.[40] He reports that 'some 256 members began to attend our services, afraid of the NPA and the uprising'.[41] They began to plant churches and hold crusades in the countryside and on haciendas.

In one of its English-speaking Sunday morning services, Pastor Tom read from the Scriptures: 'As Moses said to Joshua, taking an army of 8 million over the mountain, 'don't be afraid of the enemy, be strong and of good courage and the Lord will go before you' (Deuteronomy 31: 5-8, 23; and Psalm 27). On this particular morning in June 1992, the band warmed up the congregation to sing: 'Sound the trumpet in Zion, Sound the alarm on the Holy Mountain', and 'Rush the walls of the city'. Then Pastor Tom began preaching, addressing his formerly Catholic congregation by talking about Mary as an unwed mother, one who was scorned: 'Mary was a fine Christian, we'll see her in Heaven. There's no need to worship her, she was a real person.' He then warned against idolatry: 'Don't burn candles or incense, don't engage in rituals. Read the Bible.' O'Dowd continued to preach about the need to be strong, to take the offensive: 'You kick the devil. The devil comes to kill, steal, and destroy – you must be strong. I know you're hurting. What should I do? Cry? No, I should teach you to be strong – protect and teach you.' He also emphasized the need for obedience and moderation:

> The path of freedom is the middle road, the balanced path... You are commanded to read the Bible; it doesn't mean you'll understand it... [Furthermore] God's not on our side – He's on His side. You have to follow Him and then you'll win! You are commanded to

be strong in the Lord. We are part of God's Army.

Given the successes of the Basic Christian Communities (BCCs) in Negros and the civil war being waged between the Armed Forces of the Philippines (AFP) and the New People's Army (NPA) in the mountainous areas around Bacolod City, the slightly veiled references to Catholic idolatry and the military metaphors hit close to home. In Negros Occidental, no one escapes the conflict – the only thing to be determined is whose side you are on, and those boundaries are seldom left to individual choice or definition.

Spiritual warfare is to be employed only against the 'enemy' as defined by the spiritual elite, who in terms of influence, hail largely from the United States. The enemy is Satan, demonic spirits, communists, Islamic fundamentalists and idolatrous Catholics. The average rank and file member must be very careful; in spiritual warfare one is playing with fire, and only those who are trained and have special powers will survive. Thus, while stressing the need for each individual to fight the Good Fight and be prepared as Christian soldiers in God's Army, the majority of members are relegated to the status of the footsoldier who is expected to conform to the regulations and commands of the officers. While less hierarchical and bureaucratic than historic Catholicism and mainline Protestantism, the new or, as it is sometimes referred to, 'Third Wave' Christians nonetheless are expected to conform to collective goals as defined by the spiritual élite.

A sign, hanging from the back of a series of office buildings in Bacolod City, reads: 'REACH OUT: EQUIP AN ARMY'. The charismatic group of some seventy members reaches out to a larger group of 200 people, primarily students, through small Bible studies. Reach Out uses the cell group approach that is characteristic of many of the shepherding churches. Its director, Joberto Ramos, a sincere young man in his twenties and native to the area, describes their mission:

> We believe we are an army equipped to fight against the demons. We witness to former NPA people... The Social Gospel and liberation theology are promoted by communist sympathizers and priests. I sympathize with them because they helped people organize themselves but I can't work with them; I can only work through Jesus.[42]

Communism: incarnation of Satan

> 'Christians are the best foes of communism. Therefore, evangelism helps to create a bulwark against communism.'[43]

> 'Of particular and growing concern to many of us in the Philippines is the evident, intense and highly orchestrated fear of communism

being engineered and promoted. Among the groups promoting such paranoia are the Unification Church, its political arm, CAUSA International, the World Anti-Communist League (WACL) headed by Retired Major-General John K. Singlaub, along with its Philippine affiliates, such as the Philippine Anti-Communist Movement (PACM), as well as by several fundamentalist religious sects who are making inroads into the Philippine society.'

Some people wonder how literal fundamentalists' 'spiritual war' against 'communism' may be. But while suspicions abound about fundamentalist assistance to the armed forces, most readily admit that there is little concrete evidence. Peter Brock (quoted above), formerly with the NCCP and now on the staff of the World Council of Churches, argues:

> The reality is that the US, including the CIA, [has cooperated] and will cooperate with anyone who will advance US interests. This will include religious groups of any tradition. Fundamentalist groups who already have a pro-US orientation will be more easily co-opted, misled or even convinced to assist their cause, whilst they are also highly susceptible to the lucid US/CIA propaganda against 'Godless communism'. But the burden of proof remains with the accuser who alleges an 'imperialist conspiracy'.[44]

Both the fundamentalists and opposing camps acknowledge, however, that ideological warfare against communism is being waged by the new wave of 'Christians'. Pastor Tom uses concern about the plight of Filipinos and the threat against communism both to educate his congregation and rally supporters back home in the United States. In his summer 1991 Missions letter, he writes:

> In bondage to alcoholism, loan sharks, gambling, superstition and ignorance, [Filipinos] have little hope for a better life in this world or the next. Various communist groups have been successful in infiltrating these communities resulting in the current insurgency problems. But is this the answer? We believe there is a better one – Jesus.

He then offers news about 'Hacienda Harvest', specifying which haciendas have allowed Christian revivals on their premises, how many people came, and examples of faith healing. There is no discussion about hacienda owners being influenced to offer better wages, medical care or education for the children and workers who are trapped within a feudal system of economic exploitation. Although Pastor Tom is clearly concerned about workers and the treatment and low wages they receive – 'It's almost a master-slave relationship here [Negros] – workers get maybe $2.50 a day' – he goes on to argue that one 'has to understand the planters too – they need good workers'.

As in Guatemala, the plantation owners (who are largely Catholic) are willing, even eager at times, to have the evangelists hold camp meetings on the plantation because the Christian messages they preach are ones of obedience, loyalty, sobriety and industry:

> The Gospel teaches them [workers] not to steal, to raise self-esteem. They can become happy through redemption from God... The Gospel lifts people out of poverty and ignorance. It can help them physically and spiritually... We have to lift people up culturally... to stop them from gambling and drinking... Finally, through the Gospel they will find financial prosperity.[45]

Plantation owners as well as evangelists argue that the converted become better workers with the evangelical emphasis on hard-work, 'clean living', and individual worker responsibility; moreover, it supplies an antidote to the very successful organizing of Christian base communities where liberation theology has informed more progressive thinking about socio-economic exploitation.

Pastor Jose Rivera of Maranatha in Bacolod City argued that the BCCs were communist inspired: 'The Bible tells us we should oppose labour unions, modernism, liberalism, communism – they are all false religions.' He seemed quite uneasy talking to me, and in a tired voice, he said:

> One day Christians will rule but not now – when Christ comes back, he'll find most Christians poor... During the 1983 long drought and the sugar cane crisis, people in Negros became very responsive to the Word of God. God sends them earthquakes and typhoons, time and time again to tell them that what is important is the salvation of the soul. Let the body suffer.[46]

Both Father Niall O'Brien and Father Romeo Empestan, who have been involved in BCCs, argue that the dramatic entry and growth of Protestant fundamentalist groups in Negros occurred since Operation Thunderbolt.[47] The AFP executed Operation Thunderbolt in 1988-9, bombing people out of the mountains so that they could not support the New People's Army (NPA). Official documents report 800 dead, though others argue that thousands died. Col. Colonel, who instructed Counter Subversion and Insurgency (CIS) at the PC Training Center in Silang, Cavite, for the AFP, writes explicitly about the goals and roles of the military's 'Hearts and Soul Campaign' in the *Pro-Democracy PEOPLE's War*. He argues that the major reason for the Philippines' underdevelopment is communist insurgency. In his 768-page book, he details the strategy of the militarily inspired and directed 'Pro-Democracy People's War' in combatting communism and insurgent forces in the Philippines, and specifically in Negros Occidental. Using a multi-pronged approach including 'organizational, propaganda, political, military and ideological warfare', Colonel outlines how the 'Civil Government', the police, and the military will wage warfare... to mobilize the pro-democracy NGOs, civic groups and individuals into counter-NDF organizations...[48] Discussing the need to intensify the 'hearts, minds, and souls campaign' in Negros, he writes: 'All these [military] efforts will be reinforced by public information, education, spiritual and propaganda campaigns.'[49]

Launched on 24 April 1989 in southern Negros, Operation Thunderbolt was a massive military operation intended to avenge the 18 April killing of five soldiers and one civilian by the New People's Army. By May 1989, 35,000 Negros refugees had fled their homes – the largest single evacuation on the island since the Second World War. Military officials had announced that they were going to make a 'decisive show of strength' and invaded numerous municipalities already 'softened up' by aerial bombing. And this they did. 'Tora Tora' planes dropped bombs and Sikorsky helicopter gunships targeted rebel hideouts, hitting numerous towns and villages populated by civilians. The evacuations took public officials by surprise. Lacking even rudimentary health-care facilities, the refugee sites became centres of disease and starvation. Epidemics of measles spread through the crowded and insanitary quarters and children began to die. In places like Bacolod the coffin industry thrived.[50] So, according to Father O'Brien, did the fundamentalists: 'They arrived, carrying their Bibles and preaching in the streets: "Give up your riches for the kingdom of heaven." '

National security doctrine and low-intensity conflict

The convergence of the message, the method and the timing makes many Filipinos suspicious of the new fundamentalists. Father Tom Marti, a Maryknoll priest who has researched the politics of the Religious Right in the United States and the phenomenon of fundamentalism in the Philippines, expresses concerns about the relationship of these new groups to a stepped-up counterinsurgency programme:

> The growing intrusion of fundamentalist organizations into the Philippines fits in very well with the doctrine and strategy of the US Government's Low Intensity Conflict (LIC). Their strong anti-communist line can lend support to military efforts to define communism as the most serious problem confronting the Philippines.[51]

Even with the collapse of the communist world in the early 1990s, Filipino fundamentalists argue that communist insurgents are still the major threat to political stability since they are fuelled by Maoist ideology. Reflecting upon the 4,500 missionaries who flooded the country in the spring of 1990 for the Campus Crusade for Christ (CCC) New Life campaign, Bishop Erme Camba, general secretary of the United Church of Christ in the Philippines, expressed the concern of both Catholics and mainline Protestants in the Philippines:

> We are concerned about the issue of timing. We are wondering about the possible connection between the [U.S. military] bases talks and the arrival of these missionaries. Though we have no positive proof linking the two, fundamentalist groups are traditionally conservative and perhaps they are being used without their knowledge.[52]

Others have pointed to the fundamentalistic origins of some of the vigilante groups like the Alsa Masa and *Kaming Kristiyano Kontra Komunismo* (KKKK: We Christians Against Communism).[53] 'The strategy with the indigenous religions is to appeal to nationalism and to say that Marxism and liberative ideologies are alien, foreign, and must therefore be rejected.'[54] Professor Alice Guillermo, University of the Philippines at Diliman, questions the intentions behind the Ford Foundation's willingness to sponsor programmes to revive traditional religions which are then reoriented along conservative lines in order to safeguard US interests: 'There is one right-wing sect in Mindanao, for instance, which flies the US flag side by side with the Philippine flag because according to them, the US is a holy country like the Philippines.'[55] But mostly the vigilante groups with a religious orientation involve a syncretistic mix of indigenous and folk-Catholic elements.[56] As Suzara writes, the complexity and volatility of the politico-religious situation makes it difficult to decipher exactly what the alliances are:

> The volatile configurations of a church-blessed Aquino government, a Philippine military supported by the United States, Aquino-endorsed vigilantes, and military-assisted cultist vigilantes pose formidable theoretical and methodological challenges.[57]

What does appear clear in surveying the clusters of religious groups, and the questions that surround them, is that a broad alliance of groups exists which, on the one hand, accommodates the National Security State, whether for pragmatic or ideological reasons, and on the other resists it. Many of the new Protestant fundamentalist groups, as well as most of the vigilante groups, and the Catholic fundamentalist groups would fall into the former category. The divisions between the 5-9 per cent Protestants and the 85 per cent Catholics, or between the dominant Christian groups and the 5 per cent Muslims are in many ways less dramatic than the ones between those who believe the church has a vital role to play in challenging the structures of inequality and injustice, and those who argue that the church should 'remain neutral' or actively fight insurgency and 'communism'.

In 1991, the NCCP published The Religious Right and National Security Doctrine (NSD) which drew parallels between Father Jose Comblin's analysis of NSD in the context of Latin America and the contemporary situation in the Philippines.[58] From the perspective of NSD, communism is the primary enemy of the church and the state. Therefore, the church, which does not have the power to check the enemy alone, should collaborate with the power of the state.[59]

Writing in the context of the Philippines, Bishop Erme Camba (General Secretary of the United Church of Christ in the Philippines) sees a sympathetic relationship between US evangelical and foreign policy interests:

> The US government continues repeatedly to interfere in our national affairs and processes in order to safeguard its economic and military interests. The US has given substantial amounts of military aid to help quell the rising sentiments of our people for national sovereignty. It has used the media to portray freedom-loving Filipinos as godless ideologues who are out to grab power (as if the ideology of capitalism were godly!). More alarming, the sacred Scriptures are being used by certain evangelists to reduce our arguments for change into the terms of an other-worldly battle between good and evil.[60]

Christians, the military, and value formation

At the 1991 South Asia Pacific Conference of the Association of Christian Military Fellowships held in Manila, Col. Ernesto Sacro gave the welcoming address. Using Psalm 23 as a basis for his remarks, he reminded the military of their responsibility to shepherd the people: 'The people we are shepherding are sheep. The sheep have to be led by a shepherd, they can't by themselves exist without a shepherd.'[61] Spiritual warfare was central to the conference; Ephesians (6: 10-12) was a favourite scriptural reference:

> That our battle is not against flesh and blood, but against the rulers, against the power of this dark world, and against the spiritual forces of evil in the heavenly realms.[62]

Reporting on the 1989 Military Christian Fellowship Conference held in Seoul, Korea, Brig.-General Honesto Isleta (formerly the official spokesman for the AFP) reported on the focus of the 'Spiritual Readiness Seminar' which included subjects on Self-Image, Developing Convictions, Spiritual Growth, and Spiritual Warfare.[63]

Spiritual Warfare preoccupies the new fundamentalists whose military rhetoric fluidly crosses the boundaries between spiritual and literal warfare. Increasingly the Protestant chaplaincies of the AFP are being filled by fundamentalists.

The military has met with born-again Christian groups and, in March 1989, supported the establishment of the National Association for Democracy (NAD) which brought together conservative Christian and vigilante groups, principally to counter the progressive movements within the Catholic and Protestant churches.[64] NAD, whose stated objective is 'to fight the communist insurgency', claims a mass base that runs into millions. Father O'Brien estimates that approximately 30 – 40% of the NAD are fundamentalists, and that there is a close alliance between them and a number of vigilantes in the CAFGU units and the Army itself.[65] A NAD organizational pamphlet lists member organizations which include Benny Abante Jr. and Gavino Tica's Alliance for Democracy and Morality (ADAM).

According to the 'Religious Right and National Security Doctrine', ADAM and Tica often publish 'press releases that are true copies of military disinformation campaigns'[66] and are linked with the Philippine Ministry of Defence.[67] The 1987 U.S. – Philippine Fact-Finding Mission headed by former U.S. Attorney General Ramsey Clark found that ADAM had associations with the Philippine Defence Ministry and with John Whitehall, a U.S.-based Australian who serves as Vice-President of the World Anti-Communist Crusade (WACL).[68]

Rev. Gavino Tica, president of International Baptist Ministries (mother church for some 487 fundamentalist Baptist churches in the Philippines),[69] helped to organize ADAM, an association of over 100 groups. According to him,

> ADAM represents all shades of Protestant belief and even some Catholics... We don't discuss doctrinal details... [like] baptism. Whether we sprinkle or immerse, we are both marching and we stay together. We're united against communism.[70]

ADAM holds rallies that draw from 35,000 – 100,000 people, drawing crowds of 'regular' people, from farmers to fisherman to planters.

> We have been able to influence Congress against the non-conversion law, and we use our influence to lobby against pornography, and the liberalization of the divorce law and abortion laws... We're concerned with morality. Our primary concern, however, is communism – not Marxist but Maoist communism... Our people are deceived – [they] think Communism is falling apart when they look at Eastern Europe and Russia but Communism's a threat as long as China exists – and China's only 2 hours away. Pretty soon, China will be so strong we won't be able to resist... We need a big battle.[71]

A protégé and friend of Jerry Falwell, Tica is willing to promote much more theological compromise than Falwell in creating a Moral Majority-like organization. Describing himself as both 'a one hundred per cent Full Gospel preacher' and a 'fundamentalist Baptist' (a combination that would be out of place in the United States), Tica has been very effective in bringing together various strands of conservative Protestantism. In addition to a large network of churches ('in some areas, they've dropped the name Baptist – in Mindinao Bataan you don't want to use my name – they'll kill you', he laughs), Tica credits his ministry with sponsoring a training camp for soldiers; nineteen Christian schools (nursery – high school) enrolling some 8,000 students; 822 extension Bible schools; 178 feeding centres; an International Christian Relief Programme serving 42,000 children; and livelihood training programmes in urban areas and among various tribes (including the Balooga, Tiboli, Mangans, and Magots), training some 50,000 people at all educational levels.[72] 'I believe', he says, 'that we can turn this country around... We have a country to win – one that the Lord would be proud of [where there are] tears of compassion rather than blood; where our hills are filled with laughter of children rather than gun shots; where our young children could dream'.[73]

With a Ph.D. in psychology from Temple University, Philadelphia, as sell as seminary training from Chattanooga, Tennessee, Tica talks about using 'behavioral modification techniques in seminars given for the military: The best way to change society is to change people's minds'. In this capacity, Tica and ADAM have been quite active in organizing Value Formation Courses (VFCs) in the Armed Forces of the Philippines (AFP).

Protestant President Fidel Ramos, as former AFP chief of staff back in 1987, defended the VFCs as the 'major new component of civil military operations' that sought the

.... development, interiorization and enrichment of spiritual, moral and nationalistic values in the professional soldier in order to transform him into a God-centered, people-dedicated and nation-oriented individual... The scope of Value Formation is moral and spiritual development, socio-cultural integration, and command value orientation, information, and education... One of the specific objectives of the program is to promote acceptance by the people in insurgency-affected areas, that the AFP works for their welfare.[74]

An off-shoot of the New Armed Forces of the Philippines (NAFP) after the 1986 EDSA Revolt, Value Formation courses were underway in all AFP camps and installations by 1987.[75] According to Tica, the military is not only willing but eager for such seminars: 'One of the top military leaders has asked me for Bibles... we don't have enough time for all the requests.' Graduates of the Value Formation courses are called 'Soldiers of God', and 'those who are potential leaders will be tasked to organize a Basic Military Cell (BMC) in different areas'.[76] Once 40% of the military is born-again, Tica believes they will be able to wield the kind of power they want.

A number of new Christian groups are active in the VFCs, including Word of Life International Living Waters Fellowship (Rhema origins), Heaven's Magic, the Christian Life Fellowship, *El Shaddai*, and Joshua for Christ. Rev. Norma Tinio, President of Word of Life International, specifically thanked the Kenneth Copeland Ministries, the Flying Medical Samaritans, Women's AGLOW Fellowship (the female counterpart of the Full Gospel Business Men's Fellowship), and the AFP for their support of the seminars in the closing ceremonies for the Human Values Formation Seminar.[77]

In the maiden issue of 'Joshua for Christ: Bringing the Good News to the Military', the JFC Ministry proudly proclaims they have been conducting 'weekly Bible studies and devotions since December 22', barely days after the termination of the last coup attempt. JFC uses CCC's four Spiritual Laws in their training programmes, and is exuberant about the miraculous changes taking place within the ranks of the military where 'soldiers... keep themselves fit for physical battle as they beat their bodies too for the spiritual warfare'.[78]

Another group that is active is the Full Gospel Businessmen's Fellowship which is known for its 'SWAT' – Spiritual Warfare Attack Teams. Former Chief AFP spokesman, Colonel Honesto Isleta has contributed to the VFCs and serves as a preacher in the FGBMF.

Soldiers for Christ, the Christ Mighty Warriors Christian Fellowship, and the Christian Military Fellowship (CMF) are Christian organizations internal to the AFP. CMFP describes itself as 'an association of Believers in the Armed Forces of the Philippines who are committed to follow the teaching of Jesus Christ'. Like a number of the other groups, they hold Bible studies, prayer groups, conferences and seminars and cooperate with local Christian fellowships, churches, worldwide Christian military fellowships and ministries.

Another highly visible group in the Philippines is Wilde Almeda's Jesus Miracle Crusade International Ministry (JMC) which holds anticommunist rallies throughout the country in the name of Christ. Claiming millions of followers throughout the Philippines, Almeda regularly packs in people in a large stadium in Manila. A huge 'Communism is Satanism' banner flanks the stage, and another refers to the international embrace of JMC and its alliance with Jubilee Crusades. A charismatic group that believes in faith healing and speaking in tongues, Almeda's organization has cadres of young volunteers who live, fast, pray and work together. It appears to be a very patriarchal, authoritarian community where believers must fast for long periods of time.[79]

While the Unification Church and conservative Catholic groups, such as Opus Dei and the Knights of Malta, are also quite active in running seminars that oppose liberation theology, a report published by the Socio-Pastoral Institute of Manila suggests that 'a Protestant edge cuts through the VFCs and other AFP ethics seminars'.[80] While more research would need to be done to assess to what degree this is true,[81] it is clear that many of the new Christian groups are active. Both leaders of historic Protestant and Catholic churches are concerned about the inroads Protestant fundamentalists are making into the military via various preaching programmes and the VFCs which are distributing foreign-produced comic-books equating communist ideology with the 'Anti-Christ'.[82]

Appeal of the new fundamentalists

The growth of fundamentalism around the world is both highly organized and organic. Fundamentalists are not simply political opportunists nor are they apolitical beings. They have agendas, as do we all, which play out in various ways depending upon the group and the cultural context in which they find themselves. Therefore, we must examine a number of factors that contribute to their appeal. Certainly the attention they place on the individual person as well as the collective group is not to be underestimated – You as a person are important AND you can have a sense of belonging here with us as a child of God. Individual and group identities are set up to nurture and complement rather than compete with one another.

Much of the appeal lies in the fervour of worship, the involvement of people in small, intimate groups, and the creation of a sense of belonging, that the individual matters – to God, to Jesus, to the pastor and fellow parishioners. This is powerful stuff and it gives people a sense of power, an internal locus of control that is attributed to God, Christ, and the Holy Spirit who lives within. Moreover, in order to succeed, to be faithful and to prosper, one need not challenge the entire structure of society or protest wages or human rights violations; one must struggle (only) to control one's own habits and attitudes. One is responsible for controlling one's own behaviour (not to drink, smoke, gamble or commit adultery). It is not that this is always easy, but it is manageable. Moreover, man is recognized as weak, as a sinner who must repent and ask forgiveness, who can then once again try to 'live cleanly'.

The degree of social dislocation, and economic and political chaos that characterizes recent Philippine history, contributes to the receptivity of people to experiment with new religious forms of experience, particularly those that stress the personal and 'non-political'. For those who have been uprooted from their villages and relocated in cities where they may be squatters, living in extreme poverty; workers aspiring to the working and middle classes; or the professional middle-class wanting to exercise some social and political influence, the new fundamentalists offer a place of retreat and renewal, and a community to belong to. As in many places in the developing world, the new Christian ministries are strong in urban areas, often creating megachurches that then break people down into smaller, more intimate Bible-study and home-worship groups.

The pattern of rural-to-urban migration creates a vacuum into which the New Religious Movements are effectively moving. The upheaval of family kinship networks and traditional patterns of life make people receptive to the new Christian groups who offer a message of renewal, spiritual uplift and economic prosperity. All one has to do is to put one's faith in Christ. Torn away from one's traditional home, there is little more to sacrifice in this bargain – and if it works, much to gain. Why not try it? Those who are espousing the message are prosperous, powerful people; they must be doing something right. Attributing unemployment, landlessness, poverty, and military abuses to people's sins is a relatively safe explanation in a world turned upside down.

The irony is that along with the spiritual renewal that evangelicalism brings to people in the Philippines and throughout the world, challenging in potent ways the institutionalization of mainstream religion (both Protestant and Catholic), it also brings support of American-style capitalism that serves the interests of the affluent. While it may breathe new life into religious feeling and expression, it neglects the structural abuses of power and inequality that entrap people and sap them of their strength and vitality. If people cannot have access to land which they can harvest or find work that pays liveable wages, then the process of revitalization becomes both more necessary and progressively more futile.

Another irony is that the evangelical emphasis on obedience and loyalty is dialectically related to the emphasis on the value of personal individuality. Much of the appeal of the new fundamentalists stems precisely from the paradoxical attention played both to the individual and to the community. The ultimate submission of the individual to Christ or his embodiment in the 'transnational' Christian community of believers is striking, particularly when proselytizing takes place across national, class, gender, and racial lines. The question now is, how does it work?

Organizational strategies

The new fundamentalists put much pride in numbers – both bodies and buildings. These are the tangible fruits of their labour. Success is typically measured by the number of souls who come to Christ and the number of churches planted. In fact, church-planting is perhaps the major preoc- cupation of the new wave of Christians. International church-growth agencies such as Philippine Crusades, an affiliate of US-based Overseas Crusades, and 'Discipling A Whole Nation' (DAWN) International, financed by American church-growth experts, seek to coordinate efforts among various groups by holding seminars, pastoral conferences and crusades; they support a well-financed structure of Bible schools, mission agencies, research centres, publishing houses and broadcast ministries. DAWN actively collects data on geographical regions, specifying where there is no church, what kind of competition there is, what the socio- economic conditions are like, etc. President of DAWN International, Jim Montgomery, reported that in 1986 there were twenty-two nations with a DAWN project underway; by 1989 there were forty-three. That doubled to eighty-nine by the end of 1990, and 'there are now [1991] at least 116 countries involved in some measurable form'! The goal of DAWN 2000 Philippines is 'to plant a viable and reproducing local church in every Barangay by the year 2000 AD'.

According to Jun Vencer, the tremendous amount of church growth in the Philippines has been largely aided by the coordination of in- ternational church-planting efforts. He attributes much of this growth to organizations like DAWN. Vencer reports that by December 1990 there were 23,200 congregations in 32 per cent of the *barangays*; 54 per cent of them were planted during 1981-90, and 22 per cent were planted in the period 1971-80. 'These may be correlated to the fact that the first Church Growth Seminar took place in Baguio City in 1974 and the [National Church Growth] Strategy Congress that led to the formal organization of DAWN Philippines was held in 1985... It is evident that DAWN as a catalytic movement is a significant factor'.[83]

Although most of the new churches are 'independent') non-denomina- tional and non-centralized), they tend to be affiliated to other groups that are supported by highly coordinated national and international evan- gelistic crusades, rallies, Bible schools, missions and media.

The *Mission Handbook* for 1993-5 lists 153 US mission agencies in the Philippines, with a total number of 1,961 US Protestant personnel, and 276 US and Canadian Catholic personnel for a population of 63,700,000.[84] In 1987, there were only 5,319 priests and 7,908 nuns all over the country; in two-thirds of the 72 dioceses in the Philippines, the ration was one priest to every 10,000 Catholics. In 1990, IBON reported that there was only one priest for every 30,000 people.[85] In contrast, Villanueva's Jesus is Lord (JIL) Fellowship with some 300,000 members has 5,000 pastoral workers; Sumrall's Cathedral of Praise has 800 workers for Metro Manila alone. The new Christian churches specialize in creating a community of believers who are trained to evangelize. The Cathedral of Praise holds some 1,000 Bible studies a week for its neighbourhood cells composed of between ten and twenty people each, and the staff conducts some 7,000 home visits every month, so that each member of the church is assured a home visit once every other month. Sumrall also keeps a computer data base that includes an entry on each of the 14,000 members of his flock.

Unlike other religious groups, the new Christians have maximized the use of electronic media – both radio and television. A survey of the weekly TV guide indicates that in Metro Manila alone, a total of twenty-seven religious shows are aired on fifty-one spots for a total of forty-six hours every week, with 'fundamentalists' filling approximately thirty hours of airtime a week. It was estimated that in 1991, fundamentalists were paying at least P155,000 a week for their media blitzes.[86] TV evangelists regularly aired in the Philippines include Rex Hubbard, Jimmy Swaggart and the PTL Club.

Christian education, ranging from Sunday schools to Bible schools to elementary and secondary schools, is also a significant feature, with the Philippine Bible Directory of 1990-1 listing some 220 Christian schools, Bible Schools, and Seminaries throughout the Philippines. A number of groups, including Campus Crusade for Christ, Maranatha, Intervarsity Christian Fellowship (IVCF)[87] and the Navigators, are active on college and high-school campuses. Bishop Ben Dominquez, a priest of the Philippine Independent Church of the Risen Lord on the University of the Philippines Campus, estimates that there are twelve 'fundamentalist' groups active on campus. Out of some 12,000 students they probably have an outreach to 2,000.[88]

In the Philippines, as elsewhere, those labelled as the new 'fundamentalists' do not represent a monolithic movement. Diversity exists, especially when it comes to social concerns and political action. What the new 'Christians' do share is a fundamental belief in the need for a personal conversion experience to be saved, in the Bible as the literal and inerrant Word of God, and in the responsibility of Christians to evangelize. The dominant and more conservative groups of 'fundamentalists' embrace prosperity theology and Spiritual Warfare, which is framed in dualistic thinking about good and evil forces where 'insurgents' are identified as being the major evil force. The smaller group of more progressive born-again Christians have embraced transformation theology; allying themselves with progressive Catholic and secular forces who are concerned with human rights violations and environmental well-being.

Some of the once conservative, 'apolitical' Christian groups, like

Intervarsity Fellowship and even to some extent the PCEC, became politicized during the 1980s. In the 1987 *Ministry Digest* issue on 'Christians and the Coup', excerpts from a talk given to the PCEC by then Senate President, Sen. Jovito Salonga, appeared. While declaring his support of a democratic government, and his understanding of why President Aquino needed to request the aid of the US military forces, he said:

> I want to add that in my heart of hearts, I'm not comfortable with having to beg Uncle Sam for help every time we are in a crisis... No self-respecting nation should be in captivity to any foreign power...

But Gavino Tica made his position clear:

> We [the Philippines] are in bondage economically – but I am a very pragmatic person... being in bondage to America is preferable than being in bondage to China.

The issues are complex and the stakes high. All are aware of the crippling debt, and the political and economic instability of the Philippines. The majority of Filipinos, of any religious persuasion, resent the dependency of the Philippines on foreign powers. But their analysis and ways of accommodating and resisting such inequalities in power are played out in different ways. The new fundamentalists tend to support the *status quo* and throw their dice in with the pro-capitalist forces of the United States.

Given the status of the Philippines as a colony or semi-colony of the United States throughout most of the twentieth century, and the frequent state of internal rebellion against US domination, it is not surprising that evangelization (which is heavily influenced by US sources) uses military metaphors to maintain order along socio-political lines conducive to continued neo-colonialism, plantation economy and, until recently, US military bases. In fact, as the US bases have been voted out of the Philippines, and the US government may no longer have the will or resources to maintain military or economic force, the new conservative Christians may see an even more vital role for themselves. This may also help to explain how a faith born in the United States, can be exported as a transnational faith and implanted in diverse cultural settings. Neo-colonial successes have been able to secure sacred support for secular concerns.

In terms of receptivity, Melba Maggay (General Director of the Institute for the Study of Asian Church and Culture, ISAC) argues that the appeal is not so much about 'salvation' as power:

> Many of our people respond not to abstract social analysis but persons of power... The charismatics have grown because they are speaking

to that part of the population that is not much interested in salvation but in issues of power. We must understand that in this culture anyone who speaks for God is automatically assumed as having some kind of power.[89]

As in many other places and times, the charismatic personality can draw people to join all sorts of groups and causes. And 'if you have come to know genuine spiritual experience given to you by a missionary who has a right-wing agenda, it will be very difficult for you to distinguish your faith from its political baggage'.[90] Maggay worries that

.... a political agenda seems to be exported to us along with the charismatic faith... Questions of justice and righteousness seem to go through a process of laundering... It saddens us considerably that conversion is being used to demobilize the people.[91]

It also angers many Filipinos that 'these hordes of missionaries who neither know the political or cultural context of the country would come to us and preach to us about the gospel'.[92]

Maggay, like many other religious persons concerned about the evangelical political agenda, quite willingly acknowledges a strong religious dimension. What concerns them is either the embracing of a right-wing political agenda or a willingness to make compromises in order to protect the right to preach:

We saw in evangelicalism in the Philippines for the last 20 years under Marcos a reluctance to speak out against human rights violatious because it wants its freedom to preach assured... [There is] a very brutal pragmatism which will prop up dictators for the sake of American-style democracy. I would like some answers to that because the evangelical church in the Philippines is perhaps the most deeply colonized and dependent on American values.[93]

Filipino fundamentalists are strongly influenced by US evangelicals; at the same time, they are forging their own positions – some of which have become quite critical of the United States. While most of the new Christian groups supported the continuation of the US military bases, Butch Conde, head of the mega-church Bread of Life, came out against them and other groups articulating a desire for genuine national sovereignty. While some still claim to be 'apolitical', it has been a difficult position to maintain, particularly during the 1980s. Increasingly the new fundamentalists have become politicized, the majority in conservative directions but a significant and active minority in progressive directions. Many fundamentalist leaders argue that 'Christians' need to become socially and politically active, to transform social institutions, and serve as active Christians in all spheres of life. But one does not hear much talk about theocracy. This is not so much because it is unappealing (in fact, many of the contributors to Philippine evangelical magazines are Dominion Theologists), but because it is not pragmatic, Protestants represent a small minority of Filipinos (only 5 – 10 per cent of the population) in a context where fundamentalists are politically as well as religiously suspect. Nonetheless, they are wildly optimistic about the power of Christ to transform not only individuals but whole countries; and they plan to see to it that born-again believers have a hand in shaping, if not controlling, the directions policy takes.

Notes

1. Orosa 1989: 2.
2. Bautista 1991.
3. See Bautista 1991.
4. Orosa 1989: 2.
5. Ibid.
6. Quoted by Clark in Pimentel 1991: 7.
7. Quoted in Clymer 1986: 154.
8. Orosa, 'Unveiling of His Glory', n.d.
9. Valenzuela April 1990; 'Fundamentalism: Twist of Faith' 1991: 2.
10. DAWN 2000 is an acronym for 'Discipling a Whole Nation' which aims to plant a church in every *barangay* and people group in the Philippines by the year 2000.
11. 'DAWN Research Report' 1991.
12. Mission Handbook 1993. Note that Brazil had a population of 150 million compared to 63.7 million in the Philippines.
13. 'Catholic Guidelines' 1989: 11.
14. *Exploring NRMs* 1989: 47.
15. Nicholas and de Leon 1989: 48.
16. Valenzuela 1990.
17. Ibid.; 'Fundamentalism: Twist of Faith' 1991: 2. 'DAWN Research Report' 1991.
18. DAWN Research Report 1991: 1.
19. DAWN 1991.
20. 'Philippine Council of Evangelical Churches, Inc.' (pamphlet) n.d.
21. Valenzuela 1990.
22. Vencer 1990: 7-8.
23. Interview with Vencer, 1992.
24. Interview with Orosa, 1992.
25. Orosa 1989: 2.
26. Bautista 1991: 91-2.
27. In July 1974 the International Congress on World Evangelization was held in Lausanne, Switzerland. In July 1989 over 3,000 evangelicals from some 170 countries met in Manila for the same purpose and issued the 'Manila Manifesto'. Both the 'Lausanne Covenant' and the 'Manila Manifesto' tend to express more liberal sentiments than the average Filipino evangelical; nonetheless, the Filipino delegation helped formulate and ultimately signed the Manifesto.
28. Sumrall 1990: 182.

29. Fr. O'Brien goes on to say, however, that the landowners of Negros are more likely to be aligned with the conservative Catholic *Opus Dei* than with the Protestant fundamentalist groups. In the north of the island, *haciendaros* have organized themselves into rightist groups and favour a fundamentalistic sort of religion; in the south this is not so much the case, perhaps because of the 30 – 40-year-long history of the BCCs. (Interview with O'Brien 1992.)
30. Conde 1991: 8.
31. Vencer 1990: 7-8.
32. Aquino 1981: 8-9.
33. Wagner 1989: 42.
34. Ibid.: 45.
35. Emphasis mine. Wagner 1989: 47.
36. Excerpt from a TV address, 'A Message to the Filipino Nation', by Villanueva 1989 quoted in *Ministry Digest*, Nov./Dec. 1989: 5.
37. Quoted in *Ministry Digest*, Nov./Dec. 1989: 6.
38. Quoted in Conway and Siegelman 1982: 172.
39. Tappeiner 1989: 19.
40. Word for the World is a branch of the Church of God, Cleveland, Tennessee, and sister church of the Greenhills Christian Fellowship, an AB congregation in Makati, the wealthy business district of Manila. O'Dowd had previously worked with the Swaggart ministries for five years.
41. Interview with O'Dowd, 1992.
42. Interview with Ramos, 1992.
43. McCollister, President of CCC's Christian Embassy, quoted in 'Sojourners Critique of CCC': 10.
44. Brock 1988: 4.
45. Interview with Tom and Kaulei O'Dowd, 1992.
46. Interview with Rivera, 1992. This was one of the few interviews done through an interpreter, from Illongo into English.
47. Interviews with O'Brien, 1992; Empestan 1992; see also O'Brien 1993.
48. Colonel 1991: 523, ch. 5.
49. Ibid.: 639-40.
50. De Guzman and Craige 1990.
51. Marti 1987.
52. Camba quoted in Alibutud 1990: 3.
53. See Marti 1987: 22-5; Colonel 1989: 39-42.
54. Guillermo 1991: 230.
55. Ibid.
56. See 'Something More Than A CIA Conspiracy' 1989; Marti 1987.
57. Suzara 1993: 303.
58. The Religious Right and National Security Doctrine 1991.
59. Comblin 1979.
60. Quoted in Asedillo and Williams 1989: vii.
61. Representatives came from Korea (the largest delegation), Indonesia, Republic of China, Singapore, Australia, Japan, India, Malaysia, United Kingdom, the United States and the Philippines.
62. Cited in CMF Newsletter, Jan/Feb 1990: 5.
63. Christian Military Fellowship Philippines Newsletter, n.d.
64. Church Trends 1990.
65. Interview with O'Brien, 1992.
66. Sabug 1991: 377.
67. 'Right-Wing Vigilantes and US Involvement' 1987. The mission was headed by former US Attorney General Ramsey Clark.
68. Ibid.: 20-1.

69. Established since Tica began his ministry in the Philippines on 9 July 1974. Interview with Tica 1992.
70. Interview with Tica 1 June 1992.
71. Ibid.
72. These numbers are taken from an interview with Tica, 1 June 1992, after having attended a service at the mother church, International Baptist Ministries in Metro Manila and seeing the livelihood programme established at the same location.
73. Interview with Tica 1 June 1992.
74. According to a military publication:'Value Formation' Sept. 1987: 4.
75. Ibid.
76. Ibid.: 18.
77. Seminar held 13 Aug. 1986 at Agape Park Mission Guest House.
78. 'Joshua for Christ: Bringing Good News to the Military' n.d.: 2.
79. I was unable to secure an interview with Almeda despite several attempts, but I was able to meet his mother and talk with a young woman convert who was working full-time for him in exchange for room and board, JMC, Manila, 24 May 1992. See also, 'The Religious Right and National Security Doctrine' 1991: 372-3.
80. Clad 1987: 2.
81. Because of the highly secretive and elitist nature of *Opus Dei* and the Knights of Malta, much less research has been done on these conservative and strongly anti-communist Catholic groups than on the Protestant fundamentalist groups.
82. Clad 1987: 2.
83. Vencer in 'DAWN 2000: How many more churches to go'? n.d.
84. Siewert and Kenyon 1993.
85. Citing a Philippine *Daily Globe* article, 14 July 1990, in 'Fundamentalism' 1991: 3.
86. 'Fundamentalism' 1991: 4.
87. According to the head of intervarsity Christian Fellowship in the Philippines (IVCF), IVCF is active in some 200 universities, colleges, and high schools; although it is hard to determine the number of members, he estimates that they have 2 – 3,000 committed members. Interview with Capaque 1992.
88. Interview with Bishop Ben Dominquez 1992.
89. Maggay 1991: 234.
90. Ibid.: 235.
91. Ibid.: 234.
92. Ibid.
93. Ibid.: 235-6.

References

Alibutud, R. 1990. 'Invasion of the Soul Snatchers', *Malaya*, 15 July, 1, 3.
Alejandria, N. 1989. 'Cold War: Christian Soldiers', *Midweek*, 29 March.
Anderson, G. 1969. *Studies in Philippine Church History*. Ithaca: Cornell University Press.
Aquino, J. 1981. 'Kulturang Coke at Relihiyong Born-Again', *Kalinangan*, 1(1), 8-9.
Asedillo, R. and B.D. Williams (eds) 1989. *Rice in the Storm*. NY: Friendship Press.

Barry, T. 1986. *Low Intensity Conflict: The Battlefield in Central America*. Albuquerque: The Resource Center.

Bautista, L. 1991. *The Social Views of Evangelicals on Issues Related to the Marcos Rule 1972-1986*. Master's manuscript submitted to the College of Social Sciences and Philosophy, University of Philippines, September.

Baybay, N. (Director of Development for Ecumenical Center for Justice and Peace and UCC pastor, Bacolod) 1992. Interview with author, 1 June.

Bondoc, J. 1989. 'What are Fundamentalists Really Up To?' *Philippine Free Press*, 25 Feb.

——. 1989. 'Religious Revitalization and Politics' and 'Fundamentalist Expansion', both in *Exploring the New Religious Movements*.

Brock, P. 1988. 'Fundamentalist Expansion: An Historical Perspective', *WSCF Journal*, April, 4.

Capaque, G. (Gen. Secretary Inter-Varsity Christian Fellowship) 1992. Interview with author, Quezon City, 28 May.

Cariño, F. (Gen. Secretary NCCP) 1992. Interview with author, Manila, 6 June.

'Catholic Guidelines on Fundamentalism: Hold Fast to What is Good' 1989. Manila: Catholic Bishops' Conference of the Philippines.

Church Growth Manual 1990 (3). Seoul: Church Growth International.

Church Trends 1990. Church Data Center.

Clad, J. 1987. 'The Soldiers of God', *Far Eastern Economic Review*, 12 March.

Clymer, K. 1986. *Protestant Missionaries in the Philippines 1898-1916: An Inquiry Into the American Colonial Mentality*. Chicago: University of Illinois Press.

CMF Newsletter (Christian Military Fellowship) 1990, Jan.-Feb.

Colonel, M. 1991. *Pro-Democracy PEOPLE'S WAR*. Quezon City: Vanmarc Ventures.

Comblin, J. 1979. *The Church and the National Security State*. Maryknoll, NY: Orbis.

Conde, B. 1991. 'Touch of Glory', *Christian Journal*, Aug.

Constantino, R. and L. Constantino 1987. *The Philippines: The Continuing Past*. Quezon City: Foundation for Nationalist Studies.

Conway, F. and J. Siegelman 1982. *Holy Terror: The Fundamentalist War on America's Freedom, Religion, Politics, and Our Private Lives*. NY: Dell Publishing.

Coronel, S. 1989. 'Right-Wing Evangelicals Take Part in Politics in the Name of God', *Kalinangan* 9(2), 39-42.

Corpuz, O. 1976. *The Philippines*. NJ: Presidential.

'DAWN Research Report' 1991. Prepared by Philippine Crusades Research, 5 Nov.

De Guzman, A. and T. Craige 1990. *Handbook on Militarization*. Manila: Ecumenical Movement for Justice and Peace.

Diamond, S. 1989. *Spiritual Warfare*. Boston: South End Press.

Diaz-Laurel, C. (President of CAUSA Philippines and wife of former Vice-President Laurel) 1992. Interview with author, Manila, 27 May.

Dominquez, Bishop B. (Church of the Risen Lord at University of the Philippines) 1992. Interview with author, Quezon City, 26 May.

Empestan, Father R. 1992. Diocesan Pastoral Center. Interview with author, Bacolod, 31 May.

'Evangelicals' Manila Visit to prop up pro-bases sentiment?' 1990. *Manila Times*, 18 May, 5.

Exploring the New Religious Movements in the Philippines 1989. Quezon City: Commission on Evangelism and Ecumenical Relations, National Council of Churches, Philippines.

Flores, D. 1992. Socio-Pastoral Center. Interview with author, Bacolod, 29 May.

'Fundamentalism: Twist of Faith' 1991. *IBON: Facts and Figures* 14(9), 1-7.

Guillermo, A. 1991. 'Comments', in *The Religious Right and National Security Doctrine*, Tugon, 11(2), 230.

Henares, H. 1989. 'Who are considered right-wing Christians?', *Philippine Daily Inquirer*, 8 Sept., 1.

'Joshua for Christ: Bringing Good News to the Military' n.d. *Maiden Issue*, 2.

Kowalewski, D. 1993. 'Rejoinder on Vigilantism in the Philippines', *Sociology of Religion*. 54(3), 309-12.

Lamban, S. 'Popoy' 1992. Gen. Secretary Ecumenical Movement for Justice and Peace (EMJP). Interview with author, Bacolod, 28 May.

Maggay, M. 1991. 'Comments', in *The Religious Right and National Security*.

Marti, T. 1987. 'Fundamentalist Sects and the Political Right', *Kalinangan* 7(1), 22-5.

——. 1989. 'Doctrine and Strategy: Low Intensity Conflict'. Manila: Socio-Pastoral Institute.

Miles, S. n.d. 'Low-Intensity Conflict: US New Strategy in the Third World', reprinted by Socio-Pastoral Institute (SPI), Special Issue, Series 5.

Miller, S.C. 1982. *Benevolent Assimilation*. New Haven: Yale University Press.

Nicholas, F. and J. de Leon 1989. 'Spiritual Renewal: The Philippine Experience', in *Exploring the New Religious Movements in the Philippines*.

O'Brien, N. 1992. Interview with author, Bacolod.

——. 1993. *Island of Tears, Island of Hope: Living the Gospel in a Revolutionary Situation*. Maryknoll, NY: Orbis Books.

O'Dowd, T. and K. 1992. Interview with author, Bacolod, 31 May.

Orosa, R. 1992. Interview with author, Manila, 1 June.

——. n.d. 'Unveiling of His Glory'. Unpubl. MS.

——. 1989. 'A Voice in the Wilderness Speaks', *Ministry Digest*, Nov.-Dec., 2.

Pangilinan, N. and M. Roa 1990. 'RP clergy braces for "invasion" by US fundamentalists', *Philippine Daily Globe*, 21 April, 18.

——. 'Protestants worry over fundamentalist drive' 1990. *Philippine Daily Globe*, 3 May, 7.

'Philippine Council of Evangelical Churches, Inc.' (pamphlet).

Pimentel, B. 1991. *Rebolusyon!: A Generation of Struggle in the Philippines*. New York: Monthly Review Press.

Pineda-Ofreneo, R. 1989. *The Philippines: Debt and Poverty*. Oxford: Oxfam.

Ramos, J. 1992. Interview with author, Bacolod, 29 May.

The Religious Right and National Security Doctrine 1991. Tugon. Manila: NCCP.

'Right-Wing Vigilantes and U.S. Involvement: Report of a U.S. Fact-Finding Mission to the Philippines, May 20-30, 1987' 1987. Manila: Philippine Alliance of Human Rights Advocates (PAHRA).

Rivera, Pastor J. 1992. Maranatha. Interview with author, Bacolod City, 29 May.

The Road To Damascus: Kairos and Conversion 1989. Skotaville, Braamfontein, July, 23.

Sabug, F.T. 1991. 'The Religious Right in the Philippines: A Preliminary Study', in *The Religious Right and The National Security State.*

Schirmer, D.B. and S.R. Shalom (eds). 1987. *The Philippines Reader: A History of Colonialism, Neocolonialism, Dictatorship, and Resistance.* Boston: South End Press.

Siewert, J. and J. Kenyon (eds) 1993. *Mission Handbook 1993-95.* Monrovia, CA: MARC.

'Something More Than A CIA Conspiracy' 1989, in the *Faith and Ideology Series.* Manila, Socio-Pastoral Institute, C 4.

Sumrall, D. 1990. 'Communicating Faith', in *Church Growth Manual 3.* Seoul: Church Growth Intentional, 173-94.

Suzara, A. 1993. 'Cultist Vigilantism in the Philippines', *Sociology of Religion* 54 (3) Fall, 303-8.

Tappeiner 1989. 'Prepare War! The Spirit's Call to Spiritual Warfare', *Ministry Digest* Nov./Dec. 303-8.

Tica, G. 1993. Interview with author, Manila, 1 June.

Tiplas (Bishop, Philippines Independent Church) 1992. Interview with author, Bacolod, 29 May.

Toville, A. (Bishop, Church of the Latter Day Saints) 1992. Interview with author, Bacolod, 31 May.

Valenzuela, Mgr. B. 1992. Interview with author, Quezon, 2 June.

——. 1990. 'Update on Fundamentalist Groups in the Philippines Today'. Prepared by the Archdiocesan Office for Ecumenical and Interfaith Affairs, April.

'Value Formation' 1987. *Ang Tala*, September, 4, 18.

Vencer, J. 1992. Interview with author, Manila, 1 June.

——. 1990. 'The Church and National Recovery', *Ministry Digest* 1(5), 7-8.

——. n.d. In 'DAWN 2000: How many more churches to go?'

Vigilantism in Negros 1988. Bacolod: Task Force Detainees of the Philippines.

Villanueva, Brother E. 1989. Excerpt from TV on address on 4 December, 'A Message to the Filipino Nation', in *Ministry Digest*, Nov./Dec., 5-6.

Wagner, C.P. 1989. 'Territorial Spirits', *Ministry Digest*, Nov./Dec., 42.

Waghelstein, Col. J.W. 1985. 'Post-Vietnam Counterinsurgency Doctrine', *Military Review*, May, 42.

Wallis, J. and W. Michaelson 1976. 'Building up the Common Life', *Sojourners*, April, 1-12.

ISLAMISM IN MULTIRELIGIOUS SOCIETIES

THE EXPERIENCE OF MALAYSIA AND INDONESIA

Sven Cederroth

In the 'Malay world', which includes Malaysia and Indonesia, Islam is the dominant religion. In Malaysia it is the faith of all the Malays who comprise somewhat more than 50 per cent of the population, whereas in Indonesia some 90 per cent of the total population are registered as Muslims. In both countries, Islam arrived late and had to compete with existing animist beliefs and a long-established Hindu-Buddhist religion. Somewhat after the arrival of Islam, Christianity was also propagated and spread by missionaries arriving together with European colonialists. Moreover, among the Malays there already existed a strong and well-established system of customary law known as *adat*. In many ways the *adat* contested and conflicted with Islamic principles.

All these things together contributed to the growth of a syncretistic Malay religion which was officially designated as Islam, but in reality was a mixture, containing many pre-Islamic beliefs and practices. Even today, especially in Java, but also in other parts of the Indonesian archipelago, the *adat* continues to support syncretistic practices among a majority of the population. It was not until the early decades of the twentieth century that more strictly orthodox versions of the Islamic faith began to gain ground among broader groups of people in the Malay world. During the last few decades, however, it seems that orthodox attitudes have gained a considerable amount of ground. The Islamist wave appears to be more pronounced in the Malay peninsula than among the dominant ethnic groups of Indonesia. But here too the Islamists have recently met with a new understanding, not only among the broad layers of the population, but also in leading government circles. In this chapter we shall take a closer look at these contemporary trends in the political and religious life of the two countries.

The development of Indonesian Islam

Between mainland Asia and Australia there is a vast archipelago of almost 12,000 small and large islands. Of these, some 300 are permanently inhabited by an ethnically, culturally and linguistically heterogeneous population. In addition there is also a demographic imbalance: of a total of 180 million people, almost two-thirds live on the comparatively small island of Java which comprises less than 8 per cent of the land area. The Javanese are not only the largest ethnic group, they are also politically and economically dominant. There is a further inequality here, though, in the fact that most of the natural resources come from the peripheral islands. In many islands this situation is seen as a continuation of earlier colonial patterns of dominance and exploitation and further strengthens centrifugal tendencies in the divided archipelago. In this context the issue of religious affiliation takes on great importance. Religion as a marker of exclusiveness and separate identification is a powerful weapon in the armoury of those advocating a separation from the centre in Java. Conversely, there is an urgent need for the power elite to control the potentially divisive religious feelings in such a way that they do not lead to further disintegration among the many ethnic groups.

Since Indonesia is a country that prescribes religion as one of its five fundamental tenets – it is the first principle in the *Pancasila* constitution – it is only logical that all inhabitants are obliged to confess one of the acknowledged religions: Islam, Christianity (Catholicism or Protestantism), Hinduism and Buddhism. The identity card carried by all citizens shows the religion of its bearer. From the official point of view a huge majority, almost 90 per cent of the population, are Muslims.[1] However, as has already been mentioned, many – probably a majority – of these statistical Muslims are in fact syncretists. It would therefore have been more logical to count them as adherents of the javanese religion (*Agami Jawi* or *Kejawen*) or some other similar form of syncretism. The problem is that *Agami Jawi* is not among the acknowledged religions. Moreover, the adherents of other religions are in many cases not spread evenly among the dominant Muslim masses; rather they are concentrated in their own areas or islands, such as Hindus on Bali and Christians on Flores, Sumba and North Sulawesi.

The shores of the East Indian archipelago have from early times been a meeting point of cultures and of world religions. As early as a few centuries BCE, Hinduism and Buddhism had both arrived. In the fertile soil of the East Indian islands these religions melted together into a kind of Hindu-Buddhist civilization, the high point of which was the Majapahit empire. During the height of its power, approximately during the thirteenth century, large parts of the archipelago were united under one ruler for the first time in history. However, after only a short period, conflicts began to tear the empire apart. At about the same time as these developments took place at the centre of the empire, Islam arrived, probably with Indian merchants, on its extreme periphery: Aceh on the northern tip of Sumatra.

From there, Islam slowly spread to the central parts of the empire by way of the coastal trading ports. From the time of its first arrival in Aceh, it took at least 200 years for the new religion to penetrate the interior of Java and Sumatra. Thus, for a long time the old Hindu-Buddhist civilization was able to withstand the advance of the new religion.[2] However, even after formal conversion many of the cultural traits of the earlier epoch continued to flourish, especially in the old Hindu-Buddhist core areas of central Java. Here, new and old elements mixed, giving birth to a new and unique Javanese religion, the *Agami Jawi*. In the coastal areas, the first points of entrance for Islam, the religion took on another and more orthodox character right from the beginning. This division between a syncretistically inclined population in the interior and a more puristic Islam in the coastal regions of Java and Sumatra still persists.

Around 1500, perhaps some 200 years after the original arrival of Islam in Aceh, the first Europeans came to the shores of the archipelago. At first, the Europeans were mainly interested in trade, above all in exotic spices. Later they tried to establish their own hegemony in the archipelago. After much fighting between the colonial powers, the Dutch finally managed to conquer almost the whole archipelago and during the coming centuries they extracted fabulous riches from their colony. There were many native uprisings against the Dutch, but finally the Aceh War during the last decades of the nineteenth century paved the way for growing national consciousness and resistance in Indonesia. The first nationalistic mass movement, *Sarekat Islam* (SI), was founded in 1912 and had an Islamic foundation. It grew rapidly and soon had a large, mainly rural following. In the early 1920s, the movement was divided into two parts as a result of severe internal conflicts.

After the division of SI, the purely Muslim part of the anti-colonial resistance was represented mainly by two movements: *Muhammadiyah* and *Nahdlatul Ulama* (NU). The former organization, which was created in the central Javanese town of Yogyakarta in 1912, is usually described as orthodox and modernistic. It aims at a reformation of Indonesian Islam and a return to the Quran and the Sunna, interpreted in a way suitable for modern times. In contrast to SI and NU, this organization has always had an urban base and has mainly attracted comparatively affluent middle-class people, especially merchants. NU, which came into being about ten years after *Muhammadiyah*, is characterized as orthodox and traditionalistic. The organization has its main basis of support among conservative peasants in the Javanese villages.[3] The aim of NU is to defend the Islamic tradition as it has developed in Java. In pursuing this goal, NU has openly condemned *Muhammadiyah*, criticizing its lack of understanding for specifically Javanese traditions and values. Both organizations still exist and are of great importance in the contemporary political struggle.

The independence period: modernists and traditionalists

The terms 'modernist' and 'traditionalist' used in the above paragraph to label *Muhammadiyah* and NU refer to two orthodox *aliran*,[4] both of which oppose the syncretist *Agami Jawi* Islam. Modernist inspiration came from some Middle Eastern refórmers of Islam who sought to remove later additions and corrupt practices from the religious doctrines. The solutions to all of mankind's problems are to be found in the Quran. A return to the sources (that is, the Quran) and the interpretations (the Sunna) is therefore advocated. This will equip Islam better to meet the challenges of the modern world. However, for the modernists, the interpretations of the sacred texts are not fixed and absolute. To cope with new challenges it is necessary to refer back to the source, but the texts shall, and must, be interpreted in the light of modern conditions.

The traditionalists seem to agree with the modernists about the importance of doctrine. Where they differ is whether it is necessary to go back to the original doctrinal source, the Quran, or whether the correct doctrines are to be found in the traditions as they have developed over the centuries. Attitudes towards the syncretists are another source of difference which has given rise to much conflict between modernists and traditionalists. For the modernists it is essential to refute all 'corrupt' syncretist practices, whereas the traditionalists do not regard this as a priority. Indeed the traditionalists often participate in syncretist ceremonies, such as the *slametan*, the ritual communal meal. However, both groups of orthodox Muslims hold the view that doctrine is more important than ritual.

In the religious schools of the traditionalists, the teachers emphasize the scholastic memorizing of the religious texts and commentaries on them. In opposition to these uncritical, old-fashioned methods, the modernists argue the need for a revaluation of education. Thereby they intend to equip students with attitudes and knowledge that will enable them to confront the challenges of today's world. In line with their views on education, the modernists hold that man can determine his own fate. With hard and dedicated work, a better position in life can be achieved. Contrary to this view, the traditionalists hold the opinion that man's fate is entirely predetermined by Allah and that nothing can be done to change this.[5] Finally, the modernists recognize the importance of secular institutions, whereas for the traditionalists all aspects of life have religious significance.

Islamism in independent Indonesia

After the division and subsequent decline of *Sarekat Islam*, the leadership of the anti-colonial independence movement was assumed by secular organizations, such as the Nationalist Party (PNI) under the leadership of Sukarno. Following the declaration of independence in August 1945, there were discussions between all the *aliran* about the constitution of the new state. In the course of these negotiations, the orthodox Muslims fought hard to achieve the declaration of Indonesia as an Islamic state,[6] meaning that the *syari'at*, the Islamic law (*Sharia*), would become the basis of jurisprudence. However, Sukarno and his allies realized that such a declaration would split the nation even before it had time to constitute itself. Not only would Christians and Hindus try to withdraw, but there was also bound to be strong protests from the majority of syncretist Muslims. Thus, *Pancasila*, the five principles, was brought forward as a compromise acceptable to all the *aliran*. In *Pancasila*, the first principle declares belief in God the Almighty,[7] but without any further specification. Thereby, Indonesia was constituted as a state governed by religion in a very general sense, and which gave equal rights to all the acknowledged religions.

Faced with this setback, the orthodox Muslims tried to reorganize themselves. For the first time since the split of *Sarekat Islam*, they managed to put their differences aside and in November 1945 they were united in one party – the *Masyumi*. Only three years later, the *Partai Sarekat Islam Indonesia* (PSII), which was the successor of the original *Sarekat Islam*, left the party. After the withdrawal of PSII, there were two main groups in the *Masyumi*: the above-mentioned *Muhammadiyah* and NU. There was also a smaller group of outspoken supporters of an Islamic state. A few years later, NU also left, after repeated schisms with the other factions about which *aliran* was to represent the party in the cabinets, and formed a separate party.

Thus began the decline of *Masyumi* which culminated in its dissolution in August 1960. In the 1955 general elections, however, *Masyumi* came second with almost eight million votes as against seven millions for NU.[8] Together, the two major Muslim parties received slightly more votes than the two large secular parties, the Nationalists and the Communists. However, because of the division they had virtually no power to influence the President or his cabinet. Two years after the elections, a regional rebellion centred in Sumatra and Sulawesi broke out. A large part of *Masyumi's* sympathizers lived in the outer islands and several of its leaders seeing the uprising as an Islamic Holy War against the godless Javanese communists, joined the rebellion. When the uprising was finally defeated, Sukarno decided to ban the *Masyumi* because of the party's involvement. Shortly before this decision, the *Muhammadiyah* had withdrawn its support for *Masyumi* and so avoided being banned as well. As a whole, the orthodox Islamic forces were by now severely weakened and marginal in Indonesian politics.

The 1960s turned out to be a decade of revolutionary upheavals in Indonesian politics, the climax of course being the coup on 1 October 1965. The Communist Party was held responsible for the murder of six army generals and a gruesome massacre of party sympathizers followed. After the fall of Sukarno and the establishment of the New Order regime, many Islamists argued for a revival of the banned *Masyumi* party. However, such a move was opposed not only by the army, but also by Suharto, the new President. Instead, the Islamists were allowed to establish a new party, the *Partai Muslimin Indonesia* (*Parmusi*), which came into being in 1968. NU never joined the new party, and right from the beginning it was plagued by internal conflicts between potential leaders from the various *aliran*. In the 1971 elections, *Parmusi* made a very poor show managing less than three million votes as against ten million for NU and thirty-four million for *Golkar*, the government party.[9]

After the 1971 elections, the New Order government forced the political parties to amalgamate so that only two remained. One of these, the *Partai Persatuan Pembangunan* (PPP), United Development Party, is a fusion of the earlier Muslim parties, its major components being *Parmusi* and NU. It seems obvious that the main intention behind this and other actions by the Suharto government was to stifle the political ambitions of the Islamists and restrict their activities to the social and religious sphere. That this was indeed the intention became even clearer when, in 1985, the government ordered all social and political organizations to adhere to *Pancasila* as their sole ideological foundation. As a result of this decree, the PPP was even forced to exchange its party symbol, the *kaba*, for a star. It was argued that the earlier symbol could be interpreted as exhibiting Islamic political ambitions.

All these moves by the army and the political elite constitute in reality nothing more than the continuation of a long struggle between Javanism and Islamism. In the army as well as among the civil political elite there are many syncretistic Javanese aristocrats (*priyai*). These people are extremely suspicious about the orthodox Muslims and their struggle for an Islamic state. As a result of such opposition, the PPP has never been able to develop into a strong enough political force to challenge the *Golkar* hegemony. The party has never received more than some 27-29 per cent of the total number of votes in any election. In the 1987 election its hold on the voters dwindled to 16 per cent. The main reasons for the poor show in 1987 can be attributed to two main factors: firstly, the change of party symbol was interpreted by many Islamists as a desertion of its original Islamic cause; and secondly, and perhaps the most important, the NU decided in 1984, after they had lost a power struggle within the PPP, to leave the party and become a purely socio-religious movement.

In conclusion it can be said that since independence the Islamists have become increasingly marginalized as a political force. Having participated actively in the struggle for independence, the orthodox Muslims initially looked strong. The independence period, however, has been full of disappointments, and to date none of the Islamists' ambitions have been realized. This is partly due to internal conflicts between modernists and traditionalists which have caused repeated rifts among the Islamists. Part of the explanation can also be found in the distrust between the orthodox and other Indonesian *aliran*. The latter believe that, given a chance, the Islamists would go ahead and create an Islamic state, which would threaten the very foundation of the present state. It is therefore better to deny the Islamists any political role at all and restrict their activities to the socio-religious sphere.

However, since the orthodox Muslims agreed to accept *Pancasila* as their sole organizing principle (*azas tunggal*), relations with the government have taken a definite turn for the better. Decisions that are favourable to the Islamists have been taken and the flow of material assistance has increased. This has been viewed by observers as nothing more than the old policy of attempting to hold the balance of power. This is a game at which President Sukarno was an undisputed master and which is now being played again by President Suharto. Faced by diminishing support from the military he now turns to the Islamists, thus playing the interests of one *aliran* off against another.

The development of Malayan Islam

The Malaysian federation, which came into existence in 1963, consists of thirteen states and is divided into two separate parts:[10] the Malay peninsula (West Malaysia), the southernmost part of mainland Southeast Asia, and Sabah and Sarawak (East Malaysia) in the northwest of the island of Borneo. Compared with Indonesia, it is a small country with some seventeen million people, less than a tenth of its large southern neighbour. Today it is the western half of the country which is dominant, economically as well as politically, and when talking about Malaya (as opposed to Malaysia, the nation) it is the peninsula which is referred to. Not all Malaysian citizens are Malays. To be a Malay it is not only sufficient to be born in the country, but according to the constitution one must also habitually speak the Malay language, be a Muslim and conform to Malay customs. Therefore, when a Chinese converts to Islam it is said that he becomes a Malay (*masuk Melayu*).[11]

Malaya was first settled some 2,000 years BCE, when nomadic Proto-Malays wandered into the peninsula. Later came the Deutero-Malays, the ancestors of the present-day Malays, who were sedentary, practising fishing and agriculture. Over the centuries, many conquerors and traders came to Malaya, mainly from India but also from the powerful Hindu-

Buddhist empires of the archipelago. Thus, Hindu culture and religion greatly influenced the Malays and blended with the original animist worldview. A number of small native Hindu-influenced states arose in Malaya, but before the rise of Melaka in the early fifteenth century none was very important. At that time, Aceh in nearby Sumatra had already converted to Islam and, in 1445, Melaka also became a Muslim sultanate.

During the course of the next fifty years, Melaka grew to be an important regional power and was instrumental in the further spread of Islam, not only in the peninsula itself but to parts of the archipelago as well. The existing Hindu-animist syncretism easily embraced the Sufi-laden version of Islam which was brought to Melaka by way of India. As in Indonesia, daily life was regulated by a set of detailed customary rules, the *adat*. Even today these customs, which are deeply rooted in Malay society, display many pre-Islamic traits and are therefore often in conflict with more purely Islamic-inspired rules. For many centuries, and to some extent today, the *adat* has been of greater importance to Malays, especially to the majority in the rural areas, than the Islamic behaviour code. This has led to a situation where Malayan Islam has been dominated until recently by syncretistically inspired beliefs and practices.

After the Portuguese conquered Melaka in 1511, the city continued to be of great importance, particularly as a means of controlling the trade routes with the archipelago. It was not until the Dutch conquered the city in 1641 and destroyed the Melaka fortress that its power began to wane. In the beginning of the nineteenth century, the British managed to gain control of what they called the Straits Settlements: that is, Penang, Melaka and Singapore. After an agreement with the Malay sultans a few decades later, the British established indirect rule through a residential system over the rest of Malaya, thereby relegating the Malay sultans to a secondary position.

The agreement with the sultans stipulated that the British were not to interfere with Malay customs and religion. Despite this, British policy turned out to have several far-reaching consequences for the future of Malaya, notably with regard to education, population composition and jurisprudence. The British provided only a tiny minority of Malays, mainly the sons of the aristocracy, with any kind of higher secular education. The rest of the population was given no education at all, or at best received some religious instruction from local *ulama* (Islamic religious scholars). The British moreover introduced their own jurisprudential system in Malaya, banishing the *adat* and the Islamic law to secondary roles. Decisions by Islamic courts could be overturned by the British civil courts.

It was with regard to ethnic composition that British policy came to have its most revolutionary consequences, however. Around the middle of the nineteenth century, large tin ore deposits were found in Malaya. Because the population was small and most people were traditional agriculturalists, the British began to import large groups of Chinese coolies to work in the rapidly expanding mining industry. Over the next fifty years, the demand for rubber grew rapidly around the world. Conditions in Malaya were ideal for the growing of rubber, but neither the indigenous Malays nor the Chinese were willing to labour in the isolated plantations. Therefore, the British had to find another source of labour which came in the form of indentured Indian labourers. The Chinese and Indians kept to themselves in separate communities and did not integrate into the Malay community. Thus, within the comparatively short period of half a century, the ethnic composition of Malaya changed completely. A 1921 census showed that the Malays had become a minority in their own country.[12]

As a result of the immigration of other ethnic groups, many Malays began to become more aware of their own identity as a group with joint interests. Confrontation with other groups also gave rise to insights into the backward position – educationally, economically and politically – of their own group. During the last decades of the nineteenth century many Malays went to the Arab world – to Mecca, Medina and Cairo – for the pilgrimage or to study, and were influenced by reformist Muslim scholars such as Jamaluddin al-Afghani and Muhammad Abduh,[13] who also inspired the Indonesian modernists. Their ideas were brought back to Malaya where they laid the foundations for a modernist reform movement known as *Kaum Muda*, the Young Group.

As in the Indonesian *Muhammadiyah* movement, the Malayan reformers argued for the necessity of adapting Islam to the demands of the modern world by returning to the sources. A first requirement was to educate Malays about their own religion and its demands so that they would be able to practice it in a correct way and thus move away from the supposedly corrupt *adat*[14] practices. This reformist creed was propagated and spread through a number of newspapers and journals, such as the influential *Al-Imam*.[15] The modernist reform movement was to a large extent an urban phenomenon, mainly attracting middle-class intellectuals. Reform ideas were also discussed in the villages, but due to the influence of conservative *ulama* in these rural areas, traditionalist opinions prevailed, often in open opposition to the ideas propagated by the Young Group. As a result of this conflict, the Malayan traditionalists came to be referred to as *Kaum Tua*, the Old Group.

The controversy between the two Malayan Islamic *aliran* was most pronounced during the period between the World Wars. In contrast to events in Indonesia, the Malayan Islamic reformers never succeeded in mobilizing massive popular support for their political programme.

Therefore, the growing nationalistic movement was taken over by other, more conservative social forces, mainly from the circles of the Old Group. Instead of propagating the cause of a reformed Islam as a basis for the nationalist movement, the latter emphasized the ethnic factor. Many of the leaders of the Young Group were foreign Muslims, mainly Indians, Indonesians or Arabs, a fact which was now heavily criticized by conservatives of the Old Group. To prevent the foreigners from taking power and appropriating material resources in 'the land of the Malays', a category of pure Malays (*Melayu Jati*) was created. Only those so categorized were allowed to hold leading positions and they were also given other privileges.

Thus, instead of incorporating universalistic and humanistic Islamic principles, the anti-colonial fight was now being fought in terms of Malay rights and privileges as opposed to those of the other ethnic groups. When new ethnic Malay leaders took the initiative in the nationalist struggle, they were supported by conservative *Kaum Tua* groups as well as by the ruling feudal elite, the sultans. The power and privileges of the latter had been heavily attacked by *Kaum Muda* reformers and the sultans now willingly supported the nationalist Malay movement. In 1946 the nationalists, under the slogan of *Hidup Melayu!* (Long Live the Malays!) joined forces in the United Malays National Organization (UMNO). The primary aim of this organization can be summarized as the furtherance of the ethnic interests of the Malays: that is, to assist in the advancement of their economic, social and political position.

The independence period: nationalism and Islamist reawakening

Because of the developments discussed above, when the constitution of independent Malaysia was drawn up, organized Malay nationalist forces were eager to gain political power. They intended to use such power as a means of promoting their economic standing vis-à-vis the other ethnic groups, especially the Chinese. To be able to achieve this, it was important that the new constitution reflected the fact that Malaysia was primarily a Malay state. This aim was achieved, among other things, by preserving the Malay sultanates and by adopting Malay as the national language and Islam as the state religion. The one thing which unites all Malays and at the same time distinguishes them from other Malaysians is religion. Thus unlike Indonesia, where great care was taken to avoid identifying the state with any religion, this was exactly what was aimed at in Malaysia. At the same time it was important not to raise fears among the Chinese and Indians. Therefore, it was explicitly made clear that although Islam was the state religion, its status was mainly symbolic

– except for laws regulating marriage and divorce between Muslims, Islamic law would not be practised. Moreover, the rights of the other religions were guaranteed in the constitution. It also gave much power to the sultans who stand as the protectors of Islam and are above the law, so that whatever they do they cannot be prosecuted.[16]

The staunchly nationalist policy adopted by UMNO was opposed not only by modernist Islamic reformers, but also by many traditionalist *ulama* who rejected the largely ceremonial role of Islam. Therefore, a few years after the foundation of UMNO, some Islamic traditionalists decided to leave UMNO and form their own party to promote Islamic values more effectively. Thus the Pan Malayan Islamic Party (*Persatuan Islam Se-Malaysia*, PAS) came into being in 1951. Right from the beginning, this party opposed the symbolic role of Islam. PAS has demanded that the fact that Islam is the state religion should also be reflected in socio-economic institutions and in legislation. It has consistently claimed that if it came to power it would guarantee that Islamic administrative principles were introduced.[17] The party has always had an uncompromising anti-Chinese stand and has its main basis of support in the Malay-dominated rural areas of northern Malaya.

Thus, when independence was gained on 31 August 1957, and UMNO became the dominant socio-political force, Islam was not given a prominent role. Instead, the focus was on policies designed to uplift the Malays economically. In line with the Malay nationalist policy followed by UMNO, a lot of special privileges were granted to the *Bumiputra*, the sons of the soil, here implying the Malays. Due to such discriminative policies, communal tensions rose during the course of the 1960s. The strains came to a head at the 1969 elections which were held in an atmosphere of bitter recrimination on all sides. Immediately after the elections, on 13 May 1969, violent race riots erupted. After these riots, during which several hundred people, mainly non-Malays, were killed, the government concluded that more drastic measures were necessary to secure economic equality between the Malays and the other ethnic groups. Thus, the New Economic Policy (NEP) was introduced in July 1969. This plan aimed at restructuring the economy in such a way that the *Bumiputra* share reached at least 30 per cent by 1990.[18] Increasing Malay enrolment in education was a main strategy to reach this aim, and quotas were introduced in this and in many other fields.

After the riots, a government decree banned political activities and the public discussion of all issues that were considered sensitive. This put a stop, for instance, to student activism in the university campuses. However, the ban did not include Islam. As a result of the NEP policy, there was a rapidly increasing influx of rural Malays into the universities. The Malay intellectual elite, university professors and students, had frequent contacts with Islamic scholars in other Muslim countries. Thereby, the reform ideas of people such as Hassan al-Banna, leader of the Islamic brotherhood in Algeria and Abul Ala Mawdudi, leader of the *Jamaat-i-Islami* of Pakistan were discussed and had a considerable influence on Malays in the national universities, such as the University of Malaya (UM) and Universiti Kebangsaan Malaysia (UKM).[19]

Together these factors led to an upswing for Muslim organizations in the university campuses, especially the *Angkatan Belia Islam Malaysia* (ABIM), the Muslim Youth Movement, which coincided with a more general reawakening of interest in Islam in the Malay community. This reawakening has largely been an urban phenomenon and has been attributed to feelings of rootlessness among the masses of migrants coming from stable, religiously orthodox environments in the rural areas.[20] In this context, the assertion of traditional Islamic values became a way of securing stability in a generally chaotic world. While ABIM was the intellectualist response to the new challenges, other similar organizations also arose in the larger Malay community.

The Islamist response

In Malaysia, this Islamic reawakening of the 1970s and 1980s is referred to as the *dakwah* (*dawa*, 'mission') phenomenon. By and large, the movement has been an urban phenomenon. In the rural areas where the changes have not been so profound and pervasive, influential, traditionally-oriented *ulama* have continued to give their support to PAS. When discussing the *dakwah* movement, it is important to stress from the outset that this is not a homogeneous phenomenon, but consists rather of many organizations, all with their own inclinations, programme and strategies. On the one hand *dakwah* activities can be directed primarily towards the Muslim community. Muslims are urged to take their religion more seriously and to begin practising religious obligations within their daily routine. Such is the strategy, for instance, of the *Jamaat Tabligh*, an organization of Indian origin that works with a network of voluntary missionaries. These travel long distances at their own cost and visit people in their homes where they try to convince them of the necessity to devote themselves to the cause of Islam. This method of propagation is said to follow the way Islam was originally spread during the time of the prophet Muhammad. The *Jamaat Tabligh* is a very low-profile organization which operates without any formal leadership hierarchy. The members do not publish any literature and it seems that individual members often have differing views. This makes it difficult to determine what the official ideology of the movement actually is.

There are also *dakwah* organizations, such as *Pertubuhan Kebajikan Islam Malaysia* (PERKIM), the Welfare and Missionary Organization, that devote a major part of their resources to the conversion of non-

Muslims. The organization was originally founded in 1960 by the then Malaysian prime minister Tunku Abdul Rahman. PERKIM activities are specifically directed towards the Chinese community in peninsular Malaysia and towards the native communities in the East Malaysian states of Sabah and Sarawak. To work with the Chinese, the organization employs a team of missionaries of Chinese origin. In 1980 PERKIM estimated that it had gained a total of 160,000 converts, more than half of whom came from Sabah.[21] Drawing on his personal connections, the founder of PERKIM has managed to receive much monetary support from Arab states, especially Libya. In contrast to many other *dakwah* organizations, PERKIM has excellent connections with the government, the present prime minister Dr Mahathir being its patron.

Most of the Malaysian *dakwah* movements fall somewhere between the two already mentioned, in that they address themselves both to other Muslims and to non-Muslims whom they try to convert. Two of the most influential and well-known of these movements are the already-mentioned ABIM and *Darul Arqam*. The latter will be discussed extensively in the following case study. Because of its strong influence in Malaysian politics I shall also briefly describe the ABIM. As we have seen, ABIM originated on the university campuses and its first leader, Anwar Ibrahim, came from the student ranks. Nowadays there are ABIM groups all around Malaysia, but most of its followers still hail from the universities and the urban middle class. In 1980, ABIM estimated its members to number around 35,000.[22] To spread its message that Islam represents a superior alternative to Western materialism, the organization publishes journals and newspapers and runs a network of schools in which an alternative, higher education is provided. The ABIM leader, the charismatic Anwar Ibrahim, is a gifted orator who could greatly influence and inspire people through his speeches. It did not take long, therefore, for him to become very widely known among Malaysian Malays. In 1981 ABIM condemned the government for being un-Islamic and claimed that its nationalist policy was unable to solve the ethnic conflicts facing the country.[23] A true Islamic policy as followed in an Islamic state implies justice for all people. According to ABIM, this is the only solution for multi-ethnic Malaysia. In one of his speeches, Anwar claimed that racism is foreign to Islam and that its existence in Malaysia was due to Western influences. This was but one of many areas in which ABIM clashed with the government. The latter, being fearful of ABIM's considerable influence, has on several occasions tried to limit it by banning its newspapers and other such actions.

Given these confrontations, it came as a great surprise to most people when Anwar was 'co-opted' into the government by prime minister Mahatir in 1982. Anwar, who is now minister of finance,[24] has justified his action by saying that he believed that he could do more for the

Islamic cause from inside the government than he could by criticizing it from the outside. His decision caused severe strain within the ABIM organization and widened the gap between PAS and UMNO sympathizers.

Islamist movements: two case studies

In the following pages, the variety of Islamist movements in the Malay world will be exemplified. For this purpose, two movements of quite different character, *Muhammadiyah* of Indonesia and *Darul Arqam* of Malaysia have been chosen. The basis for classifying them as Islamist is that they both argue the necessity for a return to the original fundamentals of the religion in order to save the Muslims. However, there are many obvious differences between them: one is young and struggling and considered deviant by many establishment critics; the other is old and respected and has gained a considerable influence. The members of one withdraw from the world into their own communes, while those of the other carry on an incessant daily struggle in the midst of an uncommitted public. The members of one adhere to the teachings of a Sufi school, while the other condemns all such activities. One wants to return to fundamentals in order to arm its members with tools with which they can cope with the daily challenges of the modern world. The other attempts to change the world through the power of its example: that is, it advocates a return to the spirit of the original Islamic community in the midst of a secular society.

– Darul Arqam of Malaysia

Arqam bin Abi Arqam was a friend and companion of the prophet Muhammad whose house in Mecca became a hide-out when the Islamic revolution was planned. It is probably no coincidence that the movement, which was founded by Ustaz Ashaari Muhammad in 1968, was given the name *Darul Arqam*, the house of Arqam. It automatically brings to mind that time of heroic struggle, when the Muslims were surrounded by a hostile society which they had to convert. *Darul Arqam* was initially conceived as a religious study group. Only a few years later, Ustaz Ashaari, together with a few devoted pupils, bought a piece of land and there founded *Darul Arqam*'s first Islamic commune. Thus began a struggle to revive classical Islamic values and to recreate an ideal Islamic life style, like that of the prophet Muhammad when the first Islamic community was established. The example provided by this revived ideal society would guarantee its growth in the midst of a secular society dominated by materialistic values.

Throughout its existence, the movement has been dominated by its charismatic founder, who is addressed by the members as Sheikul Arqam. Born into a religious family in 1938, he was appointed a government religious teacher in 1956 when he was only eighteen years old. He served as such until 1972 when he left to devote himself fully to the organization he had set up a few years earlier. Reviewing the failures of other Muslim societies, Ustaz Ashaari drew the conclusion that these had been caused by their failure to apply the true Islam and could be remedied only by a revival of the original Islamic values. To achieve this, inspiration had to be sought in the Quran and in the movement led by the prophet Muhammad himself. Islamic law had to replace all Western-inspired civil codes and govern all aspects of social life. This necessary reorientation of societal norms and behaviour codes could be realized only through the creation of an actively struggling organization of dedicated Muslims. These people could set an example and persuade others to join in the struggle for a just and exemplary Islamic society.

The organizational structure of the movement is hierarchical and authoritarian. At the top there is the revered 'Sheikul Arqam', Ustaz Ashaari himself, whose advice and orders are automatically followed throughout the organization. Immediately below him there is a ministerial structure, consisting of four Deputy Sheikhs (shaykhs), four Assistant Deputy Sheikhs and three Assistant Sheikhs, all of whom have been personally appointed by the Sheikul Arqam. The organization is designed to mirror a national government structure, thus forming an Islamic shadow state. *Darul Arqam* divides peninsular Malaysia into thirty-five 'states' and East Malaysia into another nine. Each 'state' consists of a number of districts. Ideally, there should be a centre and a number of autonomous villages[25] in each district. Each *Darul Arqam* 'state' is headed by a local government leader and his assistants and there are also twelve departments, each headed by a minister, dealing with education, information, economics and trade, welfare services, Islamic propagation, agriculture, the treasury, international relations, development, security and health care.

Estimates concerning the extent of *Darul Arqam* membership vary considerably. According to an interview with Ustaz Ashaari in 1987, it was somewhere in the region of 5-6,000. Outsiders have given considerably higher figures. Nagata, for instance,[26] admits great uncertainty, but estimates the membership at approximately 10,000 in the late 1970s. These differences are probably due to the fact that *Darul Arqam* distinguishes between members and sympathizers. A person who listens to the preaching of the *dakwah* programme and eventually goes on to participate in the general Islamic circle is counted as a sympathizer.

Among these, only a few are really committed to the struggle of the movement and are thus eligible to become full members.

According to *Darul Arqam*, Muslims must develop not only their inner consciousness but also their outward behaviour. Taken together, these two roads to perfection provide the basis for development, and thus for the establishment of a true Islamic state. To be able to increase knowledge about the Islamic faith, a systematic discipline is needed. As a means to the achievement of inward purification, the *Darul Arqam* movement adheres to the doctrines of a Sufi order, the *Aurad Muham-madiah*.[27] The development of outward affairs is achieved by organizing the surrounding society according to Islamic precepts. Islam, as perceived by *Darul Arqam*, includes all-embracing rules for behaviour: these range from such personal matters as styles of dress and eating habits to the way in which the national government should function.

Thus, for *Darul Arqam* the inner and outer roads must develop hand in hand and at an even pace; the one prescribes the other. Therefore, in the long run it was unsatisfactory for the organization to continue merely as a study group. From the start, Ustaz Ashaari aimed to convert his ideas into practice. Given the structure of the Malaysian state, Islamic communities could not expect to be accommodated into it. The only alternative was to establish independent Islamic villages where Islamic law could be fully observed. The first such village was created in 1973 and by 1990 the organization ran a total of thirty-two villages and was represented in all thirteen states of the Malaysian federation. Moreover, it now has branches in many other countries, including Australia, France, Britain and the United States.

The strategy followed by *Darul Arqam* aims at gradually creating Islamic villages all over Malaysia to serve as models for the future Islamic state. The movement thereby hopes to be able to convince a growing number of people about the superiority of a religiously based life-style. The number of villages will slowly grow until finally they can form a nationwide Islamic community. It can be observed that almost all the *Darul Arqam* villages are located in relatively remote rural areas. This is partly due to the fact that land is cheaper in such locations. However, the choice of such sites is also ideologically motivated in that it dissociates the communities from negative urban influences. There is a paradox here in that the Malaysian *dakwah* movement has generally been considered to be an urban phenomenon and *Darul Arqam* also began as such. Thus, many former town-dwellers move into these remote villages, while comparatively few of the surrounding rural people are attracted to the movement.

After *Darul Arqam* has acquired a piece of land, whether as a result of donations by a few wealthy members or by the collective efforts of all the prospective settlers, the land must be developed. This is done entirely by the members themselves who contribute part, or sometimes all, of their income to a joint development pool that is administered by the movement. Sometimes members continue working outside the village in which case the income is handed over to the village administration. The ideal that the organization strives for is to find employment for the members inside the village structure. When this can be realized, the member is assigned to one of the twelve departments and provided with a task for which he is responsible. No wage is paid, but in exchange the community agrees to meet the basic housing and subsistence needs of its member families. The lifestyle is simple and the provisions handed over are calculated on the basis of need rather than on the position held. This means, for instance, that a large family of unqualified workers will receive more provisions than a small family of highly qualified teachers.

In the *Darul Arqam* villages there are also a varying number of public facilities. All the villages have public prayer places, baths and toilets and in most of them there are also one or more schools and shops. In the schools, not only members' children but also those of outsiders are educated. By 1988, the movement was running forty-one primary and twenty-two secondary schools with a total of around 7,000 pupils. In the shops, food and other daily necessities are sold to members as well as to outsiders. Most of the villages have a central office which runs village affairs and the schools. In one of the villages there is also an extensive publication unit that has produced more than seventy books and continues to issue a number of periodicals.

An important aspect of the movement's activities is concerned with its attempts to establish a usury-free Islamic economic system. The movement is thus endeavouring to demonstrate the practical viability of such a system in the midst of the surrounding secular, national economic system. The aim is to increase independence from the Malaysian state and to produce food which is appropriate (*halal*) for Muslim consumers. In the fields belonging to the communes, members produce a wide range of agricultural products, cereals as well as vegetables and fruits. The production is not solely for the members' own consumption; any surplus is sold to the general public. The movement also encourages economic schemes other than agriculture, such as cottage industries, animal rearing, tailoring and motor workshops, among its members.

Many features of the *Darul Arqam* ideology are considered alien and backward by the non-committed public, such as the style of dress – Arabic garb for the men and veil (*purdah*) for the women – and the communal eating habits. Such practices have given the movement a negative image in many circles. Since the members are expected to devote themselves fully to the movement, they often have to give up secular studies or leave their jobs. In many cases young people have decided to join the movement against the outspoken will of their parents. This has resulted in well-publicized family conflicts that have contributed to the popular image of *Darul Arqam* as a group of religious fanatics, practising a deviationist version of Islam. Furthermore, the communes have been criticized for their isolationist tendencies. A visitor to one of the villages describes how the entrance is patrolled and how visitors are viewed with great suspicion. The village is said to exhibit a 'siege mentality' towards a hostile surrounding world.[28] Another critic has claimed that the movement places an exaggerated emphasis on the character of the individual in achieving social change.

> [It has an] uncritical attachment to ideas, values and life-styles of the past often sanctioned by scriptures other than the Qur'an. Arqam is undoubtedly more traditional for it regards the restoration of the Meccan and Medinan social atmosphere associated with the prophet Muhammad as a crucial precondition for the establishment of an Islamic society in today's world... Obviously, Arqam has misunderstood what the eternal truth embodied in the Qur'an and to a lesser extent in the life of the Prophet, really means. The eternal truth cannot be bound by the time period, place-setting, the mode of dressing and food consumption. It must mean values and principles, ideas and world-views hich transcend time and place because they are intrinsically universal and eternal[29]

Among mainstream Malay Muslims, there has been extensive criticism of *Darul Arqam*. For instance, there have been repeated attacks in *Utusan Malaysia*, the largest daily Malay newspaper which is closely allied to the ruling UMNO party. The movement is accused of fanaticism and deviant Sufi practices.[30] In its editorials, *Utusan Malaysia* has regularly demanded the banning of *Darul Arqam*. Furthermore, *Darul Arqam* has not been registered, as is required of all organizations in Malaysia. On these grounds the Islamic Affairs Division of the Prime Minister's Department has accused the movement of being illegal and demanded that it should be banned. So far, the organization itself has not been banned, but some of its publications have. The main reason for all this criticism from the official Malay establishment lies in the fact that the teachings and life-style of *Darul Arqam* represent a direct challenge to the dominant liberal capitalist system. There are also ideological controversies involved. Many of the leading Islamic establishment scholars adhere to the reformist *Wahhabi* school which rejects all Sufi practices,[31] including those adopted by *Darul Arqam*.

In late August 1994, the movement was finally banned. Ustaz Ashaare, who had been living in Thailand, was extradited and arrested. At first existing communes were allowed to continue, but the government soon began trying to dissolve them.

– Muhammadiyah of Indonesia

The *Muhammadiyah* organization was created by Haji Ahmed Dahlan in 1911 in the central Javanese town of Yogyakarta. Its proclaimed aim was to enhance the religious awareness of its members. A proper education was seen as the main way of promoting this aim and from the beginning, *Muhammadiyah* has consistently stressed the importance of education. The organization can be characterized as both modernist and orthodox, whereas its main Javanese rival, the *Nahdlatul Ulama* (NU), is generally described as traditionalist and orthodox. *Muhammadiyah* is modernist in the sense that it aims to restore the vitality of the Islamic religion by returning to the original beliefs and practices as laid down in the Quran and the *Sunnah* and to use these as a tool that enables them to handle the challenges of the contemporary world in a better way. It is orthodox in the sense that it puts much stress on proper behaviour and the proper performance of ritual obligations. Its first sympathizers came from the rising urban middle class (*santri*), especially the merchants. Throughout its existence, the *Muhammadiyah* has remained essentially middle-class and urban as opposed to the mainly rural-based *Nahdlatul Ulama*. In 1970, the movement claimed to have membership of about six million.[32]

From its inception, *Muhammadiyah* saw the reinvigoration of Islamic education as one of its major tasks. Such education was already practised in traditionalist *pondok* schools, but was limited to the memorizing of relevant religious texts. The early emphasis on the importance of education can be seen as a reaction to the prevailing *pondok* system with its poor and narrowly religious education. The basis for *Muhammadiyah's* insistence on education lies in the belief that if people learn about the correct practices, they will alter their behaviour accordingly. From the beginning, the *Muhammadiyah* schools were of two types: general schools which taught not only religion but also other subjects, and supplementary schools in which only religion was taught. The aim of the latter was to complement the education given in the Dutch-operated schools which provided no religious instruction at all.

In the *Muhammadiyah* schools, the pupils are nowadays first of all taught Arabic, the language of the Quran. Knowledge of Arabic is necessary to be able to read the holy book, for even though it is now translated into Indonesian, *Muhammadiyah* claims that it has to be studied in the original language. This is necessary to prevent any divine intentions revealed in the holy book from being accidentally distorted in the process of translation. Besides learning Arabic, the students are also introduced to the content of the Quran. They are taught the basic religious obligations as well as the history of the Islamic religion. In the history courses, the times of the prophet Muhammad and his struggle are praised and held forth as an example, the social and moral content of which has to be revived in today's social life. In the basic schools, the students are merely acquainted with the content of the holy book; more thorough studies are not undertaken. This is left to those continuing their studies at higher levels where the students are taught how to interpret the Quran and the Sunna. Throughout its existence, the education system has remained the most important means for *Muhammadiyah* to influence the masses of Indonesian Muslims and foster individual devotion to the religion. *Muhammadiyah* lays great stress on the individual's active participation in religious activities. It constantly attempts to increase the piety of its members and also encourages them to influence others. Besides its noteworthy contributions to education, the *Muhammadiyah* movement operates many hundreds of health clinics and pharmacies all over the country. The movement also publishes newspapers, journals and books as a means of spreading its message.

After it came into existence in 1911, the *Muhammadiyah* movement grew slowly at first, but some twenty years later it had managed to establish more than 100 branches. The various tasks of the movement were subdivided among a number of councils, each responsible for its own area, dealing with such things as politics, economics, women's affairs, education, mission and social welfare. Because of the rapid social and technological changes, there was for some time considerable confusion about how to interpret the classical texts in a consistent and correct manner. Many *Muhammadiyah* members therefore felt the need for some guidelines and in 1927 it was decided to create a council, *Majlis Tarjih*, consisting of leading *Muhammadiyah* scholars. This council has to formulate guidelines and give recommendations about all kinds of problems regarding belief and behaviour. In order not to create a new, and definite code of jurisprudence, it is explicitly stated, however, that these decisions are not final; rather they have to be reviewed, and if necessary reconsidered, when circumstances change.

In its publications[33] and through other means, *Muhammadiyah* has repeatedly condemned what it sees as corrupt beliefs and practices among other Muslims and sought to correct these. According to *Muhammadiyah*, there are two major ways in which the correct practice of Islamic dogma can be corrupted: namely, innovation (*bida*) and superstition. The first deviation has been attributed to the traditionalist orthodox Muslims, represented mainly by the NU organization, whereas allegations of the second deviation are directed chiefly against the *abangan*, the Javanese syncretists.

When defining the concept of *bida*, *Muhammadiyah* refers to a principle of behaviour not directly sanctioned by the Quran. According to the traditionalists, such codes of jurisprudence are, nevertheless, acceptable provided that they can be deduced from the Quran. Traditionalists regard these as part of the Islamic heritage, as it has developed over the generations. Against this standpoint, the *Muhammadiyah* scholars argue that each generation of Muslims must interpret the writings of the Quran themselves and judge what is correct behaviour – they should not unreflectingly accept earlier interpretations. The conflicts have centered on a number of ritual practices, many of which have been condemned by *Muhammadiyah* on the grounds that they are later inclusions. The major target of accusations about superstition are syncretist spirit beliefs which are branded by *Muhammadiyah* as polytheism – a major sin for a Muslim. This view has led *Muhammadiyah* to attack, among other things, the activities of Javanese diviners (*dukun*), which are denounced as un-Islamic. Also a number of ceremonial practices which are common among the traditionalists as well as the syncretists have been branded as superstition.

Muhammadiyah regards followers of other orthodox movements as well as the syncretists as not yet fully enlightened about the true Muslim dogmas. The main aim of Muhammadiyah, therefore, is to teach those uninformed Muslims about correct beliefs and practices. It is assumed that as soon as they are suitably informed they will change their former attitudes in favour of the *Muhammadiyah* standpoint. As mentioned earlier, the majority of followers have always come from urban areas. This is still true, although during the last decades the movement has also begun to make inroads in the villages. As an example of contemporary *Muhammadiyah* practices, I shall describe my own experiences of the work of the movement. The data were gathered in an East Javanese village in 1986-7.

The village is situated some twenty kilometres east of Malang. Most of the villagers can be considered adherents of Javanese syncretism, *kejawen*, but there is also a strong branch of the orthodox traditional organization *Nahdlatul Ulama*. The *Muhammadiyah* presence in the village dates from the early 1970s when a few newcomers settled here. The members have since been limited to a handful of people. However, despite the limited numbers, their influence has been extensive.

The leading traditionalists in NU hold the idea that the immoral behaviour of others could corrupt their own attempts to lead a virtuous life. Conversely, they also believe that association with saintly people, such as *kyai* (teachers at *madrasa* or *pondok* schools), might have a positive effect. By closely following their advice and directives, they might themselves achieve a closer affiliation with Allah. Such beliefs have given rise to extremely authoritarian attitudes among the traditionalists; whatever the teacher says is taken as a correct interpretation. His words are never questioned but accepted blindly. What is important for the traditionalists is *who* the speaker is, not *what* he is saying. As already mentioned, the traditionalists isolate themselves and direct their efforts towards the achievement of personal perfection as a preparation for eternal life. Such attitudes lead the traditionalists to consider themselves closer to Allah and therefore more valuable than ordinary people.

The attitudes of the local *Muhammadiyah* leaders are quite different. They are not afraid to confront the ordinary people in an attempt to raise their Islamic consciousness. On the contrary, according to the *Muhammadiyah*, it is precisely those people who have been alienated from Islam that one has to convince and to change. They refer to a saying of the prophet Muhammad which states that it is as important to do the work of Allah in this world as it is to prepare for heavenly life. Thus, according to *Muhammadiyah* teachings, a person will get as much credit in the eyes of Allah for performing God's services towards his fellow human beings as he will for performing religious duties such as prayer, fasting and preaching.

Given such profoundly different attitudes, it will come as no surprise to learn that there have been many local conflicts, personal as well as ideological, between *Muhammadiyah* and NU members. A case in point has to do with conflicting attitudes towards those who participate in the popular *jaran kepang*[34] performances, whether as actors or as spectators. The NU Muslims claimed that as long as no dirty words were used or evil spirits called upon, such performances amounted to nothing more than innocent entertainment and were therefore perfectly legitimate. From the *Muhammadiyah* side, however, it was maintained that irrespective of what actually took place during the performances, such entertainment was un-Islamic. Not only the actors, but also the spectators were included in this general condemnation.

During my discussions with traditionalist Muslims, I was repeatedly told about the sinful life led by the *Muhammadiyah* leaders. Much resentment also lingered on from what in NU circles was regarded as a *Muhammadiyah* sabotage of the local NU women's organization (*dibak*). This group began to hold weekly meetings in the late 1960s. Only NU women were invited to participate. Feeling excluded, some *Muhammadiyah* women took the initiative a couple of years later to start their own *dibak* group, and invited not only *Muhammadiyah* members but any other women willing to join. NU, which had hoped to expand their membership, was now forced to watch from the sidelines while the *Muhammadiyah dibak* became increasingly popular. Other activities were also taken up by the *Muhammadiyah dibak*; a weekly savings group, an *arisan*,[35] and a volleyball club were created. By not isolating themselves in the way the NU *dibak* did, they managed to reach many new women.

Criticism of the NU was also forthcoming from the *Muhammadiyah* ranks. I was often told that although the NU people considered themselves superior to others, they in fact isolated themselves from the general public in an antisocial and arrogant manner. As an example, the *Muhammadiyah* pointed to one of the NU *kyai* who used to tell his pupils about the superior professionalism of his own *pondok*. According to him, this superiority was due to his own deep and thorough understanding of Islam, but according to *Muhammadiyah* sources, this particular *kyai* was, in fact, one of the most isolated and antisocial of all the local traditionalist Muslims. This, and other similar stories, were told as proof of the arrogance and hypocrisy of the NU people.

In addition to other differences, the two Muslim groups have also ended up on opposing sides in local politics. The village head belong to one of the families claiming descent from *kyai* Ahmod Kubro, the original founder of the village. He is the leading figure of one village faction which is at loggerheads with several others.[36] In the 1970s all the orthodox Muslims joined the United Development Party, PPP. This is one of the three parties allowed by the Suharto regime to contest the general elections. In the early 1980s there was a nationwide split in the PPP, whereupon NU left the party. As a result, the NU people in the village joined *Golkar* and took the side of the faction headed by the village head. The *Muhammadiyah* members remained in PPP and therefore supported one of the opposing factions.

Another conflict between *Muhammadiyah* and NU erupted over the use of a communal prayer house (*langgar*). This particular prayer house had been built privately by an individual family but was used freely by all families in the neighbourhood. Besides being a place for individual prayers, the house was also used for classes where children were taught elementary religious knowledge. A number of Islamic holidays, such as *maulud*, the birthday of the prophet Muhammad, and the specifically Javanese *jumat legi*[37] were also celebrated jointly by all the neighbours in the prayer house. The purpose of *jumat legi* celebrations is to forward prayers[38] to the souls of deceased family members. The saying of the prayers is followed by a joint meal, called *slametan*, to which all participants contribute their share. After finishing the meal, the whole party proceeds to the graveyard where they tidy up and scatter flowers on the graves of their ancestors.

The celebration of *jumat legi* is a specifically Javanese innovation, which is condemned by *Muhammadiyah* as *bida*, and thereby as un-Islamic. NU on the other hand, having firmer roots in Javanese traditions, not only accepts, but even encourages its members to participate in the celebrations. Some Muhammadiyah members objected to the use of a sacred prayer house for what they saw as un-Islamic activities. The case was finally referred to the village *modin*,[39] who resolved it in favour of the NU standpoint. He argued that since this was a private *langgar*, it was up to the owner to decide how it should be used. As long as it was not used in a way that was openly contradictory to the Islamic cause, nobody else could interfere.

In the village there are also two influential mystical groups (*kebatinan*). In Indonesia, a distinction is made between mystical movements which base their practices on white magic and those which practice black magic (*klenik*).[40] While real *kebatinan* mystics strive to achieve perfection of life, practitioners of *klenik* achieve supernatural power with the intention of satisfying their own, or their followers', passions.[41] Since *klenik* mysticism represents a devious practice, it is regarded as harmful and is consequently illegal. It is obvious, however, that it is very difficult to define exactly where to draw the line between *kebatinan* and *klenik*. Although they are not very happy about it, the members of the *Muhammadiyah* movement recognize that there is an acceptable Islamic mysticism (*tasawuf*). They regard all other kinds of mysticism, including the *kebatinan* variety, as *klenik*.

Islamism and the state

From what has been said above, it is obvious that there is considerable variation in the situation with which Islamists are faced in Malaysia and Indonesia. There is great cultural affinity between the Malays and the Indonesians, especially the dominant Javanese. One might therefore expect the cultural response to Islamic penetration to be similar in the two countries. The main differences in the reception and development of Islam must therefore be attributed to other factors. The immigration of other non-Islamic ethnic groups, especially the Chinese, has been such a factor. In Indonesia, the Chinese number some 2-3 per cent of the population. Although they are economically powerful, they are simply far too few to constitute a real cultural or political threat to the majority population. In Malaysia, on the other hand, the Chinese comprise some 35 per cent and, together with the Indians, they account for almost half the population.

The nationalist response of the Malays to their own depressed situation has been discussed above. In mainstream Malay political thinking (represented mainly by the UMNO party, here labelled as *bumi*-Malays) conviction developed that the indigenous community – 'the sons of the soil', the *Bumiputra* – had the right to certain advantages which would enable them to catch up with the other ethnic groups. This is seen as a question of equity and the policy has been pursued with great vigour, especially since the 1969 riots. Politically, references to Islam are of importance to the *bumi*-Malays, mainly as a unifying force; since Islam is the religion of the *Bumiputra*, the bearers of the state, it shall be the state religion. Since the sultans are the traditional Malay rulers, they shall also be the religious heads.

With the creation of the Malaysian state, this attitude resulted in Islam becoming a decoration, a symbolic ornamentation to be exhibited during festive occasions, rather than something to be seriously adhered to. Among the Malays, however, there were also those who were dissatisfied with the largely ceremonial role attributed to Islam. These people demanded that the religion should be taken more seriously – since Islam is the state religion, Islamic law should be the basis of legislation. Here, it is important to realize that those advocating a more serious role for Islam are, in most cases, as much Malay nationalists as are the *bumi*-Malays. PAS, the main political proponent of the Islamic cause, has always agreed with UMNO that Malay special privileges are justified on the basis that the Malays are the indigenous population.[42] PAS can be identified as a traditionalist orthodox party and as such, has its main basis of support among conservative *ulama* and farmers in the rural areas.

From the 1970s onwards there has been a growing challenge towards the above-mentioned traditionalist UMNO- and PAS-supported interpretations of Islam. The opposition has come from a number of quite diverse organizations which in Malaysia have been conveniently lumped together as the *dakwah* movement. There seems to be some sense in the joint classification, however, in the fact that they all propagate the necessity of reforming traditional Malaysian Islam in one way or another. Thus, despite their great internal differences, the various *dakwah* movements can all be labelled as reformist and modernist (as defined above). They all espouse reforms of traditionalist Islam and advocate a return to the original sources of the religion. Furthermore, all the *dakwah* movements are united in an effort to turn away from what is seen as Western-influenced, materialistic values in favour of emphasizing a greater role for Islam in all aspects of the Malaysian social fabric. To achieve the goal of a more personalized religious experience, these movements resort to a wide variety of tactics, ranging from education and publishing to individual persuasion.

The rise of the *dakwah* movement heightened, and is perhaps even a consequence of, a rapidly growing but hitherto latent conflict in Malay society, namely that between rural and urban areas. As indicated by the *Bumiputra* epithet, traditionally almost all Malays were farmers and lived in villages. The towns began to grow in the late nineteenth century as a result of the rapidly expanding mining industry and to begin with they were populated almost exclusively by Chinese. After independence, and as a result of *Bumiputra* privileges, more and more Malays moved into the towns. Coming from a traditional environment and being newcomers to urban life, many Malays felt insecure and often also affronted by what they encountered. This provoked a reaction against the materialistic, secular life style they met with, which in turn led to an emphasis on the exclusive traits of their own ethnic and religious background. In this context, the Islamic identity which touches upon so many facets of traditional Malay culture came to the fore.

In social terms, the emergence of the *dakwah* movements in post-colonial Malaysia can be explained as a reaction against the frustrations caused by a rapidly modernizing society. Those experiencing stress and disorientation are found mainly among the urban lower and middle classes. These are recent migrants from rural villages where life was simple and circumscribed by a strict and static value system. As social movements, the *dakwah* groups exhibit many characteristics typical of salvation movements arising when a society is in crisis,[43] and several attempts have been made to explain the growth of similar millenarian or nativistic movements.[44] Such movements have occurred all over the world – the Melanesian cargo cults being an example – and have been regarded as a reaction against colonialism and moral decay, putting forward political demands in a religious guise. Typically, these movements are dominated by a charismatic prophet who denounces Western intrusion and promises intervention by the ancestors to achieve a return to the just society of a past golden age.

In the analyses of cargo cults,[45] the pre-political character of the movements was stressed. Due to the absence of clear-cut political alternatives, the protests took on a religious character. As formerly divided tribal groups were united in these protests, the movements are seen to some extent as forerunners of later political, nationalist movements. In this context it is interesting to note that the Malaysian case may function as a counterpoint to these analyses. In contrast to the tribal societies of Melanesia, Malaysia is a post-colonial national state with functioning political parties. Despite such structural differences, however, the socio-religious reaction to a crisis situation is similar.

The Malaysian *dakwah* phenomenon has thus much in common with millenarian movements of earlier social epochs. Just like the cargo cults, they spring forth in a situation of crisis in which society experiences a rapid social change. In both cases, the main evildoer is pinpointed as Western society, against which the original values of a glorified past are held up as an ideal. For the movements to thrive there has to be a charismatic leader who has the ability to channel the paralysing feelings of frustration and injustice into politico-religious action. When the 'Good' is not delivered as promised, the leader can explain this away as a failure on the part of members to follow the divine instructions.

Not only are the reactions to a crisis situation similar, but the social consequences can also be compared. In the *dakwah* groups the believers are united by the strong bonds of a sacred common cause, strictly shielding themselves off from the infidels of the surrounding society. As a result, the social divides in Malaysian society, between various Muslim *aliran* and between ethnic groups, are reinforced. However, while increasing the scale of conflicts within society, it is also true that the *dakwah* movements assist in uniting people on a larger scale. They feel themselves to be part of an international community of believers – the *umma*. In another time and another society, the cargo cults also functioned as a means of uniting hitherto divided groups, while estranging non-believers.

Thus, it can be concluded that the growth of traditionalist orthodox Islam in the early part of this century was a reaction on the part of Malays against an externally imposed immigration of non-Malays. In a similar way, the immense upsurge for the ideals propagated by the *dakwah* organizations came as a direct consequence of the recent rapid and large-scale internal migration within Malaysian society. The first wave of Islamization was traditionalist and had its basis in the rural areas, whereas the second wave is modernist and is carried by a newly developed layer of the Malay population. A large majority of the *dakwah* reformers are urban and well educated – the movement has always had a strong basis on the university campuses. During the first *dakwah* decade, the 1970s, there were many confrontations with the government which saw the criticisms mainly as a challenge to its authority. However, since the co-optation of Anwar Ibrahim much has changed. During the last ten years, the introduction and widening scope of many Islamic institutions such as *zakat* (alms tax), insurance and banking have received wide attention. However, there is still a state of confrontation with some of the more radical *dakwah* groups, such as the *Darul Arqam* discussed above.

During the late colonial era, it looked as if the orthodox Muslim forces were well on their way to gaining one of their main goals: the creation of an Islamic state in Indonesia. As discussed above, the Islamists had taken an active part in the struggle for liberation. In many circles there were high hopes that the birth of independent Indonesia would also mean the simultaneous birth of an Islamic state.[46] Others feared that such a move would divide the nation and therefore advocated a separation of state and religion, and as a result the *Pancasila*-state was born. Thus, in the largest Muslim country in the world, there is neither an Islamic state nor is Islam a state religion. In the political life of the nation there is not even a party to defend an Islamic ideology. However, this does not imply that Indonesia is a secular state – on the contrary, belief in God is proclaimed as the first principle of *Pancasila*.

A religious pluralism and the establishment of harmonious relations between the religions are important, perhaps even crucial, for the survival of Indonesia as a unitary state. Officially, all religions[47] are equal, but in practice Islamic institutions, for instance in the field of education, are given wide-ranging support. Despite this, many Muslims appear to be wary of Christian missionary activities. In 1967 all Indonesians were required to state a religious affiliation, which was to be written on their identity card. As a result, some syncretist and animist groups chose Hinduism or Christianity instead of Islam. Of course this angered the Muslims who often complain about aggressive Christian missions directed against Muslim communities, arguing that the missionaries receive extensive support from foreign sources to back their activities.[48] In an article in al-Nahdah, the author complains about 'Indonesia's missionary imbalance',[49] and maintains that Muslim protests have been dismissed by the government and that the *Pancasila* philosophy is used to erode Islamic values.

After their initial failure, the Islamists have never regained the strength they seemed to have before independence. Official state policy towards the Muslims has varied considerably between the Old and the New Order. However, in both periods leading statesmen have been wary about Islamist influence and have employed various methods to prevent the Muslims from gaining the upper hand. Due to frequent internal conflicts and divisions, the Islamists themselves have also to some extent contributed to their own diminishing influence.

After the 1945 setback, it at first looked as if the Islamists had quickly managed to reassemble and unite their forces. However, after a series of withdrawals from the united Muslim party, *Masyumi*, the 1955 elections resulted in a deadlock between three more or less equally strong *aliran* – the Muslims, the Nationalists and the communists. When, on top of this, *Masyumi* was banned and President Sukarno guided his democracy towards a growing dependence on the Communists, Muslim frustration rapidly grew. The 1965 coup and subsequent massacres shifted the balance of power and Muslim hopes began to grow again. As a first step, many Muslims demanded a rehabilitation of the *Masyumi* party. This was denied by the New Order regime, which instead opted for the creation of a new, more easily controlled Muslim party. This was a clear indication of the intentions of the government. The New Order regime wanted to control and subsume the Muslims and other potentially disruptive *aliran* under the all-embracing *Pancasila* umbrella. As a first step, the political parties were forced to merge into two parties, the activities of which have been severely restricted. The next step came about ten years later when all parties and other organizations had to subscribe to *Pancasila* as their single ideological basis.

Thus, the official position of the Indonesian government is that *Pancasila*, not Islam, is the state ideology.[50] Therefore, all Islamic political ambitions have to be suppressed. On the other hand, the importance of Islam as a religious and socio-cultural ideology has always been fully recognized, and supported, by the Indonesian state. Consequently, when the government tried to infringe on these rights by introducing a new marriage bill in 1973, this provoked a heated Muslim reaction. The Muslims felt that the proposal was anti-Islamic in several respects. First of all, the proposed law required Muslims to register a marriage with the civil authorities in order for it to be valid. Secondly, the law forbade Muslim men to take a second wife unless they got permission from a civil court. These and other proposed regulations clearly put the civil law ahead of the Islamic law, in a way unacceptable to any orthodox Muslim. This time the government retreated and withdrew the bill.

In recent years, there seem to have been signs pointing to a willingness on the part of the government to allow a larger role for Islam in the social, although not the political, life of the nation.[51] The minister of Religious Affairs, H.M. Syadzali, for instance, has pleaded for a 're-actualization' of Islam and President Suharto himself has supported the establishment of an Islamic bank. After much controversy, the government has also finally allowed schoolgirls to wear Muslim dress instead of the formerly compulsary uniform. Recently, NU and *Muhammadiyah* have come together in a seminar on 'conceptual reorientation' held in Yogyakarta. Opening the seminar, Syadzali said that there were no problems of relations between the two organizations; in the essential questions both held similar views, and what was now important was to enhance the work ethos.[52] Obviously, the government is again downplaying existing ideological differences, using arguments similar to those that preceded the merger of the political parties in 1973. The minister's speech can be interpreted as an attempt to channel the different *aliran* into a harmonious coexistence, where all energies are directed towards the development of the country.

Allan Samson has argued that the present government policy towards the Islamists follows the guidelines drawn up by the famous Dutch Islamologist Snouck Hurgronje in the early years of this century.[53] He was an advisor to the Dutch colonial government on Islamic affairs. In this capacity he recommended that the government support Muslim religious expression while curbing any political ambitions. This has been followed not only by the Dutch, but also by their successors in independent Indonesia. Sukarno, the first President, took advantage of the rift between traditionalists and modernists in order to split the Islamic forces. The more docile NU traditionalists supported the regime and in exchange they obtained control of the Ministry of Religious Affairs. The more militant modernists were first kept at bay and then neutralized as a political force when their party, the *Masyumi*, was declared illegal. The second Indonesian President, Suharto, has followed in the footsteps of his predecessor, at least with regard to the policy towards the Muslim community. To begin with, *Masyumi* was never allowed to be revived and after that there has, in the name of *Pancasila*, been a systematic suppression of all Islamic political ambitions.

The main reason for this consistent policy followed by successive Indonesian governments is to be found in the centuries old conflict between Javanist (*priyai* and *abangan*) culture on the one hand and Islamic culture on the other. With the exception of the Javanese north coast,[54] the Islamic tradition has always been at a disadvantage compared with the Hindu-influenced *adat* of the traditional Javanese aristocracy and their peasant clients. Of course, Javanese culture is not entirely uniform: generally speaking, it is at its strongest in the region dominated by central Javanese court culture and the further away one goes, the weaker it becomes.[55] Thus, in the northern coastal areas and in the outer regions of east Java, which are influenced by Madurese culture, orthodox Islam has a comparatively stronger position.

As a general rule, however, Javanist culture has always had the upper hand, especially among the influential *priyai* aristocracy. As discussed above, the *santri* (orthodox Muslims) were mainly recruited among the rising bourgeoisie, especially the merchants. This was a new social class which was not deeply rooted in the old traditions of the ruling aristocracy. The latter continued, however, to dominate the social and political life of the nation. After liberation, and particularly during the New Order, the military has also had a growing influence, officially legitimized through the doctrine of *dwifungsi* (the double function). A majority of the military can be considered Javanists and, although formally Muslims, they are suspicious of Islamic political ambitions. Another often highly educated and influential group in the Indonesian political establishment belongs to the Christian minority. Finally, there are the mysticist, *kebatinan* groups, whose numerical strength and influence among the *priyai* aristocracy and other government officials have been constantly growing. Although these *aliran* may have different interests in many respects, they are united in their opposition towards a politicized Islam. So far, at least, they have been able to hold back any Islamist ambitions.

Malaysia and Indonesia are many similarities, culturally and otherwise. Moreover, both are multi-ethnic societies in which Islam is the most widespread faith of the politically dominant group. Comparing the position of Islam in contemporary Malaysia and Indonesia, one is nevertheless struck by glaring differences. In Indonesia, Islam is almost a political pariah, whereas in Malaysia, the two dominant Malay parties seem to compete to satisfy Muslim demands. The explanation for such differences lies for the most part in the variations in historical experiences of each country.

Until the latter part of the last century, most of Malaya was a wilderness, an 'uncivilized' outpost, whereas Indonesia, and especially Java, has a long history of great civilizations. Thus, early Hindu-Buddhist cultures put down firm roots in Java and, when blended with Islam, resulted in a syncretism which exists to this day. Furthermore the Malay sultans and their followers were influenced by syncretist ideas. However, when the Malays found themselves a minority in their own country, syncretism gave way to orthodox Islam. In a situation where the Malays had to fight hard to maintain their influence, the religion was readily accepted as a unifying ideology, a rallying point, through which they could distinguish themselves from their infidel competitors. At first, nationalism and acceptance of Western secular values seemed for many Malays to be the solution to their problems. Recently, however, more and more people have reacted against Westernization. Instead they have turned to Islamic values and the idea of an Islamic state as a suitable panacea.

In the heterogeneous Indonesian archipelago, the problems facing the young nation were perceived differently. Here, the main issue was not how the dominance of one ethnic group over the others was to be achieved, but rather the opposite; how the ethnic, social and religious rifts were to be prevented from breaking up the unitary state. Whereas in Malaysia, Islam was consciously identified with the ruling Malay ethnic group, the Indonesians were determined to avoid making religion another divisive issue. Therefore, Islamic political ambitions had to be suppressed at all costs and much of Indonesia's independence politics can be understood only in this light. Political repression coupled with strong opposition from other *aliran* has forced the Islamists to adapt themselves to the realities. Many leading Islamists, such as Nurcholis Madjid and Abdurrahman Wahid[56] have argued for a separation of religion and worldly affairs; a secularization of Islam (*sekularisasi Islam*) in a way reminiscent of Christian traditions.

Thus, historical experiences leading up to contemporary political realities have led the Islamists' struggle into different tracks in the two countries. While one of the countries seems to be well on the way to the final goal of an Islamic state, the other is heading for a more definite separation of religion and state.

Notes

1. Alluding to the use of this identity card, such statistical but non-practising Muslims

are known in Indonesia as Islam KTP, where KTP stands for *Kartu Tanda Penduduk*, i.e. the identity card.

2. The history of the arrival and subsequent spread of Islam has been much debated among historians. Opinions vary about who brought Islam to the archipelago, when it was done and how it was spread. The view opined here resembles the one subscribed to by most historians such as Vlekke (1965). For more information about the discussion on early Islam in Indonesia, see Ricklefs (1979) and Drewes (1968).

3. In recent years, NU has changed character and as a result broadened its basis of support (Mc Vey 1983: 210).

4. *Aliran* translates literally as current. In Indonesia the word is used to describe ideologically motivated currents which divide the society into opposing groups. Due to the present ideological monopoly of *Pancasila*, it is obvious that *aliran* allegiances nowadays are of a different character than during the Old Order regime. All the *aliran* have to subscribe to *pancasila* and limit their activities accordingly.

5. This is not to say that the modernists do not believe in *takdir*, predestination, only that they tend to relegate it to those things which are definitely impossible for man to control.

6. As a matter of fact there were also orthodox Muslims who rejected the notion of an Islamic state, mainly because of its implications for the unity of the nation. Adnan (1990: 446) mentions among others Mohammad Hatta, the first Vice President, and Munawir Syadzali, minister of Religious Affairs, as examples. In a document containing the first draft of the *Pancasila* constitution, presented on 22 June 1945, it was stated not only that the foundation of the republic of Indonesia was 'belief in God' but also 'with the obligation for adherents of Islam to practice Islamic law' (*dengan kewajiban menjalankan Syari'at Islam bagi pemeluk-pemeluknya*). Later, when independence was proclaimed, these seven words of what became known as the 'Jakarta Charter' were omitted, to the great chagrin of the Islamists (Johns 1987).

7. The phrase used in *Pancasila* is *Ketuhanan yang Maha Esa*.

8. Feith 1957.

9. Nishihara 1972.

10. Initially, Singapore was also part of the federation but withdrew in 1965 after less than two years of conflicts between the Chinese-dominated city and the Malay-dominated states.

11. Strictly a person must also be of the Malay race to qualify as an ethnic Malay.

12. Mutalib 1990: 15.

13. These were two nineteenth-century Islamic reformers who together inspired the *Salafiyah* movement. They advocated a return to the original teachings of Islam, i.e. the Quran and the *Sunna*. They both urged Muslims to learn from Western science and technology but without adopting Western values and materialism. Abduh, especially, pointed to the need for education and emphasized the fact that Islam was in harmony with modern science.

14. Roff (1985) discusses an article by J. de Jong (1960) about the conflict between *adat* and Islam where it is suggested that it might be fruitful to analyze the relation in a way similar to the *gumsa-gumlao* oscillation described by Edmund Leach (1954) in his book about the political systems of Highland Burma.

15. Roff 1967, ch. 3; Milner 1986: 56.

16. In *Far Eastern Economic Review* (28 Jan. 1993), it is reported that after a series of incidents the Mahatir government intends to limit the immunity of the sultans. This change of the constitution has been rejected by the latter who claim that it cannot become law without their consent.

17. At present PAS has succeeded in getting a majority in one of the states of the federation: Kelantan in the northeast. The party is now attempting to introduce Islamic criminal law (*hudud*) in the state, but these measures have met with staunch opposition from the ruling UMNO party.

18. When the NEP was introduced, Malay-owned business had a total capital of only M$ 48 million as against M$ 1,219 million owned by the other races, mainly the Chinese (Mutalib 1990: 56).
19. personal communication with Prof. Sharifah Zaleha Syed Hassan, Dept. of Anthropology and Sociology, UKM.
20. Mutalib 1990: 63.
21. Ibid.: 91.
22. Nagata 1984: 88.
23. Mutalib 1990: 83.
24. On 4 November 1993 Anwar Ibrahim was elected deputy prime minister and it is now generally expected that he will replace Mahatir as prime minister within the next few years.
25. So far villages are not established in all districts.
26. Nagata 1980: 134.
27. This Sufi order was founded in the early twentieth century by a Javanese mysticist, Sheikh Muhammad Suhaimi. He is the author of *The Book of Praises*, the ideals of which have been taken over by Ustaz Ashaari. Suhaimi also came to Malaysia where he gained many followers. Most contemporary followers of this Sufi order are found in Java and Malaysia. Reportedly, the founder predicted before his death in 1925 that before the apocalypse an *Imam Mahdi* would arise. In *Darul Arqam* circles, people have implied that Ustaz Ashaari himself would be the chosen *Imam Mahdi*. Despite the similarity in name, the Sufi order has no relationship with the Indonesian *Muhammadiyah* organization.
28. Nagata 1984: 105.
29. Muzaffar 1988: 12.
30. Abaza (1991: 225) makes an interesting comparison between Egypt and Malaysia and concludes that the governments in both countries have used similar tactics against the fundamentalists, brandishing them as deviant and extremist.
31. The *Wahhabi* school was founded in the eighteenth century by Muhammad Abdul Wahhab and advocates a return to the original sources of the religion, i.e. the Quran and the *Sunna*.
32. Peacock 1978.
33. Federspiel 1970: 64-6.
34. In this ceremony, the participants ride on bamboo horses and perform a number of dances. Suddenly one or more of the actors become possessed by the spirit of a devil (*syetan*), who takes over and controls all the actions of the possessed. The dance is performed under the guidance of a diviner (*dukun*).
35. The idea of an *arisan* is that a group of people come together to save money regularly for a specific purpose. When the goal has been reached, the *arisan* is dissolved and a new one may be formed if required. Such groups, which are very popular, may consist of any number of people and may last for short or long periods. In the village there seems to be *arisan* groups for almost any conceivable purpose and most people are members of at least one such group. The *dibak arisan* running at the time I was doing fieldwork had 70 members who contributed Rp. 100 (approximately 10 US cents) each week, until Rp. 350,000 had been collected. Thereafter the money was divided and each participant received Rp. 5,000. Then a new *arisan* could be started.
36. See Cederroth (1991) for a description of the village politics and the struggle between the factions.
37. This is a day in the Javanese calender which is a combination of a five-day week and a seven-day week. Thus, the month consists of 35 days of which *jumat legi* is the day in which *jumat* (Friday) of the seven-day week happens to coincide with *legi* of the five-day week. This day has a special significance for the Javanese.
38. On this occasion *tahlil* prayers are said plus some other specific prayers for the

salvation of the souls of deceased persons. The latter are local prayers which are said in Javanese, not in Arabic.

39. One of the *pamong desa*, the village administrators, and responsible for religious issues.

40. Mulder (1978: 34) quotes the following definition of *klenik*: 'those devious practices that are inspired by the lowly passions for earthly goods and devilish powers'.

41. Mulder 1978.

42. The Malay scholar Chandra Muzaffar has made it clear that such special privileges represent a violation of the principle of a universal Islamic brotherhood and therefore constitute an un-Islamic stance. Referring to Sura Baqara 272 he claims that the Quran itself prohibits such discrimination (Muzaffar 1985: 357).

43. Nash (1991: 730) comments that '*dakwah*, like many nativistic and fundamentalist movements arises from crises. In this case the crisis centers on a new urban middle class in tension with Western modernism in a multi-ethnic society of open and competitive politics.'

44. See e.g. Lanternari (1965); Lawrence (1964); and Worsley (1957).

45. Worsley 1957; Lawrence 1964.

46. For a detailed discussion of the struggle between the socio-political *aliran* in the period before and around independence, see Boland (1982, ch. 1).

47. All officially acknowledged religions, not the others. In practice this has meant difficulties for those who do not adhere to any of the acknowledged world religions. There are many examples of more or less severe persecutions of syncretists and others. I personally experienced this when doing fieldwork in a Sasak *Wetu Telu* community on Lombok in the 1970s. The *Wetu Telu* are Muslim syncretists whose traditional ritual practices were condemned and suppressed by orthodox Muslims on the grounds that they were Hindu-influenced.

48. Harun 1991. In fact, the Indonesian Department of Religious Affairs in 1979 issued guidelines banning conversion attempts among people already adhering to one of the acknowledged religions. This restriction is accepted by Muslims but opposed by Christians. In Malaysia there are even stronger prohibitions and the statutes of one state rule that anyone who propagates another religion than Islam among Muslims will be sentenced to one year in prison plus a fine of M$3,000 (approx. US$1,200) (Mehden 1987: 189).

49. Akoseji 1985.

50. There have been fears among Muslims that *Pancasila* itself will become a kind of New Order religion (Pranowo 1990: 493).

51. See van Dijk 1991.

52. *Indonesia Times*, 1 Feb. 1993.

53. Samson 1980: 142-9.

54. Also the Sundanese areas of western Java are more influenced by orthodox Islam, but they have a culture of their own and are therefore not included in the Javanese sphere of culture.

55. See Koentjaraningrat (1984: 21-6) for a discussion of Javanese cultural variation.

56. Madjid has been chairman of the Muslim Student Association (HMI) and Wahid is the present chairman of NU.

References

Abaza, M. 1991. 'The Discourse on Islamic Fundamentalism in the Middle East and South East Asia: A Critical Perspective', *Sojourn* 6(2), 203-39.

Adnan, Z. 1990. 'Islamic religion: Yes, Islamic (Political) Ideology: No! Islam and the State in Indonesia', in A. Budiman (ed.), *State and Civil Society in Indonesia*, 441-77. (Monash Papers on Southeast Asia, no. 22.) Glen Waverly, Australia: Aristoc Press.

Akoseji, M.S. 1985. 'Indonesia's Missionary Imbalance', *Al-Nahdah* 5(1), 33-5. Kuala Lumpur: Regional Islamic Dakwah Council of Southeast Asia and the Pacific.

Baza, M. 1991. 'The Discourse on Islamic Fundamentalism in the Middle East and Southeast Asia: A Critical Perspective', *Sojourn* 6(2), 203-39.

Boland, B.J. 1982. *The Struggle of Islam in Modern Indonesia*. (Verhandelingen van het Koninklijk Instituut voor Taal-, Land-en Volkenkunde 59.) The Hague: Martinus Nijhoff.

Cederroth, S. 1991. 'From PNI to Golkar: Indonesian Village Politics, 1955-87', in M. Mörner and T. Svensson (eds), *The Transformation of Rural Society in the Third World*, 265-94. London: Routledge.

Van Dijk, C. 1991. 'The Re-actualization of Islam in Indonesia', *Rima*, 25(2), 75-83.

Drewes, G.W.J. 1968 'New Light on the Coming of Islam to Indonesia', *Bijdragen tot de Taal-, Land- en Volkenkunde* 124(4), 433-59.

Federspiel, H.M. 1970. 'The Muhammadijah: A Study of an Orthodox Islamic Movement in Indonesia', *Indonesia* (10), 57-79.

Feith, H. 1957. *The Indonesian Elections of 1955*. Ithaca, NY: Interim Series Report. Modern Indonesia Project, Cornell University.

Harun, L. 1991. 'A Plea for Inter-Faith Harmony in Indonesia', *Al-Nahdah* 11(1-2), 43-5. Kuala Lumpur: Regional Islamic Dakwah Council of Southeast Asia and the Pacific.

Indonesia Times: 'No Principal Difference', 1 Feb. 1993.

Johns, A.H. 1987. 'Indonesia. Islam and Cultural Pluralism', in J.L. Esposito (ed.), *Islam in Asia: Religion, Politics and Society*, 202-29. Oxford University Press.

D Jong, P.E. de Josselin 1960. 'Islam Versus Adat in Negri Sembilan', *Bijdragen tot de Taal-, Land- en Volkenkunde* 116, 158-201.

Koentjaraningrat 1984. *Javanese Culture*. Singapore: Oxford University Press.

Lanternari, V. 1965. *The Religions of the Oppressed*. New York: Mentor Books.

Lawrence, P. 1964. *Road Belong Cargo*. Manchester University Press.

Leach, E.R. 1954. *Political Systems of Highland Burma: A Study of Kachin Social Structure*. Boston: Beacon Press.

McVey, R. 1983. 'Faith as the Outsider: Islam in Indonesian Politics', in J.P. Piscatori (ed.), *Islam in the Political Process*, 199-225. Cambridge University Press.

Mehden, F.R. von der 1987. 'Malaysia, Islam and Multiethnic Polities', in J.L. Esposito (ed.), *Islam in Asia: Religion, Politics and Society*, 177-201. Oxford University Press.

Milner, A.C. 1986. 'Rethinking Islamic Fundamentalism in Malaysia', *Rima* 20 (2), 48-75.

Mulder, N. 1978. *Mysticism & Everyday Life in Contemporary Java*. Singapore University Press.

Mutalib, H. 1990. *Islam and Ethnicity in Malay Politics*. Singapore: Oxford University Press.

Muzaffar, C. 1985. 'Malayism, Bumiputraism and Islam', in A. Ibrahim *et al.* (eds), *Readings on Islam in Southeast Asia*, 356-61. Singapore: Institute of Southeast Asian Studies (Social Issues in Southeast Asia).

——. 1988. 'Islamic Resurgence and the Question of Development in Malaysia', in L. T. Ghee (ed.), *Reflections on Development in Southeast Asia*, 1-25. Singapore: ASEAN Economic Research Unit, Institute of Southeast Asian Studies.

Nagata, J. 1980. 'The New Fundamentalism: Islam in Contemporary Malaysia', *Asian Thought and Society* 5(14), 128-41.

——. 1984. *The Reflowering of Malaysian Islam: Modern Radicals and their Roots*. Vancouver: University of British Columbia Press.

Nash, M. 1991. 'Islamic Resurgence in Malaysia and Indonesia', in M.E. Marty and R. Scott Appleby (eds), *Fundamentalisms Observed*, 691-739. University of Chicago Press.

Nishihara, M.i 1972. *Golkar and the Indonesian Elections of 1971*. (Monograph Series 56.) Ithaca, NY: Modern Indonesia Project, Cornell University.

Peacock, J.L. 1978. *Purifying the Faith: The Muhammadiyah Movement in Indonesian Islam*. Menlo Park: Benjamin/Cummings.

Pranowo, B. 1990. 'Which Islam and which Pancasila?', in A. Budiman (ed.), *State and Civil Society in Indonesia*, 479-502. (Monash Papers on Southeast Asia no. 22.) Glen Waverly (Australia): Aristoc Press.

Ricklefs, M.C. 1979. 'Six Centuries of Islamization in Java', in N. Levitzion (ed.), *Conversion to Islam*, 100-28. New York: Holmes and Meier.

Roff, W.R. 1967. *The Origins of Malay Nationalism*. New Haven: Yale University Press.

——. 1985. 'Islam Obscured? Some Reflections on Studies of Islam and Society in Southeast Asia', *Archipel* (29), 7-33.

Samson, A. 1980. 'The Political Strength of Indonesian Islam', *Asian Thought and Society* 5(14), 142-9.

Vlekke, B.H.M. 1965. *Nusantara: A History of Indonesia*. The Hague: W. van Hoewe.

Worsley, P. 1957. *The Trumpet Shall Sound*. London: Macgibbon and Kee.

THE ISLAMIC MOVEMENT
IN AFGHANISTAN

NATIONAL LIBERATION
AND THE CHALLENGE OF POWER

Asta Olesen

In February 1989, after close to ten years' occupation, the Soviet forces were withdrawn from Afghanistan. Contrary to the expectations of most observers this did not signal the overthrow of President Najibullah's PDPA government which displayed great resilience against attack. Najibullah's policy of national reconciliation did not, however, produce any tangible results, since all his overtures were turned down by the Afghan resistance, the *mujahedin*. These were on the other hand, due to lack of coordination and internal conflicts, unable to produce any military break through in their warfare against the PDPA regime.

Ultimately, on 18 March 1992, President Najibullah announced his willingness to resign to pave the way for a UN-negotiated settlement which was intended to re-establish peaceful conditions in the war-ridden country. Najibullah's declaration, which was the outcome of heavy pressure from the UN special envoy Benon Sevan, rather than being conducive to the establishment of a broad-based interim government (which, contrary to all advice, apparently had been anticipated by Sevan), created a power vacuum in the country which all the fighting forces tried to exploit. The armed forces were gradually disintegrating, with the *Parcham* and *Khalq* factions chosing sides in the internal power struggles among the various *mujahedin* groups.

On 15 April 1992, President Najibullah took refuge at the UN Office in Kabul whereupon rival *mujahedin* groups occupied Kabul. On 27 April, a feeble compromise was reached between the seven Peshawar-based *mujahedin* parties and a number of internal commanders. Sibghatullah Mujadidi from the moderate *Jebha-i Nejat-i Melli* was pronounced formal leader of the alliance until June 1992 when he, according to the agreement, was replaced by Burhanuddin Rabbani from *Jamiat-i Islami*. Although Gulbudin Hikmatyar's radical Islamist *Hezb-i Islami* joined the alliance at the last minute, the fighting between the various *mujahedin* groups has continued, particularly between two Islamist parties, Rabbani's *Jamiat-i Islami* and Hikmatyar's *Hezb-i Islami*.

Although the Afghans fought for fourteen years to liberate themselves from Soviet occupation and from the PDPA regime, the realization of these goals has thus paved the way for neither peaceful nor orderly conditions. On the contrary, the result has been anarchy with thousands of civilian casualties, with Kabul alone being divided between up to ten rival military groups and with looting and excesses towards the civil population being the order of the day.[1]

Today, the Afghan population has thus fallen victim to the infighting between the various resistance groups. The struggle against the PDPA regime and the Soviet occupation was almost unanimously formulated in religious terms as a *jihad* (holy war), but this definition of the liberation struggle was superimposed upon the existing ethnic, tribal, religious and political divisions within the heterogeneous population. Before the fall of the PDPA regime, the question of the national versus the religious character of the resistance was unsettled. Today, the questions of secular versus religious tendencies and what constitutes the Islamic character of the Afghan state are still not resolved. The paradox of the hard-won 'liberation' may be reflected in this Kabul graffito: 'Mujahedin brothers, you took our ox [Najibullah] and brought us seven donkeys [the party leaders from Peshawar]. Please, remove the donkeys and let us have our ox back.'[2]

Historical background

During the 1960s and 1970s Afghan society experienced a social and political crisis which culminated in the Saur Revolution of 1978, when the Peoples' Party of Afghanistan (PDPA) seized power, followed not only by the Soviet invasion in December 1979 but also by the increasingly religiously-formulated resistance to the PDPA-regime and the Soviet occupation.

Afghanistan's abortive experiment with parliamentary democracy in the period 1964-73 reflected the crisis for the legitimacy of power. During this period, political life was gradually radicalized and the Islamic and the Communist movements took root. These two numerically limited movements directly challenged the established social order, each offering a model for 'the just society', but they were also superimposed upon older deep-rooted divisions within Afghan society. These partly originated in the relationship between tribes and state, since Afghanistan had emerged in 1747 as an independent state through the confederation of Pashtun tribes. For a large part of the population, tribal affiliation still supercedes other loyalties and thus carries the seeds of the disintegration of the state.

Yet another historical condition which continues to affect political development is the ethnic heterogeneity of the population and the associated problems of domination. Modern Afghanistan, *qua* its origin in a Pashtun tribal confederacy, remains a state by and for the Pashtun majority of the population, who conquered areas inhabited by a number of other ethnic groups which today form about half of the population. These basic characteristics of the Afghan state apart, since the end of the nineteenth century there has been a conflict between religious and secular tendencies in the formulation of a legitimate basis for the exercise of state power *vis-à-vis* the population. From the 1960s onwards, this latter conflict has been aggravated by the growing gap between cities and countryside, particularly as regards level of education.

The conflict between the secular and religious interpretations of the legitimacy of power dates back at least to *Amir* Abdur Rahman's (1880-1901) centralization of the Afghan state. The ultimate aim of *Amir* Abdur Rahman's policies was the consolidation and centralization of the Afghan state: in other words, the transformation of the Afghan state from a tribal confederacy to a centralized, 'modern' state. A precondition for the success of this policy was the breaking of the independence of the traditional power-groups in society – the royal lineage, the tribal leaders and the religious establishment – and turning them into groups whose basic interests, economically and politically, coincided with those of the state. However, for the centralization policies to succeed and not to be entirely dependent upon the use of physical force, it was also essential for the *Amir* to achieve legitimacy of power in relation to the population at large. Consequently, the administrative, military and economic reforms were paralleled by attempts to establish a new ideological foundation for the state and the ruler, replacing the 'tribal model' with an 'Islamic model'. This 'Islamic model' was derived from classical *Sunni* political theory, allowing for the existence of many emirates or sultanates, provided that the ruler applied the religious law strictly and relied on it for his legal opinion. The ruler's subjects were, for their part, obliged to obey the established authority except where it required disobedience to God; every Muslim being required to 'will the good and forbid evil'. This body of political thought has been known as 'the pious sultan theory'.

Since the religious establishment, as a group, controlled all education, held monopoly over the interpretation of Islam and thus was of key importance in the legal system, it was obvious that the *Amir's* policy could not succeed without subjecting this group to state control. It was also inevitable that Islam as such would gain an even stronger position in society than it had hitherto enjoyed, since it was being utilized as the state-supporting ideology. In establishing the hegemony of the state-sanctioned interpretations of Islam, the whole educational system, as well as legal, executive and legislative powers were organized to this end. Religious beliefs and practices were controlled, and measures taken to standardize these in compliance with the officially established *Hanafi Sunni* Islam. The religious content of, or elements in, the ideological discourse sanctioning the centralizing policy of the *Amir*, as well as the absolute monarchy, had, as ultimate authority, the Quran, the Sunna, the traditions of famous Muslim scholars and orthodox Sunni jurisprudence in general. However, the discourse into which these concepts were integrated was determined by the secular, political goals of the central state, and not by any religious goals. In other words, Islamization of the state was the means to achieve centralization.[3]

By the end of his rule, *Amir* Abdur Rahman had succeeded in his policies to the extent that the power of the tribes *vis-à-vis* the state was curtailed, the *ulama* (religious scholars) as a group were strengthened through being co-opted into the state, and the ideological (Islamic) discourse in support of the centralized state and the absolute monarchy was dominant. By thus weakening the traditional ties between *ulama* and tribes, the basis for a conflict between *sharia* and *qaumwali* – that is, between the legal system of Islam and the traditional loyalities to tribe, ethnic group and locality – was also laid.

Starting with the reign of *Amir* Abdur Rahman, through the mechanisms of polity expansion and polity dominance, Islamization in the long run became a precondition for the secularization of state and society in Afghanistan.[4] Such a policy was followed by all the successors of Abdur Rahman. The ultimate expropriation of the religious domain by the state was carried out by the PDPA government. This 'desacralization' of the religious was, mainly from the 1960s, challenged by its opposite: the Islamists' demand for a 'resacralization' of the state – that is, for all spheres of life, and in particular the state, to be subjected to the religious domain. However, the absolutist and centralized structure of both models of states means that they are equally totalitarian *vis-à-vis* society and population.

The foundation of the 'modern' centralized state apparatus in Afghanistan survived the death of the 'Iron *Amir*' in 1901, and did not disintegrate in succession struggles, as had been the normal trend during the nineteenth century. It was not until his grandson, King Amanullah, resumed power in 1919 that the question of legitimacy of power became an issue again. King Amanullah was not only a fervent nationalist and pan-Islamist but also a Muslim modernizer. He launched a new ideological paradigm in Afghanistan – using Islamic ethics rather than dogma as a foundation, to develop modernist interpretations and build up Afghanistan as a modern nation state. While his views on culture and education were comparable to those of the modernist reformer in India, Sir Sayid Ahmad Khan, his political outlook was more influenced by Jamal ud-Din al-Afghani and the Young Turks. This dual heritage was reflected in the constitution of 1923, which also outlined a new model for the legitimation of political power. The ideological discourse of the Amanullah reforms signalled an attempt to revolutionize society and state through a new ideological paradigm, which defined the population's relation to the state as individual citizens rather than as tribesmen, believers or subjects. The failure of this attempt, which ended with the civil war in 1929, resulted during the following years in a constitutional structure which, however inconsistent and contradictory, reflected the distribution of power in society as well as the existence of different ideological discourses. Thus, legitimacy of power and of the ruler could be seen as emanating partly from a tribal and partly from a religious basis, as well as maintaining claims on popular sovereignty.[5]

The religious leaders were far from constituting a homogeneous bloc during this social transformation. The *Hazrat* (religious title) of Shor Bazaar, Fazl Omar Mujadidi, one of the most prominent religious leaders, heading a branch of the *Naqshbandiyya* Sufi order, was against Amanullah's reform policy from the beginning and played an important role in his overthrow. The leaders of the East Afghan *Qadiriyya* Sufi order, on the other hand, remained loyal to Amanullah on the basis of his anti-colonial and pan-Islamic attitude: that is, on the basis of his defence of the faith from onslaught from the outside. Fazl Omar Mujadidi, however, represented a new generation of religious leaders in Afghanistan, who had taken the consequence of the incorporation of the *ulama* into the state. This was also reflected in the formation of the *Jamiyat al-Ulama* in 1933, the first formation of a national council of religious scholars in Afghanistan which was to scrutinize all laws according to their compatibility with Islam. Mujadidi wanted to consolidate the power of the *ulama* (and his own family) within the state apparatus, and the success of this endeavour was reflected in the new constitution of 1931 and in the number of government posts allotted to him and his family. Compared with this, the East Afghan *Qadiriyya pirs* (shaykhs) kept aloof from the formal power structure.

With this final integration of the *ulama* into the state apparatus, plus Afghanistan's changed international situation, neither *jihad* nor the question of legitimacy were at issue for the next couple of decades, as both pan-Islamism and the activist *mullahs* belonged to the past. It was not until the 1960s that the Afghan population was presented with a new religious paradigm which brought both the question of legitimacy and *jihad* back into focus.

During the Musahiban dynasty (1930-78), two parallel developments took place: the 'bureaucratization' of Islam, initiated by *Amir* Abdur Rahman, continued, particularly within the legal and educational fields, with the codification of law based on *sharia*, and the establishment of a government-controlled religious educational system. Parallel with this was a gradual secularization of society due to the spread of secular education and the increasing secularization of urban cultural life. However, during these years, an incongruity also developed between the socio-economic and political structures of the state: that is, in the lack of representation of the urban middle class in the political sphere. This resulted in a growing challenge to the legitimacy paradigm contained in the constitution of 1931. This incongruity was to be solved through the introduction of parliamentary democracy in the new constitution of 1964. Legitimacy of power was based on the nation and popular sovereignty, while laws should not contravene the spirit of *sharia*.

The legitimacy paradigm of the 1964 constitution was thus brought into accordance with the political thinking of large parts of the new middle class which dominated the state apparatus. However, as far as the majority of the Afghan population was concerned, another incongruity developed between the ideological discourse of the state and its institutions and the still dominant ideological discourse of society, represented in a growing conflict between the outlook of the traditional power groups in society and the new, state-supporting middle class. This conflict contributed to the failure of the democratic experiment in the 1960s, resulting in political unrest and leading to Daoud Khan's *coup d'état* in 1973, whereby one section of the new middle class assumed power. Law and order returned with the authoritarian rule of President Daoud, who initially co-opted part of the left and silenced the religious opposition. However, the policy of repression, far from solving the underlying problems and conflicts, instead aggravated these, and beneath a calm surface, the ideological crisis was also deepening within the urban middle class. Meanwhile political culture was becoming ever more radicalized and militant – ultimately making Afghan society victim to the internal power struggles between the various sections of the new middle class.

Recruitment to the Islamic movement

The appearance of the new political groups of Islamists, as well as the communists, were related to this conflict; both groups were recruited from the same social strata of young educated middle-class people, reacting against their own, frequently rural and traditional background, and against social injustice, nepotism and the lack of political freedom and civil liberties. The appearance of these new political ideologies among intellectuals and students in Afghanistan in the 1950s and 1960s was closely related to the translation of the works of foreign scholars into Farsi and Pashto. While Marxist literature reached Afghanistan via the translation of the classics by the Iranian Communist Party (*Tudeh*), the Islamic movement benefitted from the translations of Sayyid Qutb and others published by *Intisharaat-i Dar al-Fikr* in Qom, *Dar al-Kutub-i Islami* in Teheran and the translations of Mawlana Abul Ala Maududi from *Al Mansoorah*, Lahore.[6] While the initial inspiration came to Afghanistan from Egypt, Maududi's influence on the Afghan Islamist movement seems to have increased greatly since the 1970s, when a number of Afghan Islamist activists went into exile in Pakistan. In the years to come, the parallels between the communist and the Islamic movements remained clear in terms of theories of revolution, subversive strategies and their concept of the state.

The first signs of the new political trend in Islam in Afghanistan – of a questioning, not only of the *modus vivendi* with the state obtained after 1930, but also of established orthodoxy – came from the *ulama*, a term understood in its literal meaning as 'religious scholars' but generally used to denote the co-opted *Jamiyat al-Ulama*. Later on, the religious opposition was divided into the two directions, with intellectuals rather than religious leaders spearheading the most radical group. This was the first time since the 'modernist Islam' of the 1920s that religion and religious interpretation had been the focal point for laymen in Afghanistan.

While the initial inspiration and leadership of the most influential and organized group within the Islamic movement originated among the professors of the Faculty of *Shariat* (Religious Law), recruitment to the movement through the 1960s and 1970s spread from this Faculty to the Polytechnic Institute, the Faculty of Engineering and the government colleges of religion (*madaris, madrasas*), with some effects also being felt in the ordinary schools. Geographically, their bastions were in the west, around Herat, and the north-east and east, particularly among civil servants operating outside the religious field.

The new political ideologies in Afghanistan, both among the Left and the Islamists, reflected the alienation and aspiration for political power of the new middle class and consequently challenged the state as well as the existing social order, while also proclaiming to represent the latent opposition between the 'People' and the 'State'. But neither the Islamists nor the Left managed to absorb the views of broader sections of the population into their discourse. An indication of this was that just as the traditional parochial identities and primordial alliances of the mass of the Afghan population have been considered a problem for successive generations of absolutists and constitutional nation-builders, so neither the Islamists nor the Left were able or willing to take account of this fact in their totalitarian political ideology.

Ideological content

The Islamic movement in Afghanistan began to develop around the

Faculty of *Shariat* in 1957 with the return from Egypt of Professor Ghulam Muhammad Niazi, later Dean of the Faculty.[7] In Egypt, Niazi had been strongly influenced by the Muslim Brotherhood, *Ikhwan al-Muslimin*. On his return to Afghanistan, and probably in view of what was considered the anti-religious policies pursued by the then Prime Minister Muhammad Daoud (1953-63), Niazi took the initiative to establish a small cell at the religious college *Madrasa-i Abu Hanifa* in Paghman, conducting clandestine meetings and lectures on the message of the Quran, and on translations of the works of Sayyid Qutb and Mawlana Maududi.

In 1965, the Islamist group around the professors at the Faculty of *Shariat* formulated its programme in a *shab-nama* (night-letter) called 'Jihad', declaring its aim to work for the establishment of an Islamic state in Afghanistan. But as in the case of the first clandestine organizational attempts of the Left, written material on the platform and programme of the Islamic movement is hard to come by as it consisted only of a few cyclostyled pamphlets and some magazines published during the liberal 1960s. The reasons are obvious: political parties were not legalized, freedom of speech and the press only existed in the sixties, and even then within narrow limits, and a 'culture of publishing' with the necessary technological facilities had not yet been established.[8]

In the late 1960s, an introductory pamphlet entitled 'Who are we and what do we want' (in Farsi) was cyclostyled to inform the wider public about the movement. The pamphlet started in a predictable way by pointing to the decay and degeneration in society, particularly among the ruling group, and the subversive effect of foreign ideologies, preachings of class war and the corruption of the young. It was stated that the remedy was to be sought in the renaissance of religion, as Islam provides justice from tyranny, exploitation, poverty and discrimination. Islam guarantees equality, freedom, prosperity, intellectual attainment, moral uplift and material improvement.[9]

In the initial stages, the common goal of the advancement of Islam was a unifying feature among the various Islamic-oriented groups, but with the increasing radicalization of politics towards the end of the 1960s, the dividing lines became more clearly defined. The main activities of the Afghan Islamists were thus geared in the beginning towards the general mobilization within university circles and educational efforts among members. But from the early 1970s onwards the strategy changed towards a systematic build-up of cadres in different sectors of society, notably central government agencies with the Ministries of Defence and Education having highest priority, with the aim of ultimately taking power.[10] Parallel with this, Edwards implies an increasing association with the *Jamaat-i Islami* of Pakistan which, however, seems to have alienated some of the other Islamic-oriented groups, particularly the

Shia groups.[11] In these strategic moves, there existed a close parallel with the leftist *Khalq* which during the 1970s also aimed at, and succeeded in, building up loyal cadres within the armed forces in preparation for a coup.

The Islamists challenged the classic *Sunni* theory of power, 'the Pious Sultan theory', which in the Afghan context led to a strong condemnation of the royal Musahiban dynasty and of the 1964 Constitution (the point of reference for the liberal educated elite) for constituting a violation of Islam in its constitutionalizion of hereditary monarchy and its definition of the king as being above the law.

The second implication of the Islamists' power model was that it excluded the religious establishment, the *ulama*, as intermediary. The argument here was that the basic principles of Islam have been rendered unalterable and that no authority, neither secular nor religious, is in a position to subvert or circumvent them – in other words, the prerogative of the religious authorities in Islam is very limited. Here also lies the explanation behind the hostility which existed between the traditionalist *ulama* and the Islamists: the *ulama* have historically been partners to 'the Pious Sultan theory' and carry part of the responsibility for what the Islamists see as the corruption of the Islamic message through the centuries, and the Islamists' solution would strip them of considerable power and influence in the future.

The elitist party concept combined with the general myth of revolution in the 1960s led the Afghan Islamists into a disastrous 'guevarist' adventurism in the 1970s. With President Daoud's coup in 1973, the suppression of them increased and they became internally divided over questions of strategy: the *Jawanan*, headed by Hikmatyar, wanted to engineer a popular uprising, while Rabbani, fearing lack of support within the population, was in favour of continued infiltration of the army in preparation for a counter-coup. However, the *Jawanan*, presumably supported by the Pakistani government, proceeded, and a series of insurrections was planned in July 1975 (Panjshir, Laghman, Badakhshan).[12] The plan failed miserably as no popular support was forthcoming – but a couple of hundred Islamist activists were imprisoned, later to be executed, in June 1979, after the PDPA takeover.[13] The movement was thus close to decimation with almost all its leaders in exile and a considerable number of activists in prison – and a clear lack of popular support. Puig sees the split in the Islamist movement between the *Jamiat* of Rabbani and the *Jawanan* of Hikmatyar also as an expression of more profound ideological disagreements: *Jamiat* aimed at a reconciliation with civil society contrary to the militant voluntarism of the *Jawanan*.[14]

The new Islamic paradigm put forward by the Islamist movement in Afghanistan has centered above anything else around the concept of the state, which has consequently raised the issue of legitimacy of power once again. In this connection, the concept of *jihad* has been reinstated in its old unapologetic form, as well as taking a prominent place within the Islamists' political strategy.[15]

The condemnation of Sufism by the Afghan Islamists have been as strong and unequivocal, and phrased in almost the same terms as that of their spiritual mentors: that Sufism is a misrepresentation of Islam and that the families of Sufi leaders have been parasites on an innocent population. Intermarriage between these hereditary Sufi families and the court have further added to the corrupting influences – here the Islamists obviously hint at the Mujaddidi and Gailani families. What the Islamists see as the shallow and defeatist pattern of thinking in Afghanistan can thus be referred to two main reasons: (1) illiteracy and (2) the prevailing Sufi mentality that neglected the realities of life and led people into doubt and mistakes. For example, the naive belief that God and *pirs* protect Afghanistan from external military might was produced by this type of mentality.[16] The declining importance of Sufism in Afghanistan in this century is explained by the increased knowledge of Islam among the people, which has led to the realization of the fact that part of Sufi learning, is not in conformity with *sharia*, the religious law.[17]

Islam in the Afghan resistance

After the failed uprisings of 1975, the Islamist leaders lived in relative obscurity in Pakistan until the overthrow of President Daoud by the Islamists' dire enemies, the Peoples' Democratic Party of Afghanistan (PDPA).

It is neither surprising nor strange that the Afghan resistance for-mulated itself in terms of religious idioms. From the first scattered uprisings in 1978, it was a broad, popular resistance, lacking organized leadership and coordination, and consequently it was formulated within the existing, predominant *Weltanschauung* which to this day for a large section of the population is mainly structured by a religious consciousness integrated with tribal, ethnic and other local values.

The comparatively low profile of 'modern' intellectuals in the Afghan resistance today, except to some extent in the Islamist parties, can partly be seen as an indication of the ideological crisis and the widening gap in cultural outlook and values between the new elite and the rest of the Afghan population. However, it is also an indication of the develop-ment of exile politics since 1978, where the ideological discourse of the Islamists and, to a far lesser extent, of the traditional *ulama* have come to dominate the scene. They claim to have fought communism for years and stress the responsibility of the royal dynasty for 'letting the communists in'; by extension all the leading politicians of that time can be discredited as the 'King's men', or 'communist lackeys'. The result of this has been the alienation of a wide section of the non-Islamist, educated middle class. A tragic example was the killing in February 1988 of one of Afghanistan's most prominent and internationally known intellectuals, Professor S.B. Majrooh, who from the Afghan Information Centre in Peshawar tried to maintain the liberal and democratic values embodied in the 1964 constitution.

Apart from the Islamists, the other parties which have managed to assert themselves in the resistance all draw on primordial relations such as tribal and other traditional affiliations, and the personalized relations between leader and followers within the spiritual, religious and secular fields – i.e. of the *pir-murid/murshid* (spiritual guide-disciple), *alim – talib* (teacher-student) and patron-client type. And superimposed on this pattern are the ethnic, sectarian and regional loyalties – which also affect the ideological parties among the Islamists and the Left.[18]

It is also important to note that the initial decentralized and strongly localized nature of the Afghan resistance meant that the exile parties neither grew out of the resistance, nor were they the origin of it – on the contrary, the situation was at first that of several 'generals without an army' who were gradually able to assume a leading role in the resistance. This situation initially caused many observers to distinguish between the internal resistance and the front commanders on the one side and the exile parties (as parasites on the resistance) on the other. However, ultimately the parties came to dominate the resistance both inside and outside Afghanistan. The main factors in this development were the parties' ability to attract funds and supplies of weapons, in which they were greatly assisted by the Pakistani government's acknowledgement of only seven parties and its favouritism towards Hikmatyar's *Hezb-i islami*. The uniform Islamic rhetoric of the resistance thus should not be interpreted as symptomatic of unity, but on the contrary can be seen as an expression of the fact that Islam served as the medium through which the various divisive forces in Afghan society were played out.

While all the resistance parties and groups agree about fighting the Kabul regime in the name of Islam, they seriously diverge as to the nature of the future of a free Afghanistan. By unfolding the banner of *jihad*, they simultaneously unleashed the ever-pertinent question in Afghanistan as to what constitutes legitimate power and authority. Agreement exists that sovereignty belongs to Allah, but as to who will be the keepers of the mandate of legitimate authority, profound disagreement remains. As discussed previously, for the Islamists there is no place for monarchy in Islam. The only legitimate rule can be through some kind of consultative body (*shura*) embodying the interests of the community of believers (*umma*). The 'traditionalists' have a somewhat different view: for example, Mujadidi has argued that Islam prescribes neither monarchy nor republic, but that it is up to the Muslims to decide who rules, and to make sure that the ruler rules in accordance with Islamic Law. He goes on to compare the election of the first caliphs with the principles embodied in the Afghan traditional tribal council, the grand *jirga*, where those in authority chose the leader.[19] *Pir* Sayyid Ahmad Gailani on the other hand 'recognizes legitimacy only to that government which is established through free and universal suffrage' and has declared the principles of 'Islam, Nationalism and Democracy' as the basis of his philosophy, activities and approach to the solution of internal problems.[20] The other points mentioned in the brief party manifesto of Gailani's *Mahaz-i Melli*, such as the safeguarding of the basic freedom of the individual, freedom of the press and of association, and the separation of the powers of the state organs indicate a wish to return to parliamentary democracy according to the constitution of 1964. However, like Mujadidid, Gailani also resurrects the tribal concept of *jirga* as a representative body. The notion of legitimacy thus revolves around the Nation, embodied in the grand *jirga*, and popular sovereignty, as well as Islam.

In practical politics, these differences meant that while the Islamist parties agreed about the goal being an Islamic state, the moderate-/traditionalist parties want rule in accordance with the principles of Islam, which seemed to imply a return to *status quo ante*, that is before the Daoud Khan coup in 1973. This was, among other things, reflected in the various overtures made to ex-King Zahir Shah in order to use him as a unifying figure for national liberation. As far as the revolutionary Islamists were concerned, any attempt to bring the ex-King back into focus confirmed and aggravated the old enmity between the Islamists and the traditional religious leaders, 'proving' that the latter always were an integral part of the establishment.[21] From *Hezb-i Islami* it was thus pointed out that during the 1950s and 1970s when the Mujadidis were harmed politically, 'it was not because they were anti-Establishment, but because they took part in the internal power struggle among the ruling élite', i.e. were in favour of Zahir Shah and Abdul Wali against Daoud Khan.[22]

The Islamists were vehemently opposed to a comeback by ex-King Zahir Shah, and Gulbuddin Hikmatyar pronounced that 'the believing and courageous people of Afghanistan will not agree to anything but an Islamic government. Otherwise, the people of Afghanistan will fight [against a Zahir Shah government] as they fought against Taraki and [Hafizullah] Amin governments.'[23] In addition, the *Hezb-i Islami* journal *Shehadat* listed the 'anti-religious' episodes during Zahir Shah's reign to prove his unacceptability from a religious point of view, and *Al-Noor*

THE PESHAWAR-BASED SUNNI *MUJAHEDIN* PARTIES[29]

The Traditionalists

Mahaz-i Melli (National Islamic Front for Afghanistan) – led by Sayyid Ahmad Gailani, leader (*pir*) of the *Qadiriyya* Sufi order. Graduate from Faculty of *Sharia*, Kabul University, and former member of parliament. Married into the royal dynasty. His following is particularly among the Pashtuns of the south.

Jebha-i Nejat-i Melli Afghanistan (Afghanistan National Liberation Front) – led by Sibghatullah Mujadidi, trained at al-Azhar University, Cairo. The Mujadidi family has been the most prominent religious family in Afghanistan during this century and the spiritual leaders of a section of the *Naqshbandiyya* Sufi order.

Harakat-i Inqilab-i Islami (Islamic Revolutionary Movement) – led by *mawlawi* Mohammad Nabi Mohammadi, former member of parliament and a religious teacher. Mohammadi is well-connected among the *ulama*, and enjoys tribal support particularly in the southeastern region.

The Islamists

Jamiat-i Islami (Islamic Society) – led by Burhanuddin Rabbani, a Tajik from Faizabad in northern Afghanistan, doctorate in Islamic philosophy from al-Azhar University, Cairo, and former dean of Faculty of *Sharia*, Kabul University. Leading figure in the Islamic movement from the early 1970s. Enjoys support mainly from non-Pashtun groups in eastern and northern Afghanistan.

Hezb-i Islami/Khales (Islamic Party/*Khales*) – led by *mawlawi* Mohammad Yunis Khales, editor and religious teacher, a Pashtun from Ningarhar province. Formed his own party after a break with *Hikmatyar* in 1979.

Hezb-i Islami/Hikmatyar (Islamic Party/*Hikmatyar*) – led by Gulbuddin Hikmatyar, a Pashtun from Kunduz in north Afghanistan. Former engineering student at Kabul University and an Islamic activist in the 1970s. Imprisoned during 1972-3, and accused of a coup attempt in 1974 after which he went into hiding.

Ittihad-i Islami (Islamic Union for the Liberation of Afghanistan) – led by Abdul Rasul Sayyaf, a Pashtun from Paghman near Kabul. Former religious teacher with a degree from al-Azhar, Cairo. Arrested in 1974 and spent more than five years in prison. After his release in 1980, he went to Pakistan and joined the resistance.

IRANIAN-SUPPORTED ALLIANCE OF
SHIA *MUJAHEDIN* PARTIES[30]

The major parties

Harakat-i Islami (Islamic Movement) – led by Shaykh Asef Mohsini, who was educated by Ayatullah Khoy in Iraq and who was formerly head of a religious school in Kandahar.

Sazman-i Nasr (Organization of Victory) – spokesman is Shaykh Abdul Karim Khalili from Behsud.

Pasdaran-i Jihad-i Islami (Guardians of Islamic Holy War) – founded in Iran in 1982. Collective leadership.

The smaller parties

Nahzat-i Islami Afghanistan (Islamic Movement of Afghanistan).

Niru-i Islami Afghanistan (Islamic Force of Afghanistan).

Dawat-i Ittihad-i Islami Afghanistan (Invitation to the Islamic Unity of Afghanistan).

Hezb-i Islami Rad-i Afghanistan (Party of Islamic Thunder of Afghanistan).

Jebha-i Mutahed (United Front).

(Khales group) quoted *mawlawi* Jalaluddin Haqqani as saying that during his forty years' reign Zahir Shah even failed to perform *hajj*, the pilgrimage to Mecca, whereby even his personal credentials as a Muslim were brought into doubt.[24] Hereby, it was once again underlined that the struggle for the Islamists was not a national liberation struggle but a struggle for Islam. Since a believer shall know no other fatherland than where *sharia* reigns, the *jihad* was for Islam and for the *umma*. Or in the words of an Afghan Islamist:[25] 'The present *jihad* is not for the *watan* [Fatherland], but for Islam. The *watan* is only *khak* [dust]'. The *Al-Noor* journal of *Hezb-i Islami* formulated it thus: The concept of 'Nation' neither refers to an ethnic/tribal group nor to a geographic entity, but only to a people of one mentality, like 'infidelity is one nation'.[26]

The revolutionary vision of the Islamists is hardly shared by the non-Islamist parties, for whom the 'primordial' loyalties and traditional leaders play an important role – and the test of the Afghan reality may prove as fateful for the Islamic Revolution as it did for the Saur Revolution. All differences apart, and after many attempts, in early May 1987 the seven parties in Peshawar (almost) reached an agreement on a charter for a joint council for *Ittihad-i Islami Mujahedin-i Afghanistan* with a view to the formation of an interim government 'for the sake of hoisting the Word of God and liberating the country from the rule of unbelief and atheism'. However, the unity immediately dissolved as far as the composition of the Revolutionary Council was concerned: five parties agreed that the Council should be selected on the basis of quality among the seven constituent organizations – while Hikmatyar and Gailani proposed that members of the Council should be elected by the *mujahedin* and refugees (*muhajirin*). Hence, the implementation of the Charter was postponed. In June 1988, the 7-party Peshawar Alliance finally announced the formation of a government-in-exile. But in the Alliance, as well as in the government-in-exile, none of the *Shia* parties representing Central Afghanistan were represented, which put extra focus on two articles in the Alliance Charter mentioning the *Hanafi* jurisprudence and centralism, which were a source of offence to a sizeable minority of the Afghan population.

In March 1990, an internal coup attempt, headed by General Tanai, failed. Partly, it illustrated the long-lasting internal split in the PDPA between its *Khalq* and *Parcham* factions, rooted in personal and ethnic rather than in ideological opposition. Moreover, it signalled other, future alliances, since General Tanai was supported by one of the most radical Islamic opponents of the PDPA regime, that is Gulbuddin Hikmatyar's *Hezb-i Islami*. This unholy alliance showed that ethnic and personal considerations among the Afghan Islamists weighed heavier than ideological differences. The other Afghan resistance parties condemned Hikmatyar's support for the coup attempt and interpreted it as yet another illustration of *Hezb-i Islami*'s urge for power.[27]

Pressurized by the Soviet leaders, President Najibullah carried on with the reconciliation policy, albeit still receiving their military assistance. An increasing number of non-communists were included in the Afghan government and in June 1990 the PDPA became the *Hezb-i Watan*, the Fatherland Party, but still without any prospects of reaching an understanding with the *mujahedin*. Ultimately, after President Najibullah's resignation, the *Parcham* faction supported the Tajik *mujahedin* commander Ahmad Shah Massoud and the Islamic *Jamiat-i Islami*, which also allied itself with General Dostum's Uzbek Jawzjani militia in northern Afghanistan and other rebel generals like Syed Jafer Naderi and the former governor of Herat, General Abdul Momin. The *Khalqis* have generally sided with Hikmatyar's Pashtun-dominated and more radical *Hezb-i Islami*.

The present struggle for power

The future of Afghanistan is still uncertain. The coalition which took power after Najibullah's resignation in April 1992, and which is currently headed by Rabbani from *Jamiat-i Islami*, has neither established peace nor managed to organize the transition to a representative system of government. Although the eight-party *Shiite* alliance *Hezb-i Wahadat* was included in the coalition in July 1992 so that it enjoys the formal support of the most significance non-Pashtun groups, the question of the right of minorities will continue to be a touchy issue. This is partly underlined by the non-Pashtun groups' military strength and fighting ability during the fourteen years of resistance and partly by the widespread reluctance and suspicion among Pashtuns towards sharing their previous monopoly of power with other ethnic groups.

The most acute problem, however, remains the relations with Hikmatyar's *Hezb-i Islami*, which in spite of several ceasefire agreements has opposed the interim government militarily both before and after being excluded from it in August 1992 – and reincluded in March 1993. Hikmatyar attacks the coalition and in particular the *Jamiat-i Islami* for not being Islamic. However, the main problem seems to be that all the involved parties and groups engage in power struggles at all levels of society, creating the most unlikely and unstable alliances in order to obtain short-term benefits, and criss-crossing major ideological differences. Extra fuel is added to this state of general anarchy by the presence of foreign volunteers or mercenaries, from Arab countries and elsewhere, who actively engage in the fighting.

Finally, it remains an open question whether the majority of the Afghan population suffered fourteen years of civil war in order to establish an Islamic regime. One of the first edicts which the new *mujahedin* government passed was that all women had to cover their heads in public and wear the traditional *shalwar kamez* or baggy trousers and long shirt.[27] This confirmed the worst expectations among that part of the Afghan population for whom the resistance against the Soviet Union and the PDPA was a national liberation struggle rather than a *jihad*, and who wanted a reestablishment of the parliamentary democracy rather than any form of Islamic republic. Such an attitude is held not only by significant parts of the educated middle class but also by common people for whom Islamism has been a foreign element at odds with their traditional loyalties. This aspect is further underlined by the fact that Amnesty International pointed out as early as 1992 that human rights violations had continued after the assumption of power by the Islamic coalition.[28]

Hence, in spite of the liberation it is still debatable when Afghanistan will have a constitution and a government that will enjoy general legitimacy in the eyes of ethnically, religiously and ideologically divided population. So far, the 'Islamic Revolution' threatens to be as fatal to the Afghan population as the Saur Revolution was.

In February 1995 the power struggle in Afghanistan took an un-expected turn with the rapid military advances of the new Islamist student militia, the *Taliban*, educated and trained in Pakistan. Reportedly, the *Taliban* has, up to the present, taken over power in five of Afghanistan's nineteen provinces. While the *Taliban*'s advances have mainly been at the expense of *Hezb-i-Islami*, they are no less radical in their call for turning Afghanistan into a 'truly Islamic' state ruled by *sharia*.

Notes

1. UN 1992.
2. Freigang 1992: 13.
3. For a discussion of the *Amir* Abdur Rahman period, see Kakar 1971, 1979; Ghani 1977, 1978; and Olesen 1987, 1995.
4. Smith 1974: pt. I.
5. For a comprehensive account of the Amanullah period, see Poullada 1973. The ideological background of the Young Afghan Movement, which was the inspiration of the reform policies in the 1920s, is discussed in Schinasi 1979.
6. Roy 1985; Grevemeyer 1987.
7. Khan 1984: 8ff; Adamec 1987: 138.
8. Grevemeyer 1987.
9. Khan 1984.
10. Roy 1985: 99.
11. Edwards 1986: 218f.
12. Amin 1984: 378.
13. Roy 1985: 101f; Marwat 1986.
14. Puig 1984: 226.
15. For a discussion of the concept of *jihad*, see Peters 1979.
16. Muzammil 1981.
17. Prof. Fadhallah Fiadh, personal communication, Peshawar, Nov. 1986.
18. For a detailed description of the recruitment to various parties according to the above networks, see Roy 1985; Puig 1984; and Ulfat 1979.
19. Mujadidi 1986.
20. Manifesto n.d.
21. See e.g. Edwards 1987.
22. Muzzamil, personal communication, Peshawar, Nov. 1986.
23. *Afghan Jihad* 1987: 8f.
24. *Shehadat*, 10 June 1987, *Al-Noor*, 29 June 1987.
25. Personal communication, Peshawar, Nov. 1986.
26. *Al-Noor*, 29 June 1987.
27. Eliot 1991.
28. Rashid 1992: 28f.
29. *Faites et Dates* 1992.
30. Sources: Canfield 1989: 641; Adamec 1987.
31. Source: Robert Canfield 1989.

References

Adamec, L.W. 1987. *A Biographical Dictionary of Contemporary Afghanistan.* Graz: Akademische Druck- und Verlagsanstalt.

Amin, T. 1984. 'Afghan Resistance: Past, Present, and Future', *Asian Survey* 24(3), 373-99.

Canfield, R. 1989. 'Afghanistan: The Trajectory of Internal Alignments', *Middle East Journal* 43/4, 635-48.

Edwards, D.B. 1986. 'Charismatic Leadership and Political Process in Afghanistan'. *Central Asian Survey* 5 (3/4).

——. 1987. 'The Political Lives of Afghan Saints: The Case of the Kabul Hazrats'. Unpublished ms.

Eliot, T.L. 1991. 'Afghanistan in 1990: Groping Toward Peace?', *Asian Survey* 31/2, 125-34.

Faites et Dates 1992. 'Faites et Dates', *Afghanistan Info*, Schweizerisches Komitee zur Unterstützung des afghanisches Volk, 32.

Freigang, K.V. 1992. 'Kabul – Beirut Zentralasiens?', *Afghanistan Info*, Schweizerisches Komitee zur Unterstützung des afghanisches Volk, 32.

Ghani, A. 1977. 'State-Building and Centralization in a Tribal Society: Afghanistan, 1880-1901'. Unpublished M.A. thesis, American University of Beirut.

Ghani, A. 1978. 'Islam and State-Building in a Tribal Society. Afghanistan 1880-1901', *Modern Asian Studies* 12(2), 269-2/84.

Grevemeyer, G. 1987. *Afghanistan. Sozialer Wandel und Staat im 20. Jahrhundert.* Berlin: Express Edition.

Kakar, M.H. 1971, *Afghanistan: A Study in Internal Political Developments, 1880-1896.* Kabul.

——. 1979. *Government and Society in Afghanistan: The Reign of Amir 'Abd al-Rahman.* Austin, Texas: University of Texas Press.

Khan, A.H. 1984.'Factional Organisation of the Afghan Mujahideens in Peshawar', *Central Asia* (Journal of area Study Centre, University of Peshawar) 14, 51-85.

Marwat, F.R. 1986. 'History of Pirs and Mullahs in Afghan Politics, I-II'. *The Frontier Post*, 26 and 27 April.

Manifesto, n.d. *Manifesto of the National Islamic Front of Afghanistan.*

Mujadedi, S. 1986. *Speech delivered by Sibghatullah Mujadidi, leader of the National Front for the Salvation of Afghanistan, in condemnation of the Saur coup d'état.* No Publisher.

Muzammil M.Z. 1981. *Reason of Russian Occupation & Dimensions of Resistance in Afghanistan.* Peshawar: Hezb-i Islami.

Olesen, A. 1987. 'The Political Use of Islam in Afghanistan during the Reign of Amir Abdur Rahman (1880-1901)' in C. Braae and K. Ferdinand (eds), *Contributions to Islamic Studies: Iran, Afghanistan and Pakistan*, Aarhus University Press, 59-115.

——. 1994. *Islam and Politics in Afghanistan.* London: Curzon Press.

Peters, R. 1979. *Islam and Colonialism: The Doctrine of Jihad in Modern History.* The Hague: Mouton.

Poullada, L.B. 1973. *Reform and Rebellion in Afghanistan, 1919-1929.* Ithaca, NY: Cornell University Press.

Puig, J.-J. 1984. 'La Résistance afghane', in P. Centlivres *et al.* (eds), *Afghanistan. La colonisation impossible.* Paris: CERF, 213-45.

Rashid, A. 1992. 'Behind the Veil, Again', *Far Eastern Economic Review*, 23 Apr., 28-9.

Roy. O. 1985. *L'Afghanistan. Islam et modernité politique.* Paris: Seuil.

Schinasi, M. 1979. *Afghanistan at the Beginning of the Twentieth Century.* Naples.

Smith, D.E. 1974. *Religion, Politics and Social Change in the Third World.* New York.

Ulfat, A. 1979. *Jihad wa dastha-i posht-i pardeh.* No publisher.

United Nations. 1992. 'UN Plan Sabotaged', *Afghan Information Centre Monthly Bulletin* 11(132-5), 1-12.

INDEX

Belov, Vasilii, 119-20

Benares, 250

Bengal, 275

Benin, 220

Benjedid, Chadli, 143

Berbers, 158

Berger, Peter, 101

Bhakti movement, 261

Bharat, 16, 239, 243-4, 247-51, 253, 255 n.31

Bharatiya Janata Party (BJP) (India), 237-9, 243, 254 n.5, 280, 285

Bharat Mata, 16, 244, 249-50, 253

Bhindranwale, Sant Jarnail Singh, 274-7, 279

BIA, *see* Bureau of Indian Affairs

Bible, 4-6, 30, 32, 35-6, 44 n.24, 198, 204, 217, 335, 337-8, 342; *see also* inerrancy

bida, 143, 150, 159, 375, 378

Bilal Ibn Rabah, 51, 58

BJP, *see Bharatiya Janata Party*

Black Panther Party, 67

blacks: in the U.S., 37, 48-72

Blyden, Edward Wilmot, 69 n.11

Bob Jones University, 36, 42

bodhisatta, 300, 303

Bolshevism, Bolsheviks, 119-20, 122, 125-6, 131-2, 135 n.4, 136 n.37

Bondarev, Jurii, 120

Bonnke, Reinhard, 199-202, 205, 223

Borneo, 362

Boumedienne, Houari, 156

Boutlimit, 184

Brahma, 241

brahmans, 246, 261

Brand Nubian, 68

Brazil, 103, 326, 350 n.12

Bread of Life Ministries (Philippines), 331, 349

Brezhnev, Leonid, 120, 122

Bright, Bill, 36, 333

Britain, Great, 8, 61, 167, 269, 273, 275, 277, 317 n.7, 351 n.61, 371

Brock, Peter, 336

Bruce, S., 36, 44 n.34

Buchanan, Pat, 39

Buddha, 249, 294, 295 n.22, 299, 306, 310, 319 n.41

Buddhism: 8, 16-7, 251; in Burma, 17-8, 297-320; in Indonesia, 356-8, 386; in Malaysia, 356, 363; in Sri Lanka, 284-96; in Thailand, 18; Theravada, 17, 284

Buddhists: 16; in Burma, 297-320; in India, 251-2, 254 n.1, 259-60; in Sri Lanka, 284-96; in Tibet, 9, 96

Buddhist World Council, 310

Bulgaria, 12

Bumiputra, 366, 379-80

Bureau of Indian Affairs (BIA), 10, 75, 80, 86

Burkina Faso, 200, 220; *see also* Upper Volta

Burma, 17-18, 297-320

Bush, George, 39

Cairo, 161 n.9, 190, 364, 404

Calvinism, Calvinists, 34

Camba Erme, 339-40

Cameroon, 220

Campaore, 200, 204

Campus Crusade for Christ (US), 36, 333, 339, 347

Canada, 267, 277

capitalism, 103, 109, 122, 131, 134, 168, 226, 245, 279, 340, 345, 373

Capps, W.H., 37

cargo cults (Melanesia), 381-2

Carter, Jimmy, 32, 106

Casariego, Mario, 104, 108

caste system, 7, 16, 238, 245-6, 251, 253-4, 256 n.67, 259-64, 269, 271-2, 278, 280

Catholic Action Movement (Guatemala), 100-1, 103-4, 112 n.16

Catholic Bishops Council of the Philippines (CBCP), 326

Catholic Episcopal Conference of Zambia, 211

Catholicism, Catholics: 12, 118, 344; in Guatemala, 10, 96-114; in Indonesia, 357; in Kenya, 207; in the Philippines, 323-6, 328, 331, 333, 335, 338-9, 341, 345-7; popular, 99, 112 n.6; in Senegal, 189, 193; in Tanzania, 221-2; in the US, 36, 49-